TODAY'S NEW INTERNATIONAL VERSION

tNIV new testament

ZONDERVAN™

GRAND RAPIDS, MICHIGAN 49530 USA

WWW.ZONDERVAN.COM

CONTENTS

THE NEW TESTAMENT

A WORD TO THE READER

A mong the many English versions of the Bible that appeared in the twentieth century, the New International Version (NIV: 1973, 1978, 1984) has gained the widest readership in all parts of the English-speaking world. The NIV was a completely new translation made by over a hundred scholars working directly from the best available Hebrew, Aramaic and Greek texts. The fact that participants from the United States, Great Britain, Canada, Australia and New Zealand worked together gave the project its international scope. That they were from many denominations—including Anglican, Assemblies of God, Baptist, Brethren, Christian Reformed, Church of Christ, Evangelical Free, Lutheran, Methodist, Nazarene, Presbyterian, Wesleyan and other churches—helped to safeguard the translation from sectarian bias. Responsibility for the NIV text is held by a self-governing body, the Committee on Bible Translation, composed of biblical scholars from colleges, universities and seminaries.

From the beginning, the translators were united in their commitment to the authority and infallibility of the Bible as God's Word in written form. They believed that it contains the divine answer to the deepest needs of humanity, that it sheds unique light on our path in a dark world, and that it sets forth the way to our eternal well-being. In light of this, the Committee held to certain goals for the NIV: that it would be an accurate translation and one that would have clarity and literary quality and so prove suitable for public and private reading, teaching, preaching, memorizing and liturgical use. The Committee also sought to preserve a measure of continuity with the long tradition of translating the Scriptures into English.

There is a sense in which the work of translating the Bible is never finally finished. This very fact has prompted the Committee to engage in an ongoing review of the text of the NIV with the assistance of many other scholars. The chief goal of this review has always been to bring the text of the NIV abreast of contemporary biblical scholarship and of shifts in English idioms and usage. Already in 1978 and again in 1984 various corrections and revisions to the NIV text were made. In Today's New International Version (TNIV) the Committee offers to the reading public the latest fruits of this review.

The first concern of the translators has been the accuracy of the translation and its faithfulness to the meaning of the biblical writers. This has moved the translators to strive for more than a word-for-word rendering of the original texts. Because thought patterns and syntax differ from language to language, accurate communication of the meaning of the biblical authors demands constant regard for the contextual meanings of words and idioms and frequent modifications in sentence structures.

To achieve clarity the translators have sometimes supplied words not in the original texts but required by the context. If there was uncertainty about such material, it is enclosed in brackets. As an aid to the reader, italicized sectional headings have been inserted. They are not to be regarded as part of the TNIV text and are not for oral reading. It is the Committee's hope that the headings may prove more helpful to the reader than the traditional chapter divisions (which come only from the thirteenth century).

The Greek text used in translating the New Testament has been an eclectic one. Where existing manuscripts differ, the translators have made their choice of readings in accordance with widely accepted principles of New Testament textual criticism. Footnotes call attention to places where there was uncertainty about what the original text was. Such footnotes are introduced by "Some manuscripts" or similar expressions.

Other footnotes in this version are of several kinds, most of which need no explanation. Those giving alternative translations begin with "Or" and generally introduce the alternative with the last word preceding it in the text, except when it is a single-word alternative. In poetry quoted in a footnote a slant mark indicates a line division.

It should be noted that references to minerals, flora and fauna, architectural details, articles of clothing and jewelry, musical instruments and other articles cannot always be identified with precision. Also measures of capacity in the biblical period are particularly uncertain.

Two changes of special note in the TNIV New Testament are the frequent substitution of "Messiah" for the more traditional "Christ" and the replacement of "saints" in most cases with alternative renderings. A word about each of these is in order.

While both "Messiah" (from the Hebrew) and "Christ" (from the Greek) mean "Anointed One," what began as a title full of meaning to the early Jewish hearers of the gospel tended in the later Greek-speaking churches to become just another name for Jesus. So where the term is clearly used to designate the God-sent deliverer of Jewish expectation (primarily in the Gospels and Acts), it was judged more appropriate to use "Messiah." However, where this sense seems less prominent (primarily in the Epistles), the transliteration of the Greek word (Christ) has been retained.

Concerning "saints," current usage (as reflected in major dictionaries of the English language) burdens it with meanings that lie outside the sense of the original. As used in the New Testament documents, the Greek term primarily designates those who have become "followers of the [Christian] Way" as people consecrated to God and thus belonging to him in a special sense—a meaning derived especially from Daniel 7:18. Hence the language of choice in most instances is now "God's people" or "the people of God"—but in some cases "believers."

While a basic core of the English language remains relatively stable, many diverse and complex cultural forces continue to bring about subtle shifts in the meanings and/or connotations of even old, well-established words and phrases. Among the more programmatic changes in the TNIV is the removal of nearly all vocative "O"s and the elimination of most instances of the generic use of masculine nouns and pronouns. Relative to the second of these, the so-called singular "they/their/them," which has been gaining acceptance among careful writers and which actually has a venerable place in English idiom, has been employed to fill in the vocabulary gap in generic nouns and pronouns referring to human beings. Where an individual emphasis is deemed to be present, "anyone" or "everyone" is generally used as the antecedent of such pronouns.

Verse numbers that marked off portions of the traditional English text not supported by the best Greek manuscripts are now set alongside the immediately preceding verse numbers and placed in brackets (see, for example, Matthew 17:20 [21]).

Mark 16:9-20 and John 7:53-8:11, although long accorded virtually equal status with the rest of the Gospels in which they stand, have a very questionable—and confused—standing in the textual history of the New Testament, as noted in the bracketed annotations with which they are set off. A different typeface has now been chosen for these passages to indicate even more clearly their uncertain status.

The Committee has again been reminded that every human effort is flawed—including this revision of the NIV. We trust, however, that many will find in it an improved representation of the Word of God, through which they hear his call to faith in our Lord Jesus Christ and his guide for service in his kingdom. We offer this version of the New Testament to him in whose name and for whose glory it has been made.

The Committee on Bible Translation
August 2001

NEW TESTAMENT

MATTHEW

The Genealogy of Jesus the Messiah

1 This is the genealogy*a* of Jesus the Messiah*b* the son of David, the son of Abraham:

2 Abraham was the father of Isaac,
Isaac the father of Jacob,
Jacob the father of Judah and his brothers,
3 Judah the father of Perez and Zerah, whose mother was Tamar,
Perez the father of Hezron,
Hezron the father of Ram,
4 Ram the father of Amminadab,
Amminadab the father of Nahshon,
Nahshon the father of Salmon,
5 Salmon the father of Boaz, whose mother was Rahab,
Boaz the father of Obed, whose mother was Ruth,
Obed the father of Jesse,
6 and Jesse the father of King David.

David was the father of Solomon, whose mother had been Uriah's wife,
7 Solomon the father of Rehoboam,
Rehoboam the father of Abijah,
Abijah the father of Asa,
8 Asa the father of Jehoshaphat,
Jehoshaphat the father of Jehoram,
Jehoram the father of Uzziah,
9 Uzziah the father of Jotham,
Jotham the father of Ahaz,
Ahaz the father of Hezekiah,
10 Hezekiah the father of Manasseh,
Manasseh the father of Amon,
Amon the father of Josiah,
11 and Josiah the father of Jeconiah*c* and his brothers at the time of the exile to Babylon.

12 After the exile to Babylon:

---

a 1 Or *is an account of the origin*   *b* 1 Or *Jesus Christ.* "Messiah" (Hebrew) and "Christ" (Greek) both mean "Anointed One."   *c* 11 That is, Jehoiachin; also in verse 12

Jeconiah was the father of Shealtiel,
Shealtiel the father of Zerubbabel,
13 Zerubbabel the father of Abiud,
Abiud the father of Eliakim,
Eliakim the father of Azor,
14 Azor the father of Zadok,
Zadok the father of Akim,
Akim the father of Eliud,
15 Eliud the father of Eleazar,
Eleazar the father of Matthan,
Matthan the father of Jacob,
16 and Jacob the father of Joseph, the husband of Mary, and Mary was the
mother of Jesus who is called the Messiah.

17 Thus there were fourteen generations in all from Abraham to David, fourteen from David to the exile to Babylon, and fourteen from the exile to the
Messiah.

Joseph Accepts Jesus as His Son

18 This is how the birth of Jesus Christ[a] came about[b]: His mother Mary was
pledged to be married to Joseph, but before they came together, she was
found to be pregnant through the Holy Spirit. 19 Because Joseph her husband
was a righteous man and did not want to expose her to public disgrace, he
had in mind to divorce her quietly.

20 But after he had considered this, an angel of the Lord appeared to him in
a dream and said, "Joseph son of David, do not be afraid to take Mary home
as your wife, because what is conceived in her is from the Holy Spirit. 21 She
will give birth to a son, and you are to give him the name Jesus,[c] because he
will save his people from their sins."

22 All this took place to fulfill what the Lord had said through the prophet:
23 "The virgin will conceive and give birth to a son, and they will call him Immanuel"[d]—which means, "God with us."

24 When Joseph woke up, he did what the angel of the Lord had commanded him and took Mary home as his wife. 25 But he had no union with her until
she gave birth to a son. And he gave him the name Jesus.

The Magi Visit the Messiah

2 After Jesus was born in Bethlehem in Judea, during the time of King
Herod, Magi[e] from the east came to Jerusalem 2 and asked, "Where is the
one who has been born king of the Jews? We saw his star when it rose and
have come to worship him."

3 When King Herod heard this he was disturbed, and all Jerusalem with
him. 4 When he had called together all the people's chief priests and teachers
of the law, he asked them where the Messiah was to be born. 5 "In Bethlehem
in Judea," they replied, "for this is what the prophet has written:

a 18 Or Jesus the Messiah   b 18 Or The origin of Jesus Christ was like this   c 21 Jesus is the Greek
form of Joshua, which means the LORD saves.   d 23 Isaiah 7:14   e 1 Traditionally wise men

6 " 'But you, Bethlehem, in the land of Judah,
    are by no means least among the rulers of Judah;
for out of you will come a ruler
    who will be the shepherd of my people Israel.'*"

[7]Then Herod called the Magi secretly and found out from them the exact time the star had appeared. [8]He sent them to Bethlehem and said, "Go and make a careful search for the child. As soon as you find him, report to me, so that I too may go and worship him."

[9]After they had heard the king, they went on their way, and the star they had seen when it rose went ahead of them until it stopped over the place where the child was. [10]When they saw the star, they were overjoyed. [11]On coming to the house, they saw the child with his mother Mary, and they bowed down and worshiped him. Then they opened their treasures and presented him with gifts of gold, frankincense and myrrh. [12]And having been warned in a dream not to go back to Herod, they returned to their country by another route.

The Escape to Egypt

[13]When they had gone, an angel of the Lord appeared to Joseph in a dream. "Get up," he said, "take the child and his mother and escape to Egypt. Stay there until I tell you, for Herod is going to search for the child to kill him." [14]So he got up, took the child and his mother during the night and left for Egypt, [15]where he stayed until the death of Herod. And so was fulfilled what the Lord had said through the prophet: "Out of Egypt I called my son."*b*

[16]When Herod realized that he had been outwitted by the Magi, he was furious, and he gave orders to kill all the boys in Bethlehem and its vicinity who were two years old and under, in accordance with the time he had learned from the Magi. [17]Then what was said through the prophet Jeremiah was fulfilled:

18 "A voice is heard in Ramah,
    weeping and great mourning,
Rachel weeping for her children
    and refusing to be comforted,
because they are no more."*c*

The Return to Nazareth

[19]After Herod died, an angel of the Lord appeared in a dream to Joseph in Egypt [20]and said, "Get up, take the child and his mother and go to the land of Israel, for those who were trying to take the child's life are dead."

[21]So he got up, took the child and his mother and went to the land of Israel. [22]But when he heard that Archelaus was reigning in Judea in place of his father Herod, he was afraid to go there. Having been warned in a dream, he withdrew to the district of Galilee, [23]and he went and lived in a town called Nazareth. So was fulfilled what was said through the prophets: "He will be called a Nazarene."

a 6 Micah 5:2   *b* 15 Hosea 11:1   *c* 18 Jer. 31:15

John the Baptist Prepares the Way

3 In those days John the Baptist came, preaching in the Desert of Judea ²and saying, "Repent, for the kingdom of heaven has come near." ³This is he who was spoken of through the prophet Isaiah:

> "A voice of one calling in the desert,
> 'Prepare the way for the Lord,
>   make straight paths for him.' " *a*

⁴John's clothes were made of camel's hair, and he had a leather belt around his waist. His food was locusts and wild honey. ⁵People went out to him from Jerusalem and all Judea and the whole region of the Jordan. ⁶Confessing their sins, they were baptized by him in the Jordan River.

⁷But when he saw many of the Pharisees and Sadducees coming to where he was baptizing, he said to them: "You brood of vipers! Who warned you to flee from the coming wrath? ⁸Produce fruit in keeping with repentance. ⁹And do not think you can say to yourselves, 'We have Abraham as our father.' I tell you that out of these stones God can raise up children for Abraham. ¹⁰The ax is already at the root of the trees, and every tree that does not produce good fruit will be cut down and thrown into the fire.

¹¹"I baptize you with *b* water for repentance. But after me comes one who is more powerful than I, whose sandals I am not fit to carry. He will baptize you with *b* the Holy Spirit and fire. ¹²His winnowing fork is in his hand, and he will clear his threshing floor, gathering his wheat into the barn and burning up the chaff with unquenchable fire."

The Baptism of Jesus

¹³Then Jesus came from Galilee to the Jordan to be baptized by John. ¹⁴But John tried to deter him, saying, "I need to be baptized by you, and do you come to me?"

¹⁵Jesus replied, "Let it be so now; it is proper for us to do this to fulfill all righteousness." Then John consented.

¹⁶As soon as Jesus was baptized, he went up out of the water. At that moment heaven was opened, and he saw the Spirit of God descending like a dove and alighting on him. ¹⁷And a voice from heaven said, "This is my Son, whom I love; with him I am well pleased."

Jesus Is Tested in the Desert

4 Then Jesus was led by the Spirit into the desert to be tempted *c* by the devil. ²After fasting forty days and forty nights, he was hungry. ³The tempter came to him and said, "If you are the Son of God, tell these stones to become bread."

⁴Jesus answered, "It is written: 'People do not live on bread alone, but on every word that comes from the mouth of God.' *d*"

⁵Then the devil took him to the holy city and had him stand on the highest point of the temple. ⁶"If you are the Son of God," he said, "throw yourself down. For it is written:

---

a 3 Isaiah 40:3   *b 11* Or *in*   *c 1* The Greek for *tempted* can also mean *tested.*   *d 4* Deut. 8:3

" 'He will command his angels concerning you,
    and they will lift you up in their hands,
so that you will not strike your foot against a stone.'*"*

7Jesus answered him, "It is also written: 'Do not put the Lord your God to the test.'*"*

8Again, the devil took him to a very high mountain and showed him all the kingdoms of the world and their splendor. 9"All this I will give you," he said, "if you will bow down and worship me."

10Jesus said to him, "Away from me, Satan! For it is written: 'Worship the Lord your God, and serve him only.'*c*"

11Then the devil left him, and angels came and attended him.

Jesus Begins to Preach

12When Jesus heard that John had been put in prison, he withdrew to Galilee. 13Leaving Nazareth, he went and lived in Capernaum, which was by the lake in the area of Zebulun and Naphtali— 14to fulfill what was said through the prophet Isaiah:

15"Land of Zebulun and land of Naphtali,
    the Way of the Sea, along the Jordan,
    Galilee of the Gentiles—
16the people living in darkness
    have seen a great light;
on those living in the land of the shadow of death
    a light has dawned."*d*

17From that time on Jesus began to preach, "Repent, for the kingdom of heaven has come near."

Jesus Calls His First Disciples

18As Jesus was walking beside the Sea of Galilee, he saw two brothers, Simon called Peter and his brother Andrew. They were casting a net into the lake, for they were fishermen. 19"Come, follow me," Jesus said, "and I will send you out to catch people." 20At once they left their nets and followed him.

21Going on from there, he saw two other brothers, James son of Zebedee and his brother John. They were in a boat with their father Zebedee, preparing their nets. Jesus called them, 22and immediately they left the boat and their father and followed him.

Jesus Heals the Sick

23Jesus went throughout Galilee, teaching in their synagogues, proclaiming the good news of the kingdom, and healing every disease and sickness among the people. 24News about him spread all over Syria, and people brought to him all who were ill with various diseases, those suffering severe pain, the demon-possessed, those having seizures, and the paralyzed, and he healed them. 25Large crowds from Galilee, the Decapolis,*e* Jerusalem, Judea and the region across the Jordan followed him.

a 6 Psalm 91:11,12   *b 7* Deut. 6:16   *c 10* Deut. 6:13   *d 16* Isaiah 9:1,2   *e 25* That is, the Ten Cities

The Beatitudes

5 Now when he saw the crowds, he went up on a mountainside and sat down. His disciples came to him, ²and he began to teach them, saying:

> ³"Blessed are the poor in spirit,
>   for theirs is the kingdom of heaven.
> ⁴Blessed are those who mourn,
>   for they will be comforted.
> ⁵Blessed are the meek,
>   for they will inherit the earth.
> ⁶Blessed are those who hunger and thirst for righteousness,
>   for they will be filled.
> ⁷Blessed are the merciful,
>   for they will be shown mercy.
> ⁸Blessed are the pure in heart,
>   for they will see God.
> ⁹Blessed are the peacemakers,
>   for they will be called children of God.
> ¹⁰Blessed are those who are persecuted because of righteousness,
>   for theirs is the kingdom of heaven.

¹¹"Blessed are you when people insult you, persecute you and falsely say all kinds of evil against you because of me. ¹²Rejoice and be glad, because great is your reward in heaven, for in the same way they persecuted the prophets who were before you.

Salt and Light

¹³"You are the salt of the earth. But if the salt loses its saltiness, how can it be made salty again? It is no longer good for anything, except to be thrown out and trampled underfoot.

¹⁴"You are the light of the world. A city on a hill cannot be hidden. ¹⁵Neither do people light a lamp and put it under a bowl. Instead they put it on its stand, and it gives light to everyone in the house. ¹⁶In the same way, let your light shine before others, that they may see your good deeds and praise your Father in heaven.

The Fulfillment of the Law

¹⁷"Do not think that I have come to abolish the Law or the Prophets; I have not come to abolish them but to fulfill them. ¹⁸Truly I tell you, until heaven and earth disappear, not the smallest letter, not the least stroke of a pen, will by any means disappear from the Law until everything is accomplished. ¹⁹Anyone who sets aside one of the least of these commandments and teaches others accordingly will be called least in the kingdom of heaven, but whoever practices and teaches these commands will be called great in the kingdom of heaven. ²⁰For I tell you that unless your righteousness surpasses that of the Pharisees and the teachers of the law, you will certainly not enter the kingdom of heaven.

Murder

21"You have heard that it was said to the people long ago, 'Do not murder,*a* and anyone who murders will be subject to judgment.' 22But I tell you that anyone who is angry with a brother or sister*b* will be subject to judgment. Again, anyone who says to a brother or sister, 'Raca,*c'* is answerable to the Sanhedrin. And anyone who says, 'You fool!' will be in danger of the fire of hell.

23"Therefore, if you are offering your gift at the altar and there remember that the brother or sister has something against you, 24leave your gift there in front of the altar. First go and be reconciled to that person; then come and offer your gift.

25"Settle matters quickly with your adversary who is taking you to court. Do it while you are still together on the way, or your adversary may hand you over to the judge, and the judge may hand you over to the officer, and you may be thrown into prison. 26Truly I tell you, you will not get out until you have paid the last penny.

Adultery

27"You have heard that it was said, 'Do not commit adultery.'*d* 28But I tell you that anyone who looks at a woman lustfully has already committed adultery with her in his heart. 29If your right eye causes you to stumble, gouge it out and throw it away. It is better for you to lose one part of your body than for your whole body to be thrown into hell. 30And if your right hand causes you to stumble, cut it off and throw it away. It is better for you to lose one part of your body than for your whole body to go into hell.

Divorce

31"It has been said, 'Anyone who divorces his wife must give her a certificate of divorce.'*e* 32But I tell you that anyone who divorces his wife, except for sexual immorality, causes her to become an adulteress, and anyone who marries the divorced woman commits adultery.

Oaths

33"Again, you have heard that it was said to the people long ago, 'Do not break your oath, but keep the oaths you have made to the Lord.' 34But I tell you, do not swear at all: either by heaven, for it is God's throne; 35or by the earth, for it is his footstool; or by Jerusalem, for it is the city of the Great King. 36And do not swear by your head, for you cannot make even one hair white or black. 37All you need to say is simply 'Yes,' or 'No'; anything beyond this comes from the evil one.*f*

An Eye for an Eye

38"You have heard that it was said, 'Eye for eye, and tooth for tooth.'*g* 39But I tell you, do not resist an evil person. If anyone slaps you on the right cheek, turn to them the other cheek also. 40And if anyone wants to sue you and take

---

a 21 Exodus 20:13　　*b* 22 Some manuscripts *brother or sister without cause*　　*c* 22 An Aramaic term of contempt　　*d* 27 Exodus 20:14　　*e* 31 Deut. 24:1　　*f* 37 Or *from evil*　　*g* 38 Exodus 21:24; Lev. 24:20; Deut. 19:21

your shirt, hand over your coat as well. [41]If anyone forces you to go one mile, go with them two miles. [42]Give to the one who asks you, and do not turn away from the one who wants to borrow from you.

Love for Enemies

[43]"You have heard that it was said, 'Love your neighbor[a] and hate your enemy.' [44]But I tell you, love your enemies and pray for those who persecute you, [45]that you may be children of your Father in heaven. He causes his sun to rise on the evil and the good, and sends rain on the righteous and the unrighteous. [46]If you love those who love you, what reward will you get? Are not even the tax collectors doing that? [47]And if you greet only your own people, what are you doing more than others? Do not even pagans do that? [48]Be perfect, therefore, as your heavenly Father is perfect.

Giving to the Needy

6 "Be careful not to do your 'acts of righteousness' in front of others, to be seen by them. If you do, you will have no reward from your Father in heaven.

[2]"So when you give to the needy, do not announce it with trumpets, as the hypocrites do in the synagogues and on the streets, to be honored by others. Truly I tell you, they have received their reward in full. [3]But when you give to the needy, do not let your left hand know what your right hand is doing, [4]so that your giving may be in secret. Then your Father, who sees what is done in secret, will reward you.

Prayer

[5]"And when you pray, do not be like the hypocrites, for they love to pray standing in the synagogues and on the street corners to be seen by others. Truly I tell you, they have received their reward in full. [6]But when you pray, go into your room, close the door and pray to your Father, who is unseen. Then your Father, who sees what is done in secret, will reward you. [7]And when you pray, do not keep on babbling like pagans, for they think they will be heard because of their many words. [8]Do not be like them, for your Father knows what you need before you ask him.

[9]"This, then, is how you should pray:

" 'Our Father in heaven,
hallowed be your name,
[10]your kingdom come,
your will be done
on earth as it is in heaven.
[11]Give us today our daily bread.
[12]And forgive us our debts,
as we also have forgiven our debtors.
[13]And lead us not into temptation,[b]
but deliver us from the evil one.[c]'

---

[a]43 Lev. 19:18   [b]13 The Greek for *temptation* can also mean *testing*.   [c]13 Or *from evil*; some late manuscripts *one, / for yours is the kingdom and the power and the glory forever. Amen.*

[14]For if you forgive others when they sin against you, your heavenly Father will also forgive you. [15]But if you do not forgive others their sins, your Father will not forgive your sins.

Fasting

[16]"When you fast, do not look somber as the hypocrites do, for they disfigure their faces to show others they are fasting. Truly I tell you, they have received their reward in full. [17]But when you fast, put oil on your head and wash your face, [18]so that it will not be obvious to others that you are fasting, but only to your Father, who is unseen; and your Father, who sees what is done in secret, will reward you.

Treasures in Heaven

[19]"Do not store up for yourselves treasures on earth, where moth and rust destroy, and where thieves break in and steal. [20]But store up for yourselves treasures in heaven, where moth and rust do not destroy, and where thieves do not break in and steal. [21]For where your treasure is, there your heart will be also.

[22]"The eye is the lamp of the body. If your eyes are healthy,[a] your whole body will be full of light. [23]But if your eyes are unhealthy,[b] your whole body will be full of darkness. If then the light within you is darkness, how great is that darkness!

[24]"No one can be a loyal servant to two masters. Either you will hate the one and love the other, or you will be devoted to the one and despise the other. You cannot faithfully serve both God and Money.

Do Not Worry

[25]"Therefore I tell you, do not worry about your life, what you will eat or drink; or about your body, what you will wear. Is not life more important than food, and the body more important than clothes? [26]Look at the birds of the air; they do not sow or reap or store away in barns, and yet your heavenly Father feeds them. Are you not much more valuable than they? [27]Can any one of you by worrying add a single hour to your life[c]?

[28]"And why do you worry about clothes? See how the lilies of the field grow. They do not labor or spin. [29]Yet I tell you that not even Solomon in all his splendor was dressed like one of these. [30]If that is how God clothes the grass of the field, which is here today and tomorrow is thrown into the fire, will he not much more clothe you—you of little faith? [31]So do not worry, saying, 'What shall we eat?' or 'What shall we drink?' or 'What shall we wear?' [32]For the pagans run after all these things, and your heavenly Father knows that you need them. [33]But seek first his kingdom and his righteousness, and all these things will be given to you as well. [34]Therefore do not worry about tomorrow, for tomorrow will worry about itself. Each day has enough trouble of its own.

[a] 22　The Greek for *healthy* here implies *generous*.　　[b] 23　The Greek for *unhealthy* here implies *stingy*.
[c] 27　Or *single cubit to your height*

Judging Others

7 "Do not judge, or you too will be judged. 2For in the same way you judge others, you will be judged, and with the measure you use, it will be measured to you.

3"Why do you look at the speck of sawdust in someone else's eye and pay no attention to the plank in your own eye? 4How can you say, 'Let me take the speck out of your eye,' when all the time there is a plank in your own eye? 5You hypocrite, first take the plank out of your own eye, and then you will see clearly to remove the speck from the other person's eye.

6"Do not give dogs what is sacred; do not throw your pearls to pigs. If you do, they may trample them under their feet, and then turn and tear you to pieces.

Ask, Seek, Knock

7"Ask and it will be given to you; seek and you will find; knock and the door will be opened to you. 8For everyone who asks receives; those who seek find; and to those who knock, the door will be opened.

9"Which of you, if your son asks for bread, will give him a stone? 10Or if he asks for a fish, will give him a snake? 11If you, then, though you are evil, know how to give good gifts to your children, how much more will your Father in heaven give good gifts to those who ask him! 12So in everything, do to others what you would have them do to you, for this sums up the Law and the Prophets.

The Narrow and Wide Gates

13"Enter through the narrow gate. For wide is the gate and broad is the road that leads to destruction, and many enter through it. 14But small is the gate and narrow the road that leads to life, and only a few find it.

Warnings About False Prophets

15"Watch out for false prophets. They come to you in sheep's clothing, but inwardly they are ferocious wolves. 16By their fruit you will recognize them. Do people pick grapes from thorn bushes, or figs from thistles? 17Likewise, every good tree bears good fruit, but a bad tree bears bad fruit. 18A good tree cannot bear bad fruit, and a bad tree cannot bear good fruit. 19Every tree that does not bear good fruit is cut down and thrown into the fire. 20Thus, by their fruit you will recognize them.

21"Not everyone who says to me, 'Lord, Lord,' will enter the kingdom of heaven, but only those who do the will of my Father who is in heaven. 22Many will say to me on that day, 'Lord, Lord, did we not prophesy in your name and in your name drive out demons and in your name perform many miracles?' 23Then I will tell them plainly, 'I never knew you. Away from me, you evildoers!'

The Wise and Foolish Builders

24"Therefore everyone who hears these words of mine and puts them into practice is like a wise man who built his house on the rock. 25The rain came down, the streams rose, and the winds blew and beat against that house; yet it did not fall, because it had its foundation on the rock. 26But everyone who hears these words of mine and does not put them into practice is like a foolish man who built his house on sand. 27The rain came down, the streams rose, and the winds blew and beat against that house, and it fell with a great crash."

28When Jesus had finished saying these things, the crowds were amazed at his teaching, 29because he taught as one who had authority, and not as their teachers of the law.

Jesus Heals a Man With Leprosy

8 When he came down from the mountainside, large crowds followed him. 2A man with leprosy*a* came and knelt before him and said, "Lord, if you are willing, you can make me clean."

3Jesus reached out his hand and touched the man. "I am willing," he said. "Be clean!" Immediately he was cleansed of his leprosy. 4Then Jesus said to him, "See that you don't tell anyone. But go, show yourself to the priest and offer the gift Moses commanded, as a testimony to them."

The Faith of the Centurion

5When Jesus had entered Capernaum, a centurion came to him, asking for help. 6"Lord," he said, "my servant lies at home paralyzed, suffering terribly."

7Jesus said to him, "Shall I come and heal him?"

8The centurion replied, "Lord, I do not deserve to have you come under my roof. But just say the word, and my servant will be healed. 9For I myself am a man under authority, with soldiers under me. I tell this one, 'Go,' and he goes; and that one, 'Come,' and he comes. I say to my servant, 'Do this,' and he does it."

10When Jesus heard this, he was amazed and said to those following him, "Truly I tell you, I have not found anyone in Israel with such great faith. 11I say to you that many will come from the east and the west, and will take their places at the feast with Abraham, Isaac and Jacob in the kingdom of heaven. 12But the subjects of the kingdom will be thrown outside, into the darkness, where there will be weeping and gnashing of teeth."

13Then Jesus said to the centurion, "Go! Let it be done just as you believed it would." And his servant was healed at that very hour.

Jesus Heals Many

14When Jesus came into Peter's house, he saw Peter's mother-in-law lying in bed with a fever. 15He touched her hand and the fever left her, and she got up and began to wait on him.

16When evening came, many who were demon-possessed were brought to him, and he drove out the spirits with a word and healed all the sick. 17This was to fulfill what was spoken through the prophet Isaiah:

> "He took up our infirmities
>   and carried our diseases."*b*

---

a 2 The Greek word was used for various diseases affecting the skin—not necessarily leprosy.
b 17 Isaiah 53:4

The Cost of Following Jesus

18When Jesus saw the crowd around him, he gave orders to cross to the other side of the lake. 19Then a teacher of the law came to him and said, "Teacher, I will follow you wherever you go."

20Jesus replied, "Foxes have holes and birds have nests, but the Son of Man has no place to lay his head."

21Another disciple said to him, "Lord, first let me go and bury my father."

22But Jesus told him, "Follow me, and let the dead bury their own dead."

Jesus Calms the Storm

23Then he got into the boat and his disciples followed him. 24Suddenly a furious storm came up on the lake, so that the waves swept over the boat. But Jesus was sleeping. 25The disciples went and woke him, saying, "Lord, save us! We're going to drown!"

26He replied, "You of little faith, why are you so afraid?" Then he got up and rebuked the winds and the waves, and it was completely calm.

27The men were amazed and asked, "What kind of man is this? Even the winds and the waves obey him!"

Jesus Restores Two Demon-Possessed Men

28When he arrived at the other side in the region of the Gadarenes,*a* two demon-possessed men coming from the tombs met him. They were so violent that no one could pass that way. 29"What do you want with us, Son of God?" they shouted. "Have you come here to torture us before the appointed time?"

30Some distance from them a large herd of pigs was feeding. 31The demons begged Jesus, "If you drive us out, send us into the herd of pigs."

32He said to them, "Go!" So they came out and went into the pigs, and the whole herd rushed down the steep bank into the lake and died in the water. 33Those tending the pigs ran off, went into the town and reported all this, including what had happened to the demon-possessed men. 34Then the whole town went out to meet Jesus. And when they saw him, they pleaded with him to leave their region.

Jesus Forgives and Heals a Paralyzed Man

9 Jesus stepped into a boat, crossed over and came to his own town. 2Some men brought to him a paralyzed man, lying on a mat. When Jesus saw their faith, he said to the man, "Take heart, son; your sins are forgiven."

3At this, some of the teachers of the law said to themselves, "This fellow is blaspheming!"

4Knowing their thoughts, Jesus said, "Why do you entertain evil thoughts in your hearts? 5Which is easier: to say, 'Your sins are forgiven,' or to say, 'Get up and walk'? 6But I want you to know that the Son of Man has authority on earth to forgive sins." So he said to the paralyzed man, "Get up, take your mat and go home." 7Then the man got up and went home. 8When the crowd saw this, they were filled with awe; and they praised God, who had given such authority to human beings.

---

a 28 Some manuscripts *Gergesenes*; other manuscripts *Gerasenes*

The Calling of Matthew

⁹As Jesus went on from there, he saw a man named Matthew sitting at the tax collector's booth. "Follow me," he told him, and Matthew got up and followed him.

¹⁰While Jesus was having dinner at Matthew's house, many tax collectors and "sinners" came and ate with him and his disciples. ¹¹When the Pharisees saw this, they asked his disciples, "Why does your teacher eat with tax collectors and 'sinners'?"

¹²On hearing this, Jesus said, "It is not the healthy who need a doctor, but the sick. ¹³But go and learn what this means: 'I desire mercy, not sacrifice.'ᵃ For I have not come to call the righteous, but sinners."

Jesus Questioned About Fasting

¹⁴Then John's disciples came and asked him, "How is it that we and the Pharisees fast, but your disciples do not fast?"

¹⁵Jesus answered, "How can the guests of the bridegroom mourn while he is with them? The time will come when the bridegroom will be taken from them; then they will fast.

¹⁶"No one sews a patch of unshrunk cloth on an old garment, for the patch will pull away from the garment, making the tear worse. ¹⁷Neither do people pour new wine into old wineskins. If they do, the skins will burst, the wine will run out and the wineskins will be ruined. No, they pour new wine into new wineskins, and both are preserved."

Jesus Raises a Dead Girl and Heals a Sick Woman

¹⁸While he was saying this, a synagogue leader came and knelt before him and said, "My daughter has just died. But come and put your hand on her, and she will live." ¹⁹Jesus got up and went with him, and so did his disciples.

²⁰Just then a woman who had been subject to bleeding for twelve years came up behind him and touched the edge of his cloak. ²¹She said to herself, "If I only touch his cloak, I will be healed."

²²Jesus turned and saw her. "Take heart, daughter," he said, "your faith has healed you." And the woman was healed from that moment.

²³When Jesus entered the synagogue leader's house and saw the flute players and the noisy crowd, ²⁴he said, "Go away. The girl is not dead but asleep." But they laughed at him. ²⁵After the crowd had been put outside, he went in and took the girl by the hand, and she got up. ²⁶News of this spread through all that region.

Jesus Heals the Blind and Mute

²⁷As Jesus went on from there, two blind men followed him, calling out, "Have mercy on us, Son of David!"

²⁸When he had gone indoors, the blind men came to him, and he asked them, "Do you believe that I am able to do this?"

"Yes, Lord," they replied.

²⁹Then he touched their eyes and said, "According to your faith let it be

ᵃ 13 Hosea 6:6

done to you"; 30and their sight was restored. Jesus warned them sternly, "See that no one knows about this." 31But they went out and spread the news about him all over that region.

32While they were going out, a man who was demon-possessed and could not talk was brought to Jesus. 33And when the demon was driven out, the man who had been mute spoke. The crowd was amazed and said, "Nothing like this has ever been seen in Israel."

34But the Pharisees said, "It is by the prince of demons that he drives out demons."

The Workers Are Few

35Jesus went through all the towns and villages, teaching in their synagogues, proclaiming the good news of the kingdom and healing every disease and sickness. 36When he saw the crowds, he had compassion on them, because they were harassed and helpless, like sheep without a shepherd. 37Then he said to his disciples, "The harvest is plentiful but the workers are few. 38Ask the Lord of the harvest, therefore, to send out workers into his harvest field."

Jesus Sends Out the Twelve

10 He called his twelve disciples to him and gave them authority to drive out evil*a* spirits and to heal every disease and sickness.

2These are the names of the twelve apostles: first, Simon (who is called Peter) and his brother Andrew; James son of Zebedee, and his brother John; 3Philip and Bartholomew; Thomas and Matthew the tax collector; James son of Alphaeus, and Thaddaeus; 4Simon the Zealot and Judas Iscariot, who betrayed him.

5These twelve Jesus sent out with the following instructions: "Do not go among the Gentiles or enter any town of the Samaritans. 6Go rather to the lost sheep of Israel. 7As you go, proclaim this message: 'The kingdom of heaven has come near.' 8Heal the sick, raise the dead, cleanse those who have leprosy,*b* drive out demons. Freely you have received, freely give.

9"Do not get any gold or silver or copper to take with you in your belts— 10no bag for the journey or extra shirt or sandals or a staff, for workers are worth their keep. 11Whatever town or village you enter, search for some worthy person there and stay at that person's house until you leave. 12As you enter the home, give it your greeting. 13If the home is deserving, let your peace rest on it; if it is not, let your peace return to you. 14If anyone will not welcome you or listen to your words, shake the dust off your feet when you leave that home or town. 15Truly I tell you, it will be more bearable for Sodom and Gomorrah on the day of judgment than for that town.

16"I am sending you out like sheep among wolves. Therefore be as shrewd as snakes and as innocent as doves. 17Be on your guard; you will be handed over to the local councils and be flogged in the synagogues. 18On my account you will be brought before governors and kings as witnesses to them and to

a 1 Greek *unclean*   *b 8* The Greek word was used for various diseases affecting the skin—not necessarily leprosy.

the Gentiles. [19]But when they arrest you, do not worry about what to say or how to say it. At that time you will be given what to say, [20]for it will not be you speaking, but the Spirit of your Father speaking through you.

[21]"Brother will betray brother to death, and a father his child; children will rebel against their parents and have them put to death. [22]Everyone will hate you because of me, but those who stand firm to the end will be saved. [23]When you are persecuted in one place, flee to another. Truly I tell you, you will not finish going through the towns of Israel before the Son of Man comes.

[24]"Students are not above their teacher, nor servants above their master. [25]It is enough for students to be like their teacher, and servants like their master. If the head of the house has been called Beelzebul, how much more the members of his household!

[26]"So do not be afraid of them. There is nothing concealed that will not be disclosed, or hidden that will not be made known. [27]What I tell you in the dark, speak in the daylight; what is whispered in your ear, proclaim from the roofs. [28]Do not be afraid of those who kill the body but cannot kill the soul. Rather, be afraid of the One who can destroy both soul and body in hell. [29]Are not two sparrows sold for a penny? Yet not one of them will fall to the ground outside your Father's care.[a] [30]And even the very hairs of your head are all numbered. [31]So don't be afraid; you are worth more than many sparrows.

[32]"Whoever publicly acknowledges me I will also acknowledge before my Father in heaven. [33]But whoever publicly disowns me I will disown before my Father in heaven.

[34]"Do not suppose that I have come to bring peace to the earth. I did not come to bring peace, but a sword. [35]For I have come to turn

" 'a man against his father,
      a daughter against her mother,
   a daughter-in-law against her mother-in-law—
[36]   your enemies will be the members of your own household.'[b]

[37]"Anyone who loves their father or mother more than me is not worthy of me; anyone who loves a son or daughter more than me is not worthy of me. [38]Those who do not take up their cross and follow me are not worthy of me. [39]Those who find their life will lose it, and those who lose their life for my sake will find it.

[40]"Anyone who welcomes you welcomes me, and anyone who welcomes me welcomes the one who sent me. [41]Anyone who welcomes someone known to be a prophet will receive a prophet's reward, and anyone who welcomes someone known to be righteous will receive a righteous person's reward. [42]And if anyone gives even a cup of cold water to one of these little ones who is known to be my disciple, truly I tell you, that person will certainly be rewarded."

Jesus and John the Baptist

11 After Jesus had finished instructing his twelve disciples, he went on from there to teach and preach in the towns of Galilee.[c]

[a] 29 Greek *ground apart from your Father*   [b] 36 Micah 7:6   [c] 1 Greek *in their towns*

2When John heard in prison what the Messiah was doing, he sent his disciples 3to ask him, "Are you the one who was to come, or should we expect someone else?"

4Jesus replied, "Go back and report to John what you hear and see: 5The blind receive sight, the lame walk, those who have leprosy[a] are cleansed, the deaf hear, the dead are raised, and the good news is proclaimed to the poor. 6Blessed is anyone who does not stumble on account of me."

7As John's disciples were leaving, Jesus began to speak to the crowd about John: "What did you go out into the desert to see? A reed swayed by the wind? 8If not, what did you go out to see? A man dressed in fine clothes? No, those who wear fine clothes are in kings' palaces. 9Then what did you go out to see? A prophet? Yes, I tell you, and more than a prophet. 10This is the one about whom it is written:

> " 'I will send my messenger ahead of you,
>   who will prepare your way before you.'[b]

11Truly I tell you, among those born of women there has not risen anyone greater than John the Baptist; yet whoever is least in the kingdom of heaven is greater than he. 12From the days of John the Baptist until now, the kingdom of heaven has been subjected to violence,[c] and violent people have been raiding it. 13For all the Prophets and the Law prophesied until John. 14And if you are willing to accept it, he is the Elijah who was to come. 15Whoever has ears, let them hear.

16"To what can I compare this generation? They are like children sitting in the marketplaces and calling out to others:

> 17" 'We played the flute for you,
>   and you did not dance;
>   we sang a dirge,
>   and you did not mourn.'

18For John came neither eating nor drinking, and they say, 'He has a demon.' 19The Son of Man came eating and drinking, and they say, 'Here is a glutton and a drunkard, a friend of tax collectors and "sinners." ' But wisdom is proved right by her actions."

Woe on Unrepentant Towns

20Then Jesus began to denounce the towns in which most of his miracles had been performed, because they did not repent. 21"Woe to you, Korazin! Woe to you, Bethsaida! If the miracles that were performed in you had been performed in Tyre and Sidon, they would have repented long ago in sackcloth and ashes. 22But I tell you, it will be more bearable for Tyre and Sidon on the day of judgment than for you. 23And you, Capernaum, will you be lifted up to the skies? No, you will go down to the depths.[d] If the miracles that were performed in you had been performed in Sodom, it would have remained to

---

a 5 The Greek word was used for various diseases affecting the skin—not necessarily leprosy.
b 10 Mal. 3:1   c 12 Or been forcefully advancing   d 23 Greek Hades

this day. [24]But I tell you that it will be more bearable for Sodom on the day of judgment than for you."

The Father Revealed in the Son

[25]At that time Jesus said, "I praise you, Father, Lord of heaven and earth, because you have hidden these things from the wise and learned, and revealed them to little children. [26]Yes, Father, for this was your good pleasure.

[27]"All things have been committed to me by my Father. No one knows the Son except the Father, and no one knows the Father except the Son and those to whom the Son chooses to reveal him.

[28]"Come to me, all you who are weary and burdened, and I will give you rest. [29]Take my yoke upon you and learn from me, for I am gentle and humble in heart, and you will find rest for your souls. [30]For my yoke is easy and my burden is light."

Jesus Is Lord of the Sabbath

12 At that time Jesus went through the grainfields on the Sabbath. His disciples were hungry and began to pick some heads of grain and eat them. [2]When the Pharisees saw this, they said to him, "Look! Your disciples are doing what is unlawful on the Sabbath."

[3]He answered, "Haven't you read what David did when he and his companions were hungry? [4]He entered the house of God, and he and his companions ate the consecrated bread—which was not lawful for them to do, but only for the priests. [5]Or haven't you read in the Law that the priests on Sabbath duty in the temple desecrate the Sabbath and yet are innocent? [6]I tell you that one[a] greater than the temple is here. [7]If you had known what these words mean, 'I desire mercy, not sacrifice,'[b] you would not have condemned the innocent. [8]For the Son of Man is Lord of the Sabbath."

[9]Going on from that place, he went into their synagogue, [10]and a man with a shriveled hand was there. Looking for a reason to accuse Jesus, they asked him, "Is it lawful to heal on the Sabbath?"

[11]He said to them, "If any of you has a sheep and it falls into a pit on the Sabbath, will you not take hold of it and lift it out? [12]How much more valuable is a human being than a sheep! Therefore it is lawful to do good on the Sabbath."

[13]Then he said to the man, "Stretch out your hand." So he stretched it out and it was completely restored, just as sound as the other. [14]But the Pharisees went out and plotted how they might kill Jesus.

God's Chosen Servant

[15]Aware of this, Jesus withdrew from that place. A large crowd followed him, and he healed all who were ill. [16]He warned them not to tell others about him. [17]This was to fulfill what was spoken through the prophet Isaiah:

[18]"Here is my servant whom I have chosen,
    the one I love, in whom I delight;
I will put my Spirit on him,

a 6 Or *something*; also in verses 41 and 42   *b* 7 Hosea 6:6

and he will proclaim justice to the nations.
19 He will not quarrel or cry out;
no one will hear his voice in the streets.
20 A bruised reed he will not break,
and a smoldering wick he will not snuff out,
till he leads justice to victory.
21   In his name the nations will put their hope." *a*

Jesus and Beelzebul

22Then they brought him a demon-possessed man who was blind and mute, and Jesus healed him, so that he could both talk and see. 23All the people were astonished and said, "Could this be the Son of David?"

24But when the Pharisees heard this, they said, "It is only by Beelzebul, the prince of demons, that this fellow drives out demons."

25Jesus knew their thoughts and said to them, "Every kingdom divided against itself will be ruined, and every city or household divided against itself will not stand. 26If Satan drives out Satan, he is divided against himself. How then can his kingdom stand? 27And if I drive out demons by Beelzebul, by whom do your people drive them out? So then, they will be your judges. 28But if it is by the Spirit of God that I drive out demons, then the kingdom of God has come upon you.

29"Or again, how can anyone enter a strong man's house and carry off his possessions without first tying up the strong man? Then his house can be plundered.

30"Whoever is not with me is against me, and whoever does not gather with me scatters. 31And so I tell you, people will be forgiven every sin and blasphemy. But blasphemy against the Spirit will not be forgiven. 32Anyone who speaks a word against the Son of Man will be forgiven, but anyone who speaks against the Holy Spirit will not be forgiven, either in this age or in the age to come.

33"Make a tree good and its fruit will be good, or make a tree bad and its fruit will be bad, for a tree is recognized by its fruit. 34You brood of vipers, how can you who are evil say anything good? For out of the overflow of the heart the mouth speaks. 35Good people bring good things out of the good stored up in them, and evil people bring evil things out of the evil stored up in them. 36But I tell you that people will have to give account on the day of judgment for every empty word they have spoken. 37For by your words you will be acquitted, and by your words you will be condemned."

The Sign of Jonah

38Then some of the Pharisees and teachers of the law said to him, "Teacher, we want to see a sign from you."

39He answered, "A wicked and adulterous generation asks for a sign! But none will be given it except the sign of the prophet Jonah. 40For as Jonah was three days and three nights in the belly of a huge fish, so the Son of Man will be three days and three nights in the heart of the earth. 41The people of

a 21 Isaiah 42:1–4

Nineveh will stand up at the judgment with this generation and condemn it; for they repented at the preaching of Jonah, and now one*[a]* greater than Jonah is here. [42]The Queen of the South will rise at the judgment with this generation and condemn it; for she came from the ends of the earth to listen to Solomon's wisdom, and now one greater than Solomon is here.

[43]"When an evil*[b]* spirit comes out of anyone, it goes through arid places seeking rest and does not find it. [44]Then it says, 'I will return to the house I left.' When it arrives, it finds the house unoccupied, swept clean and put in order. [45]Then it goes and takes with it seven other spirits more wicked than itself, and they go in and live there. And the final condition of that person is worse than the first. That is how it will be with this wicked generation."

Jesus' Mother and Brothers

[46]While Jesus was still talking to the crowd, his mother and brothers stood outside, wanting to speak to him. [47]Someone told him, "Your mother and brothers are standing outside, wanting to speak to you."*[c]*

[48]He replied to him, "Who is my mother, and who are my brothers?" [49]Pointing to his disciples, he said, "Here are my mother and my brothers. [50]For whoever does the will of my Father in heaven is my brother and sister and mother."

The Parable of the Sower

13 That same day Jesus went out of the house and sat by the lake. [2]Such large crowds gathered around him that he got into a boat and sat in it, while all the people stood on the shore. [3]Then he told them many things in parables, saying: "A farmer went out to sow his seed. [4]As he was scattering the seed, some fell along the path, and the birds came and ate it up. [5]Some fell on rocky places, where it did not have much soil. It sprang up quickly, because the soil was shallow. [6]But when the sun came up, the plants were scorched, and they withered because they had no root. [7]Other seed fell among thorns, which grew up and choked the plants. [8]Still other seed fell on good soil, where it produced a crop—a hundred, sixty or thirty times what was sown. [9]Whoever has ears, let them hear."

[10]The disciples came to him and asked, "Why do you speak to the people in parables?"

[11]He replied, "The knowledge of the secrets of the kingdom of heaven has been given to you, but not to them. [12]Those who have will be given more, and they will have an abundance. As for those who do not have, even what they have will be taken from them. [13]This is why I speak to them in parables:

"Though seeing, they do not see;
   though hearing, they do not hear or understand.

[14]In them is fulfilled the prophecy of Isaiah:

" 'You will be ever hearing but never understanding;
   you will be ever seeing but never perceiving.

---

[a] 41 Or something; also in verse 42   [b] 43 Greek unclean   [c] 47 Some manuscripts do not have verse 47.

15 For this people's heart has become calloused;
   they hardly hear with their ears,
   and they have closed their eyes.
Otherwise they might see with their eyes,
   hear with their ears,
   understand with their hearts
and turn, and I would heal them.'[a]

16 But blessed are your eyes because they see, and your ears because they hear. 17 Truly I tell you, many prophets and righteous people longed to see what you see but did not see it, and to hear what you hear but did not hear it.

18 "Listen then to what the parable of the sower means: 19 When people hear the message about the kingdom and do not understand it, the evil one comes and snatches away what was sown in their hearts. This is the seed sown along the path. 20 The seed falling on rocky ground refers to people who hear the word and at once receive it with joy. 21 But since they have no root, they last only a short time. When trouble or persecution comes because of the word, they quickly fall away. 22 The seed falling among the thorns refers to people who hear the word, but the worries of this life and the deceitfulness of wealth choke the word, making it unfruitful. 23 But the seed falling on good soil refers to people who hear the word and understand it. They produce a crop, yielding a hundred, sixty or thirty times what was sown."

The Parable of the Weeds

24 Jesus told them another parable: "The kingdom of heaven is like a man who sowed good seed in his field. 25 But while everyone was sleeping, his enemy came and sowed weeds among the wheat, and went away. 26 When the wheat sprouted and formed heads, then the weeds also appeared.

27 "The owner's servants came to him and said, 'Sir, didn't you sow good seed in your field? Where then did the weeds come from?'

28 " 'An enemy did this,' he replied.

"The servants asked him, 'Do you want us to go and pull them up?'

29 " 'No,' he answered, 'because while you are pulling the weeds, you may root up the wheat with them. 30 Let both grow together until the harvest. At that time I will tell the harvesters: First collect the weeds and tie them in bundles to be burned; then gather the wheat and bring it into my barn.' "

The Parables of the Mustard Seed and the Yeast

31 He told them another parable: "The kingdom of heaven is like a mustard seed, which a man took and planted in his field. 32 Though it is the smallest of all seeds, yet when it grows, it is the largest of garden plants and becomes a tree, so that the birds come and perch in its branches."

33 He told them still another parable: "The kingdom of heaven is like yeast that a woman took and mixed into about eighteen pounds[b] of flour until it worked all through the dough."

34 Jesus spoke all these things to the crowd in parables; he did not say any-

---

[a] 15 Isaiah 6:9,10   [b] 33 About 8 kilograms

thing to them without using a parable. [35]So was fulfilled what was spoken through the prophet:

"I will open my mouth in parables,
I will utter things hidden since the creation of the world."[a]

The Parable of the Weeds Explained

[36]Then he left the crowd and went into the house. His disciples came to him and said, "Explain to us the parable of the weeds in the field."

[37]He answered, "The one who sowed the good seed is the Son of Man. [38]The field is the world, and the good seed stands for the people of the kingdom. The weeds are the people of the evil one, [39]and the enemy who sows them is the devil. The harvest is the end of the age, and the harvesters are angels.

[40]"As the weeds are pulled up and burned in the fire, so it will be at the end of the age. [41]The Son of Man will send out his angels, and they will weed out of his kingdom everything that causes sin and all who do evil. [42]They will throw them into the blazing furnace, where there will be weeping and gnashing of teeth. [43]Then the righteous will shine like the sun in the kingdom of their Father. Whoever has ears, let them hear.

The Parables of the Hidden Treasure and the Pearl

[44]"The kingdom of heaven is like treasure hidden in a field. When a man found it, he hid it again, and then in his joy went and sold all he had and bought that field.

[45]"Again, the kingdom of heaven is like a merchant looking for fine pearls. [46]When he found one of great value, he went away and sold everything he had and bought it.

The Parable of the Net

[47]"Once again, the kingdom of heaven is like a net that was let down into the lake and caught all kinds of fish. [48]When it was full, the fishermen pulled it up on the shore. Then they sat down and collected the good fish in baskets, but threw the bad away. [49]This is how it will be at the end of the age. The angels will come and separate the wicked from the righteous [50]and throw them into the blazing furnace, where there will be weeping and gnashing of teeth.

[51]"Have you understood all these things?" Jesus asked.

"Yes," they replied.

[52]He said to them, "Therefore every teacher of the law who has been instructed about the kingdom of heaven is like the owner of a house who brings out of his storeroom new treasures as well as old."

A Prophet Without Honor

[53]When Jesus had finished these parables, he moved on from there. [54]Coming to his hometown, he began teaching the people in their synagogue, and they were amazed. "Where did this man get this wisdom and these miraculous powers?" they asked. [55]"Isn't this the carpenter's son? Isn't his mother's name Mary, and aren't his brothers James, Joseph, Simon and Judas? [56]Aren't

---

[a] 35 Psalm 78:2

all his sisters with us? Where then did this man get all these things?" 57And they took offense at him.

But Jesus said to them, "Only in their own towns and in their own homes are prophets without honor."

58And he did not do many miracles there because of their lack of faith.

John the Baptist Beheaded

14 At that time Herod the tetrarch heard the reports about Jesus, 2and he said to his attendants, "This is John the Baptist; he has risen from the dead! That is why miraculous powers are at work in him."

3Now Herod had arrested John and bound him and put him in prison because of Herodias, his brother Philip's wife, 4for John had been saying to him: "It is not lawful for you to have her." 5Herod wanted to kill John, but he was afraid of the people, because they considered him a prophet.

6On Herod's birthday the daughter of Herodias danced for them and pleased Herod so much 7that he promised with an oath to give her whatever she asked. 8Prompted by her mother, she said, "Give me here on a platter the head of John the Baptist." 9The king was distressed, but because of his oaths and his dinner guests, he ordered that her request be granted 10and had John beheaded in the prison. 11His head was brought in on a platter and given to the girl, who carried it to her mother. 12John's disciples came and took his body and buried it. Then they went and told Jesus.

Jesus Feeds the Five Thousand

13When Jesus heard what had happened, he withdrew by boat privately to a solitary place. Hearing of this, the crowds followed him on foot from the towns. 14When Jesus landed and saw a large crowd, he had compassion on them and healed their sick.

15As evening approached, the disciples came to him and said, "This is a remote place, and it's already getting late. Send the crowds away, so they can go to the villages and buy themselves some food."

16Jesus replied, "They do not need to go away. You give them something to eat."

17"We have here only five loaves of bread and two fish," they answered.

18"Bring them here to me," he said. 19And he directed the people to sit down on the grass. Taking the five loaves and the two fish and looking up to heaven, he gave thanks and broke the loaves. Then he gave them to the disciples, and the disciples gave them to the people. 20They all ate and were satisfied, and the disciples picked up twelve basketfuls of broken pieces that were left over. 21The number of those who ate was about five thousand men, besides women and children.

Jesus Walks on the Water

22Immediately Jesus made the disciples get into the boat and go on ahead of him to the other side, while he dismissed the crowd. 23After he had dismissed them, he went up on a mountainside by himself to pray. When evening came, he was there alone, 24but the boat was already a considerable distance from land, buffeted by the waves because the wind was against it.

²⁵Shortly before dawn Jesus went out to them, walking on the lake. ²⁶When the disciples saw him walking on the lake, they were terrified. "It's a ghost," they said, and cried out in fear.

²⁷But Jesus immediately said to them: "Take courage! It is I. Don't be afraid."

²⁸"Lord, if it's you," Peter replied, "tell me to come to you on the water."

²⁹"Come," he said.

Then Peter got down out of the boat, walked on the water and came toward Jesus. ³⁰But when he saw the wind, he was afraid and, beginning to sink, cried out, "Lord, save me!"

³¹Immediately Jesus reached out his hand and caught him. "You of little faith," he said, "why did you doubt?"

³²And when they climbed into the boat, the wind died down. ³³Then those who were in the boat worshiped him, saying, "Truly you are the Son of God."

³⁴When they had crossed over, they landed at Gennesaret. ³⁵And when the men of that place recognized Jesus, they sent word to all the surrounding country. People brought all their sick to him ³⁶and begged him to let the sick just touch the edge of his cloak, and all who touched him were healed.

That Which Defiles You

15 Then some Pharisees and teachers of the law came to Jesus from Jerusalem and asked, ²"Why do your disciples break the tradition of the elders? They don't wash their hands before they eat!"

³Jesus replied, "And why do you break the command of God for the sake of your tradition? ⁴For God said, 'Honor your father and mother'ᵃ and 'Anyone who curses their father or mother must be put to death.'ᵇ ⁵But you say that if anyone declares that what might have been used to help their father or mother is 'devoted to God,' ⁶they are not to 'honor their father or mother' with it. Thus you nullify the word of God for the sake of your tradition. ⁷You hypocrites! Isaiah was right when he prophesied about you:

⁸" 'These people honor me with their lips,
    but their hearts are far from me.
⁹They worship me in vain;
    their teachings are merely human rules.'ᶜ"

¹⁰Jesus called the crowd to him and said, "Listen and understand. ¹¹What goes into your mouth does not defile you, but what comes out of your mouth, that is what defiles you."

¹²Then the disciples came to him and asked, "Do you know that the Pharisees were offended when they heard this?"

¹³He replied, "Every plant that my heavenly Father has not planted will be pulled up by the roots. ¹⁴Leave them; they are blind guides.ᵈ If the blind lead the blind, both will fall into a pit."

¹⁵Peter said, "Explain the parable to us."

¹⁶"Are you still so dull?" Jesus asked them. ¹⁷"Don't you see that whatever

---

ᵃ4 Exodus 20:12; Deut. 5:16   ᵇ4 Exodus 21:17; Lev. 20:9   ᶜ9 Isaiah 29:13   ᵈ14 Some manuscripts *blind guides of the blind*

enters the mouth goes into the stomach and then out of the body? 18But the things that come out of the mouth come from the heart, and these defile you. 19For out of the heart come evil thoughts, murder, adultery, sexual immorality, theft, false testimony, slander. 20These are what defile you; but eating with unwashed hands does not defile you."

The Faith of the Canaanite Woman

21Leaving that place, Jesus withdrew to the region of Tyre and Sidon. 22A Canaanite woman from that vicinity came to him, crying out, "Lord, Son of David, have mercy on me! My daughter is demon-possessed and suffering terribly."

23Jesus did not answer a word. So his disciples came to him and urged him, "Send her away, for she keeps crying out after us."

24He answered, "I was sent only to the lost sheep of Israel."

25The woman came and knelt before him. "Lord, help me!" she said.

26He replied, "It is not right to take the children's bread and toss it to the dogs."

27"Yes it is, Lord," she said. "Even the dogs eat the crumbs that fall from their master's table."

28Then Jesus said to her, "You have great faith! Your request is granted." And her daughter was healed from that very hour.

Jesus Feeds the Four Thousand

29Jesus left there and went along the Sea of Galilee. Then he went up on a mountainside and sat down. 30Great crowds came to him, bringing the lame, the blind, the crippled, the mute and many others, and laid them at his feet; and he healed them. 31The people were amazed when they saw the mute speaking, the crippled made well, the lame walking and the blind seeing. And they praised the God of Israel.

32Jesus called his disciples to him and said, "I have compassion for these people; they have already been with me three days and have nothing to eat. I do not want to send them away hungry, or they may collapse on the way."

33His disciples answered, "Where could we get enough bread in this remote place to feed such a crowd?"

34"How many loaves do you have?" Jesus asked.

"Seven," they replied, "and a few small fish."

35He told the crowd to sit down on the ground. 36Then he took the seven loaves and the fish, and when he had given thanks, he broke them and gave them to the disciples, and they in turn to the people. 37They all ate and were satisfied. Afterward the disciples picked up seven basketfuls of broken pieces that were left over. 38The number of those who ate was four thousand men, besides women and children. 39After Jesus had sent the crowd away, he got into the boat and went to the vicinity of Magadan.

The Demand for a Sign

16 The Pharisees and Sadducees came to Jesus and tested him by asking him to show them a sign from heaven.

²He replied,ᵃ "When evening comes, you say, 'It will be fair weather, for the sky is red,' ³and in the morning, 'Today it will be stormy, for the sky is red and overcast.' You know how to interpret the appearance of the sky, but you cannot interpret the signs of the times. ⁴A wicked and adulterous generation looks for a sign, but none will be given it except the sign of Jonah." Jesus then left them and went away.

The Yeast of the Pharisees and Sadducees

⁵When they went across the lake, the disciples forgot to take bread. ⁶"Be careful," Jesus said to them. "Be on your guard against the yeast of the Pharisees and Sadducees."

⁷They discussed this among themselves and said, "It is because we didn't bring any bread."

⁸Aware of their discussion, Jesus asked, "You of little faith, why are you talking among yourselves about having no bread? ⁹Do you still not understand? Don't you remember the five loaves for the five thousand, and how many basketfuls you gathered? ¹⁰Or the seven loaves for the four thousand, and how many basketfuls you gathered? ¹¹How is it you don't understand that I was not talking to you about bread? But be on your guard against the yeast of the Pharisees and Sadducees." ¹²Then they understood that he was not telling them to guard against the yeast used in bread, but against the teaching of the Pharisees and Sadducees.

Peter Declares That Jesus Is the Messiah

¹³When Jesus came to the region of Caesarea Philippi, he asked his disciples, "Who do people say the Son of Man is?"

¹⁴They replied, "Some say John the Baptist; others say Elijah; and still others, Jeremiah or one of the prophets."

¹⁵"But what about you?" he asked. "Who do you say I am?"

¹⁶Simon Peter answered, "You are the Messiah, the Son of the living God."

¹⁷Jesus replied, "Blessed are you, Simon son of Jonah, for this was not revealed to you by flesh and blood, but by my Father in heaven. ¹⁸And I tell you that you are Peter,ᵇ and on this rock I will build my church, and the gates of deathᶜ will not overcome it. ¹⁹I will give you the keys of the kingdom of heaven; whatever you bind on earth will beᵈ bound in heaven, and whatever you loose on earth will beᵈ loosed in heaven." ²⁰Then he warned his disciples not to tell anyone that he was the Messiah.

Jesus Predicts His Death

²¹From that time on Jesus began to explain to his disciples that he must go to Jerusalem and suffer many things at the hands of the elders, the chief priests and the teachers of the law, and that he must be killed and on the third day be raised to life.

²²Peter took him aside and began to rebuke him. "Never, Lord!" he said. "This shall never happen to you!"

ᵃ2 Some early manuscripts do not have the rest of verse 2 and all of verse 3.   ᵇ18 *Peter* means rock.   ᶜ18 Greek *Hades*   ᵈ19 Or *have been*

²³Jesus turned and said to Peter, "Get behind me, Satan! You are a stumbling block to me; you do not have in mind the concerns of God, but merely human concerns."

²⁴Then Jesus said to his disciples, "Those who want to be my disciples must deny themselves and take up their cross and follow me. ²⁵For those who want to save their life^a will lose it, but those who lose their life for me will find it. ²⁶What good will it be for you to gain the whole world, yet forfeit your soul? Or what can you give in exchange for your soul? ²⁷For the Son of Man is going to come in his Father's glory with his angels, and then he will reward everyone according to what they have done. ²⁸Truly I tell you, some who are standing here will not taste death before they see the Son of Man coming in his kingdom."

The Transfiguration

17 After six days Jesus took with him Peter, James and John the brother of James, and led them up a high mountain by themselves. ²There he was transfigured before them. His face shone like the sun, and his clothes became as white as the light. ³Just then there appeared before them Moses and Elijah, talking with Jesus.

⁴Peter said to Jesus, "Lord, it is good for us to be here. If you wish, I will put up three shelters—one for you, one for Moses and one for Elijah."

⁵While he was still speaking, a bright cloud covered them, and a voice from the cloud said, "This is my Son, whom I love; with him I am well pleased. Listen to him!"

⁶When the disciples heard this, they fell facedown to the ground, terrified. ⁷But Jesus came and touched them. "Get up," he said. "Don't be afraid." ⁸When they looked up, they saw no one except Jesus.

⁹As they were coming down the mountain, Jesus instructed them, "Don't tell anyone what you have seen, until the Son of Man has been raised from the dead."

¹⁰The disciples asked him, "Why then do the teachers of the law say that Elijah must come first?"

¹¹Jesus replied, "To be sure, Elijah comes and will restore all things. ¹²But I tell you, Elijah has already come, and they did not recognize him, but have done to him everything they wished. In the same way the Son of Man is going to suffer at their hands." ¹³Then the disciples understood that he was talking to them about John the Baptist.

Jesus Heals a Demon-Possessed Boy

¹⁴When they came to the crowd, a man approached Jesus and knelt before him. ¹⁵"Lord, have mercy on my son," he said. "He has seizures and is suffering greatly. He often falls into the fire or into the water. ¹⁶I brought him to your disciples, but they could not heal him."

¹⁷"You unbelieving and perverse generation," Jesus replied, "how long shall I stay with you? How long shall I put up with you? Bring the boy here

---

^a 25 The Greek word means either *life* or *soul*; also in verse 26.

to me." ¹⁸Jesus rebuked the demon, and it came out of the boy, and he was healed from that moment.

¹⁹Then the disciples came to Jesus in private and asked, "Why couldn't we drive it out?"

²⁰[²¹]He replied, "Because you have so little faith. Truly I tell you, if you have faith as small as a mustard seed, you can say to this mountain, 'Move from here to there' and it will move. Nothing will be impossible for you."

Jesus Predicts His Death a Second Time

²²When they came together in Galilee, he said to them, "The Son of Man is going to be delivered over to human hands. ²³He will be killed, and on the third day he will be raised to life." And the disciples were filled with grief.

The Temple Tax

²⁴After Jesus and his disciples arrived in Capernaum, the collectors of the two-drachma temple tax came to Peter and asked, "Doesn't your teacher pay the temple tax?"

²⁵"Yes, he does," he replied.

When Peter came into the house, Jesus was the first to speak. "What do you think, Simon?" he asked. "From whom do the kings of the earth collect duty and taxes—from their own children or from others?"

²⁶"From others," Peter answered.

"Then the children are exempt," Jesus said to him. ²⁷"But so that we may not offend them, go to the lake and throw out your line. Take the first fish you catch; open its mouth and you will find a four-drachma coin. Take it and give it to them for my tax and yours."

The Greatest in the Kingdom of Heaven

18 At that time the disciples came to Jesus and asked, "Who, then, is the greatest in the kingdom of heaven?"

²He called a little child whom he placed among them. ³And he said: "Truly I tell you, unless you change and become like little children, you will never enter the kingdom of heaven. ⁴Therefore, whoever takes a humble place—becoming like this child—is the greatest in the kingdom of heaven. ⁵And whoever welcomes one such child in my name welcomes me.

Causing to Stumble

⁶"If anyone causes one of these little ones—those who believe in me—to stumble, it would be better for them if a large millstone were hung around their neck and they were drowned in the depths of the sea. ⁷Woe to the world because of the things that cause people to stumble! Such things must come, but woe to the person through whom they come! ⁸If your hand or your foot causes you to stumble, cut it off and throw it away. It is better for you to enter life maimed or crippled than to have two hands or two feet and be thrown into eternal fire. ⁹And if your eye causes you to stumble, gouge it out and throw it away. It is better for you to enter life with one eye than to have two eyes and be thrown into the fire of hell.

The Parable of the Wandering Sheep

10[11]"See that you do not despise one of these little ones. For I tell you that their angels in heaven always see the face of my Father in heaven.

12"What do you think? If a man owns a hundred sheep, and one of them wanders away, will he not leave the ninety-nine on the hills and go to look for the one that wandered off? 13And if he finds it, truly I tell you, he is happier about that one sheep than about the ninety-nine that did not wander off. 14In the same way your Father in heaven is not willing that any of these little ones should perish.

Dealing With Sin in the Church

15"If a brother or sister sins,*a* go and point out the fault, just between the two of you alone. If they listen to you, you have won them over. 16But if they will not listen, take one or two others along, so that 'every matter may be established by the testimony of two or three witnesses.'*b* 17If they refuse to listen to them, tell it to the church; and if they refuse to listen even to the church, treat them as you would a pagan or a tax collector.

18"Truly I tell you, whatever you bind on earth will be*c* bound in heaven, and whatever you loose on earth will be*c* loosed in heaven.

19"Again, I tell you that if two of you on earth agree about anything you ask for, it will be done for you by my Father in heaven. 20For where two or three come together in my name, there am I with them."

The Parable of the Unmerciful Servant

21Then Peter came to Jesus and asked, "Lord, how many times shall I forgive someone who sins against me? Up to seven times?"

22Jesus answered, "I tell you, not seven times, but seventy-seven times.*d*

23"Therefore, the kingdom of heaven is like a king who wanted to settle accounts with his servants. 24As he began the settlement, a man who owed him billions of dollars*e* was brought to him. 25Since he was not able to pay, the master ordered that he and his wife and his children and all that he had be sold to repay the debt.

26"The servant fell on his knees before him. 'Be patient with me,' he begged, 'and I will pay back everything.' 27The servant's master took pity on him, canceled the debt and let him go.

28"But when that servant went out, he found one of his fellow servants who owed him a few hundred dollars.*f* He grabbed him and began to choke him. 'Pay back what you owe me!' he demanded.

29"His fellow servant fell to his knees and begged him, 'Be patient with me, and I will pay you back.'

30"But he refused. Instead, he went off and had the man thrown into prison until he could pay the debt. 31When the other servants saw what had happened, they were greatly distressed and went and told their master everything that had happened.

---

a 15 Some manuscripts *sins against you* *b* 16 Deut. 19:15 *c* 18 Or *have been* *d* 22 Or *seventy times seven* *e* 24 Greek *ten thousand talents*; a talent was worth about 20 years of a day laborer's wages. *f* 28 Greek *a hundred denarii*; a denarius was the daily wage of a day laborer (see Matt. 20:2).

32"Then the master called the servant in. 'You wicked servant,' he said, 'I canceled all that debt of yours because you begged me to. 33Shouldn't you have had mercy on your fellow servant just as I had on you?' 34In anger his master handed him over to the jailers to be tortured, until he should pay back all he owed.

35"This is how my heavenly Father will treat each of you unless you forgive a brother or sister from your heart."

Divorce

19 When Jesus had finished saying these things, he left Galilee and went into the region of Judea to the other side of the Jordan. 2Large crowds followed him, and he healed them there.

3Some Pharisees came to him to test him. They asked, "Is it lawful for a man to divorce his wife for any and every reason?"

4"Haven't you read," he replied, "that at the beginning the Creator 'made them male and female,'*a* 5and said, 'For this reason a man will leave his father and mother and be united to his wife, and the two will become one flesh'*b*? 6So they are no longer two, but one. Therefore what God has joined together, let no one separate."

7"Why then," they asked, "did Moses command that a man give his wife a certificate of divorce and send her away?"

8Jesus replied, "Moses permitted you to divorce your wives because your hearts were hard. But it was not this way from the beginning. 9I tell you that anyone who divorces his wife, except for sexual immorality, and marries another woman commits adultery."

10The disciples said to him, "If this is the situation between a husband and wife, it is better not to marry."

11Jesus replied, "Not everyone can accept this word, but only those to whom it has been given. 12For some are eunuchs because they were born that way; others have been made eunuchs; and others have renounced marriage*c* because of the kingdom of heaven. The one who can accept this should accept it."

The Little Children and Jesus

13Then people brought little children to Jesus for him to place his hands on them and pray for them. But the disciples rebuked them.

14Jesus said, "Let the little children come to me, and do not hinder them, for the kingdom of heaven belongs to such as these." 15When he had placed his hands on them, he went on from there.

The Rich and the Kingdom of God

16Just then a man came up to Jesus and asked, "Teacher, what good thing must I do to get eternal life?"

17"Why do you ask me about what is good?" Jesus replied. "There is only One who is good. If you want to enter life, keep the commandments."

18"Which ones?" he inquired.

a 4 Gen. 1:27   *b* 5 Gen. 2:24   *c* 12 Or *have made themselves eunuchs*

Jesus replied, " 'Do not murder, do not commit adultery, do not steal, do not give false testimony, 19honor your father and mother,'a and 'love your neighbor as yourself.'b"

20"All these I have kept," the young man said. "What do I still lack?"

21Jesus answered, "If you want to be perfect, go, sell your possessions and give to the poor, and you will have treasure in heaven. Then come, follow me."

22When the young man heard this, he went away sad, because he had great wealth.

23Then Jesus said to his disciples, "Truly I tell you, it is hard for the rich to enter the kingdom of heaven. 24Again I tell you, it is easier for a camel to go through the eye of a needle than for the rich to enter the kingdom of God."

25When the disciples heard this, they were greatly astonished and asked, "Who then can be saved?"

26Jesus looked at them and said, "With people this is impossible, but with God all things are possible."

27Peter answered him, "We have left everything to follow you! What then will there be for us?"

28Jesus said to them, "Truly I tell you, at the renewal of all things, when the Son of Man sits on his glorious throne, you who have followed me will also sit on twelve thrones, judging the twelve tribes of Israel. 29And everyone who has left houses or brothers or sisters or father or motherc or children or fields for my sake will receive a hundred times as much and will inherit eternal life. 30But many who are first will be last, and many who are last will be first.

The Parable of the Workers in the Vineyard

20 "For the kingdom of heaven is like a landowner who went out early in the morning to hire workers for his vineyard. 2He agreed to pay them a denarius for the day and sent them into his vineyard.

3"About nine in the morning he went out and saw others standing in the marketplace doing nothing. 4He told them, 'You also go and work in my vineyard, and I will pay you whatever is right.' 5So they went.

"He went out again about noon and about three in the afternoon and did the same thing. 6About five in the afternoon he went out and found still others standing around. He asked them, 'Why have you been standing here all day long doing nothing?'

7" 'Because no one has hired us,' they answered.

"He said to them, 'You also go and work in my vineyard.'

8"When evening came, the owner of the vineyard said to his supervisor, 'Call the workers and pay them their wages, beginning with the last ones hired and going on to the first.'

9"The workers who were hired about five in the afternoon came and each received a denarius. 10So when those came who were hired first, they expected to receive more. But each one of them also received a denarius. 11When they received it, they began to grumble against the landowner. 12'These men

a 19 Exodus 20:12–16; Deut. 5:16–20   b 19 Lev. 19:18   c 29 Some manuscripts mother or wife who were hired last worked only one hour,' they said, 'and you have made them equal to us who have borne the burden of the work and the heat of the day.'

13"But he answered one of them, 'Friend, I am not being unfair to you. Didn't you agree to work for a denarius? 14Take your pay and go. I want to give the one who was hired last the same as I gave you. 15Don't I have the right to do what I want with my own money? Or are you envious because I am generous?'

16"So the last will be first, and the first will be last."

Jesus Predicts His Death a Third Time

17Now Jesus was going up to Jerusalem. On the way, he took the twelve disciples aside and said to them, 18"We are going up to Jerusalem, and the Son of Man will be delivered over to the chief priests and the teachers of the law. They will condemn him to death 19and will hand him over to the Gentiles to be mocked and flogged and crucified. On the third day he will be raised to life!"

A Mother's Request

20Then the mother of Zebedee's sons came to Jesus with her sons and, kneeling down, asked a favor of him.

21"What is it you want?" he asked.

She said, "Grant that one of these two sons of mine may sit at your right and the other at your left in your kingdom."

22"You don't know what you are asking," Jesus said to them. "Can you drink the cup I am going to drink?"

"We can," they answered.

23Jesus said to them, "You will indeed drink from my cup, but to sit at my right or left is not for me to grant. These places belong to those for whom they have been prepared by my Father."

24When the ten heard about this, they were indignant with the two brothers. 25Jesus called them together and said, "You know that the rulers of the Gentiles lord it over them, and their high officials exercise authority over them. 26Not so with you. Instead, whoever wants to become great among you must be your servant, 27and whoever wants to be first must be your slave— 28just as the Son of Man did not come to be served, but to serve, and to give his life as a ransom for many."

Two Blind Men Receive Sight

29As Jesus and his disciples were leaving Jericho, a large crowd followed him. 30Two blind men were sitting by the roadside, and when they heard that Jesus was going by, they shouted, "Lord, Son of David, have mercy on us!"

31The crowd rebuked them and told them to be quiet, but they shouted all the louder, "Lord, Son of David, have mercy on us!"

32Jesus stopped and called them. "What do you want me to do for you?" he asked.

33"Lord," they answered, "we want our sight."

34Jesus had compassion on them and touched their eyes. Immediately they received their sight and followed him.

Jesus Comes to Jerusalem as King

21 As they approached Jerusalem and came to Bethphage on the Mount of Olives, Jesus sent two disciples, ²saying to them, "Go to the village ahead of you, and at once you will find a donkey tied there, with her colt by her. Untie them and bring them to me. ³If anyone says anything to you, say that the Lord needs them, and he will send them right away."

⁴This took place to fulfill what was spoken through the prophet:

> ⁵"Say to Daughter Zion,
> 'See, your king comes to you,
> gentle and riding on a donkey,
> and on a colt, the foal of a donkey.' "*ª*

⁶The disciples went and did as Jesus had instructed them. ⁷They brought the donkey and the colt and placed their cloaks on them for Jesus to sit on. ⁸A very large crowd spread their cloaks on the road, while others cut branches from the trees and spread them on the road. ⁹The crowds that went ahead of him and those that followed shouted,

> "Hosanna*ᵇ* to the Son of David!"

> "Blessed is he who comes in the name of the Lord!"*ᶜ*

> "Hosanna*ᵇ* in the highest heaven!"

¹⁰When Jesus entered Jerusalem, the whole city was stirred and asked, "Who is this?"

¹¹The crowds answered, "This is Jesus, the prophet from Nazareth in Galilee."

Jesus at the Temple

¹²Jesus entered the temple courts and drove out all who were buying and selling there. He overturned the tables of the money changers and the benches of those selling doves. ¹³"It is written," he said to them, " 'My house will be called a house of prayer,'*ᵈ* but you are making it 'a den of robbers.'*ᵉ*"

¹⁴The blind and the lame came to him at the temple, and he healed them. ¹⁵But when the chief priests and the teachers of the law saw the wonderful things he did and the children shouting in the temple courts, "Hosanna to the Son of David," they were indignant.

¹⁶"Do you hear what these children are saying?" they asked him.

"Yes," replied Jesus, "have you never read,

> " 'From the lips of children and infants
> you have ordained praise'*ᶠ*?"

¹⁷And he left them and went out of the city to Bethany, where he spent the night.

Jesus Curses a Fig Tree

¹⁸Early in the morning, as he was on his way back to the city, he was hun-

---

ª 5 Zech. 9:9   ᵇ 9 A Hebrew expression meaning "Save!" which became an exclamation of praise; also in verse 15   ᶜ 9 Psalm 118:25,26   ᵈ 13 Isaiah 56:7   ᵉ 13 Jer. 7:11   ᶠ 16 Psalm 8:2

gry. [19]Seeing a fig tree by the road, he went up to it but found nothing on it except leaves. Then he said to it, "May you never bear fruit again!" Immediately the tree withered.

[20]When the disciples saw this, they were amazed. "How did the fig tree wither so quickly?" they asked.

[21]Jesus replied, "Truly I tell you, if you have faith and do not doubt, not only can you do what was done to the fig tree, but also you can say to this mountain, 'Go, throw yourself into the sea,' and it will be done. [22]If you believe, you will receive whatever you ask for in prayer."

The Authority of Jesus Questioned

[23]Jesus entered the temple courts, and, while he was teaching, the chief priests and the elders of the people came to him. "By what authority are you doing these things?" they asked. "And who gave you this authority?"

[24]Jesus replied, "I will also ask you one question. If you answer me, I will tell you by what authority I am doing these things. [25]John's baptism—where did it come from? Was it from heaven, or of human origin?"

They discussed it among themselves and said, "If we say, 'From heaven,' he will ask, 'Then why didn't you believe him?' [26]But if we say, 'Of human origin'—we are afraid of the people, for they all hold that John was a prophet."

[27]So they answered Jesus, "We don't know."

Then he said, "Neither will I tell you by what authority I am doing these things.

The Parable of the Two Sons

[28]"What do you think? There was a man who had two sons. He went to the first and said, 'Son, go and work today in the vineyard.'

[29] 'I will not,' he answered, but later he changed his mind and went.

[30]"Then the father went to the other son and said the same thing. He answered, 'I will, sir,' but he did not go.

[31]"Which of the two did what his father wanted?"

"The first," they answered.

Jesus said to them, "Truly I tell you, the tax collectors and the prostitutes are entering the kingdom of God ahead of you. [32]For John came to you to show you the way of righteousness, and you did not believe him, but the tax collectors and the prostitutes did. And even after you saw this, you did not repent and believe him.

The Parable of the Tenants

[33]"Listen to another parable: There was a landowner who planted a vineyard. He put a wall around it, dug a winepress in it and built a watchtower. Then he rented the vineyard to some farmers and moved to another place. [34]When the harvest time approached, he sent his servants to the tenants to collect his fruit.

[35]"The tenants seized his servants; they beat one, killed another, and stoned a third. [36]Then he sent other servants to them, more than the first time, and the tenants treated them the same way. [37]Last of all, he sent his son to them. 'They will respect my son,' he said.

³⁸"But when the tenants saw the son, they said to each other, 'This is the heir. Come, let's kill him and take his inheritance.' ³⁹So they took him and threw him out of the vineyard and killed him.

⁴⁰"Therefore, when the owner of the vineyard comes, what will he do to those tenants?"

⁴¹"He will bring those wretches to a wretched end," they replied, "and he will rent the vineyard to other tenants, who will give him his share of the crop at harvest time."

⁴²Jesus said to them, "Have you never read in the Scriptures:

" 'The stone the builders rejected
   has become the cornerstone;
the Lord has done this,
   and it is marvelous in our eyes'^a?

⁴³"Therefore I tell you that the kingdom of God will be taken away from you and given to a people who will produce its fruit. ⁴⁴Anyone who falls on this stone will be broken to pieces, but anyone on whom it falls will be crushed."^b

⁴⁵When the chief priests and the Pharisees heard Jesus' parables, they knew he was talking about them. ⁴⁶They looked for a way to arrest him, but they were afraid of the crowd because the people held that he was a prophet.

The Parable of the Wedding Banquet

22 Jesus spoke to them again in parables, saying: ²"The kingdom of heaven is like a king who prepared a wedding banquet for his son. ³He sent his servants to those who had been invited to the banquet to tell them to come, but they refused to come.

⁴"Then he sent some more servants and said, 'Tell those who have been invited that I have prepared my dinner: My oxen and fattened cattle have been butchered, and everything is ready. Come to the wedding banquet.'

⁵"But they paid no attention and went off—one to his field, another to his business. ⁶The rest seized his servants, mistreated them and killed them. ⁷The king was enraged. He sent his army and destroyed those murderers and burned their city.

⁸"Then he said to his servants, 'The wedding banquet is ready, but those I invited did not deserve to come. ⁹Go to the street corners and invite to the banquet anyone you find.' ¹⁰So the servants went out into the streets and gathered all the people they could find, the bad as well as the good, and the wedding hall was filled with guests.

¹¹"But when the king came in to see the guests, he noticed a man there who was not wearing wedding clothes. ¹²'Friend,' he asked, 'how did you get in here without wedding clothes?' The man was speechless.

¹³"Then the king told the attendants, 'Tie him hand and foot, and throw him outside, into the darkness, where there will be weeping and gnashing of teeth.'

¹⁴"For many are invited, but few are chosen."

---

^a 42 Psalm 118:22,23   ^b 44 Some manuscripts do not have verse 44.

Paying the Poll Tax to Caesar

[15]Then the Pharisees went out and laid plans to trap him in his words. [16]They sent their disciples to him along with the Herodians. "Teacher," they said, "we know that you are a man of integrity and that you teach the way of God in accordance with the truth. You aren't swayed by others, because you pay no attention to who they are. [17]Tell us then, what is your opinion? Is it right to pay the poll tax[a] to Caesar or not?"

[18]But Jesus, knowing their evil intent, said, "You hypocrites, why are you trying to trap me? [19]Show me the coin used for paying the tax." They brought him a denarius, [20]and he asked them, "Whose portrait is this? And whose inscription?"

[21]"Caesar's," they replied.

Then he said to them, "Give back to Caesar what is Caesar's, and to God what is God's."

[22]When they heard this, they were amazed. So they left him and went away.

Marriage at the Resurrection

[23]That same day the Sadducees, who say there is no resurrection, came to him with a question. [24]"Teacher," they said, "Moses told us that if a man dies without having children, his brother must marry the widow and raise up an heir for him. [25]Now there were seven brothers among us. The first one married and died, and since he had no children, he left his wife to his brother. [26]The same thing happened to the second and third brother, right on down to the seventh. [27]Finally, the woman died. [28]Now then, at the resurrection, whose wife will she be of the seven, since all of them were married to her?"

[29]Jesus replied, "You are in error because you do not know the Scriptures or the power of God. [30]At the resurrection people will neither marry nor be given in marriage; they will be like the angels in heaven. [31]But about the resurrection of the dead—have you not read what God said to you, [32]'I am the God of Abraham, the God of Isaac, and the God of Jacob'[b]? He is not the God of the dead but of the living."

[33]When the crowds heard this, they were astonished at his teaching.

The Greatest Commandment

[34]Hearing that Jesus had silenced the Sadducees, the Pharisees got together. [35]One of them, an expert in the law, tested him with this question: [36]"Teacher, which is the greatest commandment in the Law?"

[37]Jesus replied: " 'Love the Lord your God with all your heart and with all your soul and with all your mind.'[c] [38]This is the first and greatest commandment. [39]And the second is like it: 'Love your neighbor as yourself.'[d] [40]All the Law and the Prophets hang on these two commandments."

Whose Son Is the Messiah?

[41]While the Pharisees were gathered together, Jesus asked them, [42]"What do you think about the Messiah? Whose son is he?"

---

[a] 17 The poll tax was a special tax levied on subject peoples, not on Roman citizens.
[b] 32 Exodus 3:6   [c] 37 Deut. 6:5   [d] 39 Lev. 19:18

"The son of David," they replied.

⁴³He said to them, "How is it then that David, speaking by the Spirit, calls him 'Lord'? For he says,

⁴⁴" 'The Lord said to my Lord:
"Sit at my right hand
until I put your enemies
under your feet." ' *a*

⁴⁵If then David calls him 'Lord,' how can he be his son?" ⁴⁶No one could say a word in reply, and from that day on no one dared to ask him any more questions.

A Warning Against Hypocrisy

23 Then Jesus said to the crowds and to his disciples: ²"The teachers of the law and the Pharisees sit in Moses' seat. ³So you must be careful to do everything they tell you. But do not do what they do, for they do not practice what they preach. ⁴They tie up heavy, cumbersome loads and put them on other people's shoulders, but they themselves are not willing to lift a finger to move them.

⁵"Everything they do is done for people to see: They make their phylacteries *b* wide and the tassels on their garments long; ⁶they love the place of honor at banquets and the most important seats in the synagogues; ⁷they love to be greeted with respect in the marketplaces and to have people call them 'Rabbi.'

⁸"But you are not to be called 'Rabbi,' for you have only one Master and you are all brothers. ⁹And do not call anyone on earth 'father,' for you have one Father, and he is in heaven. ¹⁰Nor are you to be called 'teacher,' for you have one Teacher, the Messiah. ¹¹The greatest among you will be your servant. ¹²For those who exalt themselves will be humbled, and those who humble themselves will be exalted.

Seven Woes on the Teachers of the Law and the Pharisees

¹³[¹⁴]"Woe to you, teachers of the law and Pharisees, you hypocrites! You shut the door of the kingdom of heaven in people's faces. You yourselves do not enter, nor will you let those enter who are trying to.

¹⁵"Woe to you, teachers of the law and Pharisees, you hypocrites! You travel over land and sea to win a single convert, then you make that convert twice as much a child of hell as you are.

¹⁶"Woe to you, blind guides! You say, 'If anyone swears by the temple, it means nothing; but whoever swears by the gold of the temple is bound by the oath.' ¹⁷You blind fools! Which is greater: the gold, or the temple that makes the gold sacred? ¹⁸You also say, 'If anyone swears by the altar, it means nothing; but whoever swears by the gift on the altar is bound by the oath.' ¹⁹You blind men! Which is greater: the gift, or the altar that makes the gift sacred? ²⁰Therefore, anyone who swears by the altar swears by it and by everything on it. ²¹And anyone who swears by the temple swears by it and by the one

a 44 Psalm 110:1   *b 5* That is, boxes containing Scripture verses, worn on forehead and arm

who dwells in it. ²²And anyone who swears by heaven swears by God's throne and by the one who sits on it.

²³"Woe to you, teachers of the law and Pharisees, you hypocrites! You give a tenth of your spices—mint, dill and cumin. But you have neglected the more important matters of the law—justice, mercy and faithfulness. You should have practiced the latter, without neglecting the former. ²⁴You blind guides! You strain out a gnat but swallow a camel.

²⁵"Woe to you, teachers of the law and Pharisees, you hypocrites! You clean the outside of the cup and dish, but inside they are full of greed and self-indulgence. ²⁶Blind Pharisee! First clean the inside of the cup and dish, and then the outside also will be clean.

²⁷"Woe to you, teachers of the law and Pharisees, you hypocrites! You are like whitewashed tombs, which look beautiful on the outside but on the inside are full of the bones of the dead and everything unclean. ²⁸In the same way, on the outside you appear to people as righteous but on the inside you are full of hypocrisy and wickedness.

²⁹"Woe to you, teachers of the law and Pharisees, you hypocrites! You build tombs for the prophets and decorate the graves of the righteous. ³⁰And you say, 'If we had lived in the days of our ancestors, we would not have taken part with them in shedding the blood of the prophets.' ³¹So you testify against yourselves that you are the descendants of those who murdered the prophets. ³²Fill up, then, the measure of the sin of your ancestors!

³³"You snakes! You brood of vipers! How will you escape being condemned to hell? ³⁴Therefore I am sending you prophets and sages and teachers. Some of them you will kill and crucify; others you will flog in your synagogues and pursue from town to town. ³⁵And so upon you will come all the righteous blood that has been shed on earth, from the blood of righteous Abel to the blood of Zechariah son of Berekiah, whom you murdered between the temple and the altar. ³⁶Truly I tell you, all this will come upon this generation.

³⁷"Jerusalem, Jerusalem, you who kill the prophets and stone those sent to you, how often I have longed to gather your children together, as a hen gathers her chicks under her wings, and you were not willing. ³⁸Look, your house is left to you desolate. ³⁹For I tell you, you will not see me again until you say, 'Blessed is he who comes in the name of the Lord.'^a"

The Destruction of the Temple and Signs of the End Times

24 Jesus left the temple and was walking away when his disciples came up to him to call his attention to its buildings. ²"Do you see all these things?" he asked. "Truly I tell you, not one stone here will be left on another; every one will be thrown down."

³As Jesus was sitting on the Mount of Olives, the disciples came to him privately. "Tell us," they said, "when will this happen, and what will be the sign of your coming and of the end of the age?"

⁴Jesus answered: "Watch out that no one deceives you. ⁵For many will come in my name, claiming, 'I am the Messiah,' and will deceive many. ⁶You will hear of wars and rumors of wars, but see to it that you are not alarmed. Such

^a 39 Psalm 118:26

things must happen, but the end is still to come. [7]Nation will rise against nation, and kingdom against kingdom. There will be famines and earthquakes in various places. [8]All these are the beginning of birth pains.

[9]"Then you will be handed over to be persecuted and put to death, and you will be hated by all nations because of me. [10]At that time many will turn away from the faith and will betray and hate each other, [11]and many false prophets will appear and deceive many people. [12]Because of the increase of wickedness, the love of most will grow cold, [13]but whoever stands firm to the end will be saved. [14]And this gospel of the kingdom will be preached in the whole world as a testimony to all nations, and then the end will come.

[15]"So when you see standing in the holy place 'the abomination that causes desolation,'[a] spoken of through the prophet Daniel—let the reader understand— [16]then let those who are in Judea flee to the mountains. [17]Let no one on the housetop go down to take anything out of the house. [18]Let no one in the field go back to get their cloak. [19]How dreadful it will be in those days for pregnant women and nursing mothers! [20]Pray that your flight will not take place in winter or on the Sabbath. [21]For then there will be great distress, unequaled from the beginning of the world until now—and never to be equaled again.

[22]"If those days had not been cut short, no one would survive, but for the sake of the elect those days will be shortened. [23]At that time if anyone says to you, 'Look, here is the Messiah!' or, 'There he is!' do not believe it. [24]For false messiahs and false prophets will appear and perform great signs and wonders to deceive, if possible, even the elect. [25]See, I have told you ahead of time.

[26]"So if anyone tells you, 'There he is, out in the desert,' do not go out; or, 'Here he is, in the inner rooms,' do not believe it. [27]For as lightning that comes from the east is visible even in the west, so will be the coming of the Son of Man. [28]Wherever there is a carcass, there the vultures will gather.

[29]"Immediately after the distress of those days

" 'the sun will be darkened,
    and the moon will not give its light;
the stars will fall from the sky,
    and the heavenly bodies will be shaken.'[b]

[30]"At that time the sign of the Son of Man will appear in the sky, and all the peoples of the earth[c] will mourn. They will see the Son of Man coming on the clouds of the sky, with power and great glory. [31]And he will send his angels with a loud trumpet call, and they will gather his elect from the four winds, from one end of the heavens to the other.

[32]"Now learn this lesson from the fig tree: As soon as its twigs get tender and its leaves come out, you know that summer is near. [33]Even so, when you see all these things, you know that it[d] is near, right at the door. [34]Truly I tell you, this generation will certainly not pass away until all these things have happened. [35]Heaven and earth will pass away, but my words will never pass away.

[a] 15 Daniel 9:27; 11:31; 12:11   [b] 29 Isaiah 13:10; 34:4   [c] 30 Or *the tribes of the land*   [d] 33 Or *he*

The Day and Hour Unknown

36"But about that day or hour no one knows, not even the angels in heaven, nor the Son,ª but only the Father. 37As it was in the days of Noah, so it will be at the coming of the Son of Man. 38For in the days before the flood, people were eating and drinking, marrying and giving in marriage, up to the day Noah entered the ark; 39and they knew nothing about what would happen until the flood came and took them all away. That is how it will be at the coming of the Son of Man. 40Two men will be in the field; one will be taken and the other left. 41Two women will be grinding with a hand mill; one will be taken and the other left.

42"Therefore keep watch, because you do not know on what day your Lord will come. 43But understand this: If the owner of the house had known at what time of night the thief was coming, he would have kept watch and would not have let his house be broken into. 44So you also must be ready, because the Son of Man will come at an hour when you do not expect him.

45"Who then is the faithful and wise servant, whom the master has put in charge of the servants in his household to give them their food at the proper time? 46It will be good for that servant whose master finds him doing so when he returns. 47Truly I tell you, he will put him in charge of all his possessions. 48But suppose that servant is wicked and says to himself, 'My master is staying away a long time,' 49and he then begins to beat his fellow servants and to eat and drink with drunkards. 50The master of that servant will come on a day when he does not expect him and at an hour he is not aware of. 51He will cut him to pieces and assign him a place with the hypocrites, where there will be weeping and gnashing of teeth.

The Parable of the Ten Virgins

25 "At that time the kingdom of heaven will be like ten virgins who took their lamps and went out to meet the bridegroom. 2Five of them were foolish and five were wise. 3The foolish ones took their lamps but did not take any oil with them. 4The wise, however, took oil in jars along with their lamps. 5The bridegroom was a long time in coming, and they all became drowsy and fell asleep.

6"At midnight the cry rang out: 'Here's the bridegroom! Come out to meet him!'

7"Then all the virgins woke up and trimmed their lamps. 8The foolish ones said to the wise, 'Give us some of your oil; our lamps are going out.'

9" 'No,' they replied, 'there may not be enough for both us and you. Instead, go to those who sell oil and buy some for yourselves.'

10"But while they were on their way to buy the oil, the bridegroom arrived. The virgins who were ready went in with him to the wedding banquet. And the door was shut.

11"Later the others also came. 'Sir! Sir!' they said. 'Open the door for us!'

12"But he replied, 'Truly I tell you, I don't know you.'

13"Therefore keep watch, because you do not know the day or the hour.

ª 36 Some manuscripts do not have *nor the Son.*

The Parable of the Bags of Gold

14"Again, it will be like a man going on a journey, who called his servants and entrusted his wealth to them. 15To one he gave five bags of gold, to another two bags, and to another one bag,*a* each according to his ability. Then he went on his journey. 16The man who had received five bags of gold went at once and put his money to work and gained five bags more. 17So also, the one with two bags of gold gained two more. 18But the man who had received one bag went off, dug a hole in the ground and hid his master's money.

19"After a long time the master of those servants returned and settled accounts with them. 20The man who had received five bags of gold brought the other five. 'Master,' he said, 'you entrusted me with five bags of gold. See, I have gained five more.'

21"His master replied, 'Well done, good and faithful servant! You have been faithful with a few things; I will put you in charge of many things. Come and share your master's happiness!'

22"The man with two bags of gold also came. 'Master,' he said, 'you entrusted me with two bags of gold; see, I have gained two more.'

23"His master replied, 'Well done, good and faithful servant! You have been faithful with a few things; I will put you in charge of many things. Come and share your master's happiness!'

24"Then the man who had received one bag of gold came. 'Master,' he said, 'I knew that you are a hard man, harvesting where you have not sown and gathering where you have not scattered seed. 25So I was afraid and went out and hid your gold in the ground. See, here is what belongs to you.'

26"His master replied, 'You wicked, lazy servant! So you knew that I harvest where I have not sown and gather where I have not scattered seed? 27Well then, you should have put my money on deposit with the bankers, so that when I returned I would have received it back with interest.

28" 'Take the bag of gold from him and give it to the one who has ten bags. 29For those who have will be given more, and they will have an abundance. As for those who do not have, even what they have will be taken from them. 30And throw that worthless servant outside, into the darkness, where there will be weeping and gnashing of teeth.'

The Sheep and the Goats

31"When the Son of Man comes in his glory, and all the angels with him, he will sit on his glorious throne. 32All the nations will be gathered before him, and he will separate the people one from another as a shepherd separates the sheep from the goats. 33He will put the sheep on his right and the goats on his left.

34"Then the King will say to those on his right, 'Come, you who are blessed by my Father; take your inheritance, the kingdom prepared for you since the creation of the world. 35For I was hungry and you gave me something to eat, I was thirsty and you gave me something to drink, I was a stranger and you

---

a 15 *five talents . . . two talents . . . one talent,* and so throughout this parable; a talent was worth about 20 years of a day laborer's wage.

invited me in, [36]I needed clothes and you clothed me, I was sick and you looked after me, I was in prison and you came to visit me.'

[37]"Then the righteous will answer him, 'Lord, when did we see you hungry and feed you, or thirsty and give you something to drink? [38]When did we see you a stranger and invite you in, or needing clothes and clothe you? [39]When did we see you sick or in prison and go to visit you?'

[40]"The King will reply, 'Truly I tell you, whatever you did for one of the least of these brothers and sisters of mine, you did for me.'

[41]"Then he will say to those on his left, 'Depart from me, you who are cursed, into the eternal fire prepared for the devil and his angels. [42]For I was hungry and you gave me nothing to eat, I was thirsty and you gave me nothing to drink, [43]I was a stranger and you did not invite me in, I needed clothes and you did not clothe me, I was sick and in prison and you did not look after me.'

[44]"They also will answer, 'Lord, when did we see you hungry or thirsty or a stranger or needing clothes or sick or in prison, and did not help you?'

[45]"He will reply, 'Truly I tell you, whatever you did not do for one of the least of these, you did not do for me.'

[46]"Then they will go away to eternal punishment, but the righteous to eternal life."

The Plot Against Jesus

26 When Jesus had finished saying all these things, he said to his disciples, [2]"As you know, the Passover is two days away—and the Son of Man will be handed over to be crucified."

[3]Then the chief priests and the elders of the people assembled in the palace of the high priest, whose name was Caiaphas, [4]and they plotted to arrest Jesus in some sly way and kill him. [5]"But not during the Festival," they said, "or there may be a riot among the people."

Jesus Anointed at Bethany

[6]While Jesus was in Bethany in the home of Simon the Leper, [7]a woman came to him with an alabaster jar of very expensive perfume, which she poured on his head as he was reclining at the table.

[8]When the disciples saw this, they were indignant. "Why this waste?" they asked. [9]"This perfume could have been sold at a high price and the money given to the poor."

[10]Aware of this, Jesus said to them, "Why are you bothering this woman? She has done a beautiful thing to me. [11]The poor you will always have with you,[a] but you will not always have me. [12]When she poured this perfume on my body, she did it to prepare me for burial. [13]Truly I tell you, wherever this gospel is preached throughout the world, what she has done will also be told, in memory of her."

Judas Agrees to Betray Jesus

[14]Then one of the Twelve—the one called Judas Iscariot—went to the chief

[a] 11 See Deut. 15:11.

priests [15]and asked, "What are you willing to give me if I deliver him over to you?" So they counted out for him thirty silver coins. [16]From then on Judas watched for an opportunity to hand him over.

The Lord's Supper

[17]On the first day of the Festival of Unleavened Bread, the disciples came to Jesus and asked, "Where do you want us to make preparations for you to eat the Passover?"

[18]He replied, "Go into the city to a certain man and tell him, 'The Teacher says: My appointed time is near. I am going to celebrate the Passover with my disciples at your house.' " [19]So the disciples did as Jesus had directed them and prepared the Passover.

[20]When evening came, Jesus was reclining at the table with the Twelve. [21]And while they were eating, he said, "Truly I tell you, one of you will betray me."

[22]They were very sad and began to say to him one after the other, "Surely not I, Lord?"

[23]Jesus replied, "The one who has dipped his hand into the bowl with me will betray me. [24]The Son of Man will go just as it is written about him. But woe to that man who betrays the Son of Man! It would be better for him if he had not been born."

[25]Then Judas, the one who would betray him, said, "Surely not I, Rabbi?" Jesus answered, "You have said so."

[26]While they were eating, Jesus took bread, and when he had given thanks, he broke it and gave it to his disciples, saying, "Take and eat; this is my body."

[27]Then he took the cup, and when he had given thanks, he gave it to them, saying, "Drink from it, all of you. [28]This is my blood of the[a] covenant, which is poured out for many for the forgiveness of sins. [29]I tell you, I will not drink of this fruit of the vine from now on until that day when I drink it new with you in my Father's kingdom."

[30]When they had sung a hymn, they went out to the Mount of Olives.

Jesus Predicts Peter's Denial

[31]Then Jesus told them, "This very night you will all fall away on account of me, for it is written:

> " 'I will strike the shepherd,
>   and the sheep of the flock will be scattered.'[b]

[32]But after I have risen, I will go ahead of you into Galilee."

[33]Peter replied, "Even if all fall away on account of you, I never will."

[34]"Truly I tell you," Jesus answered, "this very night, before the rooster crows, you will disown me three times."

[35]But Peter declared, "Even if I have to die with you, I will never disown you." And all the other disciples said the same.

---

[a] 28 Some manuscripts *the new*   [b] 31 Zech. 13:7

Gethsemane

[36]Then Jesus went with his disciples to a place called Gethsemane, and he said to them, "Sit here while I go over there and pray." [37]He took Peter and the two sons of Zebedee along with him, and he began to be sorrowful and troubled. [38]Then he said to them, "My soul is overwhelmed with sorrow to the point of death. Stay here and keep watch with me."

[39]Going a little farther, he fell with his face to the ground and prayed, "My Father, if it is possible, may this cup be taken from me. Yet not as I will, but as you will."

[40]Then he returned to his disciples and found them sleeping. "Couldn't you men keep watch with me for one hour?" he asked Peter. [41]"Watch and pray so that you will not fall into temptation. The spirit is willing, but the flesh is weak."

[42]He went away a second time and prayed, "My Father, if it is not possible for this cup to be taken away unless I drink it, may your will be done."

[43]When he came back, he again found them sleeping, because their eyes were heavy. [44]So he left them and went away once more and prayed the third time, saying the same thing.

[45]Then he returned to the disciples and said to them, "Are you still sleeping and resting? Look, the hour is near, and the Son of Man is betrayed into the hands of sinners. [46]Rise! Let us go! Here comes my betrayer!"

Jesus Arrested

[47]While he was still speaking, Judas, one of the Twelve, arrived. With him was a large crowd armed with swords and clubs, sent from the chief priests and the elders of the people. [48]Now the betrayer had arranged a signal with them: "The one I kiss is the man; arrest him." [49]Going at once to Jesus, Judas said, "Greetings, Rabbi!" and kissed him.

[50]Jesus replied, "Friend, do what you came for."[a]

Then the men stepped forward, seized Jesus and arrested him. [51]With that, one of Jesus' companions reached for his sword, drew it out and struck the servant of the high priest, cutting off his ear.

[52]"Put your sword back in its place," Jesus said to him, "for all who draw the sword will die by the sword. [53]Do you think I cannot call on my Father, and he will at once put at my disposal more than twelve legions of angels? [54]But how then would the Scriptures be fulfilled that say it must happen in this way?"

[55]In that hour Jesus said to the crowd, "Am I leading a rebellion, that you have come out with swords and clubs to capture me? Every day I sat in the temple courts teaching, and you did not arrest me. [56]But this has all taken place that the writings of the prophets might be fulfilled." Then all the disciples deserted him and fled.

Jesus Before the Sanhedrin

[57]Those who had arrested Jesus took him to Caiaphas, the high priest, where the teachers of the law and the elders had assembled. [58]But Peter fol-

[a] 50 Or *"Friend, why have you come?"*

lowed him at a distance, right up to the courtyard of the high priest. He entered and sat down with the guards to see the outcome.

59The chief priests and the whole Sanhedrin were looking for false evidence against Jesus so that they could put him to death. 60But they did not find any, though many false witnesses came forward.

Finally two came forward 61and declared, "This fellow said, 'I am able to destroy the temple of God and rebuild it in three days.' "

62Then the high priest stood up and said to Jesus, "Are you not going to answer? What is this testimony that these men are bringing against you?" 63But Jesus remained silent.

The high priest said to him, "I charge you under oath by the living God: Tell us if you are the Messiah, the Son of God."

64"It is as you say," Jesus replied. "But I say to all of you: From now on you will see the Son of Man sitting at the right hand of the Mighty One and coming on the clouds of heaven."*a*

65Then the high priest tore his clothes and said, "He has spoken blasphemy! Why do we need any more witnesses? Look, now you have heard the blasphemy. 66What do you think?"

"He is worthy of death," they answered.

67Then they spit in his face and struck him with their fists. Others slapped him 68and said, "Prophesy to us, Messiah. Who hit you?"

Peter Disowns Jesus

69Now Peter was sitting out in the courtyard, and a servant girl came to him. "You also were with Jesus of Galilee," she said.

70But he denied it before them all. "I don't know what you're talking about," he said.

71Then he went out to the gateway, where another servant girl saw him and said to the people there, "This fellow was with Jesus of Nazareth."

72He denied it again, with an oath: "I don't know the man!"

73After a little while, those standing there went up to Peter and said, "Surely you are one of them; your accent gives you away."

74Then he began to call down curses, and he swore to them, "I don't know the man!"

Immediately a rooster crowed. 75Then Peter remembered the word Jesus had spoken: "Before the rooster crows, you will disown me three times." And he went outside and wept bitterly.

Judas Hangs Himself

27 Early in the morning, all the chief priests and the elders of the people came to the decision to put Jesus to death. 2They bound him, led him away and handed him over to Pilate, the governor.

3When Judas, who had betrayed him, saw that Jesus was condemned, he was seized with remorse and returned the thirty silver coins to the chief priests and the elders. 4"I have sinned," he said, "for I have betrayed innocent blood."

a 64 See Psalm 110:1; Daniel 7:13.

"What is that to us?" they replied. "That's your responsibility."

[5]So Judas threw the money into the temple and left. Then he went away and hanged himself.

[6]The chief priests picked up the coins and said, "It is against the law to put this into the treasury, since it is blood money." [7]So they decided to use the money to buy the potter's field as a burial place for foreigners. [8]That is why it has been called the Field of Blood to this day. [9]Then what was spoken by Jeremiah the prophet was fulfilled: "They took the thirty silver coins, the price set on him by the people of Israel, [10]and they used them to buy the potter's field, as the Lord commanded me."[a]

Jesus Before Pilate

[11]Meanwhile Jesus stood before the governor, and the governor asked him, "Are you the king of the Jews?"

"You have said so," Jesus replied.

[12]When he was accused by the chief priests and the elders, he gave no answer. [13]Then Pilate asked him, "Don't you hear the testimony they are bringing against you?" [14]But Jesus made no reply, not even to a single charge—to the great amazement of the governor.

[15]Now it was the governor's custom at the Festival to release a prisoner chosen by the crowd. [16]At that time they had a well-known prisoner whose name was Jesus[b] Barabbas. [17]So when the crowd had gathered, Pilate asked them, "Which one do you want me to release to you: Jesus[b] Barabbas, or Jesus who is called the Messiah?" [18]For he knew it was out of envy that they had handed Jesus over to him.

[19]While Pilate was sitting on the judge's seat, his wife sent him this message: "Don't have anything to do with that innocent man, for I have suffered a great deal today in a dream because of him."

[20]But the chief priests and the elders persuaded the crowd to ask for Barabbas and to have Jesus executed.

[21]"Which of the two do you want me to release to you?" asked the governor.

"Barabbas," they answered.

[22]"What shall I do, then, with Jesus who is called the Messiah?" Pilate asked.

They all answered, "Crucify him!"

[23]"Why? What crime has he committed?" asked Pilate.

But they shouted all the louder, "Crucify him!"

[24]When Pilate saw that he was getting nowhere, but that instead an uproar was starting, he took water and washed his hands in front of the crowd. "I am innocent of this man's blood," he said. "It is your responsibility!"

[25]All the people answered, "His blood is on us and on our children!"

[26]Then he released Barabbas to them. But he had Jesus flogged, and handed him over to be crucified.

---

[a] 10 See Zech. 11:12,13; Jer. 19:1–13; 32:6–9.   [b] 16,17 Many manuscripts do not have *Jesus*.

The Soldiers Mock Jesus

27Then the governor's soldiers took Jesus into the Praetorium and gathered the whole company of soldiers around him. 28They stripped him and put a scarlet robe on him, 29and then twisted together a crown of thorns and set it on his head. They put a staff in his right hand as a scepter. Then they knelt in front of him and mocked him. "Hail, king of the Jews!" they said. 30They spit on him, and took the staff and struck him on the head again and again. 31After they had mocked him, they took off the robe and put his own clothes on him. Then they led him away to crucify him.

The Crucifixion

32As they were going out, they met a man from Cyrene, named Simon, and they forced him to carry the cross. 33They came to a place called Golgotha (which means The Place of the Skull). 34There they offered Jesus wine to drink, mixed with gall; but after tasting it, he refused to drink it. 35When they had crucified him, they divided up his clothes by casting lots. 36And sitting down, they kept watch over him there. 37Above his head they placed the written charge against him: THIS IS JESUS, THE KING OF THE JEWS. 38Two rebels were crucified with him, one on his right and one on his left. 39Those who passed by hurled insults at him, shaking their heads 40and saying, "You who are going to destroy the temple and build it in three days, save yourself! Come down from the cross, if you are the Son of God!"

41In the same way the chief priests, the teachers of the law and the elders mocked him. 42"He saved others," they said, "but he can't save himself! He's the king of Israel! Let him come down now from the cross, and we will believe in him. 43He trusts in God. Let God rescue him now if he wants him, for he said, 'I am the Son of God.' " 44In the same way the rebels who were crucified with him also heaped insults on him.

The Death of Jesus

45From noon until three in the afternoon darkness came over all the land. 46About three in the afternoon Jesus cried out in a loud voice, *"Eli, Eli,ᵃ lema sabachthani?"*—which means, "My God, my God, why have you forsaken me?"ᵇ

47When some of those standing there heard this, they said, "He's calling Elijah."

48Immediately one of them ran and got a sponge. He filled it with wine vinegar, put it on a staff, and offered it to Jesus to drink. 49The rest said, "Now leave him alone. Let's see if Elijah comes to save him."

50And when Jesus had cried out again in a loud voice, he gave up his spirit.

51At that moment the curtain of the temple was torn in two from top to bottom. The earth shook, the rocks split 52and the tombs broke open. The bodies of many holy people who had died were raised to life. 53They came out of the tombs after Jesus' resurrection andᶜ went into the holy city and appeared to many people.

ᵃ 46 Some manuscripts *Eloi, Eloi*   ᵇ 46 Psalm 22:1   ᶜ 53 Or *tombs, and after Jesus' resurrection they*

⁵⁴When the centurion and those with him who were guarding Jesus saw the earthquake and all that had happened, they were terrified, and exclaimed, "Surely he was the Son of God!"

⁵⁵Many women were there, watching from a distance. They had followed Jesus from Galilee to care for his needs. ⁵⁶Among them were Mary Magdalene, Mary the mother of James and Joseph,ᵃ and the mother of Zebedee's sons.

The Burial of Jesus

⁵⁷As evening approached, there came a rich man from Arimathea, named Joseph, who had himself become a disciple of Jesus. ⁵⁸Going to Pilate, he asked for Jesus' body, and Pilate ordered that it be given to him. ⁵⁹Joseph took the body, wrapped it in a clean linen cloth, ⁶⁰and placed it in his own new tomb that he had cut out of the rock. He rolled a big stone in front of the entrance to the tomb and went away. ⁶¹Mary Magdalene and the other Mary were sitting there opposite the tomb.

The Guard at the Tomb

⁶²The next day, the one after Preparation Day, the chief priests and the Pharisees went to Pilate. ⁶³"Sir," they said, "we remember that while he was still alive that deceiver said, 'After three days I will rise again.' ⁶⁴So give the order for the tomb to be made secure until the third day. Otherwise, his disciples may come and steal the body and tell the people that he has been raised from the dead. This last deception will be worse than the first."

⁶⁵"Take a guard," Pilate answered. "Go, make the tomb as secure as you know how." ⁶⁶So they went and made the tomb secure by putting a seal on the stone and posting the guard.

The Empty Tomb and the Risen Jesus

28 After the Sabbath, at dawn on the first day of the week, Mary Magdalene and the other Mary went to look at the tomb.

²There was a violent earthquake, for an angel of the Lord came down from heaven and, going to the tomb, rolled back the stone and sat on it. ³His appearance was like lightning, and his clothes were white as snow. ⁴The guards were so afraid of him that they shook and became like dead men.

⁵The angel said to the women, "Do not be afraid, for I know that you are looking for Jesus, who was crucified. ⁶He is not here; he has risen, just as he said. Come and see the place where he lay. ⁷Then go quickly and tell his disciples: 'He has risen from the dead and is going ahead of you into Galilee. There you will see him.' Now I have told you."

⁸So the women hurried away from the tomb, afraid yet filled with joy, and ran to tell his disciples. ⁹Suddenly Jesus met them. "Greetings," he said. They came to him, clasped his feet and worshiped him. ¹⁰Then Jesus said to them, "Do not be afraid. Go and tell my brothers to go to Galilee; there they will see me."

ᵃ 56 Greek *Joses*, a variant of *Joseph*

The Guards' Report

[11]While the women were on their way, some of the guards went into the city and reported to the chief priests everything that had happened. [12]When the chief priests had met with the elders and devised a plan, they gave the soldiers a large sum of money, [13]telling them, "You are to say, 'His disciples came during the night and stole him away while we were asleep.' [14]If this report gets to the governor, we will satisfy him and keep you out of trouble." [15]So the soldiers took the money and did as they were instructed. And this story has been widely circulated among the Jews to this very day.

The Great Commission

[16]Then the eleven disciples went to Galilee, to the mountain where Jesus had told them to go. [17]When they saw him, they worshiped him; but some doubted. [18]Then Jesus came to them and said, "All authority in heaven and on earth has been given to me. [19]Therefore go and make disciples of all nations, baptizing them in[a] the name of the Father and of the Son and of the Holy Spirit, [20]and teaching them to obey everything I have commanded you. And surely I am with you always, to the very end of the age."

[a] 19 Or into; see Acts 8:16; 19:5; Romans 6:3; 1 Cor. 1:13; 10:2; Gal. 3:27.

MARK

John the Baptist Prepares the Way

1 The beginning of the good news about Jesus the Messiah,[a,b]

²as it is written in Isaiah the prophet:

> "I will send my messenger ahead of you,
> who will prepare your way"[c]—
> ³"a voice of one calling in the desert,
> 'Prepare the way for the Lord,
> make straight paths for him.' "[d]

⁴And so John the Baptist appeared in the desert region, preaching a baptism of repentance for the forgiveness of sins. ⁵The whole Judean countryside and all the people of Jerusalem went out to him. Confessing their sins, they were baptized by him in the Jordan River. ⁶John wore clothing made of camel's hair, with a leather belt around his waist, and he ate locusts and wild honey. ⁷And this was his message: "After me comes the one more powerful than I, the thongs of whose sandals I am not worthy to stoop down and untie. ⁸I baptize you with[e] water, but he will baptize you with[e] the Holy Spirit."

The Baptism and Testing of Jesus

⁹At that time Jesus came from Nazareth in Galilee and was baptized by John in the Jordan. ¹⁰Just as Jesus was coming up out of the water, he saw heaven being torn open and the Spirit descending on him like a dove. ¹¹And a voice came from heaven: "You are my Son, whom I love; with you I am well pleased."

¹²At once the Spirit sent him out into the desert, ¹³and he was in the desert forty days, being tempted[f] by Satan. He was with the wild animals, and angels attended him.

Jesus Announces the Good News

¹⁴After John was put in prison, Jesus went into Galilee, proclaiming the good news of God. ¹⁵"The time has come," he said. "The kingdom of God has come near. Repent and believe the good news!"

---

[a]1 Or *Jesus Christ*. "Messiah" (Hebrew) and "Christ" (Greek) both mean "Anointed One."
[b]1 Many manuscripts *Messiah, the Son of God*   [c]2 Mal. 3:1   [d]3 Isaiah 40:3   [e]8 Or *in*
[f]13 The Greek for *tempted* can also mean *tested*.

Jesus Calls His First Disciples

16As Jesus walked beside the Sea of Galilee, he saw Simon and his brother Andrew casting a net into the lake, for they were fishermen. 17"Come, follow me," Jesus said, "and I will send you out to catch people." 18At once they left their nets and followed him.

19When he had gone a little farther, he saw James son of Zebedee and his brother John in a boat, preparing their nets. 20Without delay he called them, and they left their father Zebedee in the boat with the hired men and followed him.

Jesus Drives Out an Evil Spirit

21They went to Capernaum, and when the Sabbath came, Jesus went into the synagogue and began to teach. 22The people were amazed at his teaching, because he taught them as one who had authority, not as the teachers of the law. 23Just then a man in their synagogue who was possessed by an evil*a* spirit cried out, 24"What do you want with us, Jesus of Nazareth? Have you come to destroy us? I know who you are—the Holy One of God!"

25"Be quiet!" said Jesus sternly. "Come out of him!" 26The evil spirit shook the man violently and came out of him with a shriek.

27The people were all so amazed that they asked each other, "What is this? A new teaching—and with authority! He even gives orders to evil spirits and they obey him." 28News about him spread quickly over the whole region of Galilee.

Jesus Heals Many

29As soon as they left the synagogue, they went with James and John to the home of Simon and Andrew. 30Simon's mother-in-law was in bed with a fever, and they immediately told Jesus about her. 31So he went to her, took her hand and helped her up. The fever left her and she began to wait on them.

32That evening after sunset the people brought to Jesus all the sick and demon-possessed. 33The whole town gathered at the door, 34and Jesus healed many who had various diseases. He also drove out many demons, but he would not let the demons speak because they knew who he was.

Jesus Prays in a Solitary Place

35Very early in the morning, while it was still dark, Jesus got up, left the house and went off to a solitary place, where he prayed. 36Simon and his companions went to look for him, 37and when they found him, they exclaimed: "Everyone is looking for you!"

38Jesus replied, "Let us go somewhere else—to the nearby villages—so I can preach there also. That is why I have come." 39So he traveled throughout Galilee, preaching in their synagogues and driving out demons.

Jesus Heals a Man With Leprosy

40A man with leprosy*b* came to him and begged him on his knees, "If you are willing, you can make me clean."

---

a 23 Greek *unclean*; also in verses 26 and 27   *b* 40 The Greek word was used for various diseases affecting the skin—not necessarily leprosy.

⁴¹Jesus was indignant. He*a* reached out his hand and touched the man. "I am willing," he said. "Be clean!" ⁴²Immediately the leprosy left him and he was cleansed.

⁴³Jesus sent him away at once with a strong warning: ⁴⁴"See that you don't tell this to anyone. But go, show yourself to the priest and offer the sacrifices that Moses commanded for your cleansing, as a testimony to them." ⁴⁵Instead he went out and began to talk freely, spreading the news. As a result, Jesus could no longer enter a town openly but stayed outside in lonely places. Yet the people still came to him from everywhere.

Jesus Forgives and Heals a Paralyzed Man

2 A few days later, when Jesus again entered Capernaum, the people heard that he had come home. ²So many gathered that there was no room left, not even outside the door, and he preached the word to them. ³Some men came, bringing to him a paralyzed man, carried by four of them. ⁴Since they could not get him to Jesus because of the crowd, they made an opening in the roof above Jesus by digging through it and then lowered the mat the man was lying on. ⁵When Jesus saw their faith, he said to the paralyzed man, "Son, your sins are forgiven."

⁶Now some teachers of the law were sitting there, thinking to themselves, ⁷"Why does this fellow talk like that? He's blaspheming! Who can forgive sins but God alone?"

⁸Immediately Jesus knew in his spirit that this was what they were thinking in their hearts, and he said to them, "Why are you thinking these things? ⁹Which is easier: to say to this paralyzed man, 'Your sins are forgiven,' or to say, 'Get up, take your mat and walk'? ¹⁰But I want you to know that the Son of Man has authority on earth to forgive sins." So he said to the man, ¹¹"I tell you, get up, take your mat and go home." ¹²He got up, took his mat and walked out in full view of them all. This amazed everyone and they praised God, saying, "We have never seen anything like this!"

Jesus Calls Levi and Eats With Sinners

¹³Once again Jesus went out beside the lake. A large crowd came to him, and he began to teach them. ¹⁴As he walked along, he saw Levi son of Alphaeus sitting at the tax collector's booth. "Follow me," Jesus told him, and Levi got up and followed him.

¹⁵While Jesus was having dinner at Levi's house, many tax collectors and "sinners" were eating with him and his disciples, for there were many who followed him. ¹⁶When the teachers of the law who were Pharisees saw him eating with the "sinners" and tax collectors, they asked his disciples: "Why does he eat with tax collectors and 'sinners'?"

¹⁷On hearing this, Jesus said to them, "It is not the healthy who need a doctor, but the sick. I have not come to call the righteous, but sinners."

Jesus Questioned About Fasting

¹⁸Now John's disciples and the Pharisees were fasting. Some people came

a 41 Many manuscripts *Filled with compassion, Jesus*

and asked Jesus, "How is it that John's disciples and the disciples of the Pharisees are fasting, but yours are not?"

¹⁹Jesus answered, "How can the guests of the bridegroom fast while he is with them? They cannot, so long as they have him with them. ²⁰But the time will come when the bridegroom will be taken from them, and on that day they will fast.

²¹"No one sews a patch of unshrunk cloth on an old garment. If they do, the new piece will pull away from the old, making the tear worse. ²²And people do not pour new wine into old wineskins. If they do, the wine will burst the skins, and both the wine and the wineskins will be ruined. No, they pour new wine into new wineskins."

Jesus Is Lord of the Sabbath

²³One Sabbath Jesus was going through the grainfields, and as his disciples walked along, they began to pick some heads of grain. ²⁴The Pharisees said to him, "Look, why are they doing what is unlawful on the Sabbath?"

²⁵He answered, "Have you never read what David did when he and his companions were hungry and in need? ²⁶In the days of Abiathar the high priest, he entered the house of God and ate the consecrated bread, which is lawful only for priests to eat. And he also gave some to his companions."

²⁷Then he said to them, "The Sabbath was made for people, not people for the Sabbath. ²⁸So the Son of Man is Lord even of the Sabbath."

Jesus Heals on the Sabbath

3 Another time he went into the synagogue, and a man with a shriveled hand was there. ²Some of them were looking for a reason to accuse Jesus, so they watched him closely to see if he would heal him on the Sabbath. ³Jesus said to the man with the shriveled hand, "Stand up in front of everyone."

⁴Then Jesus asked them, "Which is lawful on the Sabbath: to do good or to do evil, to save life or to kill?" But they remained silent.

⁵He looked around at them in anger and, deeply distressed at their stubborn hearts, said to the man, "Stretch out your hand." He stretched it out, and his hand was completely restored. ⁶Then the Pharisees went out and began to plot with the Herodians how they might kill Jesus.

Crowds Follow Jesus

⁷Jesus withdrew with his disciples to the lake, and a large crowd from Galilee followed. ⁸When they heard all he was doing, many people came to him from Judea, Jerusalem, Idumea, and the regions across the Jordan and around Tyre and Sidon. ⁹Because of the crowd he told his disciples to have a small boat ready for him, to keep the people from crowding him. ¹⁰For he had healed many, so that those with diseases were pushing forward to touch him. ¹¹Whenever the evil[a] spirits saw him, they fell down before him and cried out, "You are the Son of God." ¹²But he gave them strict orders not to tell others about him.

[a] 11 Greek unclean; also in verse 30

Jesus Appoints the Twelve

[13]Jesus went up on a mountainside and called to him those he wanted, and they came to him. [14]He appointed twelve[a] that they might be with him and that he might send them out to preach [15]and to have authority to drive out demons. [16]These are the twelve he appointed: Simon (to whom he gave the name Peter); [17]James son of Zebedee and his brother John (to them he gave the name Boanerges, which means Sons of Thunder); [18]Andrew, Philip, Bartholomew, Matthew, Thomas, James son of Alphaeus, Thaddaeus, Simon the Zealot [19]and Judas Iscariot, who betrayed him.

Jesus Accused by His Family and by Teachers of the Law

[20]Then Jesus entered a house, and again a crowd gathered, so that he and his disciples were not even able to eat. [21]When his family[b] heard about this, they went to take charge of him, for they said, "He is out of his mind."

[22]And the teachers of the law who came down from Jerusalem said, "He is possessed by Beelzebul! By the prince of demons he is driving out demons."

[23]So Jesus called them over to him and began to speak to them in parables: "How can Satan drive out Satan? [24]If a kingdom is divided against itself, that kingdom cannot stand. [25]If a house is divided against itself, that house cannot stand. [26]And if Satan opposes himself and is divided, he cannot stand; his end has come. [27]In fact, no one can enter a strong man's house without first tying him up. Then he can plunder the strong man's house. [28]Truly I tell you, people will be forgiven all their sins and all the blasphemies they utter. [29]But whoever blasphemes against the Holy Spirit will never be forgiven, but is guilty of an eternal sin."

[30]He said this because they were saying, "He has an evil spirit."

[31]Then Jesus' mother and brothers arrived. Standing outside, they sent someone in to call him. [32]A crowd was sitting around him, and they told him, "Your mother and brothers are outside looking for you."

[33]"Who are my mother and my brothers?" he asked.

[34]Then he looked at those seated in a circle around him and said, "Here are my mother and my brothers! [35]Whoever does God's will is my brother and sister and mother."

The Parable of the Sower

4 Again Jesus began to teach by the lake. The crowd that gathered around him was so large that he got into a boat and sat in it out on the lake, while all the people were along the shore at the water's edge. [2]He taught them many things by parables, and in his teaching said: [3]"Listen! A farmer went out to sow his seed. [4]As he was scattering the seed, some fell along the path, and the birds came and ate it up. [5]Some fell on rocky places, where it did not have much soil. It sprang up quickly, because the soil was shallow. [6]But when the sun came up, the plants were scorched, and they withered because they had no root. [7]Other seed fell among thorns, which grew up and choked the plants, so that they did not bear grain. [8]Still other seed fell on good soil. It came up,

---

[a] 14 Some manuscripts twelve—designating them apostles—   [b] 21 Or his associates

grew and produced a crop, some multiplying thirty, some sixty, some a hundred times."

9Then Jesus said, "Whoever has ears to hear, let them hear."

10When he was alone, the Twelve and the others around him asked him about the parables. 11He told them, "The secret of the kingdom of God has been given to you. But to those on the outside everything is said in parables 12so that,

> " 'they may be ever seeing but never perceiving,
>   and ever hearing but never understanding;
> otherwise they might turn and be forgiven!' a"

13Then Jesus said to them, "Don't you understand this parable? How then will you understand any parable? 14The farmer sows the word. 15Some people are like seed along the path, where the word is sown. As soon as they hear it, Satan comes and takes away the word that was sown in them. 16Others, like seed sown on rocky places, hear the word and at once receive it with joy. 17But since they have no root, they last only a short time. When trouble or persecution comes because of the word, they quickly fall away. 18Still others, like seed sown among thorns, hear the word; 19but the worries of this life, the deceitfulness of wealth and the desires for other things come in and choke the word, making it unfruitful. 20Others, like seed sown on good soil, hear the word, accept it, and produce a crop—some thirty, some sixty, some a hundred times what was sown."

A Lamp on a Stand

21He said to them, "Do you bring in a lamp to put it under a bowl or a bed? Instead, don't you put it on its stand? 22For whatever is hidden is meant to be disclosed, and whatever is concealed is meant to be brought out into the open. 23If anyone has ears to hear, let them hear."

24"Consider carefully what you hear," he continued. "With the measure you use, it will be measured to you—and even more. 25Those who have will be given more; as for those who do not have, even what they have will be taken from them."

The Parable of the Growing Seed

26He also said, "This is what the kingdom of God is like. A man scatters seed on the ground. 27Night and day, whether he sleeps or gets up, the seed sprouts and grows, though he does not know how. 28All by itself the soil produces grain—first the stalk, then the head, then the full kernel in the head. 29As soon as the grain is ripe, he puts the sickle to it, because the harvest has come."

The Parable of the Mustard Seed

30Again he said, "What shall we say the kingdom of God is like, or what parable shall we use to describe it? 31It is like a mustard seed, which is the smallest of all seeds on earth. 32Yet when planted, it grows and becomes the

a 12 Isaiah 6:9,10

largest of all garden plants, with such big branches that the birds can perch in its shade."

33With many similar parables Jesus spoke the word to them, as much as they could understand. 34He did not say anything to them without using a parable. But when he was alone with his own disciples, he explained everything.

Jesus Calms the Storm

35That day when evening came, he said to his disciples, "Let us go over to the other side." 36Leaving the crowd behind, they took him along, just as he was, in the boat. There were also other boats with him. 37A furious squall came up, and the waves broke over the boat, so that it was nearly swamped. 38Jesus was in the stern, sleeping on a cushion. The disciples woke him and said to him, "Teacher, don't you care if we drown?"

39He got up, rebuked the wind and said to the waves, "Quiet! Be still!" Then the wind died down and it was completely calm.

40He said to his disciples, "Why are you so afraid? Do you still have no faith?"

41They were terrified and asked each other, "Who is this? Even the wind and the waves obey him!"

Jesus Restores a Demon-Possessed Man

5 They went across the lake to the region of the Gerasenes.ᵃ 2When Jesus got out of the boat, a man with an evilᵇ spirit came from the tombs to meet him. 3This man lived in the tombs, and no one could bind him anymore, not even with a chain. 4For he had often been chained hand and foot, but he tore the chains apart and broke the irons on his feet. No one was strong enough to subdue him. 5Night and day among the tombs and in the hills he would cry out and cut himself with stones.

6When he saw Jesus from a distance, he ran and fell on his knees in front of him. 7He shouted at the top of his voice, "What do you want with me, Jesus, Son of the Most High God? In God's name don't torture me!" 8For Jesus had said to him, "Come out of this man, you evil spirit!"

9Then Jesus asked him, "What is your name?"

"My name is Legion," he replied, "for we are many." 10And he begged Jesus again and again not to send them out of the area.

11A large herd of pigs was feeding on the nearby hillside. 12The demons begged Jesus, "Send us among the pigs; allow us to go into them." 13He gave them permission, and the evil spirits came out and went into the pigs. The herd, about two thousand in number, rushed down the steep bank into the lake and were drowned.

14Those tending the pigs ran off and reported this in the town and countryside, and the people went out to see what had happened. 15When they came to Jesus, they saw the man who had been possessed by the legion of demons, sitting there, dressed and in his right mind; and they were afraid. 16Those who

ᵃ1 Some manuscripts *Gadarenes*; other manuscripts *Gergesenes*   ᵇ2 Greek *unclean*; also in verses 8 and 13

had seen it told the people what had happened to the demon-possessed man—and told about the pigs as well. [17]Then the people began to plead with Jesus to leave their region.

[18]As Jesus was getting into the boat, the man who had been demon-possessed begged to go with him. [19]Jesus did not let him, but said, "Go home to your own people and tell them how much the Lord has done for you, and how he has had mercy on you." [20]So the man went away and began to tell in the Decapolis[a] how much Jesus had done for him. And all the people were amazed.

Jesus Raises a Dead Girl and Heals a Sick Woman

[21]When Jesus had again crossed over by boat to the other side of the lake, a large crowd gathered around him while he was by the lake. [22]Then one of the synagogue leaders, named Jairus, came, and when he saw Jesus, he fell at his feet. [23]He pleaded earnestly with him, "My little daughter is dying. Please come and put your hands on her so that she will be healed and live." [24]So Jesus went with him.

A large crowd followed and pressed around him. [25]And a woman was there who had been subject to bleeding for twelve years. [26]She had suffered a great deal under the care of many doctors and had spent all she had, yet instead of getting better she grew worse. [27]When she heard about Jesus, she came up behind him in the crowd and touched his cloak, [28]because she thought, "If I just touch his clothes, I will be healed." [29]Immediately her bleeding stopped and she felt in her body that she was freed from her suffering.

[30]At once Jesus realized that power had gone out from him. He turned around in the crowd and asked, "Who touched my clothes?"

[31]"You see the people crowding against you," his disciples answered, "and yet you can ask, 'Who touched me?' "

[32]But Jesus kept looking around to see who had done it. [33]Then the woman, knowing what had happened to her, came and fell at his feet and, trembling with fear, told him the whole truth. [34]He said to her, "Daughter, your faith has healed you. Go in peace and be freed from your suffering."

[35]While Jesus was still speaking, some people came from the house of Jairus, the synagogue leader. "Your daughter is dead," they said. "Why bother the teacher anymore?"

[36]Overhearing[b] what they said, Jesus told him, "Don't be afraid; just believe."

[37]He did not let anyone follow him except Peter, James and John the brother of James. [38]When they came to the home of the synagogue leader, Jesus saw a commotion, with people crying and wailing loudly. [39]He went in and said to them, "Why all this commotion and wailing? The child is not dead but asleep." [40]But they laughed at him.

After he put them all out, he took the child's father and mother and the disciples who were with him, and went in where the child was. [41]He took her by the hand and said to her, *"Talitha koum!"* (which means, "Little girl, I say to you, get up!"). [42]Immediately the girl stood up and began to walk around (she

---

[a] 20 That is, the Ten Cities   [b] 36 Or *Ignoring*

was twelve years old). At this they were completely astonished. [43]He gave strict orders not to let anyone know about this, and told them to give her something to eat.

A Prophet Without Honor

6 Jesus left there and went to his hometown, accompanied by his disciples. [2]When the Sabbath came, he began to teach in the synagogue, and many who heard him were amazed.

"Where did this man get these things?" they asked. "What's this wisdom that has been given him? What are these remarkable miracles he is performing? [3]Isn't this the carpenter? Isn't this Mary's son and the brother of James, Joseph,[a] Judas and Simon? Aren't his sisters here with us?" And they took offense at him.

[4]Jesus said to them, "Only in their own towns, among their relatives and in their own homes are prophets without honor." [5]He could not do any miracles there, except lay his hands on a few sick people and heal them. [6]He was amazed at their lack of faith.

Jesus Sends Out the Twelve

Then Jesus went around teaching from village to village. [7]Calling the Twelve to him, he began to send them out two by two and gave them authority over evil[b] spirits.

[8]These were his instructions: "Take nothing for the journey except a staff—no bread, no bag, no money in your belts. [9]Wear sandals but not an extra shirt. [10]Whenever you enter a house, stay there until you leave that town. [11]And if any place will not welcome you or listen to you, shake the dust off your feet when you leave, as a testimony against them."

[12]They went out and preached that people should repent. [13]They drove out many demons and anointed many sick people with oil and healed them.

John the Baptist Beheaded

[14]King Herod heard about this, for Jesus' name had become well known. Some were saying,[c] "John the Baptist has been raised from the dead, and that is why miraculous powers are at work in him."

[15]Others said, "He is Elijah."

And still others claimed, "He is a prophet, like one of the prophets of long ago."

[16]But when Herod heard this, he said, "John, whom I beheaded, has been raised from the dead!"

[17]For Herod himself had given orders to have John arrested, and he had him bound and put in prison. He did this because of Herodias, his brother Philip's wife, whom he had married. [18]For John had been saying to Herod, "It is not lawful for you to have your brother's wife." [19]So Herodias nursed a grudge against John and wanted to kill him. But she was not able to, [20]because Herod feared John and protected him, knowing him to be a righteous

---

[a] 3 Greek *Joses*, a variant of *Joseph*   [b] 7 Greek *unclean*   [c] 14 Some early manuscripts *He was saying*

and holy man. When Herod heard John, he was greatly puzzled[a]; yet he liked to listen to him.

21 Finally the opportune time came. On his birthday Herod gave a banquet for his high officials and military commanders and the leading men of Galilee. 22 When the daughter of[b] Herodias came in and danced, she pleased Herod and his dinner guests.

The king said to the girl, "Ask me for anything you want, and I'll give it to you." 23 And he promised her with an oath, "Whatever you ask I will give you, up to half my kingdom."

24 She went out and said to her mother, "What shall I ask for?"

"The head of John the Baptist," she answered.

25 At once the girl hurried in to the king with the request: "I want you to give me right now the head of John the Baptist on a platter."

26 The king was greatly distressed, but because of his oaths and his dinner guests, he did not want to refuse her. 27 So he immediately sent an executioner with orders to bring John's head. The man went, beheaded John in the prison, 28 and brought back his head on a platter. He presented it to the girl, and she gave it to her mother. 29 On hearing of this, John's disciples came and took his body and laid it in a tomb.

Jesus Feeds the Five Thousand

30 The apostles gathered around Jesus and reported to him all they had done and taught. 31 Then, because so many people were coming and going that they did not even have a chance to eat, he said to them, "Come with me by yourselves to a quiet place and get some rest."

32 So they went away by themselves in a boat to a solitary place. 33 But many who saw them leaving recognized them and ran on foot from all the towns and got there ahead of them. 34 When Jesus landed and saw a large crowd, he had compassion on them, because they were like sheep without a shepherd. So he began teaching them many things.

35 By this time it was late in the day, so his disciples came to him. "This is a remote place," they said, "and it's already very late. 36 Send the people away so that they can go to the surrounding countryside and villages and buy themselves something to eat."

37 But he answered, "You give them something to eat."

They said to him, "That would take eight months of a man's wages[c]! Are we to go and spend that much on bread and give it to them to eat?"

38 "How many loaves do you have?" he asked. "Go and see."

When they found out, they said, "Five—and two fish."

39 Then Jesus directed them to have all the people sit down in groups on the green grass. 40 So they sat down in groups of hundreds and fifties. 41 Taking the five loaves and the two fish and looking up to heaven, he gave thanks and broke the loaves. Then he gave them to his disciples to set before the people. He also divided the two fish among them all. 42 They all ate and were satisfied,

---

[a] 20 Some early manuscripts *he did many things*   [b] 22 Some early manuscripts *When his daughter*
[c] 37 Greek *take two hundred denarii*

⁴³and the disciples picked up twelve basketfuls of broken pieces of bread and fish. ⁴⁴The number of the men who had eaten was five thousand.

Jesus Walks on the Water

⁴⁵Immediately Jesus made his disciples get into the boat and go on ahead of him to Bethsaida, while he dismissed the crowd. ⁴⁶After leaving them, he went up on a mountainside to pray.

⁴⁷When evening came, the boat was in the middle of the lake, and he was alone on land. ⁴⁸He saw the disciples straining at the oars, because the wind was against them. Shortly before dawn he went out to them, walking on the lake. He was about to pass by them, ⁴⁹but when they saw him walking on the lake, they thought he was a ghost. They cried out, ⁵⁰because they all saw him and were terrified.

Immediately he spoke to them and said, "Take courage! It is I. Don't be afraid." ⁵¹Then he climbed into the boat with them, and the wind died down. They were completely amazed, ⁵²for they had not understood about the loaves; their hearts were hardened.

⁵³When they had crossed over, they landed at Gennesaret and anchored there. ⁵⁴As soon as they got out of the boat, people recognized Jesus. ⁵⁵They ran throughout that whole region and carried the sick on mats to wherever they heard he was. ⁵⁶And wherever he went—into villages, towns or countryside—they placed the sick in the marketplaces. They begged him to let them touch even the edge of his cloak, and all who touched him were healed.

That Which Defiles You

7 The Pharisees and some of the teachers of the law who had come from Jerusalem gathered around Jesus ²and saw some of his disciples eating food with hands that were defiled, that is, unwashed. ³(The Pharisees and all the Jews do not eat unless they give their hands a ceremonial washing, holding to the tradition of the elders. ⁴When they come from the marketplace they do not eat unless they wash. And they observe many other traditions, such as the washing of cups, pitchers and kettles.ᵃ)

⁵So the Pharisees and teachers of the law asked Jesus, "Why don't your disciples live according to the tradition of the elders instead of eating their food with defiled hands?"

⁶He replied, "Isaiah was right when he prophesied about you hypocrites; as it is written:

" 'These people honor me with their lips,
    but their hearts are far from me.
⁷They worship me in vain;
    their teachings are merely human rules.'ᵇ

⁸You have let go of the commands of God and are holding on to human traditions."

⁹And he continued, "You have a fine way of setting aside the commands of

---

ᵃ 4 Some early manuscripts *pitchers, kettles and dining couches*   ᵇ 6,7 Isaiah 29:13

God in order to observe[a] your own traditions! [10]For Moses said, 'Honor your father and your mother,'[b] and, 'Anyone who curses their father or mother must be put to death.'[c] [11]But you say that if anyone declares that what might have been used to help their father or mother is Corban (that is, devoted to God)— [12]then you no longer let them do anything for their father or mother. [13]Thus you nullify the word of God by your tradition that you have handed down. And you do many things like that."

[14]Again Jesus called the crowd to him and said, "Listen to me, everyone, and understand this. [15][16]Nothing outside you can defile you by going into you. Rather, it is what comes out of you that defiles you."

[17]After he had left the crowd and entered the house, his disciples asked him about this parable. [18]"Are you so dull?" he asked. "Don't you see that nothing that enters you from the outside can defile you? [19]For it doesn't go into your heart but into your stomach, and then out of your body." (In saying this, Jesus declared all foods clean.)

[20]He went on: "What comes out of you is what defiles you. [21]For from within, out of your hearts, come evil thoughts, sexual immorality, theft, murder, [22]adultery, greed, malice, deceit, lewdness, envy, slander, arrogance and folly. [23]All these evils come from inside and defile you."

Jesus Honors a Syrophoenician Woman's Faith

[24]Jesus left that place and went to the vicinity of Tyre.[d] He entered a house and did not want anyone to know it; yet he could not keep his presence secret. [25]In fact, as soon as she heard about him, a woman whose little daughter was possessed by an evil[e] spirit came and fell at his feet. [26]The woman was a Greek, born in Syrian Phoenicia. She begged Jesus to drive the demon out of her daughter.

[27]"First let the children eat all they want," he told her, "for it is not right to take the children's bread and toss it to the dogs."

[28]"Lord," she replied, "even the dogs under the table eat the children's crumbs."

[29]Then he told her, "For such a reply, you may go; the demon has left your daughter."

[30]She went home and found her child lying on the bed, and the demon gone.

Jesus Heals a Deaf and Mute Man

[31]Then Jesus left the vicinity of Tyre and went through Sidon, down to the Sea of Galilee and into the region of the Decapolis.[f] [32]There some people brought to him a man who was deaf and could hardly talk, and they begged Jesus to place his hand on him.

[33]After he took him aside, away from the crowd, Jesus put his fingers into the man's ears. Then he spit and touched the man's tongue. [34]He looked up to heaven and with a deep sigh said to him, *"Ephphatha!"* (which means, "Be

---

[a] 9 Some manuscripts *set up*   [b] 10 Exodus 20:12; Deut. 5:16   [c] 10 Exodus 21:17; Lev. 20:9
[d] 24 Many early manuscripts *Tyre and Sidon*   [e] 25 Greek *unclean*   [f] 31 That is, the Ten Cities

opened!"). 35At this, the man's ears were opened, his tongue was loosened and he began to speak plainly.

36Jesus commanded them not to tell anyone. But the more he did so, the more they kept talking about it. 37People were overwhelmed with amazement. "He has done everything well," they said. "He even makes the deaf hear and the mute speak."

Jesus Feeds the Four Thousand

8 During those days another large crowd gathered. Since they had nothing to eat, Jesus called his disciples to him and said, 2"I have compassion for these people; they have already been with me three days and have nothing to eat. 3If I send them home hungry, they will collapse on the way, because some of them have come a long distance."

4His disciples answered, "But where in this remote place can anyone get enough bread to feed them?"

5"How many loaves do you have?" Jesus asked.

"Seven," they replied.

6He told the crowd to sit down on the ground. When he had taken the seven loaves and given thanks, he broke them and gave them to his disciples to set before the people, and they did so. 7They had a few small fish as well; he gave thanks for them also and told the disciples to distribute them. 8The people ate and were satisfied. Afterward the disciples picked up seven basketfuls of broken pieces that were left over. 9About four thousand were present. And having sent them away, 10he got into the boat with his disciples and went to the region of Dalmanutha.

11The Pharisees came and began to question Jesus. To test him, they asked him for a sign from heaven. 12He sighed deeply and said, "Why does this generation ask for a sign? Truly I tell you, no sign will be given to it." 13Then he left them, got back into the boat and crossed to the other side.

The Yeast of the Pharisees and Herod

14The disciples had forgotten to bring bread, except for one loaf they had with them in the boat. 15"Be careful," Jesus warned them. "Watch out for the yeast of the Pharisees and that of Herod."

16They discussed this with one another and said, "It is because we have no bread."

17Aware of their discussion, Jesus asked them: "Why are you talking about having no bread? Do you still not see or understand? Are your hearts hardened? 18Do you have eyes but fail to see, and ears but fail to hear? And don't you remember? 19When I broke the five loaves for the five thousand, how many basketfuls of pieces did you pick up?"

"Twelve," they replied.

20"And when I broke the seven loaves for the four thousand, how many basketfuls of pieces did you pick up?"

They answered, "Seven."

21He said to them, "Do you still not understand?"

Jesus Heals a Blind Man at Bethsaida

22They came to Bethsaida, and some people brought a blind man and begged Jesus to touch him. 23He took the blind man by the hand and led him outside the village. When he had spit on the man's eyes and put his hands on him, Jesus asked, "Do you see anything?"

24He looked up and said, "I see people; they look like trees walking around."

25Once more Jesus put his hands on the man's eyes. Then his eyes were opened, his sight was restored, and he saw everything clearly. 26Jesus sent him home, saying, "Don't even go into the village. *a*"

Peter Declares That Jesus Is the Messiah

27Jesus and his disciples went on to the villages around Caesarea Philippi. On the way he asked them, "Who do people say I am?"

28They replied, "Some say John the Baptist; others say Elijah; and still others, one of the prophets."

29"But what about you?" he asked. "Who do you say I am?"

Peter answered, "You are the Messiah."

30Jesus warned them not to tell anyone about him.

Jesus Predicts His Death

31He then began to teach them that the Son of Man must suffer many things and be rejected by the elders, the chief priests and the teachers of the law, and that he must be killed and after three days rise again. 32He spoke plainly about this, and Peter took him aside and began to rebuke him.

33But when Jesus turned and looked at his disciples, he rebuked Peter. "Get behind me, Satan!" he said. "You do not have in mind the concerns of God, but merely human concerns."

The Way of the Cross

34Then he called the crowd to him along with his disciples and said: "Those who would be my disciples must deny themselves and take up their cross and follow me. 35For those who want to save their life *b* will lose it, but those who lose their life for me and for the gospel will save it. 36What good is it for you to gain the whole world, yet forfeit your soul? 37Or what can you give in exchange for your soul? 38If any of you are ashamed of me and my words in this adulterous and sinful generation, the Son of Man will be ashamed of you when he comes in his Father's glory with the holy angels."

9 And he said to them, "Truly I tell you, some who are standing here will not taste death before they see that the kingdom of God has come with power."

The Transfiguration

2After six days Jesus took Peter, James and John with him and led them up a high mountain, where they were all alone. There he was transfigured before

---

a 26 Some manuscripts *Don't even go and tell anyone in the village*   *b* 35 The Greek word means either *life* or *soul*; also in verses 36 and 37.

them. ³His clothes became dazzling white, whiter than anyone in the world could bleach them. ⁴And there appeared before them Elijah and Moses, who were talking with Jesus.

⁵Peter said to Jesus, "Rabbi, it is good for us to be here. Let us put up three shelters—one for you, one for Moses and one for Elijah." ⁶(He did not know what to say, they were so frightened.)

⁷Then a cloud appeared and covered them, and a voice came from the cloud: "This is my Son, whom I love. Listen to him!"

⁸Suddenly, when they looked around, they no longer saw anyone with them except Jesus.

⁹As they were coming down the mountain, Jesus gave them orders not to tell anyone what they had seen until the Son of Man had risen from the dead. ¹⁰They kept the matter to themselves, discussing what "rising from the dead" meant

¹¹And they asked him, "Why do the teachers of the law say that Elijah must come first?"

¹²Jesus replied, "To be sure, Elijah does come first, and restores all things. Why then is it written that the Son of Man must suffer much and be rejected? ¹³But I tell you, Elijah has come, and they have done to him everything they wished, just as it is written about him."

Jesus Heals a Demon-Possessed Boy

¹⁴When they came to the other disciples, they saw a large crowd around them and the teachers of the law arguing with them. ¹⁵As soon as all the people saw Jesus, they were overwhelmed with wonder and ran to greet him.

¹⁶"What are you arguing with them about?" he asked.

¹⁷A man in the crowd answered, "Teacher, I brought you my son, who is possessed by a spirit that has robbed him of speech. ¹⁸Whenever it seizes him, it throws him to the ground. He foams at the mouth, gnashes his teeth and becomes rigid. I asked your disciples to drive out the spirit, but they could not."

¹⁹"You unbelieving generation," Jesus replied, "how long shall I stay with you? How long shall I put up with you? Bring the boy to me."

²⁰So they brought him. When the spirit saw Jesus, it immediately threw the boy into a convulsion. He fell to the ground and rolled around, foaming at the mouth.

²¹Jesus asked the boy's father, "How long has he been like this?"

"From childhood," he answered. ²²"It has often thrown him into fire or water to kill him. But if you can do anything, take pity on us and help us."

²³" 'If you can'?" said Jesus. "Everything is possible for one who believes."

²⁴Immediately the boy's father exclaimed, "I do believe; help me overcome my unbelief!"

²⁵When Jesus saw that a crowd was running to the scene, he rebuked the evil[a] spirit. "You deaf and mute spirit," he said, "I command you, come out of him and never enter him again."

²⁶The spirit shrieked, convulsed him violently and came out. The boy

[a] 25 Greek *unclean*

looked so much like a corpse that many said, "He's dead." ²⁷But Jesus took him by the hand and lifted him to his feet, and he stood up.

²⁸After Jesus had gone indoors, his disciples asked him privately, "Why couldn't we drive it out?"

²⁹He replied, "This kind can come out only by prayer.ᵃ"

Jesus Predicts His Death a Second Time

³⁰They left that place and passed through Galilee. Jesus did not want anyone to know where they were, ³¹because he was teaching his disciples. He said to them, "The Son of Man is going to be delivered over to human hands. He will be killed, and after three days he will rise." ³²But they did not understand what he meant and were afraid to ask him about it.

³³They came to Capernaum. When he was in the house, he asked them, "What were you arguing about on the road?" ³⁴But they kept quiet because on the way they had argued about who was the greatest.

³⁵Sitting down, Jesus called the Twelve and said, "Anyone who wants to be first must be the very last, and the servant of all."

³⁶He took a little child whom he placed among them. Taking the child in his arms, he said to them, ³⁷"Whoever welcomes one of these little children in my name welcomes me; and whoever welcomes me does not welcome me but the one who sent me."

Whoever Is Not Against Us Is for Us

³⁸"Teacher," said John, "we saw someone driving out demons in your name and we told him to stop, because he was not one of us."

³⁹"Do not stop him," Jesus said. "No one who does a miracle in my name can in the next moment say anything bad about me, ⁴⁰for whoever is not against us is for us. ⁴¹Truly I tell you, anyone who gives you a cup of water in my name because you belong to the Messiah will certainly be rewarded.

Causing to Stumble

⁴²"If anyone causes one of these little ones—those who believe in me—to stumble, it would be better for them if a large millstone were hung around their neck and they were thrown into the sea. ⁴³[⁴⁴]If your hand causes you to stumble, cut it off. It is better for you to enter life maimed than with two hands to go into hell, where the fire never goes out. ⁴⁵[⁴⁶]And if your foot causes you to stumble, cut it off. It is better for you to enter life crippled than to have two feet and be thrown into hell. ⁴⁷And if your eye causes you to stumble, pluck it out. It is better for you to enter the kingdom of God with one eye than to have two eyes and be thrown into hell, ⁴⁸where

> " 'their worm does not die,
>   and the fire is not quenched.'ᵇ

⁴⁹Everyone will be salted with fire.

⁵⁰"Salt is good, but if it loses its saltiness, how can you make it salty again? Have salt in yourselves, and be at peace with each other."

ᵃ 29 Some manuscripts *prayer and fasting*   ᵇ 48 Isaiah 66:24

Divorce

10 Jesus then left that place and went into the region of Judea and across the Jordan. Again crowds of people came to him, and as was his custom, he taught them.

2Some Pharisees came and tested him by asking, "Is it lawful for a man to divorce his wife?"

3"What did Moses command you?" he replied.

4They said, "Moses permitted a man to write a certificate of divorce and send her away."

5"It was because your hearts were hard that Moses wrote you this law," Jesus replied. 6"But at the beginning of creation God 'made them male and female.'*a* 7'For this reason a man will leave his father and mother and be united to his wife,*b* 8and the two will become one flesh.'*c* So they are no longer two, but one. 9Therefore what God has joined together, let no one separate."

10When they were in the house again, the disciples asked Jesus about this. 11He answered, "Anyone who divorces his wife and marries another woman commits adultery against her. 12And if she divorces her husband and marries another man, she commits adultery."

The Little Children and Jesus

13People were bringing little children to Jesus for him to touch them, but the disciples rebuked them. 14When Jesus saw this, he was indignant. He said to them, "Let the little children come to me, and do not hinder them, for the kingdom of God belongs to such as these. 15Truly I tell you, anyone who will not receive the kingdom of God like a little child will never enter it." 16And he took the children in his arms, put his hands on them and blessed them.

The Rich and the Kingdom of God

17As Jesus started on his way, a man ran up to him and fell on his knees before him. "Good teacher," he asked, "what must I do to inherit eternal life?"

18"Why do you call me good?" Jesus answered. "No one is good—except God alone. 19You know the commandments: 'Do not murder, do not commit adultery, do not steal, do not give false testimony, do not defraud, honor your father and mother.'*d*"

20"Teacher," he declared, "all these I have kept since I was a boy."

21Jesus looked at him and loved him. "One thing you lack," he said. "Go, sell everything you have and give to the poor, and you will have treasure in heaven. Then come, follow me."

22At this the man's face fell. He went away sad, because he had great wealth.

23Jesus looked around and said to his disciples, "How hard it is for the rich to enter the kingdom of God!"

24The disciples were amazed at his words. But Jesus said again, "Children, how hard it is*e* to enter the kingdom of God! 25It is easier for a camel to go through the eye of a needle than for the rich to enter the kingdom of God."

---

*a*6 Gen. 1:27   *b*7 Some early manuscripts do not have *and be united to his wife.*   *c*8 Gen. 2:24
*d*19 Exodus 20:12–16; Deut. 5:16–20   *e*24 Some manuscripts *is for those who trust in riches*

26The disciples were even more amazed, and said to each other, "Who then can be saved?"

27Jesus looked at them and said, "Humanly, this is impossible, but not with God; all things are possible with God."

28Then Peter spoke up, "We have left everything to follow you!"

29"Truly I tell you," Jesus replied, "no one who has left home or brothers or sisters or mother or father or children or fields for me and the gospel 30will fail to receive a hundred times as much in this present age: homes, brothers, sisters, mothers, children and fields—along with persecutions—and in the age to come eternal life. 31But many who are first will be last, and the last first."

Jesus Predicts His Death a Third Time

32They were on their way up to Jerusalem, with Jesus leading the way, and the disciples were astonished, while those who followed were afraid. Again he took the Twelve aside and told them what was going to happen to him. 33"We are going up to Jerusalem," he said, "and the Son of Man will be delivered over to the chief priests and the teachers of the law. They will condemn him to death and will hand him over to the Gentiles, 34who will mock him and spit on him, flog him and kill him. Three days later he will rise."

The Request of James and John

35Then James and John, the sons of Zebedee, came to him. "Teacher," they said, "we want you to do for us whatever we ask."

36"What do you want me to do for you?" he asked.

37They replied, "Let one of us sit at your right and the other at your left in your glory."

38"You don't know what you are asking," Jesus said. "Can you drink the cup I drink or be baptized with the baptism I am baptized with?"

39"We can," they answered.

Jesus said to them, "You will drink the cup I drink and be baptized with the baptism I am baptized with, 40but to sit at my right or left is not for me to grant. These places belong to those for whom they have been prepared."

41When the ten heard about this, they became indignant with James and John. 42Jesus called them together and said, "You know that those who are regarded as rulers of the Gentiles lord it over them, and their high officials exercise authority over them. 43Not so with you. Instead, whoever wants to become great among you must be your servant, 44and whoever wants to be first must be slave of all. 45For even the Son of Man did not come to be served, but to serve, and to give his life as a ransom for many."

Blind Bartimaeus Receives His Sight

46Then they came to Jericho. As Jesus and his disciples, together with a large crowd, were leaving the city, a blind man, Bartimaeus (that is, the Son of Timaeus), was sitting by the roadside begging. 47When he heard that it was Jesus of Nazareth, he began to shout, "Jesus, Son of David, have mercy on me!"

48Many rebuked him and told him to be quiet, but he shouted all the more, "Son of David, have mercy on me!"

49Jesus stopped and said, "Call him."

So they called to the blind man, "Cheer up! On your feet! He's calling you." 50Throwing his cloak aside, he jumped to his feet and came to Jesus.

51"What do you want me to do for you?" Jesus asked him.

The blind man said, "Rabbi, I want to see."

52"Go," said Jesus, "your faith has healed you." Immediately he received his sight and followed Jesus along the road.

Jesus Comes to Jerusalem as King

11 As they approached Jerusalem and came to Bethphage and Bethany at the Mount of Olives, Jesus sent two of his disciples, 2saying to them, "Go to the village ahead of you, and just as you enter it, you will find a colt tied there, which no one has ever ridden. Untie it and bring it here. 3If anyone asks you, 'Why are you doing this?' say, 'The Lord needs it and will send it back here shortly.' "

4They went and found a colt outside in the street, tied at a doorway. As they untied it, 5some people standing there asked, "What are you doing, untying that colt?" 6They answered as Jesus had told them to, and the people let them go. 7When they brought the colt to Jesus and threw their cloaks over it, he sat on it. 8Many people spread their cloaks on the road, while others spread branches they had cut in the fields. 9Those who went ahead and those who followed shouted,

"Hosanna!*a*"

"Blessed is he who comes in the name of the Lord!"*b*

10"Blessed is the coming kingdom of our father David!"

"Hosanna in the highest heaven!"

11Jesus entered Jerusalem and went into the temple courts. He looked around at everything, but since it was already late, he went out to Bethany with the Twelve.

Jesus Curses a Fig Tree and Clears the Temple Courts

12The next day as they were leaving Bethany, Jesus was hungry. 13Seeing in the distance a fig tree in leaf, he went to find out if it had any fruit. When he reached it, he found nothing but leaves, because it was not the season for figs. 14Then he said to the tree, "May no one ever eat fruit from you again." And his disciples heard him say it.

15On reaching Jerusalem, Jesus entered the temple courts and began driving out those who were buying and selling there. He overturned the tables of the money changers and the benches of those selling doves, 16and would not allow anyone to carry merchandise through the temple courts. 17And as he taught them, he said, "Is it not written:

a 9 A Hebrew expression meaning "Save!" which became an exclamation of praise; also in verse 10
b 9 Psalm 118:25,26

" 'My house will be called
a house of prayer for all nations' [a]?

But you have made it 'a den of robbers.' [b]"

18The chief priests and the teachers of the law heard this and began looking for a way to kill him, for they feared him, because the whole crowd was amazed at his teaching.

19When evening came, they[c] went out of the city.

20In the morning, as they went along, they saw the fig tree withered from the roots. 21Peter remembered and said to Jesus, "Rabbi, look! The fig tree you cursed has withered!"

22"Have[d] faith in God," Jesus answered. 23"Truly I tell you, if you say to this mountain, 'Go, throw yourself into the sea,' and do not doubt in your heart but believe that what you say will happen, it will be done for you. 24Therefore I tell you, whatever you ask for in prayer, believe that you have received it, and it will be yours. 25[26]And when you stand praying, if you hold anything against anyone, forgive them, so that your Father in heaven may forgive you your sins."

The Authority of Jesus Questioned

27They arrived again in Jerusalem, and while Jesus was walking in the temple courts, the chief priests, the teachers of the law and the elders came to him. 28"By what authority are you doing these things?" they asked. "And who gave you authority to do this?"

29Jesus replied, "I will ask you one question. Answer me, and I will tell you by what authority I am doing these things. 30John's baptism—was it from heaven, or of human origin? Tell me!"

31They discussed it among themselves and said, "If we say, 'From heaven,' he will ask, 'Then why didn't you believe him?' 32But if we say, 'Of human origin' . . . ." (They feared the people, for everyone held that John really was a prophet.)

33So they answered Jesus, "We don't know."

Jesus said, "Neither will I tell you by what authority I am doing these things."

The Parable of the Tenants

12 He then began to speak to them in parables: "A man planted a vineyard. He put a wall around it, dug a pit for the winepress and built a watchtower. Then he rented the vineyard to some farmers and moved to another place. 2At harvest time he sent a servant to the tenants to collect from them some of the fruit of the vineyard. 3But they seized him, beat him and sent him away empty-handed. 4Then he sent another servant to them; they struck this man on the head and treated him shamefully. 5He sent still another, and that one they killed. He sent many others; some of them they beat, others they killed.

---

[a] 17 Isaiah 56:7   [b] 17 Jer. 7:11   [c] 19 Some early manuscripts *he*   [d] 22 Some early manuscripts *If you have*

[6]"He had one left to send, a son, whom he loved. He sent him last of all, saying, 'They will respect my son.'

[7]"But the tenants said to one another, 'This is the heir. Come, let's kill him, and the inheritance will be ours.' [8]So they took him and killed him, and threw him out of the vineyard.

[9]"What then will the owner of the vineyard do? He will come and kill those tenants and give the vineyard to others. [10]Haven't you read this passage of Scripture:

> " 'The stone the builders rejected
>   has become the cornerstone;
> [11] the Lord has done this,
>   and it is marvelous in our eyes'[a]?"

[12]Then the chief priests, the teachers of the law and the elders looked for a way to arrest him because they knew he had spoken the parable against them. But they were afraid of the crowd; so they left him and went away.

Paying the Poll Tax to Caesar

[13]Later they sent some of the Pharisees and Herodians to Jesus to catch him in his words. [14]They came to him and said, "Teacher, we know that you are a man of integrity. You aren't swayed by others, because you pay no attention to who they are; but you teach the way of God in accordance with the truth. Is it right to pay the poll tax[b] to Caesar or not? [15]Should we pay or shouldn't we?"

But Jesus knew their hypocrisy. "Why are you trying to trap me?" he asked. "Bring me a denarius and let me look at it." [16]They brought the coin, and he asked them, "Whose portrait is this? And whose inscription?"

"Caesar's," they replied.

[17]Then Jesus said to them, "Give back to Caesar what is Caesar's and to God what is God's."

And they were amazed at him.

Marriage at the Resurrection

[18]Then the Sadducees, who say there is no resurrection, came to him with a question. [19]"Teacher," they said, "Moses wrote for us that if a man's brother dies and leaves a wife but no children, the man must marry the widow and raise up an heir for his brother. [20]Now there were seven brothers. The first one married and died without leaving any children. [21]The second one married the widow, but he also died, leaving no child. It was the same with the third. [22]In fact, none of the seven left any children. Last of all, the woman died too. [23]At the resurrection[c] whose wife will she be, since the seven were married to her?"

[24]Jesus replied, "Are you not in error because you do not know the Scriptures or the power of God? [25]When the dead rise, they will neither marry nor be given in marriage; they will be like the angels in heaven. [26]Now about the dead rising—have you not read in the Book of Moses, in the account of the

---

[a]11 Psalm 118:22,23   [b]14 The poll tax was a special tax levied on subject peoples, not on Roman citizens.   [c]23 Some manuscripts *resurrection, when people rise from the dead,*

burning bush, how God said to him, 'I am the God of Abraham, the God of Isaac, and the God of Jacob'ᵃ? ²⁷He is not the God of the dead, but of the living. You are badly mistaken!"

The Greatest Commandment

²⁸One of the teachers of the law came and heard them debating. Noticing that Jesus had given them a good answer, he asked him, "Of all the commandments, which is the most important?"

²⁹"The most important one," answered Jesus, "is this: 'Hear, O Israel, the Lord our God, the Lord is one.ᵇ ³⁰Love the Lord your God with all your heart and with all your soul and with all your mind and with all your strength.'ᶜ ³¹The second is this: 'Love your neighbor as yourself.'ᵈ There is no commandment greater than these."

³²"Well said, teacher," the man replied. "You are right in saying that God is one and there is no other but him. ³³To love him with all your heart, with all your understanding and with all your strength, and to love your neighbor as yourself is more important than all burnt offerings and sacrifices."

³⁴When Jesus saw that he had answered wisely, he said to him, "You are not far from the kingdom of God." And from then on no one dared ask him any more questions.

Whose Son Is the Messiah?

³⁵While Jesus was teaching in the temple courts, he asked, "Why do the teachers of the law say that the Messiah is the son of David? ³⁶David himself, speaking by the Holy Spirit, declared:

" 'The Lord said to my Lord:
"Sit at my right hand
until I put your enemies
under your feet." 'ᵉ

³⁷David himself calls him 'Lord.' How then can he be his son?"
The large crowd listened to him with delight.

Warning Against the Teachers of the Law

³⁸As he taught, Jesus said, "Watch out for the teachers of the law. They like to walk around in flowing robes and be greeted with respect in the marketplaces, ³⁹and have the most important seats in the synagogues and the places of honor at banquets. ⁴⁰They devour widows' houses and for a show make lengthy prayers. These men will be punished most severely."

The Widow's Offering

⁴¹Jesus sat down opposite the place where the offerings were put and watched the crowd putting their money into the temple treasury. Many rich people threw in large amounts. ⁴²But a poor widow came and put in two very small copper coins, worth only a fraction of a penny.

ᵃ 26 Exodus 3:6   ᵇ 29 Or the Lord our God is one Lord   ᶜ 30 Deut. 6:4,5   ᵈ 31 Lev. 19:18
ᵉ 36 Psalm 110:1

43Calling his disciples to him, Jesus said, "Truly I tell you, this poor widow has put more into the treasury than all the others. 44They all gave out of their wealth; but she, out of her poverty, put in everything—all she had to live on."

The Destruction of the Temple and Signs of the End Times

13 As he was leaving the temple, one of his disciples said to him, "Look, Teacher! What massive stones! What magnificent buildings!"

2"Do you see all these great buildings?" replied Jesus. "Not one stone here will be left on another; every one will be thrown down."

3As Jesus was sitting on the Mount of Olives opposite the temple, Peter, James, John and Andrew asked him privately, 4"Tell us, when will these things happen? And what will be the sign that they are all about to be fulfilled?"

5Jesus said to them: "Watch out that no one deceives you. 6Many will come in my name, claiming, 'I am he,' and will deceive many. 7When you hear of wars and rumors of wars, do not be alarmed. Such things must happen, but the end is still to come. 8Nation will rise against nation, and kingdom against kingdom. There will be earthquakes in various places, and famines. These are the beginning of birth pains.

9"You must be on your guard. You will be handed over to the local councils and flogged in the synagogues. On account of me you will stand before governors and kings as witnesses to them. 10And the gospel must first be preached to all nations. 11Whenever you are arrested and brought to trial, do not worry beforehand about what to say. Just say whatever is given you at the time, for it is not you speaking, but the Holy Spirit.

12"Brother will betray brother to death, and a father his child. Children will rebel against their parents and have them put to death. 13Everyone will hate you because of me, but those who stand firm to the end will be saved.

14"When you see 'the abomination that causes desolation'*a* standing where it*b* does not belong—let the reader understand—then let those who are in Judea flee to the mountains. 15Let no one on the housetop go down or enter the house to take anything out. 16Let no one in the field go back to get their cloak. 17How dreadful it will be in those days for pregnant women and nursing mothers! 18Pray that this will not take place in winter, 19because those will be days of distress unequaled from the beginning, when God created the world, until now—and never to be equaled again.

20"If the Lord had not cut short those days, no one would survive. But for the sake of the elect, whom he has chosen, he has shortened them. 21At that time if anyone says to you, 'Look, here is the Messiah!' or, 'Look, there he is!' do not believe it. 22For false messiahs and false prophets will appear and perform signs and wonders to deceive, if possible, even the elect. 23So be on your guard; I have told you everything ahead of time.

24"But in those days, following that distress,

> " 'the sun will be darkened,
>   and the moon will not give its light;
> 25the stars will fall from the sky,
>   and the heavenly bodies will be shaken.'*c*

a 14 Daniel 9:27; 11:31; 12:11   *b 14* Or *he*   *c 25* Isaiah 13:10; 34:4

[26]"At that time people will see the Son of Man coming in clouds with great power and glory. [27]And he will send his angels and gather his elect from the four winds, from the ends of the earth to the ends of the heavens.

[28]"Now learn this lesson from the fig tree: As soon as its twigs get tender and its leaves come out, you know that summer is near. [29]Even so, when you see these things happening, you know that it[a] is near, right at the door. [30]Truly I tell you, this generation will certainly not pass away until all these things have happened. [31]Heaven and earth will pass away, but my words will never pass away.

The Day and Hour Unknown

[32]"But about that day or hour no one knows, not even the angels in heaven, nor the Son, but only the Father. [33]Be on guard! Be alert[b]! You do not know when that time will come. [34]It's like a man going away: He leaves his house and puts his servants in charge, each with an assigned task, and tells the one at the door to keep watch.

[35]"Therefore keep watch because you do not know when the owner of the house will come back—whether in the evening, or at midnight, or when the rooster crows, or at dawn. [36]If he comes suddenly, do not let him find you sleeping. [37]What I say to you, I say to everyone: 'Watch!' "

Jesus Anointed at Bethany

14 Now the Passover and the Festival of Unleavened Bread were only two days away, and the chief priests and the teachers of the law were looking for some sly way to arrest Jesus and kill him. [2]"But not during the Festival," they said, "or the people may riot."

[3]While he was in Bethany, reclining at the table in the home of Simon the Leper, a woman came with an alabaster jar of very expensive perfume, made of pure nard. She broke the jar and poured the perfume on his head.

[4]Some of those present were saying indignantly to one another, "Why this waste of perfume? [5]It could have been sold for more than a year's wages[c] and the money given to the poor." And they rebuked her harshly.

[6]"Leave her alone," said Jesus. "Why are you bothering her? She has done a beautiful thing to me. [7]The poor you will always have with you,[d] and you can help them any time you want. But you will not always have me. [8]She did what she could. She poured perfume on my body beforehand to prepare for my burial. [9]Truly I tell you, wherever the gospel is preached throughout the world, what she has done will also be told, in memory of her."

[10]Then Judas Iscariot, one of the Twelve, went to the chief priests to betray Jesus to them. [11]They were delighted to hear this and promised to give him money. So he watched for an opportunity to hand him over.

The Lord's Supper

[12]On the first day of the Festival of Unleavened Bread, when it was cus-

---

[a] 29 Or he   [b] 33 Some manuscripts *alert and pray*   [c] 5 Greek *than three hundred denarii*   [d] 7 See Deut. 15:11.

tomary to sacrifice the Passover lamb, Jesus' disciples asked him, "Where do you want us to go and make preparations for you to eat the Passover?"

[13]So he sent two of his disciples, telling them, "Go into the city, and a man carrying a jar of water will meet you. Follow him. [14]Say to the owner of the house he enters, 'The Teacher asks: Where is my guest room, where I may eat the Passover with my disciples?' [15]He will show you a large room upstairs, furnished and ready. Make preparations for us there."

[16]The disciples left, went into the city and found things just as Jesus had told them. So they prepared the Passover.

[17]When evening came, Jesus arrived with the Twelve. [18]While they were reclining at the table eating, he said, "Truly I tell you, one of you will betray me—one who is eating with me."

[19]They were saddened, and one by one they said to him, "Surely not I?"

[20]"It is one of the Twelve," he replied, "one who dips bread into the bowl with me. [21]The Son of Man will go just as it is written about him. But woe to that man who betrays the Son of Man! It would be better for him if he had not been born."

[22]While they were eating, Jesus took bread, and when he had given thanks, he broke it and gave it to his disciples, saying, "Take it; this is my body."

[23]Then he took the cup, and when he had given thanks, he gave it to them, and they all drank from it.

[24]"This is my blood of the[a] covenant, which is poured out for many," he said to them. [25]"Truly I tell you, I will not drink again of the fruit of the vine until that day when I drink it new in the kingdom of God."

[26]When they had sung a hymn, they went out to the Mount of Olives.

Jesus Predicts Peter's Denial

[27]"You will all fall away," Jesus told them, "for it is written:

" 'I will strike the shepherd,
and the sheep will be scattered.'[b]

[28]But after I have risen, I will go ahead of you into Galilee."

[29]Peter declared, "Even if all fall away, I will not."

[30]"Truly I tell you," Jesus answered, "today—yes, tonight—before the rooster crows twice[c] you yourself will disown me three times."

[31]But Peter insisted emphatically, "Even if I have to die with you, I will never disown you." And all the others said the same.

Gethsemane

[32]They went to a place called Gethsemane, and Jesus said to his disciples, "Sit here while I pray." [33]He took Peter, James and John along with him, and he began to be deeply distressed and troubled. [34]"My soul is overwhelmed with sorrow to the point of death," he said to them. "Stay here and keep watch."

[35]Going a little farther, he fell to the ground and prayed that if possible the

[a] 24 Some manuscripts *the new*   [b] 27 Zech. 13:7   [c] 30 Some early manuscripts do not have *twice*.

hour might pass from him. 36"*Abba*,^a Father," he said, "everything is possible for you. Take this cup from me. Yet not what I will, but what you will."

37Then he returned to his disciples and found them sleeping. "Simon," he said to Peter, "are you asleep? Could you not keep watch for one hour? 38Watch and pray so that you will not fall into temptation. The spirit is willing, but the flesh is weak."

39Once more he went away and prayed the same thing. 40When he came back, he again found them sleeping, because their eyes were heavy. They did not know what to say to him.

41Returning the third time, he said to them, "Are you still sleeping and resting? Enough! The hour has come. Look, the Son of Man is delivered into the hands of sinners. 42Rise! Let us go! Here comes my betrayer!"

Jesus Arrested

43Just as he was speaking, Judas, one of the Twelve, appeared. With him was a crowd armed with swords and clubs, sent from the chief priests, the teachers of the law, and the elders.

44Now the betrayer had arranged a signal with them: "The one I kiss is the man; arrest him and lead him away under guard." 45Going at once to Jesus, Judas said, "Rabbi!" and kissed him. 46The men seized Jesus and arrested him. 47Then one of those standing near drew his sword and struck the servant of the high priest, cutting off his ear.

48"Am I leading a rebellion," said Jesus, "that you have come out with swords and clubs to capture me? 49Every day I was with you, teaching in the temple courts, and you did not arrest me. But the Scriptures must be fulfilled." 50Then everyone deserted him and fled.

51A young man, wearing nothing but a linen garment, was following Jesus. When they seized him, 52he fled naked, leaving his garment behind.

Jesus Before the Sanhedrin

53They took Jesus to the high priest, and all the chief priests, the elders and the teachers of the law came together. 54Peter followed him at a distance, right into the courtyard of the high priest. There he sat with the guards and warmed himself at the fire.

55The chief priests and the whole Sanhedrin were looking for evidence against Jesus so that they could put him to death, but they did not find any. 56Many testified falsely against him, but their statements did not agree.

57Then some stood up and gave this false testimony against him: 58"We heard him say, 'I will destroy this temple made with human hands and in three days will build another, not made with hands.' " 59Yet even then their testimony did not agree.

60Then the high priest stood up before them and asked Jesus, "Are you not going to answer? What is this testimony that these men are bringing against you?" 61But Jesus remained silent and gave no answer.

Again the high priest asked him, "Are you the Messiah, the Son of the Blessed One?"

^a 36 Aramaic for *Father*

62"I am," said Jesus. "And you will see the Son of Man sitting at the right hand of the Mighty One and coming on the clouds of heaven."

63The high priest tore his clothes. "Why do we need any more witnesses?" he asked. 64"You have heard the blasphemy. What do you think?"

They all condemned him as worthy of death. 65Then some began to spit at him; they blindfolded him, struck him with their fists, and said, "Prophesy!" And the guards took him and beat him.

Peter Disowns Jesus

66While Peter was below in the courtyard, one of the servant girls of the high priest came by. 67When she saw Peter warming himself, she looked closely at him.

"You also were with that Nazarene, Jesus," she said.

68But he denied it. "I don't know or understand what you're talking about," he said, and went out into the entryway.*ᵃ*

69When the servant girl saw him there, she said again to those standing around, "This fellow is one of them." 70Again he denied it.

After a little while, those standing near said to Peter, "Surely you are one of them, for you are a Galilean."

71He began to call down curses, and he swore to them, "I don't know this man you're talking about."

72Immediately the rooster crowed the second time.*ᵇ* Then Peter remembered the word Jesus had spoken to him: "Before the rooster crows twice*ᶜ* you will disown me three times." And he broke down and wept.

Jesus Before Pilate

15 Very early in the morning, the chief priests, with the elders, the teachers of the law and the whole Sanhedrin, reached a decision. They bound Jesus, led him away and handed him over to Pilate.

2"Are you the king of the Jews?" asked Pilate.

"You have said so," Jesus replied.

3The chief priests accused him of many things. 4So again Pilate asked him, "Aren't you going to answer? See how many things they are accusing you of."

5But Jesus still made no reply, and Pilate was amazed.

6Now it was the custom at the Festival to release a prisoner whom the people requested. 7A man called Barabbas was in prison with the insurrectionists who had committed murder in the uprising. 8The crowd came up and asked Pilate to do for them what he usually did.

9"Do you want me to release to you the king of the Jews?" asked Pilate, 10knowing it was out of envy that the chief priests had handed Jesus over to him. 11But the chief priests stirred up the crowd to have Pilate release Barabbas instead.

12"What shall I do, then, with the one you call the king of the Jews?" Pilate asked them.

13"Crucify him!" they shouted.

ᵃ 68 Some early manuscripts *entryway and the rooster crowed*   *ᵇ 72* Some early manuscripts do not have *the second time.*   *ᶜ 72* Some early manuscripts do not have *twice.*

14"Why? What crime has he committed?" asked Pilate.

But they shouted all the louder, "Crucify him!"

15Wanting to satisfy the crowd, Pilate released Barabbas to them. He had Jesus flogged, and handed him over to be crucified.

The Soldiers Mock Jesus

16The soldiers led Jesus away into the palace (that is, the Praetorium) and called together the whole company of soldiers. 17They put a purple robe on him, then twisted together a crown of thorns and set it on him. 18And they began to call out to him, "Hail, king of the Jews!" 19Again and again they struck him on the head with a staff and spit on him. Falling on their knees, they paid homage to him. 20And when they had mocked him, they took off the purple robe and put his own clothes on him. Then they led him out to crucify him.

The Crucifixion

21A certain man from Cyrene, Simon, the father of Alexander and Rufus, was passing by on his way in from the country, and they forced him to carry the cross. 22They brought Jesus to the place called Golgotha (which means The Place of the Skull). 23Then they offered him wine mixed with myrrh, but he did not take it. 24And they crucified him. Dividing up his clothes, they cast lots to see what each would get.

25It was nine in the morning when they crucified him. 26The written notice of the charge against him read: THE KING OF THE JEWS. 27[28]They crucified two rebels with him, one on his right and one on his left. 29Those who passed by hurled insults at him, shaking their heads and saying, "So! You who are going to destroy the temple and build it in three days, 30come down from the cross and save yourself!"

31In the same way the chief priests and the teachers of the law mocked him among themselves. "He saved others," they said, "but he can't save himself! 32Let this Messiah, this king of Israel, come down now from the cross, that we may see and believe." Those crucified with him also heaped insults on him.

The Death of Jesus

33At noon, darkness came over the whole land until three in the afternoon. 34And at three in the afternoon Jesus cried out in a loud voice, *"Eloi, Eloi, lema sabachthani?"*—which means, "My God, my God, why have you forsaken me?"[a]

35When some of those standing near heard this, they said, "Listen, he's calling Elijah."

36Someone ran, filled a sponge with wine vinegar, put it on a staff, and offered it to Jesus to drink. "Now leave him alone. Let's see if Elijah comes to take him down," he said.

37With a loud cry, Jesus breathed his last.

38The curtain of the temple was torn in two from top to bottom. 39And when

a 34 Psalm 22:1

the centurion, who stood there in front of Jesus, saw how he died,[a] he said, "Surely this man was the Son of God!" [40]Some women were watching from a distance. Among them were Mary Magdalene, Mary the mother of James the younger and of Joseph,[b] and Salome. [41]In Galilee these women had followed him and cared for his needs. Many other women who had come up with him to Jerusalem were also there.

The Burial of Jesus

[42]It was Preparation Day (that is, the day before the Sabbath). So as evening approached, [43]Joseph of Arimathea, a prominent member of the Council, who was himself waiting for the kingdom of God, went boldly to Pilate and asked for Jesus' body. [44]Pilate was surprised to hear that he was already dead. Summoning the centurion, he asked him if Jesus had already died. [45]When he learned from the centurion that it was so, he gave the body to Joseph. [46]So Joseph bought some linen cloth, took down the body, wrapped it in the linen, and placed it in a tomb cut out of rock. Then he rolled a stone against the entrance of the tomb. [47]Mary Magdalene and Mary the mother of Joseph[b] saw where he was laid.

He Has Risen!

16 When the Sabbath was over, Mary Magdalene, Mary the mother of James, and Salome bought spices so that they might go to anoint Jesus' body. [2]Very early on the first day of the week, just after sunrise, they were on their way to the tomb [3]and they asked each other, "Who will roll the stone away from the entrance of the tomb?"

[4]But when they looked up, they saw that the stone, which was very large, had been rolled away. [5]As they entered the tomb, they saw a young man dressed in a white robe sitting on the right side, and they were alarmed.

[6]"Don't be alarmed," he said. "You are looking for Jesus the Nazarene, who was crucified. He has risen! He is not here. See the place where they laid him. [7]But go, tell his disciples and Peter, 'He is going ahead of you into Galilee. There you will see him, just as he told you.' "

[8]Trembling and bewildered, the women went out and fled from the tomb. They said nothing to anyone, because they were afraid.

[The earliest manuscripts and some other ancient witnesses
do not have Mark 16:9–20.]

[9]*When Jesus rose early on the first day of the week, he appeared first to Mary Magdalene, out of whom he had driven seven demons. [10]She went and told those who had been with him and who were mourning and weeping. [11]When they heard that Jesus was alive and that she had seen him, they did not believe it.*

[12]*Afterward Jesus appeared in a different form to two of them while they were walking in the country. [13]These returned and reported it to the rest; but they did not believe them either.*

[a] 39 Some manuscripts *saw that he died with such a cry*   [b] 40,47 Greek *Joses*, a variant of *Joseph*

¹⁴*Later Jesus appeared to the Eleven as they were eating; he rebuked them for their lack of faith and their stubborn refusal to believe those who had seen him after he had risen.*

¹⁵*He said to them, "Go into all the world and preach the gospel to all creation.* ¹⁶*Whoever believes and is baptized will be saved, but whoever does not believe will be condemned.* ¹⁷*And these signs will accompany those who believe: In my name they will drive out demons; they will speak in new tongues;* ¹⁸*they will pick up snakes with their hands; and when they drink deadly poison, it will not hurt them at all; they will place their hands on sick people, and they will get well."*

¹⁹*After the Lord Jesus had spoken to them, he was taken up into heaven and he sat at the right hand of God.* ²⁰*Then the disciples went out and preached everywhere, and the Lord worked with them and confirmed his word by the signs that accompanied it.*

LUKE

Introduction

1 Many have undertaken to draw up an account of the things that have been fulfilled[a] among us, 2just as they were handed down to us by those who from the first were eyewitnesses and servants of the word. 3With this in mind, since I myself have carefully investigated everything from the beginning, I too decided to write an orderly account for you, most excellent Theophilus, 4so that you may know the certainty of the things you have been taught.

The Birth of John the Baptist Foretold

5In the time of Herod king of Judea there was a priest named Zechariah, who belonged to the priestly division of Abijah; his wife Elizabeth was also a descendant of Aaron. 6Both of them were righteous in the sight of God, observing all the Lord's commands and decrees blamelessly. 7But they were childless because Elizabeth was not able to conceive, and they were both well advanced in years.

8Once when Zechariah's division was on duty and he was serving as priest before God, 9he was chosen by lot, according to the custom of the priesthood, to go into the temple of the Lord and burn incense. 10And when the time for the burning of incense came, all the assembled worshipers were praying outside.

11Then an angel of the Lord appeared to him, standing at the right side of the altar of incense. 12When Zechariah saw him, he was startled and was gripped with fear. 13But the angel said to him: "Do not be afraid, Zechariah; your prayer has been heard. Your wife Elizabeth will bear you a son, and you are to call him John. 14He will be a joy and delight to you, and many will rejoice because of his birth, 15for he will be great in the sight of the Lord. He is never to take wine or other fermented drink, and he will be filled with the Holy Spirit even before he is born. 16Many of the people of Israel will he bring back to the Lord their God. 17And he will go on before the Lord, in the spirit and power of Elijah, to turn the hearts of the parents to their children and the disobedient to the wisdom of the righteous—to make ready a people prepared for the Lord."

18Zechariah asked the angel, "How can I be sure of this? I am an old man and my wife is well along in years."

a 1 Or been surely believed

¹⁹The angel said to him, "I am Gabriel. I stand in the presence of God, and I have been sent to speak to you and to tell you this good news. ²⁰And now you will be silent and not able to speak until the day this happens, because you did not believe my words, which will come true at their appointed time."

²¹Meanwhile, the people were waiting for Zechariah and wondering why he stayed so long in the temple. ²²When he came out, he could not speak to them. They realized he had seen a vision in the temple, for he kept making signs to them but remained unable to speak.

²³When his time of service was completed, he returned home. ²⁴After this his wife Elizabeth became pregnant and for five months remained in seclusion. ²⁵"The Lord has done this for me," she said. "In these days he has shown his favor and taken away my disgrace among the people."

The Birth of Jesus Foretold

²⁶In the sixth month of Elizabeth's pregnancy, God sent the angel Gabriel to Nazareth, a town in Galilee, ²⁷to a virgin pledged to be married to a man named Joseph, a descendant of David. The virgin's name was Mary. ²⁸The angel went to her and said, "Greetings, you who are highly favored! The Lord is with you."

²⁹Mary was greatly troubled at his words and wondered what kind of greeting this might be. ³⁰But the angel said to her, "Do not be afraid, Mary, you have found favor with God. ³¹You will conceive and give birth to a son, and you are to call him Jesus. ³²He will be great and will be called the Son of the Most High. The Lord God will give him the throne of his father David, ³³and he will reign over the house of Jacob forever; his kingdom will never end."

³⁴"How will this be," Mary asked the angel, "since I am a virgin?"

³⁵The angel answered, "The Holy Spirit will come upon you, and the power of the Most High will overshadow you. So the holy one to be born will be called*ᵃ* the Son of God. ³⁶Even Elizabeth your relative is going to have a child in her old age, and she who was said to be unable to conceive is in her sixth month. ³⁷For no word from God will ever fail."

³⁸"I am the Lord's servant," Mary answered. "May it be to me according to your word." Then the angel left her.

Mary Visits Elizabeth

³⁹At that time Mary got ready and hurried to a town in the hill country of Judea, ⁴⁰where she entered Zechariah's home and greeted Elizabeth. ⁴¹When Elizabeth heard Mary's greeting, the baby leaped in her womb, and Elizabeth was filled with the Holy Spirit. ⁴²In a loud voice she exclaimed: "Blessed are you among women, and blessed is the child you will bear! ⁴³But why am I so favored, that the mother of my Lord should come to me? ⁴⁴As soon as the sound of your greeting reached my ears, the baby in my womb leaped for joy. ⁴⁵Blessed is she who has believed that the Lord would fulfill his promises to her!"

ᵃ 35 Or So the child to be born will be called holy,

Mary's Song

46And Mary said:

> "My soul glorifies the Lord
> 47   and my spirit rejoices in God my Savior,
> 48for he has been mindful
>   of the humble state of his servant.
> From now on all generations will call me blessed,
> 49   for the Mighty One has done great things for me—
>   holy is his name.
> 50His mercy extends to those who fear him,
>   from generation to generation.
> 51He has performed mighty deeds with his arm;
>   he has scattered those who are proud in their inmost thoughts.
> 52He has brought down rulers from their thrones
>   but has lifted up the humble.
> 53He has filled the hungry with good things
>   but has sent the rich away empty.
> 54He has helped his servant Israel,
>   remembering to be merciful
> 55to Abraham and his descendants forever,
>   just as he promised our ancestors."

56Mary stayed with Elizabeth for about three months and then returned home.

The Birth of John the Baptist

57When it was time for Elizabeth to have her baby, she gave birth to a son. 58Her neighbors and relatives heard that the Lord had shown her great mercy, and they shared her joy.

59On the eighth day they came to circumcise the child, and they were going to name him after his father Zechariah, 60but his mother spoke up and said, "No! He is to be called John."

61They said to her, "There is no one among your relatives who has that name."

62Then they made signs to his father, to find out what he would like to name the child. 63He asked for a writing tablet, and to everyone's astonishment he wrote, "His name is John." 64Immediately his mouth was opened and his tongue was loosed, and he began to speak, praising God. 65The neighbors were all filled with awe, and throughout the hill country of Judea people were talking about all these things. 66Everyone who heard this wondered about it, asking, "What then is this child going to be?" For the Lord's hand was with him.

Zechariah's Song

67His father Zechariah was filled with the Holy Spirit and prophesied:

> 68"Praise be to the Lord, the God of Israel,
>   because he has come to his people and redeemed them.

69 He has raised up a horn*a* of salvation for us
  in the house of his servant David
70 (as he said through his holy prophets of long ago),
71 salvation from our enemies
  and from the hand of all who hate us—
72 to show mercy to our ancestors
  and to remember his holy covenant,
73   the oath he swore to our father Abraham:
74 to rescue us from the hand of our enemies,
  and to enable us to serve him without fear
75   in holiness and righteousness before him all our days.

76 And you, my child, will be called a prophet of the Most High;
  for you will go on before the Lord to prepare the way for him,
77 to give his people the knowledge of salvation
  through the forgiveness of their sins,
78 because of the tender mercy of our God,
  by which the rising sun will come to us from heaven
79 to shine on those living in darkness
  and in the shadow of death,
  to guide our feet into the path of peace."

80 And the child grew and became strong in spirit;*b* and he lived in the desert until he appeared publicly to Israel.

The Birth of Jesus

2 In those days Caesar Augustus issued a decree that a census should be taken of the entire Roman world. 2(This was the first census that took place while Quirinius was governor of Syria.) 3And everyone went to their own town to register.

4So Joseph also went up from the town of Nazareth in Galilee to Judea, to Bethlehem the town of David, because he belonged to the house and line of David. 5He went there to register with Mary, who was pledged to be married to him and was expecting a child. 6While they were there, the time came for the baby to be born, 7and she gave birth to her firstborn, a son. She wrapped him in cloths and placed him in a manger, because there was no guest room available for them.

The Shepherds and the Angels

8And there were shepherds living out in the fields nearby, keeping watch over their flocks at night. 9An angel of the Lord appeared to them, and the glory of the Lord shone around them, and they were terrified. 10But the angel said to them, "Do not be afraid. I bring you good news of great joy that will be for all the people. 11Today in the town of David a Savior has been born to you; he is the Messiah, the Lord. 12This will be a sign to you: You will find a baby wrapped in cloths and lying in a manger."

---

a 69 Horn here symbolizes a strong king.   *b 80* Or *in the Spirit*

¹³Suddenly a great company of the heavenly host appeared with the angel, praising God and saying,

¹⁴"Glory to God in the highest heaven,
　and on earth peace to those on whom his favor rests."

¹⁵When the angels had left them and gone into heaven, the shepherds said to one another, "Let's go to Bethlehem and see this thing that has happened, which the Lord has told us about."

¹⁶So they hurried off and found Mary and Joseph, and the baby, who was lying in the manger. ¹⁷When they had seen him, they spread the word concerning what had been told them about this child, ¹⁸and all who heard it were amazed at what the shepherds said to them. ¹⁹But Mary treasured up all these things and pondered them in her heart. ²⁰The shepherds returned, glorifying and praising God for all the things they had heard and seen, which were just as they had been told.

Jesus Presented in the Temple

²¹On the eighth day, when it was time to circumcise the child, he was named Jesus, the name the angel had given him before he was conceived.

²²When the time came for the purification rites required by the Law of Moses, Joseph and Mary took him to Jerusalem to present him to the Lord ²³(as it is written in the Law of the Lord, "Every firstborn male is to be consecrated to the Lord" ᵃ), ²⁴and to offer a sacrifice in keeping with what is said in the Law of the Lord: "a pair of doves or two young pigeons." ᵇ

²⁵Now there was a man in Jerusalem called Simeon, who was righteous and devout. He was waiting for the consolation of Israel, and the Holy Spirit was upon him. ²⁶It had been revealed to him by the Holy Spirit that he would not die before he had seen the Lord's Messiah. ²⁷Moved by the Spirit, he went into the temple courts. When the parents brought in the child Jesus to do for him what the custom of the Law required, ²⁸Simeon took him in his arms and praised God, saying:

²⁹"Sovereign Lord, as you have promised,
　you may now dismissᶜ your servant in peace.
³⁰For my eyes have seen your salvation,
³¹　which you have prepared in the sight of all nations:
³²a light for revelation to the Gentiles,
　and the glory of your people Israel."

³³The child's father and mother marveled at what was said about him. ³⁴Then Simeon blessed them and said to Mary, his mother: "This child is destined to cause the falling and rising of many in Israel, and to be a sign that will be spoken against, ³⁵so that the thoughts of many hearts will be revealed. And a sword will pierce your own soul too."

³⁶There was also a prophet, Anna, the daughter of Phanuel, of the tribe of Asher. She was very old; she had lived with her husband seven years after her

---

ᵃ 23 Exodus 13:2,12　　ᵇ 24 Lev. 12:8　　ᶜ 29 *Or promised, / now dismiss*

marriage, 37and then had been a widow for eighty-four years.*a* She never left the temple but worshiped night and day, fasting and praying. 38Coming up to them at that very moment, she gave thanks to God and spoke about the child to all who were looking forward to the redemption of Jerusalem.

39When Joseph and Mary had done everything required by the Law of the Lord, they returned to Galilee to their own town of Nazareth. 40And the child grew and became strong; he was filled with wisdom, and the grace of God was upon him.

The Boy Jesus at the Temple

41Every year his parents went to Jerusalem for the Festival of the Passover. 42When he was twelve years old, they went up to the Festival, according to the custom. 43After the Festival was over, while his parents were returning home, the boy Jesus stayed behind in Jerusalem, but they were unaware of it. 44Thinking he was in their company, they traveled on for a day. Then they began looking for him among their relatives and friends. 45When they did not find him, they went back to Jerusalem to look for him. 46After three days they found him in the temple courts, sitting among the teachers, listening to them and asking them questions. 47Everyone who heard him was amazed at his understanding and his answers. 48When his parents saw him, they were astonished. His mother said to him, "Son, why have you treated us like this? Your father and I have been anxiously searching for you."

49"Why were you searching for me?" he asked. "Didn't you know I had to be in my Father's house?"*b* 50But they did not understand what he was saying to them.

51Then he went down to Nazareth with them and was obedient to them. But his mother treasured all these things in her heart. 52And as Jesus grew up, he increased in wisdom and in favor with God and people.

John the Baptist Prepares the Way

3 In the fifteenth year of the reign of Tiberius Caesar—when Pontius Pilate was governor of Judea, Herod tetrarch of Galilee, his brother Philip tetrarch of Iturea and Traconitis, and Lysanias tetrarch of Abilene— 2during the high priesthood of Annas and Caiaphas, the word of God came to John son of Zechariah in the desert. 3He went into all the country around the Jordan, preaching a baptism of repentance for the forgiveness of sins. 4As it is written in the book of the words of Isaiah the prophet:

"A voice of one calling in the desert,
   'Prepare the way for the Lord,
      make straight paths for him.
5Every valley shall be filled in,
      every mountain and hill made low.
   The crooked roads shall become straight,
      the rough ways smooth.
6And all people will see God's salvation.' "*c*

---

a 37 Or *then was a widow until she was eighty-four*   *b* 49 Or *be about my Father's business*
c 6 Isaiah 40:3–5

[7]John said to the crowds coming out to be baptized by him, "You brood of vipers! Who warned you to flee from the coming wrath? [8]Produce fruit in keeping with repentance. And do not begin to say to yourselves, 'We have Abraham as our father.' For I tell you that out of these stones God can raise up children for Abraham. [9]The ax is already at the root of the trees, and every tree that does not produce good fruit will be cut down and thrown into the fire."

[10]"What should we do then?" the crowd asked.

[11]John answered, "Anyone who has two shirts should share with the one who has none, and anyone who has food should do the same."

[12]Even tax collectors came to be baptized. "Teacher," they asked, "what should we do?"

[13]"Don't collect any more than you are required to," he told them.

[14]Then some soldiers asked him, "And what should we do?"

He replied, "Don't extort money and don't accuse people falsely—be content with your pay."

[15]The people were waiting expectantly and were all wondering in their hearts if John might possibly be the Messiah. [16]John answered them all, "I baptize you with[a] water. But one who is more powerful than I will come, the thongs of whose sandals I am not worthy to untie. He will baptize you with[a] the Holy Spirit and fire. [17]His winnowing fork is in his hand to clear his threshing floor and to gather the wheat into his barn, but he will burn up the chaff with unquenchable fire." [18]And with many other words John exhorted the people and proclaimed the good news to them.

[19]But when John rebuked Herod the tetrarch because of his marriage to Herodias, his brother's wife, and all the other evil things he had done, [20]Herod added this to them all: He locked John up in prison.

The Baptism and Genealogy of Jesus

[21]When all the people were being baptized, Jesus was baptized too. And as he was praying, heaven was opened [22]and the Holy Spirit descended on him in bodily form like a dove. And a voice came from heaven: "You are my Son, whom I love; with you I am well pleased."

[23]Now Jesus himself was about thirty years old when he began his ministry. He was the son, so it was thought, of Joseph,

the son of Heli, [24]the son of Matthat,
the son of Levi, the son of Melki,
the son of Jannai, the son of Joseph,
[25]the son of Mattathias, the son of Amos,
the son of Nahum, the son of Esli,
the son of Naggai, [26]the son of Maath,
the son of Mattathias, the son of Semein,
the son of Josech, the son of Joda,
[27]the son of Joanan, the son of Rhesa,
the son of Zerubbabel, the son of Shealtiel,
the son of Neri, [28]the son of Melki,

[a] 16 Or in

the son of Addi, the son of Cosam,
the son of Elmadam, the son of Er,
29 the son of Joshua, the son of Eliezer,
the son of Jorim, the son of Matthat,
the son of Levi, 30 the son of Simeon,
the son of Judah, the son of Joseph,
the son of Jonam, the son of Eliakim,
31 the son of Melea, the son of Menna,
the son of Mattatha, the son of Nathan,
the son of David, 32 the son of Jesse,
the son of Obed, the son of Boaz,
the son of Salmon,ᵃ the son of Nahshon,
33 the son of Amminadab, the son of Ram,ᵇ
the son of Hezron, the son of Perez,
the son of Judah, 34 the son of Jacob,
the son of Isaac, the son of Abraham,
the son of Terah, the son of Nahor,
35 the son of Serug, the son of Reu,
the son of Peleg, the son of Eber,
the son of Shelah, 36 the son of Cainan,
the son of Arphaxad, the son of Shem,
the son of Noah, the son of Lamech,
37 the son of Methuselah, the son of Enoch,
the son of Jared, the son of Mahalalel,
the son of Kenan, 38 the son of Enosh,
the son of Seth, the son of Adam,
the son of God.

Jesus Is Tested in the Desert

4 Jesus, full of the Holy Spirit, left the Jordan and was led by the Spirit in the desert, 2where for forty days he was temptedᶜ by the devil. He ate nothing during those days, and at the end of them he was hungry.

3The devil said to him, "If you are the Son of God, tell this stone to become bread."

4Jesus answered, "It is written: 'People do not live on bread alone.'ᵈ"

5The devil led him up to a high place and showed him in an instant all the kingdoms of the world. 6And he said to him, "I will give you all their authority and splendor; it has been given to me, and I can give it to anyone I want to. 7If you worship me, it will all be yours."

8Jesus answered, "It is written: 'Worship the Lord your God and serve him only.'ᵉ"

9The devil led him to Jerusalem and had him stand on the highest point of the temple. "If you are the Son of God," he said, "throw yourself down from here. 10For it is written:

ᵃ 32 Some early manuscripts *Sala*   ᵇ 33 Some manuscripts *Amminadab, the son of Admin, the son of Arni*; other manuscripts vary widely.   ᶜ 2 The Greek for *tempted* can also mean *tested.*
ᵈ 4 Deut. 8:3   ᵉ 8 Deut. 6:13

" 'He will command his angels concerning you
    to guard you carefully;
11 they will lift you up in their hands,
    so that you will not strike your foot against a stone.' a"

12Jesus answered, "It is said: 'Do not put the Lord your God to the test.' b"

13When the devil had finished all this tempting, he left him until an opportune time.

Jesus Rejected at Nazareth

14Jesus returned to Galilee in the power of the Spirit, and news about him spread through the whole countryside. 15He was teaching in their synagogues, and everyone praised him.

16He went to Nazareth, where he had been brought up, and on the Sabbath day he went into the synagogue, as was his custom. He stood up to read, 17and the scroll of the prophet Isaiah was handed to him. Unrolling it, he found the place where it is written:

18 "The Spirit of the Lord is on me,
    because he has anointed me
    to proclaim good news to the poor.
He has sent me to proclaim freedom for the prisoners
    and recovery of sight for the blind,
to release the oppressed,
19   to proclaim the year of the Lord's favor." c

20Then he rolled up the scroll, gave it back to the attendant and sat down. The eyes of everyone in the synagogue were fastened on him, 21He began by saying to them, "Today this scripture is fulfilled in your hearing."

22All spoke well of him and were amazed at the gracious words that came from his lips. "Isn't this Joseph's son?" they asked.

23Jesus said to them, "Surely you will quote this proverb to me: 'Physician, heal yourself!' And you will tell me, 'Do here in your hometown what we have heard that you did in Capernaum.' "

24"Truly I tell you," he continued, "prophets are not accepted in their hometowns. 25I assure you that there were many widows in Israel in Elijah's time, when the sky was shut for three and a half years and there was a severe famine throughout the land. 26Yet Elijah was not sent to any of them, but to a widow in Zarephath in the region of Sidon. 27And there were many in Israel with leprosy d in the time of Elisha the prophet, yet not one of them was cleansed—only Naaman the Syrian."

28All the people in the synagogue were furious when they heard this. 29They got up, drove him out of the town, and took him to the brow of the hill on which the town was built, in order to throw him off the cliff. 30But he walked right through the crowd and went on his way.

---

a 11 Psalm 91:11,12   b 12 Deut. 6:16   c 19 Isaiah 61:1,2   d 27 The Greek word was used for various diseases affecting the skin—not necessarily leprosy.

Jesus Drives Out an Evil Spirit

31Then he went down to Capernaum, a town in Galilee, and on the Sabbath he taught the people. 32They were amazed at his teaching, because his words had authority.

33In the synagogue there was a man possessed by a demon, an evil[a] spirit. He cried out at the top of his voice, 34"Go away! What do you want with us, Jesus of Nazareth? Have you come to destroy us? I know who you are—the Holy One of God!"

35"Be quiet!" Jesus said sternly. "Come out of him!" Then the demon threw the man down before them all and came out without injuring him.

36All the people were amazed and said to each other, "What words these are! With authority and power he gives orders to evil spirits and they come out!" 37And the news about him spread throughout the surrounding area.

Jesus Heals Many

38Jesus left the synagogue and went to the home of Simon. Now Simon's mother-in-law was suffering from a high fever, and they asked Jesus to help her. 39So he bent over her and rebuked the fever, and it left her. She got up at once and began to wait on them.

40At sunset, the people brought to Jesus all who had various kinds of sickness, and laying his hands on each one, he healed them. 41Moreover, demons came out of many people, shouting, "You are the Son of God!" But he rebuked them and would not allow them to speak, because they knew he was the Messiah.

42At daybreak, Jesus went out to a solitary place. The people were looking for him and when they came to where he was, they tried to keep him from leaving them. 43But he said, "I must proclaim the good news of the kingdom of God to the other towns also, because that is why I was sent." 44And he kept on preaching in the synagogues of Judea.

Jesus Calls His First Disciples

5 One day as Jesus was standing by the Lake of Gennesaret,[b] the people were crowding around him and listening to the word of God. 2He saw at the water's edge two boats, left there by the fishermen, who were washing their nets. 3He got into one of the boats, the one belonging to Simon, and asked him to put out a little from shore. Then he sat down and taught the people from the boat.

4When he had finished speaking, he said to Simon, "Put out into deep water, and let down[c] the nets for a catch."

5Simon answered, "Master, we've worked hard all night and haven't caught anything. But because you say so, I will let down the nets."

6When they had done so, they caught such a large number of fish that their nets began to break. 7So they signaled their partners in the other boat to come and help them, and they came and filled both boats so full that they began to sink.

8When Simon Peter saw this, he fell at Jesus' knees and said, "Go away

---

a 33 Greek *unclean*; also in verse 36   *b 1* That is, Sea of Galilee   *c 4* The Greek verb is plural.

from me, Lord; I am a sinful man!" ⁹For he and all his companions were astonished at the catch of fish they had taken, ¹⁰and so were James and John, the sons of Zebedee, Simon's partners.

Then Jesus said to Simon, "Don't be afraid; from now on you will catch people." ¹¹So they pulled their boats up on shore, left everything and followed him.

Jesus Heals a Man With Leprosy

¹²While Jesus was in one of the towns, a man came along who was covered with leprosy.ᵃ When he saw Jesus, he fell with his face to the ground and begged him, "Lord, if you are willing, you can make me clean."

¹³Jesus reached out his hand and touched the man. "I am willing," he said. "Be clean!" And immediately the leprosy left him.

¹⁴Then Jesus ordered him, "Don't tell anyone, but go, show yourself to the priest and offer the sacrifices that Moses commanded for your cleansing, as a testimony to them."

¹⁵Yet the news about him spread all the more, so that crowds of people came to hear him and to be healed of their sicknesses. ¹⁶But Jesus often withdrew to lonely places and prayed.

Jesus Forgives and Heals a Paralyzed Man

¹⁷One day Jesus was teaching, and Pharisees and teachers of the law were sitting there. They had come from every village of Galilee and from Judea and Jerusalem. And the power of the Lord was with Jesus to heal the sick. ¹⁸Some men came carrying a paralyzed man on a mat and tried to take him into the house to lay him before Jesus. ¹⁹When they could not find a way to do this because of the crowd, they went up on the roof and lowered him on his mat through the tiles into the middle of the crowd, right in front of Jesus.

²⁰When Jesus saw their faith, he said, "Friend, your sins are forgiven."

²¹The Pharisees and the teachers of the law began thinking to themselves, "Who is this fellow who speaks blasphemy? Who can forgive sins but God alone?"

²²Jesus knew what they were thinking and asked, "Why are you thinking these things in your hearts? ²³Which is easier: to say, 'Your sins are forgiven,' or to say, 'Get up and walk'? ²⁴But I want you to know that the Son of Man has authority on earth to forgive sins." So he said to the paralyzed man, "I tell you, get up, take your mat and go home." ²⁵Immediately he stood up in front of them, took what he had been lying on and went home praising God. ²⁶Everyone was amazed and gave praise to God. They were filled with awe and said, "We have seen remarkable things today."

Jesus Calls Levi and Eats With Sinners

²⁷After this, Jesus went out and saw a tax collector by the name of Levi sitting at his tax booth. "Follow me," Jesus said to him, ²⁸and Levi got up, left everything and followed him.

²⁹Then Levi held a great banquet for Jesus at his house, and a large crowd

---

ᵃ 12 The Greek word was used for various diseases affecting the skin—not necessarily leprosy.

of tax collectors and others were eating with them. ³⁰But the Pharisees and the teachers of the law who belonged to their sect complained to his disciples, "Why do you eat and drink with tax collectors and 'sinners'?"

³¹Jesus answered them, "It is not the healthy who need a doctor, but the sick. ³²I have not come to call the righteous, but sinners to repentance."

Jesus Questioned About Fasting

³³They said to him, "John's disciples often fast and pray, and so do the disciples of the Pharisees, but yours go on eating and drinking."

³⁴Jesus answered, "Can you make the friends of the bridegroom fast while he is with them? ³⁵But the time will come when the bridegroom will be taken from them; in those days they will fast."

³⁶He told them this parable: "No one tears a piece out of a new garment to patch an old one. If they do, they will have torn the new garment, and the patch from the new will not match the old. ³⁷And people do not pour new wine into old wineskins. If they do, the new wine will burst the skins, the wine will run out and the wineskins will be ruined. ³⁸No, new wine must be poured into new wineskins. ³⁹And none of you, after drinking old wine, wants the new, for you say, 'The old is better.' "

Jesus Is Lord of the Sabbath

6 One Sabbath Jesus was going through the grainfields, and his disciples began to pick some heads of grain, rub them in their hands and eat the kernels. ²Some of the Pharisees asked, "Why are you doing what is unlawful on the Sabbath?"

³Jesus answered them, "Have you never read what David did when he and his companions were hungry? ⁴He entered the house of God, and taking the consecrated bread, he ate what is lawful only for priests to eat. And he also gave some to his companions." ⁵Then Jesus said to them, "The Son of Man is Lord of the Sabbath."

⁶On another Sabbath he went into the synagogue and was teaching, and a man was there whose right hand was shriveled. ⁷The Pharisees and the teachers of the law were looking for a reason to accuse Jesus, so they watched him closely to see if he would heal on the Sabbath. ⁸But Jesus knew what they were thinking and said to the man with the shriveled hand, "Get up and stand in front of everyone." So he got up and stood there.

⁹Then Jesus said to them, "I ask you, which is lawful on the Sabbath: to do good or to do evil, to save life or to destroy it?"

¹⁰He looked around at them all, and then said to the man, "Stretch out your hand." He did so, and his hand was completely restored. ¹¹But the Pharisees and the teachers of the law were furious and began to discuss with one another what they might do to Jesus.

The Twelve Apostles

¹²One of those days Jesus went out to a mountainside to pray, and spent the night praying to God. ¹³When morning came, he called his disciples to him and chose twelve of them, whom he also designated apostles: ¹⁴Simon (whom he named Peter), his brother Andrew, James, John, Philip, Bartholomew,

15Matthew, Thomas, James son of Alphaeus, Simon who was called the Zealot, 16Judas son of James, and Judas Iscariot, who became a traitor.

Blessings and Woes

17He went down with them and stood on a level place. A large crowd of his disciples was there and a great number of people from all over Judea, from Jerusalem, and from the coastal region around Tyre and Sidon, 18who had come to hear him and to be healed of their diseases. Those troubled by evil*a* spirits were cured, 19and the people all tried to touch him, because power was coming from him and healing them all.

20Looking at his disciples, he said:

> "Blessed are you who are poor,
>   for yours is the kingdom of God.
> 21 Blessed are you who hunger now,
>   for you will be satisfied.
> Blessed are you who weep now,
>   for you will laugh.
> 22 Blessed are you when people hate you,
>   when they exclude you and insult you
>   and reject your name as evil,
>   because of the Son of Man.

23"Rejoice in that day and leap for joy, because great is your reward in heaven. For that is how their ancestors treated the prophets.

> 24 "But woe to you who are rich,
>   for you have already received your comfort
> 25 Woe to you who are well fed now,
>   for you will go hungry.
> Woe to you who laugh now,
>   for you will mourn and weep.
> 26 Woe to you when everyone speaks well of you,
>   for that is how their ancestors treated the false prophets.

Love for Enemies

27"But to you who are listening I say: Love your enemies, do good to those who hate you, 28bless those who curse you, pray for those who mistreat you. 29If someone slaps you on one cheek, turn the other also. If someone takes your coat, do not withhold your shirt. 30Give to everyone who asks you, and if anyone takes what belongs to you, do not demand it back. 31Do to others as you would have them do to you.

32"If you love those who love you, what credit is that to you? Even 'sinners' love those who love them. 33And if you do good to those who are good to you, what credit is that to you? Even 'sinners' do that. 34And if you lend to those from whom you expect repayment, what credit is that to you? Even 'sinners' lend to 'sinners,' expecting to be repaid in full. 35But love your enemies, do good to them, and lend to them without expecting to get anything back. Then

---

a 18 Greek *unclean*

your reward will be great, and you will be children of the Most High, because he is kind to the ungrateful and wicked. 36Be merciful, just as your Father is merciful.

Judging Others

37"Do not judge, and you will not be judged. Do not condemn, and you will not be condemned. Forgive, and you will be forgiven. 38Give, and it will be given to you. A good measure, pressed down, shaken together and running over, will be poured into your lap. For with the measure you use, it will be measured to you."

39He also told them this parable: "Can the blind lead the blind? Will they not both fall into a pit? 40Students are not above their teacher, but all who are fully trained will be like their teacher.

41"Why do you look at the speck of sawdust in someone else's eye and pay no attention to the plank in your own eye? 42How can you say, 'Friend, let me take the speck out of your eye,' when you yourself fail to see the plank in your own eye? You hypocrite, first take the plank out of your eye, and then you will see clearly to remove the speck from the other person's eye.

A Tree and Its Fruit

43"No good tree bears bad fruit, nor does a bad tree bear good fruit. 44Each tree is recognized by its own fruit. People do not pick figs from thornbushes, or grapes from briers. 45Good people bring good things out of the good stored up in their heart, and evil people bring evil things out of the evil stored up in their heart. For out of the overflow of the heart the mouth speaks.

The Wise and Foolish Builders

46"Why do you call me, 'Lord, Lord,' and do not do what I say? 47As for those who come to me and hear my words and put them into practice, I will show you what they are like. 48They are like a man building a house, who dug down deep and laid the foundation on rock. When a flood came, the torrent struck that house but could not shake it, because it was well built. 49But those who hear my words and do not put them into practice are like a man who built a house on the ground without a foundation. The moment the torrent struck that house, it collapsed and its destruction was complete."

The Faith of the Centurion

7 When Jesus had finished saying all this to the people who were listening, he entered Capernaum. 2There a centurion's servant, whom his master valued highly, was sick and about to die. 3The centurion heard of Jesus and sent some elders of the Jews to him, asking him to come and heal his servant. 4When they came to Jesus, they pleaded earnestly with him, "This man deserves to have you do this, 5because he loves our nation and has built our synagogue." 6So Jesus went with them.

He was not far from the house when the centurion sent friends to say to him: "Lord, don't trouble yourself, for I do not deserve to have you come under my roof. 7That is why I did not even consider myself worthy to come to you. But say the word, and my servant will be healed. 8For I myself am a man under authority, with soldiers under me. I tell this one, 'Go,' and he goes; and that one, 'Come,' and he comes. I say to my servant, 'Do this,' and he does it."

9When Jesus heard this, he was amazed at him, and turning to the crowd following him, he said, "I tell you, I have not found such great faith even in Israel." 10Then the men who had been sent returned to the house and found the servant well.

Jesus Raises a Widow's Son

11Soon afterward, Jesus went to a town called Nain, and his disciples and a large crowd went along with him. 12As he approached the town gate, a dead person was being carried out—the only son of his mother, and she was a widow. And a large crowd from the town was with her. 13When the Lord saw her, his heart went out to her and he said, "Don't cry."

14Then he went up and touched the bier they were carrying him on, and the bearers stood still. He said, "Young man, I say to you, get up!" 15The dead man sat up and began to talk, and Jesus gave him back to his mother.

16They were all filled with awe and praised God. "A great prophet has appeared among us," they said. "God has come to help his people." 17This news about Jesus spread throughout Judea and the surrounding country.

Jesus and John the Baptist

18John's disciples told him about all these things. Calling two of them, 19he sent them to the Lord to ask, "Are you the one who was to come, or should we expect someone else?"

20When the men came to Jesus, they said, "John the Baptist sent us to you to ask, 'Are you the one who was to come, or should we expect someone else?' "

21At that very time Jesus cured many who had diseases, sicknesses and evil spirits, and gave sight to many who were blind. 22So he replied to the messengers, "Go back and report to John what you have seen and heard: The blind receive sight, the lame walk, those who have leprosy*a* are cleansed, the deaf hear, the dead are raised, and the good news is proclaimed to the poor. 23Blessed is anyone who does not stumble on account of me."

24After John's messengers left, Jesus began to speak to the crowd about John: "What did you go out into the desert to see? A reed swayed by the wind? 25If not, what did you go out to see? A man dressed in fine clothes? No, those who wear expensive clothes and indulge in luxury are in palaces. 26But what did you go out to see? A prophet? Yes, I tell you, and more than a prophet. 27This is the one about whom it is written:

> " 'I will send my messenger ahead of you,
> who will prepare your way before you.'*b*

28I tell you, among those born of women there is no one greater than John; yet the one who is least in the kingdom of God is greater than he."

a 22 The Greek word was used for various diseases affecting the skin—not necessarily leprosy.
b 27 Mal. 3:1

29(All the people, even the tax collectors, when they heard Jesus' words, acknowledged that God's way was right, because they had been baptized by John. 30But the Pharisees and the experts in the law rejected God's purpose for themselves, because they had not been baptized by John.)

31Jesus went on to say, "To what, then, can I compare the people of this generation? What are they like? 32They are like children sitting in the marketplace and calling out to each other:

> " 'We played the flute for you,
>   and you did not dance;
> we sang a dirge,
>   and you did not cry.'

33For John the Baptist came neither eating bread nor drinking wine, and you say, 'He has a demon.' 34The Son of Man came eating and drinking, and you say, 'Here is a glutton and a drunkard, a friend of tax collectors and "sinners." ' 35But wisdom is proved right by all her children."

Jesus Anointed by a Sinful Woman

36When one of the Pharisees invited Jesus to have dinner with him, he went to the Pharisee's house and reclined at the table. 37A woman in that town who lived a sinful life learned that Jesus was eating at the Pharisee's house, so she came there with an alabaster jar of perfume. 38As she stood behind him at his feet weeping, she began to wet his feet with her tears. Then she wiped them with her hair, kissed them and poured perfume on them.

39When the Pharisee who had invited him saw this, he said to himself, "If this man were a prophet, he would know who is touching him and what kind of woman she is—that she is a sinner."

40Jesus answered him, "Simon, I have something to tell you."

"Tell me, teacher," he said.

41"Two people owed money to a certain moneylender. One owed him five hundred denarii,a and the other fifty. 42Neither of them had the money to pay him back, so he forgave the debts of both. Now which of them will love him more?"

43Simon replied, "I suppose the one who had the bigger debt forgiven."

"You have judged correctly," Jesus said.

44Then he turned toward the woman and said to Simon, "Do you see this woman? I came into your house. You did not give me any water for my feet, but she wet my feet with her tears and wiped them with her hair. 45You did not give me a kiss, but this woman, from the time I entered, has not stopped kissing my feet. 46You did not put oil on my head, but she has poured perfume on my feet. 47Therefore, I tell you, her many sins have been forgiven— as her great love has shown. But whoever has been forgiven little loves little."

48Then Jesus said to her, "Your sins are forgiven."

49The other guests began to say among themselves, "Who is this who even forgives sins?"

50Jesus said to the woman, "Your faith has saved you; go in peace."

---

a 41 A denarius was the daily wage of a day laborer (see Matt. 20:2).

The Parable of the Sower

8 After this, Jesus traveled about from one town and village to another, proclaiming the good news of the kingdom of God. The Twelve were with him, ²and also some women who had been cured of evil spirits and diseases: Mary (called Magdalene) from whom seven demons had come out; ³Joanna the wife of Chuza, the manager of Herod's household; Susanna; and many others. These women were helping to support them out of their own means.

⁴While a large crowd was gathering and people were coming to Jesus from town after town, he told this parable: ⁵"A farmer went out to sow his seed. As he was scattering the seed, some fell along the path; it was trampled on, and the birds ate it up. ⁶Some fell on rock, and when it came up, the plants withered because they had no moisture. ⁷Other seed fell among thorns, which grew up with it and choked the plants. ⁸Still other seed fell on good soil. It came up and yielded a crop, a hundred times more than was sown."

When he said this, he called out, "Whoever has ears to hear, let them hear."

⁹His disciples asked him what this parable meant. ¹⁰He said, "The knowledge of the secrets of the kingdom of God has been given to you, but to others I speak in parables, so that,

> " 'though seeing, they may not see;
> though hearing, they may not understand.'ᵃ

¹¹"This is the meaning of the parable: The seed is the word of God. ¹²Those along the path are the ones who hear, and then the devil comes and takes away the word from their hearts, so that they may not believe and be saved. ¹³Those on the rock are the ones who receive the word with joy when they hear it, but they have no root. They believe for a while, but in the time of testing they fall away. ¹⁴The seed that fell among thorns stands for those who hear, but as they go on their way they are choked by life's worries, riches and pleasures, and they do not mature. ¹⁵But the seed on good soil stands for those with a noble and good heart, who hear the word, retain it, and by persevering produce a crop.

A Lamp on a Stand

¹⁶"No one lights a lamp and hides it in a clay jar or puts it under a bed. Instead, they put it on a stand, so that those who come in can see the light. ¹⁷For there is nothing hidden that will not be disclosed, and nothing concealed that will not be known or brought out into the open. ¹⁸Therefore consider carefully how you listen. Those who have will be given more; as for those who do not have, even what they think they have will be taken from them."

Jesus' Mother and Brothers

¹⁹Now Jesus' mother and brothers came to see him, but they were not able to get near him because of the crowd. ²⁰Someone told him, "Your mother and brothers are standing outside, wanting to see you."

²¹He replied, "My mother and brothers are those who hear God's word and put it into practice."

ᵃ 10 Isaiah 6:9

Jesus Calms the Storm

²²One day Jesus said to his disciples, "Let us go over to the other side of the lake." So they got into a boat and set out. ²³As they sailed, he fell asleep. A squall came down on the lake, so that the boat was being swamped, and they were in great danger.

²⁴The disciples went and woke him, saying, "Master, Master, we're going to drown!"

He got up and rebuked the wind and the raging waters; the storm subsided, and all was calm. ²⁵"Where is your faith?" he asked his disciples.

In fear and amazement they asked one another, "Who is this? He commands even the winds and the water, and they obey him."

Jesus Restores a Demon-Possessed Man

²⁶They sailed to the region of the Gerasenes,ᵃ which is across the lake from Galilee. ²⁷When Jesus stepped ashore, he was met by a demon-possessed man from the town. For a long time this man had not worn clothes or lived in a house, but had lived in the tombs. ²⁸When he saw Jesus, he cried out and fell at his feet, shouting at the top of his voice, "What do you want with me, Jesus, Son of the Most High God? I beg you, don't torture me!" ²⁹For Jesus had commanded the evilᵇ spirit to come out of the man. Many times it had seized him, and though he was chained hand and foot and kept under guard, he had broken his chains and had been driven by the demon into solitary places.

³⁰Jesus asked him, "What is your name?"

"Legion," he replied, because many demons had gone into him. ³¹And they begged Jesus repeatedly not to order them to go into the Abyss.

³²A large herd of pigs was feeding there on the hillside. The demons begged Jesus to let them go into the pigs, and he gave them permission. ³³When the demons came out of the man, they went into the pigs, and the herd rushed down the steep bank into the lake and was drowned.

³⁴When those tending the pigs saw what had happened, they ran off and reported this in the town and countryside, ³⁵and the people went out to see what had happened. When they came to Jesus, they found the man from whom the demons had gone out, sitting at Jesus' feet, dressed and in his right mind; and they were afraid. ³⁶Those who had seen it told the people how the demon-possessed man had been cured. ³⁷Then all the people of the region of the Gerasenes asked Jesus to leave them, because they were overcome with fear. So he got into the boat and left.

³⁸The man from whom the demons had gone out begged to go with him, but Jesus sent him away, saying, ³⁹"Return home and tell how much God has done for you." So the man went away and told all over town how much Jesus had done for him.

Jesus Raises a Dead Girl and Heals a Sick Woman

⁴⁰Now when Jesus returned, a crowd welcomed him, for they were all expecting him. ⁴¹Then a man named Jairus, a synagogue leader, came and fell at

---

ᵃ 26 Some manuscripts *Gadarenes*; other manuscripts *Gergesenes*; also in verse 37   ᵇ 29 Greek *unclean*

Jesus' feet, pleading with him to come to his house ⁴²because his only daughter, a girl of about twelve, was dying.

As Jesus was on his way, the crowds almost crushed him. ⁴³And a woman was there who had been subject to bleeding for twelve years,ᵃ but no one could heal her. ⁴⁴She came up behind him and touched the edge of his cloak, and immediately her bleeding stopped.

⁴⁵"Who touched me?" Jesus asked.

When they all denied it, Peter said, "Master, the people are crowding and pressing against you."

⁴⁶But Jesus said, "Someone touched me; I know that power has gone out from me."

⁴⁷Then the woman, seeing that she could not go unnoticed, came trembling and fell at his feet. In the presence of all the people, she told why she had touched him and how she had been instantly healed. ⁴⁸Then he said to her, "Daughter, your faith has healed you. Go in peace."

⁴⁹While Jesus was still speaking, someone came from the house of Jairus, the synagogue leader. "Your daughter is dead," he said. "Don't bother the teacher anymore."

⁵⁰Hearing this, Jesus said to Jairus, "Don't be afraid; just believe, and she will be healed."

⁵¹When he arrived at the house of Jairus, he did not let anyone go in with him except Peter, John and James, and the child's father and mother. ⁵²Meanwhile, all the people were wailing and mourning for her. "Stop wailing," Jesus said. "She is not dead but asleep."

⁵³They laughed at him, knowing that she was dead. ⁵⁴But he took her by the hand and said, "My child, get up!" ⁵⁵Her spirit returned, and at once she stood up. Then Jesus told them to give her something to eat. ⁵⁶Her parents were astonished, but he ordered them not to tell anyone what had happened.

Jesus Sends Out the Twelve

9 When Jesus had called the Twelve together, he gave them power and authority to drive out all demons and to cure diseases, ²and he sent them out to proclaim the kingdom of God and to heal the sick. ³He told them: "Take nothing for the journey—no staff, no bag, no bread, no money, no extra shirt. ⁴Whatever house you enter, stay there until you leave that town. ⁵If people do not welcome you, shake the dust off your feet when you leave their town, as a testimony against them." ⁶So they set out and went from village to village, proclaiming the good news and healing people everywhere.

⁷Now Herod the tetrarch heard about all that was going on. And he was perplexed because some were saying that John had been raised from the dead, ⁸others that Elijah had appeared, and still others that one of the prophets of long ago had come back to life. ⁹But Herod said, "I beheaded John. Who, then, is this I hear such things about?" And he tried to see him.

Jesus Feeds the Five Thousand

¹⁰When the apostles returned, they reported to Jesus what they had done.

ᵃ 43 Many manuscripts *years, and she had spent all she had on doctors*

Then he took them with him and they withdrew by themselves to a town called Bethsaida, 11but the crowds learned about it and followed him. He welcomed them and spoke to them about the kingdom of God, and healed those who needed healing.

12Late in the afternoon the Twelve came to him and said, "Send the crowd away so they can go to the surrounding villages and countryside and find food and lodging, because we are in a remote place here."

13He replied, "You give them something to eat."

They answered, "We have only five loaves of bread and two fish—unless we go and buy food for all this crowd." 14(About five thousand men were there.)

But he said to his disciples, "Have them sit down in groups of about fifty each." 15The disciples did so, and everyone sat down. 16Taking the five loaves and the two fish and looking up to heaven, he gave thanks and broke them. Then he gave them to the disciples to set before the people. 17They all ate and were satisfied, and the disciples picked up twelve basketfuls of broken pieces that were left over.

Peter Declares That Jesus Is the Messiah

18Once when Jesus was praying in private and his disciples were with him, he asked them, "Who do the crowds say I am?"

19They replied, "Some say John the Baptist; others say Elijah; and still others, that one of the prophets of long ago has come back to life."

20"But what about you?" he asked. "Who do you say I am?"

Peter answered, "God's Messiah."

Jesus Predicts His Death

21Jesus strictly warned them not to tell this to anyone. 22And he said, "The Son of Man must suffer many things and be rejected by the elders, the chief priests and the teachers of the law, and he must be killed and on the third day be raised to life."

23Then he said to them all: "Those who would be my disciples must deny themselves and take up their cross daily and follow me. 24For those who want to save their life will lose it, but those who lose their life for me will save it. 25What good is it for you to gain the whole world, and yet lose or forfeit your very self? 26If any of you are ashamed of me and my words, the Son of Man will be ashamed of you when he comes in his glory and in the glory of the Father and of the holy angels. 27Truly I tell you, some who are standing here will not taste death before they see the kingdom of God."

The Transfiguration

28About eight days after Jesus said this, he took Peter, John and James with him and went up onto a mountain to pray. 29As he was praying, the appearance of his face changed, and his clothes became as bright as a flash of lightning. 30Two men, Moses and Elijah, 31appeared in glorious splendor, talking with Jesus. They spoke about his departure,a which he was about to bring to fulfillment at Jerusalem. 32Peter and his companions were very sleepy, but

a 31 Greek his exodus

when they became fully awake, they saw his glory and the two men standing with him. 33As the men were leaving Jesus, Peter said to him, "Master, it is good for us to be here. Let us put up three shelters—one for you, one for Moses and one for Elijah." (He did not know what he was saying.)

34While he was speaking, a cloud appeared and covered them, and they were afraid as they entered the cloud. 35A voice came from the cloud, saying, "This is my Son, whom I have chosen; listen to him." 36When the voice had spoken, they found that Jesus was alone. The disciples kept this to themselves and did not tell anyone at that time what they had seen.

Jesus Heals a Demon-Possessed Boy

37The next day, when they came down from the mountain, a large crowd met him. 38A man in the crowd called out, "Teacher, I beg you to look at my son, for he is my only child. 39A spirit seizes him and he suddenly screams; it throws him into convulsions so that he foams at the mouth. It scarcely ever leaves him and is destroying him. 40I begged your disciples to drive it out, but they could not."

41"You unbelieving and perverse generation," Jesus replied, "how long shall I stay with you and put up with you? Bring your son here."

42Even while the boy was coming, the demon threw him to the ground in a convulsion. But Jesus rebuked the evil*a* spirit, healed the boy and gave him back to his father. 43And they were all amazed at the greatness of God.

Jesus Predicts His Death a Second Time

While everyone was marveling at all that Jesus did, he said to his disciples, 44"Listen carefully to what I am about to tell you: The Son of Man is going to be delivered over to human hands." 45But they did not understand what this meant. It was hidden from them, so that they did not grasp it, and they were afraid to ask him about it.

46An argument started among the disciples as to which of them would be the greatest. 47Jesus, knowing their thoughts, took a little child and had him stand beside him. 48Then he said to them, "Whoever welcomes this little child in my name welcomes me; and whoever welcomes me welcomes the one who sent me. For whoever is least among you all is the greatest."

49"Master," said John, "we saw someone driving out demons in your name and we tried to stop him, because he is not one of us."

50"Do not stop him," Jesus said, "for whoever is not against you is for you."

Samaritan Opposition

51As the time approached for him to be taken up to heaven, Jesus resolutely set out for Jerusalem. 52And he sent messengers on ahead, who went into a Samaritan village to get things ready for him; 53but the people there did not welcome him, because he was heading for Jerusalem. 54When the disciples James and John saw this, they asked, "Lord, do you want us to call fire down from heaven to destroy them*b*?" 55But Jesus turned and rebuked them. 56Then he and his disciples went to another village.

---

a 42 Greek unclean   *b* 54 Some manuscripts them, even as Elijah did

The Cost of Following Jesus

⁵⁷As they were walking along the road, a man said to him, "I will follow you wherever you go."

⁵⁸Jesus replied, "Foxes have holes and birds have nests, but the Son of Man has no place to lay his head."

⁵⁹He said to another man, "Follow me."

But he replied, "Lord, first let me go and bury my father."

⁶⁰Jesus said to him, "Let the dead bury their own dead, but you go and proclaim the kingdom of God."

⁶¹Still another said, "I will follow you, Lord; but first let me go back and say good-by to my family."

⁶²Jesus replied, "No one who puts a hand to the plow and looks back is fit for service in the kingdom of God."

Jesus Sends Out the Seventy-Two

10 After this the Lord appointed seventy-two[a] others and sent them two by two ahead of him to every town and place where he was about to go. ²He told them, "The harvest is plentiful, but the workers are few. Ask the Lord of the harvest, therefore, to send out workers into his harvest field. ³Go! I am sending you out like lambs among wolves. ⁴Do not take a purse or bag or sandals; and do not greet anyone on the road.

⁵"When you enter a house, first say, 'Peace to this house.' ⁶If the head of the house loves peace, your peace will rest on that house; if not, it will return to you. ⁷Stay there, eating and drinking whatever they give you, for workers deserve their wages. Do not move around from house to house.

⁸"When you enter a town and are welcomed, eat what is set before you. ⁹Heal the sick who are there and tell them, 'The kingdom of God has come near to you.' ¹⁰But when you enter a town and are not welcomed, go into its streets and say, ¹¹'Even the dust of your town we wipe from our feet as a warning to you. Yet be sure of this: The kingdom of God has come near.' ¹²I tell you, it will be more bearable on that day for Sodom than for that town.

¹³"Woe to you, Korazin! Woe to you, Bethsaida! For if the miracles that were performed in you had been performed in Tyre and Sidon, they would have repented long ago, sitting in sackcloth and ashes. ¹⁴But it will be more bearable for Tyre and Sidon at the judgment than for you. ¹⁵And you, Capernaum, will you be lifted up to the skies? No, you will go down to the depths.[b]

¹⁶"Whoever listens to you listens to me; whoever rejects you rejects me; but whoever rejects me rejects him who sent me."

¹⁷The seventy-two returned with joy and said, "Lord, even the demons submit to us in your name."

¹⁸He replied, "I saw Satan fall like lightning from heaven. ¹⁹I have given you authority to trample on snakes and scorpions and to overcome all the power of the enemy; nothing will harm you. ²⁰However, do not rejoice that the spirits submit to you, but rejoice that your names are written in heaven."

²¹At that time Jesus, full of joy through the Holy Spirit, said, "I praise you, Father, Lord of heaven and earth, because you have hidden these things from

---

the wise and learned, and revealed them to little children. Yes, Father, for this was your good pleasure.

22"All things have been committed to me by my Father. No one knows who the Son is except the Father, and no one knows who the Father is except the Son and those to whom the Son chooses to reveal him."

23Then he turned to his disciples and said privately, "Blessed are the eyes that see what you see. 24For I tell you that many prophets and kings wanted to see what you see but did not see it, and to hear what you hear but did not hear it."

The Parable of the Good Samaritan

25On one occasion an expert in the law stood up to test Jesus. "Teacher," he asked, "what must I do to inherit eternal life?"

26"What is written in the Law?" he replied. "How do you read it?"

27He answered: " 'Love the Lord your God with all your heart and with all your soul and with all your strength and with all your mind'ª; and, 'Love your neighbor as yourself.'ᵇ"

28"You have answered correctly," Jesus replied. "Do this and you will live."

29But he wanted to justify himself, so he asked Jesus, "And who is my neighbor?"

30In reply Jesus said: "A man was going down from Jerusalem to Jericho, when he fell into the hands of robbers. They stripped him of his clothes, beat him and went away, leaving him half dead. 31A priest happened to be going down the same road, and when he saw the man, he passed by on the other side. 32So too, a Levite, when he came to the place and saw him, passed by on the other side. 33But a Samaritan, as he traveled, came where the man was; and when he saw him, he took pity on him. 34He went to him and bandaged his wounds, pouring on oil and wine. Then he put the man on his own donkey, brought him to an inn and took care of him. 35The next day he took out two silver coinsᶜ and gave them to the innkeeper. 'Look after him,' he said, 'and when I return, I will reimburse you for any extra expense you may have.'

36"Which of these three do you think was a neighbor to the man who fell into the hands of robbers?"

37The expert in the law replied, "The one who had mercy on him."

Jesus told him, "Go and do likewise."

At the Home of Martha and Mary

38As Jesus and his disciples were on their way, he came to a village where a woman named Martha opened her home to him. 39She had a sister called Mary, who sat at the Lord's feet listening to what he said. 40But Martha was distracted by all the preparations that had to be made. She came to him and asked, "Lord, don't you care that my sister has left me to do the work by myself? Tell her to help me!"

41"Martha, Martha," the Lord answered, "you are worried and upset about

ª27 Deut. 6:5   ᵇ27 Lev. 19:18   ᶜ35 Greek *two denarii;* a denarius was the daily wage of a day laborer (see Matt. 20:2).

many things, [42]but few things are needed—or indeed only one.[a] Mary has chosen what is better, and it will not be taken away from her."

Jesus' Teaching on Prayer

11 One day Jesus was praying in a certain place. When he finished, one of his disciples said to him, "Lord, teach us to pray, just as John taught his disciples."

[2]He said to them, "When you pray, say:

" 'Father,[b]
hallowed be your name,
your kingdom come.[c]
[3]Give us each day our daily bread.
[4]Forgive us our sins,
    for we also forgive everyone who sins against us.[d]
And lead us not into temptation.[e]' "

[5]Then Jesus said to them, "Suppose you have a friend, and you go to him at midnight and say, 'Friend, lend me three loaves of bread; [6]a friend of mine on a journey has come to me, and I have nothing to set before him.' [7]And suppose the one inside answers, 'Don't bother me. The door is already locked, and my children and I are in bed. I can't get up and give you anything.' [8]I tell you, even though he will not get up and give you the bread because of friendship, yet because of your shameless audacity[f] he will surely get up and give you as much as you need.

[9]"So I say to you: Ask and it will be given to you; seek and you will find; knock and the door will be opened to you. [10]For everyone who asks receives; those who seek find; and to those who knock, the door will be opened.

[11]"Which of you fathers, if your son asks for[g] a fish, will give him a snake instead? [12]Or if he asks for an egg, will give him a scorpion? [13]If you then, though you are evil, know how to give good gifts to your children, how much more will your Father in heaven give the Holy Spirit to those who ask him!"

Jesus and Beelzebul

[14]Jesus was driving out a demon that was mute. When the demon left, the man who had been mute spoke, and the crowd was amazed. [15]But some of them said, "By Beelzebul, the prince of demons, he is driving out demons." [16]Others tested him by asking for a sign from heaven.

[17]Jesus knew their thoughts and said to them: "Any kingdom divided against itself will be ruined, and a house divided against itself will fall. [18]If Satan is divided against himself, how can his kingdom stand? I say this because you claim that I drive out demons by Beelzebul. [19]Now if I drive out demons by Beelzebul, by whom do your followers drive them out? So then, they will be your judges. [20]But if I drive out demons by the finger of God, then the kingdom of God has come to you.

---

[a] 42 Some manuscripts *but only one thing is needed*   [b] 2 Some manuscripts *Our Father in heaven*   [c] 2 Some manuscripts *come. May your will be done on earth as it is in heaven.*   [d] 4 Greek *everyone who is indebted to us*   [e] 4 Some manuscripts *temptation, but deliver us from the evil one*   [f] 8 Or *yet to preserve his good name*   [g] 11 Some manuscripts *for bread, will give him a stone? Or if he asks for*

²¹"When a strong man, fully armed, guards his own house, his possessions are safe. ²²But when someone stronger attacks and overpowers him, he takes away the armor in which the man trusted and divides up his plunder.

²³"Whoever is not with me is against me, and whoever does not gather with me scatters.

²⁴"When an evilᵃ spirit comes out of anyone, it goes through arid places seeking rest and does not find it. Then it says, 'I will return to the house I left.' ²⁵When it arrives, it finds the house swept clean and put in order. ²⁶Then it goes and takes seven other spirits more wicked than itself, and they go in and live there. And the final condition of that person is worse than the first."

²⁷As Jesus was saying these things, a woman in the crowd called out, "Blessed is the mother who gave you birth and nursed you."

²⁸He replied, "Blessed rather are those who hear the word of God and obey it."

The Sign of Jonah

²⁹As the crowds increased, Jesus said, "This is a wicked generation. It asks for a sign, but none will be given it except the sign of Jonah. ³⁰For as Jonah was a sign to the Ninevites, so also will the Son of Man be to this generation. ³¹The Queen of the South will rise at the judgment with the people of this generation and condemn them, for she came from the ends of the earth to listen to Solomon's wisdom; and now oneᵇ greater than Solomon is here. ³²The people of Nineveh will stand up at the judgment with this generation and condemn it, for they repented at the preaching of Jonah; and now one greater than Jonah is here.

The Lamp of the Body

³³"None of you lights a lamp and puts it in a place where it will be hidden, or under a bowl. Instead you put it on its stand, so that those who come in may see the light. ³⁴Your eye is the lamp of your body. When your eyes are healthy,ᶜ your whole body also is full of light. But when they are unhealthy,ᵈ your body also is full of darkness. ³⁵See to it, then, that the light within you is not darkness. ³⁶Therefore, if your whole body is full of light, and no part of it dark, it will be completely lighted, as when the light of a lamp shines on you."

Woes on the Pharisees and the Experts in the Law

³⁷When Jesus had finished speaking, a Pharisee invited him to eat with him; so he went in and reclined at the table. ³⁸But the Pharisee was surprised when he noticed that Jesus did not first wash before the meal.

³⁹Then the Lord said to him, "Now then, you Pharisees clean the outside of the cup and dish, but inside you are full of greed and wickedness. ⁴⁰You foolish people! Did not the one who made the outside make the inside also? ⁴¹But now as for what is inside you—be generous to the poor, and everything will be clean for you.

⁴²"Woe to you Pharisees, because you give God a tenth of your mint, rue

---

ᵃ 24 Greek *unclean*   ᵇ 31 Or *something*; also in verse 32   ᶜ 34 The Greek for *healthy* here implies *generous.*   ᵈ 34 The Greek for *unhealthy* here implies *stingy.*

and all other kinds of garden herbs, but you neglect justice and the love of God. You should have practiced the latter without leaving the former undone.

⁴³"Woe to you Pharisees, because you love the most important seats in the synagogues and respectful greetings in the marketplaces.

⁴⁴"Woe to you, because you are like unmarked graves, which people walk over without knowing it."

⁴⁵One of the experts in the law answered him, "Teacher, when you say these things, you insult us also."

⁴⁶Jesus replied, "And you experts in the law, woe to you, because you load people down with burdens they can hardly carry, and you yourselves will not lift one finger to help them.

⁴⁷"Woe to you, because you build tombs for the prophets, and it was your ancestors who killed them. ⁴⁸So you testify that you approve of what your ancestors did; they killed the prophets, and you build their tombs. ⁴⁹Because of this, God in his wisdom said, 'I will send them prophets and apostles, some of whom they will kill and others they will persecute.' ⁵⁰Therefore this generation will be held responsible for the blood of all the prophets that has been shed since the beginning of the world, ⁵¹from the blood of Abel to the blood of Zechariah, who was killed between the altar and the sanctuary. Yes, I tell you, this generation will be held responsible for it all.

⁵²"Woe to you experts in the law, because you have taken away the key to knowledge. You yourselves have not entered, and you have hindered those who were entering."

⁵³When Jesus went outside, the Pharisees and the teachers of the law began to oppose him fiercely and to besiege him with questions, ⁵⁴waiting to catch him in something he might say.

Warnings and Encouragements

12 Meanwhile, when a crowd of many thousands had gathered, so that they were trampling on one another, Jesus began to speak first to his disciples, saying: "Be*ᵃ* on your guard against the yeast of the Pharisees, which is hypocrisy. ²There is nothing concealed that will not be disclosed, or hidden that will not be made known. ³What you have said in the dark will be heard in the daylight, and what you have whispered in the ear in the inner rooms will be proclaimed from the roofs.

⁴"I tell you, my friends, do not be afraid of those who kill the body and after that can do no more. ⁵But I will show you whom you should fear: Fear him who, after your body has been killed, has authority to throw you into hell. Yes, I tell you, fear him. ⁶Are not five sparrows sold for two pennies? Yet not one of them is forgotten by God. ⁷Indeed, the very hairs of your head are all numbered. Don't be afraid; you are worth more than many sparrows.

⁸"I tell you, whoever publicly acknowledges me, the Son of Man will also acknowledge before the angels of God. ⁹But whoever publicly disowns me will be disowned before the angels of God. ¹⁰And everyone who speaks a word against the Son of Man will be forgiven, but anyone who blasphemes against the Holy Spirit will not be forgiven.

ᵃ 1 Or speak to his disciples, saying: "First of all, be

[11]"When you are brought before synagogues, rulers and authorities, do not worry about how you will defend yourselves or what you will say, [12]for the Holy Spirit will teach you at that time what you should say."

The Parable of the Rich Fool

[13]Someone in the crowd said to him, "Teacher, tell my brother to divide the inheritance with me."

[14]Jesus replied, "Man, who appointed me a judge or an arbiter between you?" [15]Then he said to them, "Watch out! Be on your guard against all kinds of greed; life does not consist in an abundance of possessions."

[16]And he told them this parable: "The ground of a certain rich man yielded an abundant harvest. [17]He thought to himself, 'What shall I do? I have no place to store my crops.'

[18]"Then he said, 'This is what I'll do. I will tear down my barns and build bigger ones, and there I will store my surplus grain. [19]And I'll say to myself, "You have plenty of grain laid up for many years. Take life easy; eat, drink and be merry." '

[20]"But God said to him, 'You fool! This very night your life will be demanded from you. Then who will get what you have prepared for yourself?'

[21]"This is how it will be with those who store up things for themselves but are not rich toward God."

Do Not Worry

[22]Then Jesus said to his disciples: "Therefore I tell you, do not worry about your life, what you will eat; or about your body, what you will wear. [23]Life is more than food, and the body more than clothes. [24]Consider the ravens: They do not sow or reap, they have no storeroom or barn; yet God feeds them. And how much more valuable you are than birds! [25]Who of you by worrying can add a single hour to your life[a]? [26]Since you cannot do this very little thing, why do you worry about the rest?

[27]"Consider how the lilies grow. They do not labor or spin. Yet I tell you, not even Solomon in all his splendor was dressed like one of these. [28]If that is how God clothes the grass of the field, which is here today, and tomorrow is thrown into the fire, how much more will he clothe you—you of little faith! [29]And do not set your heart on what you will eat or drink; do not worry about it. [30]For the pagan world runs after all such things, and your Father knows that you need them. [31]But seek his kingdom, and these things will be given to you as well.

[32]"Do not be afraid, little flock, for your Father has been pleased to give you the kingdom. [33]Sell your possessions and give to the poor. Provide purses for yourselves that will not wear out, a treasure in heaven that will never fail, where no thief comes near and no moth destroys. [34]For where your treasure is, there your heart will be also.

Watchfulness

[35]"Be dressed ready for service and keep your lamps burning, [36]like

[a] 25 Or *single cubit to your height*

servants waiting for their master to return from a wedding banquet, so that when he comes and knocks they can immediately open the door for him. [37]It will be good for those servants whose master finds them watching when he comes. Truly I tell you, he will dress himself to serve, will have them recline at the table and will come and wait on them. [38]It will be good for those servants whose master finds them ready, even if he comes in the middle of the night or toward daybreak. [39]But understand this: If the owner of the house had known at what hour the thief was coming, he would not have let his house be broken into. [40]You also must be ready, because the Son of Man will come at an hour when you do not expect him."

[41]Peter asked, "Lord, are you telling this parable to us, or to everyone?"

[42]The Lord answered, "Who then is the faithful and wise manager, whom the master puts in charge of his servants to give them their food allowance at the proper time? [43]It will be good for that servant whom the master finds doing so when he returns. [44]Truly I tell you, he will put him in charge of all his possessions. [45]But suppose the servant says to himself, 'My master is taking a long time in coming,' and he then begins to beat the other servants, both men and women, and to eat and drink and get drunk. [46]The master of that servant will come on a day when he does not expect him and at an hour he is not aware of. He will cut him to pieces and assign him a place with the unbelievers.

[47]"The servant who knows the master's will and does not get ready or does not do what the master wants will be beaten with many blows. [48]But the one who does not know and does things deserving punishment will be beaten with few blows. From everyone who has been given much, much will be demanded; and from the one who has been entrusted with much, much more will be asked.

Not Peace but Division

[49]"I have come to bring fire on the earth, and how I wish it were already kindled! [50]But I have a baptism to undergo, and what constraint I am under until it is completed! [51]Do you think I came to bring peace on earth? No, I tell you, but division. [52]From now on there will be five in one family divided against each other, three against two and two against three. [53]They will be divided, father against son and son against father, mother against daughter and daughter against mother, mother-in-law against daughter-in-law and daughter-in-law against mother-in-law."

Interpreting the Times

[54]He said to the crowd: "When you see a cloud rising in the west, immediately you say, 'It's going to rain,' and it does. [55]And when the south wind blows, you say, 'It's going to be hot,' and it is. [56]Hypocrites! You know how to interpret the appearance of the earth and the sky. How is it that you don't know how to interpret this present time?

[57]"Why don't you judge for yourselves what is right? [58]As you are going with your adversary to the magistrate, try hard to be reconciled on the way, or your adversary may drag you off to the judge, and the judge turn you over to the officer, and the officer throw you into prison. [59]I tell you, you will not get out until you have paid the last penny."

Repent or Perish

13 Now there were some present at that time who told Jesus about the Galileans whose blood Pilate had mixed with their sacrifices. ²Jesus answered, "Do you think that these Galileans were worse sinners than all the other Galileans because they suffered this way? ³I tell you, no! But unless you repent, you too will all perish. ⁴Or those eighteen who died when the tower in Siloam fell on them—do you think they were more guilty than all the others living in Jerusalem? ⁵I tell you, no! But unless you repent, you too will all perish."

⁶Then he told this parable: "A man had a fig tree growing in his vineyard, and he went to look for fruit on it but did not find any. ⁷So he said to the man who took care of the vineyard, 'For three years now I've been coming to look for fruit on this fig tree and haven't found any. Cut it down! Why should it use up the soil?'

⁸" 'Sir,' the man replied, 'leave it alone for one more year, and I'll dig around it and fertilize it. ⁹If it bears fruit next year, fine! If not, then cut it down.' "

Jesus Heals a Crippled Woman on the Sabbath

¹⁰On a Sabbath Jesus was teaching in one of the synagogues, ¹¹and a woman was there who had been crippled by a spirit for eighteen years. She was bent over and could not straighten up at all. ¹²When Jesus saw her, he called her forward and said to her, "You are set free from your infirmity." ¹³Then he put his hands on her, and immediately she straightened up and praised God.

¹⁴Indignant because Jesus had healed on the Sabbath, the synagogue leader said to the people, "There are six days for work. So come and be healed on those days, not on the Sabbath."

¹⁵The Lord answered him, "You hypocrites! Doesn't each of you on the Sabbath untie his ox or donkey from the stall and lead it out to give it water? ¹⁶Then should not this woman, a daughter of Abraham, whom Satan has kept bound for eighteen long years, be set free on the Sabbath day from what bound her?"

¹⁷When he said this, all his opponents were humiliated, but the people were delighted with all the wonderful things he was doing.

The Parables of the Mustard Seed and the Yeast

¹⁸Then Jesus asked, "What is the kingdom of God like? What shall I compare it to? ¹⁹It is like a mustard seed, which a man took and planted in his garden. It grew and became a tree, and the birds of the air perched in its branches."

²⁰Again he asked, "What shall I compare the kingdom of God to? ²¹It is like yeast that a woman took and mixed into about eighteen pounds*a* of flour until it worked all through the dough."

The Narrow Door

²²Then Jesus went through the towns and villages, teaching as he made his

a 21 About 8 kilograms

way to Jerusalem. 23Someone asked him, "Lord, are only a few people going to be saved?"

He said to them, 24"Make every effort to enter through the narrow door, because many, I tell you, will try to enter and will not be able to. 25Once the owner of the house gets up and closes the door, you will stand outside knocking and pleading, 'Sir, open the door for us.'

"But he will answer, 'I don't know you or where you come from.'

26"Then you will say, 'We ate and drank with you, and you taught in our streets.'

27"But he will reply, 'I don't know you or where you come from. Away from me, all you evildoers!'

28"There will be weeping there, and gnashing of teeth, when you see Abraham, Isaac and Jacob and all the prophets in the kingdom of God, but you yourselves thrown out. 29People will come from east and west and north and south, and will take their places at the feast in the kingdom of God. 30Indeed there are those who are last who will be first, and first who will be last."

Jesus' Sorrow for Jerusalem

31At that time some Pharisees came to Jesus and said to him, "Leave this place and go somewhere else. Herod wants to kill you."

32He replied, "Go tell that fox, 'I will keep on driving out demons and healing people today and tomorrow, and on the third day I will reach my goal.' 33In any case, I must press on today and tomorrow and the next day—for surely no prophet can die outside Jerusalem!

34"Jerusalem, Jerusalem, you who kill the prophets and stone those sent to you, how often I have longed to gather your children together, as a hen gathers her chicks under her wings, and you were not willing. 35Look, your house is left to you desolate. I tell you, you will not see me again until you say, 'Blessed is he who comes in the name of the Lord.'ᵃ"

Jesus at a Pharisee's House

14 One Sabbath, when Jesus went to eat in the house of a prominent Pharisee, he was being carefully watched. 2There in front of him was a man suffering from abnormal swelling of his body. 3Jesus asked the Pharisees and experts in the law, "Is it lawful to heal on the Sabbath or not?" 4But they remained silent. So taking hold of the man, he healed him and sent him on his way.

5Then he asked them, "If one of you has a childᵇ or an ox that falls into a well on the Sabbath day, will you not immediately pull it out?" 6And they had nothing to say.

7When he noticed how the guests picked the places of honor at the table, he told them this parable: 8"When someone invites you to a wedding feast, do not take the place of honor, for a person more distinguished than you may have been invited. 9If so, the host who invited both of you will come and say to you, 'Give this person your seat.' Then, humiliated, you will have to take the least important place. 10But when you are invited, take the lowest place,

ᵃ 35 Psalm 118:26   ᵇ 5 Some manuscripts donkey

so that when your host comes, he will say to you, 'Friend, move up to a better place.' Then you will be honored in the presence of all the other guests. [11]For all those who exalt themselves will be humbled, and those who humble themselves will be exalted."

[12]Then Jesus said to his host, "When you give a luncheon or dinner, do not invite your friends, your brothers or sisters, your relatives, or your rich neighbors; if you do, they may invite you back and so you will be repaid. [13]But when you give a banquet, invite the poor, the crippled, the lame, the blind, [14]and you will be blessed. Although they cannot repay you, you will be repaid at the resurrection of the righteous."

The Parable of the Great Banquet

[15]When one of those at the table with him heard this, he said to Jesus, "Blessed are those who will eat at the feast in the kingdom of God."

[16]Jesus replied: "A certain man was preparing a great banquet and invited many guests. [17]At the time of the banquet he sent his servant to tell those who had been invited, 'Come, for everything is now ready.'

[18]"But they all alike began to make excuses. The first said, 'I have just bought a field, and I must go and see it. Please excuse me.'

[19]"Another said, 'I have just bought five yoke of oxen, and I'm on my way to try them out. Please excuse me.'

[20]"Still another said, 'I just got married, so I can't come.'

[21]"The servant came back and reported this to his master. Then the owner of the house became angry and ordered his servant, 'Go out quickly into the streets and alleys of the town and bring in the poor, the crippled, the blind and the lame.'

[22]" 'Sir,' the servant said, 'what you ordered has been done, but there is still room.'

[23]"Then the master told his servant, 'Go out to the roads and country lanes and compel them to come in, so that my house will be full. [24]I tell you, not one of those who were invited will get a taste of my banquet.' "

The Cost of Being a Disciple

[25]Large crowds were traveling with Jesus, and turning to them he said: [26]"If anyone comes to me and does not hate father and mother, wife and children, brothers and sisters—yes, even life itself—such a person cannot be my disciple. [27]And those who do not carry their cross and follow me cannot be my disciples.

[28]"Suppose one of you wants to build a tower. Won't you first sit down and estimate the cost to see if you have enough money to complete it? [29]For if you lay the foundation and are not able to finish it, everyone who sees it will ridicule you, [30]saying, 'This person began to build and wasn't able to finish.'

[31]"Or suppose a king is about to go to war against another king. Won't he first sit down and consider whether he is able with ten thousand men to oppose the one coming against him with twenty thousand? [32]If he is not able, he will send a delegation while the other is still a long way off and will ask for terms of peace. [33]In the same way, those of you who do not give up everything you have cannot be my disciples.

³⁴"Salt is good, but if it loses its saltiness, how can it be made salty again? ³⁵It is fit neither for the soil nor for the manure pile; it is thrown out.

"Whoever has ears to hear, let them hear."

The Parable of the Lost Sheep

15 Now the tax collectors and "sinners" were all gathering around to hear him. ²But the Pharisees and the teachers of the law muttered, "This man welcomes sinners and eats with them."

³Then Jesus told them this parable: ⁴"Suppose one of you has a hundred sheep and loses one of them. Doesn't he leave the ninety-nine in the open country and go after the lost sheep until he finds it? ⁵And when he finds it, he joyfully puts it on his shoulders ⁶and goes home. Then he calls his friends and neighbors together and says, 'Rejoice with me; I have found my lost sheep.' ⁷I tell you that in the same way there will be more rejoicing in heaven over one sinner who repents than over ninety-nine righteous persons who do not need to repent.

The Parable of the Lost Coin

⁸"Or suppose a woman has ten silver coins[a] and loses one. Doesn't she light a lamp, sweep the house and search carefully until she finds it? ⁹And when she finds it, she calls her friends and neighbors together and says, 'Rejoice with me; I have found my lost coin.' ¹⁰In the same way, I tell you, there is rejoicing in the presence of the angels of God over one sinner who repents."

The Parable of the Lost Son

¹¹Jesus continued: "There was a man who had two sons. ¹²The younger one said to his father, 'Father, give me my share of the estate.' So he divided his property between them.

¹³"Not long after that, the younger son got together all he had, set off for a distant country and there squandered his wealth in wild living. ¹⁴After he had spent everything, there was a severe famine in that whole country, and he began to be in need. ¹⁵So he went and hired himself out to a citizen of that country, who sent him to his fields to feed pigs. ¹⁶He longed to fill his stomach with the pods that the pigs were eating, but no one gave him anything.

¹⁷"When he came to his senses, he said, 'How many of my father's hired servants have food to spare, and here I am starving to death! ¹⁸I will set out and go back to my father and say to him: Father, I have sinned against heaven and against you. ¹⁹I am no longer worthy to be called your son; make me like one of your hired servants.' ²⁰So he got up and went to his father.

"But while he was still a long way off, his father saw him and was filled with compassion for him; he ran to his son, threw his arms around him and kissed him.

²¹"The son said to him, 'Father, I have sinned against heaven and against you. I am no longer worthy to be called your son.'

²²"But the father said to his servants, 'Quick! Bring the best robe and put it on him. Put a ring on his finger and sandals on his feet. ²³Bring the fattened

---

a 8 Greek *ten drachmas*, each worth about a day's wages

calf and kill it. Let's have a feast and celebrate. 24For this son of mine was dead and is alive again; he was lost and is found.' So they began to celebrate.

25"Meanwhile, the older son was in the field. When he came near the house, he heard music and dancing. 26So he called one of the servants and asked him what was going on. 27'Your brother has come,' he replied, 'and your father has killed the fattened calf because he has him back safe and sound.'

28"The older brother became angry and refused to go in. So his father went out and pleaded with him. 29But he answered his father, 'Look! All these years I've been slaving for you and never disobeyed your orders. Yet you never gave me even a young goat so I could celebrate with my friends. 30But when this son of yours who has squandered your property with prostitutes comes home, you kill the fattened calf for him!'

31" 'My son,' the father said, 'you are always with me, and everything I have is yours. 32But we had to celebrate and be glad, because this brother of yours was dead and is alive again; he was lost and is found.' "

The Parable of the Shrewd Manager

16 Jesus told his disciples: "There was a rich man whose manager was accused of wasting his possessions. 2So he called him in and asked him, 'What is this I hear about you? Give an account of your management, because you cannot be manager any longer.'

3"The manager said to himself, 'What shall I do now? My master is taking away my job. I'm not strong enough to dig, and I'm ashamed to beg— 4I know what I'll do so that, when I lose my job here, people will welcome me into their houses.'

5"So he called in each one of his master's debtors. He asked the first, 'How much do you owe my master?'

6" 'Eight hundred gallons*a* of olive oil,' he replied.

"The manager told him, 'Take your bill, sit down quickly, and make it four hundred.'

7"Then he asked the second, 'And how much do you owe?'

" 'A thousand bushels*b* of wheat,' he replied.

"He told him, 'Take your bill and make it eight hundred.'

8"The master commended the dishonest manager because he had acted shrewdly. For the people of this world are more shrewd in dealing with their own kind than are the people of the light. 9I tell you, use worldly wealth to gain friends for yourselves, so that when it is gone, you will be welcomed into eternal dwellings.

10"Whoever can be trusted with very little can also be trusted with much, and whoever is dishonest with very little will also be dishonest with much. 11So if you have not been trustworthy in handling worldly wealth, who will trust you with true riches? 12And if you have not been trustworthy with someone else's property, who will give you property of your own?

13"No one can be a slave to two masters. Either you will hate the one and love the other, or you will be devoted to the one and despise the other. You cannot be a slave to both God and Money."

*a*6 About 3 kiloliters   *b*7 About 35 kiloliters

¹⁴The Pharisees, who loved money, heard all this and were sneering at Jesus. ¹⁵He said to them, "You are the ones who justify yourselves in the eyes of others, but God knows your hearts. What people value highly is detestable in God's sight.

Additional Teachings

¹⁶"The Law and the Prophets were proclaimed until John. Since that time, the good news of the kingdom of God is being preached, and people are forcing their way into it. ¹⁷It is easier for heaven and earth to disappear than for the least stroke of a pen to drop out of the Law.

¹⁸"Anyone who divorces his wife and marries another woman commits adultery, and the man who marries a divorced woman commits adultery.

The Rich Man and Lazarus

¹⁹"There was a rich man who was dressed in purple and fine linen and lived in luxury every day. ²⁰At his gate was laid a beggar named Lazarus, covered with sores ²¹and longing to eat what fell from the rich man's table. Even the dogs came and licked his sores.

²²"The time came when the beggar died and the angels carried him to Abraham's side. The rich man also died and was buried. ²³In Hades, where he was in torment, he looked up and saw Abraham far away, with Lazarus by his side. ²⁴So he called to him, 'Father Abraham, have pity on me and send Lazarus to dip the tip of his finger in water and cool my tongue, because I am in agony in this fire.'

²⁵"But Abraham replied, 'Son, remember that in your lifetime you received your good things, while Lazarus received bad things, but now he is comforted here and you are in agony. ²⁶And besides all this, between us and you a great chasm has been set in place, so that those who want to go from here to you cannot, nor can anyone cross over from there to us.'

²⁷"He answered, 'Then I beg you, father, send Lazarus to my family, ²⁸for I have five brothers. Let him warn them, so that they will not also come to this place of torment.'

²⁹"Abraham replied, 'They have Moses and the Prophets; let them listen to them.'

³⁰" 'No, father Abraham,' he said, 'but if someone from the dead goes to them, they will repent.'

³¹"He said to him, 'If they do not listen to Moses and the Prophets, they will not be convinced even if someone rises from the dead.' "

Sin, Faith, Duty

17 Jesus said to his disciples: "Things that cause people to stumble are bound to come, but woe to anyone through whom they come. ²It would be better for you to be thrown into the sea with a millstone tied around your neck than for you to cause one of these little ones to stumble. ³So watch yourselves.

"If any brother or sister sins against you, rebuke the offender; and if they repent, forgive them. ⁴Even if they sin against you seven times in a day and seven times come back to you saying 'I repent,' you must forgive them."

5The apostles said to the Lord, "Increase our faith!"

6He replied, "If you have faith as small as a mustard seed, you can say to this mulberry tree, 'Be uprooted and planted in the sea,' and it will obey you.

7"Suppose one of you has a servant plowing or looking after the sheep. Will he say to the servant when he comes in from the field, 'Come along now and sit down to eat'? 8Won't he rather say, 'Prepare my supper, get yourself ready and wait on me while I eat and drink; after that you may eat and drink'? 9Will he thank the servant because he did what he was told to do? 10So you also, when you have done everything you were told to do, should say, 'We are unworthy servants; we have only done our duty.' "

Jesus Heals Ten Men With Leprosy

11Now on his way to Jerusalem, Jesus traveled along the border between Samaria and Galilee. 12As he was going into a village, ten men who had leprosy*a* met him. They stood at a distance 13and called out in a loud voice, "Jesus, Master, have pity on us!"

14When he saw them, he said, "Go, show yourselves to the priests." And as they went, they were cleansed.

15One of them, when he saw he was healed, came back, praising God in a loud voice. 16He threw himself at Jesus' feet and thanked him—and he was a Samaritan.

17Jesus asked, "Were not all ten cleansed? Where are the other nine? 18Was no one found to return and give praise to God except this foreigner?" 19Then he said to him, "Rise and go, your faith has made you well."

The Coming of the Kingdom of God

20Once, having been asked by the Pharisees when the kingdom of God would come, Jesus replied, "The coming of the kingdom of God is not something that can be observed, 21nor will people say, 'Here it is,' or 'There it is,' because the kingdom of God is in your midst."*b*

22Then he said to his disciples, "The time is coming when you will long to see one of the days of the Son of Man, but you will not see it. 23People will tell you, 'There he is!' or 'Here he is!' Do not go running off after them. 24For the Son of Man in his day*c* will be like the lightning, which flashes and lights up the sky from one end to the other. 25But first he must suffer many things and be rejected by this generation.

26"Just as it was in the days of Noah, so also will it be in the days of the Son of Man. 27People were eating, drinking, marrying and being given in marriage up to the day Noah entered the ark. Then the flood came and destroyed them all.

28"It was the same in the days of Lot. People were eating and drinking, buying and selling, planting and building. 29But the day Lot left Sodom, fire and sulfur rained down from heaven and destroyed them all.

---

a 12 The Greek word was used for various diseases affecting the skin—not necessarily leprosy.
b 21 Or is within you   *c* 24 Some manuscripts do not have in his day.

³⁰"It will be just like this on the day the Son of Man is revealed. ³¹On that day no one who is on the housetop, with possessions inside, should go down to get them. Likewise, no one in the field should go back for anything. ³²Remember Lot's wife! ³³Those who try to keep their life will lose it, and those who lose their life will preserve it. ³⁴I tell you, on that night two people will be in one bed; one will be taken and the other left. ³⁵[³⁶]Two women will be grinding grain together; one will be taken and the other left."

³⁷"Where, Lord?" they asked.

He replied, "Where there is a dead body, there the vultures will gather."

The Parable of the Persistent Widow

18 Then Jesus told his disciples a parable to show them that they should always pray and not give up. ²He said: "In a certain town there was a judge who neither feared God nor cared what people thought. ³And there was a widow in that town who kept coming to him with the plea, 'Grant me justice against my adversary.'

⁴"For some time he refused. But finally he said to himself, 'Even though I don't fear God or care what people think, ⁵yet because this widow keeps bothering me, I will see that she gets justice, so that she won't eventually come and attack me!' "

⁶And the Lord said, "Listen to what the unjust judge says. ⁷And will not God bring about justice for his chosen ones, who cry out to him day and night? Will he keep putting them off? ⁸I tell you, he will see that they get justice, and quickly. However, when the Son of Man comes, will he find faith on the earth?"

The Parable of the Pharisee and the Tax Collector

⁹To some who were confident of their own righteousness and looked down on everyone else, Jesus told this parable: ¹⁰"Two men went up to the temple to pray, one a Pharisee and the other a tax collector. ¹¹The Pharisee stood by himself and prayed: 'God, I thank you that I am not like other people—robbers, evildoers, adulterers—or even like this tax collector. ¹²I fast twice a week and give a tenth of all I get.'

¹³"But the tax collector stood at a distance. He would not even look up to heaven, but beat his breast and said, 'God, have mercy on me, a sinner.'

¹⁴"I tell you that this man, rather than the other, went home justified before God. For all those who exalt themselves will be humbled, and those who humble themselves will be exalted."

The Little Children and Jesus

¹⁵People were also bringing babies to Jesus to have him touch them. When the disciples saw this, they rebuked them. ¹⁶But Jesus called the children to him and said, "Let the little children come to me, and do not hinder them, for the kingdom of God belongs to such as these. ¹⁷Truly I tell you, anyone who will not receive the kingdom of God like a little child will never enter it."

The Rich and the Kingdom of God

¹⁸A certain ruler asked him, "Good teacher, what must I do to inherit eternal life?"

19"Why do you call me good?" Jesus answered. "No one is good—except God alone. 20You know the commandments: 'Do not commit adultery, do not murder, do not steal, do not give false testimony, honor your father and mother.'ᵃ"

21"All these I have kept since I was a boy," he said.

22When Jesus heard this, he said to him, "You still lack one thing. Sell everything you have and give to the poor, and you will have treasure in heaven. Then come, follow me."

23When he heard this, he became very sad, because he was very wealthy. 24Jesus looked at him and said, "How hard it is for the rich to enter the kingdom of God! 25Indeed, it is easier for a camel to go through the eye of a needle than for the rich to enter the kingdom of God."

26Those who heard this asked, "Who then can be saved?"

27Jesus replied, "What is humanly impossible is possible with God."

28Peter said to him, "We have left all we had to follow you!"

29"Truly I tell you," Jesus said to them, "no one who has left home or wife or brothers or sisters or parents or children for the sake of the kingdom of God 30will fail to receive many times as much in this age, and in the age to come eternal life."

Jesus Predicts His Death a Third Time

31Jesus took the Twelve aside and told them, "We are going up to Jerusalem, and everything that is written by the prophets about the Son of Man will be fulfilled. 32He will be delivered over to the Gentiles. They will mock him, insult him, spit on him, flog him and kill him. 33On the third day he will rise again."

34The disciples did not understand any of this. Its meaning was hidden from them, and they did not know what he was talking about.

A Blind Beggar Receives His Sight

35As Jesus approached Jericho, a blind man was sitting by the roadside begging. 36When he heard the crowd going by, he asked what was happening. 37They told him, "Jesus of Nazareth is passing by."

38He called out, "Jesus, Son of David, have mercy on me!"

39Those who led the way rebuked him and told him to be quiet, but he shouted all the more, "Son of David, have mercy on me!"

40Jesus stopped and ordered the man to be brought to him. When he came near, Jesus asked him, 41"What do you want me to do for you?"

"Lord, I want to see," he replied.

42Jesus said to him, "Receive your sight; your faith has healed you." 43Immediately he received his sight and followed Jesus, praising God. When all the people saw it, they also praised God.

Zacchaeus the Tax Collector

19 Jesus entered Jericho and was passing through. 2A man was there by the name of Zacchaeus; he was a chief tax collector and was wealthy.

ᵃ 20 Exodus 20:12–16; Deut. 5:16–20

³He wanted to see who Jesus was, but because he was short he could not see over the crowd. ⁴So he ran ahead and climbed a sycamore-fig tree to see him, since Jesus was coming that way.

⁵When Jesus reached the spot, he looked up and said to him, "Zacchaeus, come down immediately. I must stay at your house today." ⁶So he came down at once and welcomed him gladly.

⁷All the people saw this and began to mutter, "He has gone to be the guest of a 'sinner.' "

⁸But Zacchaeus stood up and said to the Lord, "Look, Lord! Here and now I give half of my possessions to the poor, and if I have cheated anybody out of anything, I will pay back four times the amount."

⁹Jesus said to him, "Today salvation has come to this house, because this man, too, is a son of Abraham. ¹⁰For the Son of Man came to seek and to save what was lost."

The Parable of the Ten Minas

¹¹While they were listening to this, he went on to tell them a parable, because he was near Jerusalem and the people thought that the kingdom of God was going to appear at once. ¹²He said: "A man of noble birth went to a distant country to have himself appointed king and then to return. ¹³So he called ten of his servants and gave them ten minas.ᵃ 'Put this money to work,' he said, 'until I come back.'

¹⁴"But his subjects hated him and sent a delegation after him to say, 'We don't want this man to be our king.'

¹⁵"He was made king, however, and returned home. Then he sent for the servants to whom he had given the money, in order to find out what they had gained with it.

¹⁶"The first one came and said, 'Sir, your mina has earned ten more.'

¹⁷" 'Well done, my good servant!' his master replied. 'Because you have been trustworthy in a very small matter, take charge of ten cities.'

¹⁸"The second came and said, 'Sir, your mina has earned five more.'

¹⁹"His master answered, 'You take charge of five cities.'

²⁰"Then another servant came and said, 'Sir, here is your mina; I have kept it laid away in a piece of cloth. ²¹I was afraid of you, because you are a hard man. You take out what you did not put in and reap what you did not sow.'

²²"His master replied, 'I will judge you by your own words, you wicked servant! You knew, did you, that I am a hard man, taking out what I did not put in, and reaping what I did not sow? ²³Why then didn't you put my money on deposit, so that when I came back, I could have collected it with interest?'

²⁴"Then he said to those standing by, 'Take his mina away from him and give it to the one who has ten minas.'

²⁵" 'Sir,' they said, 'he already has ten!'

²⁶"He replied, 'I tell you that to everyone who has, more will be given, but as for those who have nothing, even what they have will be taken away. ²⁷But those enemies of mine who did not want me to be king over them—bring them here and kill them in front of me.' "

ᵃ 13 A mina was about three months' wages.

Jesus Comes to Jerusalem as King

28After Jesus had said this, he went on ahead, going up to Jerusalem. 29As he approached Bethphage and Bethany at the hill called the Mount of Olives, he sent two of his disciples, saying to them, 30"Go to the village ahead of you, and as you enter it, you will find a colt tied there, which no one has ever ridden. Untie it and bring it here. 31If anyone asks you, 'Why are you untying it?' say, 'The Lord needs it.' "

32Those who were sent ahead went and found it just as he had told them. 33As they were untying the colt, its owners asked them, "Why are you untying the colt?"

34They replied, "The Lord needs it."

35They brought it to Jesus, threw their cloaks on the colt and put Jesus on it. 36As he went along, people spread their cloaks on the road.

37When he came near the place where the road goes down the Mount of Olives, the whole crowd of disciples began joyfully to praise God in loud voices for all the miracles they had seen:

38"Blessed is the king who comes in the name of the Lord!"*a*

"Peace in heaven and glory in the highest!"

39Some of the Pharisees in the crowd said to Jesus, "Teacher, rebuke your disciples!"

40"I tell you," he replied, "if they keep quiet, the stones will cry out."

41As he approached Jerusalem and saw the city, he wept over it 42and said, "If you, even you, had only known on this day what would bring you peace— but now it is hidden from your eyes. 43The days will come upon you when your enemies will build an embankment against you and encircle you and hem you in on every side. 44They will dash you to the ground, you and the children within your walls. They will not leave one stone on another, because you did not recognize the time of God's coming to you."

Jesus at the Temple

45When Jesus entered the temple courts, he began to drive out those who were selling. 46"It is written," he said to them, " 'My house will be a house of prayer'*b*; but you have made it 'a den of robbers.'*c*"

47Every day he was teaching at the temple. But the chief priests, the teachers of the law and the leaders among the people were trying to kill him. 48Yet they could not find any way to do it, because all the people hung on his words.

The Authority of Jesus Questioned

20 One day as he was teaching the people in the temple courts and proclaiming the good news, the chief priests and the teachers of the law, together with the elders, came up to him. 2"Tell us by what authority you are doing these things," they said. "Who gave you this authority?"

3He replied, "I will also ask you a question. Tell me, 4John's baptism—was it from heaven, or of human origin?"

a 38 Psalm 118:26   *b 46* Isaiah 56:7   *c 46* Jer. 7:11

5They discussed it among themselves and said, "If we say, 'From heaven,' he will ask, 'Why didn't you believe him?' 6But if we say, 'Of human origin,' all the people will stone us, because they are persuaded that John was a prophet."

7So they answered, "We don't know where it was from."

8Jesus said, "Neither will I tell you by what authority I am doing these things."

The Parable of the Tenants

9He went on to tell the people this parable: "A man planted a vineyard, rented it to some farmers and went away for a long time. 10At harvest time he sent a servant to the tenants so they would give him some of the fruit of the vineyard. But the tenants beat him and sent him away empty-handed. 11He sent another servant, but that one also they beat and treated shamefully and sent away empty-handed. 12He sent still a third, and they wounded him and threw him out.

13"Then the owner of the vineyard said, 'What shall I do? I will send my son, whom I love; perhaps they will respect him.'

14"But when the tenants saw him, they talked the matter over. 'This is the heir,' they said. 'Let's kill him, and the inheritance will be ours.' 15So they threw him out of the vineyard and killed him.

"What then will the owner of the vineyard do to them? 16He will come and kill those tenants and give the vineyard to others."

When the people heard this, they said, "May this never be!"

17Jesus looked directly at them and asked, "Then what is the meaning of that which is written:

" 'The stone the builders rejected
has become the cornerstone'ª?

18Everyone who falls on that stone will be broken to pieces, but anyone on whom it falls will be crushed."

19The teachers of the law and the chief priests looked for a way to arrest him immediately, because they knew he had spoken this parable against them. But they were afraid of the people.

Paying Taxes to Caesar

20Keeping a close watch on him, they sent spies, who pretended to be sincere. They hoped to catch Jesus in something he said so that they might hand him over to the power and authority of the governor. 21So the spies questioned him: "Teacher, we know that you speak and teach what is right, and that you do not show partiality but teach the way of God in accordance with the truth. 22Is it right for us to pay taxes to Caesar or not?"

23He saw through their duplicity and said to them, 24"Show me a denarius. Whose portrait and inscription are on it?"

"Caesar's," they replied.

25He said to them, "Then give back to Caesar what is Caesar's, and to God what is God's."

ª 17 Psalm 118:22

²⁶They were unable to trap him in what he had said there in public. And astonished by his answer, they became silent.

The Resurrection and Marriage

²⁷Some of the Sadducees, who say there is no resurrection, came to Jesus with a question. ²⁸"Teacher," they said, "Moses wrote for us that if a man's brother dies and leaves a wife but no children, the man must marry the widow and raise up an heir for his brother. ²⁹Now there were seven brothers. The first one married a woman and died childless. ³⁰The second ³¹and then the third married her, and in the same way the seven died, leaving no children. ³²Finally, the woman died too. ³³Now then, at the resurrection whose wife will she be, since the seven were married to her?"

³⁴Jesus replied, "The people of this age marry and are given in marriage. ³⁵But those who are considered worthy of taking part in the age to come and in the resurrection from the dead will neither marry nor be given in marriage, ³⁶and they can no longer die; for they are like the angels. They are God's children, since they are children of the resurrection. ³⁷But in the account of the burning bush, even Moses showed that the dead rise, for he calls the Lord 'the God of Abraham, and the God of Isaac, and the God of Jacob.'ᵃ ³⁸He is not the God of the dead, but of the living, for to him all are alive."

³⁹Some of the teachers of the law responded, "Well said, teacher!" ⁴⁰And no one dared to ask him any more questions.

Whose Son Is the Messiah?

⁴¹Then Jesus said to them, "Why is it said that the Messiah is the son of David? ⁴²David himself declares in the Book of Psalms:

" 'The Lord said to my Lord:
   "Sit at my right hand
⁴³until I make your enemies
   a footstool for your feet." 'ᵇ

⁴⁴David calls him 'Lord.' How then can he be his son?"

Warning Against the Teachers of the Law

⁴⁵While all the people were listening, Jesus said to his disciples, ⁴⁶"Beware of the teachers of the law. They like to walk around in flowing robes and love to be greeted with respect in the marketplaces and have the most important seats in the synagogues and the places of honor at banquets. ⁴⁷They devour widows' houses and for a show make lengthy prayers. These men will be punished most severely."

The Widow's Offering

21 As Jesus looked up, he saw the rich putting their gifts into the temple treasury. ²He also saw a poor widow put in two very small copper coins. ³"Truly I tell you," he said, "this poor widow has put in more than all

ᵃ37 Exodus 3:6   ᵇ43 Psalm 110:1

the others. 4All these people gave their gifts out of their wealth; but she out of her poverty put in all she had to live on."

The Destruction of the Temple and Signs of the End Times

5Some of his disciples were remarking about how the temple was adorned with beautiful stones and with gifts dedicated to God. But Jesus said, 6"As for what you see here, the time will come when not one stone will be left on another; every one of them will be thrown down."

7"Teacher," they asked, "when will these things happen? And what will be the sign that they are about to take place?"

8He replied: "Watch out that you are not deceived. For many will come in my name, claiming, 'I am he,' and, 'The time is near.' Do not follow them. 9When you hear of wars and uprisings, do not be frightened. These things must happen first, but the end will not come right away."

10Then he said to them: "Nation will rise against nation, and kingdom against kingdom. 11There will be great earthquakes, famines and pestilences in various places, and fearful events and great signs from heaven.

12"But before all this, they will lay hands on you and persecute you. They will deliver you to synagogues and prisons, and you will be brought before kings and governors, and all on account of my name. 13And so you will bear testimony to me. 14But make up your mind not to worry beforehand how you will defend yourselves. 15For I will give you words and wisdom that none of your adversaries will be able to resist or contradict. 16You will be betrayed even by parents, brothers, sisters, relatives and friends, and they will put some of you to death. 17Everyone will hate you because of me. 18But not a hair of your head will perish. 19Stand firm, and you will win life.

20"When you see Jerusalem being surrounded by armies, you will know that its desolation is near. 21Then let those who are in Judea flee to the mountains, let those in the city get out, and let those in the country not enter the city. 22For this is the time of punishment in fulfillment of all that has been written. 23How dreadful it will be in those days for pregnant women and nursing mothers! There will be great distress in the land and wrath against this people. 24They will fall by the sword and will be taken as prisoners to all the nations. Jerusalem will be trampled on by the Gentiles until the times of the Gentiles are fulfilled.

25"There will be signs in the sun, moon and stars. On the earth, nations will be in anguish and perplexity at the roaring and tossing of the sea. 26People will faint from terror, apprehensive of what is coming on the world, for the heavenly bodies will be shaken. 27At that time they will see the Son of Man coming in a cloud with power and great glory. 28When these things begin to take place, stand up and lift up your heads, because your redemption is drawing near."

29He told them this parable: "Look at the fig tree and all the trees. 30When they sprout leaves, you can see for yourselves and know that summer is near. 31Even so, when you see these things happening, you know that the kingdom of God is near.

32"Truly I tell you, this generation will certainly not pass away until all these things have happened. [33]Heaven and earth will pass away, but my words will never pass away.

[34]"Be careful, or your hearts will be weighed down with dissipation, drunkenness and the anxieties of life, and that day will close on you suddenly like a trap. [35]For it will come upon all those who live on the face of the whole earth. [36]Be always on the watch, and pray that you may be able to escape all that is about to happen, and that you may be able to stand before the Son of Man."

[37]Each day Jesus was teaching at the temple, and each evening he went out to spend the night on the hill called the Mount of Olives, [38]and all the people came early in the morning to hear him at the temple.

Judas Agrees to Betray Jesus

22 Now the Festival of Unleavened Bread, called the Passover, was approaching, [2]and the chief priests and the teachers of the law were looking for some way to get rid of Jesus, for they were afraid of the people. [3]Then Satan entered Judas, called Iscariot, one of the Twelve. [4]And Judas went to the chief priests and the officers of the temple guard and discussed with them how he might betray Jesus. [5]They were delighted and agreed to give him money. [6]He consented, and watched for an opportunity to hand Jesus over to them when no crowd was present.

The Last Supper

[7]Then came the day of Unleavened Bread on which the Passover lamb had to be sacrificed. [8]Jesus sent Peter and John, saying, "Go and make preparations for us to eat the Passover."

[9]"Where do you want us to prepare for it?" they asked.

[10]He replied, "As you enter the city, a man carrying a jar of water will meet you. Follow him to the house that he enters, [11]and say to the owner of the house, 'The Teacher asks: Where is the guest room, where I may eat the Passover with my disciples?' [12]He will show you a large room upstairs, all furnished. Make preparations there."

[13]They left and found things just as Jesus had told them. So they prepared the Passover.

[14]When the hour came, Jesus and his apostles reclined at the table. [15]And he said to them, "I have eagerly desired to eat this Passover with you before I suffer. [16]For I tell you, I will not eat it again until it finds fulfillment in the kingdom of God."

[17]After taking the cup, he gave thanks and said, "Take this and divide it among you. [18]For I tell you I will not drink again of the fruit of the vine until the kingdom of God comes."

[19]And he took bread, gave thanks and broke it, and gave it to them, saying, "This is my body given for you; do this in remembrance of me."

[20]In the same way, after the supper he took the cup, saying, "This cup is the new covenant in my blood, which is poured out for you. [21]But the hand of him who is going to betray me is with mine on the table. [22]The Son of Man will go as it has been decreed. But woe to that man who betrays him!" [23]They

began to question among themselves which of them it might be who would do this.

²⁴A dispute also arose among them as to which of them was considered to be greatest. ²⁵Jesus said to them, "The kings of the Gentiles lord it over them; and those who exercise authority over them call themselves Benefactors. ²⁶But you are not to be like that. Instead, the greatest among you should be like the youngest, and the one who rules like the one who serves. ²⁷For who is greater, the one who is at the table or the one who serves? Is it not the one who is at the table? But I am among you as one who serves. ²⁸You are those who have stood by me in my trials. ²⁹And I confer on you a kingdom, just as my Father conferred one on me, ³⁰so that you may eat and drink at my table in my kingdom and sit on thrones, judging the twelve tribes of Israel.

³¹"Simon, Simon, Satan has asked to sift all of you as wheat. ³²But I have prayed for you, Simon, that your faith may not fail. And when you have turned back, strengthen your brothers."

³³But he replied, "Lord, I am ready to go with you to prison and to death."

³⁴Jesus answered, "I tell you, Peter, before the rooster crows today, you will deny three times that you know me."

³⁵Then Jesus asked them, "When I sent you without purse, bag or sandals, did you lack anything?"

"Nothing," they answered.

³⁶He said to them, "But now if you have a purse, take it, and also a bag; and if you don't have a sword, sell your cloak and buy one. ³⁷It is written: 'And he was numbered with the transgressors'ᵃ; and I tell you that this must be fulfilled in me. Yes, what is written about me is reaching its fulfillment."

³⁸The disciples said, "See, Lord, here are two swords."

"That is enough," he replied.

Jesus Prays on the Mount of Olives

³⁹Jesus went out as usual to the Mount of Olives, and his disciples followed him. ⁴⁰On reaching the place, he said to them, "Pray that you will not fall into temptation." ⁴¹He withdrew about a stone's throw beyond them, knelt down and prayed, ⁴²"Father, if you are willing, take this cup from me; yet not my will, but yours be done." ⁴³An angel from heaven appeared to him and strengthened him. ⁴⁴And being in anguish, he prayed more earnestly, and his sweat was like drops of blood falling to the ground.ᵇ

⁴⁵When he rose from prayer and went back to the disciples, he found them asleep, exhausted from sorrow. ⁴⁶"Why are you sleeping?" he asked them. "Get up and pray so that you will not fall into temptation."

Jesus Arrested

⁴⁷While he was still speaking a crowd came up, and the man who was called Judas, one of the Twelve, was leading them. He approached Jesus to kiss him, ⁴⁸but Jesus asked him, "Judas, are you betraying the Son of Man with a kiss?"

⁴⁹When Jesus' followers saw what was going to happen, they said, "Lord,

ᵃ 37 Isaiah 53:12   ᵇ 43,44 Some early manuscripts do not have verses 43 and 44.

should we strike with our swords?" ⁵⁰And one of them struck the servant of the high priest, cutting off his right ear.

⁵¹But Jesus answered, "No more of this!" And he touched the man's ear and healed him.

⁵²Then Jesus said to the chief priests, the officers of the temple guard, and the elders, who had come for him, "Am I leading a rebellion, that you have come with swords and clubs? ⁵³Every day I was with you in the temple courts, and you did not lay a hand on me. But this is your hour—when darkness reigns."

Peter Disowns Jesus

⁵⁴Then seizing him, they led him away and took him into the house of the high priest. Peter followed at a distance. ⁵⁵And when some there had kindled a fire in the middle of the courtyard and had sat down together, Peter sat down with them. ⁵⁶A servant girl saw him seated there in the firelight. She looked closely at him and said, "This man was with him."

⁵⁷But he denied it. "Woman, I don't know him," he said.

⁵⁸A little later someone else saw him and said, "You also are one of them."

"Man, I am not!" Peter replied.

⁵⁹About an hour later another asserted, "Certainly this fellow was with him, for he is a Galilean."

⁶⁰Peter replied, "Man, I don't know what you're talking about!" Just as he was speaking, the rooster crowed. ⁶¹The Lord turned and looked straight at Peter. Then Peter remembered the word the Lord had spoken to him: "Before the rooster crows today, you will disown me three times." ⁶²And he went outside and wept bitterly.

The Guards Mock Jesus

⁶³The men who were guarding Jesus began mocking and beating him. ⁶⁴They blindfolded him and demanded, "Prophesy! Who hit you?" ⁶⁵And they said many other insulting things to him.

Jesus Before Pilate and Herod

⁶⁶At daybreak the council of the elders of the people, both the chief priests and teachers of the law, met together, and Jesus was led before them. ⁶⁷"If you are the Messiah," they said, "tell us."

Jesus answered, "If I tell you, you will not believe me, ⁶⁸and if I asked you, you would not answer. ⁶⁹But from now on, the Son of Man will be seated at the right hand of the mighty God."

⁷⁰They all asked, "Are you then the Son of God?"

He replied, "You say that I am."

⁷¹Then they said, "Why do we need any more testimony? We have heard it from his own lips."

23 Then the whole assembly rose and led him off to Pilate. ²And they began to accuse him, saying, "We have found this man subverting our nation. He opposes payment of taxes to Caesar and claims to be Messiah, a king."

³So Pilate asked Jesus, "Are you the king of the Jews?"

"You have said so," Jesus replied.

⁴Then Pilate announced to the chief priests and the crowd, "I find no basis for a charge against this man."

⁵But they insisted, "He stirs up the people all over Judea by his teaching. He started in Galilee and has come all the way here."

⁶On hearing this, Pilate asked if the man was a Galilean. ⁷When he learned that Jesus was under Herod's jurisdiction, he sent him to Herod, who was also in Jerusalem at that time.

⁸When Herod saw Jesus, he was greatly pleased, because for a long time he had been wanting to see him. From what he had heard about him, he hoped to see him perform some miracle. ⁹He plied him with many questions, but Jesus gave him no answer. ¹⁰The chief priests and the teachers of the law were standing there, vehemently accusing him. ¹¹Then Herod and his soldiers ridiculed and mocked him. Dressing him in an elegant robe, they sent him back to Pilate. ¹²That day Herod and Pilate became friends—before this they had been enemies.

¹³Pilate called together the chief priests, the rulers and the people, ¹⁴and said to them, "You brought me this man as one who was inciting the people to rebellion. I have examined him in your presence and have found no basis for your charges against him. ¹⁵Neither has Herod, for he sent him back to us; as you can see, he has done nothing to deserve death. ¹⁶[¹⁷]Therefore, I will punish him and then release him."

¹⁸With one voice they cried out, "Away with this man! Release Barabbas to us!" ¹⁹(Barabbas had been thrown into prison for an insurrection in the city, and for murder.)

²⁰Wanting to release Jesus, Pilate appealed to them again. ²¹But they kept shouting, "Crucify him! Crucify him!"

²²For the third time he spoke to them: "Why? What crime has this man committed? I have found in him no grounds for the death penalty. Therefore I will have him punished and then release him."

²³But with loud shouts they insistently demanded that he be crucified, and their shouts prevailed. ²⁴So Pilate decided to grant their demand. ²⁵He released the man who had been thrown into prison for insurrection and murder, the one they asked for, and surrendered Jesus to their will.

The Crucifixion

²⁶As the soldiers led him away, they seized Simon from Cyrene, who was on his way in from the country, and put the cross on him and made him carry it behind Jesus. ²⁷A large number of people followed him, including women who mourned and wailed for him. ²⁸Jesus turned and said to them, "Daughters of Jerusalem, do not weep for me; weep for yourselves and for your children. ²⁹For the time will come when you will say, 'Blessed are the childless women, the wombs that never bore and the breasts that never nursed!' ³⁰Then

> " 'they will say to the mountains, "Fall on us!"
>   and to the hills, "Cover us!" '[a]

[a] 30 Hosea 10:8

³¹For if people do these things when the tree is green, what will happen when it is dry?"

³²Two other men, both criminals, were also led out with him to be executed. ³³When they came to the place called the Skull, they crucified him there, along with the criminals—one on his right, the other on his left. ³⁴Jesus said, "Father, forgive them, for they do not know what they are doing." ᵃ And they divided up his clothes by casting lots.

³⁵The people stood watching, and the rulers even sneered at him. They said, "He saved others; let him save himself if he is God's Messiah, the Chosen One."

³⁶The soldiers also came up and mocked him. They offered him wine vinegar ³⁷and said, "If you are the king of the Jews, save yourself."

³⁸There was a written notice above him, which read: THIS IS THE KING OF THE JEWS.

³⁹One of the criminals who hung there hurled insults at him: "Aren't you the Messiah? Save yourself and us!"

⁴⁰But the other criminal rebuked him. "Don't you fear God," he said, "since you are under the same sentence? ⁴¹We are punished justly, for we are getting what our deeds deserve. But this man has done nothing wrong."

⁴²Then he said, "Jesus, remember me when you come into your kingdom. ᵇ"

⁴³Jesus answered him, "Truly I tell you, today you will be with me in paradise."

Jesus' Death

⁴⁴It was now about noon, and darkness came over the whole land until three in the afternoon, ⁴⁵for the sun stopped shining. And the curtain of the temple was torn in two. ⁴⁶Jesus called out with a loud voice, "Father, into your hands I commit my spirit." ᶜ When he had said this, he breathed his last.

⁴⁷The centurion, seeing what had happened, praised God and said, "Surely this was a righteous man." ⁴⁸When all the people who had gathered to witness this sight saw what took place, they beat their breasts and went away. ⁴⁹But all those who knew him, including the women who had followed him from Galilee, stood at a distance, watching these things.

Jesus' Burial

⁵⁰Now there was a man named Joseph, a member of the Council, a good and upright man, ⁵¹who had not consented to their decision and action. He came from the Judean town of Arimathea and he was waiting for the kingdom of God. ⁵²Going to Pilate, he asked for Jesus' body. ⁵³Then he took it down, wrapped it in linen cloth and placed it in a tomb cut in the rock, one in which no one had yet been laid. ⁵⁴It was Preparation Day, and the Sabbath was about to begin.

⁵⁵The women who had come with Jesus from Galilee followed Joseph and saw the tomb and how his body was laid in it. ⁵⁶Then they went home and prepared spices and perfumes. But they rested on the Sabbath in obedience to the commandment.

ᵃ 34 Some early manuscripts do not have this sentence.   ᵇ 42 Some manuscripts *come with your kingly power*   ᶜ 46 Psalm 31:5

The Resurrection

24 On the first day of the week, very early in the morning, the women took the spices they had prepared and went to the tomb. ²They found the stone rolled away from the tomb, ³but when they entered, they did not find the body of the Lord Jesus. ⁴While they were wondering about this, suddenly two men in clothes that gleamed like lightning stood beside them. ⁵In their fright the women bowed down with their faces to the ground, but the men said to them, "Why do you look for the living among the dead? ⁶He is not here; he has risen! Remember how he told you, while he was still with you in Galilee: ⁷'The Son of Man must be delivered into the hands of sinful men, be crucified and on the third day be raised again.' " ⁸Then they remembered his words.

⁹When they came back from the tomb, they told all these things to the Eleven and to all the others. ¹⁰It was Mary Magdalene, Joanna, Mary the mother of James, and the others with them who told this to the apostles. ¹¹But they did not believe the women, because their words seemed to them like nonsense. ¹²Peter, however, got up and ran to the tomb. Bending over, he saw the strips of linen lying by themselves, and he went away, wondering to himself what had happened.

On the Road to Emmaus

¹³Now that same day two of them were going to a village called Emmaus, about seven miles*ª* from Jerusalem. ¹⁴They were talking with each other about everything that had happened. ¹⁵As they talked and discussed these things with each other, Jesus himself came up and walked along with them; ¹⁶but they were kept from recognizing him.

¹⁷He asked them, "What are you discussing together as you walk along?"

They stood still, their faces downcast. ¹⁸One of them, named Cleopas, asked him, "Are you only a visitor to Jerusalem and do not know the things that have happened there in these days?"

¹⁹"What things?" he asked.

"About Jesus of Nazareth," they replied. "He was a prophet, powerful in word and deed before God and all the people. ²⁰The chief priests and our rulers handed him over to be sentenced to death, and they crucified him; ²¹but we had hoped that he was the one who was going to redeem Israel. And what is more, it is the third day since all this took place. ²²In addition, some of our women amazed us. They went to the tomb early this morning ²³but didn't find his body. They came and told us that they had seen a vision of angels, who said he was alive. ²⁴Then some of our companions went to the tomb and found it just as the women had said, but him they did not see."

²⁵He said to them, "How foolish you are, and how slow to believe all that the prophets have spoken! ²⁶Did not the Messiah have to suffer these things and then enter his glory?" ²⁷And beginning with Moses and all the Prophets, he explained to them what was said in all the Scriptures concerning himself.

²⁸As they approached the village to which they were going, Jesus continued on as if he were going farther. ²⁹But they urged him strongly, "Stay with us,

---

ª 13 About 11 kilometers

for it is nearly evening; the day is almost over." So he went in to stay with them.

³⁰When he was at the table with them, he took bread, gave thanks, broke it and began to give it to them. ³¹Then their eyes were opened and they recognized him, and he disappeared from their sight. ³²They asked each other, "Were not our hearts burning within us while he talked with us on the road and opened the Scriptures to us?"

³³They got up and returned at once to Jerusalem. There they found the Eleven and those with them, assembled together ³⁴and saying, "It is true! The Lord has risen and has appeared to Simon." ³⁵Then the two told what had happened on the way, and how Jesus was recognized by them when he broke the bread.

Jesus Appears to the Disciples

³⁶While they were still talking about this, Jesus himself stood among them and said to them, "Peace be with you."

³⁷They were startled and frightened, thinking they saw a ghost. ³⁸He said to them, "Why are you troubled, and why do doubts rise in your minds? ³⁹Look at my hands and my feet. It is I myself! Touch me and see; a ghost does not have flesh and bones, as you see I have."

⁴⁰When he had said this, he showed them his hands and feet. ⁴¹And while they still did not believe it because of joy and amazement, he asked them, "Do you have anything here to eat?" ⁴²They gave him a piece of broiled fish, ⁴³and he took it and ate it in their presence.

⁴⁴He said to them, "This is what I told you while I was still with you: Everything must be fulfilled that is written about me in the Law of Moses, the Prophets and the Psalms."

⁴⁵Then he opened their minds so they could understand the Scriptures. ⁴⁶He told them, "This is what is written: The Messiah will suffer and rise from the dead on the third day, ⁴⁷and repentance for the forgiveness of sins will be preached in his name to all nations, beginning at Jerusalem. ⁴⁸You are witnesses of these things. ⁴⁹I am going to send you what my Father has promised; but stay in the city until you have been clothed with power from on high."

The Ascension

⁵⁰When he had led them out to the vicinity of Bethany, he lifted up his hands and blessed them. ⁵¹While he was blessing them, he left them and was taken up into heaven. ⁵²Then they worshiped him and returned to Jerusalem with great joy. ⁵³And they stayed continually at the temple, praising God.

JOHN

The Word Became Flesh

1 In the beginning was the Word, and the Word was with God, and the Word was God. ²He was with God in the beginning.

³Through him all things were made; without him nothing was made that has been made. ⁴In him was life, and that life was the light of all people. ⁵The light shines in the darkness, and the darkness has not overcome*ᵃ* it.

⁶There was a man sent from God whose name was John. ⁷He came as a witness to testify concerning that light, so that through him all might believe. ⁸He himself was not the light; he came only as a witness to the light.

⁹The true light that gives light to everyone was coming into the world. ¹⁰He was in the world, and though the world was made through him, the world did not recognize him. ¹¹He came to that which was his own, but his own did not receive him. ¹²Yet to all who did receive him, to those who believed in his name, he gave the right to become children of God— ¹³children born not of natural descent, nor of human decision or a husband's will, but born of God.

¹⁴The Word became flesh and made his dwelling among us. We have seen his glory, the glory of the one and only ⌐Son⌐, who came from the Father, full of grace and truth.

¹⁵(John testified concerning him. He cried out, saying, "This is he of whom I said, 'He who comes after me has surpassed me because he was before me.' ") ¹⁶Out of his fullness we have all received grace in place of grace already given. ¹⁷For the law was given through Moses; grace and truth came through Jesus Christ. ¹⁸No one has ever seen God, but the one and only ⌐Son⌐, who is himself God and*ᵇ* is in closest relationship with the Father, has made him known.

John the Baptist Denies Being the Messiah

¹⁹Now this was John's testimony when the Jewish leaders in Jerusalem sent priests and Levites to ask him who he was. ²⁰He did not fail to confess, but confessed freely, "I am not the Messiah."

²¹They asked him, "Then who are you? Are you Elijah?"

He said, "I am not."

"Are you the Prophet?"

He answered, "No."

ᵃ 5 Or *understood*   *ᵇ 18* Some manuscripts *but the only Son, who*

²²Finally they said, "Who are you? Give us an answer to take back to those who sent us. What do you say about yourself?"

²³John replied in the words of Isaiah the prophet, "I am the voice of one calling in the desert, 'Make straight the way for the Lord.' "ᵃ

²⁴Now the Pharisees who had been sent ²⁵questioned him, "Why then do you baptize if you are not the Messiah, nor Elijah, nor the Prophet?"

²⁶"I baptize withᵇ water," John replied, "but among you stands one you do not know. ²⁷He is the one who comes after me, the thongs of whose sandals I am not worthy to untie."

²⁸This all happened at Bethany on the other side of the Jordan, where John was baptizing.

John's Testimony About Jesus

²⁹The next day John saw Jesus coming toward him and said, "Look, the Lamb of God, who takes away the sin of the world! ³⁰This is the one I meant when I said, 'A man who comes after me has surpassed me because he was before me.' ³¹I myself did not know him, but the reason I came baptizing with water was that he might be revealed to Israel."

³²Then John gave this testimony: "I saw the Spirit come down from heaven as a dove and remain on him. ³³And I myself did not know him, but the one who sent me to baptize with water told me, 'The man on whom you see the Spirit come down and remain is the one who will baptize with the Holy Spirit.' ³⁴I have seen and I testify that this is God's Chosen One."ᶜ

John's Disciples Follow Jesus

³⁵The next day John was there again with two of his disciples. ³⁶When he saw Jesus passing by, he said, "Look, the Lamb of God!"

³⁷When the two disciples heard him say this, they followed Jesus. ³⁸Turning around, Jesus saw them following and asked, "What do you want?"

They said, "Rabbi" (which means Teacher), "where are you staying?"

³⁹"Come," he replied, "and you will see."

So they went and saw where he was staying, and they spent that day with him. It was about four in the afternoon.

⁴⁰Andrew, Simon Peter's brother, was one of the two who heard what John had said and who had followed Jesus. ⁴¹The first thing Andrew did was to find his brother Simon and tell him, "We have found the Messiah" (that is, the Christ). ⁴²And he brought him to Jesus.

Jesus looked at him and said, "You are Simon son of John. You will be called Cephas" (which, when translated, is Peterᵈ).

Jesus Calls Philip and Nathanael

⁴³The next day Jesus decided to leave for Galilee. Finding Philip, he said to him, "Follow me."

⁴⁴Philip, like Andrew and Peter, was from the town of Bethsaida. ⁴⁵Philip found Nathanael and told him, "We have found the one Moses wrote about

ᵃ 23 Isaiah 40:3   ᵇ 26 Or in; also in verses 31 and 33   ᶜ 34 See Isaiah 42:1; many manuscripts is the Son of God.   ᵈ 42 Both Cephas (Aramaic) and Peter (Greek) mean rock.

in the Law, and about whom the prophets also wrote—Jesus of Nazareth, the son of Joseph."

46"Nazareth! Can anything good come from there?" Nathanael asked.

"Come and see," said Philip.

47When Jesus saw Nathanael approaching, he said of him, "Here truly is an Israelite in whom there is no deceit."

48"How do you know me?" Nathanael asked.

Jesus answered, "I saw you while you were still under the fig tree before Philip called you."

49Then Nathanael declared, "Rabbi, you are the Son of God; you are the king of Israel."

50Jesus said, "You believe[a] because I told you I saw you under the fig tree. You shall see greater things than that." 51He then added, "Very truly I tell you,[b] you[b] shall see 'heaven open, and the angels of God ascending and descending on'[c] the Son of Man."

Jesus Changes Water to Wine

2 On the third day a wedding took place at Cana in Galilee. Jesus' mother was there, 2and Jesus and his disciples had also been invited to the wedding. 3When the wine was gone, Jesus' mother said to him, "They have no more wine."

4"Mother,[d] why do you involve me?" Jesus replied. "My hour has not yet come."

5His mother said to the servants, "Do whatever he tells you."

6Nearby stood six stone water jars, the kind used by the Jews for ceremonial washing, each holding from twenty to thirty gallons.[e]

7Jesus said to the servants, "Fill the jars with water"; so they filled them to the brim.

8Then he told them, "Now draw some out and take it to the master of the banquet."

They did so, 9and the master of the banquet tasted the water that had been turned into wine. He did not realize where it had come from, though the servants who had drawn the water knew. Then he called the bridegroom aside 10and said, "Everyone brings out the choice wine first and then the cheaper wine after the guests have had too much to drink; but you have saved the best till now."

11This, the first of his miraculous signs, Jesus performed at Cana in Galilee. He thus revealed his glory, and his disciples put their faith in him.

12After this he went down to Capernaum with his mother and brothers and his disciples. There they stayed for a few days.

Jesus Clears the Temple Courts

13When it was almost time for the Jewish Passover, Jesus went up to Jerusalem. 14In the temple courts he found people selling cattle, sheep and doves, and others sitting at tables exchanging money. 15So he made a whip

---

[a] 50 Or Do you believe . . . ?   [b] 51 The Greek is plural.   [c] 51 Gen. 28:12   [d] 4 Or Woman; the Greek term does not denote any disrespect.   [e] 6 From 75 to 115 liters

out of cords, and drove all from the temple courts, both sheep and cattle; he scattered the coins of the money changers and overturned their tables. ¹⁶To those who sold doves he said, "Get these out of here! Stop turning my Father's house into a market!" ¹⁷His disciples remembered that it is written: "Zeal for your house will consume me."ᵃ

¹⁸The Jews then responded to him, "What sign can you show us to prove your authority to do all this?"

¹⁹Jesus answered them, "Destroy this temple, and I will raise it again in three days."

²⁰They replied, "It has taken forty-six years to build this temple, and you are going to raise it in three days?" ²¹But the temple he had spoken of was his body. ²²After he was raised from the dead, his disciples recalled what he had said. Then they believed the scripture and the words that Jesus had spoken.

²³Now while he was in Jerusalem at the Passover Festival, many people saw the miraculous signs he was doing and believed in his name.ᵇ ²⁴But Jesus would not entrust himself to them, for he knew all people. ²⁵He did not need human testimony about them, for he knew what was in them.

Jesus Teaches Nicodemus

3 Now there was a Pharisee, a man named Nicodemus who was a member of the Jewish ruling council. ²He came to Jesus at night and said, "Rabbi, we know you are a teacher who has come from God. For no one could perform the miraculous signs you are doing if God were not with them."

³Jesus replied, "Very truly I tell you, no one can see the kingdom of God without being born again.ᶜ"

⁴"How can anyone be born when they are old?" Nicodemus asked. "Surely they cannot enter a second time into their mother's womb to be born!"

⁵Jesus answered, "Very truly I tell you, no one can enter the kingdom of God without being born of water and the Spirit. ⁶Flesh gives birth to flesh, but the Spiritᵈ gives birth to spirit. ⁷You should not be surprised at my saying, 'Youᵉ must be born again.' ⁸The wind blows wherever it pleases. You hear its sound, but you cannot tell where it comes from or where it is going. So it is with everyone born of the Spirit."ᶠ

⁹"How can this be?" Nicodemus asked.

¹⁰"You are Israel's teacher," said Jesus, "and do you not understand these things? ¹¹Very truly I tell you, we speak of what we know, and we testify to what we have seen, but still you people do not accept our testimony. ¹²I have spoken to you of earthly things and you do not believe; how then will you believe if I speak of heavenly things? ¹³No one has ever gone into heaven except the one who came from heaven—the Son of Man.ᵍ ¹⁴Just as Moses lifted up the snake in the desert, so the Son of Man must be lifted up,ʰ ¹⁵that everyone who believes may have eternal life in him."ⁱ

¹⁶For God so loved the world that he gave his one and only Son, that whoever believes in him shall not perish but have eternal life. ¹⁷For God did not

---

ᵃ 17 Psalm 69:9   ᵇ 23 Or *and believed in him*   ᶜ 3 The Greek for *again* also means *from above*; also in verse 7.   ᵈ 6 Or *but spirit*   ᵉ 7 The Greek is plural.   ᶠ 8 The Greek for *Spirit* is the same as that for *wind*.   ᵍ 13 Some manuscripts *Man, who is in heaven*   ʰ 14 The Greek for *lifted up* also means *exalted*.   ⁱ 15 Some interpreters end the quotation with verse 21.

send his Son into the world to condemn the world, but to save the world through him. 18Whoever believes in him is not condemned, but whoever does not believe stands condemned already because they have not believed in the name of God's one and only Son. 19This is the verdict: Light has come into the world, but people loved darkness instead of light because their deeds were evil. 20All those who do evil hate the light, and will not come into the light for fear that their deeds will be exposed. 21But those who live by the truth come into the light, so that it may be seen plainly that what they have done has been done in the sight of God.

John Testifies Again About Jesus

22After this, Jesus and his disciples went out into the Judean countryside, where he spent some time with them, and baptized. 23Now John also was baptizing at Aenon near Salim, because there was plenty of water, and people were coming and being baptized. 24(This was before John was put in prison.) 25An argument developed between some of John's disciples and a certain Jew over the matter of ceremonial washing. 26They came to John and said to him, "Rabbi, that man who was with you on the other side of the Jordan—the one you testified about—well, he is baptizing, and everyone is going to him."

27To this John replied, "A person can receive only what is given from heaven. 28You yourselves can testify that I said, 'I am not the Messiah but am sent ahead of him.' 29The bride belongs to the bridegroom. The friend who attends the bridegroom waits and listens for him, and is full of joy when he hears the bridegroom's voice. That joy is mine, and it is now complete. 30He must become greater; I must become less."a

31The one who comes from above is above all; the one who is from the earth belongs to the earth, and speaks as one from the earth. The one who comes from heaven is above all. 32He testifies to what he has seen and heard, but no one accepts his testimony. 33The person who has accepted it has certified that God is truthful. 34For the one whom God has sent speaks the words of God, for Godb gives the Spirit without limit. 35The Father loves the Son and has placed everything in his hands. 36Whoever believes in the Son has eternal life, but whoever rejects the Son will not see life, for God's wrath remains on them.

Jesus Talks With a Samaritan Woman

4 Now Jesus learned that the Pharisees had heard that he was gaining and baptizing more disciples than John— 2although in fact it was not Jesus who baptized, but his disciples. 3So he left Judea and went back once more to Galilee.

4Now he had to go through Samaria. 5So he came to a town in Samaria called Sychar, near the plot of ground Jacob had given to his son Joseph. 6Jacob's well was there, and Jesus, tired as he was from the journey, sat down by the well. It was about noon.

7When a Samaritan woman came to draw water, Jesus said to her, "Will you give me a drink?" 8(His disciples had gone into the town to buy food.)

9The Samaritan woman said to him, "You are a Jew and I am a Samaritan

---

a 30 Some interpreters end the quotation with verse 36.   b 34 Greek he woman. How can you ask me for a drink?" (For Jews do not associate with Samaritans.*)

¹⁰Jesus answered her, "If you knew the gift of God and who it is that asks you for a drink, you would have asked him and he would have given you living water."

¹¹"Sir," the woman said, "you have nothing to draw with and the well is deep. Where can you get this living water? ¹²Are you greater than our father Jacob, who gave us the well and drank from it himself, as did also his sons and his flocks and herds?"

¹³Jesus answered, "Everyone who drinks this water will be thirsty again, ¹⁴but those who drink the water I give them will never thirst. Indeed, the water I give them will become in them a spring of water welling up to eternal life."

¹⁵The woman said to him, "Sir, give me this water so that I won't get thirsty and have to keep coming here to draw water."

¹⁶He told her, "Go, call your husband and come back."

¹⁷"I have no husband," she replied.

Jesus said to her, "You are right when you say you have no husband. ¹⁸The fact is, you have had five husbands, and the man you now have is not your husband. What you have just said is quite true."

¹⁹"Sir," the woman said, "I can see that you are a prophet. ²⁰Our ancestors worshiped on this mountain, but you Jews claim that the place where we must worship is in Jerusalem."

²¹Jesus said to her, "Believe me, a time is coming when you will worship the Father neither on this mountain nor in Jerusalem. ²²You Samaritans worship what you do not know; we worship what we do know, for salvation is from the Jews. ²³Yet a time is coming and has now come when the true worshipers will worship the Father in the Spirit and in truth, for they are the kind of worshipers the Father seeks. ²⁴God is spirit, and his worshipers must worship in the Spirit and in truth."

²⁵The woman said, "I know that Messiah" (called Christ) "is coming. When he comes, he will explain everything to us."

²⁶Then Jesus declared, "I, the one speaking to you—I am he."

The Disciples Rejoin Jesus

²⁷Just then his disciples returned and were surprised to find him talking with a woman. But no one asked, "What do you want?" or "Why are you talking with her?"

²⁸Then, leaving her water jar, the woman went back to the town and said to the people, ²⁹"Come, see a man who told me everything I ever did. Could this be the Messiah?" ³⁰They came out of the town and made their way toward him.

³¹Meanwhile his disciples urged him, "Rabbi, eat something."

³²But he said to them, "I have food to eat that you know nothing about."

³³Then his disciples said to each other, "Could someone have brought him food?"

³⁴"My food," said Jesus, "is to do the will of him who sent me and to finish his work. ³⁵Don't you have a saying, 'It's still four months until harvest'? I tell

9 Or do not use dishes Samaritans have used

you, open your eyes and look at the fields! They are ripe for harvest. 36Even now those who reap draw their wages, even now they harvest the crop for eternal life, so that the sower and the reaper may be glad together. 37Thus the saying 'One sows and another reaps' is true. 38I sent you to reap what you have not worked for. Others have done the hard work, and you have reaped the benefits of their labor."

Many Samaritans Believe

39Many of the Samaritans from that town believed in him because of the woman's testimony, "He told me everything I ever did." 40So when the Samaritans came to him, they urged him to stay with them, and he stayed two days. 41And because of his words many more became believers.

42They said to the woman, "We no longer believe just because of what you said; now we have heard for ourselves, and we know that this man really is the Savior of the world."

Jesus Heals the Official's Son

43After the two days he left for Galilee. 44(Now Jesus himself had pointed out that prophets have no honor in their own country.) 45When he arrived in Galilee, the Galileans welcomed him. They had seen all that he had done in Jerusalem at the Passover Festival, for they also had been there.

46Once more he visited Cana in Galilee, where he had turned the water into wine. And there was a certain royal official whose son lay sick at Capernaum. 47When this man heard that Jesus had arrived in Galilee from Judea, he went to him and begged him to come and heal his son, who was close to death.

48"Unless you people see miraculous signs and wonders," Jesus told him, "you will never believe."

49The royal official said, "Sir, come down before my child dies."

50"Go," Jesus replied, "your son will live."

The man took Jesus at his word and departed. 51While he was still on the way, his servants met him with the news that his boy was living. 52When he inquired as to the time when his son got better, they said to him, "Yesterday, at one in the afternoon, the fever left him."

53Then the father realized that this was the exact time at which Jesus had said to him, "Your son will live." So he and his whole household believed.

54This was the second miraculous sign that Jesus performed after coming from Judea to Galilee.

The Healing at the Pool

5 Some time later, Jesus went up to Jerusalem for one of the Jewish festivals. 2Now there is in Jerusalem near the Sheep Gate a pool, which in Aramaic is called Bethesda*a* and which is surrounded by five covered colonnades. 3[4]Here a great number of disabled people used to lie—the blind, the lame, the paralyzed.*b* 5One who was there had been an invalid for thirty-eight

---

a 2 Some manuscripts *Bethzatha*; other manuscripts *Bethsaida*   *b* 3 Some later manuscripts and some ancient witnesses, wholly or in part, *paralyzed—and they waited for the moving of the waters.* *4From time to time an angel of the Lord would come down and stir up the waters. The first one into the pool after each such disturbance would be cured of whatever disease he had.*

years. 6When Jesus saw him lying there and learned that he had been in this condition for a long time, he asked him, "Do you want to get well?"

7"Sir," the invalid replied, "I have no one to help me into the pool when the water is stirred. While I am trying to get in, someone else goes down ahead of me."

8Then Jesus said to him, "Get up! Pick up your mat and walk." 9At once the man was cured; he picked up his mat and walked.

The day on which this took place was a Sabbath, 10and so the Jewish leaders said to the man who had been healed, "It is the Sabbath; the law forbids you to carry your mat."

11But he replied, "The man who made me well said to me, 'Pick up your mat and walk.' "

12So they asked him, "Who is this fellow who told you to pick it up and walk?"

13The man who was healed had no idea who it was, for Jesus had slipped away into the crowd that was there.

14Later Jesus found him at the temple and said to him, "See, you are well again. Stop sinning or something worse may happen to you." 15The man went away and told the Jewish leaders that it was Jesus who had made him well.

The Authority of the Son

16So, because Jesus was doing these things on the Sabbath, the Jewish leaders began to persecute him. 17In his defense Jesus said to them, "My Father is always at his work to this very day, and I too am working." 18For this reason they tried all the more to kill him; not only was he breaking the Sabbath, but he was even calling God his own Father, making himself equal with God.

19Jesus gave them this answer: "Very truly I tell you, the Son can do nothing by himself; he can do only what he sees his Father doing, because whatever the Father does the Son also does. 20For the Father loves the Son and shows him all he does. Yes, and he will show him even greater works than these, so that you will be amazed. 21For just as the Father raises the dead and gives them life, even so the Son gives life to whom he is pleased to give it. 22Moreover, the Father judges no one, but has entrusted all judgment to the Son, 23that all may honor the Son just as they honor the Father. Whoever does not honor the Son does not honor the Father, who sent him.

24"Very truly I tell you, whoever hears my word and believes him who sent me has eternal life and will not be judged but has crossed over from death to life. 25Very truly I tell you, a time is coming and has now come when the dead will hear the voice of the Son of God and those who hear will live. 26For as the Father has life in himself, so he has granted the Son also to have life in himself. 27And he has given him authority to judge because he is the Son of Man.

28"Do not be amazed at this, for a time is coming when all who are in their graves will hear his voice 29and come out—those who have done good will rise to live, and those who have done evil will rise to be condemned. 30By myself I can do nothing; I judge only as I hear, and my judgment is just, for I seek not to please myself but him who sent me.

Testimonies About Jesus

31"If I testify about myself, my testimony is not true. 32There is another who testifies in my favor, and I know that his testimony about me is true.

33"You have sent to John and he has testified to the truth. 34Not that I accept human testimony; but I mention it that you may be saved. 35John was a lamp that burned and gave light, and you chose for a time to enjoy his light.

36"I have testimony weightier than that of John. For the works that the Father has given me to finish—the very works that I am doing—testify that the Father has sent me. 37And the Father who sent me has himself testified concerning me. You have never heard his voice nor seen his form, 38nor does his word dwell in you, for you do not believe the one he sent. 39You diligently study*a* the Scriptures because you think that in them you possess eternal life. These are the very Scriptures that testify about me, 40yet you refuse to come to me to have life.

41"I do not accept glory from human beings, 42but I know you. I know that you do not have the love of God in your hearts. 43I have come in my Father's name, and you do not accept me; but if someone else comes in his own name, you will accept him. 44How can you believe since you accept glory from one another but do not seek the glory that comes from the only God*b*?

45"But do not think I will accuse you before the Father. Your accuser is Moses, on whom your hopes are set. 46If you believed Moses, you would believe me, for he wrote about me. 47But since you do not believe what he wrote, how are you going to believe what I say?"

Jesus Feeds the Five Thousand

6 Some time after this, Jesus crossed to the far shore of the Sea of Galilee (that is, the Sea of Tiberias), 2and a great crowd of people followed him because they saw the miraculous signs he had performed on the sick. 3Then Jesus went up on a mountainside and sat down with his disciples. 4The Jewish Passover Festival was near.

5When Jesus looked up and saw a great crowd coming toward him, he said to Philip, "Where shall we buy bread for these people to eat?" 6He asked this only to test him, for he already had in mind what he was going to do.

7Philip answered him, "Eight months' wages*c* would not buy enough bread for each one to have a bite!"

8Another of his disciples, Andrew, Simon Peter's brother, spoke up, 9"Here is a boy with five small barley loaves and two small fish, but how far will they go among so many?"

10Jesus said, "Have the people sit down." There was plenty of grass in that place, and they sat down (about five thousand men were there). 11Jesus then took the loaves, gave thanks, and distributed to those who were seated as much as they wanted. He did the same with the fish.

12When they had all had enough to eat, he said to his disciples, "Gather the pieces that are left over. Let nothing be wasted." 13So they gathered them and

---

a 39 Or *Study diligently* (the imperative)   *b* 44 Some early manuscripts *the Only One*   *c* 7 Greek *two hundred denarii*

filled twelve baskets with the pieces of the five barley loaves left over by those who had eaten.

[14]After the people saw the miraculous sign that Jesus did, they began to say, "Surely this is the Prophet who is to come into the world." [15]Jesus, knowing that they intended to come and make him king by force, withdrew again to a mountain by himself.

Jesus Walks on the Water

[16]When evening came, his disciples went down to the lake, [17]where they got into a boat and set off across the lake for Capernaum. By now it was dark, and Jesus had not yet joined them. [18]A strong wind was blowing and the waters grew rough. [19]When they had rowed about three or three and a half miles,[a] they saw Jesus approaching the boat, walking on the water; and they were frightened. [20]But he said to them, "It is I; don't be afraid." [21]Then they were willing to take him into the boat, and immediately the boat reached the shore where they were heading.

[22]The next day the crowd that had stayed on the opposite shore of the lake realized that only one boat had been there, and that Jesus had not entered it with his disciples, but that they had gone away alone. [23]Then some boats from Tiberias landed near the place where the people had eaten the bread after the Lord had given thanks. [24]Once the crowd realized that neither Jesus nor his disciples were there, they got into the boats and went to Capernaum in search of Jesus.

Jesus the Bread of Life

[25]When they found him on the other side of the lake, they asked him, "Rabbi, when did you get here?"

[26]Jesus answered, "Very truly I tell you, you are looking for me, not because you saw miraculous signs but because you ate the loaves and had your fill. [27]Do not work for food that spoils, but for food that endures to eternal life, which the Son of Man will give you. On him God the Father has placed his seal of approval."

[28]Then they asked him, "What must we do to do the works God requires?"

[29]Jesus answered, "The work of God is this: to believe in the one he has sent."

[30]So they asked him, "What miraculous sign then will you give that we may see it and believe you? What will you do? [31]Our ancestors ate the manna in the desert; as it is written: 'He gave them bread from heaven to eat.'[b]"

[32]Jesus said to them, "Very truly I tell you, it is not Moses who has given you the bread from heaven, but it is my Father who gives you the true bread from heaven. [33]For the bread of God is that which[c] comes down from heaven and gives life to the world."

[34]"Sir," they said, "always give us this bread."

[35]Then Jesus declared, "I am the bread of life. Whoever comes to me will never go hungry, and whoever believes in me will never be thirsty. [36]But as I

---

[a]19 About 5 or 6 kilometers   [b]31 Exodus 16:4; Neh. 9:15; Psalm 78:24,25   [c]33 The Greek for *that which* can also mean *he who.*

told you, you have seen me and still you do not believe. 37All whom the Father gives me will come to me, and whoever comes to me I will never drive away. 38For I have come down from heaven not to do my will but to do the will of him who sent me. 39And this is the will of him who sent me, that I shall lose none of all those he has given me, but raise them up at the last day. 40For my Father's will is that everyone who looks to the Son and believes in him shall have eternal life, and I will raise them up at the last day."

41At this the Jews there began to grumble about him because he said, "I am the bread that came down from heaven." 42They said, "Is this not Jesus, the son of Joseph, whose father and mother we know? How can he now say, 'I came down from heaven'?"

43"Stop grumbling among yourselves," Jesus answered. 44"No one can come to me unless the Father who sent me draws them, and I will raise them up at the last day. 45It is written in the Prophets: 'They will all be taught by God.'a Everyone who has heard the Father and learned from him comes to me. 46No one has seen the Father except the one who is from God; only he has seen the Father. 47Very truly I tell you, whoever believes has eternal life. 48I am the bread of life. 49Your ancestors ate the manna in the desert, yet they died. 50But here is the bread that comes down from heaven, which people may eat and not die. 51I am the living bread that came down from heaven. Whoever eats of this bread will live forever. This bread is my flesh, which I will give for the life of the world."

52Then the Jews began to argue sharply among themselves, "How can this man give us his flesh to eat?"

53Jesus said to them, "Very truly I tell you, unless you eat the flesh of the Son of Man and drink his blood, you have no life in you. 54Whoever eats my flesh and drinks my blood has eternal life, and I will raise them up at the last day. 55For my flesh is real food and my blood is real drink. 56Whoever eats my flesh and drinks my blood remains in me, and I in them. 57Just as the living Father sent me and I live because of the Father, so the one who feeds on me will live because of me. 58This is the bread that came down from heaven. Your ancestors ate manna and died, but whoever feeds on this bread will live forever." 59He said this while teaching in the synagogue in Capernaum.

Many Disciples Desert Jesus

60On hearing it, many of his disciples said, "This is a hard teaching. Who can accept it?"

61Aware that his disciples were grumbling about this, Jesus said to them, "Does this offend you? 62Then what if you see the Son of Man ascend to where he was before! 63The Spirit gives life; the flesh counts for nothing. The words I have spoken to you—they are full of the Spiritb and life. 64Yet there are some of you who do not believe." For Jesus had known from the beginning which of them did not believe and who would betray him. 65He went on to say, "This is why I told you that no one can come to me unless the Father has enabled them."

66From this time many of his disciples turned back and no longer followed him.

a 45 Isaiah 54:13   b 63 Or are Spirit; or are spirit

⁶⁷"You do not want to leave too, do you?" Jesus asked the Twelve.

⁶⁸Simon Peter answered him, "Lord, to whom shall we go? You have the words of eternal life. ⁶⁹We have come to believe and to know that you are the Holy One of God."

⁷⁰Then Jesus replied, "Have I not chosen you, the Twelve? Yet one of you is a devil!" ⁷¹(He meant Judas, the son of Simon Iscariot, who, though one of the Twelve, was later to betray him.)

Jesus Goes to the Festival of Tabernacles

7 After this, Jesus went around in Galilee. He did not want*a* to go about in Judea because the Jewish leaders there were looking for a way to kill him. ²But when the Jewish Festival of Tabernacles was near, ³Jesus' brothers said to him, "Leave Galilee and go to Judea, so that your disciples there may see the works you do. ⁴No one who wants to become a public figure acts in secret. Since you are doing these things, show yourself to the world." ⁵For even his own brothers did not believe in him.

⁶Therefore Jesus told them, "My time is not yet here; for you any time will do. ⁷The world cannot hate you, but it hates me because I testify that its works are evil. ⁸You go to the Festival. I am not*b* going up to this Festival, because my time has not yet fully come." ⁹Having said this, he stayed in Galilee.

¹⁰However, after his brothers had left for the Festival, he went also, not publicly, but in secret. ¹¹Now at the Festival the Jewish leaders were watching for Jesus and asking, "Where is he?"

¹²Among the crowds there was widespread whispering about him. Some said, "He is a good man."

Others replied, "No, he deceives the people." ¹³But no one would say anything publicly about him for fear of the leaders.

Jesus Teaches at the Festival

¹⁴Not until halfway through the Festival did Jesus go up to the temple courts and begin to teach. ¹⁵The Jews there were amazed and asked, "How did this man get such learning without having been taught?"

¹⁶Jesus answered, "My teaching is not my own. It comes from him who sent me. ¹⁷Anyone who chooses to do the will of God will find out whether my teaching comes from God or whether I speak on my own. ¹⁸Those who speak on their own do so to gain glory for themselves, but he who seeks the glory of the one who sent him is a man of truth; there is nothing false about him. ¹⁹Has not Moses given you the law? Yet not one of you keeps the law. Why are you trying to kill me?"

²⁰"You are demon-possessed," the crowd answered. "Who is trying to kill you?"

²¹Jesus said to them, "I did one miracle, and you are all amazed. ²²Yet, because Moses gave you circumcision (though actually it did not come from Moses, but from the patriarchs), you circumcise a boy on the Sabbath. ²³Now if a boy can be circumcised on the Sabbath so that the law of Moses may not

---

a 1 Some manuscripts *not have authority*   *b* 8 Some manuscripts *not yet*

be broken, why are you angry with me for healing a man's whole body on the Sabbath? 24Stop judging by mere appearances, but instead judge correctly."

Division Over Who Jesus Is

25At that point some of the people of Jerusalem began to ask, "Isn't this the man they are trying to kill? 26Here he is, speaking publicly, and they are not saying a word to him. Have the authorities really concluded that he is the Messiah? 27But we know where this man is from; when the Messiah comes, no one will know where he is from."

28Then Jesus, still teaching in the temple courts, cried out, "Yes, you know me, and you know where I am from. I am not here on my own authority, but he who sent me is true. You do not know him, 29but I know him because I am from him and he sent me."

30At this they tried to seize him, but no one laid a hand on him, because his hour had not yet come. 31Still, many in the crowd put their faith in him. They said, "When the Messiah comes, will he do more miraculous signs than this man?"

32The Pharisees heard the crowd whispering such things about him. Then the chief priests and the Pharisees sent temple guards to arrest him.

33Jesus said, "I am with you for only a short time, and then I go to the one who sent me. 34You will look for me, but you will not find me; and where I am, you cannot come."

35The Jews said to one another, "Where does this man intend to go that we cannot find him? Will he go where our people live scattered among the Greeks, and teach the Greeks? 36What did he mean when he said, 'You will look for me, but you will not find me,' and 'Where I am, you cannot come'?"

37On the last and greatest day of the Festival, Jesus stood and said in a loud voice, "Let anyone who is thirsty come to me and drink. 38Whoever believes in me, as Scripture has said, streams of living water will flow from within them." *a* 39By this he meant the Spirit, whom those who believed in him were later to receive. Up to that time the Spirit had not been given, since Jesus had not yet been glorified.

40On hearing his words, some of the people said, "Surely this man is the Prophet."

41Others said, "He is the Messiah."

Still others asked, "How can the Messiah come from Galilee? 42Does not Scripture say that the Messiah will come from David's family *b* and from Bethlehem, the town where David lived?" 43Thus the people were divided because of Jesus. 44Some wanted to seize him, but no one laid a hand on him.

Unbelief of the Jewish Leaders

45Finally the temple guards went back to the chief priests and the Pharisees, who asked them, "Why didn't you bring him in?"

46"No one ever spoke the way this man does," the guards replied.

47"You mean he has deceived you also?" the Pharisees retorted. 48"Have

a 37,38 Or *me. And let anyone drink,* 38*who believes in me. As Scripture has said, 'Out of them will flow rivers of living water.' "   *b* 42 Greek *seed*

any of the rulers or of the Pharisees believed in him? 49No! But this mob that knows nothing of the law—there is a curse on them."

50Nicodemus, who had gone to Jesus earlier and who was one of their own number, asked, 51"Does our law condemn a man without first hearing him to find out what he has been doing?"

52They replied, "Are you from Galilee, too? Look into it, and you will find that a prophet does not come out of Galilee."

[The earliest manuscripts and many other ancient witnesses
do not have John 7:53–8:11.]

8 53Then they all went home, 1but Jesus went to the Mount of Olives. 2At dawn he appeared again in the temple courts, where all the people gathered around him, and he sat down to teach them. 3The teachers of the law and the Pharisees brought in a woman caught in adultery. They made her stand before the group 4and said to Jesus, "Teacher, this woman was caught in the act of adultery. 5In the Law Moses commanded us to stone such women. Now what do you say?" 6They were using this question as a trap, in order to have a basis for accusing him.

But Jesus bent down and started to write on the ground with his finger. 7When they kept on questioning him, he straightened up and said to them, "Let any one of you who is without sin be the first to throw a stone at her." 8Again he stooped down and wrote on the ground.

9At this, those who heard began to go away one at a time, the older ones first, until only Jesus was left, with the woman still standing there. 10Jesus straightened up and asked her, "Woman, where are they? Has no one condemned you?"

11"No one, sir," she said.

"Then neither do I condemn you," Jesus declared. "Go now and leave your life of sin."

Dispute Over Jesus' Testimony

12When Jesus spoke again to the people, he said, "I am the light of the world. Whoever follows me will never walk in darkness, but will have the light of life."

13The Pharisees challenged him, "Here you are, appearing as your own witness; your testimony is not valid."

14Jesus answered, "Even if I testify on my own behalf, my testimony is valid, for I know where I came from and where I am going. But you have no idea where I come from or where I am going. 15You judge by human standards; I pass judgment on no one. 16But if I do judge, my decisions are true, because I am not alone. I stand with the Father, who sent me. 17In your own Law it is written that the testimony of two witnesses is true. 18I am one who testifies for myself; my other witness is the Father, who sent me."

19Then they asked him, "Where is your father?"

"You do not know me or my Father," Jesus replied. "If you knew me, you would know my Father also." 20He spoke these words while teaching in the temple courts near the place where the offerings were put. Yet no one seized him, because his hour had not yet come.

Dispute Over Who Jesus Is

21Once more Jesus said to them, "I am going away, and you will look for me, and you will die in your sin. Where I go, you cannot come."

22This made the Jews ask, "Will he kill himself? Is that why he says, 'Where I go, you cannot come'?"

23But he continued, "You are from below; I am from above. You are of this world; I am not of this world. 24I told you that you would die in your sins; if you do not believe that I am he, you will indeed die in your sins."

25"Who are you?" they asked.

"Just what I have been telling you from the beginning," Jesus replied. 26"I have much to say in judgment of you. But he who sent me is reliable, and what I have heard from him I tell the world."

27They did not understand that he was telling them about his Father. 28So Jesus said, "When you have lifted up[a] the Son of Man, then you will know that I am he and that I do nothing on my own but speak just what the Father has taught me. 29The one who sent me is with me; he has not left me alone, for I always do what pleases him." 30Even as he spoke, many put their faith in him.

Dispute Over Whose Children Jesus' Opponents Are

31To the Jews who had believed him, Jesus said, "If you hold to my teaching, you are really my disciples. 32Then you will know the truth, and the truth will set you free."

33They answered him, "We are Abraham's descendants[b] and have never been slaves of anyone. How can you say that we shall be set free?"

34Jesus replied, "Very truly I tell you, everyone who sins is a slave to sin. 35Now a slave has no permanent place in the family, but a son belongs to it forever. 36So if the Son sets you free, you will be free indeed. 37I know you are Abraham's descendants. Yet you are looking for a way to kill me, because you have no room for my word. 38I am telling you what I have seen in the Father's presence, and you are doing what you have heard from your father.[c]"

39"Abraham is our father," they answered.

"If you were Abraham's children," said Jesus, "then you would[d] do what Abraham did. 40As it is, you are looking for a way to kill me, a man who has told you the truth that I heard from God. Abraham did not do such things. 41You are doing the works of your own father."

"We are not illegitimate children," they protested. "The only Father we have is God himself."

42Jesus said to them, "If God were your Father, you would love me, for I came from God and now am here. I have not come on my own; but he sent me. 43Why is my language not clear to you? Because you are unable to hear what I say. 44You belong to your father, the devil, and you want to carry out

---

[a] 28 The Greek for *lifted up* also means *exalted.* Therefore do what you have heard from the Father.　　[b] 33 Greek *seed*; also in verse 37　　[c] 38 Or *presence.*　　[d] 39 Some early manuscripts "If you are Abraham's children," said Jesus, "then

your father's desires. He was a murderer from the beginning, not holding to the truth, for there is no truth in him. When he lies, he speaks his native language, for he is a liar and the father of lies. 45Yet because I tell the truth, you do not believe me! 46Can any of you prove me guilty of sin? If I am telling the truth, why don't you believe me? 47Whoever belongs to God hears what God says. The reason you do not hear is that you do not belong to God."

Jesus' Claims About Himself

48The Jews answered him, "Aren't we right in saying that you are a Samaritan and demon-possessed?"

49"I am not possessed by a demon," said Jesus, "but I honor my Father and you dishonor me. 50I am not seeking glory for myself; but there is one who seeks it, and he is the judge. 51Very truly I tell you, whoever obeys my word will never see death."

52At this they exclaimed, "Now we know that you are demon-possessed! Abraham died and so did the prophets, yet you say that whoever obeys your word will never taste death. 53Are you greater than our father Abraham? He died, and so did the prophets. Who do you think you are?"

54Jesus replied, "If I glorify myself, my glory means nothing. My Father, whom you claim as your God, is the one who glorifies me. 55Though you do not know him, I know him. If I said I did not, I would be a liar like you, but I do know him and obey his word. 56Your father Abraham rejoiced at the thought of seeing my day; he saw it and was glad."

57"You are not yet fifty years old," they said to him, "and you have seen Abraham!"

58"Very truly I tell you," Jesus answered, "before Abraham was born, I am!" 59At this, they picked up stones to stone him, but Jesus hid himself, slipping away from the temple grounds.

Jesus Heals a Man Born Blind

9 As he went along, he saw a man blind from birth. 2His disciples asked him, "Rabbi, who sinned, this man or his parents, that he was born blind?"

3"Neither this man nor his parents sinned," said Jesus, "but this happened so that the works of God might be displayed in him. 4As long as it is day, we must do the works of him who sent me. Night is coming, when no one can work. 5While I am in the world, I am the light of the world."

6Having said this, he spit on the ground, made some mud with the saliva, and put it on the man's eyes. 7"Go," he told him, "wash in the Pool of Siloam" (this word means Sent). So the man went and washed, and came home seeing.

8His neighbors and those who had formerly seen him begging asked, "Isn't this the same man who used to sit and beg?" 9Some claimed that he was.

Others said, "No, he only looks like him."

But he himself insisted, "I am the man."

10"How then were your eyes opened?" they asked.

11He replied, "The man they call Jesus made some mud and put it on my eyes. He told me to go to Siloam and wash. So I went and washed, and then I could see."

12"Where is this man?" they asked him.

"I don't know," he said.

The Pharisees Investigate the Healing

13They brought to the Pharisees the man who had been blind. 14Now the day on which Jesus had made the mud and opened the man's eyes was a Sabbath. 15Therefore the Pharisees also asked him how he had received his sight. "He put mud on my eyes," the man replied, "and I washed, and now I see."

16Some of the Pharisees said, "This man is not from God, for he does not keep the Sabbath."

But others asked, "How can a sinner do such miraculous signs?" So they were divided.

17Then they turned again to the blind man, "What have you to say about him? It was your eyes he opened."

The man replied, "He is a prophet."

18They still did not believe that he had been blind and had received his sight until they sent for the man's parents. 19"Is this your son?" they asked. "Is this the one you say was born blind? How is it that now he can see?"

20"We know he is our son," the parents answered, "and we know he was born blind. 21But how he can see now, or who opened his eyes, we don't know. Ask him. He is of age; he will speak for himself." 22His parents said this because they were afraid of the Jewish leaders, who already had decided that anyone who acknowledged that Jesus was the Messiah would be put out of the synagogue. 23That was why his parents said, "He is of age; ask him."

24A second time they summoned the man who had been blind. "Give glory to God,*a*" they said. "We know this man is a sinner."

25He replied, "Whether he is a sinner or not, I don't know. One thing I do know. I was blind but now I see!"

26Then they asked him, "What did he do to you? How did he open your eyes?"

27He answered, "I have told you already and you did not listen. Why do you want to hear it again? Do you want to become his disciples too?"

28Then they hurled insults at him and said, "You are this fellow's disciple! We are disciples of Moses! 29We know that God spoke to Moses, but as for this fellow, we don't even know where he comes from."

30The man answered, "Now that is remarkable! You don't know where he comes from, yet he opened my eyes. 31We know that God does not listen to sinners. He listens to the godly person who does his will. 32Nobody has ever heard of opening the eyes of a man born blind. 33If this man were not from God, he could do nothing."

34To this they replied, "You were steeped in sin at birth; how dare you lecture us!" And they threw him out.

a 24 A solemn charge to tell the truth (see Joshua 7:19)

Spiritual Blindness

35Jesus heard that they had thrown him out, and when he found him, he said, "Do you believe in the Son of Man?"

36"Who is he, sir?" the man asked. "Tell me so that I may believe in him."

37Jesus said, "You have now seen him; in fact, he is the one speaking with you."

38Then the man said, "Lord, I believe," and he worshiped him.

39Jesus said,*a* "For judgment I have come into this world, so that the blind will see and those who see will become blind."

40Some Pharisees who were with him heard him say this and asked, "What? Are we blind too?"

41Jesus said, "If you were blind, you would not be guilty of sin; but now that you claim you can see, your guilt remains.

The Good Shepherd and His Sheep

10 "Very truly I tell you Pharisees, anyone who does not enter the sheep pen by the gate, but climbs in by some other way, is a thief and a robber. 2The one who enters by the gate is the shepherd of the sheep. 3The gatekeeper opens the gate for him, and the sheep listen to his voice. He calls his own sheep by name and leads them out. 4When he has brought out all his own, he goes on ahead of them, and his sheep follow him because they know his voice. 5But they will never follow a stranger; in fact, they will run away from him because they do not recognize a stranger's voice." 6Jesus used this figure of speech, but the Pharisees did not understand what he was telling them.

7Therefore Jesus said again, "Very truly I tell you, I am the gate for the sheep. 8All who have come before me are thieves and robbers, but the sheep have not listened to them. 9I am the gate; whoever enters through me will be saved.*b* They will come in and go out, and find pasture. 10The thief comes only to steal and kill and destroy; I have come that they may have life, and have it to the full.

11"I am the good shepherd. The good shepherd lays down his life for the sheep. 12The hired hand is not the shepherd and does not own the sheep. So when he sees the wolf coming, he abandons the sheep and runs away. Then the wolf attacks the flock and scatters it. 13The man runs away because he is a hired hand and cares nothing for the sheep.

14"I am the good shepherd; I know my sheep and my sheep know me— 15just as the Father knows me and I know the Father—and I lay down my life for the sheep. 16I have other sheep that are not of this sheep pen. I must bring them also. They too will listen to my voice, and there shall be one flock and one shepherd. 17The reason my Father loves me is that I lay down my life— only to take it up again. 18No one takes it from me, but I lay it down of my own accord. I have authority to lay it down and authority to take it up again. This command I received from my Father."

19The Jews who heard these words were again divided. 20Many of them said, "He is demon-possessed and raving mad. Why listen to him?"

a 38,39 Some early manuscripts do not have verses 38 and 39a.   *b 9* Or *kept safe*

21But others said, "These are not the sayings of someone possessed by a demon. Can a demon open the eyes of the blind?"

Further Conflict Over Jesus' Claims

22Then came the Festival of Dedication[a] at Jerusalem. It was winter, 23and Jesus was in the temple courts walking in Solomon's Colonnade. 24The Jews who were there gathered around him, saying, "How long will you keep us in suspense? If you are the Messiah, tell us plainly."

25Jesus answered, "I did tell you, but you do not believe. The works I do in my Father's name testify about me, 26but you do not believe because you are not my sheep. 27My sheep listen to my voice; I know them, and they follow me. 28I give them eternal life, and they shall never perish; no one will snatch them out of my hand. 29My Father, who has given them to me, is greater than all[b]; no one can snatch them out of my Father's hand. 30I and the Father are one."

31Again the Jews picked up stones to stone him, 32but Jesus said to them, "I have shown you many good works from the Father. For which of these do you stone me?"

33"We are not stoning you for any good work," they replied, "but for blasphemy, because you, a mere man, claim to be God."

34Jesus answered them, "Is it not written in your Law, 'I have said you are "gods" '[c]? 35If he called them 'gods,' to whom the word of God came—and Scripture cannot be broken— 36what about the one whom the Father set apart as his very own and sent into the world? Why then do you accuse me of blasphemy because I said, 'I am God's Son'? 37Do not believe me unless I do the works of my Father. 38But if I do them, even though you do not believe me, believe the works, that you may know and understand that the Father is in me, and I in the Father." 39Again they tried to seize him, but he escaped their grasp.

40Then Jesus went back across the Jordan to the place where John had been baptizing in the early days. Here he stayed 41and many people came to him. They said, "Though John never performed a miraculous sign, all that John said about this man was true." 42And in that place many believed in Jesus.

The Death of Lazarus

11 Now a man named Lazarus was sick. He was from Bethany, the village of Mary and her sister Martha. 2(This Mary, whose brother Lazarus now lay sick, was the same one who poured perfume on the Lord and wiped his feet with her hair.) 3So the sisters sent word to Jesus, "Lord, the one you love is sick."

4When he heard this, Jesus said, "This sickness will not end in death. No, it is for God's glory so that God's Son may be glorified through it." 5Now Jesus loved Martha and her sister and Lazarus; 6and yet when he heard that Lazarus was sick, he stayed where he was two more days.

7Then he said to his disciples, "Let us go back to Judea."

8"But Rabbi," they said, "a short while ago the Jews there tried to stone you, and yet you are going back?"

---

a 22 That is, Hanukkah　　b 29 Many early manuscripts *What my Father has given me is greater than all*　　c 34 Psalm 82:6

⁹Jesus answered, "Are there not twelve hours of daylight? Those who walk in the daytime will not stumble, for they see by this world's light. ¹⁰It is when people walk at night that they stumble, for they have no light."

¹¹After he had said this, he went on to tell them, "Our friend Lazarus has fallen asleep; but I am going there to wake him up."

¹²His disciples replied, "Lord, if he sleeps, he will get better." ¹³Jesus had been speaking of his death, but his disciples thought he meant natural sleep.

¹⁴So then he told them plainly, "Lazarus is dead, ¹⁵and for your sake I am glad I was not there, so that you may believe. But let us go to him."

¹⁶Then Thomas (called Didymus) said to the rest of the disciples, "Let us also go, that we may die with him."

Jesus Comforts the Sisters of Lazarus

¹⁷On his arrival, Jesus found that Lazarus had already been in the tomb for four days. ¹⁸Now Bethany was less than two miles*ᵃ* from Jerusalem, ¹⁹and many Jews had come to Martha and Mary to comfort them in the loss of their brother. ²⁰When Martha heard that Jesus was coming, she went out to meet him, but Mary stayed at home.

²¹"Lord," Martha said to Jesus, "if you had been here, my brother would not have died. ²²But I know that even now God will give you whatever you ask."

²³Jesus said to her, "Your brother will rise again."

²⁴Martha answered, "I know he will rise again in the resurrection at the last day."

²⁵Jesus said to her, "I am the resurrection and the life. Anyone who believes in me will live, even though they die; ²⁶and whoever lives and believes in me will never die. Do you believe this?"

²⁷"Yes, Lord," she told him, "I believe that you are the Messiah, the Son of God, who was to come into the world."

²⁸And after she had said this, she went back and called her sister Mary aside. "The Teacher is here," she said, "and is asking for you." ²⁹When Mary heard this, she got up quickly and went to him. ³⁰Now Jesus had not yet entered the village, but was still at the place where Martha had met him. ³¹When the Jews who had been with Mary in the house, comforting her, noticed how quickly she got up and went out, they followed her, supposing she was going to the tomb to mourn there.

³²When Mary reached the place where Jesus was and saw him, she fell at his feet and said, "Lord, if you had been here, my brother would not have died."

³³When Jesus saw her weeping, and the Jews who had come along with her also weeping, he was deeply moved in spirit and troubled. ³⁴"Where have you laid him?" he asked.

"Come and see, Lord," they replied.

³⁵Jesus wept.

³⁶Then the Jews said, "See how he loved him!"

³⁷But some of them said, "Could not he who opened the eyes of the blind man have kept this man from dying?"

ᵃ 18 About 3 kilometers

Jesus Raises Lazarus From the Dead

38Jesus, once more deeply moved, came to the tomb. It was a cave with a stone laid across the entrance. 39"Take away the stone," he said.

"But, Lord," said Martha, the sister of the dead man, "by this time there is a bad odor, for he has been there four days."

40Then Jesus said, "Did I not tell you that if you believe, you will see the glory of God?"

41So they took away the stone. Then Jesus looked up and said, "Father, I thank you that you have heard me. 42I knew that you always hear me, but I said this for the benefit of the people standing here, that they may believe that you sent me."

43When he had said this, Jesus called in a loud voice, "Lazarus, come out!" 44The dead man came out, his hands and feet wrapped with strips of linen, and a cloth around his face.

Jesus said to them, "Take off the grave clothes and let him go."

The Plot to Kill Jesus

45Therefore many of the Jews who had come to visit Mary, and had seen what Jesus did, put their faith in him. 46But some of them went to the Pharisees and told them what Jesus had done. 47Then the chief priests and the Pharisees called a meeting of the Sanhedrin.

"What are we accomplishing?" they asked. "Here is this man performing many miraculous signs. 48If we let him go on like this, everyone will believe in him, and then the Romans will come and take away both our temple and our nation."

49Then one of them, named Caiaphas, who was high priest that year, spoke up, "You know nothing at all! 50You do not realize that it is better for you that one man die for the people than that the whole nation perish."

51He did not say this on his own, but as high priest that year he prophesied that Jesus would die for the Jewish nation, 52and not only for that nation but also for the scattered children of God, to bring them together and make them one. 53So from that day on they plotted to take his life.

54Therefore Jesus no longer moved about publicly among the Jews. Instead he withdrew to a region near the desert, to a village called Ephraim, where he stayed with his disciples.

55When it was almost time for the Jewish Passover, many went up from the country to Jerusalem for their ceremonial cleansing before the Passover. 56They kept looking for Jesus, and as they stood in the temple courts they asked one another, "What do you think? Isn't he coming to the Festival at all?" 57But the chief priests and the Pharisees had given orders that anyone who found out where Jesus was should report it so that they might arrest him.

Jesus Anointed at Bethany

12 Six days before the Passover, Jesus came to Bethany, where Lazarus lived, whom Jesus had raised from the dead. 2Here a dinner was given in Jesus' honor. Martha served, while Lazarus was among those reclining at the table with him. 3Then Mary took about a pint*a* of pure nard, an expensive

a 3 About half a liter

perfume; she poured it on Jesus' feet and wiped his feet with her hair. And the house was filled with the fragrance of the perfume.

⁴But one of his disciples, Judas Iscariot, who was later to betray him, objected, ⁵"Why wasn't this perfume sold and the money given to the poor? It was worth a year's wages.ᵃ" ⁶He did not say this because he cared about the poor but because he was a thief; as keeper of the money bag, he used to help himself to what was put into it.

⁷"Leave her alone," Jesus replied. "⌐It was intended⌐ that she should save this perfume for the day of my burial. ⁸You will always have the poor among you,ᵇ but you will not always have me."

⁹Meanwhile a large crowd of Jews found out that Jesus was there and came, not only because of him but also to see Lazarus, whom he had raised from the dead. ¹⁰So the chief priests made plans to kill Lazarus as well, ¹¹for on account of him many of the Jews were going over to Jesus and putting their faith in him.

Jesus Comes to Jerusalem as King

¹²The next day the great crowd that had come for the Festival heard that Jesus was on his way to Jerusalem. ¹³They took palm branches and went out to meet him, shouting,

"Hosanna!ᶜ"

"Blessed is he who comes in the name of the Lord!"ᵈ

"Blessed is the king of Israel!"

¹⁴Jesus found a young donkey and sat on it, as it is written:

¹⁵"Do not be afraid, Daughter Zion;
    see, your king is coming,
    seated on a donkey's colt."ᵉ

¹⁶At first his disciples did not understand all this. Only after Jesus was glorified did they realize that these things had been written about him and that they had done these things to him.

¹⁷Now the crowd that was with him when he called Lazarus from the tomb and raised him from the dead continued to spread the word. ¹⁸Many people, because they had heard that he had performed this miraculous sign, went out to meet him. ¹⁹So the Pharisees said to one another, "See, this is getting us nowhere. Look how the whole world has gone after him!"

Jesus Predicts His Death

²⁰Now there were some Greeks among those who went up to worship at the Festival. ²¹They came to Philip, who was from Bethsaida in Galilee, with a request. "Sir," they said, "we would like to see Jesus." ²²Philip went to tell Andrew; Andrew and Philip in turn told Jesus.

²³Jesus replied, "The hour has come for the Son of Man to be glorified.

ᵃ5 Greek *three hundred denarii*   ᵇ8 See Deut. 15:11.   ᶜ13 A Hebrew expression meaning "Save!" which became an exclamation of praise   ᵈ13 Psalm 118:25,26   ᵉ15 Zech. 9:9

24Very truly I tell you, unless a kernel of wheat falls to the ground and dies, it remains only a single seed. But if it dies, it produces many seeds. 25Those who love their life will lose it, while those who hate their life in this world will keep it for eternal life. 26Whoever serves me must follow me; and where I am, my servant also will be. My Father will honor the one who serves me.

27"Now my heart is troubled, and what shall I say? 'Father, save me from this hour'? No, it was for this very reason I came to this hour. 28Father, glorify your name!"

Then a voice came from heaven, "I have glorified it, and will glorify it again." 29The crowd that was there and heard it said it had thundered; others said an angel had spoken to him.

30Jesus said, "This voice was for your benefit, not mine. 31Now is the time for judgment on this world; now the prince of this world will be driven out. 32And I, when I am lifted up*a* from the earth, will draw all people to myself." 33He said this to show the kind of death he was going to die.

34The crowd spoke up, "We have heard from the Law that the Messiah will remain forever, so how can you say, 'The Son of Man must be lifted up'? Who is this 'Son of Man'?"

35Then Jesus told them, "You are going to have the light just a little while longer. Walk while you have the light, before darkness overtakes you. Those who walk in the dark do not know where they are going. 36Put your trust in the light while you have the light, so that you may become children of light." When he had finished speaking, Jesus left and hid himself from them.

Belief and Unbelief Among the Jews

37Even after Jesus had done so many miraculous signs in their presence, they still would not believe in him. 38This was to fulfill the word of Isaiah the prophet:

> "Lord, who has believed our message
> and to whom has the arm of the Lord been revealed?"*b*

39For this reason they could not believe, because, as Isaiah says elsewhere:

> 40"He has blinded their eyes
> and hardened their hearts,
> so they can neither see with their eyes,
> nor understand with their hearts,
> nor turn—and I would heal them."*c*

41Isaiah said this because he saw Jesus' glory and spoke about him.

42Yet at the same time many even among the leaders believed in him. But because of the Pharisees they would not openly acknowledge their faith for fear they would be put out of the synagogue; 43for they loved human glory more than the glory of God.

44Then Jesus cried out, "Those who believe in me do not believe in me only, but in the one who sent me. 45When they look at me, they see the one who

a 32 The Greek for lifted up also means exalted.   b 38 Isaiah 53:1   c 40 Isaiah 6:10 sent me. 46I have come into the world as a light, so that no one who believes in me should stay in darkness.

47"As for those who hear my words but do not keep them, I do not judge them. For I did not come to judge the world, but to save the world. 48There is a judge for those who reject me and do not accept my words; the very words I have spoken will condemn them at the last day. 49For I did not speak on my own, but the Father who sent me commanded me to say all that I have spoken. 50I know that his command leads to eternal life. So whatever I say is just what the Father has told me to say."

Jesus Washes His Disciples' Feet

13 It was just before the Passover Festival. Jesus knew that the hour had come for him to leave this world and go to the Father. Having loved his own who were in the world, he loved them to the end.

2The evening meal was in progress, and the devil had already prompted Judas, the son of Simon Iscariot, to betray Jesus. 3Jesus knew that the Father had put all things under his power, and that he had come from God and was returning to God; 4so he got up from the meal, took off his outer clothing, and wrapped a towel around his waist. 5After that, he poured water into a basin and began to wash his disciples' feet, drying them with the towel that was wrapped around him.

6He came to Simon Peter, who said to him, "Lord, are you going to wash my feet?"

7Jesus replied, "You do not realize now what I am doing, but later you will understand."

8"No," said Peter, "you shall never wash my feet."

Jesus answered, "Unless I wash you, you have no part with me."

9"Then, Lord," Simon Peter replied, "not just my feet but my hands and my head as well!"

10Jesus answered, "Those who have had a bath need only to wash their feet; their whole body is clean. And you are clean, though not every one of you." 11For he knew who was going to betray him, and that was why he said not every one was clean.

12When he had finished washing their feet, he put on his clothes and returned to his place. "Do you understand what I have done for you?" he asked them. 13"You call me 'Teacher' and 'Lord,' and rightly so, for that is what I am. 14Now that I, your Lord and Teacher, have washed your feet, you also should wash one another's feet. 15I have set you an example that you should do as I have done for you. 16Very truly I tell you, servants are not greater than their master, nor are messengers greater than the one who sent them. 17Now that you know these things, you will be blessed if you do them.

Jesus Predicts His Betrayal

18"I am not referring to all of you; I know those I have chosen. But this is to fulfill this passage of Scripture: 'He who shared my bread has lifted up his heel against me.'a

a 18 Psalm 41:9

19"I am telling you now before it happens, so that when it does happen you will believe that I am who I am. 20Very truly I tell you, whoever accepts anyone I send accepts me; and whoever accepts me accepts the one who sent me."

21After he had said this, Jesus was troubled in spirit and testified, "Very truly I tell you, one of you is going to betray me."

22His disciples stared at one another, at a loss to know which of them he meant. 23One of them, the disciple whom Jesus loved, was reclining next to him. 24Simon Peter motioned to this disciple and said, "Ask him which one he means."

25Leaning back against Jesus, he asked him, "Lord, who is it?"

26Jesus answered, "It is the one to whom I will give this piece of bread when I have dipped it in the dish." Then, dipping the piece of bread, he gave it to Judas, the son of Simon Iscariot. 27As soon as Judas took the bread, Satan entered into him.

So Jesus told him, "What you are about to do, do quickly." 28But no one at the meal understood why Jesus said this to him. 29Since Judas had charge of the money, some thought Jesus was telling him to buy what was needed for the Festival, or to give something to the poor. 30As soon as Judas had taken the bread, he went out. And it was night.

Jesus Predicts Peter's Denial

31When he was gone, Jesus said, "Now is the Son of Man glorified and God is glorified in him. 32If God is glorified in him,*a* God will glorify the Son in himself, and will glorify him at once.

33"My children, I will be with you only a little longer. You will look for me, and just as I told the Jews, so I tell you now: Where I am going, you cannot come.

34"A new command I give you: Love one another. As I have loved you, so you must love one another. 35By this everyone will know that you are my disciples, if you love one another."

36Simon Peter asked him, "Lord, where are you going?"

Jesus replied, "Where I am going, you cannot follow now, but you will follow later."

37Peter asked, "Lord, why can't I follow you now? I will lay down my life for you."

38Then Jesus answered, "Will you really lay down your life for me? Very truly I tell you, before the rooster crows, you will disown me three times!

Jesus Comforts His Disciples

14 "Do not let your hearts be troubled. Trust in God*b*; trust also in me. 2My Father's house has plenty of room; if that were not so, would I have told you that I am going there to prepare a place for you? 3And if I go and prepare a place for you, I will come back and take you to be with me that you also may be where I am. 4You know the way to the place where I am going."

a 32 Many early manuscripts do not have *If God is glorified in him.*   *b* 1 Or *You trust in God*

Jesus the Way to the Father

⁵Thomas said to him, "Lord, we don't know where you are going, so how can we know the way?"

⁶Jesus answered, "I am the way and the truth and the life. No one comes to the Father except through me. ⁷If you really know me, you will know*a* my Father as well. From now on, you do know him and have seen him."

⁸Philip said, "Lord, show us the Father and that will be enough for us."

⁹Jesus answered: "Don't you know me, Philip, even after I have been among you such a long time? Anyone who has seen me has seen the Father. How can you say, 'Show us the Father'? ¹⁰Don't you believe that I am in the Father, and that the Father is in me? The words I say to you I do not speak on my own authority. Rather, it is the Father, living in me, who is doing his work. ¹¹Believe me when I say that I am in the Father and the Father is in me; or at least believe on the evidence of the works themselves. ¹²Very truly I tell you, all who have faith in me will do the works I have been doing, and they will do even greater things than these, because I am going to the Father. ¹³And I will do whatever you ask in my name, so that the Father may be glorified in the Son. ¹⁴You may ask me for anything in my name, and I will do it.

Jesus Promises the Holy Spirit

¹⁵"If you love me, keep my commands. ¹⁶And I will ask the Father, and he will give you another advocate to help you and be with you forever— ¹⁷the Spirit of truth. The world cannot accept him, because it neither sees him nor knows him. But you know him, for he lives with you and will be*b* in you. ¹⁸I will not leave you as orphans; I will come to you. ¹⁹Before long, the world will not see me anymore, but you will see me. Because I live, you also will live. ²⁰On that day you will realize that I am in my Father, and you are in me, and I am in you. ²¹Whoever has my commands and keeps them is the one who loves me. Anyone who loves me will be loved by my Father, and I too will love them and show myself to them."

²²Then Judas (not Judas Iscariot) said, "But, Lord, why do you intend to show yourself to us and not to the world?"

²³Jesus replied, "Anyone who loves me will obey my teaching. My Father will love them, and we will come to them and make our home with them. ²⁴Anyone who does not love me will not obey my teaching. These words you hear are not my own; they belong to the Father who sent me.

²⁵"All this I have spoken while still with you. ²⁶But the Advocate, the Holy Spirit, whom the Father will send in my name, will teach you all things and will remind you of everything I have said to you. ²⁷Peace I leave with you; my peace I give you. I do not give to you as the world gives. Do not let your hearts be troubled and do not be afraid.

²⁸"You heard me say, 'I am going away and I am coming back to you.' If you loved me, you would be glad that I am going to the Father, for the Father is greater than I. ²⁹I have told you now before it happens, so that when it does happen you will believe. ³⁰I will not say much more to you, for the prince of this world is coming. He has no hold over me, ³¹but he comes so that the

a 7 Some manuscripts If you really knew me, you would know   b 17 Some early manuscripts and is world may learn that I love the Father and do exactly what my Father has commanded me.

"Come now; let us leave.

The Vine and the Branches

15 "I am the true vine, and my Father is the gardener. [2]He cuts off every branch in me that bears no fruit, while every branch that does bear fruit he prunes[a] so that it will be even more fruitful. [3]You are already clean because of the word I have spoken to you. [4]Remain in me, as I also remain in you. No branch can bear fruit by itself; it must remain in the vine. Neither can you bear fruit unless you remain in me.

[5]"I am the vine; you are the branches. If you remain in me and I in you, you will bear much fruit; apart from me you can do nothing. [6]If you do not remain in me, you are like a branch that is thrown away and withers; such branches are picked up, thrown into the fire and burned. [7]If you remain in me and my words remain in you, ask whatever you wish, and it will be done for you. [8]This is to my Father's glory, that you bear much fruit, showing yourselves to be my disciples.

[9]"As the Father has loved me, so have I loved you. Now remain in my love. [10]If you keep my commands, you will remain in my love, just as I have kept my Father's commands and remain in his love. [11]I have told you this so that my joy may be in you and that your joy may be complete. [12]My command is this: Love each other as I have loved you. [13]Greater love has no one than this: to lay down one's life for one's friends. [14]You are my friends if you do what I command. [15]I no longer call you servants, because servants do not know their master's business. Instead, I have called you friends, for everything that I learned from my Father I have made known to you. [16]You did not choose me, but I chose you and appointed you so that you might go and bear fruit—fruit that will last—and so that whatever you ask in my name the Father will give you. [17]This is my command: Love each other.

The World Hates the Disciples

[18]"If the world hates you, keep in mind that it hated me first. [19]If you belonged to the world, it would love you as its own. As it is, you do not belong to the world, but I have chosen you out of the world. That is why the world hates you. [20]Remember what I told you: 'Servants are not greater than their master.'[b] If they persecuted me, they will persecute you also. If they obeyed my teaching, they will obey yours also. [21]They will treat you this way because of my name, for they do not know the One who sent me. [22]If I had not come and spoken to them, they would not be guilty of sin; but now they have no excuse for their sin. [23]Those who hate me hate my Father as well. [24]If I had not done among them the works no one else did, they would not be guilty of sin. As it is, they have seen, and yet they have hated both me and my Father. [25]But this is to fulfill what is written in their Law: 'They hated me without reason.'[c]

---

[a] 2 The Greek for *prunes* also means *cleans.*   [b] 20 John 13:16   [c] 25 Psalms 35:19; 69:4

The Work of the Holy Spirit

26"When the Advocate comes, whom I will send to you from the Father—the Spirit of truth who goes out from the Father—he will testify about me. 27And you also must testify, for you have been with me from the beginning.

16 "All this I have told you so that you will not fall away. 2They will put you out of the synagogue; in fact, the hour is coming when those who kill you will think they are offering a service to God. 3They will do such things because they have not known the Father or me. 4I have told you this, so that when their hour comes you will remember that I warned you about them. I did not tell you this from the beginning because I was with you, 5but now I am going to him who sent me. None of you asks me, 'Where are you going?' 6Rather, you are filled with grief because I have said these things. 7But very truly I tell you, it is for your good that I am going away. Unless I go away, the Advocate will not come to you; but if I go, I will send him to you. 8When he comes, he will prove the world to be in the wrong about sin and righteousness and judgment: 9about sin, because people do not believe in me; 10about righteousness, because I am going to the Father, where you can see me no longer; 11and about judgment, because the prince of this world now stands condemned.

12"I have much more to say to you, more than you can now bear. 13But when he, the Spirit of truth, comes, he will guide you into all the truth. He will not speak on his own; he will speak only what he hears, and he will tell you what is yet to come. 14He will glorify me because it is from me that he will receive what he will make known to you. 15All that belongs to the Father is mine. That is why I said the Spirit will receive from me what he will make known to you."

The Disciples' Grief Will Turn to Joy

16Jesus went on to say, "In a little while you will see me no more, and then after a little while you will see me."

17At this, some of his disciples said to one another, "What does he mean by saying, 'In a little while you will see me no more, and then after a little while you will see me,' and 'Because I am going to the Father'?" 18They kept asking, "What does he mean by 'a little while'? We don't understand what he is saying."

19Jesus saw that they wanted to ask him about this, so he said to them, "Are you asking one another what I meant when I said, 'In a little while you will see me no more, and then after a little while you will see me'? 20Very truly I tell you, you will weep and mourn while the world rejoices. You will grieve, but your grief will turn to joy. 21A woman giving birth to a child has pain because her time has come; but when her baby is born she forgets the anguish because of her joy that a child is born into the world. 22So with you: Now is your time of grief, but I will see you again and you will rejoice, and no one will take away your joy. 23In that day you will no longer ask me anything. Very truly I tell you, my Father will give you whatever you ask in my name. 24Until now you have not asked for anything in my name. Ask and you will receive, and your joy will be complete.

25"Though I have been speaking figuratively, a time is coming when I will no longer use this kind of language but will tell you plainly about my Father. 26In that day you will ask in my name. I am not saying that I will ask the Father on your behalf. 27No, the Father himself loves you because you have loved me and have believed that I came from God. 28I came from the Father and entered the world; now I am leaving the world and going back to the Father."

29Then Jesus' disciples said, "Now you are speaking clearly and without figures of speech. 30Now we can see that you know all things and that you do not even need to have anyone ask you questions. This makes us believe that you came from God."

31"Do you now believe?" Jesus replied. 32"A time is coming and in fact has come when you will be scattered, each to your own home. You will leave me all alone. Yet I am not alone, for my Father is with me.

33"I have told you these things, so that in me you may have peace. In this world you will have trouble. But take heart! I have overcome the world."

Jesus Prays to Be Glorified

17 After Jesus said this, he looked toward heaven and prayed:

"Father, the hour has come. Glorify your Son, that your Son may glorify you. 2For you granted him authority over all people that he might give eternal life to all those you have given him. 3Now this is eternal life: that they know you, the only true God, and Jesus Christ, whom you have sent. 4I have brought you glory on earth by finishing the work you gave me to do. 5And now, Father, glorify me in your presence with the glory I had with you before the world began.

Jesus Prays for His Disciples

6"I have revealed you[a] to those whom you gave me out of the world. They were yours; you gave them to me and they have obeyed your word. 7Now they know that everything you have given me comes from you. 8For I gave them the words you gave me and they accepted them. They knew with certainty that I came from you, and they believed that you sent me. 9I pray for them. I am not praying for the world, but for those you have given me, for they are yours. 10All I have is yours, and all you have is mine. And glory has come to me through them. 11I will remain in the world no longer, but they are still in the world, and I am coming to you. Holy Father, protect them by the power of[b] your name, the name you gave me, so that they may be one as we are one. 12While I was with them, I protected them and kept them safe by[c] that name you gave me. None has been lost except the one doomed to destruction so that Scripture would be fulfilled.

13"I am coming to you now, but I say these things while I am still in the world, so that they may have the full measure of my joy within them. 14I have given them your word and the world has hated them, for they are

a 6 Greek *your name*; also in verse 26   b 11 Or *Father, keep them faithful to*   c 12 Or *kept them faithful to*

not of the world any more than I am of the world. [15]My prayer is not that you take them out of the world but that you protect them from the evil one. [16]They are not of the world, even as I am not of it. [17]Sanctify them by[a] the truth; your word is truth. [18]As you sent me into the world, I have sent them into the world. [19]For them I sanctify myself, that they too may be truly sanctified.

Jesus Prays for All Believers

[20]"My prayer is not for them alone. I pray also for those who will believe in me through their message, [21]that all of them may be one, Father, just as you are in me and I am in you. May they also be in us so that the world may believe that you have sent me. [22]I have given them the glory that you gave me, that they may be one as we are one— [23]I in them and you in me—so that they may be brought to complete unity. Then the world will know that you sent me and have loved them even as you have loved me.

[24]"Father, I want those you have given me to be with me where I am, and to see my glory, the glory you have given me because you loved me before the creation of the world.

[25]"Righteous Father, though the world does not know you, I know you, and they know that you have sent me. [26]I have made you[b] known to them, and will continue to make you known in order that the love you have for me may be in them and that I myself may be in them."

Jesus Arrested

18 When he had finished praying, Jesus left with his disciples and crossed the Kidron Valley. On the other side there was a garden, and he and his disciples went into it.

[2]Now Judas, who betrayed him, knew the place, because Jesus had often met there with his disciples. [3]So Judas came to the garden, guiding a detachment of soldiers and some officials from the chief priests and the Pharisees. They were carrying torches, lanterns and weapons.

[4]Jesus, knowing all that was going to happen to him, went out and asked them, "Who is it you want?"

[5]"Jesus of Nazareth," they replied.

"I am he," Jesus said. (And Judas the traitor was standing there with them.) [6]When Jesus said, "I am he," they drew back and fell to the ground.

[7]Again he asked them, "Who is it you want?"

"Jesus of Nazareth," they said.

[8]Jesus answered, "I told you that I am he. If you are looking for me, then let these men go." [9]This happened so that the words he had spoken would be fulfilled: "I have not lost one of those you gave me."[c]

[10]Then Simon Peter, who had a sword, drew it and struck the high priest's servant, cutting off his right ear. (The servant's name was Malchus.)

[11]Jesus commanded Peter, "Put your sword away! Shall I not drink the cup the Father has given me?"

[a] 17 Or *them to live in accordance with*   [b] 26 Greek *your name*   [c] 9 John 6:39

¹²Then the detachment of soldiers with its commander and the Jewish officials arrested Jesus. They bound him ¹³and brought him first to Annas, who was the father-in-law of Caiaphas, the high priest that year. ¹⁴Caiaphas was the one who had advised the Jewish leaders that it would be good if one man died for the people.

Peter's First Denial

¹⁵Simon Peter and another disciple were following Jesus. Because this disciple was known to the high priest, he went with Jesus into the high priest's courtyard, ¹⁶but Peter had to wait outside at the door. The other disciple, who was known to the high priest, came back, spoke to the servant girl on duty there and brought Peter in.

¹⁷"You aren't one of this man's disciples too, are you?" she asked Peter.

He replied, "I am not."

¹⁸It was cold, and the servants and officials stood around a fire they had made to keep warm. Peter also was standing with them, warming himself.

The High Priest Questions Jesus

¹⁹Meanwhile, the high priest questioned Jesus about his disciples and his teaching.

²⁰"I have spoken openly to the world," Jesus replied. "I always taught in synagogues or at the temple, where all the Jews come together. I said nothing in secret. ²¹Why question me? Ask those who heard me. Surely they know what I said."

²²When Jesus said this, one of the officials nearby slapped him in the face. "Is this the way you answer the high priest?" he demanded.

²³"If I said something wrong," Jesus replied, "testify as to what is wrong. But if I spoke the truth, why did you strike me?" ²⁴Then Annas sent him bound to Caiaphas the high priest.

Peter's Second and Third Denials

²⁵Meanwhile Simon Peter was still standing there warming himself. So they asked him, "You aren't one of his disciples too, are you?"

He denied it, saying, "I am not."

²⁶One of the high priest's servants, a relative of the man whose ear Peter had cut off, challenged him, "Didn't I see you with him in the garden?" ²⁷Again Peter denied it, and at that moment a rooster began to crow.

Jesus Before Pilate

²⁸Then the Jewish leaders took Jesus from Caiaphas to the palace of the Roman governor. By now it was early morning, and to avoid ceremonial uncleanness they did not enter the palace, because they wanted to be able to eat the Passover. ²⁹So Pilate came out to them and asked, "What charges are you bringing against this man?"

³⁰"If he were not a criminal," they replied, "we would not have handed him over to you."

³¹Pilate said, "Take him yourselves and judge him by your own law."

"But we have no right to execute anyone," they objected. ³²This took place to fulfill what Jesus had said about the kind of death he was going to die.

³³Pilate then went back inside the palace, summoned Jesus and asked him, "Are you the king of the Jews?"

³⁴"Is that your own idea," Jesus asked, "or did others talk to you about me?"

³⁵"Am I a Jew?" Pilate replied. "Your own people and chief priests handed you over to me. What is it you have done?"

³⁶Jesus said, "My kingdom is not of this world. If it were, my servants would fight to prevent my arrest by the Jewish leaders. But now my kingdom is from another place."

³⁷"You are a king, then!" said Pilate.

Jesus answered, "You say I am a king. In fact, the reason I was born and came into the world is to testify to the truth. Everyone on the side of truth listens to me."

³⁸"What is truth?" retorted Pilate. With this he went out again to the Jews gathered there and said, "I find no basis for a charge against him. ³⁹But it is your custom for me to release to you one prisoner at the time of the Passover. Do you want me to release 'the king of the Jews'?"

⁴⁰They shouted back, "No, not him! Give us Barabbas!" Now Barabbas had taken part in an uprising.

Jesus Sentenced to Be Crucified

19 Then Pilate took Jesus and had him flogged. ²The soldiers twisted together a crown of thorns and put it on his head. They clothed him in a purple robe ³and went up to him again and again, saying, "Hail, king of the Jews!" And they slapped him in the face.

⁴Once more Pilate came out and said to the Jews, "Look, I am bringing him out to you to let you know that I find no basis for a charge against him." ⁵When Jesus came out wearing the crown of thorns and the purple robe, Pilate said to them, "Here is the man!"

⁶As soon as the chief priests and their officials saw him, they shouted, "Crucify! Crucify!"

But Pilate answered, "You take him and crucify him. As for me, I find no basis for a charge against him."

⁷They insisted, "We have a law, and according to that law he must die, because he claimed to be the Son of God."

⁸When Pilate heard this, he was even more afraid, ⁹and he went back inside the palace. "Where do you come from?" he asked Jesus, but Jesus gave him no answer. ¹⁰"Do you refuse to speak to me?" Pilate said. "Don't you realize I have power either to free you or to crucify you?"

¹¹Jesus answered, "You would have no power over me if it were not given to you from above. Therefore the one who handed me over to you is guilty of a greater sin."

¹²From then on, Pilate tried to set Jesus free, but the Jewish leaders kept shouting, "If you let this man go, you are no friend of Caesar. Anyone who claims to be a king opposes Caesar."

¹³When Pilate heard this, he brought Jesus out and sat down on the judge's

seat at a place known as the Stone Pavement (which in Aramaic is Gabbatha). 14It was the day of Preparation of the Passover; it was about noon.

"Here is your king," Pilate said to the Jews.

15But they shouted, "Take him away! Take him away! Crucify him!"

"Shall I crucify your king?" Pilate asked.

"We have no king but Caesar," the chief priests answered.

16Finally Pilate handed him over to them to be crucified.

The Crucifixion

So the soldiers took charge of Jesus. 17Carrying his own cross, he went out to the place of the Skull (which in Aramaic is called Golgotha). 18Here they crucified him, and with him two others—one on each side and Jesus in the middle.

19Pilate had a notice prepared and fastened to the cross. It read: JESUS OF NAZARETH, THE KING OF THE JEWS. 20Many of the Jews read this sign, for the place where Jesus was crucified was near the city, and the sign was written in Aramaic, Latin and Greek. 21The chief priests of the Jews protested to Pilate, "Do not write 'The King of the Jews,' but that this man claimed to be king of the Jews."

22Pilate answered, "What I have written, I have written."

23When the soldiers crucified Jesus, they took his clothes, dividing them into four shares, one for each of them, with the undergarment remaining. This garment was seamless, woven in one piece from top to bottom.

24"Let's not tear it," they said to one another. "Let's decide by lot who will get it."

This happened that the scripture might be fulfilled which said,

> "They divided my clothes among them
>   and cast lots for my garment."[a]

So this is what the soldiers did.

25Near the cross of Jesus stood his mother, his mother's sister, Mary the wife of Clopas, and Mary Magdalene. 26When Jesus saw his mother there, and the disciple whom he loved standing nearby, he said to her, "Mother,[b] here is your son," 27and to the disciple, "Here is your mother." From that time on, this disciple took her into his home.

The Death of Jesus

28Later, knowing that everything had now been finished, and so that Scripture would be fulfilled, Jesus said, "I am thirsty." 29A jar of wine vinegar was there, so they soaked a sponge in it, put the sponge on a stalk of the hyssop plant, and lifted it to Jesus' lips. 30When he had received the drink, Jesus said, "It is finished." With that, he bowed his head and gave up his spirit.

31Now it was the day of Preparation, and the next day was to be a special Sabbath. Because the Jewish leaders did not want the bodies left on the crosses during the Sabbath, they asked Pilate to have the legs broken and the bodies taken down. 32The soldiers therefore came and broke the legs of the

---

a 24 Psalm 22:18   b 26 Or *Woman*; the Greek term does not denote any disrespect.

first man who had been crucified with Jesus, and then those of the other. ³³But when they came to Jesus and found that he was already dead, they did not break his legs. ³⁴Instead, one of the soldiers pierced Jesus' side with a spear, bringing a sudden flow of blood and water. ³⁵The man who saw it has given testimony, and his testimony is true. He knows that he tells the truth, and he testifies so that you also may believe. ³⁶These things happened so that the scripture would be fulfilled: "Not one of his bones will be broken,"ᵃ ³⁷and, as another scripture says, "They will look on the one they have pierced."ᵇ

The Burial of Jesus

³⁸Later, Joseph of Arimathea asked Pilate for the body of Jesus. Now Joseph was a disciple of Jesus, but secretly because he feared the Jewish leaders. With Pilate's permission, he came and took the body away. ³⁹He was accompanied by Nicodemus, the man who earlier had visited Jesus at night. Nicodemus brought a mixture of myrrh and aloes, about seventy-five pounds.ᶜ ⁴⁰Taking Jesus' body, the two of them wrapped it, with the spices, in strips of linen. This was in accordance with Jewish burial customs. ⁴¹At the place where Jesus was crucified, there was a garden, and in the garden a new tomb, in which no one had ever been laid. ⁴²Because it was the Jewish day of Preparation and since the tomb was nearby, they laid Jesus there.

The Empty Tomb

20 Early on the first day of the week, while it was still dark, Mary Magdalene went to the tomb and saw that the stone had been removed from the entrance. ²So she came running to Simon Peter and the other disciple, the one Jesus loved, and said, "They have taken the Lord out of the tomb, and we don't know where they have put him!"

³So Peter and the other disciple started for the tomb. ⁴Both were running, but the other disciple outran Peter and reached the tomb first. ⁵He bent over and looked in at the strips of linen lying there but did not go in. ⁶Then Simon Peter came along behind him and went straight into the tomb. He saw the strips of linen lying there, ⁷as well as the cloth that had been wrapped around Jesus' head. The cloth was still lying in its place, separate from the linen. ⁸Finally the other disciple, who had reached the tomb first, also went inside. He saw and believed. ⁹(They still did not understand from Scripture that Jesus had to rise from the dead.) ¹⁰Then the disciples went back to where they were staying.

Jesus Appears to Mary Magdalene

¹¹Now Mary stood outside the tomb crying. As she wept, she bent over to look into the tomb ¹²and saw two angels in white, seated where Jesus' body had been, one at the head and the other at the foot.

¹³They asked her, "Why are you crying?"

"They have taken my Lord away," she said, "and I don't know where they have put him." ¹⁴At this, she turned around and saw Jesus standing there, but she did not realize that it was Jesus.

¹⁵He said to her, "Why are you crying? Who is it you are looking for?"

ᵃ36 Exodus 12:46; Num. 9:12; Psalm 34:20   ᵇ37 Zech. 12:10   ᶜ39 About 34 kilograms

Thinking he was the gardener, she said, "Sir, if you have carried him away, tell me where you have put him, and I will get him."

16Jesus said to her, "Mary."

She turned toward him and cried out in Aramaic, "Rabboni!" (which means Teacher).

17Jesus said, "Do not hold on to me, for I have not yet ascended to the Father. Go instead to my brothers and tell them, 'I am ascending to my Father and your Father, to my God and your God.' "

18Mary Magdalene went to the disciples with the news: "I have seen the Lord!" And she told them that he had said these things to her.

Jesus Appears to His Disciples

19On the evening of that first day of the week, when the disciples were together, with the doors locked for fear of the Jewish leaders, Jesus came and stood among them and said, "Peace be with you!" 20After he said this, he showed them his hands and side. The disciples were overjoyed when they saw the Lord.

21Again Jesus said, "Peace be with you! As the Father has sent me, I am sending you." 22And with that he breathed on them and said, "Receive the Holy Spirit. 23If you forgive the sins of anyone, their sins are forgiven; if you do not forgive them, they are not forgiven."

Jesus Appears to Thomas

24Now Thomas (called Didymus), one of the Twelve, was not with the disciples when Jesus came. 25So the other disciples told him, "We have seen the Lord!"

But he said to them, "Unless I see the nail marks in his hands and put my finger where the nails were, and put my hand into his side, I will not believe."

26A week later his disciples were in the house again, and Thomas was with them. Though the doors were locked, Jesus came and stood among them and said, "Peace be with you!" 27Then he said to Thomas, "Put your finger here; see my hands. Reach out your hand and put it into my side. Stop doubting and believe."

28Thomas said to him, "My Lord and my God!"

29Then Jesus told him, "Because you have seen me, you have believed; blessed are those who have not seen and yet have believed."

The Purpose of John's Gospel

30Jesus did many other miraculous signs in the presence of his disciples, which are not recorded in this book. 31But these are written that you may believea that Jesus is the Messiah, the Son of God, and that by believing you may have life in his name.

Jesus and the Miraculous Catch of Fish

21 Afterward Jesus appeared again to his disciples, by the Sea of Tiberias.b It happened this way: 2Simon Peter, Thomas (called Didymus),

a 31 The original Greek text may imply continue to believe.   b 1 That is, Sea of Galilee

Nathanael from Cana in Galilee, the sons of Zebedee, and two other disciples were together. ³"I'm going out to fish," Simon Peter told them, and they said, "We'll go with you." So they went out and got into the boat, but that night they caught nothing.

⁴Early in the morning, Jesus stood on the shore, but the disciples did not realize that it was Jesus.

⁵He called out to them, "Friends, haven't you any fish?"

"No," they answered.

⁶He said, "Throw your net on the right side of the boat and you will find some." When they did, they were unable to haul the net in because of the large number of fish.

⁷Then the disciple whom Jesus loved said to Peter, "It is the Lord!" As soon as Simon Peter heard him say, "It is the Lord," he wrapped his outer garment around him (for he had taken it off) and jumped into the water. ⁸The other disciples followed in the boat, towing the net full of fish, for they were not far from shore, about a hundred yards.^a ⁹When they landed, they saw a fire of burning coals there with fish on it, and some bread.

¹⁰Jesus said to them, "Bring some of the fish you have just caught."

¹¹Simon Peter climbed aboard and dragged the net ashore. It was full of large fish, 153, but even with so many the net was not torn. ¹²Jesus said to them, "Come and have breakfast." None of the disciples dared ask him, "Who are you?" They knew it was the Lord. ¹³Jesus came, took the bread and gave it to them, and did the same with the fish. ¹⁴This was now the third time Jesus appeared to his disciples after he was raised from the dead.

Jesus Reinstates Peter

¹⁵When they had finished eating, Jesus said to Simon Peter, "Simon son of John, do you love me more than these?"

"Yes, Lord," he said, "you know that I love you."

Jesus said, "Feed my lambs."

¹⁶Again Jesus said, "Simon son of John, do you love me?"

He answered, "Yes, Lord, you know that I love you."

Jesus said, "Take care of my sheep."

¹⁷The third time he said to him, "Simon son of John, do you love me?"

Peter was hurt because Jesus asked him the third time, "Do you love me?" He said, "Lord, you know all things; you know that I love you."

Jesus said, "Feed my sheep. ¹⁸Very truly I tell you, when you were younger you dressed yourself and went where you wanted; but when you are old you will stretch out your hands, and someone else will dress you and lead you where you do not want to go." ¹⁹Jesus said this to indicate the kind of death by which Peter would glorify God. Then he said to him, "Follow me!"

²⁰Peter turned and saw that the disciple whom Jesus loved was following them. (This was the one who had leaned back against Jesus at the supper and had said, "Lord, who is going to betray you?") ²¹When Peter saw him, he asked, "Lord, what about him?"

²²Jesus answered, "If I want him to remain alive until I return, what is that

^a 8 About 90 meters

to you? You must follow me." 23Because of this, the rumor spread among the believers that this disciple would not die. But Jesus did not say that he would not die; he only said, "If I want him to remain alive until I return, what is that to you?"

24This is the disciple who testifies to these things and who wrote them down. We know that his testimony is true.

25Jesus did many other things as well. If every one of them were written down, I suppose that even the whole world would not have room for the books that would be written.

ACTS

Jesus Taken Up Into Heaven

1 In my former book, Theophilus, I wrote about all that Jesus began to do and to teach ²until the day he was taken up to heaven, after giving instructions through the Holy Spirit to the apostles he had chosen. ³After his suffering, he presented himself to them and gave many convincing proofs that he was alive. He appeared to them over a period of forty days and spoke about the kingdom of God. ⁴On one occasion, while he was eating with them, he gave them this command: "Do not leave Jerusalem, but wait for the gift my Father promised, which you have heard me speak about. ⁵For John baptized with*a* water, but in a few days you will be baptized with*a* the Holy Spirit."

⁶So when they met together, they asked him, "Lord, are you at this time going to restore the kingdom to Israel?"

⁷He said to them: "It is not for you to know the times or dates the Father has set by his own authority. ⁸But you will receive power when the Holy Spirit comes on you; and you will be my witnesses in Jerusalem, and in all Judea and Samaria, and to the ends of the earth."

⁹After he said this, he was taken up before their very eyes, and a cloud hid him from their sight.

¹⁰They were looking intently up into the sky as he was going, when suddenly two men dressed in white stood beside them. ¹¹"Men of Galilee," they said, "why do you stand here looking into the sky? This same Jesus, who has been taken from you into heaven, will come back in the same way you have seen him go into heaven."

Matthias Chosen to Replace Judas

¹²Then the apostles returned to Jerusalem from the hill called the Mount of Olives, a Sabbath day's walk*b* from the city. ¹³When they arrived, they went upstairs to the room where they were staying. Those present were Peter, John, James and Andrew; Philip and Thomas, Bartholomew and Matthew; James son of Alphaeus and Simon the Zealot, and Judas son of James. ¹⁴They all joined together constantly in prayer, along with the women and Mary the mother of Jesus, and with his brothers.

¹⁵In those days Peter stood up among the believers (a group numbering about a hundred and twenty) ¹⁶and said, "Brothers and sisters, long ago the Holy Spirit spoke through the mouth of David concerning Judas, who served

a 5 Or *in*   *b* 12 That is, about 3/4 mile (about 1,100 meters)

as guide for those who arrested Jesus, and that Scripture had to be fulfilled. [17]Judas was one of our number and shared in this ministry."

[18](With the reward he got for his wickedness, Judas bought a field; there he fell headlong, his body burst open and all his intestines spilled out. [19]Everyone in Jerusalem heard about this, so they called that field in their language Akeldama, that is, Field of Blood.)

[20]"For," said Peter, "it is written in the Book of Psalms:

> " 'May his place be deserted;
> let there be no one to dwell in it,'[a]

and,

> " 'May another take his place of leadership.'[b]

[21]Therefore it is necessary to choose one of the men who have been with us the whole time the Lord Jesus went in and out among us, [22]beginning from John's baptism to the time when Jesus was taken up from us. For one of these must become a witness with us of his resurrection."

[23]So they proposed the names of two men: Joseph called Barsabbas (also known as Justus) and Matthias. [24]Then they prayed, "Lord, you know everyone's heart. Show us which of these two you have chosen [25]to take over this apostolic ministry, which Judas left to go where he belongs." [26]Then they cast lots, and the lot fell to Matthias; so he was added to the eleven apostles.

The Holy Spirit Comes at Pentecost

2 When the day of Pentecost came, they were all together in one place. [2]Suddenly a sound like the blowing of a violent wind came from heaven and filled the whole house where they were sitting. [3]They saw what seemed to be tongues of fire that separated and came to rest on each of them. [4]All of them were filled with the Holy Spirit and began to speak in other tongues[c] as the Spirit enabled them.

[5]Now there were staying in Jerusalem God-fearing Jews from every nation under heaven. [6]When they heard this sound, a crowd came together in bewilderment, because each one heard their own language being spoken. [7]Utterly amazed, they asked: "Aren't all these who are speaking Galileans? [8]Then how is it that each of us hears them in our native language? [9]Parthians, Medes and Elamites; residents of Mesopotamia, Judea and Cappadocia, Pontus and Asia,[d] [10]Phrygia and Pamphylia, Egypt and the parts of Libya near Cyrene; visitors from Rome [11](both Jews and converts to Judaism); Cretans and Arabs—we hear them declaring the wonders of God in our own tongues!" [12]Amazed and perplexed, they asked one another, "What does this mean?"

[13]Some, however, made fun of them and said, "They have had too much wine.[e]"

Peter Addresses the Crowd

[14]Then Peter stood up with the Eleven, raised his voice and addressed the

---

[a] 20 Psalm 69:25   [b] 20 Psalm 109:8   [c] 4 Or *languages*; also in verse 11   [d] 9 That is, the Roman province by that name   [e] 13 Or *sweet wine*

crowd: "Fellow Jews and all of you who live in Jerusalem, let me explain this to you; listen carefully to what I say. 15These people are not drunk, as you suppose. It's only nine in the morning! 16No, this is what was spoken by the prophet Joel:

17" 'In the last days, God says,
I will pour out my Spirit on all people.
Your sons and daughters will prophesy,
your young men will see visions,
your old men will dream dreams.
18Even on my servants, both men and women,
I will pour out my Spirit in those days,
and they will prophesy.
19I will show wonders in the heaven above
and signs on the earth below,
blood and fire and billows of smoke.
20The sun will be turned to darkness
and the moon to blood
before the coming of the great and glorious day of the Lord.
21And everyone who calls
on the name of the Lord will be saved.'a

22"People of Israel, listen to this: Jesus of Nazareth was a man accredited by God to you by miracles, wonders and signs, which God did among you through him, as you yourselves know. 23This man was handed over to you by God's deliberate plan and foreknowledge; and you, with the help of wicked men,b put him to death by nailing him to the cross. 24But God raised him from the dead, freeing him from the agony of death, because it was impossible for death to keep its hold on him. 25David said about him:

" 'I saw the Lord always before me.
Because he is at my right hand,
I will not be shaken.
26Therefore my heart is glad and my tongue rejoices;
my body also will rest in hope,
27because you will not abandon me to the grave,
you will not let your Holy One see decay.
28You have made known to me the paths of life;
you will fill me with joy in your presence.'c

29"Brothers and sisters, we all know that the patriarch David died and was buried, and his tomb is here to this day. 30But he was a prophet and knew that God had promised him on oath that he would place one of his descendants on his throne. 31Seeing what was to come, he spoke of the resurrection of the Messiah, that he was not abandoned to the grave, nor did his body see decay. 32God has raised this Jesus to life, and we are all witnesses of the fact. 33Exalted to the right hand of God, he has received from the Father the promised

a 21 Joel 2:28–32   b 23 Or of those not having the law (that is, Gentiles)   c 28 Psalm 16:8–11

Holy Spirit and has poured out what you now see and hear. [34]For David did not ascend to heaven, and yet he said,

> " 'The Lord said to my Lord:
> "Sit at my right hand
> [35]until I make your enemies
> a footstool for your feet." ' [a]

[36]"Therefore let all Israel be assured of this: God has made this Jesus, whom you crucified, both Lord and Messiah."

[37]When the people heard this, they were cut to the heart and said to Peter and the other apostles, "Brothers, what shall we do?"

[38]Peter replied, "Repent and be baptized, every one of you, in the name of Jesus Christ for the forgiveness of your sins. And you will receive the gift of the Holy Spirit. [39]The promise is for you and your children and for all who are far off—for all whom the Lord our God will call."

[40]With many other words he warned them; and he pleaded with them, "Save yourselves from this corrupt generation." [41]Those who accepted his message were baptized, and about three thousand were added to their number that day.

The Fellowship of the Believers

[42]They devoted themselves to the apostles' teaching and to fellowship, to the breaking of bread and to prayer. [43]Everyone was filled with awe at the many wonders and miraculous signs done by the apostles. [44]All the believers were together and had everything in common. [45]They sold property and possessions to give to anyone who had need. [46]Every day they continued to meet together in the temple courts. They broke bread in their homes and ate together with glad and sincere hearts, [47]praising God and enjoying the favor of all the people. And the Lord added to their number daily those who were being saved.

Peter Heals a Lame Beggar

3 One day Peter and John were going up to the temple at the time of prayer—at three in the afternoon. [2]Now a man who was lame from birth was being carried to the temple gate called Beautiful, where he was put every day to beg from those going into the temple courts. [3]When he saw Peter and John about to enter, he asked them for money. [4]Peter looked straight at him, as did John. Then Peter said, "Look at us!" [5]So the man gave them his attention, expecting to get something from them.

[6]Then Peter said, "Silver or gold I do not have, but what I do have I give you. In the name of Jesus Christ of Nazareth, walk." [7]Taking him by the right hand, he helped him up, and instantly the man's feet and ankles became strong. [8]He jumped to his feet and began to walk. Then he went with them into the temple courts, walking and jumping, and praising God. [9]When all the people saw him walking and praising God, [10]they recognized him as the same

[a] 35 Psalm 110:1

man who used to sit begging at the temple gate called Beautiful, and they were filled with wonder and amazement at what had happened to him.

Peter Speaks to the Onlookers

[11]While the man held on to Peter and John, all the people were astonished and came running to them in the place called Solomon's Colonnade. [12]When Peter saw this, he said to them: "People of Israel, why does this surprise you? Why do you stare at us as if by our own power or godliness we had made this man walk? [13]The God of Abraham, Isaac and Jacob, the God of our fathers, has glorified his servant Jesus. You handed him over to be killed, and you disowned him before Pilate, though he had decided to let him go. [14]You disowned the Holy and Righteous One and asked that a murderer be released to you. [15]You killed the author of life, but God raised him from the dead. We are witnesses of this. [16]By faith in the name of Jesus, this man whom you see and know was made strong. It is Jesus' name and the faith that comes through him that has completely healed him, as you can all see.

[17]"Now, brothers and sisters, I know that you acted in ignorance, as did your leaders. [18]But this is how God fulfilled what he had foretold through all the prophets, saying that his Messiah would suffer. [19]Repent, then, and turn to God, so that your sins may be wiped out, that times of refreshing may come from the Lord, [20]and that he may send the Messiah, who has been appointed for you—even Jesus. [21]Heaven must receive him until the time comes for God to restore everything, as he promised long ago through his holy prophets. [22]For Moses said, 'The Lord your God will raise up for you a prophet like me from among your own people; you must listen to everything he tells you. [23]Anyone who does not listen to him will be completely cut off from the people.'[a]

[24]"Indeed, beginning with Samuel, all the prophets who have spoken have foretold these days. [25]And you are heirs of the prophets and of the covenant God made with your fathers. He said to Abraham, 'Through your offspring all peoples on earth will be blessed.'[b] [26]When God raised up his servant, he sent him first to you to bless you by turning each of you from your wicked ways."

Peter and John Before the Sanhedrin

4 The priests and the captain of the temple guard and the Sadducees came up to Peter and John while they were speaking to the people. [2]They were greatly disturbed because the apostles were teaching the people, proclaiming in Jesus the resurrection of the dead. [3]They seized Peter and John, and because it was evening, they put them in jail until the next day. [4]But many who heard the message believed, and the number of believers[c] grew to about five thousand.

[5]The next day the rulers, the elders and the teachers of the law met in Jerusalem. [6]Annas the high priest was there, and so were Caiaphas, John, Alexander and others of the high priest's family. [7]They had Peter and John brought

[a] 23 Deut. 18:15,18,19   [b] 25 Gen. 22:18; 26:4   [c] 4 Or men

before them and began to question them: "By what power or what name did you do this?"

[8]Then Peter, filled with the Holy Spirit, said to them: "Rulers and elders of the people! [9]If we are being called to account today for an act of kindness shown to a man who was lame and are being asked how he was healed, [10]then know this, you and all the people of Israel: It is by the name of Jesus Christ of Nazareth, whom you crucified but whom God raised from the dead, that this man stands before you healed. [11]Jesus is

> " 'the stone you builders rejected,
> which has become the cornerstone.'[a]

[12]Salvation is found in no one else, for there is no other name given under heaven by which we must be saved."

[13]When they saw the courage of Peter and John and realized that they were unschooled, ordinary men, they were astonished and they took note that these men had been with Jesus. [14]But since they could see the man who had been healed standing there with them, there was nothing they could say. [15]So they ordered them to withdraw from the Sanhedrin and then conferred together. [16]"What are we going to do with these men?" they asked. "Everyone living in Jerusalem knows they have done an outstanding miracle, and we cannot deny it. [17]But to stop this thing from spreading any further among the people, we must warn them to speak no longer to anyone in this name."

[18]Then they called them in again and commanded them not to speak or teach at all in the name of Jesus. [19]But Peter and John replied, "Which is right in God's eyes: to listen to you, or to him? You be the judges! [20]As for us, we cannot help speaking about what we have seen and heard."

[21]After further threats they let them go. They could not decide how to punish them, because all the people were praising God for what had happened. [22]For the man who was miraculously healed was over forty years old.

The Believers' Prayer

[23]On their release, Peter and John went back to their own people and reported all that the chief priests and the elders had said to them. [24]When they heard this, they raised their voices together in prayer to God. "Sovereign Lord," they said, "you made the heaven and the earth and the sea, and everything in them. [25]You spoke by the Holy Spirit through the mouth of your servant, our father David:

> " 'Why do the nations rage
> and the peoples plot in vain?
> [26]The kings of the earth take their stand
> and the rulers gather together
> against the Lord
> and against his Anointed One.[b'c]

[27]Indeed Herod and Pontius Pilate met together with the Gentiles and the people[d] of Israel in this city to conspire against your holy servant Jesus,

---

[a]11 Psalm 118:22   [b]26 That is, Messiah or Christ   [c]26 Psalm 2:1,2   [d]27 The Greek is plural.

whom you anointed. ²⁸They did what your power and will had decided beforehand should happen. ²⁹Now, Lord, consider their threats and enable your servants to speak your word with great boldness. ³⁰Stretch out your hand to heal and perform miraculous signs and wonders through the name of your holy servant Jesus."

³¹After they prayed, the place where they were meeting was shaken. And they were all filled with the Holy Spirit and spoke the word of God boldly.

The Believers Share Their Possessions

³²All the believers were one in heart and mind. No one claimed that any of their possessions was their own, but they shared everything they had. ³³With great power the apostles continued to testify to the resurrection of the Lord Jesus. And God's grace was so powerfully at work in them all ³⁴that there were no needy persons among them. For from time to time those who owned lands or houses sold them, brought the money from the sales ³⁵and put it at the apostles' feet, and it was distributed to anyone who had need.

³⁶Joseph, a Levite from Cyprus, whom the apostles called Barnabas (which means Son of Encouragement), ³⁷sold a field he owned and brought the money and put it at the apostles' feet.

Ananias and Sapphira

5 Now a man named Ananias, together with his wife Sapphira, also sold a piece of property. ²With his wife's full knowledge he kept back part of the money for himself, but brought the rest and put it at the apostles' feet.

³Then Peter said, "Ananias, how is it that Satan has so filled your heart that you have lied to the Holy Spirit and have kept for yourself some of the money you received for the land? ⁴Didn't it belong to you before it was sold? And after it was sold, wasn't the money at your disposal? What made you think of doing such a thing? You have not lied just to human beings but to God."

⁵When Ananias heard this, he fell down and died. And great fear seized all who heard what had happened. ⁶Then some young men came forward, wrapped up his body, and carried him out and buried him.

⁷About three hours later his wife came in, not knowing what had happened. ⁸Peter asked her, "Tell me, is this the price you and Ananias got for the land?"

"Yes," she said, "that is the price."

⁹Peter said to her, "How could you conspire to test the Spirit of the Lord? Listen! The feet of those who buried your husband are at the door, and they will carry you out also."

¹⁰At that moment she fell down at his feet and died. Then the young men came in and, finding her dead, carried her out and buried her beside her husband. ¹¹Great fear seized the whole church and all who heard about these events.

The Apostles Heal Many

¹²The apostles performed many miraculous signs and wonders among the people. And all the believers used to meet together in Solomon's Colonnade. ¹³No one else dared join them, even though they were highly regarded by the

people. [14]Nevertheless, more and more men and women believed in the Lord and were added to their number. [15]As a result, people brought the sick into the streets and laid them on beds and mats so that at least Peter's shadow might fall on some of them as he passed by. [16]Crowds gathered also from the towns around Jerusalem, bringing their sick and those tormented by evil[a] spirits, and all of them were healed.

The Apostles Persecuted

[17]Then the high priest and all his associates, who were members of the party of the Sadducees, were filled with jealousy. [18]They arrested the apostles and put them in the public jail. [19]But during the night an angel of the Lord opened the doors of the jail and brought them out. [20]"Go, stand in the temple courts," he said, "and tell the people all about this new life."

[21]At daybreak they entered the temple courts, as they had been told, and began to teach the people.

When the high priest and his associates arrived, they called together the Sanhedrin—the full assembly of the elders of Israel—and sent to the jail for the apostles. [22]But on arriving at the jail, the officers did not find them there. So they went back and reported, [23]"We found the jail securely locked, with the guards standing at the doors; but when we opened them, we found no one inside." [24]On hearing this report, the captain of the temple guard and the chief priests were puzzled, wondering what this might lead to.

[25]Then someone came and said, "Look! The men you put in jail are standing in the temple courts teaching the people." [26]At that, the captain went with his officers and brought the apostles. They did not use force, because they feared that the people would stone them.

[27]The apostles were brought in and made to appear before the Sanhedrin to be questioned by the high priest. [28]"We gave you strict orders not to teach in this name," he said. "Yet you have filled Jerusalem with your teaching and are determined to make us guilty of this man's blood."

[29]Peter and the other apostles replied: "We must obey God rather than human beings! [30]The God of our ancestors raised Jesus from the dead—whom you killed by hanging him on a tree. [31]God exalted him to his own right hand as Prince and Savior that he might bring Israel to repentance and forgive their sins. [32]We are witnesses of these things, and so is the Holy Spirit, whom God has given to those who obey him."

[33]When they heard this, they were furious and wanted to put them to death. [34]But a Pharisee named Gamaliel, a teacher of the law, who was honored by all the people, stood up in the Sanhedrin and ordered that the men be put outside for a little while. [35]Then he addressed the Sanhedrin: "Men of Israel, consider carefully what you intend to do to these men. [36]Some time ago Theudas appeared, claiming to be somebody, and about four hundred men rallied to him. He was killed, all his followers were dispersed, and it all came to nothing. [37]After him, Judas the Galilean appeared in the days of the census and led a band of people in revolt. He too was killed, and all his followers were scattered. [38]Therefore, in the present case I advise you: Leave these men alone! Let

[a] 16 Greek unclean

them go! For if their purpose or activity is of human origin, it will fail. ³⁹But if it is from God, you will not be able to stop these men; you will only find yourselves fighting against God."

⁴⁰His speech persuaded them. They called the apostles in and had them flogged. Then they ordered them not to speak in the name of Jesus, and let them go.

⁴¹The apostles left the Sanhedrin, rejoicing because they had been counted worthy of suffering disgrace for the Name. ⁴²Day after day, in the temple courts and from house to house, they never stopped teaching and proclaiming the good news that Jesus is the Messiah.

The Choosing of the Seven

6 In those days when the number of disciples was increasing, the Hellenistic Jews[a] among them complained against the Hebraic Jews because their widows were being overlooked in the daily distribution of food. ²So the Twelve gathered all the disciples together and said, "It would not be right for us to neglect the ministry of the word of God in order to wait on tables. ³Brothers and sisters, choose seven men from among you who are known to be full of the Spirit and wisdom. We will turn this responsibility over to them ⁴and will give our attention to prayer and the ministry of the word."

⁵This proposal pleased the whole group. They chose Stephen, a man full of faith and of the Holy Spirit; also Philip, Procorus, Nicanor, Timon, Parmenas, and Nicolas from Antioch, a convert to Judaism. ⁶They presented them to the apostles, who prayed and laid their hands on them.

⁷So the word of God spread. The number of disciples in Jerusalem increased rapidly, and a large number of priests became obedient to the faith.

Stephen Seized

⁸Now Stephen, a man full of God's grace and power, did great wonders and miraculous signs among the people. ⁹Opposition arose, however, from members of the Synagogue of the Freedmen (as it was called)—Jews of Cyrene and Alexandria as well as the provinces of Cilicia and Asia—who began to argue with Stephen. ¹⁰But they could not stand up against the wisdom the Spirit gave him as he spoke.

¹¹Then they secretly persuaded some men to say, "We have heard Stephen speak blasphemous words against Moses and against God."

¹²So they stirred up the people and the elders and the teachers of the law. They seized Stephen and brought him before the Sanhedrin. ¹³They produced false witnesses, who testified, "This fellow never stops speaking against this holy place and against the law. ¹⁴For we have heard him say that this Jesus of Nazareth will destroy this place and change the customs Moses handed down to us."

¹⁵All who were sitting in the Sanhedrin looked intently at Stephen, and they saw that his face was like the face of an angel.

---

*a 1 That is, Jews who had adopted the Greek language and culture

Stephen's Speech to the Sanhedrin

7 Then the high priest asked Stephen, "Are these charges true?"
²To this he replied: "Brothers and fathers, listen to me! The God of glory appeared to our father Abraham while he was still in Mesopotamia, before he lived in Haran. ³'Leave your country and your people,' God said, 'and go to the land I will show you.'ᵃ

⁴"So he left the land of the Chaldeans and settled in Haran. After the death of his father, God sent him to this land where you are now living. ⁵He gave him no inheritance here, not even enough ground to set his foot on. But God promised him that he and his descendants after him would possess the land, even though at that time Abraham had no child. ⁶God spoke to him in this way: 'Your descendants will be strangers in a country not their own, and they will be enslaved and mistreated four hundred years. ⁷But I will punish the nation they serve as slaves,' God said, 'and afterward they will come out of that country and worship me in this place.'ᵇ ⁸Then he gave Abraham the covenant of circumcision. And Abraham became the father of Isaac and circumcised him eight days after his birth. Later Isaac became the father of Jacob, and Jacob became the father of the twelve patriarchs.

⁹"Because the patriarchs were jealous of Joseph, they sold him as a slave into Egypt. But God was with him ¹⁰and rescued him from all his troubles. He gave Joseph wisdom and enabled him to gain the goodwill of Pharaoh king of Egypt. So Pharaoh made him ruler over Egypt and all his palace.

¹¹"Then a famine struck all Egypt and Canaan, bringing great suffering, and our people could not find food. ¹²When Jacob heard that there was grain in Egypt, he sent our ancestors on their first visit. ¹³On their second visit, Joseph told his brothers who he was, and Pharaoh learned about Joseph's family. ¹⁴After this, Joseph sent for his father Jacob and his whole family, seventy-five in all. ¹⁵Then Jacob went down to Egypt, where he and our ancestors died. ¹⁶Their bodies were brought back to Shechem and placed in the tomb that Abraham had bought from the sons of Hamor at Shechem for a certain sum of money.

¹⁷"As the time drew near for God to fulfill his promise to Abraham, the number of our people in Egypt had greatly increased. ¹⁸Then 'a new king, to whom Joseph meant nothing, came to power in Egypt.'ᶜ ¹⁹He dealt treacherously with our people and oppressed our ancestors by forcing them to throw out their newborn babies so that they would die.

²⁰"At that time Moses was born, and he was no ordinary child.ᵈ For three months he was cared for in his parents' home. ²¹When he was placed outside, Pharaoh's daughter took him and brought him up as her own son. ²²Moses was educated in all the wisdom of the Egyptians and was powerful in speech and action.

²³"When Moses was forty years old, he decided to visit his own people, the Israelites. ²⁴He saw one of them being mistreated by an Egyptian, so he went to his defense and avenged him by killing the Egyptian. ²⁵Moses thought that his own people would realize that God was using him to rescue them, but they did not. ²⁶The next day Moses came upon two Israelites who were fight-

ᵃ3 Gen. 12:1　ᵇ7 Gen. 15:13,14　ᶜ18 Exodus 1:8　ᵈ20 Or *was fair in the sight of God*

ing. He tried to reconcile them by saying, 'Men, you are brothers; why do you want to hurt each other?'

[27]"But the man who was mistreating the other pushed Moses aside and said, 'Who made you ruler and judge over us? [28]Do you want to kill me as you killed the Egyptian yesterday?'[a] [29]When Moses heard this, he fled to Midian, where he settled as a foreigner and had two sons.

[30]"After forty years had passed, an angel appeared to Moses in the flames of a burning bush in the desert near Mount Sinai. [31]When he saw this, he was amazed at the sight. As he went over to get a closer look, he heard the Lord say: [32]'I am the God of your fathers, the God of Abraham, Isaac and Jacob.'[b] Moses trembled with fear and did not dare to look.

[33]"Then the Lord said to him, 'Take off your sandals; the place where you are standing is holy ground. [34]I have indeed seen the oppression of my people in Egypt. I have heard their groaning and have come down to set them free. Now come, I will send you back to Egypt.'[c]

[35]"This is the same Moses they had rejected with the words, 'Who made you ruler and judge?' He was sent to be their ruler and deliverer by God himself, through the angel who appeared to him in the bush. [36]He led them out of Egypt and did wonders and miraculous signs in Egypt, at the Red Sea[d] and for forty years in the desert.

[37]"This is the Moses who told the Israelites, 'God will send you a prophet like me from your own people.'[e] [38]He was in the assembly in the desert, with the angel who spoke to him on Mount Sinai, and with our ancestors; and he received living words to pass on to us.

[39]"But our ancestors refused to obey him. Instead, they rejected him and in their hearts turned back to Egypt. [40]They told Aaron, 'Make us gods who will go before us. As for this fellow Moses who led us out of Egypt—we don't know what has happened to him!'[f] [41]That was the time they made an idol in the form of a calf. They brought sacrifices to it and reveled in what their own hands had made. [42]But God turned away from them and gave them over to the worship of the sun, moon and stars. This agrees with what is written in the book of the prophets:

> " 'Did you bring me sacrifices and offerings
>   forty years in the desert, house of Israel?
> [43]You have taken up the tabernacle of Molech
>   and the star of your god Rephan,
>   the idols you made to worship.
> Therefore I will send you into exile'[g] beyond Babylon.

[44]"Our ancestors had the tabernacle of the covenant law with them in the desert. It had been made as God directed Moses, according to the pattern he had seen. [45]Having received the tabernacle, our ancestors under Joshua brought it with them when they took the land from the nations God drove out before them. It remained in the land until the time of David, [46]who enjoyed

---

[a] 28 Exodus 2:14   [b] 32 Exodus 3:6   [c] 34 Exodus 3:5,7,8,10   [d] 36 That is, Sea of Reeds
[e] 37 Deut. 18:15   [f] 40 Exodus 32:1   [g] 43 Amos 5:25–27

God's favor and asked that he might provide a dwelling place for the God of Jacob.*ª* [47]But it was Solomon who built a house for him.

[48]"However, the Most High does not live in houses made by human hands. As the prophet says:

> [49]" 'Heaven is my throne,
> and the earth is my footstool.
> What kind of house will you build for me?
>
> says the Lord.
>
> Or where will my resting place be?
> [50]Has not my hand made all these things?'*ᵇ*

[51]"You stiff-necked people! Your hearts and ears are still uncircumcised. You are just like your ancestors: You always resist the Holy Spirit! [52]Was there ever a prophet your ancestors did not persecute? They even killed those who predicted the coming of the Righteous One. And now you have betrayed and murdered him— [53]you who have received the law that was given through angels but have not obeyed it."

The Stoning of Stephen

[54]When the members of the Sanhedrin heard this, they were furious and gnashed their teeth at him. [55]But Stephen, full of the Holy Spirit, looked up to heaven and saw the glory of God, and Jesus standing at the right hand of God. [56]"Look," he said, "I see heaven open and the Son of Man standing at the right hand of God."

[57]At this they covered their ears and, yelling at the top of their voices, they all rushed at him, [58]dragged him out of the city and began to stone him. Meanwhile, the witnesses laid their coats at the feet of a young man named Saul.

[59]While they were stoning him, Stephen prayed, "Lord Jesus, receive my spirit." [60]Then he fell on his knees and cried out, "Lord, do not hold this sin against them." When he had said this, he fell asleep.

8 And Saul approved of their killing him.

The Church Persecuted and Scattered

On that day a great persecution broke out against the church in Jerusalem, and all except the apostles were scattered throughout Judea and Samaria. [2]Godly men buried Stephen and mourned deeply for him. [3]But Saul began to destroy the church. Going from house to house, he dragged off both men and women and put them in prison.

Philip in Samaria

[4]Those who had been scattered preached the word wherever they went. [5]Philip went down to a city in Samaria and proclaimed the Messiah there. [6]When the crowds heard Philip and saw the miraculous signs he did, they all paid close attention to what he said. [7]With shrieks, evil*ᶜ* spirits came out of

---

ª 46 Some early manuscripts *the house of Jacob*   *ᵇ* 50 Isaiah 66:1,2   *ᶜ* 7 Greek *unclean*

many, and many who were paralyzed or lame were healed. [8]So there was great joy in that city.

Simon the Sorcerer

[9]Now for some time a man named Simon had practiced sorcery in the city and amazed all the people of Samaria. He boasted that he was someone great, [10]and all the people, both high and low, gave him their attention and exclaimed, "This man is rightly called the Great Power of God." [11]They followed him because he had amazed them for a long time with his sorcery. [12]But when they believed Philip as he proclaimed the good news of the kingdom of God and the name of Jesus Christ, they were baptized, both men and women. [13]Simon himself believed and was baptized. And he followed Philip everywhere, astonished by the great signs and miracles he saw

[14]When the apostles in Jerusalem heard that Samaria had accepted the word of God, they sent Peter and John to Samaria. [15]When they arrived, they prayed for the new believers there that they might receive the Holy Spirit, [16]because the Holy Spirit had not yet come upon any of them; they had simply been baptized into[a] the name of the Lord Jesus. [17]Then Peter and John placed their hands on them, and they received the Holy Spirit.

[18]When Simon saw that the Spirit was given at the laying on of the apostles' hands, he offered them money [19]and said, "Give me also this ability so that everyone on whom I lay my hands may receive the Holy Spirit."

[20]Peter answered: "May your money perish with you, because you thought you could buy the gift of God with money! [21]You have no part or share in this ministry, because your heart is not right before God [22]Repent of this wickedness and pray to the Lord in the hope that he may forgive you for having such a thought in your heart. [23]For I see that you are full of bitterness and captive to sin."

[24]Then Simon answered, "Pray to the Lord for me so that nothing you have said may happen to me."

[25]After they had further proclaimed the word of the Lord and testified about Jesus, Peter and John returned to Jerusalem, preaching the gospel in many Samaritan villages.

Philip and the Ethiopian

[26]Now an angel of the Lord said to Philip, "Go south to the road—the desert road—that goes down from Jerusalem to Gaza." [27]So he started out, and on his way he met an Ethiopian[b] eunuch, an important official in charge of all the treasury of Candace, queen of the Ethiopians. This man had gone to Jerusalem to worship, [28]and on his way home was sitting in his chariot reading the Book of Isaiah the prophet. [29]The Spirit told Philip, "Go to that chariot and stay near it."

[30]Then Philip ran up to the chariot and heard the man reading Isaiah the prophet. "Do you understand what you are reading?" Philip asked.

[31]"How can I," he said, "unless someone explains it to me?" So he invited Philip to come up and sit with him.

[a]16 Or in   [b]27 That is, from the southern Nile region

32This is the passage of Scripture the eunuch was reading:

"He was led like a sheep to the slaughter,
and as a lamb before the shearer is silent,
so he did not open his mouth.
33 In his humiliation he was deprived of justice.
Who can speak of his descendants?
For his life was taken from the earth."*a*

34The eunuch asked Philip, "Tell me, please, who is the prophet talking about, himself or someone else?" 35Then Philip began with that very passage of Scripture and told him the good news about Jesus.

36[37]As they traveled along the road, they came to some water and the eunuch said, "Look, here is water. What can stand in the way of my being baptized?"*b* 38And he gave orders to stop the chariot. Then both Philip and the eunuch went down into the water and Philip baptized him. 39When they came up out of the water, the Spirit of the Lord suddenly took Philip away, and the eunuch did not see him again, but went on his way rejoicing. 40Philip, however, appeared at Azotus and traveled about, preaching the gospel in all the towns until he reached Caesarea.

Saul's Conversion

9 Meanwhile, Saul was still breathing out murderous threats against the Lord's disciples. He went to the high priest 2and asked him for letters to the synagogues in Damascus, so that if he found any there who belonged to the Way, whether men or women, he might take them as prisoners to Jerusalem. 3As he neared Damascus on his journey, suddenly a light from heaven flashed around him. 4He fell to the ground and heard a voice say to him, "Saul, Saul, why do you persecute me?"

5"Who are you, Lord?" Saul asked.

"I am Jesus, whom you are persecuting," he replied. 6"Now get up and go into the city, and you will be told what you must do."

7The men traveling with Saul stood there speechless; they heard the sound but did not see anyone. 8Saul got up from the ground, but when he opened his eyes he could see nothing. So they led him by the hand into Damascus. 9For three days he was blind, and did not eat or drink anything.

10In Damascus there was a disciple named Ananias. The Lord called to him in a vision, "Ananias!"

"Yes, Lord," he answered.

11The Lord told him, "Go to the house of Judas on Straight Street and ask for a man from Tarsus named Saul, for he is praying. 12In a vision he has seen a man named Ananias come and place his hands on him to restore his sight."

13"Lord," Ananias answered, "I have heard many reports about this man and all the harm he has done to those in Jerusalem who believe in you. 14And he has come here with authority from the chief priests to arrest all who call on your name."

a 33 Isaiah 53:7,8   *b* 36 Some late manuscripts *baptized?" 37Philip said, "If you believe with all your heart, you may." The eunuch answered, "I believe that Jesus Christ is the Son of God."*

¹⁵But the Lord said to Ananias, "Go! This man is my chosen instrument to proclaim my name to the Gentiles and their kings and to the people of Israel. ¹⁶I will show him how much he must suffer for my name."

¹⁷Then Ananias went to the house and entered it. Placing his hands on Saul, he said, "Brother Saul, the Lord—Jesus, who appeared to you on the road as you were coming here—has sent me so that you may see again and be filled with the Holy Spirit." ¹⁸Immediately, something like scales fell from Saul's eyes, and he could see again. He got up and was baptized, ¹⁹and after taking some food, he regained his strength.

Saul in Damascus and Jerusalem

Saul spent several days with the disciples in Damascus. ²⁰At once he began to preach in the synagogues that Jesus is the Son of God. ²¹All those who heard him were astonished and asked, "Isn't he the man who raised havoc in Jerusalem among those who call on this name? And hasn't he come here to take them as prisoners to the chief priests?" ²²Yet Saul grew more and more powerful and baffled the Jews living in Damascus by proving that Jesus is the Messiah.

²³After many days had gone by, there was a conspiracy among the Jews to kill him, ²⁴but Saul learned of their plan. Day and night they kept close watch on the city gates in order to kill him. ²⁵But his followers took him by night and lowered him in a basket through an opening in the wall.

²⁶When he came to Jerusalem, he tried to join the disciples, but they were all afraid of him, not believing that he really was a disciple. ²⁷But Barnabas took him and brought him to the apostles. He told them how Saul on his journey had seen the Lord and that the Lord had spoken to him, and how in Damascus he had preached fearlessly in the name of Jesus. ²⁸So Saul stayed with them and moved about freely in Jerusalem, speaking boldly in the name of the Lord. ²⁹He talked and debated with the Hellenistic Jews,[a] but they tried to kill him. ³⁰When the believers learned of this, they took him down to Caesarea and sent him off to Tarsus.

³¹Then the church throughout Judea, Galilee and Samaria enjoyed a time of peace and was strengthened. Living in the fear of the Lord and encouraged by the Holy Spirit, it increased in numbers.

Aeneas and Dorcas

³²As Peter traveled about the country, he went to visit the believers in Lydda. ³³There he found a man named Aeneas, who was paralyzed and had been confined to bed for eight years. ³⁴"Aeneas," Peter said to him, "Jesus Christ heals you. Get up and take care of your mat." Immediately Aeneas got up. ³⁵All those who lived in Lydda and Sharon saw him and turned to the Lord.

³⁶In Joppa there was a disciple named Tabitha (in Greek her name is Dorcas); she was always doing good and helping the poor. ³⁷About that time she became sick and died, and her body was washed and placed in an upstairs room. ³⁸Lydda was near Joppa; so when the disciples heard that Peter was in Lydda, they sent two men to him and urged him, "Please come at once!"

[a] 29 That is, Jews who had adopted the Greek language and culture

39Peter went with them, and when he arrived he was taken upstairs to the room. All the widows stood around him, crying and showing him the robes and other clothing that Dorcas had made while she was still with them. 40Peter sent them all out of the room; then he got down on his knees and prayed. Turning toward the dead woman, he said, "Tabitha, get up." She opened her eyes, and seeing Peter she sat up. 41He took her by the hand and helped her to her feet. Then he called the believers and the widows and presented her to them alive. 42This became known all over Joppa, and many people believed in the Lord. 43Peter stayed in Joppa for some time with a tanner named Simon.

Cornelius Calls for Peter

10 At Caesarea there was a man named Cornelius, a centurion in what was known as the Italian Regiment. 2He and all his family were devout and God-fearing; he gave generously to those in need and prayed to God regularly. 3One day at about three in the afternoon he had a vision. He distinctly saw an angel of God, who came to him and said, "Cornelius!"

4Cornelius stared at him in fear. "What is it, Lord?" he asked.

The angel answered, "Your prayers and gifts to the poor have come up as a memorial offering before God. 5Now send men to Joppa to bring back a man named Simon who is called Peter. 6He is staying with Simon the tanner, whose house is by the sea."

7When the angel who spoke to him had gone, Cornelius called two of his servants and a devout soldier who was one of his attendants. 8He told them everything that had happened and sent them to Joppa.

Peter's Vision

9About noon the following day as they were on their journey and approaching the city, Peter went up on the roof to pray. 10He became hungry and wanted something to eat, and while the meal was being prepared, he fell into a trance. 11He saw heaven opened and something like a large sheet being let down to earth by its four corners. 12It contained all kinds of four-footed animals, as well as reptiles and birds. 13Then a voice told him, "Get up, Peter. Kill and eat."

14"Surely not, Lord!" Peter replied. "I have never eaten anything impure or unclean."

15The voice spoke to him a second time, "Do not call anything impure that God has made clean."

16This happened three times, and immediately the sheet was taken back to heaven.

17While Peter was wondering about the meaning of the vision, the men sent by Cornelius found out where Simon's house was and stopped at the gate. 18They called out, asking if Simon who was known as Peter was staying there.

19While Peter was still thinking about the vision, the Spirit said to him, "Simon, three*a* men are looking for you. 20So get up and go downstairs. Do not hesitate to go with them, for I have sent them."

a 19 One early manuscript *two*; other manuscripts do not have the number.

²¹Peter went down and said to the men, "I'm the one you're looking for. Why have you come?"

²²The men replied, "We have come from Cornelius the centurion. He is a righteous and God-fearing man, who is respected by all the Jewish people. A holy angel told him to ask you to come to his house so that he could hear what you have to say." ²³Then Peter invited the men into the house to be his guests.

Peter at Cornelius's House

The next day Peter started out with them, and some of the believers from Joppa went along. ²⁴The following day he arrived in Caesarea. Cornelius was expecting them and had called together his relatives and close friends. ²⁵As Peter entered the house, Cornelius met him and fell at his feet in reverence. ²⁶But Peter made him get up. "Stand up," he said, "I am only human myself."

²⁷While talking with him, Peter went inside and found a large gathering of people. ²⁸He said to them: "You are well aware that it is against our law for a Jew to associate with Gentiles or visit them. But God has shown me that I should not call anyone impure or unclean. ²⁹So when I was sent for, I came without raising any objection. May I ask why you sent for me?"

³⁰Cornelius answered: "Three days ago I was in my house praying at this hour, at three in the afternoon. Suddenly a man in shining clothes stood before me ³¹and said, 'Cornelius, God has heard your prayer and remembered your gifts to the poor. ³²Send to Joppa for Simon who is called Peter. He is a guest in the home of Simon the tanner, who lives by the sea.' ³³So I sent for you immediately, and it was good of you to come. Now we are all here in the presence of God to listen to everything the Lord has commanded you to tell us."

³⁴Then Peter began to speak: "I now realize how true it is that God does not show favoritism ³⁵but accepts those from every nation who fear him and do what is right. ³⁶You know the message God sent to the people of Israel, announcing the good news of peace through Jesus Christ, who is Lord of all. ³⁷You know what has happened throughout the province of Judea, beginning in Galilee after the baptism that John preached— ³⁸how God anointed Jesus of Nazareth with the Holy Spirit and power, and how he went around doing good and healing all who were under the power of the devil, because God was with him.

³⁹"We are witnesses of everything he did in the country of the Jews and in Jerusalem. They killed him by hanging him on a tree, ⁴⁰but God raised him from the dead on the third day and caused him to be seen. ⁴¹He was not seen by all the people, but by witnesses whom God had already chosen—by us who ate and drank with him after he rose from the dead. ⁴²He commanded us to preach to the people and to testify that he is the one whom God appointed as judge of the living and the dead. ⁴³All the prophets testify about him that everyone who believes in him receives forgiveness of sins through his name."

⁴⁴While Peter was still speaking these words, the Holy Spirit came on all who heard the message. ⁴⁵The circumcised believers who had come with Peter were astonished that the gift of the Holy Spirit had been poured out even on Gentiles. ⁴⁶For they heard them speaking in tongues*a* and praising God.

a 46 Or other languages

Then Peter said, [47]"Surely no one can stand in the way of their being baptized with water. They have received the Holy Spirit just as we have." [48]So he ordered that they be baptized in the name of Jesus Christ. Then they asked Peter to stay with them for a few days.

Peter Explains His Actions

11 The apostles and the believers throughout Judea heard that the Gentiles also had received the word of God. [2]So when Peter went up to Jerusalem, the circumcised believers criticized him [3]and said, "You went into the house of uncircumcised men and ate with them."

[4]Starting from the beginning, Peter told them the whole story: [5]"I was in the city of Joppa praying, and in a trance I saw a vision. I saw something like a large sheet being let down from heaven by its four corners, and it came down to where I was. [6]I looked into it and saw four-footed animals of the earth, wild beasts, reptiles and birds. [7]Then I heard a voice telling me, 'Get up, Peter. Kill and eat.'

[8]"I replied, 'Surely not, Lord! Nothing impure or unclean has ever entered my mouth.'

[9]"The voice spoke from heaven a second time, 'Do not call anything impure that God has made clean.' [10]This happened three times, and then it was all pulled up to heaven again.

[11]"Right then three men who had been sent to me from Caesarea stopped at the house where I was staying. [12]The Spirit told me to have no hesitation about going with them. These six brothers also went with me, and we entered the man's house. [13]He told us how he had seen an angel appear in his house and say, 'Send to Joppa for Simon who is called Peter. [14]He will bring you a message through which you and all your household will be saved.'

[15]"As I began to speak, the Holy Spirit came on them as he had come on us at the beginning. [16]Then I remembered what the Lord had said: 'John baptized with[a] water, but you will be baptized with[a] the Holy Spirit.' [17]So if God gave them the same gift as he gave us who believed in the Lord Jesus Christ, who was I to think that I could stand in God's way?"

[18]When they heard this, they had no further objections and praised God, saying, "So then, even to Gentiles God has granted repentance that leads to life."

The Church in Antioch

[19]Now those who had been scattered by the persecution that broke out when Stephen was killed traveled as far as Phoenicia, Cyprus and Antioch, spreading the word only among Jews. [20]Some of them, however, men from Cyprus and Cyrene, went to Antioch and began to speak to Greeks also, telling them the good news about the Lord Jesus. [21]The Lord's hand was with them, and a great number of people believed and turned to the Lord.

[22]News of this reached the ears of the church in Jerusalem, and they sent Barnabas to Antioch. [23]When he arrived and saw what the grace of God had done, he was glad and encouraged them all to remain true to the Lord with

[a] 16 Or *in*

all their hearts. 24He was a good man, full of the Holy Spirit and faith, and a great number of people were brought to the Lord.

25Then Barnabas went to Tarsus to look for Saul, 26and when he found him, he brought him to Antioch. So for a whole year Barnabas and Saul met with the church and taught great numbers of people. The disciples were called Christians first at Antioch.

27During this time some prophets came down from Jerusalem to Antioch. 28One of them, named Agabus, stood up and through the Spirit predicted that a severe famine would spread over the entire Roman world. (This happened during the reign of Claudius.) 29The disciples, as each one was able, decided to provide help for the believers living in Judea. 30This they did, sending their gift to the elders by Barnabas and Saul.

Peter's Miraculous Escape From Prison

12 It was about this time that King Herod arrested some who belonged to the church, intending to persecute them. 2He had James, the brother of John, put to death with the sword. 3When he saw that this met with approval among the Jews, he proceeded to seize Peter also. This happened during the Festival of Unleavened Bread. 4After arresting him, he put him in prison, handing him over to be guarded by four squads of four soldiers each. Herod intended to bring him out for public trial after the Passover.

5So Peter was kept in prison, but the church was earnestly praying to God for him.

6The night before Herod was to bring him to trial, Peter was sleeping between two soldiers, bound with two chains, and sentries stood guard at the entrance. 7Suddenly an angel of the Lord appeared and a light shone in the cell. He struck Peter on the side and woke him up. "Quick, get up!" he said, and the chains fell off Peter's wrists.

8Then the angel said to him, "Put on your clothes and sandals." And Peter did so. "Wrap your cloak around you and follow me," the angel told him. 9Peter followed him out of the prison, but he had no idea that what the angel was doing was really happening; he thought he was seeing a vision. 10They passed the first and second guards and came to the iron gate leading to the city. It opened for them by itself, and they went through it. When they had walked the length of one street, suddenly the angel left him.

11Then Peter came to himself and said, "Now I know without a doubt that the Lord has sent his angel and rescued me from Herod's clutches and from everything the Jewish people were hoping would happen."

12When this had dawned on him, he went to the house of Mary the mother of John, also called Mark, where many people had gathered and were praying. 13Peter knocked at the outer entrance, and a servant named Rhoda came to answer the door. 14When she recognized Peter's voice, she was so overjoyed she ran back without opening it and exclaimed, "Peter is at the door!"

15"You're out of your mind," they told her. When she kept insisting that it was so, they said, "It must be his angel."

16But Peter kept on knocking, and when they opened the door and saw him, they were astonished. 17Peter motioned with his hand for them to be quiet and described how the Lord had brought him out of prison. "Tell James and the other brothers and sisters about this," he said, and then he left for another place.

[18]In the morning, there was no small commotion among the soldiers as to what had become of Peter. [19]After Herod had a thorough search made for him and did not find him, he cross-examined the guards and ordered that they be executed.

Herod's Death

Then Herod went from Judea to Caesarea and stayed there. [20]He had been quarreling with the people of Tyre and Sidon; they now joined together and sought an audience with him. Having secured the support of Blastus, a trusted personal servant of the king, they asked for peace, because they depended on the king's country for their food supply.

[21]On the appointed day Herod, wearing his royal robes, sat on his throne and delivered a public address to the people. [22]They shouted, "This is the voice of a god, not of a mere mortal." [23]Immediately, because Herod did not give praise to God, an angel of the Lord struck him down, and he was eaten by worms and died.

[24]But the word of God continued to increase and spread.

Barnabas and Saul Sent Off

[25]When Barnabas and Saul had finished their mission, they returned from[a] Jerusalem, taking with them John, also called Mark. **13** [1]Now in the church at Antioch there were prophets and teachers: Barnabas, Simeon called Niger, Lucius of Cyrene, Manaen (who had been brought up with Herod the tetrarch) and Saul. [2]While they were worshiping the Lord and fasting, the Holy Spirit said, "Set apart for me Barnabas and Saul for the work to which I have called them." [3]So after they had fasted and prayed, they placed their hands on them and sent them off.

On Cyprus

[4]The two of them, sent on their way by the Holy Spirit, went down to Seleucia and sailed from there to Cyprus. [5]When they arrived at Salamis, they proclaimed the word of God in the Jewish synagogues. John was with them as their helper.

[6]They traveled through the whole island until they came to Paphos. There they met a Jewish sorcerer and false prophet named Bar-Jesus, [7]who was an attendant of the proconsul, Sergius Paulus. The proconsul, an intelligent man, sent for Barnabas and Saul because he wanted to hear the word of God. [8]But Elymas the sorcerer (for that is what his name means) opposed them and tried to turn the proconsul from the faith. [9]Then Saul, who was also called Paul, filled with the Holy Spirit, looked straight at Elymas and said, [10]"You are a child of the devil and an enemy of everything that is right! You are full of all kinds of deceit and trickery. Will you never stop perverting the right ways of the Lord? [11]Now the hand of the Lord is against you. You are going to be blind for a time, not even able to see the light of the sun."

[a] 25 Some manuscripts *to*

Immediately mist and darkness came over him, and he groped about, seeking someone to lead him by the hand. ¹²When the proconsul saw what had happened, he believed, for he was amazed at the teaching about the Lord.

In Pisidian Antioch

¹³From Paphos, Paul and his companions sailed to Perga in Pamphylia, where John left them to return to Jerusalem. ¹⁴From Perga they went on to Pisidian Antioch. On the Sabbath they entered the synagogue and sat down. ¹⁵After the reading from the Law and the Prophets, the leaders of the synagogue sent word to them, saying, "Brothers, if you have a message of encouragement for the people, please speak."

¹⁶Standing up, Paul motioned with his hand and said: "People of Israel and you Gentiles who worship God, listen to me! ¹⁷The God of the people of Israel chose our ancestors, he made the people prosper during their stay in Egypt; with mighty power he led them out of that country; ¹⁸for about forty years he endured their conduct*ᵃ* in the desert; ¹⁹he overthrew seven nations in Canaan, giving their land to his people as their inheritance. ²⁰All this took about 450 years.

"After this, God gave them judges until the time of Samuel the prophet. ²¹Then the people asked for a king, and he gave them Saul son of Kish, of the tribe of Benjamin, who ruled forty years. ²²After removing Saul, he made David their king. God testified concerning him: 'I have found David son of Jesse a man after my own heart; he will do everything I want him to do.'

²³"From this man's descendants God has brought to Israel the Savior Jesus, as he promised. ²⁴Before the coming of Jesus, John preached repentance and baptism to all the people of Israel. ²⁵As John was completing his work, he said: 'Who do you suppose I am? I am not the one you are looking for. But there is someone coming after me whose sandals I am not worthy to untie.'

²⁶"Brothers and sisters from the children of Abraham and you God-fearing Gentiles, it is to us that this message of salvation has been sent. ²⁷The people of Jerusalem and their rulers did not recognize Jesus, yet in condemning him they fulfilled the words of the prophets that are read every Sabbath. ²⁸Though they found no proper ground for a death sentence, they asked Pilate to have him executed. ²⁹When they had carried out all that was written about him, they took him down from the tree and laid him in a tomb. ³⁰But God raised him from the dead, ³¹and for many days he was seen by those who had traveled with him from Galilee to Jerusalem. They are now his witnesses to our people.

³²"We tell you the good news: What God promised our ancestors ³³he has fulfilled for us, their children, by raising up Jesus. As it is written in the second Psalm:

" 'You are my Son;
        today I have become your Father.*ᵇ ᶜ*

³⁴God raised him from the dead so that he will never be subject to decay. As God has said,

ᵃ 18 Some manuscripts *and cared for them*   *ᵇ 33* Or *have begotten you*   *ᶜ 33* Psalm 2:7

" 'I will give you the holy and sure blessings promised to David.'[a]

35So it is also stated elsewhere:

" 'You will not let your Holy One see decay.'[b]

36"For when David had served God's purpose in his own generation, he fell asleep; he was buried with his ancestors and his body decayed. 37But the one whom God raised from the dead did not see decay.

38"Therefore, my brothers and sisters, I want you to know that through Jesus the forgiveness of sins is proclaimed to you. 39Through him everyone who believes is set free from every sin, a justification you were not able to obtain under the law of Moses. 40Take care that what the prophets have said does not happen to you:

41" 'Look, you scoffers,
    wonder and perish,
  for I am going to do something in your days
    that you would never believe,
    even if someone told you.'[c]"

42As Paul and Barnabas were leaving the synagogue, the people invited them to speak further about these things on the next Sabbath. 43When the congregation was dismissed, many of the Jews and devout converts to Judaism followed Paul and Barnabas, who talked with them and urged them to continue in the grace of God.

44On the next Sabbath almost the whole city gathered to hear the word of the Lord. 45When the Jews saw the crowds, they were filled with jealousy. They began to contradict what Paul was saying and heaped abuse on him.

46Then Paul and Barnabas answered them boldly: "We had to speak the word of God to you first. Since you reject it and do not consider yourselves worthy of eternal life, we now turn to the Gentiles. 47For this is what the Lord has commanded us:

" 'I have made you[d] a light for the Gentiles,
    that you[d] may bring salvation to the ends of the earth.'[e]"

48When the Gentiles heard this, they were glad and honored the word of the Lord; and all who were appointed for eternal life believed.

49The word of the Lord spread through the whole region. 50But the Jewish leaders incited the God-fearing women of high standing and the leading men of the city. They stirred up persecution against Paul and Barnabas and expelled them from their region. 51So they shook the dust off their feet as a warning to them and went to Iconium. 52And the disciples were filled with joy and with the Holy Spirit.

In Iconium

14 At Iconium Paul and Barnabas went as usual into the Jewish synagogue. There they spoke so effectively that a great number of Jews and Gentiles believed. 2But the Jews who refused to believe stirred up the Gentiles

---

[a] 34 Isaiah 55:3   [b] 35 Psalm 16:10   [c] 41 Hab. 1:5   [d] 47 The Greek is singular.   [e] 47 Isaiah 49:6

and poisoned their minds against the brothers. [3]So Paul and Barnabas spent considerable time there, speaking boldly for the Lord, who confirmed the message of his grace by enabling them to do miraculous signs and wonders. [4]The people of the city were divided; some sided with the Jews, others with the apostles. [5]There was a plot afoot among both Gentiles and Jews, together with their leaders, to mistreat them and stone them. [6]But they found out about it and fled to the Lycaonian cities of Lystra and Derbe and to the surrounding country, [7]where they continued to preach the gospel.

In Lystra and Derbe

[8]In Lystra there sat a man who was lame. He had been that way from birth and had never walked. [9]He listened to Paul as he was speaking. Paul looked directly at him, saw that he had faith to be healed [10]and called out, "Stand up on your feet!" At that, the man jumped up and began to walk.

[11]When the crowd saw what Paul had done, they shouted in the Lycaonian language, "The gods have come down to us in human form!" [12]Barnabas they called Zeus, and Paul they called Hermes because he was the chief speaker. [13]The priest of Zeus, whose temple was just outside the city, brought bulls and wreaths to the city gates because he and the crowd wanted to offer sacrifices to them.

[14]But when the apostles Barnabas and Paul heard of this, they tore their clothes and rushed out into the crowd, shouting: [15]"Friends, why are you doing this? We too are only human, like you. We are bringing you good news, telling you to turn from these worthless things to the living God, who made heaven and earth and sea and everything in them. [16]In the past, he let all nations go their own way. [17]Yet he has not left himself without testimony: He has shown kindness by giving you rain from heaven and crops in their seasons; he provides you with plenty of food and fills your hearts with joy." [18]Even with these words, they had difficulty keeping the crowd from sacrificing to them.

[19]Then some Jews came from Antioch and Iconium and won the crowd over. They stoned Paul and dragged him outside the city, thinking he was dead. [20]But after the disciples had gathered around him, he got up and went back into the city. The next day he and Barnabas left for Derbe.

The Return to Antioch in Syria

[21]They preached the gospel in that city and won a large number of disciples. Then they returned to Lystra, Iconium and Antioch, [22]strengthening the disciples and encouraging them to remain true to the faith. "We must go through many hardships to enter the kingdom of God," they said. [23]Paul and Barnabas appointed elders[a] for them in each church and, with prayer and fasting, committed them to the Lord, in whom they had put their trust. [24]After going through Pisidia, they came into Pamphylia, [25]and when they had preached the word in Perga, they went down to Attalia.

[26]From Attalia they sailed back to Antioch, where they had been committed to the grace of God for the work they had now completed. [27]On arriving there,

[a] 23 Or *Barnabas ordained elders; or Barnabas had elders elected*

they gathered the church together and reported all that God had done through them and how he had opened a door of faith to the Gentiles. [28]And they stayed there a long time with the disciples.

The Council at Jerusalem

15 Certain individuals came down from Judea to Antioch and were teaching the believers: "Unless you are circumcised, according to the custom taught by Moses, you cannot be saved." [2]This brought Paul and Barnabas into sharp dispute and debate with them. So Paul and Barnabas were appointed, along with some other believers, to go up to Jerusalem to see the apostles and elders about this question. [3]The church sent them on their way, and as they traveled through Phoenicia and Samaria, they told how the Gentiles had been converted. This news made all the believers very glad. [4]When they came to Jerusalem, they were welcomed by the church and the apostles and elders, to whom they reported everything God had done through them.

[5]Then some of the believers who belonged to the party of the Pharisees stood up and said, "The Gentiles must be circumcised and required to keep the law of Moses."

[6]The apostles and elders met to consider this question. [7]After much discussion, Peter got up and addressed them: "Brothers, you know that some time ago God made a choice among you that the Gentiles might hear from my lips the message of the gospel and believe. [8]God, who knows the heart, showed that he accepted them by giving the Holy Spirit to them, just as he did to us. [9]He did not discriminate between us and them, for he purified their hearts by faith. [10]Now then, why do you try to test God by putting on the necks of Gentiles a yoke that neither we nor our ancestors have been able to bear? [11]No! We believe it is through the grace of our Lord Jesus that we are saved, just as they are."

[12]The whole assembly became silent as they listened to Barnabas and Paul telling about the miraculous signs and wonders God had done among the Gentiles through them. [13]When they finished, James spoke up. "Brothers," he said, "listen to me. [14]Simon[a] has described to us how God first intervened to choose a people for his name from the Gentiles. [15]The words of the prophets are in agreement with this, as it is written:

[16]" 'After this I will return
          and rebuild David's fallen tent.
      Its ruins I will rebuild,
          and I will restore it,
  [17]that the rest of humanity may seek the Lord,
          even all the Gentiles who bear my name,
      says the Lord, who does these things'[b]—
  [18]   things known from long ago.[c]

[19]"It is my judgment, therefore, that we should not make it difficult for the Gentiles who are turning to God. [20]Instead we should write to them, telling

---

[a] 14 Greek *Simeon*, a variant of *Simon*; that is, Peter   [b] 17 Amos 9:11,12   [c] 17,18 Some manuscripts *things'— / 18known to the Lord from long ago is his work*

them to abstain from food polluted by idols, from sexual immorality, from the meat of strangled animals and from blood. 21For the law of Moses has been preached in every city from the earliest times and is read in the synagogues on every Sabbath."

The Council's Letter to Gentile Believers

22Then the apostles and elders, with the whole church, decided to choose some of their own men and send them to Antioch with Paul and Barnabas. They chose Judas (called Barsabbas) and Silas, who were leaders among the believers. 23With them they sent the following letter:

The apostles and elders, your brothers,

To the Gentile believers in Antioch, Syria and Cilicia:

Greetings.

24We have heard that some went out from us without our authorization and disturbed you, troubling your minds by what they said. 25So we all agreed to choose some men and send them to you with our dear friends Barnabas and Paul— 26men who have risked their lives for the name of our Lord Jesus Christ. 27Therefore we are sending Judas and Silas to confirm by word of mouth what we are writing. 28It seemed good to the Holy Spirit and to us not to burden you with anything beyond the following requirements: 29You are to abstain from food sacrificed to idols, from blood, from the meat of strangled animals and from sexual immorality. You will do well to avoid these things.

Farewell.

30So they were sent off and went down to Antioch, where they gathered the church together and delivered the letter. 31The people read it and were glad for its encouraging message. 32Judas and Silas, who themselves were prophets, said much to encourage and strengthen the believers. 33[34]After spending some time there, they were sent off by the believers with the blessing of peace to return to those who had sent them. 35But Paul and Barnabas remained in Antioch, where they and many others taught and preached the word of the Lord.

Disagreement Between Paul and Barnabas

36Some time later Paul said to Barnabas, "Let us go back and visit the believers in all the towns where we preached the word of the Lord and see how they are doing." 37Barnabas wanted to take John, also called Mark, with them, 38but Paul did not think it wise to take him, because he had deserted them in Pamphylia and had not continued with them in the work. 39They had such a sharp disagreement that they parted company. Barnabas took Mark and sailed for Cyprus, 40but Paul chose Silas and left, commended by the believers to the grace of the Lord. 41He went through Syria and Cilicia, strengthening the churches.

Timothy Joins Paul and Silas

16 Paul came to Derbe and then to Lystra, where a disciple named Timo- thy lived, whose mother was Jewish and a believer but whose father was a Greek. 2The believers at Lystra and Iconium spoke well of him. 3Paul wanted to take him along on the journey, so he circumcised him because of the Jews who lived in that area, for they all knew that his father was a Greek. 4As they traveled from town to town, they delivered the decisions reached by the apostles and elders in Jerusalem for the people to obey. 5So the churches were strengthened in the faith and grew daily in numbers.

Paul's Vision of the Man of Macedonia

6Paul and his companions traveled throughout the region of Phrygia and Galatia, having been kept by the Holy Spirit from preaching the word in the province of Asia. 7When they came to the border of Mysia, they tried to enter Bithynia, but the Spirit of Jesus would not allow them to. 8So they passed by Mysia and went down to Troas. 9During the night Paul had a vision of a man of Macedonia standing and begging him, "Come over to Macedonia and help us." 10After Paul had seen the vision, we got ready at once to leave for Mace- donia, concluding that God had called us to preach the gospel to them.

Lydia's Conversion in Philippi

11From Troas we put out to sea and sailed straight for Samothrace, and the next day we went on to Neapolis. 12From there we traveled to Philippi, a Roman colony and the leading city of that district*a* of Macedonia. And we stayed there several days.

13On the Sabbath we went outside the city gate to the river, where we ex- pected to find a place of prayer. We sat down and began to speak to the women who had gathered there. 14One of those listening was a woman from the city of Thyatira named Lydia, a dealer in purple cloth. She was a wor- shiper of God. The Lord opened her heart to respond to Paul's message. 15When she and the members of her household were baptized, she invited us to her home. "If you consider me a believer in the Lord," she said, "come and stay at my house." And she persuaded us.

Paul and Silas in Prison

16Once when we were going to the place of prayer, we were met by a female slave who had a spirit by which she predicted the future. She earned a great deal of money for her owners by fortune-telling. 17She followed Paul and the rest of us, shouting, "These men are servants of the Most High God, who are telling you the way to be saved." 18She kept this up for many days. Finally Paul became so annoyed that he turned around and said to the spirit, "In the name of Jesus Christ I command you to come out of her!" At that moment the spirit left her.

19When her owners realized that their hope of making money was gone, they seized Paul and Silas and dragged them into the marketplace to face the authorities. 20They brought them before the magistrates and said, "These men

---

a 12 The text and meaning of the Greek for *the leading city of that district* are uncertain.

are Jews, and are throwing our city into an uproar [21]by advocating customs unlawful for us Romans to accept or practice."

[22]The crowd joined in the attack against Paul and Silas, and the magistrates ordered them to be stripped and beaten with rods. [23]After they had been severely flogged, they were thrown into prison, and the jailer was commanded to guard them carefully. [24]Upon receiving such orders, he put them in the inner cell and fastened their feet in the stocks.

[25]About midnight Paul and Silas were praying and singing hymns to God, and the other prisoners were listening to them. [26]Suddenly there was such a violent earthquake that the foundations of the prison were shaken. At once all the prison doors flew open, and everyone's chains came loose. [27]The jailer woke up, and when he saw the prison doors open, he drew his sword and was about to kill himself because he thought the prisoners had escaped. [28]But Paul shouted, "Don't harm yourself! We are all here!"

[29]The jailer called for lights, rushed in and fell trembling before Paul and Silas. [30]He then brought them out and asked, "Sirs, what must I do to be saved?"

[31]They replied, "Believe in the Lord Jesus, and you will be saved—you and your household." [32]Then they spoke the word of the Lord to him and to all the others in his house. [33]At that hour of the night the jailer took them and washed their wounds; then immediately he and all his household were baptized. [34]The jailer brought them into his house and set a meal before them; he was filled with joy because he had come to believe in God—he and his whole household.

[35]When it was daylight, the magistrates sent their officers to the jailer with the order: "Release those men." [36]The jailer told Paul, "The magistrates have ordered that you and Silas be released. Now you can leave. Go in peace."

[37]But Paul said to the officers: "They beat us publicly without a trial, even though we are Roman citizens, and threw us into prison. And now do they want to get rid of us quietly? No! Let them come themselves and escort us out."

[38]The officers reported this to the magistrates, and when they heard that Paul and Silas were Roman citizens, they were alarmed. [39]They came to appease them and escorted them from the prison, requesting them to leave the city. [40]After Paul and Silas came out of the prison, they went to Lydia's house, where they met with the believers and encouraged them. Then they left.

In Thessalonica

17 When Paul and his companions had passed through Amphipolis and Apollonia, they came to Thessalonica, where there was a Jewish synagogue. [2]As his custom was, Paul went into the synagogue, and on three Sabbath days he reasoned with them from the Scriptures, [3]explaining and proving that the Messiah had to suffer and rise from the dead. "This Jesus I am proclaiming to you is the Messiah," he said. [4]Some of the Jews were persuaded and joined Paul and Silas, as did a large number of God-fearing Greeks and not a few prominent women.

[5]But other Jews were jealous; so they rounded up some bad characters from the marketplace, formed a mob and started a riot in the city. They rushed to

Jason's house in search of Paul and Silas in order to bring them out to the crowd.*⁶But when they did not find them, they dragged Jason and some other believers before the city officials, shouting: "These men who have caused trouble all over the world have now come here, ⁷and Jason has welcomed them into his house. They are all defying Caesar's decrees, saying that there is another king, one called Jesus." ⁸When they heard this, the crowd and the city officials were thrown into turmoil. ⁹Then they made Jason and the others post bond and let them go.

In Berea

¹⁰As soon as it was night, the believers sent Paul and Silas away to Berea. On arriving there, they went to the Jewish synagogue. ¹¹Now the Berean Jews were of more noble character than those in Thessalonica, for they received the message with great eagerness and examined the Scriptures every day to see if what Paul said was true. ¹²Many of them believed, as did also a number of prominent Greek women and many Greek men.

¹³But when the Jews in Thessalonica learned that Paul was preaching the word of God at Berea, some of them went there too, agitating the crowds and stirring them up. ¹⁴The believers immediately sent Paul to the coast, but Silas and Timothy stayed at Berea. ¹⁵Those who escorted Paul brought him to Athens and then left with instructions for Silas and Timothy to join him as soon as possible.

In Athens

¹⁶While Paul was waiting for them in Athens, he was greatly distressed to see that the city was full of idols. ¹⁷So he reasoned in the synagogue with both Jews and God-fearing Greeks, as well as in the marketplace day by day with those who happened to be there. ¹⁸A group of Epicurean and Stoic philosophers began to debate with him. Some of them asked, "What is this babbler trying to say?" Others remarked, "He seems to be advocating foreign gods." They said this because Paul was preaching the good news about Jesus and the resurrection. ¹⁹Then they took him and brought him to a meeting of the Areopagus, where they said to him, "May we know what this new teaching is that you are presenting? ²⁰You are bringing some strange ideas to our ears, and we would like to know what they mean." ²¹(All the Athenians and the foreigners who lived there spent their time doing nothing but talking about and listening to the latest ideas.)

²²Paul then stood up in the meeting of the Areopagus and said: "People of Athens! I see that in every way you are very religious. ²³For as I walked around and looked carefully at your objects of worship, I even found an altar with this inscription: TO AN UNKNOWN GOD. So you are ignorant of the very thing you worship—and this is what I am going to proclaim to you.

²⁴"The God who made the world and everything in it is the Lord of heaven and earth and does not live in temples built by hands. ²⁵And he is not served by human hands, as if he needed anything. Rather, he himself gives everyone life and breath and everything else. ²⁶From one man he made all the nations,

ᵃ 5 Or the assembly of the people

that they should inhabit the whole earth; and he marked out their appointed times in history and the boundaries of their lands. 27God did this so that they would seek him and perhaps reach out for him and find him, though he is not far from any one of us. 28'For in him we live and move and have our being.'ᵃ As some of your own poets have said, 'We are his offspring.'ᵇ

29"Therefore since we are God's offspring, we should not think that the divine being is like gold or silver or stone—an image made by human design and skill. 30In the past God overlooked such ignorance, but now he commands all people everywhere to repent. 31For he has set a day when he will judge the world with justice by the man he has appointed. He has given proof of this to everyone by raising him from the dead."

32When they heard about the resurrection of the dead, some of them sneered, but others said, "We want to hear you again on this subject." 33At that, Paul left the Council. 34Some of the people became followers of Paul and believed. Among them was Dionysius, a member of the Areopagus, also a woman named Damaris, and a number of others.

In Corinth

18 After this, Paul left Athens and went to Corinth. 2There he met a Jew named Aquila, a native of Pontus, who had recently come from Italy with his wife Priscilla, because Claudius had ordered all Jews to leave Rome. Paul went to see them, 3and because he was a tentmaker as they were, he stayed and worked with them. 4Every Sabbath he reasoned in the synagogue, trying to persuade Jews and Greeks.

5When Silas and Timothy came from Macedonia, Paul devoted himself exclusively to preaching, testifying to the Jews that Jesus was the Messiah. 6But when they opposed Paul and became abusive, he shook out his clothes in protest and said to them, "Your blood be on your own heads! I am innocent of it. From now on I will go to the Gentiles."

7Then Paul left the synagogue and went next door to the house of Titius Justus, a worshiper of God. 8Crispus, the synagogue leader, and his entire household believed in the Lord; and many of the Corinthians who heard Paul believed and were baptized.

9One night the Lord spoke to Paul in a vision: "Do not be afraid; keep on speaking, do not be silent. 10For I am with you, and no one is going to attack and harm you, because I have many people in this city." 11So Paul stayed in Corinth for a year and a half, teaching them the word of God.

12While Gallio was proconsul of Achaia, the Jews of Corinth made a united attack on Paul and brought him to the place of judgment. 13"This man," they charged, "is persuading the people to worship God in ways contrary to the law."

14Just as Paul was about to speak, Gallio said to them, "If you Jews were making a complaint about some misdemeanor or serious crime, it would be reasonable for me to listen to you. 15But since it involves questions about words and names and your own law—settle the matter yourselves. I will not be a judge of such things." 16So he drove them off. 17Then the crowd there

ᵃ 28 From the Cretan philosopher Epimenides   ᵇ 28 From the Cilician Stoic philosopher Aratus

turned on Sosthenes the synagogue leader and beat him in front of the proconsul; and Gallio showed no concern whatever.

Priscilla, Aquila and Apollos

18Paul stayed on in Corinth for some time. Then he left the believers and sailed for Syria, accompanied by Priscilla and Aquila. Before he sailed, he had his hair cut off at Cenchrea because of a vow he had taken. 19They arrived at Ephesus, where Paul left Priscilla and Aquila. He himself went into the synagogue and reasoned with the Jews. 20When they asked him to spend more time with them, he declined. 21But as he left, he promised, "I will come back if it is God's will." Then he set sail from Ephesus. 22When he landed at Caesarea, he went up to Jerusalem and greeted the church and then went down to Antioch.

23After spending some time in Antioch, Paul set out from there and traveled from place to place throughout the region of Galatia and Phrygia, strengthening all the disciples.

24Meanwhile a Jew named Apollos, a native of Alexandria, came to Ephesus. He was a learned man, with a thorough knowledge of the Scriptures. 25He had been instructed in the way of the Lord, and he spoke with great fervor[a] and taught about Jesus accurately, though he knew only the baptism of John. 26He began to speak boldly in the synagogue. When Priscilla and Aquila heard him, they invited him to their home and explained to him the way of God more adequately.

27When Apollos wanted to go to Achaia, the believers encouraged him and wrote to the disciples there to welcome him. When he arrived, he was a great help to those who by grace had believed. 28For he vigorously refuted the Jews in public debate, proving from the Scriptures that Jesus was the Messiah.

Paul in Ephesus

19 While Apollos was at Corinth, Paul took the road through the interior and arrived at Ephesus. There he found some disciples 2and asked them, "Did you receive the Holy Spirit when[b] you believed?"

They answered, "No, we have not even heard that there is a Holy Spirit."

3So Paul asked, "Then what baptism did you receive?"

"John's baptism," they replied.

4Paul said, "John's baptism was a baptism of repentance. He told the people to believe in the one coming after him, that is, in Jesus." 5On hearing this, they were baptized into[c] the name of the Lord Jesus. 6When Paul placed his hands on them, the Holy Spirit came on them, and they spoke in tongues[d] and prophesied. 7There were about twelve men in all.

8Paul entered the synagogue and spoke boldly there for three months, arguing persuasively about the kingdom of God. 9But some of them became obstinate; they refused to believe and publicly maligned the Way. So Paul left them. He took the disciples with him and had discussions daily in the lecture hall of Tyrannus. 10This went on for two years, so that all the Jews and Greeks who lived in the province of Asia heard the word of the Lord.

---

a 25 Or with fervor in the Spirit   *b 2 Or after*   *c 5 Or in*   *d 6 Or other languages*

[11]God did extraordinary miracles through Paul, [12]so that even handker-chiefs and aprons that had touched him were taken to the sick, and their ill-nesses were cured and the evil spirits left them.

[13]Some Jews who went around driving out evil spirits tried to invoke the name of the Lord Jesus over those who were demon-possessed. They would say, "In the name of the Jesus whom Paul preaches, I command you to come out." [14]Seven sons of Sceva, a Jewish chief priest, were doing this. [15]One day, the evil spirit answered them, "Jesus I know, and I know about Paul, but who are you?" [16]Then the man who had the evil spirit jumped on them and over-powered them all. He gave them such a beating that they ran out of the house naked and bleeding.

[17]When this became known to the Jews and Greeks living in Ephesus, they were all seized with fear, and the name of the Lord Jesus was held in high honor. [18]Many of those who believed now came and openly confessed what they had done. [19]A number who had practiced sorcery brought their scrolls together and burned them publicly. When they calculated the value of the scrolls, the total came to fifty thousand drachmas.[a] [20]In this way the word of the Lord spread widely and grew in power.

[21]After all this had happened, Paul decided[b] to go to Jerusalem, passing through Macedonia and Achaia. "After I have been there," he said, "I must visit Rome also." [22]He sent two of his helpers, Timothy and Erastus, to Mace-donia, while he stayed in the province of Asia a little longer.

The Riot in Ephesus

[23]About that time there arose a great disturbance about the Way. [24]A silver-smith named Demetrius, who made silver shrines of Artemis, brought in no little business for the skilled workers there. [25]He called them together, along with the workers in related trades, and said: "You know, my friends, that we receive a good income from this business. [26]And you see and hear how this fellow Paul has convinced and led astray large numbers of people here in Ephesus and in practically the whole province of Asia. He says that gods made by human hands are no gods at all. [27]There is danger not only that our trade will lose its good name, but also that the temple of the great goddess Ar-temis will be discredited, and the goddess herself, who is worshiped through-out the province of Asia and the world, will be robbed of her divine majesty."

[28]When they heard this, they were furious and began shouting: "Great is Artemis of the Ephesians!" [29]Soon the whole city was in an uproar. The peo-ple seized Gaius and Aristarchus, Paul's traveling companions from Macedo-nia, and they all rushed together into the theater. [30]Paul wanted to appear be-fore the crowd, but the disciples would not let him. [31]Even some of the officials of the province, friends of Paul, sent him a message begging him not to venture into the theater.

[32]The assembly was in confusion: Some were shouting one thing, some an-other. Most of the people did not even know why they were there. [33]The Jews in the crowd pushed Alexander to the front, and they shouted instructions to him. He motioned for silence in order to make a defense before the people.

[a] 19 A drachma was a silver coin worth about a day's wages.   [b] 21 Or decided in the Spirit

34But when they realized he was a Jew, they all shouted in unison for about two hours: "Great is Artemis of the Ephesians!"

35The city clerk quieted the crowd and said: "People of Ephesus, doesn't all the world know that the city of Ephesus is the guardian of the temple of the great Artemis and of her image, which fell from heaven? 36Therefore, since these facts are undeniable, you ought to calm down and not do anything rash. 37You have brought these men here, though they have neither robbed temples nor blasphemed our goddess. 38If, then, Demetrius and his associates have a grievance against anybody, the courts are open and there are proconsuls. They can press charges. 39If there is anything further you want to bring up, it must be settled in a legal assembly. 40As it is, we are in danger of being charged with rioting because of what happened today. In that case we would not be able to account for this commotion, since there is no reason for it." 41After he had said this, he dismissed the assembly.

Through Macedonia and Greece

20 When the uproar had ended, Paul sent for the disciples and, after encouraging them, said good-by and set out for Macedonia. 2He traveled through that area, speaking many words of encouragement to the people, and finally arrived in Greece, 3where he stayed three months. Because some Jews had plotted against him just as he was about to sail for Syria, he decided to go back through Macedonia. 4He was accompanied by Sopater son of Pyrrhus from Berea, Aristarchus and Secundus from Thessalonica, Gaius from Derbe, Timothy also, and Tychicus and Trophimus from the province of Asia. 5These men went on ahead and waited for us at Troas. 6But we sailed from Philippi after the Festival of Unleavened Bread, and five days later joined the others at Troas, where we stayed seven days.

Eutychus Raised From the Dead at Troas

7On the first day of the week we came together to break bread. Paul spoke to the people and, because he intended to leave the next day, kept on talking until midnight. 8There were many lamps in the upstairs room where we were meeting. 9Seated in a window was a young man named Eutychus, who was sinking into a deep sleep as Paul talked on and on. When he was sound asleep, he fell to the ground from the third story and was picked up dead. 10Paul went down, threw himself on the young man and put his arms around him. "Don't be alarmed," he said. "He's alive!" 11Then he went upstairs again and broke bread and ate. After talking until daylight, he left. 12The people took the young man home alive and were greatly comforted.

Paul's Farewell to the Ephesian Elders

13We went on ahead to the ship and sailed for Assos, where we were going to take Paul aboard. He had made this arrangement because he was going there on foot. 14When he met us at Assos, we took him aboard and went on to Mitylene. 15The next day we set sail from there and arrived off Kios. The day after that we crossed over to Samos, and on the following day arrived at Miletus. 16Paul had decided to sail past Ephesus to avoid spending time in the province of Asia, for he was in a hurry to reach Jerusalem, if possible, by the day of Pentecost.

[17]From Miletus, Paul sent to Ephesus for the elders of the church. [18]When they arrived, he said to them: "You know how I lived the whole time I was with you, from the first day I came into the province of Asia. [19]I served the Lord with great humility and with tears and in the midst of severe testing by the plots of the Jews. [20]You know that I have not hesitated to preach anything that would be helpful to you but have taught you publicly and from house to house. [21]I have declared to both Jews and Greeks that they must turn to God in repentance and have faith in our Lord Jesus.

[22]"And now, compelled by the Spirit, I am going to Jerusalem, not knowing what will happen to me there. [23]I only know that in every city the Holy Spirit warns me that prison and hardships are facing me. [24]However, I consider my life worth nothing to me; my only aim is to finish the race and complete the task the Lord Jesus has given me—the task of testifying to the good news of God's grace.

[25]"Now I know that none of you among whom I have gone about preaching the kingdom will ever see me again. [26]Therefore, I declare to you today that I am innocent of the blood of everyone. [27]For I have not hesitated to proclaim to you the whole will of God. [28]Keep watch over yourselves and all the flock of which the Holy Spirit has made you overseers.[a] Be shepherds of the church of God,[b] which he bought with his own blood. [29]I know that after I leave, savage wolves will come in among you and will not spare the flock. [30]Even from your own number some will arise and distort the truth in order to draw away disciples after them. [31]So be on your guard! Remember that for three years I never stopped warning each of you night and day with tears.

[32]"Now I commit you to God and to the word of his grace, which can build you up and give you an inheritance among all those who are sanctified. [33]I have not coveted anyone's silver or gold or clothing. [34]You yourselves know that these hands of mine have supplied my own needs and the needs of my companions. [35]In everything I did, I showed you that by this kind of hard work we must help the weak, remembering the words the Lord Jesus himself said: 'It is more blessed to give than to receive.' "

[36]When Paul had finished speaking, he knelt down with all of them and prayed. [37]They all wept as they embraced him and kissed him. [38]What grieved them most was his statement that they would never see his face again. Then they accompanied him to the ship.

On to Jerusalem

21 After we had torn ourselves away from them, we put out to sea and sailed straight to Cos. The next day we went to Rhodes and from there to Patara. [2]We found a ship crossing over to Phoenicia, went on board and set sail. [3]After sighting Cyprus and passing to the south of it, we sailed on to Syria. We landed at Tyre, where our ship was to unload its cargo. [4]We sought out the disciples there and stayed with them seven days. Through the Spirit they urged Paul not to go on to Jerusalem. [5]When it was time to leave, we left

---

[a]28 Traditionally *bishops*   [b]28 Many manuscripts *of the Lord*

and continued on our way. All of them, including wives and children, accompanied us out of the city, and there on the beach we knelt to pray. 6After saying good-by to each other, we went aboard the ship, and they returned home.

7We continued our voyage from Tyre and landed at Ptolemais, where we greeted the believers and stayed with them for a day. 8Leaving the next day, we reached Caesarea and stayed at the house of Philip the evangelist, one of the Seven. 9He had four unmarried daughters who prophesied.

10After we had been there a number of days, a prophet named Agabus came down from Judea. 11Coming over to us, he took Paul's belt, tied his own hands and feet with it and said, "The Holy Spirit says, 'In this way the Jewish leaders in Jerusalem will bind the owner of this belt and will hand him over to the Gentiles.' "

12When we heard this, we and the people there pleaded with Paul not to go up to Jerusalem. 13Then Paul answered, "Why are you weeping and breaking my heart? I am ready not only to be bound, but also to die in Jerusalem for the name of the Lord Jesus." 14When he would not be dissuaded, we gave up and said, "The Lord's will be done."

15After this, we started on our way up to Jerusalem. 16Some of the disciples from Caesarea accompanied us and brought us to the home of Mnason, where we were to stay. He was a man from Cyprus and one of the early disciples.

Paul's Arrival at Jerusalem

17When we arrived at Jerusalem, the believers received us warmly. 18The next day Paul and the rest of us went to see James, and all the elders were present. 19Paul greeted them and reported in detail what God had done among the Gentiles through his ministry.

20When they heard this, they praised God. Then they said to Paul: "You see, brother, how many thousands of Jews have believed, and all of them are zealous for the law. 21They have been informed that you teach all the Jews who live among the Gentiles to turn away from Moses, telling them not to circumcise their children or live according to our customs. 22What shall we do? They will certainly hear that you have come, 23so do what we tell you. There are four men with us who have made a vow. 24Take these men, join in their purification rites and pay their expenses, so that they can have their heads shaved. Then everyone will know there is no truth in these reports about you, but that you yourself are living in obedience to the law. 25As for the Gentile believers, we have written to them our decision that they should abstain from food sacrificed to idols, from blood, from the meat of strangled animals and from sexual immorality."

26The next day Paul took the men and purified himself along with them. Then he went to the temple to give notice of the date when the days of purification would end and the offering would be made for each of them.

Paul Arrested

27When the seven days were nearly over, some Jews from the province of Asia saw Paul at the temple. They stirred up the whole crowd and seized him, 28shouting, "People of Israel, help us! This is the man who teaches everyone everywhere against our people and our law and this place. And besides, he has brought Greeks into the temple and defiled this holy place." ²⁹(They had previously seen Trophimus the Ephesian in the city with Paul and assumed that Paul had brought him into the temple.)

³⁰The whole city was aroused, and the people came running from all directions. Seizing Paul, they dragged him from the temple, and immediately the gates were shut. ³¹While they were trying to kill him, news reached the commander of the Roman troops that the whole city of Jerusalem was in an uproar. ³²He at once took some officers and soldiers and ran down to the crowd. When the rioters saw the commander and his soldiers, they stopped beating Paul.

³³The commander came up and arrested him and ordered him to be bound with two chains. Then he asked who he was and what he had done. ³⁴Some in the crowd shouted one thing and some another, and since the commander could not get at the truth because of the uproar, he ordered that Paul be taken into the barracks. ³⁵When Paul reached the steps, the violence of the mob was so great he had to be carried by the soldiers. ³⁶The crowd that followed kept shouting, "Get rid of him!"

Paul Speaks to the Crowd

³⁷As the soldiers were about to take Paul into the barracks, he asked the commander, "May I say something to you?"

"Do you speak Greek?" he replied. ³⁸"Aren't you the Egyptian who started a revolt and led four thousand terrorists out into the desert some time ago?"

³⁹Paul answered, "I am a Jew, from Tarsus in Cilicia, a citizen of no ordinary city. Please let me speak to the people."

⁴⁰Having received the commander's permission, Paul stood on the steps and motioned to the crowd. When they were all silent, he said to them in

22 Aramaic*ᵃ*: ¹"Brothers and fathers, listen now to my defense." ²When they heard him speak to them in Aramaic, they became very quiet.

Then Paul said: ³"I am a Jew, born in Tarsus of Cilicia, but brought up in this city. I studied under Gamaliel and was thoroughly trained in the law of our ancestors. I was just as zealous for God as any of you are today. ⁴I persecuted the followers of this Way to their death, arresting both men and women and throwing them into prison, ⁵as the high priest and all the Council can themselves testify. I even obtained letters from them to their associates in Damascus, and went there to bring these people as prisoners to Jerusalem to be punished.

⁶"About noon as I came near Damascus, suddenly a bright light from heaven flashed around me. ⁷I fell to the ground and heard a voice say to me, 'Saul! Saul! Why do you persecute me?'

⁸" 'Who are you, Lord?' I asked.

" 'I am Jesus of Nazareth, whom you are persecuting,' he replied. ⁹My companions saw the light, but they did not understand the voice of him who was speaking to me.

ᵃ *40* Or possibly *Hebrew*; also in 22:2

[10]" 'What shall I do, Lord?' I asked.

" 'Get up,' the Lord said, 'and go into Damascus. There you will be told all that you have been assigned to do.' [11]My companions led me by the hand into Damascus, because the brilliance of the light had blinded me.

[12]"A man named Ananias came to see me. He was a devout observer of the law and highly respected by all the Jews living there. [13]He stood beside me and said, 'Brother Saul, receive your sight!' And at that very moment I was able to see him.

[14]"Then he said: 'The God of our ancestors has chosen you to know his will and to see the Righteous One and to hear words from his mouth. [15]You will be his witness to all people of what you have seen and heard. [16]And now what are you waiting for? Get up, be baptized and wash your sins away, calling on his name.'

[17]"When I returned to Jerusalem and was praying at the temple, I fell into a trance [18]and saw the Lord speaking to me. 'Quick!' he said. 'Leave Jerusalem immediately, because the people here will not accept your testimony about me.'

[19]" 'Lord,' I replied, 'these people know that I went from one synagogue to another to imprison and beat those who believe in you. [20]And when the blood of your martyr[a] Stephen was shed, I stood there giving my approval and guarding the clothes of those who were killing him.'

[21]"Then the Lord said to me, 'Go; I will send you far away to the Gentiles.' "

Paul the Roman Citizen

[22]The crowd listened to Paul until he said this. Then they raised their voices and shouted, "Rid the earth of him! He's not fit to live!"

[23]As they were shouting and throwing off their cloaks and flinging dust into the air, [24]the commander ordered that Paul be taken into the barracks. He directed that he be flogged and interrogated in order to find out why the people were shouting at him like this. [25]As they stretched him out to flog him, Paul said to the centurion standing there, "Is it legal for you to flog a Roman citizen who hasn't even been found guilty?"

[26]When the centurion heard this, he went to the commander and reported it. "What are you going to do?" he asked. "This man is a Roman citizen."

[27]The commander went to Paul and asked, "Tell me, are you a Roman citizen?"

"Yes, I am," he answered.

[28]Then the commander said, "I had to pay a lot of money for my citizenship."

"But I was born a citizen," Paul replied.

[29]Those who were about to interrogate him withdrew immediately. The commander himself was alarmed when he realized that he had put Paul, a Roman citizen, in chains.

Paul Before the Sanhedrin

[30]The commander wanted to find out exactly why Paul was being accused by the Jews. So the next day he released him and ordered the chief priests and

[a] 20 Or *witness*

all the members of the Sanhedrin to assemble. Then he brought Paul and had him stand before them.

23 Paul looked straight at the Sanhedrin and said, "My brothers, I have fulfilled my duty to God in all good conscience to this day." ²At this the high priest Ananias ordered those standing near Paul to strike him on the mouth. ³Then Paul said to him, "God will strike you, you whitewashed wall! You sit there to judge me according to the law, yet you yourself violate the law by commanding that I be struck!"

⁴Those who were standing near Paul said, "How dare you insult God's high priest!"

⁵Paul replied, "Brothers, I did not realize that he was the high priest; for it is written: 'Do not speak evil about the ruler of your people.'ᵃ"

⁶Then Paul, knowing that some of them were Sadducees and the others Pharisees, called out in the Sanhedrin, "My brothers, I am a Pharisee, the son of a Pharisee. I stand on trial because of the hope of the resurrection of the dead." ⁷When he said this, a dispute broke out between the Pharisees and the Sadducees, and the assembly was divided. ⁸(The Sadducees say that there is no resurrection, and that there are neither angels nor spirits, but the Pharisees believe all these things.)

⁹There was a great uproar, and some of the teachers of the law who were Pharisees stood up and argued vigorously. "We find nothing wrong with this man," they said. "What if a spirit or an angel has spoken to him?" ¹⁰The dispute became so violent that the commander was afraid Paul would be torn to pieces by them. He ordered the troops to go down and take him away from them by force and bring him into the barracks.

¹¹The following night the Lord stood near Paul and said, "Take courage! As you have testified about me in Jerusalem, so you must also testify in Rome."

The Plot to Kill Paul

¹²The next morning the Jews formed a conspiracy and bound themselves with an oath not to eat or drink until they had killed Paul. ¹³More than forty men were involved in this plot. ¹⁴They went to the chief priests and the elders and said, "We have taken a solemn oath not to eat anything until we have killed Paul. ¹⁵Now then, you and the Sanhedrin petition the commander to bring him before you on the pretext of wanting more accurate information about his case. We are ready to kill him before he gets here."

¹⁶But when the son of Paul's sister heard of this plot, he went into the barracks and told Paul.

¹⁷Then Paul called one of the centurions and said, "Take this young man to the commander; he has something to tell him." ¹⁸So he took him to the commander.

The centurion said, "Paul, the prisoner, sent for me and asked me to bring this young man to you because he has something to tell you."

¹⁹The commander took the young man by the hand, drew him aside and asked, "What is it you want to tell me?"

²⁰He said: "The Jews have agreed to ask you to bring Paul before the San-

ᵃ 5 Exodus 22:28

hedrin tomorrow on the pretext of wanting more accurate information about him. 21Don't give in to them, because more than forty of them are waiting in ambush for him. They have taken an oath not to eat or drink until they have killed him. They are ready now, waiting for your consent to their request."

22The commander dismissed the young man with this warning: "Don't tell anyone that you have reported this to me."

Paul Transferred to Caesarea

23Then he called two of his centurions and ordered them, "Get ready a detachment of two hundred soldiers, seventy horsemen and two hundred spearmen*a* to go to Caesarea at nine tonight. 24Provide horses for Paul so that he may be taken safely to Governor Felix."

25He wrote a letter as follows:

26Claudius Lysias,

To His Excellency, Governor Felix:

Greetings.

27This man was seized by the Jews and they were about to kill him, but I came with my troops and rescued him, for I had learned that he is a Roman citizen. 28I wanted to know why they were accusing him, so I brought him to their Sanhedrin. 29I found that the accusation had to do with questions about their law, but there was no charge against him that deserved death or imprisonment. 30When I was informed of a plot to be carried out against the man, I sent him to you at once. I also ordered his accusers to present to you their case against him.

31So the soldiers, carrying out their orders, took Paul with them during the night and brought him as far as Antipatris. 32The next day they let the cavalry go on with him, while they returned to the barracks. 33When the cavalry arrived in Caesarea, they delivered the letter to the governor and handed Paul over to him. 34The governor read the letter and asked what province he was from. Learning that he was from Cilicia, 35he said, "I will hear your case when your accusers get here." Then he ordered that Paul be kept under guard in Herod's palace.

Paul's Trial Before Felix

24 Five days later the high priest Ananias went down to Caesarea with some of the elders and a lawyer named Tertullus, and they brought their charges against Paul before the governor. 2When Paul was called in, Tertullus presented his case before Felix: "We have enjoyed a long period of peace under you, and your foresight has brought about reforms in this nation. 3Everywhere and in every way, most excellent Felix, we acknowledge this with profound gratitude. 4But in order not to weary you further, I would request that you be kind enough to hear us briefly.

a 23 The meaning of the Greek for this word is uncertain.

5"We have found this man to be a troublemaker, stirring up riots among the Jews all over the world. He is a ringleader of the Nazarene sect 6[7]and even tried to desecrate the temple; so we seized him. 8By examining him yourself you will be able to learn the truth about all these charges we are bringing against him."

9The other Jews joined in the accusation, asserting that these things were true.

10When the governor motioned for him to speak, Paul replied: "I know that for a number of years you have been a judge over this nation; so I gladly make my defense. 11You can easily verify that no more than twelve days ago I went up to Jerusalem to worship. 12My accusers did not find me arguing with anyone at the temple, or stirring up a crowd in the synagogues or anywhere else in the city. 13And they cannot prove to you the charges they are now making against me. 14However, I admit that I worship the God of our ancestors as a follower of the Way, which they call a sect. I believe everything that is in accordance with the Law and that is written in the Prophets, 15and I have the same hope in God as these people themselves have, that there will be a resurrection of both the righteous and the wicked. 16So I strive always to keep my conscience clear before God and all people.

17"After an absence of several years, I came to Jerusalem to bring my people gifts for the poor and to present offerings. 18I was ceremonially clean when they found me in the temple courts doing this. There was no crowd with me, nor was I involved in any disturbance. 19But there are some Jews from the province of Asia, who ought to be here before you and bring charges if they have anything against me. 20Or these who are here should state what crime they found in me when I stood before the Sanhedrin 21unless it was this one thing I shouted as I stood in their presence: 'It is concerning the resurrection of the dead that I am on trial before you today.' "

22Then Felix, who was well acquainted with the Way, adjourned the proceedings. "When Lysias the commander comes," he said, "I will decide your case." 23He ordered the centurion to keep Paul under guard but to give him some freedom and permit his friends to take care of his needs.

24Several days later Felix came with his wife Drusilla, who was Jewish. He sent for Paul and listened to him as he spoke about faith in Christ Jesus. 25As Paul talked about righteousness, self-control and the judgment to come, Felix was afraid and said, "That's enough for now! You may leave. When I find it convenient, I will send for you." 26At the same time he was hoping that Paul would offer him a bribe, so he sent for him frequently and talked with him.

27When two years had passed, Felix was succeeded by Porcius Festus, but because Felix wanted to grant a favor to the Jews, he left Paul in prison.

Paul's Trial Before Festus

25 Three days after arriving in the province, Festus went up from Caesarea to Jerusalem, 2where the chief priests and the Jewish leaders appeared before him and presented the charges against Paul. 3They requested Festus, as a favor to them, to have Paul transferred to Jerusalem, for they were preparing an ambush to kill him along the way. 4Festus answered, "Paul is being held at Caesarea, and I myself am going there soon. 5Let some of your

leaders come with me, and if the man has done anything wrong, they can press charges against him there."

⁶After spending eight or ten days with them, Festus went down to Caesarea. The next day he convened the court and ordered that Paul be brought before him. ⁷When Paul came in, the Jews who had come down from Jerusalem stood around him. They brought many serious charges against him, but they could not prove them.

⁸Then Paul made his defense: "I have done nothing wrong against the Jewish law or against the temple or against Caesar."

⁹Festus, wishing to do the Jews a favor, said to Paul, "Are you willing to go up to Jerusalem and stand trial before me there on these charges?"

¹⁰Paul answered: "I am now standing before Caesar's court, where I ought to be tried. I have not done any wrong to the Jews, as you yourself know very well. ¹¹If, however, I am guilty of doing anything deserving death, I do not refuse to die. But if the charges brought against me by these Jews are not true, no one has the right to hand me over to them. I appeal to Caesar!"

¹²After Festus had conferred with his council, he declared: "You have appealed to Caesar. To Caesar you will go!"

Festus Consults King Agrippa

¹³A few days later King Agrippa and Bernice arrived at Caesarea to pay their respects to Festus. ¹⁴Since they were spending many days there, Festus discussed Paul's case with the king. He said: "There is a man here whom Felix left as a prisoner. ¹⁵When I went to Jerusalem, the chief priests and the elders of the Jews brought charges against him and asked that he be condemned.

¹⁶"I told them that it is not the Roman custom to hand over anyone before they have faced their accusers and have had an opportunity to defend themselves against the charges. ¹⁷When they came here with me, I did not delay the case, but convened the court the next day and ordered the man to be brought in. ¹⁸When his accusers got up to speak, they did not charge him with any of the crimes I had expected. ¹⁹Instead, they had some points of dispute with him about their own religion and about a dead man named Jesus who Paul claimed was alive. ²⁰I was at a loss how to investigate such matters; so I asked if he would be willing to go to Jerusalem and stand trial there on these charges. ²¹But when Paul made his appeal to be held over for the Emperor's decision, I ordered him held until I could send him to Caesar."

²²Then Agrippa said to Festus, "I would like to hear this man myself."

He replied, "Tomorrow you will hear him."

Paul Before Agrippa

²³The next day Agrippa and Bernice came with great pomp and entered the audience room with the high-ranking military officers and the prominent men of the city. At the command of Festus, Paul was brought in. ²⁴Festus said: "King Agrippa, and all who are present with us, you see this man! The whole Jewish community has petitioned me about him in Jerusalem and here in Caesarea, shouting that he ought not to live any longer. ²⁵I found he had done nothing deserving of death, but because he made his appeal to the Emperor I decided to send him to Rome. ²⁶But I have nothing definite to write to His

Majesty about him. Therefore I have brought him before all of you, and especially before you, King Agrippa, so that as a result of this investigation I may have something to write. 27For I think it is unreasonable to send a prisoner on to Rome without specifying the charges against him."

26 Then Agrippa said to Paul, "You have permission to speak for yourself."

So Paul motioned with his hand and began his defense: 2"King Agrippa, I consider myself fortunate to stand before you today as I make my defense against all the accusations of the Jews, 3and especially so because you are well acquainted with all the Jewish customs and controversies. Therefore, I beg you to listen to me patiently.

4"The Jewish people all know the way I have lived ever since I was a child, from the beginning of my life in my own country, and also in Jerusalem. 5They have known me for a long time and can testify, if they are willing, that I conformed to the strictest sect of our religion, living as a Pharisee. 6And now it is because of my hope in what God has promised our ancestors that I am on trial today. 7This is the promise our twelve tribes are hoping to see fulfilled as they earnestly serve God day and night. King Agrippa, it is because of this hope that the Jews are accusing me. 8Why should any of you consider it incredible that God raises the dead?

9"I too was convinced that I ought to do all that was possible to oppose the name of Jesus of Nazareth. 10And that is just what I did in Jerusalem. On the authority of the chief priests I put many of the believers in prison, and when they were put to death, I cast my vote against them. 11Many a time I went from one synagogue to another to have them punished, and I tried to force them to blaspheme. I was so obsessed with persecuting them that I even hunted them down in foreign cities.

12"On one of these journeys I was going to Damascus with the authority and commission of the chief priests. 13About noon, King Agrippa, as I was on the road, I saw a light from heaven, brighter than the sun, blazing around me and my companions. 14We all fell to the ground, and I heard a voice saying to me in Aramaic,ᵃ 'Saul, Saul, why do you persecute me? It is hard for you to kick against the goads.'

15"Then I asked, 'Who are you, Lord?'

" 'I am Jesus, whom you are persecuting,' the Lord replied. 16'Now get up and stand on your feet. I have appeared to you to appoint you as a servant and as a witness of what you have seen and will see of me. 17I will rescue you from your own people and from the Gentiles. I am sending you to them 18to open their eyes and turn them from darkness to light, and from the power of Satan to God, so that they may receive forgiveness of sins and a place among those who are sanctified by faith in me.'

19"So then, King Agrippa, I was not disobedient to the vision from heaven. 20First to those in Damascus, then to those in Jerusalem and in all Judea, and then to the Gentiles, I preached that they should repent and turn to God and demonstrate their repentance by their deeds. 21That is why some Jews seized me in the temple courts and tried to kill me. 22But God has helped me to this

ᵃ 14 Or *Hebrew*

very day; so I stand here and testify to small and great alike. I am saying nothing beyond what the prophets and Moses said would happen— 23that the Messiah would suffer and, as the first to rise from the dead, would bring the message of light to his own people and to the Gentiles."

24At this point Festus interrupted Paul's defense. "You are out of your mind, Paul!" he shouted. "Your great learning is driving you insane."

25"I am not insane, most excellent Festus," Paul replied. "What I am saying is true and reasonable. 26The king is familiar with these things, and I can speak freely to him. I am convinced that none of this has escaped his notice, because it was not done in a corner. 27King Agrippa, do you believe the prophets? I know you do."

28Then Agrippa said to Paul, "Do you think that in such a short time you can persuade me to be a Christian?"

29Paul replied, "Short time or long—I pray God that not only you but all who are listening to me today may become what I am, except for these chains."

30The king rose, and with him the governor and Bernice and those sitting with them. 31After they left the room, they began saying to one another, "This man is not doing anything that deserves death or imprisonment."

32Agrippa said to Festus, "This man could have been set free if he had not appealed to Caesar."

Paul Sails for Rome

27 When it was decided that we would sail for Italy, Paul and some other prisoners were handed over to a centurion named Julius, who belonged to the Imperial Regiment. 2We boarded a ship from Adramyttium about to sail for ports along the coast of the province of Asia, and we put out to sea. Aristarchus, a Macedonian from Thessalonica, was with us.

3The next day we landed at Sidon; and Julius, in kindness to Paul, allowed him to go to his friends so they might provide for his needs. 4From there we put out to sea again and passed to the lee of Cyprus because the winds were against us. 5When we had sailed across the open sea off the coast of Cilicia and Pamphylia, we landed at Myra in Lycia. 6There the centurion found an Alexandrian ship sailing for Italy and put us on board. 7We made slow headway for many days and had difficulty arriving off Cnidus. When the wind did not allow us to hold our course, we sailed to the lee of Crete, opposite Salmone. 8We moved along the coast with difficulty and came to a place called Fair Havens, near the town of Lasea.

9Much time had been lost, and sailing had already become dangerous because by now it was after the Day of Atonement.*a* So Paul warned them, 10"Men, I can see that our voyage is going to be disastrous and bring great loss to ship and cargo, and to our own lives also." 11But the centurion, instead of listening to what Paul said, followed the advice of the pilot and of the owner of the ship. 12Since the harbor was unsuitable to winter in, the majority decided that we should sail on, hoping to reach Phoenix and winter there. This was a harbor in Crete, facing both southwest and northwest.

a 9 That is, Yom Kippur

The Storm

13When a gentle south wind began to blow, they saw their opportunity; so they weighed anchor and sailed along the shore of Crete. 14Before very long, a wind of hurricane force, called the "Northeaster," swept down from the island. 15The ship was caught by the storm and could not head into the wind; so we gave way to it and were driven along. 16As we passed to the lee of a small island called Cauda, we were hardly able to make the lifeboat secure, 17so the men hoisted it aboard. Then they passed ropes under the ship itself to hold it together. Because they were afraid they would run aground on the sandbars of Syrtis, they lowered the sea anchor and let the ship be driven along. 18We took such a violent battering from the storm that the next day they began to throw the cargo overboard. 19On the third day, they threw the ship's tackle overboard with their own hands. 20When neither sun nor stars appeared for many days and the storm continued raging, we finally gave up all hope of being saved.

21After they had gone a long time without food, Paul stood up before them and said: "Men, you should have taken my advice not to sail from Crete; then you would have spared yourselves this damage and loss. 22But now I urge you to keep up your courage, because not one of you will be lost; only the ship will be destroyed. 23Last night an angel of the God whose I am and whom I serve stood beside me 24and said, 'Do not be afraid, Paul. You must stand trial before Caesar; and God has graciously given you the lives of all who sail with you.' 25So keep up your courage, men, for I have faith in God that it will happen just as he told me. 26Nevertheless, we must run aground on some island."

The Shipwreck

27On the fourteenth night we were still being driven across the Adriatic[a] Sea, when about midnight the sailors sensed they were approaching land. 28They took soundings and found that the water was a hundred and twenty feet[b] deep. A short time later they took soundings again and found it was ninety feet[c] deep. 29Fearing that we would be dashed against the rocks, they dropped four anchors from the stern and prayed for daylight. 30In an attempt to escape from the ship, the sailors let the lifeboat down into the sea, pretending they were going to lower some anchors from the bow. 31Then Paul said to the centurion and the soldiers, "Unless these men stay with the ship, you cannot be saved." 32So the soldiers cut the ropes that held the lifeboat and let it drift away.

33Just before dawn Paul urged them all to eat. "For the last fourteen days," he said, "you have been in constant suspense and have gone without food— you haven't eaten anything. 34Now I urge you to take some food. You need it to survive. Not one of you will lose a single hair from his head." 35After he said this, he took some bread and gave thanks to God in front of them all. Then he broke it and began to eat. 36They were all encouraged and ate some food themselves. 37Altogether there were 276 of us on board. 38When they had

---

[a] 27 In ancient times the name referred to an area extending well south of Italy.   [b] 28 About 37 meters   [c] 28 About 27 meters

eaten as much as they wanted, they lightened the ship by throwing the grain into the sea.

39When daylight came, they did not recognize the land, but they saw a bay with a sandy beach, where they decided to run the ship aground if they could. 40Cutting loose the anchors, they left them in the sea and at the same time untied the ropes that held the rudders. Then they hoisted the foresail to the wind and made for the beach. 41But the ship struck a sandbar and ran aground. The bow stuck fast and would not move, and the stern was broken to pieces by the pounding of the surf.

42The soldiers planned to kill the prisoners to prevent any of them from swimming away and escaping. 43But the centurion wanted to spare Paul's life and kept them from carrying out their plan. He ordered those who could swim to jump overboard first and get to land. 44The rest were to get there on planks or on other pieces of the ship. In this way everyone reached land safely.

Paul Ashore on Malta

28 Once safely on shore, we found out that the island was called Malta. 2The islanders showed us unusual kindness. They built a fire and welcomed us all because it was raining and cold. 3Paul gathered a pile of brushwood and, as he put it on the fire, a viper, driven out by the heat, fastened itself on his hand. 4When the islanders saw the snake hanging from his hand, they said to each other, "This man must be a murderer; for though he escaped from the sea, the goddess Justice has not allowed him to live." 5But Paul shook the snake off into the fire and suffered no ill effects. 6The people expected him to swell up or suddenly fall dead; but after waiting a long time and seeing nothing unusual happen to him, they changed their minds and said he was a god.

7There was an estate nearby that belonged to Publius, the chief official of the island. He welcomed us to his home and showed us generous hospitality for three days. 8His father was sick in bed, suffering from fever and dysentery. Paul went in to see him and, after prayer, placed his hands on him and healed him. 9When this had happened, the rest of the sick on the island came and were cured. 10They honored us in many ways; and when we were ready to sail, they furnished us with the supplies we needed.

Paul's Arrival at Rome

11After three months we put out to sea in a ship that had wintered in the island—it was an Alexandrian ship with the figurehead of the twin gods Castor and Pollux. 12We put in at Syracuse and stayed there three days. 13From there we set sail and arrived at Rhegium. The next day the south wind came up, and on the following day we reached Puteoli. 14There we found some believers who invited us to spend a week with them. And so we came to Rome. 15The believers there had heard that we were coming, and they traveled as far as the Forum of Appius and the Three Taverns to meet us. At the sight of these people Paul thanked God and was encouraged. 16When we got to Rome, Paul was allowed to live by himself, with a soldier to guard him.

Paul Preaches at Rome Under Guard

[17]Three days later he called together the local Jewish leaders. When they had assembled, Paul said to them: "My brothers, although I have done nothing against our people or against the customs of our ancestors, I was arrested in Jerusalem and handed over to the Romans. [18]They examined me and wanted to release me, because I was not guilty of any crime deserving death. [19]The Jews objected, so I was compelled to make an appeal to Caesar. I certainly did not intend to bring any charge against my own people. [20]For this reason I have asked to see you and talk with you. It is because of the hope of Israel that I am bound with this chain."

[21]They replied, "We have not received any letters from Judea concerning you, and none of our people who have come from there has reported or said anything bad about you. [22]But we want to hear what your views are, for we know that people everywhere are talking against this sect."

[23]They arranged to meet Paul on a certain day, and came in even larger numbers to the place where he was staying. He witnessed to them from morning till evening, explaining about the kingdom of God, and from the Law of Moses and from the Prophets he tried to persuade them about Jesus. [24]Some were convinced by what he said, but others would not believe. [25]They disagreed among themselves and began to leave after Paul had made this final statement: "The Holy Spirit spoke the truth to your ancestors when he said through Isaiah the prophet:

[26]" 'Go to this people and say,
"You will be ever hearing but never understanding;
    you will be ever seeing but never perceiving."
[27]For this people's heart has become calloused,
    they hardly hear with their ears,
    and they have closed their eyes.
Otherwise they might see with their eyes,
    hear with their ears,
    understand with their hearts
and turn, and I would heal them.'[a]

[28][29]"Therefore I want you to know that God's salvation has been sent to the Gentiles, and they will listen!"

[30]For two whole years Paul stayed there in his own rented house and welcomed all who came to see him. [31]He proclaimed the kingdom of God and taught about the Lord Jesus Christ—with all boldness and without hindrance!

---

[a] 27 Isaiah 6:9,10

ROMANS

1 Paul, a servant of Christ Jesus, called to be an apostle and set apart for the gospel of God— [2]the gospel he promised beforehand through his prophets in the Holy Scriptures [3]regarding his Son, who as to his earthly life[a] was a descendant of David, [4]and who through the Spirit of holiness was appointed the Son of God in power[b] by his resurrection from the dead: Jesus Christ our Lord. [5]Through him we received grace and apostleship to call all the Gentiles to faith and obedience for his name's sake. [6]And you also are among those Gentiles who are called to belong to Jesus Christ.

[7]To all in Rome who are loved by God and called to be saints:

Grace and peace to you from God our Father and from the Lord Jesus Christ.

Paul's Longing to Visit Rome

[8]First, I thank my God through Jesus Christ for all of you, because your faith is being reported all over the world. [9]God, whom I serve in my spirit in preaching the gospel of his Son, is my witness how constantly I remember you [10]in my prayers at all times; and I pray that now at last by God's will the way may be opened for me to come to you.

[11]I long to see you so that I may impart to you some spiritual gift to make you strong— [12]that is, that you and I may be mutually encouraged by each other's faith. [13]I do not want you to be unaware, brothers and sisters, that I planned many times to come to you (but have been prevented from doing so until now) in order that I might have a harvest among you, just as I have had among the other Gentiles.

[14]I am obligated both to Greeks and non-Greeks, both to the wise and the foolish. [15]That is why I am so eager to preach the gospel also to you who are in Rome.

[16]I am not ashamed of the gospel, because it is the power of God that brings salvation to everyone who believes: first to the Jew, then to the Gentile. [17]For in the gospel the righteousness of God is revealed—a righteousness that is by faith from first to last,[c] just as it is written: "The righteous will live by faith."[d]

God's Wrath Against Sinful Humanity

[18]The wrath of God is being revealed from heaven against all the godless-

---

[a]3 Or *who according to the flesh*   [b]4 Or *was declared with power to be the Son of God*   [c]17 Or *is from faith to faith*   [d]17 Hab. 2:4

ness and wickedness of human beings who suppress the truth by their wickedness, [19]since what may be known about God is plain to them, because God has made it plain to them. [20]For since the creation of the world God's invisible qualities—his eternal power and divine nature—have been clearly seen, being understood from what has been made, so that people are without excuse.

[21]For although they knew God, they neither glorified him as God nor gave thanks to him, but their thinking became futile and their foolish hearts were darkened. [22]Although they claimed to be wise, they became fools [23]and exchanged the glory of the immortal God for images made to look like mortal human beings and birds and animals and reptiles.

[24]Therefore God gave them over in the sinful desires of their hearts to sexual impurity for the degrading of their bodies with one another. [25]They exchanged the truth about God for a lie, and worshiped and served created things rather than the Creator—who is forever praised. Amen.

[26]Because of this, God gave them over to shameful lusts. Even their women exchanged natural sexual relations for unnatural ones. [27]In the same way the men also abandoned natural relations with women and were inflamed with lust for one another. Men committed shameful acts with other men, and received in themselves the due penalty for their error.

[28]Furthermore, just as they did not think it worthwhile to retain the knowledge of God, so God gave them over to a depraved mind, so that they do what ought not to be done. [29]They have become filled with every kind of wickedness, evil, greed and depravity. They are full of envy, murder, strife, deceit and malice. They are gossips, [30]slanderers, God-haters, insolent, arrogant and boastful; they invent ways of doing evil; they disobey their parents; [31]they have no understanding, no fidelity, no love, no mercy. [32]Although they know God's righteous decree that those who do such things deserve death, they not only continue to do these very things but also approve of those who practice them.

God's Righteous Judgment

2 You, therefore, have no excuse, you who pass judgment on someone else, for at whatever point you judge the other, you are condemning yourself, because you who pass judgment do the same things. [2]Now we know that God's judgment against those who do such things is based on truth. [3]So when you, a mere human, pass judgment on them and yet do the same things, do you think you will escape God's judgment? [4]Or do you show contempt for the riches of his kindness, tolerance and patience, not realizing that God's kindness is intended to lead you to repentance?

[5]But because of your stubbornness and your unrepentant heart, you are storing up wrath against yourself for the day of God's wrath, when his righteous judgment will be revealed. [6]God "will repay everyone according to what they have done."[a] [7]To those who by persistence in doing good seek glory, honor and immortality, he will give eternal life. [8]But for those who are self-seeking and who reject the truth and follow evil, there will be wrath and

[a] 6 Psalm 62:12; Prov. 24:12

anger. [9]There will be trouble and distress for every human being who does evil: first for the Jew, then for the Gentile; [10]but glory, honor and peace for everyone who does good: first for the Jew, then for the Gentile. [11]For God does not show favoritism.

[12]All who sin apart from the law will also perish apart from the law, and all who sin under the law will be judged by the law. [13]For it is not those who hear the law who are righteous in God's sight, but it is those who obey the law who will be declared righteous. [14](Indeed, when Gentiles, who do not have the law, do by nature things required by the law, they are a law for themselves, even though they do not have the law. [15]They show that the requirements of the law are written on their hearts, their consciences also bearing witness, and their thoughts now accusing, now even defending them.) [16]This will take place on the day when God judges everyone's secrets through Jesus Christ, as my gospel declares.

The Jews and the Law

[17]Now you, if you call yourself a Jew; if you rely on the law and boast in God; [18]if you know his will and approve of what is superior because you are instructed by the law; [19]if you are convinced that you are a guide for the blind, a light for those who are in the dark, [20]an instructor of the foolish, a teacher of infants, because you have in the law the embodiment of knowledge and truth— [21]you, then, who teach others, do you not teach yourself? You who preach against stealing, do you steal? [22]You who say that people should not commit adultery, do you commit adultery? You who abhor idols, do you rob temples? [23]You who boast in the law, do you dishonor God by breaking the law? [24]As it is written: "God's name is blasphemed among the Gentiles because of you." [a]

[25]Circumcision has value if you observe the law, but if you break the law, you have become as though you had not been circumcised. [26]If those who are not circumcised keep the law's requirements, will they not be regarded as though they were circumcised? [27]The one who is not circumcised physically and yet obeys the law will condemn you who, even though you have the[b] written code and circumcision, are a lawbreaker.

[28]A person is not a Jew who is one only outwardly, nor is circumcision merely outward and physical. [29]No, a person is a Jew who is one inwardly; and circumcision is circumcision of the heart, by the Spirit, not by the written code. Such a person's praise is not from other people, but from God.

God's Faithfulness

3 What advantage, then, is there in being a Jew, or what value is there in circumcision? [2]Much in every way! First of all, they have been entrusted with the very words of God.

[3]What if some were unfaithful? Will their unfaithfulness nullify God's faithfulness? [4]Not at all! Let God be true, and every human being a liar. As it is written:

[a] 24 Isaiah 52:5; Ezek. 36:22   [b] 27 Or *who, by means of a*

"So that you may be proved right when you speak
and prevail when you judge."*a*

5But if our unrighteousness brings out God's righteousness more clearly, what shall we say? That God is unjust in bringing his wrath on us? (I am using a human argument.) 6Certainly not! If that were so, how could God judge the world? 7Someone might argue, "If my falsehood enhances God's truthfulness and so increases his glory, why am I still condemned as a sinner?" 8Why not say—as we are being slanderously reported as saying and as some claim that we say—"Let us do evil that good may result"? Their condemnation is just!

No One Is Righteous

9What shall we conclude then? Do we have any advantage? Not at all! We have already made the charge that Jews and Gentiles alike are all under the power of sin. 10As it is written:

"There is no one righteous, not even one;
11   there is no one who understands;
there is no one who seeks God.
12 All have turned away,
they have together become worthless;
there is no one who does good,
not even one."*b*
13 "Their throats are open graves;
their tongues practice deceit."*c*
"The poison of vipers is on their lips."*d*
14   "Their mouths are full of cursing and bitterness."*e*
15 "Their feet are swift to shed blood;
16   ruin and misery mark their ways,
17 and the way of peace they do not know."*f*
18   "There is no fear of God before their eyes."*g*

19Now we know that whatever the law says, it says to those who are under the law, so that every mouth may be silenced and the whole world held accountable to God. 20Therefore no one will be declared righteous in his sight by observing the law; rather, through the law we become conscious of our sin.

Righteousness Through Faith

21But now apart from the law the righteousness of God has been made known, to which the Law and the Prophets testify. 22This righteousness is given through faith in*h* Jesus Christ to all who believe. There is no difference between Jew and Gentile, 23for all have sinned and fall short of the glory of God, 24and all are justified freely by his grace through the redemption that came by Christ Jesus. 25God presented Christ as a sacrifice of atonement, through the shedding of his blood—to be received by faith. He did this to demonstrate his justice, because in his forbearance he had left the sins com-

*a*4 Psalm 51:4   *b*12 Psalms 14:1–3; 53:1–3; Eccles. 7:20   *c*13 Psalm 5:9   *d*13 Psalm 140:3
*e*14 Psalm 10:7   *f*17 Isaiah 59:7,8   *g*18 Psalm 36:1   *h*22 Or *through the faithfulness of*

mitted beforehand unpunished— 26he did it to demonstrate his justice at the present time, so as to be just and the one who justifies those who have faith in Jesus.

27Where, then, is boasting? It is excluded. Because of what law? The law that requires works? No, because of the "law" that requires faith. 28For we maintain that a person is justified by faith apart from observing the law. 29Is God the God of Jews only? Is he not the God of Gentiles too? Yes, of Gentiles too, 30since there is only one God, who will justify the circumcised by faith and the uncircumcised through that same faith. 31Do we, then, nullify the law by this faith? Not at all! Rather, we uphold the law.

Abraham Justified by Faith

4 What then shall we say that Abraham, the forefather of us Jews, discovered in this matter? 2If, in fact, Abraham was justified by works, he had something to boast about—but not before God. 3What does Scripture say? "Abraham believed God, and it was credited to him as righteousness."[a]

4Now to anyone who works, their wages are not credited to them as a gift, but as an obligation. 5However, to anyone who does not work but trusts God who justifies the ungodly, their faith is credited as righteousness. 6David says the same thing when he speaks of the blessedness of those to whom God credits righteousness apart from works:

7"Blessed are those
  whose transgressions are forgiven,
  whose sins are covered.
8Blessed are those
  whose sin the Lord will never count against them."[b]

9Is this blessedness only for the circumcised, or also for the uncircumcised? We have been saying that Abraham's faith was credited to him as righteousness. 10Under what circumstances was it credited? Was it after he was circumcised, or before? It was not after, but before! 11And he received circumcision as a sign, a seal of the righteousness that he had by faith while he was still uncircumcised. So then, he is the father of all who believe but have not been circumcised, in order that righteousness might be credited to them. 12And he is then also the father of the circumcised who not only are circumcised but who also follow in the footsteps of the faith that our father Abraham had before he was circumcised.

13It was not through the law that Abraham and his offspring received the promise that he would be heir of the world, but through the righteousness that comes by faith. 14For if those who depend on the law are heirs, faith means nothing and the promise is worthless, 15because the law brings wrath. And where there is no law there is no transgression.

16Therefore, the promise comes by faith, so that it may be by grace and may be guaranteed to all Abraham's offspring—not only to those who are of the law but also to those who have the faith of Abraham. He is the father of us all. 17As it is written: "I have made you a father of many nations."[c] He is our fa-

a 3 Gen. 15:6; also in verse 22   b 8 Psalm 32:1,2   c 17 Gen. 17:5

ther in the sight of God, in whom he believed—the God who gives life to the dead and calls into being things that were not.

[18]Against all hope, Abraham in hope believed and so became the father of many nations, just as it had been said to him, "So shall your offspring be."[a] [19]Without weakening in his faith, he faced the fact that his body was as good as dead—since he was about a hundred years old—and that Sarah's womb was also dead. [20]Yet he did not waver through unbelief regarding the promise of God, but was strengthened in his faith and gave glory to God, [21]being fully persuaded that God had power to do what he had promised. [22]This is why "it was credited to him as righteousness." [23]The words "it was credited to him" were written not for him alone, [24]but also for us, to whom God will credit righteousness—for us who believe in him who raised Jesus our Lord from the dead. [25]He was delivered over to death for our sins and was raised to life for our justification.

Peace and Hope

5 Therefore, since we have been justified through faith, we[b] have peace with God through our Lord Jesus Christ, [2]through whom we have gained access by faith into this grace in which we now stand. And we[c] boast in the hope of the glory of God. [3]Not only so, but we[c] also glory in our sufferings, because we know that suffering produces perseverance; [4]perseverance, character; and character, hope. [5]And hope does not put us to shame, because God's love has been poured out into our hearts through the Holy Spirit, who has been given to us.

[6]You see, at just the right time, when we were still powerless, Christ died for the ungodly. [7]Very rarely will anyone die for a righteous person, though for a good person someone might possibly dare to die. [8]But God demonstrates his own love for us in this: While we were still sinners, Christ died for us.

[9]Since we have now been justified by his blood, how much more shall we be saved from God's wrath through him! [10]For if, while we were God's enemies, we were reconciled to him through the death of his Son, how much more, having been reconciled, shall we be saved through his life! [11]Not only is this so, but we also boast in God through our Lord Jesus Christ, through whom we have now received reconciliation.

Death Through Adam, Life Through Christ

[12]Therefore, just as sin entered the world through one man, and death through sin, and in this way death came to all people, because all sinned—

[13]To be sure, sin was in the world before the law was given, but sin is not charged against anyone's account where there is no law. [14]Nevertheless, death reigned from the time of Adam to the time of Moses, even over those who did not sin by breaking a command, as did Adam, who is a pattern of the one to come.

[15]But the gift is not like the trespass. For if the many died by the trespass of the one man, how much more did God's grace and the gift that came by the

---

[a] 18 Gen. 15:5   [b] 1 Many manuscripts *let us*   [c] 2,3 Or *let us*

grace of the one man, Jesus Christ, overflow to the many! 16Nor can the gift of God be compared with the result of one man's sin: The judgment followed one sin and brought condemnation, but the gift followed many trespasses and brought justification. 17For if, by the trespass of the one man, death reigned through that one man, how much more will those who receive God's abundant provision of grace and of the gift of righteousness reign in life through the one man, Jesus Christ!

18Consequently, just as one trespass resulted in condemnation for all people, so also one righteous act resulted in justification and life for all. 19For just as through the disobedience of the one man the many were made sinners, so also through the obedience of the one man the many will be made righteous.

20The law was brought in so that the trespass might increase. But where sin increased, grace increased all the more, 21so that, just as sin reigned in death, so also grace might reign through righteousness to bring eternal life through Jesus Christ our Lord.

Dead to Sin, Alive in Christ

6 What shall we say, then? Shall we go on sinning so that grace may increase? 2By no means! We are those who have died to sin; how can we live in it any longer? 3Or don't you know that all of us who were baptized into Christ Jesus were baptized into his death? 4We were therefore buried with him through baptism into death in order that, just as Christ was raised from the dead through the glory of the Father, we too may live a new life.

5If we have been united with him in a death like his, we will certainly also be united with him in a resurrection like his. 6For we know that our old self was crucified with him so that the body ruled by sin might be done away with,a that we should no longer be slaves to sin— 7because anyone who has died has been set free from sin.

8Now if we died with Christ, we believe that we will also live with him. 9For we know that since Christ was raised from the dead, he cannot die again; death no longer has mastery over him. 10The death he died, he died to sin once for all; but the life he lives, he lives to God.

11In the same way, count yourselves dead to sin but alive to God in Christ Jesus. 12Therefore do not let sin reign in your mortal body so that you obey its evil desires. 13Do not offer any part of yourself to sin as an instrument of wickedness, but rather offer yourselves to God as those who have been brought from death to life; and offer every part of yourself to him as an instrument of righteousness. 14For sin shall no longer be your master, because you are not under the law, but under grace.

Slaves to Righteousness

15What then? Shall we sin because we are not under the law but under grace? By no means! 16Don't you know that when you offer yourselves to someone as obedient slaves, you are slaves of the one you obey—whether you are slaves to sin, which leads to death, or to obedience, which leads to righteousness? 17But thanks be to God that, though you used to be slaves to sin,

a 6 Or be rendered powerless

you have come to obey from your heart the pattern of teaching that has now claimed your allegiance. [18]You have been set free from sin and have become slaves to righteousness.

[19]I am using an example from everyday life because of your human limitations. Just as you used to offer yourselves as slaves to impurity and to ever-increasing wickedness, so now offer yourselves as slaves to righteousness leading to holiness. [20]When you were slaves to sin, you were free from the control of righteousness. [21]What benefit did you reap at that time from the things you are now ashamed of? Those things result in death! [22]But now that you have been set free from sin and have become slaves of God, the benefit you reap leads to holiness, and the result is eternal life. [23]For the wages of sin is death, but the gift of God is eternal life in[a] Christ Jesus our Lord.

Released from the Law, Bound to Christ

7 Do you not know, brothers and sisters—for I am speaking to those who know the law—that the law has authority over someone only as long as that person lives? [2]For example, by law a married woman is bound to her husband as long as he is alive, but if her husband dies, she is released from the law that binds her to him. [3]So then, if she marries another man while her husband is still alive, she is called an adulteress. But if her husband dies, she is released from that law and is not an adulteress if she marries another man.

[4]So, my brothers and sisters, you also died to the law through the body of Christ, that you might belong to another, to him who was raised from the dead, in order that we might bear fruit for God. [5]For when we were controlled by our sinful nature,[b] the sinful passions aroused by the law were at work in us, so that we bore fruit for death. [6]But now, by dying to what once bound us, we have been released from the law so that we serve in the new way of the Spirit, and not in the old way of the written code.

The Law and Sin

[7]What shall we say, then? Is the law sinful? Certainly not! Nevertheless, I would not have known what sin was had it not been for the law. For I would not have known what coveting really was if the law had not said, "Do not covet."[c] [8]But sin, seizing the opportunity afforded by the commandment, produced in me every kind of coveting. For apart from the law, sin was dead. [9]Once I was alive apart from the law; but when the commandment came, sin sprang to life and I died. [10]I found that the very commandment that was intended to bring life actually brought death. [11]For sin, seizing the opportunity afforded by the commandment, deceived me, and through the commandment put me to death. [12]So then, the law is holy, and the commandment is holy, righteous and good.

[13]Did that which is good, then, become death to me? By no means! Nevertheless, in order that sin might be recognized as sin, it used what is good to bring about my death, so that through the commandment sin might become utterly sinful.

[14]We know that the law is spiritual; but I am unspiritual, sold as a slave to

[a] 23 Or *through*   [b] 5 Or *by the flesh*   [c] 7 Exodus 20:17; Deut. 5:21

sin. [15]I do not understand what I do. For what I want to do I do not do, but what I hate I do. [16]And if I do what I do not want to do, I agree that the law is good. [17]As it is, it is no longer I myself who do it, but it is sin living in me. [18]I know that good itself does not dwell in me, that is, in my sinful nature.[a] For I have the desire to do what is good, but I cannot carry it out. [19]For I do not do the good I want to do, but the evil I do not want to do—this I keep on doing. [20]Now if I do what I do not want to do, it is no longer I who do it, but it is sin living in me that does it.

[21]So I find this law at work: Although I want to do good, evil is right there with me. [22]For in my inner being I delight in God's law; [23]but I see another law at work in me, waging war against the law of my mind and making me a prisoner of the law of sin at work within me. [24]What a wretched man I am! Who will rescue me from this body of death? [25]Thanks be to God, who delivers me through Jesus Christ our Lord!

So then, I myself in my mind am a slave to God's law, but in my sinful nature[b] a slave to the law of sin.

Life Through the Spirit

8 Therefore, there is now no condemnation for those who are in Christ Jesus, [2]because through Christ Jesus the law of the Spirit who gives life has set you[c] free from the law of sin and death. [3]For what the law was powerless to do because it was weakened by the sinful nature,[d] God did by sending his own Son in the likeness of sinful humanity to be a sin offering.[e] And so he condemned sin in human flesh, [4]in order that the righteous requirement of the law might be fully met in us, who do not live according to the sinful nature but according to the Spirit.

[5]Those who live according to the sinful nature have their minds set on what that nature desires; but those who live in accordance with the Spirit have their minds set on what the Spirit desires. [6]The mind controlled by the sinful nature[f] is death, but the mind controlled by the Spirit is life and peace; [7]the sinful mind[g] is hostile to God. It does not submit to God's law, nor can it do so. [8]Those controlled by the sinful nature cannot please God.

[9]You, however, are not controlled by the sinful nature but are in the Spirit, if indeed the Spirit of God lives in you. And if anyone does not have the Spirit of Christ, they do not belong to Christ. [10]But if Christ is in you, then even though your body is subject to death because of sin, the Spirit gives life[h] because of righteousness. [11]And if the Spirit of him who raised Jesus from the dead is living in you, he who raised Christ from the dead will also give life to your mortal bodies because of[i] his Spirit who lives in you.

[12]Therefore, brothers and sisters, we have an obligation—but it is not to the sinful nature, to live according to it. [13]For if you live according to the sinful nature, you will die; but if by the Spirit you put to death the misdeeds of the body, you will live.

[14]For those who are led by the Spirit of God are the children of God. [15]The

---

[a] 18 Or *my flesh*   [b] 25 Or *in the flesh*   [c] 2 Some manuscripts *me*   [d] 3 Or *the flesh*; also in verses 4, 5, 8, 9, 12 and 13   [e] 3 Or *humanity, for sin*   [f] 6 Or *mind set on the flesh*   [g] 7 Or *the mind set on the flesh*   [h] 10 Or *you, your body is dead because of sin, yet your spirit is alive*   [i] 11 Some manuscripts *bodies through*

Spirit you received does not make you slaves, so that you live in fear again; rather, the Spirit you received brought about your adoption to sonship.[a] And by him we cry, "*Abba,*[b] Father." [16]The Spirit himself testifies with our spirit that we are God's children. [17]Now if we are children, then we are heirs—heirs of God and co-heirs with Christ, if indeed we share in his sufferings in order that we may also share in his glory.

Present Suffering and Future Glory

[18]I consider that our present sufferings are not worth comparing with the glory that will be revealed in us. [19]The creation waits in eager expectation for the children of God to be revealed. [20]For the creation was subjected to frustration, not by its own choice, but by the will of the one who subjected it, in hope [21]that[c] the creation itself will be liberated from its bondage to decay and brought into the freedom and glory of the children of God.

[22]We know that the whole creation has been groaning as in the pains of childbirth right up to the present time. [23]Not only so, but we ourselves, who have the firstfruits of the Spirit, groan inwardly as we wait eagerly for our adoption, the redemption of our bodies. [24]For in this hope we were saved. But hope that is seen is no hope at all. Who hopes for what they already have? [25]But if we hope for what we do not yet have, we wait for it patiently.

[26]In the same way, the Spirit helps us in our weakness. We do not know what we ought to pray for, but the Spirit himself intercedes for us through wordless groans. [27]And he who searches our hearts knows the mind of the Spirit, because the Spirit intercedes for God's people in accordance with the will of God.

[28]And we know that in all things God works for the good of those who love him, who[d] have been called according to his purpose. [29]For those God foreknew he also predestined to be conformed to the likeness of his Son, that he might be the firstborn among many brothers and sisters. [30]And those he predestined, he also called; those he called, he also justified; those he justified, he also glorified.

More Than Conquerors

[31]What, then, shall we say in response to these things? If God is for us, who can be against us? [32]He who did not spare his own Son, but gave him up for us all—how will he not also, along with him, graciously give us all things? [33]Who will bring any charge against those whom God has chosen? It is God who justifies. [34]Who then can condemn? No one. Christ Jesus who died—more than that, who was raised to life—is at the right hand of God and is also interceding for us. [35]Who shall separate us from the love of Christ? Shall trouble or hardship or persecution or famine or nakedness or danger or sword? [36]As it is written:

> "For your sake we face death all day long;
> we are considered as sheep to be slaughtered."[e]

---

[a] 15 The Greek word for *adoption to sonship* is a term referring to the full legal standing of an adopted male heir in Roman culture.   [b] 15 Aramaic for *Father*   [c] 20,21 Or *subjected it in hope.* [21]*For* [d] 28 Or *that all things work together for good to those who love God, who;* or *that in all things God works together with those who love him to bring about what is good—with those who* [e] 36 Psalm 44:22

37No, in all these things we are more than conquerors through him who loved us. 38For I am convinced that neither death nor life, neither angels nor demons,*a* neither the present nor the future, nor any powers, 39neither height nor depth, nor anything else in all creation, will be able to separate us from the love of God that is in Christ Jesus our Lord.

Paul's Anguish Over Israel

9 I speak the truth in Christ—I am not lying, my conscience confirms it through the Holy Spirit— 2I have great sorrow and unceasing anguish in my heart. 3For I could wish that I myself were cursed and cut off from Christ for the sake of my people, those of my own race, 4the people of Israel. Theirs is the adoption; theirs the divine glory, the covenants, the receiving of the law, the temple worship and the promises. 5Theirs are the patriarchs, and from them is traced the human ancestry of the Messiah, who is God over all, forever praised!*b* Amen.

God's Sovereign Choice

6It is not as though God's word had failed. For not all who are descended from Israel are Israel. 7Nor because they are his descendants are they all Abraham's children. On the contrary, "It is through Isaac that your offspring will be reckoned."*c* 8In other words, it is not the natural children who are God's children, but it is the children of the promise who are regarded as Abraham's offspring. 9For this was how the promise was stated: "At the appointed time I will return, and Sarah will have a son."*d*

10Not only that, but Rebekah's children were conceived at the same time by our father Isaac. 11Yet, before the twins were born or had done anything good or bad—in order that God's purpose in election might stand: 12not by works but by him who calls—she was told, "The older will serve the younger."*e* 13Just as it is written: "Jacob I loved, but Esau I hated."*f*

14What then shall we say? Is God unjust? Not at all! 15For he says to Moses,

"I will have mercy on whom I have mercy,
    and I will have compassion on whom I have compassion."*g*

16It does not, therefore, depend on human desire or effort, but on God's mercy. 17For Scripture says to Pharaoh: "I raised you up for this very purpose, that I might display my power in you and that my name might be proclaimed in all the earth."*h* 18Therefore God has mercy on whom he wants to have mercy, and he hardens whom he wants to harden.

19One of you will say to me: "Then why does God still blame us? For who is able to resist his will?" 20But who are you, a mere human being, to talk back to God? "Shall what is formed say to the one who formed it, 'Why did you make me like this?' "*i* 21Does not the potter have the right to make out of the same lump of clay some pottery for noble purposes and some for disposal of refuse? 22What if God, although choosing to show his wrath and make his power known, bore with great patience the objects of his wrath—prepared for de-

---

a 38 Or *nor heavenly rulers*   *b 5* Or *Messiah, who is over all. God be forever praised! Or Messiah. God who is over all be forever praised!*   *c 7* Gen. 21:12   *d 9* Gen. 18:10,14   *e 12* Gen. 25:23   *f 13* Mal. 1:2,3   *g 15* Exodus 33:19   *h 17* Exodus 9:16   *i 20* Isaiah 29:16; 45:9

struction? 23What if he did this to make the riches of his glory known to the objects of his mercy, whom he prepared in advance for glory— 24even us, whom he also called, not only from the Jews but also from the Gentiles? 25As he says in Hosea:

> "I will call them 'my people' who are not my people;
>   and I will call her 'my loved one' who is not my loved one,"ᵃ

26and,

> "In the very place where it was said to them,
>   'You are not my people,'
> they will be called 'children of the living God.' "ᵇ

27Isaiah cries out concerning Israel:

> "Though the number of the Israelites be like the sand by the sea,
>   only the remnant will be saved.
> 28For the Lord will carry out
>   his sentence on earth with speed and finality."ᶜ

29It is just as Isaiah said previously:

> "Unless the Lord Almighty
>   had left us descendants,
> we would have become like Sodom,
>   we would have been like Gomorrah."ᵈ

Israel's Unbelief

30What then shall we say? That the Gentiles, who did not pursue righteousness, have obtained it, a righteousness that is by faith; 31but the people of Israel, who pursued the law as the way of righteousness, have not attained their goal. 32Why not? Because they pursued it not by faith but as if it were by works. They stumbled over the "stumbling stone." 33As it is written:

> "See, I lay in Zion a stone that causes people to stumble
>   and a rock that makes them fall,
>   and the one who believes in him will never be put to shame."ᵉ

10 Brothers and sisters, my heart's desire and prayer to God for the Israelites is that they may be saved. 2For I can testify about them that they are zealous for God, but their zeal is not based on knowledge. 3Since they did not know the righteousness of God and sought to establish their own, they did not submit to God's righteousness. 4Christ is the culmination of the law so that there may be righteousness for everyone who believes.

5Moses writes this about the righteousness that is by the law: "The one who does these things will live by them."ᶠ 6But the righteousness that is by faith says: "Do not say in your heart, 'Who will ascend into heaven?'ᵍ" (that is, to bring Christ down) 7"or 'Who will descend into the deep?'ʰ" (that is, to bring Christ up from the dead). 8But what does it say? "The word is near you; it is in

ᵃ25 Hosea 2:23   ᵇ26 Hosea 1:10   ᶜ28 Isaiah 10:22,23   ᵈ29 Isaiah 1:9   ᵉ33 Isaiah 8:14; 28:16   ᶠ5 Lev. 18:5   ᵍ6 Deut. 30:12   ʰ7 Deut. 30:13

your mouth and in your heart,"[a] that is, the message concerning faith that we proclaim: [9]If you declare with your mouth, "Jesus is Lord," and believe in your heart that God raised him from the dead, you will be saved. [10]For it is with your heart that you believe and are justified, and it is with your mouth that you profess your faith and are saved. [11]As Scripture says, "Anyone who believes in him will never be put to shame."[b] [12]For there is no difference between Jew and Gentile—the same Lord is Lord of all and richly blesses all who call on him, [13]for, "Everyone who calls on the name of the Lord will be saved."[c]

[14]How, then, can they call on the one they have not believed in? And how can they believe in the one of whom they have not heard? And how can they hear without someone preaching to them? [15]And how can anyone preach unless they are sent? As it is written: "How beautiful are the feet of those who bring good news!"[d]

[16]But not all the Israelites accepted the good news. For Isaiah says, "Lord, who has believed our message?"[e] [17]Consequently, faith comes from hearing the message, and the message is heard through the word about Christ. [18]But I ask: Did they not hear? Of course they did:

> "Their voice has gone out into all the earth,
>   their words to the ends of the world."[f]

[19]Again I ask: Did Israel not understand? First, Moses says,

> "I will make you envious by those who are not a nation;
>   I will make you angry by a nation that has no understanding."[g]

[20]And Isaiah boldly says,

> "I was found by those who did not seek me;
>   I revealed myself to those who did not ask for me."[h]

[21]But concerning Israel he says,

> "All day long I have held out my hands
>   to a disobedient and obstinate people."[i]

The Remnant of Israel

11 I ask then: Did God reject his people? By no means! I am an Israelite myself, a descendant of Abraham, from the tribe of Benjamin. [2]God did not reject his people, whom he foreknew. Don't you know what Scripture says in the passage about Elijah—how he appealed to God against Israel: [3]"Lord, they have killed your prophets and torn down your altars; I am the only one left, and they are trying to kill me"[j]? [4]And what was God's answer to him? "I have reserved for myself seven thousand who have not bowed the knee to Baal."[k] [5]So too, at the present time there is a remnant chosen by grace. [6]And if by grace, then it cannot be based on works; if it were, grace would no longer be grace.

[7]What then? What the people of Israel sought so earnestly they did not obtain. The elect among them did, but the others were hardened, [8]as it is written:

[a]8 Deut. 30:14　　[b]11 Isaiah 28:16　　[c]13 Joel 2:32　　[d]15 Isaiah 52:7　　[e]16 Isaiah 53:1
[f]18 Psalm 19:4　　[g]19 Deut. 32:21　　[h]20 Isaiah 65:1　　[i]21 Isaiah 65:2　　[j]3 1 Kings 19:10,14
[k]4 1 Kings 19:18

"God gave them a spirit of stupor,
  eyes that could not see
  and ears that could not hear,
to this very day." [a]

9And David says:

"May their table become a snare and a trap,
  a stumbling block and a retribution for them.
10May their eyes be darkened so they cannot see,
  and their backs be bent forever." [b]

Ingrafted Branches

11Again I ask: Did they stumble so as to fall beyond recovery? Not at all! Rather, because of their transgression, salvation has come to the Gentiles to make Israel envious. 12But if their transgression means riches for the world, and their loss means riches for the Gentiles, how much greater riches will their fullness bring!

13I am talking to you Gentiles. Inasmuch as I am the apostle to the Gentiles, I make much of my ministry 14in the hope that I may somehow arouse my own people to envy and save some of them. 15For if their rejection brought reconciliation to the world, what will their acceptance be but life from the dead? 16If the part of the dough offered as firstfruits is holy, then the whole batch is holy; if the root is holy, so are the branches.

17If some of the branches have been broken off, and you, though a wild olive shoot, have been grafted in among the others and now share in the nourishing sap from the olive root, 18do not consider yourself to be superior to those other branches. If you do, consider this: You do not support the root, but the root supports you. 19You will say then, "Branches were broken off so that I could be grafted in." 20Granted. But they were broken off because of unbelief, and you stand by faith. Do not be arrogant, but tremble. 21For if God did not spare the natural branches, he will not spare you either.

22Consider therefore the kindness and sternness of God: sternness to those who fell, but kindness to you, provided that you continue in his kindness. Otherwise, you also will be cut off. 23And if they do not persist in unbelief, they will be grafted in, for God is able to graft them in again. 24After all, if you were cut out of an olive tree that is wild by nature, and contrary to nature were grafted into a cultivated olive tree, how much more readily will these, the natural branches, be grafted into their own olive tree!

All Israel Will Be Saved

25I do not want you to be ignorant of this mystery, brothers and sisters, so that you may not think you are superior: Israel has experienced a hardening in part until the full number of the Gentiles has come in, 26and in this way[c] all Israel will be saved. As it is written:

"The deliverer will come from Zion;
  he will turn godlessness away from Jacob.

[a] 8 Deut. 29:4; Isaiah 29:10   [b] 10 Psalm 69:22,23   [c] 26 Or and so

²⁷ And this is^a my covenant with them
    when I take away their sins."^b

²⁸As far as the gospel is concerned, they are enemies for your sake; but as far as election is concerned, they are loved on account of the patriarchs, ²⁹for God's gifts and his call are irrevocable. ³⁰Just as you who were at one time disobedient to God have now received mercy as a result of their disobedience, ³¹so they too have now become disobedient in order that they too may now^c receive mercy as a result of God's mercy to you. ³²For God has bound everyone over to disobedience so that he may have mercy on them all.

Doxology

³³Oh, the depth of the riches of the wisdom and^d knowledge of God!
    How unsearchable his judgments,
        and his paths beyond tracing out!
³⁴"Who has known the mind of the Lord?
    Or who has been his counselor?"^e
³⁵"Who has ever given to God,
    that God should repay them?"^f
³⁶For from him and through him and to him are all things.
    To him be the glory forever! Amen.

Living Sacrifices

12 Therefore, I urge you, brothers and sisters, in view of God's mercy, to offer your bodies as living sacrifices, holy and pleasing to God—this is your proper worship as rational beings. ²Do not conform to the pattern of this world, but be transformed by the renewing of your mind. Then you will be able to test and approve what God's will is—his good, pleasing and perfect will.

Humble Service in the Body of Christ

³For by the grace given me I say to every one of you: Do not think of yourself more highly than you ought, but rather think of yourself with sober judgment, in accordance with the faith God has distributed to each of you. ⁴For just as each of us has one body with many members, and these members do not all have the same function, ⁵so in Christ we, though many, form one body, and each member belongs to all the others. ⁶We have different gifts, according to the grace given to each of us. If your gift is prophesying, then prophesy in accordance with your^g faith; ⁷if it is serving, then serve; if it is teaching, then teach; ⁸if it is to encourage, then give encouragement; if it is giving, then give generously; if it is to lead,^h do it diligently; if it is to show mercy, do it cheerfully.

Love in Action

⁹Love must be sincere. Hate what is evil; cling to what is good. ¹⁰Be devoted to one another in love. Honor one another above yourselves. ¹¹Never be lacking in zeal, but keep your spiritual fervor, serving the Lord. ¹²Be joyful in

---

^a 27 Or will be   ^b 27 Isaiah 59:20,21; 27:9; Jer. 31:33,34   ^c 31 Some manuscripts do not have now.
^d 33 Or riches and the wisdom and the   ^e 34 Isaiah 40:13   ^f 35 Job 41:11   ^g 6 Or the   ^h 8 Or to provide for others

hope, patient in affliction, faithful in prayer. [13]Share with God's people who are in need. Practice hospitality.

[14]Bless those who persecute you; bless and do not curse. [15]Rejoice with those who rejoice; mourn with those who mourn. [16]Live in harmony with one another. Do not be proud, but be willing to associate with people of low position.[a] Do not think you are superior.

[17]Do not repay anyone evil for evil. Be careful to do what is right in the eyes of everyone. [18]If it is possible, as far as it depends on you, live at peace with everyone. [19]Do not take revenge, my dear friends, but leave room for God's wrath, for it is written: "It is mine to avenge; I will repay,"[b] says the Lord. [20]On the contrary:

> "If your enemy is hungry, feed him;
>   if he is thirsty, give him something to drink.
> In doing this, you will heap burning coals on his head."[c]

[21]Do not be overcome by evil, but overcome evil with good.

Submission to Governing Authorities

13 Let everyone be subject to the governing authorities, for there is no authority except that which God has established. The authorities that exist have been established by God. [2]Consequently, whoever rebels against the authority is rebelling against what God has instituted, and those who do so will bring judgment on themselves. [3]For rulers hold no terror for those who do right, but for those who do wrong. Do you want to be free from fear of the one in authority? Then do what is right and you will be commended. [4]For the one in authority is God's servant for your good. But if you do wrong, be afraid, for rulers do not bear the sword for no reason. They are God's servants, agents of wrath to bring punishment on the wrongdoer. [5]Therefore, it is necessary to submit to the authorities, not only because of possible punishment but also as a matter of conscience.

[6]This is also why you pay taxes, for the authorities are God's servants, who give their full time to governing. [7]Give to everyone what you owe: If you owe taxes, pay taxes; if revenue, then revenue; if respect, then respect; if honor, then honor.

Love Fulfills the Law

[8]Let no debt remain outstanding, except the continuing debt to love one another, for whoever loves others has fulfilled the law. [9]The commandments, "Do not commit adultery," "Do not murder," "Do not steal," "Do not covet,"[d] and whatever other commandment there may be, are summed up in this one command: "Love your neighbor as yourself."[e] [10]Love does no harm to its neighbor. Therefore love is the fulfillment of the law.

The Day Is Near

[11]And do this, understanding the present time. The hour has already come

[a]16 Or willing to do menial work   [b]19 Deut. 32:35   [c]20 Prov. 25:21,22   [d]9 Exodus 20:13–15,17; Deut. 5:17–19,21   [e]9 Lev. 19:18

for you to wake up from your slumber, because our salvation is nearer now than when we first believed. [12]The night is nearly over; the day is almost here. So let us put aside the deeds of darkness and put on the armor of light. [13]Let us behave decently, as in the daytime, not in carousing and drunkenness, not in sexual immorality and debauchery, not in dissension and jealousy. [14]Rather, clothe yourselves with the Lord Jesus Christ, and do not think about how to gratify the desires of the sinful nature. [a]

The Weak and the Strong

14 Accept those whose faith is weak, without passing judgment in disputable matters. [2]One person's faith allows him to eat everything, but another person, whose faith is weak, eats only vegetables. [3]The one who eats everything must not look down on the one who does not, and the one who does not eat everything must not condemn the one who does, for God has accepted that person. [4]Who are you to judge someone else's servants? To their own master they stand or fall. And they will stand, for the Lord is able to make them stand.

[5]Some consider one day more sacred than another; others consider every day alike. Everyone should be fully convinced in their own mind. [6]Those who regard one day as special do so to the Lord. Those who eat meat do so to the Lord, for they give thanks to God; and those who abstain do so to the Lord and give thanks to God. [7]For we do not live to ourselves alone and we do not die to ourselves alone. [8]If we live, we live to the Lord; and if we die, we die to the Lord. So, whether we live or die, we belong to the Lord. [9]For this very reason, Christ died and returned to life so that he might be the Lord of both the dead and the living.

[10]You, then, why do you judge your brother or sister? Or why do you look down on your brother or sister? For we will all stand before God's judgment seat. [11]It is written:

" 'As surely as I live,' says the Lord,
'every knee will bow before me;
every tongue will confess to God.' " [b]

[12]So then, we will all give an account of ourselves to God.

[13]Therefore let us stop passing judgment on one another. Instead, make up your mind not to put any stumbling block or obstacle in the way of a brother or sister. [14]I am convinced, being fully persuaded in the Lord Jesus, that nothing is unclean in itself. But if anyone regards something as unclean, then for that person it is unclean. [15]If your brother or sister is distressed because of what you eat, you are no longer acting in love. Do not by your eating destroy your brother or sister for whom Christ died. [16]Therefore do not let what you know is good be spoken of as evil. [17]For the kingdom of God is not a matter of eating and drinking, but of righteousness, peace and joy in the Holy Spirit, [18]because anyone who serves Christ in this way is pleasing to God and receives human approval.

[19]Let us therefore make every effort to do what leads to peace and to mu-

[a] 14 Or *the flesh*   [b] 11 Isaiah 45:23

tual edification. 20Do not destroy the work of God for the sake of food. All food is clean, but it is wrong for a person to eat anything that causes someone else to stumble. 21It is better not to eat meat or drink wine or to do anything else that will cause your brother or sister to fall.

22So whatever you believe about these things keep between yourself and God. Blessed are those who do not condemn themselves by what they approve. 23But those who have doubts are condemned if they eat, because their eating is not from faith; and everything that does not come from faith is sin.

15 We who are strong ought to bear with the failings of the weak and not to please ourselves. 2We should all please our neighbors for their good, to build them up. 3For even Christ did not please himself but, as it is written: "The insults of those who insult you have fallen on me."a 4For everything that was written in the past was written to teach us, so that through the endurance taught in the Scriptures and the encouragement they provide we might have hope.

5May the God who gives endurance and encouragement give you the same attitude of mind toward each other that Christ Jesus had, 6so that with one mind and one voice you may glorify the God and Father of our Lord Jesus Christ.

7Accept one another, then, just as Christ accepted you, in order to bring praise to God. 8For I tell you that Christ has become a servant of the Jewsb on behalf of God's truth, so that the promises made to the patriarchs might be confirmed 9and, moreover, that the Gentiles might glorify God for his mercy. As it is written:

> "Therefore I will praise you among the Gentiles;
>   I will sing hymns to your name."c

10Again, it says,

> "Rejoice, you Gentiles, with his people."d

11And again,

> "Praise the Lord, all you Gentiles,
>   and sing praises to him, all you peoples."e

12And again, Isaiah says,

> "The Root of Jesse will spring up,
>   one who will arise to rule over the nations;
>   in him the Gentiles will hope."f

13May the God of hope fill you with all joy and peace as you trust in him, so that you may overflow with hope by the power of the Holy Spirit.

Paul the Minister to the Gentiles

14I myself am convinced, my brothers and sisters, that you yourselves are full of goodness, filled with knowledge and competent to instruct one another. 15Yet I have written you quite boldly on some points to remind you of them

---

a 3 Psalm 69:9   b 8 Greek *circumcision*   c 9 2 Samuel 22:50; Psalm 18:49   d 10 Deut. 32:43
e 11 Psalm 117:1   f 12 Isaiah 11:10

again, because of the grace God gave me [16]to be a minister of Christ Jesus to the Gentiles. He gave me the priestly duty of proclaiming the gospel of God, so that the Gentiles might become an offering acceptable to God, sanctified by the Holy Spirit.

[17]Therefore I glory in Christ Jesus in my service to God. [18]I will not venture to speak of anything except what Christ has accomplished through me in leading the Gentiles to obey God by what I have said and done— [19]by the power of signs and wonders, through the power of the Spirit of God. So from Jerusalem all the way around to Illyricum, I have fully proclaimed the gospel of Christ. [20]It has always been my ambition to preach the gospel where Christ was not known, so that I would not be building on someone else's foundation. [21]Rather, as it is written:

> "Those who were not told about him will see,
>   and those who have not heard will understand." [a]

[22]This is why I have often been hindered from coming to you.

Paul's Plan to Visit Rome

[23]But now that there is no more place for me to work in these regions, and since I have been longing for many years to visit you, [24]I plan to do so when I go to Spain. I hope to see you while passing through and to have you assist me on my journey there, after I have enjoyed your company for a while. [25]Now, however, I am on my way to Jerusalem in the service of the Lord's people there. [26]For Macedonia and Achaia were pleased to make a contribution for the poor among the saints in Jerusalem. [27]They were pleased to do it, and indeed they owe it to them. For if the Gentiles have shared in the Jews' spiritual blessings, they owe it to the Jews to share with them their material blessings. [28]So after I have completed this task and have made sure that they have received this fruit, I will go to Spain and visit you on the way. [29]I know that when I come to you, I will come in the full measure of the blessing of Christ.

[30]I urge you, brothers and sisters, by our Lord Jesus Christ and by the love of the Spirit, to join me in my struggle by praying to God for me. [31]Pray that I may be kept safe from the unbelievers in Judea and that the contribution I take to Jerusalem may be favorably received by the believers there, [32]so that by God's will I may come to you with joy and together with you be refreshed. [33]The God of peace be with you all. Amen.

Personal Greetings

16 I commend to you our sister Phoebe, a deacon [b] of the church in Cenchrea. [2]I ask you to receive her in the Lord in a way worthy of God's people and to give her any help she may need from you, for she has been the benefactor of many people, including me.

[3]Greet Priscilla [c] and Aquila, my co-workers in Christ Jesus. [4]They risked their lives for me. Not only I but all the churches of the Gentiles are grateful to them.

[5]Greet also the church that meets at their house.

[a] 21 Isaiah 52:15   [b] 1 Or *servant*   [c] 3 Greek *Prisca*, a variant of *Priscilla*

Greet my dear friend Epenetus, who was the first convert to Christ in the province of Asia.

6 Greet Mary, who worked very hard for you.

7 Greet Andronicus and Junia, my fellow Jews who have been in prison with me. They are outstanding among the apostles, and they were in Christ before I was.

8 Greet Ampliatus, my dear friend in the Lord.

9 Greet Urbanus, our co-worker in Christ, and my dear friend Stachys.

10 Greet Apelles, whose fidelity to Christ has stood the test.

Greet those who belong to the household of Aristobulus.

11 Greet Herodion, my fellow Jew.

Greet those in the household of Narcissus who are in the Lord.

12 Greet Tryphena and Tryphosa, those women who work hard in the Lord.

Greet my dear friend Persis, another woman who has worked very hard in the Lord.

13 Greet Rufus, chosen in the Lord, and his mother, who has been a mother to me, too.

14 Greet Asyncritus, Phlegon, Hermes, Patrobas, Hermas and the other brothers and sisters with them.

15 Greet Philologus, Julia, Nereus and his sister, and Olympas and all the believers with them.

16 Greet one another with a holy kiss.

All the churches of Christ send greetings.

17 I urge you, brothers and sisters, to watch out for those who cause divisions and put obstacles in your way that are contrary to the teaching you have learned. Keep away from them. 18 For such people are not serving our Lord Christ, but their own appetites. By smooth talk and flattery they deceive the minds of naive people. 19 Everyone has heard about your obedience, so I rejoice because of you; but I want you to be wise about what is good, and innocent about what is evil.

20 The God of peace will soon crush Satan under your feet.

The grace of our Lord Jesus be with you.

21 Timothy, my co-worker, sends his greetings to you, as do Lucius, Jason and Sosipater, my fellow Jews.

22 I, Tertius, who wrote down this letter, greet you in the Lord.

23 [24] Gaius, whose hospitality I and the whole church here enjoy, sends you his greetings.

Erastus, who is the city's director of public works, and our brother Quartus send you their greetings. a

25 Now to him who is able to establish you in accordance with my gospel, the message I proclaim about Jesus Christ, in keeping with the revelation of the mystery hidden for long ages past, 26 but now revealed and made known through the prophetic writings by the command of the eternal God, so that all the Gentiles might come to faith and obedience— 27 to the only wise God be glory forever through Jesus Christ! Amen.

a 23 Some manuscripts *their greetings.* 24 *May the grace of our Lord Jesus Christ be with all of you. Amen.*

1 CORINTHIANS

1 Paul, called to be an apostle of Christ Jesus by the will of God, and our brother Sosthenes,

2To the church of God in Corinth, to those sanctified in Christ Jesus and called to be saints, together with all those everywhere who call on the name of our Lord Jesus Christ—their Lord and ours:

3Grace and peace to you from God our Father and the Lord Jesus Christ.

Thanksgiving

4I always thank my God for you because of his grace given you in Christ Jesus. 5For in him you have been enriched in every way—with all kinds of speech and with all knowledge— 6God thus confirming our testimony about Christ among you. 7Therefore you do not lack any spiritual gift as you eagerly wait for our Lord Jesus Christ to be revealed. 8He will also keep you firm to the end, so that you will be blameless on the day of our Lord Jesus Christ. 9God is faithful, who has called you into fellowship with his Son, Jesus Christ our Lord.

A Church Divided Over Leaders

10I appeal to you, brothers and sisters, in the name of our Lord Jesus Christ, that all of you agree with one another in what you say and that there be no divisions among you, but that you be perfectly united in mind and thought. 11My brothers and sisters, some from Chloe's household have informed me that there are quarrels among you. 12What I mean is this: One of you says, "I follow Paul"; another, "I follow Apollos"; another, "I follow Cephas[a]"; still another, "I follow Christ."

13Is Christ divided? Was Paul crucified for you? Were you baptized into[b] the name of Paul? 14I thank God that I did not baptize any of you except Crispus and Gaius, 15so no one can say that you were baptized into my name. 16(Yes, I also baptized the household of Stephanas; beyond that, I don't remember if I baptized anyone else.) 17For Christ did not send me to baptize, but to preach the gospel—not with wisdom and eloquence, lest the cross of Christ be emptied of its power.

Christ Crucified Is God's Power and Wisdom

18For the message of the cross is foolishness to those who are perishing, but to us who are being saved it is the power of God. 19For it is written:

_a 12_ That is, Peter   _b 13_ Or _in_; also in verse 15

"I will destroy the wisdom of the wise;
    the intelligence of the intelligent I will frustrate."[a]

20Where are the wise? Where is the teacher of the law? Where is the philosopher of this age? Has not God made foolish the wisdom of the world? 21For since in the wisdom of God the world through its wisdom did not know him, God was pleased through the foolishness of what was preached to save those who believe. 22Jews demand signs and Greeks look for wisdom, 23but we preach Christ crucified: a stumbling block to Jews and foolishness to Gentiles, 24but to those whom God has called, both Jews and Greeks, Christ the power of God and the wisdom of God. 25For the foolishness of God is wiser than human wisdom, and the weakness of God is stronger than human strength.

26Brothers and sisters, think of what you were when you were called. Not many of you were wise by human standards; not many were influential; not many were of noble birth. 27But God chose the foolish things of the world to shame the wise; God chose the weak things of the world to shame the strong. 28He chose the lowly things of this world and the despised things—and the things that are not—to nullify the things that are, 29so that no one may boast before him. 30It is because of him that you are in Christ Jesus, who has become for us wisdom from God—that is, our righteousness, holiness and redemption. 31Therefore, as it is written: "Let those who boast boast in the Lord."[b]

2 And so it was with me, brothers and sisters. When I came to you, I did not come with eloquence or human wisdom as I proclaimed to you the testimony about God.[c] 2For I resolved to know nothing while I was with you except Jesus Christ and him crucified. 3I came to you in weakness with great fear and trembling. 4My message and my preaching were not with wise and persuasive words, but with a demonstration of the Spirit's power, 5so that your faith might not rest on human wisdom, but on God's power.

God's Wisdom Revealed by the Spirit

6We do, however, speak a message of wisdom among the mature, but not the wisdom of this age or of the rulers of this age, who are coming to nothing. 7No, we declare God's wisdom, a mystery that has been hidden and that God destined for our glory before time began. 8None of the rulers of this age understood it, for if they had, they would not have crucified the Lord of glory. 9However, as it is written:

"What no eye has seen,
    what no ear has heard,
    and what no human mind has conceived—
        these things God has prepared for those who love him"[d]—

10for God has revealed them to us by his Spirit.

The Spirit searches all things, even the deep things of God. 11For who knows a person's thoughts except that person's own spirit within? In the same way no one knows the thoughts of God except the Spirit of God. 12We have not received the spirit of the world but the Spirit who is from God, that

---

a 19 Isaiah 29:14   b 31 Jer. 9:24   c 1 Some manuscripts as I proclaimed to you God's mystery
d 9 Isaiah 64:4

we may understand what God has freely given us. [13]This is what we speak, not in words taught us by human wisdom but in words taught by the Spirit, explaining spiritual realities with Spirit-taught words.[a] [14]The person without the Spirit does not accept the things that come from the Spirit of God but considers them foolishness, and cannot understand them because they are discerned only through the Spirit. [15]The person with the Spirit makes judgments about all things, but such a person is not subject to merely human judgments, [16]for,

> "Who has known the mind of the Lord
>   so as to instruct him?"[b]

But we have the mind of Christ.

The Church and Its Leaders

3 Brothers and sisters, I could not address you as spiritual but as worldly— mere infants in Christ. [2]I gave you milk, not solid food, for you were not yet ready for it. Indeed, you are still not ready. [3]You are still worldly. For since there is jealousy and quarreling among you, are you not worldly? Are you not acting like mere human beings? [4]For when one says, "I follow Paul," and another, "I follow Apollos," are you not mere human beings?

[5]What, after all, is Apollos? And what is Paul? Only servants, through whom you came to believe—as the Lord has assigned to each his task. [6]I planted the seed, Apollos watered it, but God has been making it grow. [7]So neither the one who plants nor the one who waters is anything, but only God, who makes things grow. [8]The one who plants and the one who waters have one purpose, and they will each be rewarded according to their own labor. [9]For we are God's co-workers; you are God's field, God's building.

[10]By the grace God has given me, I laid a foundation as a wise builder, and someone else is building on it. But each one should build with care. [11]For no one can lay any foundation other than the one already laid, which is Jesus Christ. [12]If anyone builds on this foundation using gold, silver, costly stones, wood, hay or straw, [13]their work will be shown for what it is, because the Day will bring it to light. It will be revealed with fire, and the fire will test the quality of each person's work. [14]If what has been built survives, the builder will receive a reward. [15]If it is burned up, the builder will suffer loss but yet will be saved—even though only as one escaping through the flames.

[16]Don't you know that you yourselves are God's temple and that God's Spirit dwells in your midst? [17]If anyone destroys God's temple, God will destroy that person; for God's temple is sacred, and you together are that temple.

[18]Do not deceive yourselves. If any of you think you are wise by the standards of this age, you should become "fools" so that you may become wise. [19]For the wisdom of this world is foolishness in God's sight. As it is written: "He catches the wise in their craftiness"[c]; [20]and again, "The Lord knows that the thoughts of the wise are futile."[d] [21]So then, no more boasting about

---

[a] 13 Or *Spirit, interpreting spiritual truths to those who are spiritual*   [b] 16 Isaiah 40:13   [c] 19 Job 5:13
[d] 20 Psalm 94:11

human leaders! All things are yours, [22]whether Paul or Apollos or Cephas[a] or the world or life or death or the present or the future—all are yours, [23]and you are of Christ, and Christ is of God.

The Nature of True Apostleship

4 This, then, is how you ought to regard us: as servants of Christ and as those entrusted with the mysteries God has revealed. [2]Now it is required that those who have been given a trust must prove faithful. [3]I care very little if I am judged by you or by any human court; indeed, I do not even judge myself. [4]My conscience is clear, but that does not make me innocent. It is the Lord who judges me. [5]Therefore judge nothing before the appointed time; wait till the Lord comes. He will bring to light what is hidden in darkness and will expose the motives of people's hearts. At that time each will receive their praise from God.

[6]Now, brothers and sisters, I have applied these things to myself and Apollos for your benefit, so that you may learn from us the meaning of the saying, "Do not go beyond what is written." Then you will not be puffed up in being a follower of one of us over against the other. [7]For who makes you different from anyone else? What do you have that you did not receive? And if you did receive it, why do you boast as though you did not?

[8]Already you have all you want! Already you have become rich! You have begun to reign—and that without us! How I wish that you really had begun to reign so that we also might reign with you! [9]For it seems to me that God has put us apostles on display at the end of the procession, like those condemned to die in the arena. We have been made a spectacle to the whole universe, to angels as well as to human beings. [10]We are fools for Christ, but you are so wise in Christ! We are weak, but you are strong! You are honored, we are dishonored! [11]To this very hour we go hungry and thirsty, we are in rags, we are brutally treated, we are homeless. [12]We work hard with our own hands. When we are cursed, we bless; when we are persecuted, we endure it; [13]when we are slandered, we answer kindly. We have become the scum of the earth, the garbage of the world—right up to this moment.

Paul's Appeal and Warning

[14]I am writing this not to shame you but to warn you as my dear children. [15]Even if you had ten thousand guardians in Christ, you do not have many fathers, for in Christ Jesus I became your father through the gospel. [16]Therefore I urge you to imitate me. [17]For this reason I have sent to you Timothy, my son whom I love, who is faithful in the Lord. He will remind you of my way of life in Christ Jesus, which agrees with what I teach everywhere in every church.

[18]Some of you have become arrogant, as if I were not coming to you. [19]But I will come to you very soon, if the Lord is willing, and then I will find out not only how these arrogant people are talking, but what power they have. [20]For the kingdom of God is not a matter of talk but of power. [21]What do you prefer? Shall I come to you with a rod of discipline, or shall I come in love and with a gentle spirit?

[a] 22 That is, Peter

Dealing With a Case of Incest

5 It is actually reported that there is sexual immorality among you, and of a kind that even pagans do not tolerate: A man has his father's wife. 2And you are proud! Shouldn't you rather have gone into mourning and have put out of your fellowship the man who has been doing this? 3For my part, even though I am not physically present, I am with you in spirit. As one who is present with you in this way, I have already passed judgment in the name of our Lord Jesus on the one who has been doing this. 4So when you are assembled and I am with you in spirit, and the power of our Lord Jesus is present, 5hand this man over to Satan, for the destruction of the sinful nature,[a] so that his spirit may be saved on the day of the Lord.

6Your boasting is not good. Don't you know that a little yeast leavens the whole batch of dough? 7Get rid of the old yeast, so that you may be a new unleavened batch—as you really are. For Christ, our Passover lamb, has been sacrificed. 8Therefore let us keep the Festival, not with the old bread leavened with malice and wickedness, but with the unleavened bread of sincerity and truth.

9I wrote to you in my letter not to associate with sexually immoral people— 10not at all meaning the people of this world who are immoral, or the greedy and swindlers, or idolaters. In that case you would have to leave this world. 11But now I am writing to you that you must not associate with any who claim to be fellow believers but are sexually immoral or greedy, idolaters or slanderers, drunkards or swindlers. With such persons do not even eat.

12What business is it of mine to judge those outside the church? Are you not to judge those inside? 13God will judge those outside. "Expel the wicked person from among you."[b]

Lawsuits Among Believers

6 If any of you has a dispute with another, dare you take it before the ungodly for judgment instead of before God's people? 2Or do you not know that God's people will judge the world? And if you are to judge the world, are you not competent to judge trivial cases? 3Do you not know that we will judge angels? How much more the things of this life! 4Therefore, if you have disputes about such matters, do you ask for a ruling from those whose way of life is scorned in the church? 5I say this to shame you. Is it possible that there is nobody among you wise enough to judge a dispute between believers? 6But instead, one brother goes to law against another—and this in front of unbelievers!

7The very fact that you have lawsuits among you means you have been completely defeated already. Why not rather be wronged? Why not rather be cheated? 8Instead, you yourselves cheat and do wrong, and you do this to your brothers and sisters. 9Or do you not know that wrongdoers will not inherit the kingdom of God? Do not be deceived: Neither the sexually immoral nor idolaters nor adulterers nor male prostitutes nor practicing homosexuals 10nor thieves nor the greedy nor drunkards nor slanderers nor swindlers will inherit the kingdom of God. 11And that is what some of you were. But you

---

[a] 5 Or of his body; or of the flesh   [b] 13 Deut. 13:5; 17:7; 19:19; 21:21; 22:21,24; 24:7

were washed, you were sanctified, you were justified in the name of the Lord Jesus Christ and by the Spirit of our God.

Sexual Immorality

[12]"I have the right to do anything," you say—but not everything is beneficial. "I have the right to do anything"—but I will not be mastered by anything. [13]You say, "Food for the stomach and the stomach for food, and God will destroy them both." The body, however, is not meant for sexual immorality but for the Lord, and the Lord for the body. [14]By his power God raised the Lord from the dead, and he will raise us also. [15]Do you not know that your bodies are members of Christ himself? Shall I then take the members of Christ and unite them with a prostitute? Never! [16]Do you not know that he who unites himself with a prostitute is one with her in body? For it is said, "The two will become one flesh." [a] [17]But whoever is united with the Lord is one with him in spirit. [b]

[18]Flee from sexual immorality. All other sins people commit are outside their bodies, but those who sin sexually sin against their own bodies. [19]Do you not know that your bodies are temples of the Holy Spirit, who is in you, whom you have received from God? You are not your own; [20]you were bought at a price. Therefore honor God with your bodies.

Concerning Married Life

7 Now for the matters you wrote about: "It is good for a man not to have sexual relations with a woman." [2]But since sexual immorality is occurring, each man should have sexual relations with his own wife, and each woman with her own husband. [3]The husband should fulfill his marital duty to his wife, and likewise the wife to her husband. [4]The wife does not have authority over her own body but yields it to her husband. In the same way, the husband does not have authority over his own body but yields it to his wife. [5]Do not deprive each other except perhaps by mutual consent and for a time, so that you may devote yourselves to prayer. Then come together again so that Satan will not tempt you because of your lack of self-control. [6]I say this as a concession, not as a command. [7]I wish that all of you were as I am. But each of you has your own gift from God; one has this gift, another has that.

[8]Now to the unmarried [c] and the widows I say: It is good for them to stay unmarried, as I do. [9]But if they cannot control themselves, they should marry, for it is better to marry than to burn with passion.

[10]To the married I give this command (not I, but the Lord): A wife must not separate from her husband. [11]But if she does, she must remain unmarried or else be reconciled to her husband. And a husband must not divorce his wife. [12]To the rest I say this (I, not the Lord): If any brother has a wife who is not a believer and she is willing to live with him, he must not divorce her. [13]And if a woman has a husband who is not a believer and he is willing to live with her, she must not divorce him. [14]For the unbelieving husband has been sanctified through his wife, and the unbelieving wife has been sanctified through

[a] 16 Gen. 2:24   [b] 17 Or in the Spirit   [c] 8 Or widowers

her believing husband. Otherwise your children would be unclean, but as it is, they are holy.

15But if the unbeliever leaves, let it be so. The brother or sister is not bound in such circumstances; God has called us to live in peace. 16How do you know, wife, whether you will save your husband? Or, how do you know, husband, whether you will save your wife?

Concerning Change of Status

17Nevertheless, each of you should live as a believer in whatever situation the Lord has assigned to you, just as God has called you. This is the rule I lay down in all the churches. 18Was a man already circumcised when he was called? He should not become uncircumcised. Was a man uncircumcised when he was called? He should not be circumcised. 19Circumcision is nothing and uncircumcision is nothing. Keeping God's commands is what counts. 20Each of you should remain in the situation you were in when God called you.

21Were you a slave when you were called? Don't let it trouble you—although if you can gain your freedom, do so. 22For those who were slaves when called to faith in the Lord are the Lord's freed people; similarly, those who were free when called are Christ's slaves. 23You were bought at a price; do not become slaves of human beings. 24Brothers and sisters, all of you, as responsible to God, should remain in the situation in which God called you.

Concerning the Unmarried

25Now about virgins: I have no command from the Lord, but I give a judgment as one who by the Lord's mercy is trustworthy. 26Because of the present crisis, I think that it is good for a man to remain as he is. 27Are you pledged to a woman? Do not seek to be released. Are you free from such a commitment? Do not look for a wife. 28But if you do marry, you have not sinned; and if a virgin marries, she has not sinned. But those who marry will face many troubles in this life, and I want to spare you this.

29What I mean, brothers and sisters, is that the time is short. From now on those who have a husband or wife should live as if they did not; 30those who mourn, as if they did not; those who are happy, as if they were not; those who buy something, as if it were not theirs to keep; 31those who use the things of the world, as if not engrossed in them. For this world in its present form is passing away.

32I would like you to be free from concern. An unmarried man is concerned about the Lord's affairs—how he can please the Lord. 33But a married man is concerned about the affairs of this world—how he can please his wife— 34and his interests are divided. An unmarried woman or virgin is concerned about the Lord's affairs: Her aim is to be devoted to the Lord in both body and spirit. But a married woman is concerned about the affairs of this world—how she can please her husband. 35I am saying this for your own good, not to restrict you, but that you may live in a right way in undivided devotion to the Lord.

36If anyone is worried that he might not be acting honorably toward the virgin he is engaged to, and if she is getting beyond the usual age for marrying and he feels he ought to marry, he should do as he wants. He is not sinning. They should get married. [37]But the man who has settled the matter in his own mind, who is under no compulsion but has control over his own will, and who has made up his mind not to marry the virgin—this man also does the right thing. [38]So then, he who marries the virgin does right, but he who does not marry her does better.

[39]A woman is bound to her husband as long as he lives. But if her husband dies, she is free to marry anyone she wishes, but he must belong to the Lord. [40]In my judgment, she is happier if she stays as she is—and I think that I too have the Spirit of God.

Concerning Food Sacrificed to Idols

8 Now about food sacrificed to idols: We know that "We all possess knowledge." But knowledge puffs up while love builds up. [2]Those who think they know something do not yet know as they ought to know. [3]But whoever loves God is known by God.[a]

[4]So then, about eating food sacrificed to idols: We know that "An idol is nothing at all in the world" and that "There is no God but one." [5]For even if there are so-called gods, whether in heaven or on earth (as indeed there are many "gods" and many "lords"), [6]yet for us there is but one God, the Father, from whom all things came and for whom we live; and there is but one Lord, Jesus Christ, through whom all things came and through whom we live.

[7]But not everyone possesses this knowledge. Some people are still so accustomed to idols that when they eat food in a temple they think of it as having been sacrificed to an idol, and since their conscience is weak, it is defiled. [8]But food does not bring us near to God; we are no worse if we do not eat, and no better if we do.

[9]Be careful, however, that the exercise of your rights does not become a stumbling block to the weak. [10]For if anyone with a weak conscience sees you, with all your knowledge, eating in an idol's temple, won't they be emboldened to eat what is sacrificed to idols? [11]So this weak brother or sister, for whom Christ died, is destroyed by your knowledge. [12]When you sin against them in this way and wound their weak conscience, you sin against Christ. [13]Therefore, if what I eat causes my brother or sister to fall into sin, I will never eat meat again, so that I will not cause them to fall.

Paul's Rights as an Apostle

9 Am I not free? Am I not an apostle? Have I not seen Jesus our Lord? Are you not the result of my work in the Lord? [2]Even though I may not be an apostle to others, surely I am to you! For you are the seal of my apostleship in the Lord.

[3]This is my defense to those who sit in judgment on me. [4]Don't we have the right to food and drink? [5]Don't we have the right to take a believing wife along with us, as do the other apostles and the Lord's brothers and Cephas[b]?

---

[a] 2,3 An early manuscript and another ancient witness *think they have knowledge do not yet know as they ought to know. 3But whoever loves truly knows.*   [b] 5 That is, Peter

6Or is it only I and Barnabas who don't have the right not to work for a living?

7Who serves as a soldier at his own expense? Who plants a vineyard and does not eat of its grapes? Who tends a flock and does not drink of the milk? 8Do I say this merely on human authority? Doesn't the Law say the same thing? 9For it is written in the Law of Moses: "Do not muzzle an ox while it is treading out the grain."[a] Is it about oxen that God is concerned? 10Surely he says this for us, doesn't he? Yes, this was written for us, because when farmers plow and thresh, they should be able to do so in the hope of sharing in the harvest. 11If we have sown spiritual seed among you, is it too much if we reap a material harvest from you? 12If others have this right of support from you, shouldn't we have it all the more?

But we did not use this right. On the contrary, we put up with anything rather than hinder the gospel of Christ.

13Don't you know that those who serve in the temple get their food from the temple, and that those who serve at the altar share in what is offered on the altar? 14In the same way, the Lord has commanded that those who preach the gospel should receive their living from the gospel.

15But I have not used any of these rights. And I am not writing this in the hope that you will do such things for me, for I would rather die than allow anyone to deprive me of this boast. 16For when I preach the gospel, I cannot boast, since I am compelled to preach. Woe to me if I do not preach the gospel! 17If I preach voluntarily, I have a reward; if not voluntarily, I am simply discharging the trust committed to me. 18What then is my reward? Just this: that in preaching the gospel I may offer it free of charge, and so not misuse my rights as a preacher of the gospel.

Paul's Use of His Freedom

19Though I am free and belong to no one, I have made myself a slave to everyone, to win as many as possible. 20To the Jews I became like a Jew, to win the Jews. To those under the law I became like one under the law (though I myself am not under the law), so as to win those under the law. 21To those not having the law I became like one not having the law (though I am not free from God's law but am under Christ's law), so as to win those not having the law. 22To the weak I became weak, to win the weak. I have become all things to all people so that by all possible means I might save some. 23I do all this for the sake of the gospel, that I may share in its blessings.

The Need for Self-Discipline

24Do you not know that in a race all the runners run, but only one gets the prize? Run in such a way as to get the prize. 25Everyone who competes in the games goes into strict training. They do it to get a crown that will not last; but we do it to get a crown that will last forever. 26Therefore I do not run like someone running aimlessly; I do not fight like a boxer beating the air. 27No, I strike a blow to my body and make it my slave so that after I have preached to others, I myself will not be disqualified for the prize.

a 9 Deut. 25:4

Warnings From Israel's History

10 For I do not want you to be ignorant of the fact, brothers and sisters, that our ancestors were all under the cloud and that they all passed through the sea. ²They were all baptized into Moses in the cloud and in the sea. ³They all ate the same spiritual food ⁴and drank the same spiritual drink; for they drank from the spiritual rock that accompanied them, and that rock was Christ. ⁵Nevertheless, God was not pleased with most of them; their bodies were scattered over the desert.

⁶Now these things occurred as examples*a* to keep us from setting our hearts on evil things as they did. ⁷Do not be idolaters, as some of them were; as it is written: "The people sat down to eat and drink and got up to indulge in pagan revelry."*b* ⁸We should not commit sexual immorality, as some of them did—and in one day twenty-three thousand of them died. ⁹We should not test Christ,*c* as some of them did—and were killed by snakes. ¹⁰And do not grumble, as some of them did—and were killed by the destroying angel.

¹¹These things happened to them as examples and were written down as warnings for us, on whom the culmination of the ages has come. ¹²So, if you think you are standing firm, be careful that you don't fall! ¹³No temptation*d* has overtaken you except what is common to us all. And God is faithful; he will not let you be tempted*d* beyond what you can bear. But when you are tempted,*d* he will also provide a way out so that you can endure it.

Idol Feasts and the Lord's Supper

¹⁴Therefore, my dear friends, flee from idolatry. ¹⁵I speak to sensible people; judge for yourselves what I say. ¹⁶Is not the cup of thanksgiving for which we give thanks a participation in the blood of Christ? And is not the bread that we break a participation in the body of Christ? ¹⁷Because there is one loaf, we, who are many, are one body, for we all partake of the one loaf.

¹⁸Consider the people of Israel: Do not those who eat the sacrifices participate in the altar? ¹⁹Do I mean then that food sacrificed to an idol is anything, or that an idol is anything? ²⁰No, but the sacrifices of pagans are offered to demons, not to God, and I do not want you to be participants with demons. ²¹You cannot drink the cup of the Lord and the cup of demons too; you cannot have a part in both the Lord's table and the table of demons. ²²Are we trying to arouse the Lord's jealousy? Are we stronger than he?

The Believer's Freedom

²³"I have the right to do anything," you say—but not everything is beneficial. "I have the right to do anything"—but not everything is constructive. ²⁴No one should seek their own good, but the good of others.

²⁵Eat anything sold in the meat market without raising questions of conscience, ²⁶for, "The earth is the Lord's, and everything in it."*e*

²⁷If an unbeliever invites you to a meal and you want to go, eat whatever is put before you without raising questions of conscience. ²⁸But if someone says to you, "This has been offered in sacrifice," then do not eat it, both for the sake

---

a 6 Or *types*; also in verse 11   *b* 7 Exodus 32:6   *c* 9 Some manuscripts *test the Lord*
d 13 The Greek for *temptation* and *tempted* can also mean *testing* and *tested*.   *e* 26 Psalm 24:1

of the one who told you and for conscience' sake. 29I am referring to the other person's conscience, not yours. For why is my freedom being judged by another's conscience? 30If I take part in the meal with thankfulness, why am I denounced because of something I thank God for?

31So whether you eat or drink or whatever you do, do it all for the glory of God. 32Do not cause anyone to stumble, whether Jews, Greeks or the church of God— 33even as I try to please everyone in every way. For I am not seeking my own good but the good of many, so that they may be saved. 1Follow my example, as I follow the example of Christ.

11

On Covering the Head in Worship

2I praise you for remembering me in everything and for holding to the traditions just as I passed them on to you. 3But I want you to realize that the head of every man is Christ, and the head of the woman is man,*a* and the head of Christ is God. 4Every man who prays or prophesies with his head covered dishonors his head. 5But every woman who prays or prophesies with her head uncovered dishonors her head—it is the same as having her head shaved. 6For if a woman does not cover her head, she might as well have her hair cut off; but if it is a disgrace for a woman to have her hair cut off or her head shaved, then she should cover her head.

7A man ought not to cover his head, since he is the image and glory of God; but the woman is the glory of man. 8For man did not come from woman, but woman from man; 9neither was man created for woman, but woman for man. 10For this reason, and because of the angels, the woman ought to have authority over her own*b* head. 11Nevertheless, in the Lord woman is not independent of man, nor is man independent of woman. 12For as woman came from man, so also man is born of woman. But everything comes from God.

13Judge for yourselves: Is it proper for a woman to pray to God with her head uncovered? 14Does not the very nature of things teach you that if a man has long hair, it is a disgrace to him, 15but that if a woman has long hair, it is her glory? For long hair is given to her as a covering. 16If anyone wants to be contentious about this, we have no other practice—nor do the churches of God.

Correcting an Abuse of the Lord's Supper

17In the following directives I have no praise for you, for your meetings do more harm than good. 18In the first place, I hear that when you come together as a church, there are divisions among you, and to some extent I believe it. 19No doubt there have to be differences among you to show which of you have God's approval. 20So then, when you come together, it is not the Lord's Supper you eat, 21for when you are eating, some of you go ahead with your own private suppers. As a result, one person remains hungry and another gets drunk. 22Don't you have homes to eat and drink in? Or do you despise the church of God by humiliating those who have nothing? What shall I say to you? Shall I praise you? Certainly not in this matter!

23For I received from the Lord what I also passed on to you: The Lord Jesus,

a 3 Or *of the wife is her husband*   *b 10* Or *have a sign of authority on her*

on the night he was betrayed, took bread, 24and when he had given thanks, he broke it and said, "This is my body, which is for you; do this in remembrance of me." 25In the same way, after supper he took the cup, saying, "This cup is the new covenant in my blood; do this, whenever you drink it, in remembrance of me." 26For whenever you eat this bread and drink this cup, you proclaim the Lord's death until he comes.

27So then, whoever eats the bread or drinks the cup of the Lord in an unworthy manner will be guilty of sinning against the body and blood of the Lord. 28We ought to examine ourselves before we eat of the bread and drink of the cup. 29For those who eat and drink without discerning the body of Christ eat and drink judgment on themselves. 30That is why many among you are weak and sick, and a number of you have fallen asleep. 31But if we were more discerning with regard to ourselves, we would not come under such judgment. 32Nevertheless, when we are judged in this way by the Lord, we are being disciplined so that we will not be finally condemned with the world.

33So then, my brothers and sisters, when you come together to eat, make everyone equally welcome. 34Those who are hungry should eat at home, so that when you meet together it may not result in judgment.

And when I come I will give further directions.

Concerning Spiritual Gifts

12 Now about the gifts of the Spirit, brothers and sisters, I do not want you to be uninformed. 2You know that when you were pagans, somehow or other you were influenced and led astray to mute idols. 3Therefore I want you to know that no one who is speaking by the Spirit of God says, "Jesus be cursed," and no one can say, "Jesus is Lord," except by the Holy Spirit.

4There are different kinds of gifts, but the same Spirit distributes them. 5There are different kinds of service, but the same Lord. 6There are different kinds of working, but in all of them and in everyone it is the same God at work.

7Now to each one the manifestation of the Spirit is given for the common good. 8To one there is given through the Spirit a message of wisdom, to another a message of knowledge by means of the same Spirit, 9to another faith by the same Spirit, to another gifts of healing by that one Spirit, 10to another· miraculous powers, to another prophecy, to another distinguishing between spirits, to another speaking in different kinds of tongues,ᵃ and to still another the interpretation of tongues.ᵃ 11All these are the work of one and the same Spirit, and he distributes them to each one, just as he determines.

Unity and Diversity in the Body

12Just as a body, though one, has many parts, but all its many parts form one body, so it is with Christ. 13For we were all baptized byᵇ one Spirit so as to form one body—whether Jews or Greeks, slave or free—and we were all given the one Spirit to drink. 14Even so the body is not made up of one part but of many.

ᵃ 10 Or *languages*; also in verse 28   ᵇ 13 Or *with*; or *in*

¹⁵Now if the foot should say, "Because I am not a hand, I do not belong to the body," it would not for that reason cease to be part of the body. ¹⁶And if the ear should say, "Because I am not an eye, I do not belong to the body," it would not for that reason cease to be part of the body. ¹⁷If the whole body were an eye, where would the sense of hearing be? If the whole body were an ear, where would the sense of smell be? ¹⁸But in fact God has placed the parts in the body, every one of them, just as he wanted them to be. ¹⁹If they were all one part, where would the body be? ²⁰As it is, there are many parts, but one body.

²¹The eye cannot say to the hand, "I don't need you!" And the head cannot say to the feet, "I don't need you!" ²²On the contrary, those parts of the body that seem to be weaker are indispensable, ²³and the parts that we think are less honorable we treat with special honor. And the parts that are unpresentable are treated with special modesty, ²⁴while our presentable parts need no special treatment. But God has put the body together, giving greater honor to the parts that lacked it, ²⁵so that there should be no division in the body, but that its parts should have equal concern for each other. ²⁶If one part suffers, every part suffers with it; if one part is honored, every part rejoices with it.

²⁷Now you are the body of Christ, and each one of you is a part of it. ²⁸And God has placed in the church first of all apostles, second prophets, third teachers, then miracles, then gifts of healing, of helping, of guidance, and of different kinds of tongues. ²⁹Are all apostles? Are all prophets? Are all teachers? Do all work miracles? ³⁰Do all have gifts of healing? Do all speak in tongues*ᵃ*? Do all interpret? ³¹Now eagerly desire*ᵇ* the greater gifts.

Love Is Indispensable

And yet I will show you the most excellent way.

13 If I speak in human or angelic tongues,*ᶜ* but do not have love, I am only a resounding gong or a clanging cymbal. ²If I have the gift of prophecy and can fathom all mysteries and all knowledge, and if I have a faith that can move mountains, but do not have love, I am nothing. ³If I give all I possess to the poor and give over my body ⌊to hardship⌋ that I may boast,*ᵈ* but do not have love, I gain nothing.

⁴Love is patient, love is kind. It does not envy, it does not boast, it is not proud. ⁵It does not dishonor others, it is not self-seeking, it is not easily angered, it keeps no record of wrongs. ⁶Love does not delight in evil but rejoices with the truth. ⁷It always protects, always trusts, always hopes, always perseveres.

⁸Love never fails. But where there are prophecies, they will cease; where there are tongues, they will be stilled; where there is knowledge, it will pass away. ⁹For we know in part and we prophesy in part, ¹⁰but when completeness comes, what is in part disappears. ¹¹When I was a child, I talked like a child, I thought like a child, I reasoned like a child. When I became a man, I put the ways of childhood behind me. ¹²For now we see only a reflection as in a mirror; then we shall see face to face. Now I know in part; then I shall know fully, even as I am fully known.

ᵃ 30 Or *other languages*   *ᵇ 31* Or *But you are eagerly desiring*   *ᶜ 1* Or *languages*   *ᵈ 3* Some manuscripts *body to the flames*

¹³And now these three remain: faith, hope and love. But the greatest of these is love.

Intelligibility in Worship

14 Follow the way of love and eagerly desire spiritual gifts, especially the gift of prophecy. ²For those who speak in a tongue*a* do not speak to other people but to God. Indeed, no one understands them; they utter mysteries by the Spirit. ³But those who prophesy speak to people for their strengthening, encouragement and comfort. ⁴Those who speak in a tongue edify themselves, but those who prophesy edify the church. ⁵I would like every one of you to speak in tongues,*b* but I would rather have you prophesy. Those who prophesy are greater than those who speak in tongues,*b* unless they interpret, so that the church may be edified.

⁶Now, brothers and sisters, if I come to you and speak in tongues, what good will I be to you, unless I bring you some revelation or knowledge or prophecy or word of instruction? ⁷Even in the case of lifeless things that make sounds, such as the flute or harp, how will anyone know what tune is being played unless there is a distinction in the notes? ⁸Again, if the trumpet does not sound a clear call, who will get ready for battle? ⁹So it is with you. Unless you speak intelligible words with your tongue, how will anyone know what you are saying? You will just be speaking into the air. ¹⁰Undoubtedly there are all sorts of languages in the world, yet none of them is without meaning. ¹¹If then I do not grasp the meaning of what someone is saying, I am a foreigner to the speaker, and the speaker is a foreigner to me. ¹²So it is with you. Since you are eager for gifts of the Spirit, try to excel in those that build up the church.

¹³For this reason those who speak in a tongue should pray that they may interpret what they say. ¹⁴For if I pray in a tongue, my spirit prays, but my mind is unfruitful. ¹⁵So what shall I do? I will pray with my spirit, but I will also pray with my understanding; I will sing with my spirit, but I will also sing with my understanding. ¹⁶Otherwise when you are praising God in the Spirit, how can the others, who are now put in the same situation as an inquirer,*c* say "Amen" to your thanksgiving, since they do not know what you are saying? ¹⁷You are giving thanks well enough, but the others are not edified.

¹⁸I thank God that I speak in tongues more than all of you. ¹⁹But in the church I would rather speak five intelligible words to instruct others than ten thousand words in a tongue.

²⁰Brothers and sisters, stop thinking like children. In regard to evil be infants, but in your thinking be adults. ²¹In the Law it is written:

> "With other tongues
>   and through the lips of foreigners
> I will speak to this people,
>   but even then they will not listen to me,

> says the Lord."*d*

---

a 2 Or *in another language*; also in verses 4, 13, 14, 19, 26 and 27   *b 5* Or *in other languages*; also in verses 6, 18, 22, 23 and 39   *c 16* The Greek word for *inquirer* is a technical term for someone not fully initiated into a religion; also in verses 23 and 24.   *d 21* Isaiah 28:11,12

22Tongues, then, are a sign, not for believers but for unbelievers; prophecy, however, is not for unbelievers but for believers. 23So if the whole church comes together and everyone speaks in tongues, and inquirers or unbelievers come in, will they not say that you are out of your mind? 24But if an unbeliever or an inquirer comes in while everyone is prophesying, they are convicted of sin and are brought under judgment by all, 25as the secrets of their hearts are laid bare. So they will fall down and worship God, exclaiming, "God is really among you!"

Good Order in Worship

26What then shall we say, brothers and sisters? When you come together, each of you has a hymn, or a word of instruction, a revelation, a tongue or an interpretation. Everything must be done so that the church may be built up. 27If anyone speaks in a tongue, two—or at the most three—should speak, one at a time, and someone must interpret. 28If there is no interpreter, the speaker should keep quiet in the church and speak to God when alone.

29Two or three prophets should speak, and the others should weigh carefully what is said. 30And if a revelation comes to someone who is sitting down, the first speaker should stop. 31For you can all prophesy in turn so that everyone may be instructed and encouraged. 32The spirits of prophets are subject to the control of prophets. 33For God is not a God of disorder but of peace—as in all the congregations of the people of God.

34Women should remain silent in the churches. They are not allowed to speak, but must be in submission, as the law says. 35If they want to inquire about something, they should ask their own husbands at home; for it is disgraceful for a woman to speak in the church.*a*

36Or did the word of God originate with you? Or are you the only people it has reached? 37If any think they are prophets or otherwise gifted by the Spirit, let them acknowledge that what I am writing to you is the Lord's command. 38Those who ignore this will themselves be ignored.*b*

39Therefore, my brothers and sisters, be eager to prophesy, and do not forbid speaking in tongues. 40But everything should be done in a fitting and orderly way.

The Resurrection of Christ

15 Now, brothers and sisters, I want to remind you of the gospel I preached to you, which you received and on which you have taken your stand. 2By this gospel you are saved, if you hold firmly to the word I preached to you. Otherwise, you have believed in vain.

3For what I received I passed on to you as of first importance*c*: that Christ died for our sins according to the Scriptures, 4that he was buried, that he was raised on the third day according to the Scriptures, 5and that he appeared to Cephas,*d* and then to the Twelve. 6After that, he appeared to more than five hundred of the brothers and sisters at the same time, most of whom are still living, though some have fallen asleep. 7Then he appeared to James, then to

---

a 34,35 In some manuscripts these verses come after verse 40. b 38 Some manuscripts Those who are ignorant of this will be ignorant c 3 Or you at the first d 5 That is, Peter

all the apostles, [8]and last of all he appeared to me also, as to one abnormally born.

[9]For I am the least of the apostles and do not even deserve to be called an apostle, because I persecuted the church of God. [10]But by the grace of God I am what I am, and his grace to me was not without effect. No, I worked harder than all of them—yet not I, but the grace of God that was with me. [11]Whether, then, it is I or they, this is what we preach, and this is what you believed.

The Resurrection of the Dead

[12]But if it is preached that Christ has been raised from the dead, how can some of you say that there is no resurrection of the dead? [13]If there is no resurrection of the dead, then not even Christ has been raised. [14]And if Christ has not been raised, our preaching is useless and so is your faith. [15]More than that, we are then found to be false witnesses about God, for we have testified about God that he raised Christ from the dead. But he did not raise him if in fact the dead are not raised. [16]For if the dead are not raised, then Christ has not been raised either. [17]And if Christ has not been raised, your faith is futile; you are still in your sins. [18]Then those also who have fallen asleep in Christ are lost. [19]If only for this life we have hope in Christ, we are to be pitied more than all others.

[20]But Christ has indeed been raised from the dead, the firstfruits of those who have fallen asleep. [21]For since death came through a human being, the resurrection of the dead comes also through a human being. [22]For as in Adam all die, so in Christ all will be made alive. [23]But in this order: Christ, the firstfruits; then, when he comes, those who belong to him. [24]Then the end will come, when he hands over the kingdom to God the Father after he has destroyed all dominion, authority and power. [25]For he must reign until he has put all his enemies under his feet. [26]The last enemy to be destroyed is death. [27]For he "has put everything under his feet." [a] Now when it says that "everything" has been put under him, it is clear that this does not include God himself, who put everything under Christ. [28]When he has done this, then the Son himself will be made subject to him who put everything under him, so that God may be all in all.

[29]Now if there is no resurrection, what will those do who are baptized for the dead? If the dead are not raised at all, why are people baptized for them? [30]And as for us, why do we endanger ourselves every hour? [31]I face death every day—yes, just as surely as I boast about you in Christ Jesus our Lord. [32]If I fought wild beasts in Ephesus with no more than human hopes, what have I gained? If the dead are not raised,

> "Let us eat and drink,
>   for tomorrow we die." [b]

[33]Do not be misled: "Bad company corrupts good character." [c] [34]Come back to your senses as you ought, and stop sinning; for there are some who are ignorant of God—I say this to your shame.

---

[a] 27 Psalm 8:6   [b] 32 Isaiah 22:13   [c] 33 From the Greek poet Menander

The Resurrection Body

³⁵But someone will ask, "How are the dead raised? With what kind of body will they come?" ³⁶How foolish! What you sow does not come to life unless it dies. ³⁷When you sow, you do not plant the body that will be, but just a seed, perhaps of wheat or of something else. ³⁸But God gives it a body as he has determined, and to each kind of seed he gives its own body. ³⁹All flesh is not the same: Human beings have one kind of flesh, animals have another, birds another and fish another. ⁴⁰There are also heavenly bodies and there are earthly bodies; but the splendor of the heavenly bodies is one kind, and the splendor of the earthly bodies is another. ⁴¹The sun has one kind of splendor, the moon another and the stars another; and star differs from star in splendor.

⁴²So will it be with the resurrection of the dead. The body that is sown is perishable, it is raised imperishable; ⁴³it is sown in dishonor, it is raised in glory; it is sown in weakness, it is raised in power; ⁴⁴it is sown a natural body, it is raised a spiritual body.

If there is a natural body, there is also a spiritual body. ⁴⁵So it is written: "The first Adam became a living being"ᵃ; the last Adam, a life-giving spirit. ⁴⁶The spiritual did not come first, but the natural, and after that the spiritual. ⁴⁷The first man was of the dust of the earth; the second man is of heaven. ⁴⁸As was the earthly man, so are those who are of the earth; and as is the heavenly man, so also are those who are of heaven. ⁴⁹And just as we have borne the likeness of the earthly man, so shall weᵇ bear the likeness of the heavenly man.

⁵⁰I declare to you, brothers and sisters, that flesh and blood cannot inherit the kingdom of God, nor does the perishable inherit the imperishable. ⁵¹Listen, I tell you a mystery: We will not all sleep, but we will all be changed— ⁵²in a flash, in the twinkling of an eye, at the last trumpet. For the trumpet will sound, the dead will be raised imperishable, and we will be changed. ⁵³For the perishable must clothe itself with the imperishable, and the mortal with immortality. ⁵⁴When the perishable has been clothed with the imperishable, and the mortal with immortality, then the saying that is written will come true: "Death has been swallowed up in victory."ᶜ

⁵⁵"Where, O death, is your victory?
    Where, O death, is your sting?"ᵈ

⁵⁶The sting of death is sin, and the power of sin is the law. ⁵⁷But thanks be to God! He gives us the victory through our Lord Jesus Christ.

⁵⁸Therefore, my dear brothers and sisters, stand firm. Let nothing move you. Always give yourselves fully to the work of the Lord, because you know that your labor in the Lord is not in vain.

The Collection for God's People

16 Now about the collection for God's people: Do what I told the Galatian churches to do. ²On the first day of every week, each one of you should set aside a sum of money in keeping with your income, saving it up, so that when I come no collections will have to be made. ³Then, when I arrive, I will

---

ᵃ 45 Gen. 2:7   ᵇ 49 Some early manuscripts *so let us*   ᶜ 54 Isaiah 25:8   ᵈ 55 Hosea 13:14

give letters of introduction to the men you approve and send them with your gift to Jerusalem. [4]If it seems advisable for me to go also, they will accompany me.

Personal Requests

[5]After I go through Macedonia, I will come to you—for I will be going through Macedonia. [6]Perhaps I will stay with you awhile, or even spend the winter, so that you can help me on my journey, wherever I go. [7]For I do not want to see you now and make only a passing visit; I hope to spend some time with you, if the Lord permits. [8]But I will stay on at Ephesus until Pentecost, [9]because a great door for effective work has opened to me, and there are many who oppose me.

[10]When Timothy comes, see to it that he has nothing to fear while he is with you, for he is carrying on the work of the Lord, just as I am. [11]No one, then, should treat him with contempt. Send him on his way in peace so that he may return to me. I am expecting him along with the brothers.

[12]Now about our brother Apollos: I strongly urged him to go to you with the brothers. He was quite unwilling to go now, but he will go when he has the opportunity.

[13]Be on your guard; stand firm in the faith; be courageous; be strong. [14]Do everything in love.

[15]You know that the household of Stephanas were the first converts in Achaia, and they have devoted themselves to the service of God's people. I urge you, brothers and sisters, [16]to submit to such as these and to everyone who joins in the work and labors at it. [17]I was glad when Stephanas, Fortunatus and Achaicus arrived, because they have supplied what was lacking from you. [18]For they refreshed my spirit and yours also. Such men deserve recognition.

Final Greetings

[19]The churches in the province of Asia send you greetings. Aquila and Priscilla[a] greet you warmly in the Lord, and so does the church that meets at their house. [20]All the brothers and sisters here send you greetings. Greet one another with a holy kiss.

[21]I, Paul, write this greeting in my own hand.

[22]If anyone does not love the Lord, let that person be cursed! Come, Lord[b]!

[23]The grace of the Lord Jesus be with you.

[24]My love to all of you in Christ Jesus. Amen.[c]

---

[a] 19 Greek *Prisca*, a variant of *Priscilla*   [b] 22 The Greek for *Come, Lord* reproduces an Aramaic expression (*Marana tha*) used by early Christians.   [c] 24 Some manuscripts do not have *Amen*.

2 CORINTHIANS

1 Paul, an apostle of Christ Jesus by the will of God, and Timothy our brother,

To the church of God in Corinth, together with all the saints throughout Achaia:

2Grace and peace to you from God our Father and the Lord Jesus Christ.

Praise to the God of All Comfort

3Praise be to the God and Father of our Lord Jesus Christ, the Father of compassion and the God of all comfort, 4who comforts us in all our troubles, so that we can comfort those in any trouble with the comfort we ourselves receive from God. 5For just as we share abundantly in the sufferings of Christ, so also our comfort abounds through Christ. 6If we are distressed, it is for your comfort and salvation; if we are comforted, it is for your comfort, which produces in you patient endurance of the same sufferings we suffer. 7And our hope for you is firm, because we know that just as you share in our sufferings, so also you share in our comfort.

8We do not want you to be uninformed, brothers and sisters, about the troubles we experienced in the province of Asia. We were under great pressure, far beyond our ability to endure, so that we despaired of life itself. 9Indeed, we felt we had received the sentence of death. But this happened that we might not rely on ourselves but on God, who raises the dead. 10He has delivered us from such a deadly peril, and he will deliver us again. On him we have set our hope that he will continue to deliver us, 11as you help us by your prayers. Then many will give thanks on our behalf for the gracious favor granted us in answer to the prayers of many.

Paul's Change of Plans

12Now this is our boast: Our conscience testifies that we have conducted ourselves in the world, and especially in our relations with you, with integrity*a* and godly sincerity. We have done so, relying not on worldly wisdom but on God's grace. 13For we do not write you anything you cannot read or understand. And I hope that, 14as you have understood us in part, you will come to understand fully that you can boast of us just as we will boast of you in the day of the Lord Jesus.

15Because I was confident of this, I wanted to visit you first so that you

a 12 Many manuscripts *holiness*

might benefit twice. [16]I wanted to visit you on my way to Macedonia and to come back to you from Macedonia, and then to have you send me on my way to Judea. [17]Was I fickle when I intended to do this? Or do I make my plans in a worldly manner so that in the same breath I say both "Yes, yes" and "No, no"?

[18]But as surely as God is faithful, our message to you is not "Yes" and "No." [19]For the Son of God, Jesus Christ, who was preached among you by us—by me and Silas[a] and Timothy—was not "Yes" and "No," but in him it has always been "Yes." [20]For no matter how many promises God has made, they are "Yes" in Christ. And so through him the "Amen" is spoken by us to the glory of God. [21]Now it is God who makes both us and you stand firm in Christ. He anointed us, [22]set his seal of ownership on us, and put his Spirit in our hearts as a deposit, guaranteeing what is to come.

[23]I call God as my witness—and I stake my life on it—that it was in order to spare you that I did not return to Corinth. [24]Not that we lord it over your faith, but we work with you for your joy, because it is by faith you stand firm. 2 [1]So I made up my mind that I would not make another painful visit to you. [2]For if I grieve you, who is left to make me glad but you whom I have grieved? [3]I wrote as I did, so that when I came I would not be distressed by those who should have made me rejoice. I had confidence in all of you, that you would all share my joy. [4]For I wrote you out of great distress and anguish of heart and with many tears, not to grieve you but to let you know the depth of my love for you.

Forgiveness for the Offender

[5]If anyone has caused grief, he has not so much grieved me as he has grieved all of you, to some extent—not to put it too severely. [6]The punishment inflicted on him by the majority is sufficient. [7]Now instead, you ought to forgive and comfort him, so that he will not be overwhelmed by excessive sorrow. [8]I urge you, therefore, to reaffirm your love for him. [9]Another reason I wrote you was to see if you would stand the test and be obedient in everything. [10]Anyone you forgive, I also forgive. And what I have forgiven—if there was anything to forgive—I have forgiven in the sight of Christ for your sake, [11]in order that Satan might not outwit us. For we are not unaware of his schemes.

Ministers of the New Covenant

[12]Now when I went to Troas to preach the gospel of Christ and found that the Lord had opened a door for me, [13]I still had no peace of mind, because I did not find my brother Titus there. So I said good-by to them and went on to Macedonia.

[14]But thanks be to God, who always leads us as captives in Christ's triumphal procession and uses us to spread the aroma of the knowledge of him everywhere. [15]For we are to God the pleasing aroma of Christ among those who are being saved and those who are perishing. [16]To the one we are an aroma that brings death; to the other, an aroma that brings life. And who is

[a] 19 Greek *Silvanus*, a variant of *Silas*

equal to such a task? [17]Unlike so many, we do not peddle the word of God for profit. On the contrary, in Christ we speak before God with sincerity, as those sent from God.

3 Are we beginning to commend ourselves again? Or do we need, like some people, letters of recommendation to you or from you? [2]You yourselves are our letter, written on our hearts, known and read by everyone. [3]You show that you are a letter from Christ, the result of our ministry, written not with ink but with the Spirit of the living God, not on tablets of stone but on tablets of human hearts.

[4]Such confidence we have through Christ before God. [5]Not that we are competent in ourselves to claim anything for ourselves, but our competence comes from God. [6]He has made us competent as ministers of a new covenant—not of the letter but of the Spirit; for the letter kills, but the Spirit gives life.

The Greater Glory of the New Covenant

[7]Now if the ministry that brought death, which was engraved in letters on stone, came with glory, so that the Israelites could not look steadily at the face of Moses because of its glory, transitory though it was, [8]will not the ministry of the Spirit be even more glorious? [9]If the ministry that brought condemnation was glorious, how much more glorious is the ministry that brings righteousness! [10]For what was glorious has no glory now in comparison with the surpassing glory. [11]And if what was transitory came with glory, how much greater is the glory of that which lasts!

[12]Therefore, since we have such a hope, we are very bold. [13]We are not like Moses, who would put a veil over his face to prevent the Israelites from seeing the end of what was passing away. [14]But their minds were made dull, for to this day the same veil remains when the old covenant is read. It has not been removed, because only in Christ is it taken away. [15]Even to this day when Moses is read, a veil covers their hearts. [16]But whenever anyone turns to the Lord, the veil is taken away. [17]Now the Lord is the Spirit, and where the Spirit of the Lord is, there is freedom. [18]And we all, who with unveiled faces contemplate[a] the Lord's glory, are being transformed into his likeness with ever-increasing glory, which comes from the Lord, who is the Spirit.

Present Weakness and Resurrection Life

4 Therefore, since through God's mercy we have this ministry, we do not lose heart. [2]Rather, we have renounced secret and shameful ways; we do not use deception, nor do we distort the word of God. On the contrary, by setting forth the truth plainly we commend ourselves to everyone's conscience in the sight of God. [3]And even if our gospel is veiled, it is veiled to those who are perishing. [4]The god of this age has blinded the minds of unbelievers, so that they cannot see the light of the gospel that displays the glory of Christ, who is the image of God. [5]For what we preach is not ourselves, but Jesus Christ as Lord, and ourselves as your servants for Jesus' sake. [6]For God, who said, "Let light shine out of darkness,"[b] made his light shine in our hearts to give us the light of the knowledge of God's glory displayed in the face of Christ.

---

[a] 18 Or reflect   [b] 6 Gen. 1:3

7But we have this treasure in jars of clay to show that this all-surpassing power is from God and not from us. 8We are hard pressed on every side, but not crushed; perplexed, but not in despair; 9persecuted, but not abandoned; struck down, but not destroyed. 10We always carry around in our body the death of Jesus, so that the life of Jesus may also be revealed in our body. 11For we who are alive are always being given over to death for Jesus' sake, so that his life may also be revealed in our mortal body. 12So then, death is at work in us, but life is at work in you.

13It is written: "I believed; therefore I have spoken."*a* Since we have that same spirit of*b* faith, we also believe and therefore speak, 14because we know that the one who raised the Lord Jesus from the dead will also raise us with Jesus and present us with you to himself. 15All this is for your benefit, so that the grace that is reaching more and more people may cause thanksgiving to overflow to the glory of God.

16Therefore we do not lose heart. Though outwardly we are wasting away, yet inwardly we are being renewed day by day. 17For our light and momentary troubles are achieving for us an eternal glory that far outweighs them all. 18So we fix our eyes not on what is seen, but on what is unseen, since what is seen is temporary, but what is unseen is eternal.

Awaiting the New Body

5 For we know that if the earthly tent we live in is destroyed, we have a building from God, an eternal house in heaven, not built by human hands. 2Meanwhile we groan, longing to be clothed with our heavenly dwelling, 3because when we are clothed, we will not be found naked. 4For while we are in this tent, we groan and are burdened, because we do not wish to be unclothed but to be clothed with our heavenly dwelling, so that what is mortal may be swallowed up by life. 5Now the one who has fashioned us for this very purpose is God, who has given us the Spirit as a deposit, guaranteeing what is to come.

6Therefore we are always confident and know that as long as we are at home in the body we are away from the Lord. 7We live by faith, not by sight. 8We are confident, I say, and would prefer to be away from the body and at home with the Lord. 9So we make it our goal to please him, whether we are at home in the body or away from it. 10For we must all appear before the judgment seat of Christ, that everyone may receive what is due them for the things done while in the body, whether good or bad.

The Ministry of Reconciliation

11Since, then, we know what it is to fear the Lord, we try to persuade people. What we are is plain to God, and I hope it is also plain to your conscience. 12We are not trying to commend ourselves to you again, but are giving you an opportunity to take pride in us, so that you can answer those who take pride in what is seen rather than in what is in the heart. 13If we are "out of our mind," as some say, it is for God; if we are in our right mind, it is for you. 14For Christ's love compels us, because we are convinced that one died for all, and

---

a 13 Psalm 116:10   *b* 13 Or *Spirit-given*

therefore all died. [15]And he died for all, that those who live should no longer live for themselves but for him who died for them and was raised again.

[16]So from now on we regard no one from a worldly point of view. Though we once regarded Christ in this way, we do so no longer. [17]Therefore, if anyone is in Christ, there is a new creation: The old has gone, the new has come! [18]All this is from God, who reconciled us to himself through Christ and gave us the ministry of reconciliation: [19]that God was reconciling the world to himself in Christ, not counting people's sins against them. And he has committed to us the message of reconciliation. [20]We are therefore Christ's ambassadors, as though God were making his appeal through us. We implore you on Christ's behalf: Be reconciled to God. [21]God made him who had no sin to be sin[a] for us, so that in him we might become the righteousness of God.

6 As God's co-workers we urge you not to receive God's grace in vain. [2]For he says,

> "In the time of my favor I heard you,
> and in the day of salvation I helped you."[b]

I tell you, now is the time of God's favor, now is the day of salvation.

Paul's Hardships

[3]We put no stumbling block in anyone's path, so that our ministry will not be discredited. [4]Rather, as servants of God we commend ourselves in every way: in great endurance; in troubles, hardships and distresses; [5]in beatings, imprisonments and riots; in hard work, sleepless nights and hunger; [6]in purity, understanding, patience and kindness; in the Holy Spirit and in sincere love; [7]in truthful speech and in the power of God; with weapons of righteousness in the right hand and in the left; [8]through glory and dishonor, bad report and good report; genuine, yet regarded as impostors; [9]known, yet regarded as unknown; dying, and yet we live on; beaten, and yet not killed; [10]sorrowful, yet always rejoicing; poor, yet making many rich; having nothing, and yet possessing everything.

[11]We have spoken freely to you, Corinthians, and opened wide our hearts to you. [12]We are not withholding our affection from you, but you are withholding yours from us. [13]As a fair exchange—I speak as to my children—open wide your hearts also.

Warning Against Idolatry

[14]Do not be yoked together with unbelievers. For what do righteousness and wickedness have in common? Or what fellowship can light have with darkness? [15]What harmony is there between Christ and Belial[c]? Or what does a believer have in common with an unbeliever? [16]What agreement is there between the temple of God and idols? For we are the temple of the living God. As God has said:

> "I will live with them
> and walk among them,

---

[a] 21 Or *be a sin offering*　　[b] 2 Isaiah 49:8　　[c] 15 Greek *Beliar*, a variant of *Belial*

> and I will be their God,
> and they will be my people."[a]

[17]Therefore,

> "Come out from them
> and be separate,
>
> says the Lord.
>
> Touch no unclean thing,
> and I will receive you."[b]

[18]And,

> "I will be a Father to you,
> and you will be my sons and daughters,
>
> says the Lord Almighty."[c]

7 Since we have these promises, dear friends, let us purify ourselves from everything that contaminates body and spirit, perfecting holiness out of reverence for God.

Paul's Joy Over the Church's Repentance

[2]Make room for us in your hearts. We have wronged no one, we have corrupted no one, we have exploited no one. [3]I do not say this to condemn you; I have said before that you have such a place in our hearts that we would live or die with you. [4]I have spoken to you with great frankness; I take great pride in you. I am greatly encouraged; in all our troubles my joy knows no bounds.

[5]For when we came into Macedonia, this body of ours had no rest, but we were harassed at every turn—conflicts on the outside, fears within. [6]But God, who comforts the downcast, comforted us by the coming of Titus, [7]and not only by his coming but also by the comfort you had given him. He told us about your longing for me, your deep sorrow, your ardent concern for me, so that my joy was greater than ever.

[8]Even if I caused you sorrow by my letter, I do not regret it. Though I did regret it—I see that my letter hurt you, but only for a little while— [9]yet now I am happy, not because you were made sorry, but because your sorrow led you to repentance. For you became sorrowful as God intended and so were not harmed in any way by us. [10]Godly sorrow brings repentance that leads to salvation and leaves no regret, but worldly sorrow brings death. [11]See what this godly sorrow has produced in you: what earnestness, what eagerness to clear yourselves, what indignation, what alarm, what longing, what concern, what readiness to see justice done. At every point you have proved yourselves to be innocent in this matter. [12]So even though I wrote to you, it was neither on account of the one who did the wrong nor on account of the injured party, but rather that before God you could see for yourselves how devoted to us you are. [13]By all this we are encouraged.

In addition to our own encouragement, we were especially delighted to see how happy Titus was, because his spirit has been refreshed by all of you. [14]I had boasted to him about you, and you have not embarrassed me. But just as

---

[a]16 Lev. 26:12; Jer. 32:38; Ezek. 37:27   [b]17 Isaiah 52:11; Ezek. 20:34,41   [c]18 2 Samuel 7:14; 7:8

everything we said to you was true, so our boasting about you to Titus has proved to be true as well. [15]And his affection for you is all the greater when he remembers that you were all obedient, receiving him with fear and trembling. [16]I am glad I can have complete confidence in you.

The Collection for God's People

8 And now, brothers and sisters, we want you to know about the grace that God has given the Macedonian churches. [2]In the midst of a very severe trial, their overflowing joy and their extreme poverty welled up in rich generosity. [3]For I testify that they gave as much as they were able, and even beyond their ability. Entirely on their own, [4]they urgently pleaded with us for the privilege of sharing in this service to God's people. [5]And they went beyond our expectations; having given themselves first of all to the Lord, they gave themselves by the will of God also to us. [6]So we urged Titus, just as he had earlier made a beginning, to bring also to completion this act of grace on your part. [7]But since you excel in everything—in faith, in speech, in knowledge, in complete earnestness and in the love we have kindled in you[a]—see that you also excel in this grace of giving.

[8]I am not commanding you, but I want to test the sincerity of your love by comparing it with the earnestness of others. [9]For you know the grace of our Lord Jesus Christ, that though he was rich, yet for your sake he became poor, so that you through his poverty might become rich.

[10]And here is my judgment about what is best for you in this matter. Last year you were the first not only to give but also to have the desire to do so. [11]Now finish the work, so that your eager willingness to do it may be matched by your completion of it, according to your means. [12]For if the willingness is there, the gift is acceptable according to what one has, not according to what one does not have.

[13]Our desire is not that others might be relieved while you are hard pressed, but that there might be equality. [14]At the present time your plenty will supply what they need, so that in turn their plenty will supply what you need. The goal is equality, [15]as it is written: "The one who gathered much did not have too much, and the one who gathered little did not have too little."[b]

Titus Sent to Receive the Collection

[16]Thanks be to God, who put into the heart of Titus the same concern I have for you. [17]For Titus not only welcomed our appeal, but he is coming to you with much enthusiasm and on his own initiative. [18]And we are sending along with him the brother who is praised by all the churches for his service to the gospel. [19]What is more, he was chosen by the churches to accompany us as we carry the offering, which we administer in order to honor the Lord himself and to show our eagerness to help. [20]We want to avoid any criticism of the way we administer this liberal gift. [21]For we are taking pains to do what is right, not only in the eyes of the Lord but also in the eyes of others.

[22]In addition, we are sending with them our brother who has often proved to us in many ways that he is zealous, and now even more so because of his

[a] 7 Some manuscripts *in your love for us*   [b] 15 Exodus 16:18

great confidence in you. 23As for Titus, he is my partner and co-worker among you; as for our brothers, they are representatives of the churches and an honor to Christ. 24Therefore show these men the proof of your love and the reason for our pride in you, so that the churches can see it.

9 There is no need for me to write to you about this service to God's people. 2For I know your eagerness to help, and I have been boasting about it to the Macedonians, telling them that since last year you in Achaia were ready to give; and your enthusiasm has stirred most of them to action. 3But I am sending the brothers in order that our boasting about you in this matter should not prove hollow, but that you may be ready, as I said you would be. 4For if any Macedonians come with me and find you unprepared, we—not to say anything about you—would be ashamed of having been so confident. 5So I thought it necessary to urge the brothers to visit you in advance and finish the arrangements for the generous gift you had promised. Then it will be ready as a generous gift, not as one grudgingly given.

Generosity Encouraged

6Remember this: Whoever sows sparingly will also reap sparingly, and whoever sows generously will also reap generously. 7Each of you should give what you have decided in your heart to give, not reluctantly or under compulsion, for God loves a cheerful giver. 8And God is able to bless you abundantly, so that in all things at all times, having all that you need, you will abound in every good work. 9As it is written:

> "They have scattered abroad their gifts to the poor;
>   their righteousness endures forever." [a]

10Now he who supplies seed to the sower and bread for food will also supply and increase your store of seed and will enlarge the harvest of your righteousness. 11You will be made rich in every way so that you can be generous on every occasion, and through us your generosity will result in thanksgiving to God.

12This service that you perform is not only supplying the needs of God's people but is also overflowing in many expressions of thanks to God. 13Because of the service by which you have proved yourselves, people will praise God for the obedience that accompanies your confession of the gospel of Christ, and for your generosity in sharing with them and with everyone else. 14And in their prayers for you their hearts will go out to you, because of the surpassing grace God has given you. 15Thanks be to God for his indescribable gift!

Paul's Defense of His Ministry

10 By the meekness and gentleness of Christ, I appeal to you—I, Paul, who am "timid" when face to face with you, but "bold" toward you when away! 2I beg you that when I come I may not have to be as bold as I expect to be toward some people who think that we live by the standards of this world. 3For though we live in the world, we do not wage war as the world

---

a 9 Psalm 112:9

does. ⁴The weapons we fight with are not the weapons of the world. On the contrary, they have divine power to demolish strongholds. ⁵We demolish arguments and every pretension that sets itself up against the knowledge of God, and we take captive every thought to make it obedient to Christ. ⁶And we will be ready to punish every act of disobedience, once your obedience is complete.

⁷You are judging by appearances.ᵃ If any are confident that they belong to Christ, they should consider again that we belong to Christ just as much as they do. ⁸So even if I boast somewhat freely about the authority the Lord gave us for building you up rather than tearing you down, I will not be ashamed of it. ⁹I do not want to seem to be trying to frighten you with my letters. ¹⁰For some say, "His letters are weighty and forceful, but in person he is unimpressive and his speaking amounts to nothing." ¹¹Such people should realize that what we are in our letters when we are absent, we will be in our actions when we are present.

¹²We do not dare to classify or compare ourselves with some who commend themselves. When they measure themselves by themselves and compare themselves with themselves, they are not wise. ¹³We, however, will not boast beyond proper limits, but will confine our boasting to the sphere of service God himself has assigned to us, a sphere that also includes you. ¹⁴We are not going too far in our boasting, as would be the case if we had not come to you, for we did get as far as you with the gospel of Christ. ¹⁵Neither do we go beyond our limits by boasting of work done by others. Our hope is that, as your faith continues to grow, our sphere of activity among you will greatly expand, ¹⁶so that we can preach the gospel in the regions beyond you. For we do not want to boast about work already done in someone else's territory. ¹⁷But, "Let those who boast boast in the Lord."ᵇ ¹⁸For it is not those who commend themselves who are approved, but those whom the Lord commends.

Paul and the False Apostles

11 I hope you will put up with me in a little foolishness. Yes, please put up with me! ²I am jealous for you with a godly jealousy. I promised you to one husband, to Christ, so that I might present you as a pure virgin to him. ³But I am afraid that just as Eve was deceived by the serpent's cunning, your minds may somehow be led astray from your sincere and pure devotion to Christ. ⁴For if someone comes to you and preaches a Jesus other than the Jesus we preached, or if you receive a different spirit from the Spirit you received, or a different gospel from the one you accepted, you put up with it easily enough.

⁵I do not think I am in the least inferior to those "super-apostles."ᶜ ⁶I may indeed be untrained as a speaker, but I do have knowledge. We have made this perfectly clear to you in every way. ⁷Was it a sin for me to lower myself in order to elevate you by preaching the gospel of God to you free of charge? ⁸I robbed other churches by receiving support from them so as to serve you. ⁹And when I was with you and needed something, I was not a burden to anyone, for the brothers and sisters who came from Macedonia supplied what I

ᵃ 7 Or *Look at the obvious facts*　　ᵇ 17 Jer. 9:24　　ᶜ 5 Or *to the most eminent apostles*

needed. I have kept myself from being a burden to you in any way, and will continue to do so. ¹⁰As surely as the truth of Christ is in me, nobody in the regions of Achaia will stop this boasting of mine. ¹¹Why? Because I do not love you? God knows I do!

¹²And I will keep on doing what I am doing in order to cut the ground from under those who want an opportunity to be considered equal with us in the things they boast about. ¹³For such persons are false apostles, deceitful workers, masquerading as apostles of Christ. ¹⁴And no wonder, for Satan himself masquerades as an angel of light. ¹⁵It is not surprising, then, if his servants also masquerade as servants of righteousness. Their end will be what their actions deserve.

Paul Boasts About His Sufferings

¹⁶I repeat: Let no one take me for a fool. But if you do, then tolerate me just as you would a fool, so that I may do a little boasting. ¹⁷In this self-confident boasting I am not talking as the Lord would, but as a fool. ¹⁸Since many are boasting in the way the world does, I too will boast. ¹⁹You gladly put up with fools since you are so wise! ²⁰In fact, you even put up with any who enslave you or exploit you or take advantage of you or push themselves forward or slap you in the face. ²¹To my shame I admit that we were too weak for that!

Whatever anyone else dares to boast about—I am speaking as a fool—I also dare to boast about. ²²Are they Hebrews? So am I. Are they Israelites? So am I. Are they Abraham's descendants? So am I. ²³Are they servants of Christ? (I am out of my mind to talk like this.) I am more. I have worked much harder, been in prison more frequently, been flogged more severely, and been exposed to death again and again. ²⁴Five times I received from the Jews the forty lashes minus one. ²⁵Three times I was beaten with rods, once I was stoned, three times I was shipwrecked, I spent a night and a day in the open sea, ²⁶I have been constantly on the move. I have been in danger from rivers, in danger from bandits, in danger from my own people, in danger from Gentiles; in danger in the city, in danger in the country, in danger at sea; and in danger from false believers. ²⁷I have labored and toiled and have often gone without sleep; I have known hunger and thirst and have often gone without food; I have been cold and naked. ²⁸Besides everything else, I face daily the pressure of my concern for all the churches. ²⁹Who is weak, and I do not feel weak? Who is led into sin, and I do not inwardly burn?

³⁰If I must boast, I will boast of the things that show my weakness. ³¹The God and Father of the Lord Jesus, who is to be praised forever, knows that I am not lying. ³²In Damascus the governor under King Aretas had the city of the Damascenes guarded in order to arrest me. ³³But I was lowered in a basket from a window in the wall and slipped through his hands.

Paul's Vision and His Thorn

12 I must go on boasting. Although there is nothing to be gained, I will go on to visions and revelations from the Lord. ²I know a man in Christ who fourteen years ago was caught up to the third heaven. Whether it was in the body or out of the body I do not know—God knows. ³And I know that this man—whether in the body or apart from the body I do not know, but God knows— [4]was caught up to paradise and heard inexpressible things, things that no one is permitted to tell. [5]I will boast about someone like that, but I will not boast about myself, except about my weaknesses. [6]Even if I should choose to boast, I would not be a fool, because I would be speaking the truth. But I refrain, so no one will think more of me than is warranted by what I do or say, [7]or because of these surpassingly great revelations. Therefore, in order to keep me from becoming conceited, I was given a thorn in my flesh, a messenger of Satan, to torment me. [8]Three times I pleaded with the Lord to take it away from me. [9]But he said to me, "My grace is sufficient for you, for my power is made perfect in weakness." Therefore I will boast all the more gladly about my weaknesses, so that Christ's power may rest on me. [10]That is why, for Christ's sake, I delight in weaknesses, in insults, in hardships, in persecutions, in difficulties. For when I am weak, then I am strong.

Paul's Concern for the Corinthians

[11]I have made a fool of myself, but you drove me to it. I ought to have been commended by you, for I am not in the least inferior to the "super-apostles," [a] even though I am nothing. [12]I persevered in demonstrating among you the marks of a true apostle, including signs, wonders and miracles. [13]How were you inferior to the other churches, except that I was never a burden to you? Forgive me this wrong!

[14]Now I am ready to visit you for the third time, and I will not be a burden to you, because what I want is not your possessions but you. After all, children should not have to save up for their parents, but parents for their children. [15]So I will very gladly spend for you everything I have and expend myself as well. If I love you more, will you love me less? [16]Be that as it may, I have not been a burden to you. Yet, crafty fellow that I am, I caught you by trickery! [17]Did I exploit you through any of the men I sent to you? [18]I urged Titus to go to you and I sent our brother with him. Titus did not exploit you, did he? Did we not walk in the same footsteps by the same Spirit?

[19]Have you been thinking all along that we have been defending ourselves to you? We have been speaking in the sight of God as those in Christ; and everything we do, dear friends, is for your strengthening. [20]For I am afraid that when I come I may not find you as I want you to be, and you may not find me as you want me to be. I fear that there may be quarreling, jealousy, outbursts of anger, factions, slander, gossip, arrogance and disorder. [21]I am afraid that when I come again my God will humble me before you, and I will be grieved over many who have sinned earlier and have not repented of the impurity, sexual sin and debauchery in which they have indulged.

Final Warnings

13 This will be my third visit to you. "Every matter must be established by the testimony of two or three witnesses." [b] [2]I already gave you a warning when I was with you the second time. I now repeat it while absent: On my return I will not spare those who sinned earlier or any of the others, [3]since you are demanding proof that Christ is speaking through me. He is not

[a] 11 Or *the most eminent apostles*   [b] 1 Deut. 19:15

weak in dealing with you, but is powerful among you. [4]For to be sure, he was crucified in weakness, yet he lives by God's power. Likewise, we are weak in him, yet by God's power we will live with him in our dealing with you.

[5]Examine yourselves to see whether you are in the faith; test yourselves. Do you not realize that Christ Jesus is in you—unless, of course, you fail the test? [6]And I trust that you will discover that we have not failed the test. [7]Now we pray to God that you will not do anything wrong. Not that people will see that we have stood the test but that you will do what is right even though we may seem to have failed. [8]For we cannot do anything against the truth, but only for the truth. [9]We are glad whenever we are weak but you are strong; and our prayer is that you may be fully restored. [10]This is why I write these things when I am absent, that when I come I may not have to be harsh in my use of authority—the authority the Lord gave me for building you up, not for tearing you down.

Final Greetings

[11]Finally, brothers and sisters, rejoice! Strive for full restoration, encourage one another, be of one mind, live in peace. And the God of love and peace will be with you.

[12]Greet one another with a holy kiss. [13]All God's people here send their greetings.

[14]May the grace of the Lord Jesus Christ, and the love of God, and the fellowship of the Holy Spirit be with you all.

GALATIANS

1 Paul, an apostle—sent not with a human commission nor by human authority, but by Jesus Christ and God the Father, who raised him from the dead— 2and all the brothers and sisters with me,

To the churches in Galatia:

3Grace and peace to you from God our Father and the Lord Jesus Christ, 4who gave himself for our sins to rescue us from the present evil age, according to the will of our God and Father, 5to whom be glory for ever and ever. Amen.

No Other Gospel

6I am astonished that you are so quickly deserting the one who called you by the grace of Christ and are turning to a different gospel— 7which is really no gospel at all. Evidently some people are throwing you into confusion and are trying to pervert the gospel of Christ. 8But even if we or an angel from heaven should preach a gospel other than the one we preached to you, let that person be under God's curse! 9As we have already said, so now I say again: If anybody is preaching to you a gospel other than what you accepted, let that person be under God's curse!

10Am I now trying to win human approval, or God's approval? Or am I trying to please people? If I were still trying to please people, I would not be a servant of Christ.

Paul Called by God

11I want you to know, brothers and sisters, that the gospel I preached is not of human origin. 12I did not receive it from any human source, nor was I taught it; rather, I received it by revelation from Jesus Christ.

13For you have heard of my previous way of life in Judaism, how intensely I persecuted the church of God and tried to destroy it. 14I was advancing in Judaism beyond many of my own age among my people and was extremely zealous for the traditions of my fathers. 15But when God, who set me apart from birth*a* and called me by his grace, was pleased 16to reveal his Son in me so that I might preach him among the Gentiles, my immediate response was not to consult any human being. 17I did not go up to Jerusalem to see those who were apostles before I was, but I went into Arabia. Later I returned to Damascus.

a 15 Or from my mother's womb

[18]Then after three years, I went up to Jerusalem to get acquainted with Cephas[a] and stayed with him fifteen days. [19]I saw none of the other apostles—only James, the Lord's brother. [20]I assure you before God that what I am writing you is no lie.

[21]Then I went to Syria and Cilicia. [22]I was personally unknown to the churches of Judea that are in Christ. [23]They only heard the report: "The man who formerly persecuted us is now preaching the faith he once tried to destroy." [24]And they praised God because of me.

Paul Accepted by the Apostles

2 Then after fourteen years, I went up again to Jerusalem, this time with Barnabas. I took Titus along also. [2]I went in response to a revelation and, meeting privately with those esteemed as leaders, I set before them the gospel that I preach among the Gentiles. I wanted to be sure I was not running and had not been running my race in vain. [3]Yet not even Titus, who was with me, was compelled to be circumcised, even though he was a Greek. [4]This matter arose because some false believers had infiltrated our ranks to spy on the freedom we have in Christ Jesus and to make us slaves. [5]We did not give in to them for a moment, so that the truth of the gospel might remain with you.

[6]As for those who were held in high esteem—whatever they were makes no difference to me; God does not show favoritism—they added nothing to my message. [7]On the contrary, they saw that I had been entrusted with the task of preaching the gospel to the Gentiles,[b] just as Peter had been to the Jews.[c] [8]For God, who was at work in Peter as an apostle to the Jews, was also at work in me as an apostle to the Gentiles. [9]James, Cephas[d] and John, those esteemed as pillars, gave me and Barnabas the right hand of fellowship when they recognized the grace given to me. They agreed that we should go to the Gentiles, and they to the Jews. [10]All they asked was that we should continue to remember the poor, the very thing I had been eager to do all along.

Paul Opposes Cephas

[11]When Cephas came to Antioch, I opposed him to his face, because he stood condemned. [12]For before certain people came from James, he used to eat with the Gentiles. But when they arrived, he began to draw back and separate himself from the Gentiles because he was afraid of those who belonged to the circumcision group. [13]The other Jews joined him in his hypocrisy, so that by their hypocrisy even Barnabas was led astray.

[14]When I saw that they were not acting in line with the truth of the gospel, I said to Cephas in front of them all, "You are a Jew, yet you live like a Gentile and not like a Jew. How is it, then, that you force Gentiles to follow Jewish customs?

[15]"We who are Jews by birth and not 'Gentile sinners' [16]know that a person is not justified by observing the law, but by faith in Jesus Christ. So we, too, have put our faith in Christ Jesus that we may be justified by faith in[e] Christ

---

[a] 18 That is, Peter   [b] 7 Greek *uncircumcised*   [c] 7 Greek *circumcised*; also in verses 8 and 9
[d] 9 That is, Peter; also in verses 11 and 14   [e] 16 Or *but through the faithfulness of . . . justified on the basis of the faithfulness of*

and not by observing the law, because by observing the law no one will be justified.

[17]"But if, in seeking to be justified in Christ, we Jews find ourselves also among the 'sinners,' doesn't that mean that Christ promotes sin? Absolutely not! [18]If I rebuild what I destroyed, then I really would be a lawbreaker.

[19]"For through the law I died to the law so that I might live for God. [20]I have been crucified with Christ and I no longer live, but Christ lives in me. The life I now live in the body, I live by faith in the Son of God, who loved me and gave himself for me. [21]I do not set aside the grace of God, for if righteousness could be gained through the law, Christ died for nothing!"[a]

Faith or Observance of the Law

3 You foolish Galatians! Who has bewitched you? Before your very eyes Jesus Christ was clearly portrayed as crucified. [2]I would like to learn just one thing from you: Did you receive the Spirit by observing the law, or by believing what you heard? [3]Are you so foolish? After beginning with the Spirit, are you now trying to finish by human effort? [4]Have you experienced[b] so much in vain—if it really was in vain? [5]Does God give you his Spirit and work miracles among you by your observing the law, or by your believing what you heard? [6]So also Abraham "believed God, and it was credited to him as righteousness."[c]

[7]Understand, then, that those who have faith are children of Abraham. [8]Scripture foresaw that God would justify the Gentiles by faith, and announced the gospel in advance to Abraham: "All nations will be blessed through you."[d] [9]So those who rely on faith are blessed along with Abraham, the man of faith.

[10]All who rely on observing the law are under a curse, for it is written: "Cursed is everyone who does not continue to do everything written in the Book of the Law."[e] [11]Clearly no one is justified before God by the law, because "the righteous will live by faith."[f] [12]The law is not based on faith; on the contrary, it says, "The one who does these things will live by them."[g] [13]Christ redeemed us from the curse of the law by becoming a curse for us, for it is written: "Cursed is everyone who is hung on a tree."[h] [14]He redeemed us in order that the blessing given to Abraham might come to the Gentiles through Christ Jesus, so that by faith we might receive the promise of the Spirit.

The Law and the Promise

[15]Brothers and sisters, let me take an example from everyday life. Just as no one can set aside or add to a human covenant that has been duly established, so it is in this case. [16]The promises were spoken to Abraham and to his seed. Scripture does not say "and to seeds," meaning many people, but "and to your seed,"[i] meaning one person, who is Christ. [17]What I mean is this: The law, introduced 430 years later, does not set aside the covenant previously established by God and thus do away with the promise. [18]For if the inheritance

---

[a] 21 Some interpreters end the quotation after verse 14.   [b] 4 Or *suffered*   [c] 6 Gen. 15:6
[d] 8 Gen. 12:3; 18:18; 22:18   [e] 10 Deut. 27:26   [f] 11 Hab. 2:4   [g] 12 Lev. 18:5   [h] 13 Deut. 21:23
[i] 16 Gen. 12:7; 13:15; 24:7

depends on the law, then it no longer depends on the promise; but God in his grace gave it to Abraham through a promise.

[19]What, then, was the purpose of the law? It was added because of transgressions until the Seed to whom the promise referred had come. The law was given through angels and entrusted to a mediator. [20]A mediator, however, implies more than one party; but God is one.

[21]Is the law, therefore, opposed to the promises of God? Absolutely not! For if a law had been given that could impart life, then righteousness would certainly have come by the law. [22]But Scripture has locked up everything under the control of sin, so that what was promised, being given through faith in Jesus Christ, might be given to those who believe.

Children of God

[23]Before the coming of this faith,[a] we were held in custody under the law, locked up until the faith that was to come would be revealed. [24]So the law was put in charge of us until Christ came that we might be justified by faith. [25]Now that this faith has come, we are no longer under the supervision of the law.

[26]So in Christ Jesus you are all children of God through faith, [27]for all of you who were baptized into Christ have clothed yourselves with Christ. [28]There is neither Jew nor Greek, neither slave nor free, neither male nor female, for you are all one in Christ Jesus. [29]If you belong to Christ, then you are Abraham's seed, and heirs according to the promise.

4 What I am saying is that as long as heirs are underage they are no different from slaves, although they own the whole estate. [2]They are subject to guardians and trustees until the time set by their fathers. [3]So also, when we were underage, we were in slavery under the elemental spiritual forces[b] of the world. [4]But when the set time had fully come, God sent his Son, born of a woman, born under the law, [5]to redeem those under the law, that we might receive adoption to sonship.[c] [6]Because you are his sons, God sent the Spirit of his Son into our hearts, the Spirit who calls out, "Abba,[d] Father." [7]So you are no longer slaves, but God's children; and since you are his children, he has made you also heirs.

Paul's Concern for the Galatians

[8]Formerly, when you did not know God, you were slaves to those who by nature are not gods. [9]But now that you know God—or rather are known by God—how is it that you are turning back to those weak and miserable forces[e]? Do you wish to be enslaved by them all over again? [10]You are observing special days and months and seasons and years! [11]I fear for you, that somehow I have wasted my efforts on you.

[12]I plead with you, brothers and sisters, become like me, for I became like you. You have done me no wrong. [13]As you know, it was because of an illness that I first preached the gospel to you. [14]Even though my illness was a trial to you, you did not treat me with contempt or scorn. Instead, you welcomed me

---

[a] 22,23 Or *through the faithfulness of Jesus* . . . . [23]*Before faith came*   [b] 3 Or *under the basic principles*
[c] 5 The Greek word for *adoption to sonship* is a legal term referring to the full legal standing of an adopted male heir in Roman culture.   [d] 6 Aramaic for *Father*   [e] 9 Or *principles*

as if I were an angel of God, as if I were Christ Jesus himself. 15What has happened to all your joy? I can testify that, if you could have done so, you would have torn out your eyes and given them to me. 16Have I now become your enemy by telling you the truth?

17Those people are zealous to win you over, but for no good. What they want is to alienate you from us, so that you may have zeal for them. 18It is fine to be zealous, provided the purpose is good, and to be so always, not just when I am with you. 19My dear children, for whom I am again in the pains of childbirth until Christ is formed in you, 20how I wish I could be with you now and change my tone, because I am perplexed about you!

Hagar and Sarah

21Tell me, you who want to be under the law, are you not aware of what the law says? 22For it is written that Abraham had two sons, one by the slave woman and the other by the free woman. 23His son by the slave woman was born as the result of human effort,*a* but his son by the free woman was born as the result of a divine promise.

24I am taking these things figuratively, for the women represent two covenants. One covenant is from Mount Sinai and bears children who are to be slaves: This is Hagar. 25Now Hagar stands for Mount Sinai in Arabia and corresponds to the present city of Jerusalem, because she is in slavery with her children. 26But the Jerusalem that is above is free, and she is our mother. 27For it is written:

> "Be glad, barren woman,
>   you who bear no children;
> break forth and cry aloud,
>   you who have no labor pains;
> because more are the children of the desolate woman
>   than of her who has a husband."*b*

28Now you, brothers and sisters, like Isaac, are children of promise. 29At that time the son born by human effort persecuted the son born by the power of the Spirit. It is the same now. 30But what does Scripture say? "Get rid of the slave woman and her son, for the slave woman's son will never share in the inheritance with the free woman's son."*c* 31Therefore, brothers and sisters, we are not children of the slave woman, but of the free woman.

Freedom in Christ

5 It is for freedom that Christ has set us free. Stand firm, then, and do not let yourselves be burdened again by a yoke of slavery.

2Mark my words! I, Paul, tell you that if you let yourselves be circumcised, Christ will be of no value to you at all. 3Again I declare to every man who lets himself be circumcised that he is obligated to obey the whole law. 4You who are trying to be justified by law have been alienated from Christ; you have fallen away from grace. 5But by faith we eagerly await through the Spirit the righteousness for which we hope. 6For in Christ Jesus neither circumcision

a 23 Or *born according to the flesh*; also in verse 29   *b 27* Isaiah 54:1   *c 30* Gen. 21:10

nor uncircumcision has any value. The only thing that counts is faith expressing itself through love.

[7]You were running a good race. Who cut in on you to keep you from obeying the truth? [8]That kind of persuasion does not come from the one who calls you. [9]"A little yeast works through the whole batch of dough." [10]I am confident in the Lord that you will take no other view. The one who is throwing you into confusion will have to pay the penalty, whoever that may be. [11]Brothers and sisters, if I am still preaching circumcision, why am I still being persecuted? In that case the offense of the cross has been abolished. [12]As for those agitators, I wish they would go the whole way and emasculate themselves!

Life by the Spirit

[13]You, my brothers and sisters, were called to be free. But do not use your freedom to indulge the sinful nature[a]; rather, serve one another humbly in love. [14]For the entire law is fulfilled in keeping this one command: "Love your neighbor as yourself."[b] [15]If you keep on biting and devouring each other, watch out or you will be destroyed by each other.

[16]So I say, walk by the Spirit, and you will not gratify the desires of the sinful nature. [17]For the sinful nature desires what is contrary to the Spirit, and the Spirit what is contrary to the sinful nature. They are in conflict with each other, so that you are not to do whatever[c] you want. [18]But if you are led by the Spirit, you are not under the law.

[19]The acts of the sinful nature are obvious: sexual immorality, impurity and debauchery; [20]idolatry and witchcraft; hatred, discord, jealousy, fits of rage, selfish ambition, dissensions, factions [21]and envy; drunkenness, orgies, and the like. I warn you, as I did before, that those who live like this will not inherit the kingdom of God.

[22]But the fruit of the Spirit is love, joy, peace, patience, kindness, goodness, faithfulness, [23]gentleness and self-control. Against such things there is no law. [24]Those who belong to Christ Jesus have crucified the sinful nature with its passions and desires. [25]Since we live by the Spirit, let us keep in step with the Spirit. [26]Let us not become conceited, provoking and envying each other.

Doing Good to All

6 Brothers and sisters, if someone is caught in a sin, you who live by the Spirit should restore that person gently. But watch yourselves, or you also may be tempted. [2]Carry each other's burdens, and in this way you will fulfill the law of Christ. [3]If any of you think you are something when you are nothing, you deceive yourselves. [4]Each of you should test your own actions. Then you can take pride in yourself, without comparing yourself to somebody else, [5]for each of you should carry your own load. [6]Nevertheless, those who receive instruction in the word should share all good things with their instructor.

[7]Do not be deceived: God cannot be mocked. People reap what they sow. [8]Those who sow to please their sinful nature, from that nature[d] will reap destruction; those who sow to please the Spirit, from the Spirit will reap eternal

---

[a] 13 Or *the flesh*; also in verses 16, 17, 19 and 24   [b] 14 Lev. 19:18   [c] 17 Or *you do not do what*
[d] 8 Or *their flesh, from the flesh*

life. ⁹Let us not become weary in doing good, for at the proper time we will reap a harvest if we do not give up. ¹⁰Therefore, as we have opportunity, let us do good to all people, especially to those who belong to the family of believers.

Not Circumcision but a New Creation

¹¹See what large letters I use as I write to you with my own hand!

¹²Those who want to impress others by means of the flesh are trying to compel you to be circumcised. The only reason they do this is to avoid being persecuted for the cross of Christ. ¹³Not even those who are circumcised keep the law, yet they want you to be circumcised that they may boast about your circumcision in the flesh. ¹⁴May I never boast except in the cross of our Lord Jesus Christ, through which*ᵃ* the world has been crucified to me, and I to the world. ¹⁵Neither circumcision nor uncircumcision means anything; what counts is a new creation. ¹⁶Peace and mercy to all who follow this rule—to*ᵇ* the Israel of God.

¹⁷From now on, let no one cause me trouble, for I bear on my body the marks of Jesus.

¹⁸The grace of our Lord Jesus Christ be with your spirit, brothers and sisters. Amen.

ᵃ 14 Or *whom*   *ᵇ* 16 Or *rule and to*

EPHESIANS

1 Paul, an apostle of Christ Jesus by the will of God,

To the saints in Ephesus,[a] the believers who are[b] in Christ Jesus:

[2]Grace and peace to you from God our Father and the Lord Jesus Christ.

Praise for Spiritual Blessings in Christ

[3]Praise be to the God and Father of our Lord Jesus Christ, who has blessed us in the heavenly realms with every spiritual blessing in Christ. [4]For he chose us in him before the creation of the world to be holy and blameless in his sight. In love [5]he[c] predestined us for adoption to sonship[d] through Jesus Christ, in accordance with his pleasure and will— [6]to the praise of his glorious grace, which he has freely given us in the One he loves. [7]In him we have redemption through his blood, the forgiveness of sins, in accordance with the riches of God's grace [8]that he lavished on us. With all wisdom and understanding, [9]he[e] made known to us the mystery of his will according to his good pleasure, which he purposed in Christ, [10]to be put into effect when the times reach their fulfillment—to bring unity to all things in heaven and on earth under Christ.

[11]In him we were also chosen,[f] having been predestined according to the plan of him who works out everything in conformity with the purpose of his will, [12]in order that we, who were the first to put our hope in Christ, might be for the praise of his glory. [13]And you also were included in Christ when you heard the word of truth, the gospel of your salvation. When you believed, you were marked in him with a seal, the promised Holy Spirit, [14]who is a deposit guaranteeing our inheritance until the redemption of those who are God's possession—to the praise of his glory.

Thanksgiving and Prayer

[15]For this reason, ever since I heard about your faith in the Lord Jesus and your love for all God's people, [16]I have not stopped giving thanks for you, remembering you in my prayers. [17]I keep asking that the God of our Lord Jesus Christ, the glorious Father, may give you the Spirit[g] of wisdom and revelation, so that you may know him better. [18]I pray that the eyes of your heart

---

[a]1 Some early manuscripts do not have *in Ephesus*.   [b]1 Or *the faithful*   [c]4,5 Or *sight in love.* [5]*He*
[d]5 The Greek word for *adoption to sonship* is a legal term referring to the full legal standing of an adopted male heir in Roman culture.   [e]8,9 Or *us with all wisdom and understanding.* [9]*And he*
[f]11 Or *were made heirs*   [g]17 Or *a spirit*

may be enlightened in order that you may know the hope to which he has called you, the riches of his glorious inheritance in his people, [19]and his incomparably great power for us who believe. That power is the same as the mighty strength [20]he exerted when he raised Christ from the dead and seated him at his right hand in the heavenly realms, [21]far above all rule and authority, power and dominion, and every name that can be invoked, not only in the present age but also in the one to come. [22]And God placed all things under his feet and appointed him to be head over everything for the church, [23]which is his body, the fullness of him who fills everything in every way.

Made Alive in Christ

2 As for you, you were dead in your transgressions and sins, [2]in which you used to live when you followed the ways of this world and of the ruler of the kingdom of the air, the spirit who is now at work in those who are disobedient. [3]All of us also lived among them at one time, gratifying the cravings of our sinful nature[a] and following its desires and thoughts. Like the rest, we were by nature deserving of wrath. [4]But because of his great love for us, God, who is rich in mercy, [5]made us alive with Christ even when we were dead in transgressions—it is by grace you have been saved. [6]And God raised us up with Christ and seated us with him in the heavenly realms in Christ Jesus, [7]in order that in the coming ages he might show the incomparable riches of his grace, expressed in his kindness to us in Christ Jesus. [8]For it is by grace you have been saved, through faith—and this is not from yourselves, it is the gift of God— [9]not by works, so that no one can boast. [10]For we are God's handiwork, created in Christ Jesus to do good works, which God prepared in advance for us to do.

Jew and Gentile Reconciled Through Christ

[11]Therefore, remember that formerly you who are Gentiles by birth and called "uncircumcised" by those who call themselves "the circumcision" (which is done in the body by human hands)— [12]remember that at that time you were separate from Christ, excluded from citizenship in Israel and foreigners to the covenants of the promise, without hope and without God in the world. [13]But now in Christ Jesus you who once were far away have been brought near by the blood of Christ.

[14]For he himself is our peace, who has made the two one and has destroyed the barrier, the dividing wall of hostility, [15]by setting aside in his flesh the law with its commandments and regulations. His purpose was to create in himself one new humanity out of the two, thus making peace, [16]and in one body to reconcile both of them to God through the cross, by which he put to death their hostility. [17]He came and preached peace to you who were far away and peace to those who were near. [18]For through him we both have access to the Father by one Spirit.

[19]Consequently, you are no longer foreigners and strangers, but fellow citizens with God's people and members of God's household, [20]built on the foundation of the apostles and prophets, with Christ Jesus himself as the chief cor-

a 3 Or our flesh

nerstone. 21In him the whole building is joined together and rises to become a holy temple in the Lord. 22And in him you too are being built together to become a dwelling in which God lives by his Spirit.

God's Marvelous Plan for the Gentiles

3 For this reason I, Paul, the prisoner of Christ Jesus for the sake of you Gentiles—

2Surely you have heard about the administration of God's grace that was given to me for you, 3that is, the mystery made known to me by revelation, as I have already written briefly. 4In reading this, then, you will be able to understand my insight into the mystery of Christ, 5which was not made known to people in other generations as it has now been revealed by the Spirit to God's holy apostles and prophets. 6This mystery is that through the gospel the Gentiles are heirs together with Israel, members together of one body, and sharers together in the promise in Christ Jesus.

7I became a servant of this gospel by the gift of God's grace given me through the working of his power. 8Although I am less than the least of all God's people, this grace was given me: to preach to the Gentiles the boundless riches of Christ, 9and to make plain to everyone the administration of this mystery, which for ages past was kept hidden in God, who created all things. 10His intent was that now, through the church, the manifold wisdom of God should be made known to the rulers and authorities in the heavenly realms, 11according to his eternal purpose that he accomplished in Christ Jesus our Lord. 12In him and through faith in him we may approach God with freedom and confidence. 13I ask you, therefore, not to be discouraged because of my sufferings for you, which are your glory.

A Prayer for the Ephesians

14For this reason I kneel before the Father, 15from whom every family*a* in heaven and on earth derives its name. 16I pray that out of his glorious riches he may strengthen you with power through his Spirit in your inner being, 17so that Christ may dwell in your hearts through faith. And I pray that you, being rooted and established in love, 18may have power, together with all God's people, to grasp how wide and long and high and deep is the love of Christ, 19and to know this love that surpasses knowledge—that you may be filled to the measure of all the fullness of God.

20Now to him who is able to do immeasurably more than all we ask or imagine, according to his power that is at work within us, 21to him be glory in the church and in Christ Jesus throughout all generations, for ever and ever! Amen.

Unity and Maturity in the Body of Christ

4 As a prisoner for the Lord, then, I urge you to live a life worthy of the calling you have received. 2Be completely humble and gentle; be patient, bearing with one another in love. 3Make every effort to keep the unity of the Spirit through the bond of peace. 4There is one body and one Spirit, just as

a 15 The Greek for family (patria) is derived from the Greek for father (pater).

you were called to one hope when you were called; ⁵one Lord, one faith, one baptism; ⁶one God and Father of all, who is over all and through all and in all.

⁷But to each one of us grace has been given as Christ apportioned it. ⁸This is why it*ᵃ* says:

> "When he ascended on high,
>   he led captives in his train
>   and gave gifts to his people."*ᵇ*

⁹(What does "he ascended" mean except that he also descended to the lower, earthly regions*ᶜ*? ¹⁰He who descended is the very one who ascended higher than all the heavens, in order to fill the whole universe.) ¹¹It was he who gave the apostles, the prophets, the evangelists, the pastors and teachers, ¹²to equip God's people for works of service, so that the body of Christ may be built up ¹³until we all reach unity in the faith and in the knowledge of the Son of God and become mature, attaining to the whole measure of the fullness of Christ.

¹⁴Then we will no longer be infants, tossed back and forth by the waves, and blown here and there by every wind of teaching and by the cunning and craftiness of people in their deceitful scheming. ¹⁵Instead, speaking the truth in love, we will in all things grow up into him who is the Head, that is, Christ. ¹⁶From him the whole body, joined and held together by every supporting ligament, grows and builds itself up in love, as each part does its work.

Instructions for Christian Living

¹⁷So I tell you this, and insist on it in the Lord, that you must no longer live as the Gentiles do, in the futility of their thinking. ¹⁸They are darkened in their understanding and separated from the life of God because of the ignorance that is in them due to the hardening of their hearts. ¹⁹Having lost all sensitivity, they have given themselves over to sensuality so as to indulge in every kind of impurity, and they are full of greed.

²⁰That, however, is not the way of life you learned ²¹when you heard about Christ and were taught in him in accordance with the truth that is in Jesus. ²²You were taught, with regard to your former way of life, to put off your old self, which is being corrupted by its deceitful desires; ²³to be made new in the attitude of your minds; ²⁴and to put on the new self, created to be like God in true righteousness and holiness.

²⁵Therefore each of you must put off falsehood and speak truthfully to your neighbor, for we are all members of one body. ²⁶"In your anger do not sin"*ᵈ*: Do not let the sun go down while you are still angry, ²⁷and do not give the devil a foothold. ²⁸Those who have been stealing must steal no longer, but must work, doing something useful with their own hands, that they may have something to share with those in need.

²⁹Do not let any unwholesome talk come out of your mouths, but only what is helpful for building others up according to their needs, that it may benefit those who listen. ³⁰And do not grieve the Holy Spirit of God, with whom you were sealed for the day of redemption. ³¹Get rid of all bitterness,

---

*ᵃ*8 Or *God*   *ᵇ*8 Psalm 68:18   *ᶜ*9 Or *the depths of the earth*   *ᵈ*26 Psalm 4:4

rage and anger, brawling and slander, along with every form of malice. 32Be kind and compassionate to one another, forgiving each other, just as in Christ God forgave you. 1Follow God's example, therefore, as dearly loved children 2and walk in the way of love, just as Christ loved us and gave himself up for us as a fragrant offering and sacrifice to God.

3But among you there must not be even a hint of sexual immorality, or of any kind of impurity, or of greed, because these are improper for God's holy people. 4Nor should there be obscenity, foolish talk or coarse joking, which are out of place, but rather thanksgiving. 5For of this you can be sure: No immoral, impure or greedy person—such a person is an idolater—has any inheritance in the kingdom of Christ and of God.ᵃ 6Let no one deceive you with empty words, for because of such things God's wrath comes on those who are disobedient. 7Therefore do not be partners with them.

8For you were once darkness, but now you are light in the Lord. Live as children of light 9(for the fruit of the light consists in all goodness, righteousness and truth) 10and find out what pleases the Lord. 11Have nothing to do with the fruitless deeds of darkness, but rather expose them. 12It is shameful even to mention what the disobedient do in secret. 13But everything exposed by the light becomes visible—and everything that is illuminated becomes a light. 14This is why it is said:

> "Wake up, sleeper,
> rise from the dead,
> and Christ will shine on you."

15Be very careful, then, how you live—not as unwise but as wise, 16making the most of every opportunity, because the days are evil. 17Therefore do not be foolish, but understand what the Lord's will is. 18Do not get drunk on wine, which leads to debauchery. Instead, be filled with the Spirit, 19speaking to one another with psalms, hymns and songs from the Spirit. Sing and make music from your heart to the Lord, 20always giving thanks to God the Father for everything, in the name of our Lord Jesus Christ.

Instructions for Christian Households

21Submit to one another out of reverence for Christ.

22Wives, submit yourselves to your own husbands as you do to the Lord. 23For the husband is the head of the wife as Christ is the head of the church, his body, of which he is the Savior. 24Now as the church submits to Christ, so also wives should submit to their husbands in everything.

25Husbands, love your wives, just as Christ loved the church and gave himself up for her 26to make her holy, cleansingᵇ her by the washing with water through the word, 27and to present her to himself as a radiant church, without stain or wrinkle or any other blemish, but holy and blameless. 28In this same way, husbands ought to love their wives as their own bodies. He who loves his wife loves himself. 29After all, people have never hated their own bodies, but they feed and care for them, just as Christ does the church— 30for we are members of his body. 31"For this reason a man will leave his father and

ᵃ 5 Or *kingdom of the Christ and God*   ᵇ 26 Or *having cleansed*

mother and be united to his wife, and the two will become one flesh."*a* 32This is a profound mystery—but I am talking about Christ and the church. 33However, each one of you also must love his wife as he loves himself, and the wife must respect her husband.

6 Children, obey your parents in the Lord, for this is right. 2"Honor your father and mother"—which is the first commandment with a promise— 3"so that it may go well with you and that you may enjoy long life on the earth."*b*

4Fathers,*c* do not exasperate your children; instead, bring them up in the training and instruction of the Lord.

5Slaves, obey your earthly masters with respect and fear, and with sincerity of heart, just as you would obey Christ. 6Obey them not only to win their favor when their eye is on you, but as slaves of Christ, doing the will of God from your heart. 7Serve wholeheartedly, as if you were serving the Lord, not people, 8because you know that the Lord will reward each one of you for whatever good you do, whether you are slave or free.

9And masters, treat your slaves in the same way. Do not threaten them, since you know that he who is both their Master and yours is in heaven, and there is no favoritism with him.

The Armor of God

10Finally, be strong in the Lord and in his mighty power. 11Put on the full armor of God, so that you can take your stand against the devil's schemes. 12For our struggle is not against flesh and blood, but against the rulers, against the authorities, against the powers of this dark world and against the spiritual forces of evil in the heavenly realms. 13Therefore put on the full armor of God, so that when the day of evil comes, you may be able to stand your ground, and after you have done everything, to stand. 14Stand firm then, with the belt of truth buckled around your waist, with the breastplate of righteousness in place, 15and with your feet fitted with the readiness that comes from the gospel of peace. 16In addition to all this, take up the shield of faith, with which you can extinguish all the flaming arrows of the evil one. 17Take the helmet of salvation and the sword of the Spirit, which is the word of God.

18And pray in the Spirit on all occasions with all kinds of prayers and requests. With this in mind, be alert and always keep on praying for all God's people. 19Pray also for me, that whenever I speak, words may be given me so that I will fearlessly make known the mystery of the gospel, 20for which I am an ambassador in chains. Pray that I may declare it fearlessly, as I should.

Final Greetings

21Tychicus, the dear brother and faithful servant in the Lord, will tell you everything, so that you also may know how I am and what I am doing. 22I am sending him to you for this very purpose, that you may know how we are, and that he may encourage you.

23Peace to the brothers and sisters, and love with faith from God the Father and the Lord Jesus Christ. 24Grace to all who love our Lord Jesus Christ with an undying love.*d*

---

a 31 Gen. 2:24   *b* 3 Deut. 5:16   *c* 4 Or *Parents*   *d* 24 Or *Grace and immortality to all who love our Lord Jesus Christ.*

PHILIPPIANS

1 Paul and Timothy, servants of Christ Jesus,

To all the saints in Christ Jesus at Philippi, together with the overseers[a] and deacons:

²Grace and peace to you from God our Father and the Lord Jesus Christ.

Thanksgiving and Prayer

³I thank my God every time I remember you. ⁴In all my prayers for all of you, I always pray with joy ⁵because of your partnership in the gospel from the first day until now, ⁶being confident of this, that he who began a good work in you will carry it on to completion until the day of Christ Jesus.

⁷It is right for me to feel this way about all of you, since I have you in my heart and, whether I am in chains or defending and confirming the gospel, all of you share in God's grace with me. ⁸God can testify how I long for all of you with the affection of Christ Jesus.

⁹And this is my prayer: that your love may abound more and more in knowledge and depth of insight, ¹⁰so that you may be able to discern what is best and may be pure and blameless for the day of Christ, ¹¹filled with the fruit of righteousness that comes through Jesus Christ—to the glory and praise of God.

Paul's Chains Advance the Gospel

¹²Now I want you to know, brothers and sisters, that what has happened to me has actually served to advance the gospel. ¹³As a result, it has become clear throughout the whole palace guard[b] and to everyone else that I am in chains for Christ. ¹⁴And because of my chains, most of the brothers and sisters have become confident in the Lord and dare all the more to proclaim the gospel without fear.

¹⁵It is true that some preach Christ out of envy and rivalry, but others out of goodwill. ¹⁶The latter do so out of love, knowing that I am put here for the defense of the gospel. ¹⁷The former preach Christ out of selfish ambition, not sincerely, supposing that they can stir up trouble for me while I am in chains. ¹⁸But what does it matter? The important thing is that in every way, whether from false motives or true, Christ is preached. And because of this I rejoice.

Yes, and I will continue to rejoice, ¹⁹for I know that through your prayers and God's provision of the Spirit of Jesus Christ what has happened to me

a 1 Traditionally *bishops*   *b 13* Or *whole palace*

will turn out for my deliverance.[a] [20]I eagerly expect and hope that I will in no way be ashamed, but will have sufficient courage so that now as always Christ will be exalted in my body, whether by life or by death. [21]For to me, to live is Christ and to die is gain. [22]If I am to go on living in the body, this will mean fruitful labor for me. Yet what shall I choose? I do not know! [23]I am torn between the two: I desire to depart and be with Christ, which is better by far; [24]but it is more necessary for you that I remain in the body. [25]Convinced of this, I know that I will remain, and I will continue with all of you for your progress and joy in the faith, [26]so that through my being with you again your boasting in Christ Jesus will abound on account of me.

Life Worthy of the Gospel

[27]Whatever happens, as citizens of heaven live in a manner worthy of the gospel of Christ. Then, whether I come and see you or only hear about you in my absence, I will know that you stand firm in the one Spirit,[b] striving together with one accord for the faith of the gospel [28]without being frightened in any way by those who oppose you. This is a sign to them that they will be destroyed, but that you will be saved—and that by God. [29]For it has been granted to you on behalf of Christ not only to believe on him, but also to suffer for him, [30]since you are going through the same struggle you saw I had, and now hear that I still have.

Imitating Christ's Humility

2 Therefore if you have any encouragement from being united with Christ, if any comfort from his love, if any common sharing in the Spirit, if any tenderness and compassion, [2]then make my joy complete by being like-minded, having the same love, being one in spirit and of one mind. [3]Do nothing out of selfish ambition or vain conceit. Rather, in humility value others above yourselves, [4]not looking to your own interests but each of you to the interests of the others.

[5]In your relationships with one another, have the same attitude of mind Christ Jesus had:

> [6]Who, being in very nature[c] God,
> did not consider equality with God something to be used to his
> own advantage;
> [7]rather he made himself nothing
> by taking the very nature[d] of a servant,
> being made in human likeness.
> [8]And being found in appearance as a human being,
> he humbled himself
> by becoming obedient to death—
> even death on a cross!
> [9]Therefore God exalted him to the highest place
> and gave him the name[e] that is above every name,

[a] 19 Or *vindication*; or *salvation*   [b] 27 Or *in one spirit*   [c] 6 Or *in the form of*   [d] 7 Or *the form*
[e] 9 That is, Lord (see verse 11)

¹⁰that at the name of Jesus every knee should bow,
in heaven and on earth and under the earth,
¹¹and every tongue acknowledge that Jesus Christ is Lord,
to the glory of God the Father.

Do Everything Without Grumbling

¹²Therefore, my dear friends, as you have always obeyed—not only in my presence, but now much more in my absence—continue to work out your salvation with fear and trembling, ¹³for it is God who works in you to will and to act to fulfill his good purpose.

¹⁴Do everything without grumbling or arguing, ¹⁵so that you may become blameless and pure, "children of God without fault in a warped and crooked generation."ᵃ Then you will shine among them like stars in the sky ¹⁶as you hold firmly to the word of life. And then I will be able to boast on the day of Christ that I did not run or labor in vain. ¹⁷But even if I am being poured out like a drink offering on the sacrifice and service coming from your faith, I am glad and rejoice with all of you. ¹⁸So you too should be glad and rejoice with me.

Timothy and Epaphroditus

¹⁹I hope in the Lord Jesus to send Timothy to you soon, that I also may be cheered when I receive news about you. ²⁰I have no one else like him, who will show genuine concern for your welfare. ²¹For everyone looks out for their own interests, not those of Jesus Christ. ²²But you know that Timothy has proved himself, because as a son with his father he has served with me in the work of the gospel. ²³I hope, therefore, to send him as soon as I see how things go with me. ²⁴And I am confident in the Lord that I myself will come soon.

²⁵But I think it is necessary to send back to you Epaphroditus, my brother, co-worker and fellow soldier, who is also your messenger, whom you sent to take care of my needs. ²⁶For he longs for all of you and is distressed because you heard he was ill. ²⁷Indeed he was ill, and almost died. But God had mercy on him, and not on him only but also on me, to spare me sorrow upon sorrow. ²⁸Therefore I am all the more eager to send him, so that when you see him again you may be glad and I may have less anxiety. ²⁹Welcome him in the Lord with great joy, and honor people like him, ³⁰because he almost died for the work of Christ. He risked his life to make up for the help you yourselves could not give me.

No Confidence in the Flesh

3 Further, my brothers and sisters, rejoice in the Lord! It is no trouble for me to write the same things to you again, and it is a safeguard for you. ²Watch out for those dogs, those evildoers, those mutilators of the flesh. ³For it is we who are the circumcision, we who serve God by his Spirit, who boast in Christ Jesus, and who put no confidence in the flesh— ⁴though I myself have reasons for such confidence.

If others think they have reasons to put confidence in the flesh, I have more:

ᵃ 15 See Deut. 32:5.

5circumcised on the eighth day, of the people of Israel, of the tribe of Benjamin, a Hebrew of Hebrews; in regard to the law, a Pharisee; 6as for zeal, persecuting the church; as for righteousness based on the law, faultless.

7But whatever were gains to me I now consider loss for the sake of Christ. 8What is more, I consider everything a loss because of the surpassing worth of knowing Christ Jesus my Lord, for whose sake I have lost all things. I consider them garbage, that I may gain Christ 9and be found in him, not having a righteousness of my own that comes from the law, but that which is through faith in*a* Christ—the righteousness that comes from God on the basis of faith. 10I want to know Christ—yes, to know the power of his resurrection and participation in his sufferings, becoming like him in his death, 11and so, somehow, attaining to the resurrection from the dead.

12Not that I have already obtained all this, or have already arrived at my goal, but I press on to take hold of that for which Christ Jesus took hold of me. 13Brothers and sisters, I do not consider myself yet to have taken hold of it. But one thing I do: Forgetting what is behind and straining toward what is ahead, 14I press on toward the goal to win the prize for which God has called me heavenward in Christ Jesus.

Following Paul's Example

15All of us, then, who are mature should take such a view of things. And if on some point you think differently, that too God will make clear to you. 16Only let us live up to what we have already attained.

17Join together in following my example, brothers and sisters, and just as you have us as a model, keep your eyes on those who live as we do. 18For, as I have often told you before and now tell you again even with tears, many live as enemies of the cross of Christ. 19Their destiny is destruction, their god is their stomach, and their glory is in their shame. Their mind is set on earthly things. 20But our citizenship is in heaven. And we eagerly await a Savior from there, the Lord Jesus Christ, 21who, by the power that enables him to bring everything under his control, will transform our lowly bodies so that they will be like his glorious body.

Closing Appeal for Steadfastness and Unity

4 Therefore, my brothers and sisters, you whom I love and long for, my joy and crown, stand firm in the Lord in this way, dear friends!

2I plead with Euodia and I plead with Syntyche to be of the same mind in the Lord. 3Yes, and I ask you, my true companion, help these women since they have contended at my side in the cause of the gospel, along with Clement and the rest of my co-workers, whose names are in the book of life.

Final Exhortations

4Rejoice in the Lord always. I will say it again: Rejoice! 5Let your gentleness be evident to all. The Lord is near. 6Do not be anxious about anything, but in every situation, by prayer and petition, with thanksgiving, present your re-

a 9 Or *through the faithfulness of*

quests to God. [7]And the peace of God, which transcends all understanding, will guard your hearts and your minds in Christ Jesus.

[8]Finally, brothers and sisters, whatever is true, whatever is noble, whatever is right, whatever is pure, whatever is lovely, whatever is admirable—if anything is excellent or praiseworthy—think about such things. [9]Whatever you have learned or received or heard from me, or seen in me—put it into practice. And the God of peace will be with you.

Thanks for Their Gifts

[10]I rejoiced greatly in the Lord that at last you renewed your concern for me. Indeed, you were concerned, but you had no opportunity to show it. [11]I am not saying this because I am in need, for I have learned to be content whatever the circumstances. [12]I know what it is to be in need, and I know what it is to have plenty. I have learned the secret of being content in any and every situation, whether well fed or hungry, whether living in plenty or in want. [13]I can do all this through him who gives me strength.

[14]Yet it was good of you to share in my troubles. [15]Moreover, as you Philippians know, in the early days of your acquaintance with the gospel, when I set out from Macedonia, not one church shared with me in the matter of giving and receiving, except you only; [16]for even when I was in Thessalonica, you sent me aid more than once when I was in need. [17]Not that I desire your gifts; what I desire is that more be credited to your account. [18]I have received full payment and have more than enough. I am amply supplied, now that I have received from Epaphroditus the gifts you sent. They are a fragrant offering, an acceptable sacrifice, pleasing to God. [19]And my God will meet all your needs according to the riches of his glory in Christ Jesus.

[20]To our God and Father be glory for ever and ever. Amen.

Final Greetings

[21]Greet all God's people in Christ Jesus. The brothers and sisters who are with me send greetings. [22]All God's people here send you greetings, especially those who belong to Caesar's household.

[23]The grace of the Lord Jesus Christ be with your spirit. Amen.[a]

---

[a] 23 Some manuscripts do not have *Amen*.

COLOSSIANS

1 Paul, an apostle of Christ Jesus by the will of God, and Timothy our
  brother,

2To the saints, the faithful*a* brothers and sisters in Christ at Colosse:

Grace and peace to you from God our Father.*b*

Thanksgiving and Prayer
3We always thank God, the Father of our Lord Jesus Christ, when we pray
for you, 4because we have heard of your faith in Christ Jesus and of the love
you have for all God's people— 5the faith and love that spring from the hope
stored up for you in heaven and about which you have already heard in the
true word of the gospel 6that has come to you. In the same way, it is bearing
fruit and growing throughout the whole world— just as it has been doing
among you since the day you heard it and truly understood God's grace. 7You
learned it from Epaphras, our dear fellow servant,*c* who is a faithful minister
of Christ on our*d* behalf, 8and who also told us of your love in the Spirit.

9For this reason, since the day we heard about you, we have not stopped
praying for you. We continually ask God to fill you with the knowledge of his
will through all the wisdom and understanding that the Spirit gives,*e* 10so that
you may live a life worthy of the Lord and please him in every way: bearing
fruit in every good work, growing in the knowledge of God, 11being strengthened with all power according to his glorious might so that you may have
great endurance and patience, 12and giving joyful thanks to the Father, who
has qualified you*f* to share in the inheritance of his people in the kingdom of
light. 13For he has rescued us from the dominion of darkness and brought us
into the kingdom of the Son he loves, 14in whom we have redemption, the forgiveness of sins.

The Supremacy of the Son of God
15The Son is the image of the invisible God, the firstborn over all creation.
16For in him all things were created: things in heaven and on earth, visible and
invisible, whether thrones or powers or rulers or authorities; all things have
been created through him and for him. 17He is before all things, and in him all
things hold together. 18And he is the head of the body, the church; he is the
beginning and the firstborn from among the dead, so that in everything he

---

a 2 Or *believing*   *b* 2 Some manuscripts *Father and the Lord Jesus Christ*   *c* 7 Or *slave*   *d* 7 Some
manuscripts *your*   *e* 9 Or *all spiritual wisdom and understanding*   *f* 12 Some manuscripts *us*

might have the supremacy. [19]For God was pleased to have all his fullness dwell in him, [20]and through him to reconcile to himself all things, whether things on earth or things in heaven, by making peace through his blood, shed on the cross.

[21]Once you were alienated from God and were enemies in your minds because of[a] your evil behavior. [22]But now he has reconciled you by Christ's physical body through death to present you holy in his sight, without blemish and free from accusation— [23]if you continue in your faith, established and firm, and do not move from the hope held out in the gospel. This is the gospel that you heard and that has been proclaimed to every creature under heaven, and of which I, Paul, have become a servant.

Paul's Labor for the Church

[24]Now I rejoice in what I am suffering for you, and I fill up in my flesh what is still lacking in regard to Christ's afflictions, for the sake of his body, which is the church. [25]I have become its servant by the commission God gave me to present to you the word of God in its fullness— [26]the mystery that has been kept hidden for ages and generations, but is now disclosed to God's people. [27]To them God has chosen to make known among the Gentiles the glorious riches of this mystery, which is Christ in you, the hope of glory.

[28]We proclaim him, admonishing and teaching everyone with all wisdom, so that we may present everyone fully mature in Christ. [29]To this end I strenuously contend with all the energy Christ so powerfully works in me.

2 I want you to know how hard I am contending for you and for those at Laodicea, and for all who have not met me personally. [2]My goal is that they may be encouraged in heart and united in love, so that they may have the full riches of complete understanding, in order that they may know the mystery of God, namely, Christ, [3]in whom are hidden all the treasures of wisdom and knowledge. [4]I tell you this so that no one may deceive you by fine-sounding arguments. [5]For though I am absent from you in body, I am present with you in spirit and delight to see how disciplined you are and how firm your faith in Christ is.

Spiritual Fullness in Christ

[6]So then, just as you received Christ Jesus as Lord, continue to live your lives in him, [7]rooted and built up in him, strengthened in the faith as you were taught, and overflowing with thankfulness.

[8]See to it that no one takes you captive through hollow and deceptive philosophy, which depends on human tradition and the elemental spiritual forces[b] of this world rather than on Christ.

[9]For in Christ all the fullness of the Deity lives in bodily form, [10]and in Christ you have been brought to fullness. He is the head over every power and authority. [11]In him you were also circumcised with a circumcision not performed by human hands. Your sinful nature[c] was put off when you were circumcised by[d] Christ, [12]having been buried with him in baptism, in which

you were also raised with him through your faith in the working of God, who raised him from the dead.

13When you were dead in your sins and in the uncircumcision of your sinful nature,*a* God made you*b* alive with Christ. He forgave us all our sins, 14having canceled the statement of indebtedness, with its particulars, that was against us and that stood opposed to us; he has taken it away, nailing it to the cross. 15And having disarmed the powers and authorities, he made a public spectacle of them, triumphing over them by the cross.*c*

Freedom From Human Rules

16Therefore do not let anyone judge you by what you eat or drink, or with regard to a religious festival, a New Moon celebration or a Sabbath day. 17These are a shadow of the things that were to come; the reality, however, is found in Christ. 18Do not let anyone who delights in false humility and the worship of angels disqualify you. Such people also go into great detail about what they have seen, and their unspiritual minds puff them up with idle notions. 19They have lost connection with the Head, from whom the whole body, supported and held together by its ligaments and sinews, grows as God causes it to grow.

20Since you died with Christ to the elemental spiritual forces of this world, why, as though you still belonged to the world, do you submit to its rules: 21"Do not handle! Do not taste! Do not touch!"? 22These rules, which have to do with things that are all destined to perish with use, are based on merely human commands and teachings. 23Such regulations indeed have an appearance of wisdom, with their self-imposed worship, their false humility and their harsh treatment of the body, but they lack any value in restraining sensual indulgence.

Living as Those Made Alive in Christ

3 Since, then, you have been raised with Christ, set your hearts on things above, where Christ is seated at the right hand of God. 2Set your minds on things above, not on earthly things. 3For you died, and your life is now hidden with Christ in God. 4When Christ, who is your*d* life, appears, then you also will appear with him in glory.

5Put to death, therefore, whatever belongs to your earthly nature: sexual immorality, impurity, lust, evil desires and greed, which is idolatry. 6Because of these, the wrath of God is coming.*e* 7You used to walk in these ways, in the life you once lived. 8But now you must also rid yourselves of all such things as these: anger, rage, malice, slander, and filthy language from your lips. 9Do not lie to each other, since you have taken off your old self with its practices 10and have put on the new self, which is being renewed in knowledge in the image of its Creator. 11Here there is no Greek or Jew, circumcised or uncircumcised, barbarian, Scythian, slave or free, but Christ is all, and is in all.

12Therefore, as God's chosen people, holy and dearly loved, clothe yourselves with compassion, kindness, humility, gentleness and patience. 13Bear

---

a 13 Or *your flesh*   *b* 13 Some manuscripts *us*   *c* 15 Or *them in him*   *d* 4 Some manuscripts *our*
e 6 Some early manuscripts *coming on those who are disobedient*

with each other and forgive one another if any of you has a grievance against someone. Forgive as the Lord forgave you. ¹⁴And over all these virtues put on love, which binds them all together in perfect unity.

¹⁵Let the peace of Christ rule in your hearts, since as members of one body you were called to peace. And be thankful. ¹⁶Let the message of Christ dwell among you richly as you teach and admonish one another with all wisdom through psalms, hymns and songs from the Spirit, singing to God with gratitude in your hearts. ¹⁷And whatever you do, whether in word or deed, do it all in the name of the Lord Jesus, giving thanks to God the Father through him.

Instructions for Christian Households

¹⁸Wives, submit yourselves to your own husbands, as is fitting in the Lord. ¹⁹Husbands, love your wives and do not be harsh with them.

²⁰Children, obey your parents in everything, for this pleases the Lord.

²¹Fathers,ᵃ do not embitter your children, or they will become discouraged.

²²Slaves, obey your earthly masters in everything; and do it, not only when their eye is on you and to curry their favor, but with sincerity of heart and reverence for the Lord. ²³Whatever you do, work at it with all your heart, as working for the Lord, not for human masters, ²⁴since you know that you will receive an inheritance from the Lord as a reward. It is the Lord Christ you are serving. ²⁵Those who do wrong will be repaid for their wrongs, and there is no favoritism.

4 Masters, provide your slaves with what is right and fair, because you know that you also have a Master in heaven.

Further Instructions

²Devote yourselves to prayer, being watchful and thankful. ³And pray for us, too, that God may open a door for our message, so that we may proclaim the mystery of Christ, for which I am in chains. ⁴Pray that I may proclaim it clearly, as I should. ⁵Be wise in the way you act toward outsiders; make the most of every opportunity. ⁶Let your conversation be always full of grace, seasoned with salt, so that you may know how to answer everyone.

Final Greetings

⁷Tychicus will tell you all the news about me. He is a dear brother, a faithful minister and fellow servantᵇ in the Lord. ⁸I am sending him to you for the express purpose that you may know about ourᶜ circumstances and that he may encourage your hearts. ⁹He is coming with Onesimus, our faithful and dear brother, who is one of you. They will tell you everything that is happening here.

¹⁰My fellow prisoner Aristarchus sends you his greetings, as does Mark, the cousin of Barnabas. (You have received instructions about him; if he comes to you, welcome him.) ¹¹Jesus, who is called Justus, also sends greetings. These are the only Jewsᵈ among my co-workers for the kingdom of God, and they

---

ᵃ 21 Or Parents   ᵇ 7 Or slave; also in verse 12   ᶜ 8 Some manuscripts that he may know about your
ᵈ 11 Greek only ones of the circumcision group

have proved a comfort to me. [12]Epaphras, who is one of you and a servant of Christ Jesus, sends greetings. He is always wrestling in prayer for you, that you may stand firm in all the will of God, mature and fully assured. [13]I vouch for him that he is working hard for you and for those at Laodicea and Hierapolis. [14]Our dear friend Luke, the doctor, and Demas send greetings. [15]Give my greetings to the brothers and sisters at Laodicea, and to Nympha and the church in her house.

[16]After this letter has been read to you, see that it is also read in the church of the Laodiceans and that you in turn read the letter from Laodicea.

[17]Tell Archippus: "See to it that you complete the work you have received in the Lord."

[18]I, Paul, write this greeting in my own hand. Remember my chains. Grace be with you.

1 THESSALONIANS

1 Paul, Silas[a] and Timothy,

To the church of the Thessalonians in God the Father and the Lord Jesus Christ:

Grace and peace to you.

Thanksgiving for the Thessalonians' Faith

2We always thank God for all of you and continually mention you in our prayers. 3We remember before our God and Father your work produced by faith, your labor prompted by love, and your endurance inspired by hope in our Lord Jesus Christ.

4For we know, brothers and sisters loved by God, that he has chosen you, 5because our gospel came to you not simply with words but also with power, with the Holy Spirit and deep conviction. You know how we lived among you for your sake. 6You became imitators of us and of the Lord, for you welcomed the message in the midst of severe suffering with the joy given by the Holy Spirit. 7And so you became a model to all the believers in Macedonia and Achaia. 8The Lord's message rang out from you not only in Macedonia and Achaia—your faith in God has become known everywhere. Therefore we do not need to say anything about it, 9for they themselves report what happened when we visited you. They tell how you turned to God from idols to serve the living and true God, 10and to wait for his Son from heaven, whom he raised from the dead—Jesus, who rescues us from the coming wrath.

Paul's Ministry in Thessalonica

2 You know, brothers and sisters, that our visit to you was not without results. 2We had previously suffered and been treated outrageously in Philippi, as you know, but with the help of our God we dared to tell you his gospel in the face of strong opposition. 3For the appeal we make does not spring from error or impure motives, nor are we trying to trick you. 4On the contrary, we speak as those approved by God to be entrusted with the gospel. We are not trying to please people but God, who tests our hearts. 5You know we never used flattery, nor did we put on a mask to cover up greed—God is our witness. 6We were not looking for praise from any human being, not from

a 1 Greek *Silvanus*, a variant of *Silas*

you or anyone else, even though as apostles of Christ we could have asserted our prerogatives. [7]Instead, we were like young children among you.

Just as a nursing mother cares for her children, [8]so we cared for you. Because we loved you so much, we were delighted to share with you not only the gospel of God but our lives as well. [9]Surely you remember, brothers and sisters, our toil and hardship; we worked night and day in order not to be a burden to anyone while we preached the gospel of God to you.

[10]You are witnesses, and so is God, of how holy, righteous and blameless we were among you who believed. [11]For you know that we dealt with each of you as a father deals with his own children, [12]encouraging, comforting and urging you to live lives worthy of God, who calls you into his kingdom and glory.

[13]And we also thank God continually because, when you received the word of God, which you heard from us, you accepted it not as a human word, but as it actually is, the word of God, which is indeed at work in you who believe. [14]For you, brothers and sisters, became imitators of God's churches in Judea, which are in Christ Jesus: You suffered from your fellow Gentiles the same things those churches suffered from the Jews, [15]who killed the Lord Jesus and the prophets and also drove us out. They displease God and are hostile to everyone [16]in their effort to keep us from speaking to the Gentiles so that they may be saved. In this way they always heap up their sins to the limit. The wrath of God has come upon them at last.[a]

Paul's Longing to See the Thessalonians

[17]But, brothers and sisters, when we were orphaned by being separated from you for a short time (in person, not in thought), out of our intense longing we made every effort to see you. [18]For we wanted to come to you—certainly I, Paul, did, again and again—but Satan blocked our way. [19]For what is our hope, our joy, or the crown in which we will glory in the presence of our Lord Jesus when he comes? Is it not you? [20]Indeed, you are our glory and joy.

3 So when we could stand it no longer, we thought it best to be left by ourselves in Athens. [2]We sent Timothy, who is our brother and co-worker in God's service in spreading the gospel of Christ, to strengthen and encourage you in your faith, [3]so that no one would be unsettled by these trials. You know quite well that we are destined for them. [4]In fact, when we were with you, we kept telling you that we would be persecuted. And it turned out that way, as you well know. [5]For this reason, when I could stand it no longer, I sent to find out about your faith. I was afraid that in some way the tempter had tempted you and that our labors might have been in vain.

Timothy's Encouraging Report

[6]But Timothy has just now come to us from you and has brought good news about your faith and love. He has told us that you always have pleasant memories of us and that you long to see us, just as we also long to see you. [7]Therefore, brothers and sisters, in all our distress and persecution we were encouraged about you because of your faith. [8]For now we really live, since you are

[a] 16 Or *them fully*

standing firm in the Lord. [9]How can we thank God enough for you in return for all the joy we have in the presence of our God because of you? [10]Night and day we pray most earnestly that we may see you again and supply what is lacking in your faith.

[11]Now may our God and Father himself and our Lord Jesus clear the way for us to come to you. [12]May the Lord make your love increase and overflow for each other and for everyone else, just as ours does for you. [13]May he strengthen your hearts so that you will be blameless and holy in the presence of our God and Father when our Lord Jesus comes with all his holy ones.

Living to Please God

4 As for other matters, brothers and sisters, we instructed you how to live in order to please God, as in fact you are living. Now we ask you and urge you in the Lord Jesus to do this more and more. [2]For you know what instructions we gave you by the authority of the Lord Jesus.

[3]It is God's will that you should be sanctified: that you should avoid sexual immorality; [4]that each of you should learn to control your own body[a] in a way that is holy and honorable, [5]not in passionate lust like the pagans, who do not know God; [6]and that in this matter no one should wrong or take advantage of a brother or sister. The Lord will punish all those who commit such sins, as we told you and warned you before. [7]For God did not call us to be impure, but to live a holy life. [8]Therefore, anyone who rejects this instruction does not reject a human being but God, the very God who gives you his Holy Spirit.

[9]Now about your love for one another we do not need to write to you, for you yourselves have been taught by God to love each other. [10]And in fact, you do love all the brothers and sisters throughout Macedonia. Yet we urge you, dear friends, to do so more and more, [11]and to make it your ambition to lead a quiet life: You should mind your own business and work with your hands, just as we told you, [12]so that your daily life may win the respect of outsiders and so that you will not be dependent on anybody.

Believers Who Have Died

[13]Brothers and sisters, we do not want you to be uninformed about those who sleep in death, so that you do not grieve like the rest, who have no hope. [14]We believe that Jesus died and rose again, and so we believe that God will bring with Jesus those who have fallen asleep in him. [15]According to the Lord's word, we tell you that we who are still alive, who are left till the coming of the Lord, will certainly not precede those who have fallen asleep. [16]For the Lord himself will come down from heaven, with a loud command, with the voice of the archangel and with the trumpet call of God, and the dead in Christ will rise first. [17]After that, we who are still alive and are left will be caught up together with them in the clouds to meet the Lord in the air. And so we will be with the Lord forever. [18]Therefore encourage one another with these words.

[a] 4 Or *learn to live with his own wife;* or *learn to acquire a wife*

The Day of the Lord

5 Now, brothers and sisters, about times and dates we do not need to write to you, [2]for you know very well that the day of the Lord will come like a thief in the night. [3]While people are saying, "Peace and safety," destruction will come on them suddenly, as labor pains on a pregnant woman, and they will not escape.

[4]But you, brothers and sisters, are not in darkness so that this day should surprise you like a thief. [5]You are all children of the light and children of the day. We do not belong to the night or to the darkness. [6]So then, let us not be like others, who are asleep, but let us be awake and sober. [7]For those who sleep, sleep at night, and those who get drunk, get drunk at night. [8]But since we belong to the day, let us be sober, putting on faith and love as a breastplate, and the hope of salvation as a helmet. [9]For God did not appoint us to suffer wrath but to receive salvation through our Lord Jesus Christ. [10]He died for us so that, whether we are awake or asleep, we may live together with him. [11]Therefore encourage one another and build each other up, just as in fact you are doing.

Final Instructions

[12]Now we ask you, brothers and sisters, to acknowledge those who work hard among you, who care for you in the Lord and who admonish you. [13]Hold them in the highest regard in love because of their work. Live in peace with each other. [14]And we urge you, brothers and sisters, warn those who are idle and disruptive, encourage the disheartened, help the weak, be patient with everyone. [15]Make sure that nobody pays back wrong for wrong, but always strive to do what is good for each other and for everyone else.

[16]Rejoice always, [17]pray continually, [18]give thanks in all circumstances; for this is God's will for you in Christ Jesus.

[19]Do not put out the Spirit's fire. [20]Do not treat prophecies with contempt [21]but test them all; hold on to what is good, [22]reject whatever is harmful.

[23]May God himself, the God of peace, sanctify you through and through. May your whole spirit, soul and body be kept blameless at the coming of our Lord Jesus Christ. [24]The one who calls you is faithful, and he will do it.

[25]Brothers and sisters, pray for us. [26]Greet all God's people with a holy kiss. [27]I charge you before the Lord to have this letter read to all the brothers and sisters.

[28]The grace of our Lord Jesus Christ be with you.

2 THESSALONIANS

1 Paul, Silas[a] and Timothy,

To the church of the Thessalonians in God our Father and the Lord Jesus Christ:

²Grace and peace to you from God the Father and the Lord Jesus Christ.

Thanksgiving and Prayer

³We ought always to thank God for you, brothers and sisters, and rightly so, because your faith is growing more and more, and the love all of you have for one another is increasing. ⁴Therefore, among God's churches we boast about your perseverance and faith in all the persecutions and trials you are enduring.

⁵All this is evidence that God's judgment is right, and as a result you will be counted worthy of the kingdom of God, for which you are suffering. ⁶God is just: He will pay back trouble to those who trouble you ⁷and give relief to you who are troubled, and to us as well. This will happen when the Lord Jesus is revealed from heaven in blazing fire with his powerful angels. ⁸He will punish those who do not know God and do not obey the gospel of our Lord Jesus. ⁹They will be punished with everlasting destruction and shut out from the presence of the Lord and from the glory of his might ¹⁰on the day he comes to be glorified in his holy people and to be marveled at among all those who have believed. This includes you, because you believed our testimony to you.

¹¹With this in mind, we constantly pray for you, that our God may make you worthy of his calling, and that by his power he may bring to fruition your every desire for goodness and your every deed prompted by faith. ¹²We pray this so that the name of our Lord Jesus may be glorified in you, and you in him, according to the grace of our God and the Lord Jesus Christ.[b]

The Man of Lawlessness

2 Concerning the coming of our Lord Jesus Christ and our being gathered to him, we ask you, brothers and sisters, ²not to become easily unsettled or alarmed by the teaching allegedly from us—whether by a prophecy or by word of mouth or by letter—asserting that the day of the Lord has already come. ³Don't let anyone deceive you in any way, for ⌊that day will not come⌋

---

[a] 1 Greek *Silvanus*, a variant of *Silas*   [b] 12 Or *God and Lord, Jesus Christ*

until the rebellion occurs and the man of lawlessness[a] is revealed, the man doomed to destruction. [4]He will oppose and will exalt himself over everything that is called God or is worshiped, so that he sets himself up in God's temple, proclaiming himself to be God.

[5]Don't you remember that when I was with you I used to tell you these things? [6]And now you know what is holding him back, so that he may be revealed at the proper time. [7]For the secret power of lawlessness is already at work; but the one who now holds it back will continue to do so till he is taken out of the way. [8]And then the lawless one will be revealed, whom the Lord Jesus will overthrow with the breath of his mouth and destroy by the splendor of his coming. [9]The coming of the lawless one will be in accordance with how Satan works. He will use all sorts of displays of power through signs and wonders that serve the lie, [10]and all the ways that wickedness deceives those who are perishing. They perish because they refused to love the truth and so be saved. [11]For this reason God sends them a powerful delusion so that they will believe the lie [12]and so that all will be condemned who have not believed the truth but have delighted in wickedness.

Stand Firm

[13]But we ought always to thank God for you, brothers and sisters loved by the Lord, because God chose you as firstfruits[b] to be saved through the sanctifying work of the Spirit and through belief in the truth. [14]He called you to this through our gospel, that you might share in the glory of our Lord Jesus Christ.

[15]So then, brothers and sisters, stand firm and hold fast to the teachings[c] we passed on to you, whether by word of mouth or by letter.

[16]May our Lord Jesus Christ himself and God our Father, who loved us and by his grace gave us eternal encouragement and good hope, [17]encourage your hearts and strengthen you in every good deed and word.

Request for Prayer

3 As for other matters, brothers and sisters, pray for us that the message of the Lord may spread rapidly and be honored, just as it was with you. [2]And pray that we may be delivered from wicked and evil people, for not everyone has faith. [3]But the Lord is faithful, and he will strengthen you and protect you from the evil one. [4]We have confidence in the Lord that you are doing and will continue to do the things we command. [5]May the Lord direct your hearts into God's love and Christ's perseverance.

Warning Against Idleness

[6]In the name of the Lord Jesus Christ, we command you, brothers and sisters, to keep away from every believer who is idle and disruptive and does not live according to the teaching[d] you received from us. [7]For you yourselves know how you ought to follow our example. We were not idle when we were with you, [8]nor did we eat anyone's food without paying for it. On the con-

---

[a] 3 Some manuscripts *sin*   [b] 13 Some manuscripts *because from the beginning God chose you*
[c] 15 Or *traditions*   [d] 6 Or *tradition*

trary, we worked night and day, laboring and toiling so that we would not be a burden to any of you. ⁹We did this, not because we do not have the right to such help, but in order to offer ourselves as a model for you to imitate. ¹⁰For even when we were with you, we gave you this rule: "Anyone who will not work shall not eat."

¹¹We hear that some among you are idle and disruptive. They are not busy; they are busybodies. ¹²Such people we command and urge in the Lord Jesus Christ to settle down and earn the bread they eat. ¹³And as for you, brothers and sisters, never tire of doing what is good.

¹⁴Take special note of those who do not obey our instruction in this letter. Do not associate with them, in order that they may feel ashamed. ¹⁵Yet do not regard them as enemies, but warn them as fellow believers.

Final Greetings

¹⁶Now may the Lord of peace himself give you peace at all times and in every way. The Lord be with all of you.

¹⁷I, Paul, write this greeting in my own hand, which is the distinguishing mark in all my letters. This is how I write.

¹⁸The grace of our Lord Jesus Christ be with you all.

1 TIMOTHY

1 Paul, an apostle of Christ Jesus by the command of God our Savior and of Christ Jesus our hope,

2To Timothy my true son in the faith:

Grace, mercy and peace from God the Father and Christ Jesus our Lord.

Timothy Charged to Oppose False Teachers

3As I urged you when I went into Macedonia, stay there in Ephesus so that you may command certain persons not to teach false doctrines any longer 4or to devote themselves to myths and endless genealogies. Such things promote controversial speculations rather than advancing God's work—which is by faith. 5The goal of this command is love, which comes from a pure heart and a good conscience and a sincere faith. 6Some have departed from these and have turned to meaningless talk. 7They want to be teachers of the law, but they do not know what they are talking about or what they so confidently affirm.

8We know that the law is good if one uses it properly. 9We also know that the law is made not for the righteous but for lawbreakers and rebels, the ungodly and sinful, the unholy and irreligious; for those who kill their fathers or mothers, for murderers, 10for the sexually immoral, for those practicing homosexuality, for slave traders and liars and perjurers. And it is for whatever else is contrary to the sound doctrine 11that conforms to the gospel concerning the glory of the blessed God, which he entrusted to me.

The Lord's Grace to Paul

12I thank Christ Jesus our Lord, who has given me strength, that he considered me trustworthy, appointing me to his service. 13Even though I was once a blasphemer and a persecutor and a violent man, I was shown mercy because I acted in ignorance and unbelief. 14The grace of our Lord was poured out on me abundantly, along with the faith and love that are in Christ Jesus.

15Here is a trustworthy saying that deserves full acceptance: Christ Jesus came into the world to save sinners—of whom I am the worst. 16But for that very reason I was shown mercy so that in me, the worst of sinners, Christ Jesus might display his immense patience as an example for those who would believe on him and receive eternal life. 17Now to the King eternal, immortal, invisible, the only God, be honor and glory for ever and ever. Amen.

The Charge to Timothy Renewed

[18]Timothy, my son, I am giving you this command in keeping with the prophecies once made about you, so that by recalling them you may fight the battle well, [19]holding on to faith and a good conscience. Some have rejected these and so have suffered shipwreck with regard to the faith. [20]Among them are Hymenaeus and Alexander, whom I have handed over to Satan to be taught not to blaspheme.

Instructions on Worship

2 I urge, then, first of all, that petitions, prayers, intercession and thanksgiving be made for everyone— [2]for kings and all those in authority, that we may live peaceful and quiet lives in all godliness and holiness. [3]This is good, and pleases God our Savior, [4]who wants all people to be saved and to come to a knowledge of the truth. [5]For there is one God and one mediator between God and human beings, Christ Jesus, himself human, [6]who gave himself as a ransom for all people. This has now been witnessed to at the proper time. [7]And for this purpose I was appointed a herald and an apostle — I am telling the truth, I am not lying—and a true and faithful teacher of the Gentiles.

[8]Therefore I want the men everywhere to pray, lifting up holy hands without anger or disputing. [9]I also want the women to dress modestly, with decency and propriety, adorning themselves, not with elaborate hairstyles or gold or pearls or expensive clothes, [10]but with good deeds, appropriate for women who profess to worship God.

[11]A woman[a] should learn in quietness and full submission. [12]I do not permit a woman to teach or to have authority over[b] a man,[c] she must be quiet. [13]For Adam was formed first, then Eve. [14]And Adam was not the one deceived; it was the woman who was deceived and became a sinner. [15]But women[d] will be saved through childbearing—if they continue in faith, love and holiness with propriety.

Qualifications for Overseers and Deacons

3 Here is a trustworthy saying: Whoever aspires to be an overseer[e] desires a noble task. [2]Now the overseer is to be above reproach, faithful to his wife, temperate, self-controlled, respectable, hospitable, able to teach, [3]not given to drunkenness, not violent but gentle, not quarrelsome, not a lover of money. [4]He must manage his own family well and see that his children obey him, and he must do so in a manner worthy of full[f] respect. [5](If anyone does not know how to manage his own family, how can he take care of God's church?) [6]He must not be a recent convert, or he may become conceited and fall under the same judgment as the devil. [7]He must also have a good reputation with outsiders, so that he will not fall into disgrace and into the devil's trap.

[8]In the same way, deacons are to be worthy of respect, sincere, not indulging in much wine, and not pursuing dishonest gain. [9]They must keep

---

[a] 11 Or *wife*; also in verse 12   [b] 12 Or *to exercise authority over*; or *to dominate*   [c] 12 Or *her husband*
[d] 15 Greek *she*   [e] 1 Traditionally *bishop*; also in verse 2   [f] 4 Or *him with proper*

hold of the deep truths of the faith with a clear conscience. [10]They must first be tested; and then if there is nothing against them, let them serve as deacons.

[11]In the same way, women ˻who are deacons˼[a] are to be worthy of respect, not malicious talkers but temperate and trustworthy in everything.

[12]A deacon must be faithful to his wife and must manage his children and his household well. [13]Those who have served well gain an excellent standing and great assurance in their faith in Christ Jesus.

Reasons for Paul's Instructions

[14]Although I hope to come to you soon, I am writing you these instructions so that, [15]if I am delayed, you will know how people ought to conduct themselves in God's household, which is the church of the living God, the pillar and foundation of the truth. [16]Beyond all question, the mystery from which true godliness springs is great:

> He appeared in a body,
>   was vindicated by the Spirit,[b]
> was seen by angels,
>   was preached among the nations,
> was believed on in the world,
>   was taken up in glory.

4 The Spirit clearly says that in later times some will abandon the faith and follow deceiving spirits and things taught by demons. [2]Such teachings come through hypocritical liars, whose consciences have been seared as with a hot iron. [3]They forbid people to marry and order them to abstain from certain foods, which God created to be received with thanksgiving by those who believe and who know the truth. [4]For everything God created is good, and nothing is to be rejected if it is received with thanksgiving, [5]because it is consecrated by the word of God and prayer.

[6]If you point these things out to the brothers and sisters, you will be a good minister of Christ Jesus, nourished on the truths of the faith and of the good teaching that you have followed. [7]Have nothing to do with godless myths and old wives' tales; rather, train yourself to be godly. [8]For physical training is of some value, but godliness has value for all things, holding promise for both the present life and the life to come. [9]This is a trustworthy saying that deserves full acceptance. [10]That is why we labor and strive, because we have put our hope in the living God, who is the Savior of all people, and especially of those who believe.

[11]Command and teach these things. [12]Don't let anyone look down on you because you are young, but set an example for the believers in speech, in conduct, in love, in faith and in purity. [13]Until I come, devote yourself to the public reading of Scripture, to preaching and to teaching. [14]Do not neglect your gift, which was given you through prophecy when the body of elders laid their hands on you.

[15]Be diligent in these matters; give yourself wholly to them, so that every-

---

a 11 Or *way,* ˻*deacons'*˼ *wives*   *b 16* Or *vindicated in spirit* one may see your progress. ¹⁶Watch your life and doctrine closely. Persevere in them, because if you do, you will save both yourself and your hearers.

Widows, Elders and Slaves

5 Do not rebuke an older man harshly, but exhort him as if he were your father. Treat younger men as brothers, ²older women as mothers, and younger women as sisters, with absolute purity.

³Give proper recognition to those widows who are really in need. ⁴But if a widow has children or grandchildren, these should learn first of all to put their religion into practice by caring for their own family and so repaying their parents and grandparents, for this is pleasing to God. ⁵The widow who is really in need and left all alone puts her hope in God and continues night and day to pray and to ask God for help. ⁶But the widow who lives for pleasure is dead even while she lives. ⁷Give the people these instructions, so that no one may be open to blame. ⁸Anyone who does not provide for their relatives, and especially for their immediate family members, has denied the faith and is worse than an unbeliever.

⁹No widow may be put on the list of widows unless she is over sixty, has been faithful to her husband, ¹⁰and is well known for her good deeds, such as bringing up children, showing hospitality, washing the feet of God's people, helping those in trouble and devoting herself to all kinds of good deeds.

¹¹As for younger widows, do not put them on such a list. For when their sensual desires overcome their dedication to Christ, they want to marry. ¹²Thus they bring judgment on themselves, because they have broken their first pledge. ¹³Besides, they get into the habit of being idle and going about from house to house. And not only do they become idlers, but also busybodies who talk nonsense, saying things they ought not to. ¹⁴So I counsel younger widows to marry, to have children, to manage their homes and to give the enemy no opportunity for slander. ¹⁵Some have in fact already turned away to follow Satan.

¹⁶If any woman who is a believer has widows in her care, she should continue to help them and not let the church be burdened with them, so that the church can help those widows who are really in need.

¹⁷The elders who direct the affairs of the church well are worthy of double honor, especially those whose work is preaching and teaching. ¹⁸For Scripture says, "Do not muzzle the ox while it is treading out the grain,"ᵃ and "Workers deserve their wages."ᵇ ¹⁹Do not entertain an accusation against an elder unless it is brought by two or three witnesses. ²⁰Those who sin are to be rebuked publicly, so that the others may take warning. ²¹I charge you, in the sight of God and Christ Jesus and the elect angels, to keep these instructions without partiality, and to do nothing out of favoritism.

²²Do not be hasty in the laying on of hands, and do not share in the sins of others. Keep yourself pure.

²³Stop drinking only water, and use a little wine because of your stomach and your frequent illnesses.

²⁴The sins of some are obvious, reaching the place of judgment ahead of

ᵃ 18 Deut. 25:4   ᵇ 18 Luke 10:7

them; the sins of others trail behind them. 25In the same way, good deeds are obvious, and even those that are not obvious cannot remain hidden forever.

6 All who are under the yoke of slavery should consider their masters worthy of full respect, so that God's name and our teaching may not be slandered. 2Those who have believing masters should not show them disrespect just because they are fellow believers. Instead, they should serve them even better because their masters are dear to them as fellow believers and are devoted to the welfareᵃ of their slaves.

False Teachers and the Love of Money

These are the things you are to teach and insist on. 3If anyone teaches otherwise and does not agree to the sound instruction of our Lord Jesus Christ and to godly teaching, 4they are conceited and understand nothing. They have an unhealthy interest in controversies and quarrels about words that result in envy, strife, malicious talk, evil suspicions 5and constant friction between people of corrupt mind, who have been robbed of the truth and who think that godliness is a means to financial gain.

6But godliness with contentment is great gain. 7For we brought nothing into the world, and we can take nothing out of it. 8But if we have food and clothing, we will be content with that. 9Those who want to get rich fall into temptation and a trap and into many foolish and harmful desires that plunge people into ruin and destruction. 10For the love of money is a root of all kinds of evil. Some people, eager for money, have wandered from the faith and pierced themselves with many griefs.

Final Charge to Timothy

11But you, man of God, flee from all this, and pursue righteousness, godliness, faith, love, endurance and gentleness. 12Fight the good fight of the faith. Take hold of the eternal life to which you were called when you made your good confession in the presence of many witnesses. 13In the sight of God, who gives life to everything, and of Christ Jesus, who while testifying before Pontius Pilate made the good confession, I charge you 14to keep this command without spot or blame until the appearing of our Lord Jesus Christ, 15which God will bring about in his own time—God, the blessed and only Ruler, the King of kings and Lord of lords, 16who alone is immortal and who lives in unapproachable light, whom no one has seen or can see. To him be honor and might forever. Amen.

17Command those who are rich in this present world not to be arrogant nor to put their hope in wealth, which is so uncertain, but to put their hope in God, who richly provides us with everything for our enjoyment. 18Command them to do good, to be rich in good deeds, and to be generous and willing to share. 19In this way they will lay up treasure for themselves as a firm foundation for the coming age, so that they may take hold of the life that is truly life.

20Timothy, guard what has been entrusted to your care. Turn away from godless chatter and the opposing ideas of what is falsely called knowledge, 21which some have professed and in so doing have departed from the faith.

Grace be with you all.

ᵃ2 Or *and benefit from the service*

2 TIMOTHY

1 Paul, an apostle of Christ Jesus by the will of God, in keeping with the promise of life that is in Christ Jesus,

2To Timothy, my dear son:

Grace, mercy and peace from God the Father and Christ Jesus our Lord.

Thanksgiving
3I thank God, whom I serve, as my ancestors did, with a clear conscience, as night and day I constantly remember you in my prayers. 4Recalling your tears, I long to see you, so that I may be filled with joy. 5I have been reminded of your sincere faith, which first lived in your grandmother Lois and in your mother Eunice and, I am persuaded, now lives in you also.

Appeal for Loyalty to Paul and the Gospel
6For this reason I remind you to fan into flame the gift of God, which is in you through the laying on of my hands. 7For the Spirit God gave us does not make us timid, but gives us power, love and self-discipline. 8So do not be ashamed of the testimony about our Lord or of me his prisoner. But join with me in suffering for the gospel, by the power of God, 9who has saved us and called us to a holy life—not because of anything we have done but because of his own purpose and grace. This grace was given us in Christ Jesus before the beginning of time, 10but it has now been revealed through the appearing of our Savior, Christ Jesus, who has destroyed death and has brought life and immortality to light through the gospel. 11And of this gospel I was appointed a herald and an apostle and a teacher. 12That is why I am suffering as I am. Yet I am not ashamed, because I know whom I have believed, and am convinced that he is able to guard what I have entrusted to him until that day.

13What you heard from me, keep as the pattern of sound teaching, with faith and love in Christ Jesus. 14Guard the good deposit that was entrusted to you—guard it with the help of the Holy Spirit who lives in us.

Examples of Disloyalty and Loyalty
15You know that everyone in the province of Asia has deserted me, including Phygelus and Hermogenes.

16May the Lord show mercy to the household of Onesiphorus, because he often refreshed me and was not ashamed of my chains. 17On the contrary, when he was in Rome, he searched hard for me until he found me. 18May the

Lord grant that he will find mercy from the Lord on that day! You know very well in how many ways he helped me in Ephesus.

The Appeal Renewed

2 You then, my son, be strong in the grace that is in Christ Jesus. [2]And the things you have heard me say in the presence of many witnesses entrust to reliable people[a] who will also be qualified to teach others. [3]Join with me in suffering, like a good soldier of Christ Jesus. [4]No one serving as a soldier gets involved in civilian affairs; rather, they try to please their commanding officer. [5]Similarly, anyone who competes as an athlete does not receive the victor's crown except by competing according to the rules. [6]The hardworking farmer should be the first to receive a share of the crops. [7]Reflect on what I am saying, for the Lord will give you insight into all this.

[8]Remember Jesus Christ, raised from the dead, descended from David. This is my gospel, [9]for which I am suffering even to the point of being chained like a criminal. But God's word is not chained. [10]Therefore I endure everything for the sake of the elect, that they too may obtain the salvation that is in Christ Jesus, with eternal glory.

[11]Here is a trustworthy saying:

> If we died with him,
>   we will also live with him;
> [12]if we endure,
>   we will also reign with him.
> If we disown him,
>   he will also disown us;
> [13]if we are faithless,
>   he remains faithful,
>   for he cannot disown himself.

Dealing With False Teachers

[14]Keep reminding God's people of these things. Warn them before God against quarreling about words; it is of no value, and only ruins those who listen. [15]Do your best to present yourself to God as one approved, a worker who does not need to be ashamed and who correctly handles the word of truth. [16]Avoid godless chatter, because those who indulge in it will become more and more ungodly. [17]Their teaching will spread like gangrene. Among them are Hymenaeus and Philetus, [18]who have departed from the truth. They say that the resurrection has already taken place, and they destroy the faith of some. [19]Nevertheless, God's solid foundation stands firm, sealed with this inscription: "The Lord knows those who are his," and, "Everyone who confesses the name of the Lord must turn away from wickedness."

[20]In a large house there are articles not only of gold and silver, but also of wood and clay; some are for noble purposes and some for disposal of refuse. [21]Any who cleanse themselves from the latter will be instruments for noble purposes, made holy, useful to the Master and prepared to do any good work. [22]Flee the evil desires of youth and pursue righteousness, faith, love and

[a] 2 Or *men*

peace, along with those who call on the Lord out of a pure heart. 23Don't have anything to do with foolish and stupid arguments, because you know they produce quarrels. 24And the Lord's servant must not be quarrelsome but must be kind to everyone, able to teach, not resentful. 25Opponents must be gently instructed, in the hope that God will grant them repentance leading them to a knowledge of the truth, 26and that they will come to their senses and escape from the trap of the devil, who has taken them captive to do his will.

3 But mark this: There will be terrible times in the last days. 2People will be lovers of themselves, lovers of money, boastful, proud, abusive, disobedient to their parents, ungrateful, unholy, 3without love, unforgiving, slanderous, without self-control, brutal, not lovers of the good, 4treacherous, rash, conceited, lovers of pleasure rather than lovers of God— 5having a form of godliness but denying its power. Have nothing to do with such people.

6They are the kind who worm their way into homes and gain control over gullible women, who are loaded down with sins and are swayed by all kinds of evil desires, 7always learning but never able to acknowledge the truth. 8Just as Jannes and Jambres opposed Moses, so also these teachers oppose the truth. They are men of depraved minds, who, as far as the faith is concerned, are rejected. 9But they will not get very far because, as in the case of those men, their folly will be clear to everyone.

A Final Charge to Timothy

10You, however, know all about my teaching, my way of life, my purpose, faith, patience, love, endurance, 11persecutions, sufferings—what kinds of things happened to me in Antioch, Iconium and Lystra, the persecutions I endured. Yet the Lord rescued me from all of them. 12In fact, everyone who wants to live a godly life in Christ Jesus will be persecuted, 13while evildoers and impostors will go from bad to worse, deceiving and being deceived. 14But as for you, continue in what you have learned and have become convinced of, because you know those from whom you learned it, 15and how from infancy you have known the Holy Scriptures, which are able to make you wise for salvation through faith in Christ Jesus. 16All Scripture is God-breathed and is useful for teaching, rebuking, correcting and training in righteousness, 17so that all God's people[a] may be thoroughly equipped for every good work.

4 In the presence of God and of Christ Jesus, who will judge the living and the dead, and in view of his appearing and his kingdom, I give you this charge: 2Preach the word; be prepared in season and out of season; correct, rebuke and encourage—with great patience and careful instruction. 3For the time will come when people will not put up with sound doctrine. Instead, to suit their own desires, they will gather around them a great number of teachers to say what their itching ears want to hear. 4They will turn their ears away from the truth and turn aside to myths. 5But you, keep your head in all situations, endure hardship, do the work of an evangelist, discharge all the duties of your ministry.

6For I am already being poured out like a drink offering, and the time for my departure is near. 7I have fought the good fight, I have finished the race, I

a 17 Or *that the servant of God*

have kept the faith. [8]Now there is in store for me the crown of righteousness, which the Lord, the righteous Judge, will award to me on that day—and not only to me, but also to all who have longed for his appearing.

Personal Remarks

[9]Do your best to come to me quickly, [10]for Demas, because he loved this world, has deserted me and has gone to Thessalonica. Crescens has gone to Galatia, and Titus to Dalmatia. [11]Only Luke is with me. Get Mark and bring him with you, because he is helpful to me in my ministry. [12]I sent Tychicus to Ephesus. [13]When you come, bring the cloak that I left with Carpus at Troas, and my scrolls, especially the parchments.

[14]Alexander the metalworker did me a great deal of harm. The Lord will repay him for what he has done. [15]You too should be on your guard against him, because he strongly opposed our message.

[16]At my first defense, no one came to my support, but everyone deserted me. May it not be held against them. [17]But the Lord stood at my side and gave me strength, so that through me the message might be fully proclaimed and all the Gentiles might hear it. And I was delivered from the lion's mouth. [18]The Lord will rescue me from every evil attack and will bring me safely to his heavenly kingdom. To him be glory for ever and ever. Amen.

Final Greetings

[19]Greet Priscilla[a] and Aquila and the household of Onesiphorus. [20]Erastus stayed in Corinth, and I left Trophimus sick in Miletus. [21]Do your best to get here before winter. Eubulus greets you, and so do Pudens, Linus, Claudia and all the brothers and sisters.

[22]The Lord be with your spirit. Grace be with you all.

[a] 19 Greek *Prisca*, a variant of *Priscilla*

TITUS

1 Paul, a servant of God and an apostle of Jesus Christ to further the faith of God's elect and their knowledge of the truth that leads to godliness— [2]in the hope of eternal life, which God, who does not lie, promised before the beginning of time, [3]and which now at his appointed season he has brought to light through the preaching entrusted to me by the command of God our Savior.

[4]To Titus, my true son in our common faith:

Grace and peace from God the Father and Christ Jesus our Savior.

Appointing Elders Who Love What Is Good

[5]The reason I left you in Crete was that you might put in order what was left unfinished and appoint[a] elders in every town, as I directed you. [6]An elder must be blameless, faithful to his wife, a man whose children believe and are not open to the charge of being wild and disobedient. [7]Since an overseer[b] manages God's household, he must be blameless—not overbearing, not quick tempered, not given to drunkenness, not violent, not pursuing dishonest gain. [8]Rather, he must be hospitable, one who loves what is good, who is self-controlled, upright, holy and disciplined. [9]He must hold firmly to the trustworthy message as it has been taught, so that he can encourage others by sound doctrine and refute those who oppose it.

Rebuking Those Who Fail to Do Good

[10]For there are many rebellious people, full of meaningless talk and deception, especially those of the circumcision group. [11]They must be silenced, because they are disrupting whole households by teaching things they ought not to teach—and that for the sake of dishonest gain. [12]One of Crete's own prophets has said it: "Cretans are always liars, evil brutes, lazy gluttons."[c] [13]He has surely told the truth! Therefore rebuke them sharply, so that they will be sound in the faith [14]and will pay no attention to Jewish myths or to the merely human commands of those who reject the truth. [15]To the pure, all things are pure, but to those who are corrupted and do not believe, nothing is pure. In fact, both their minds and consciences are corrupted. [16]They claim to know God, but by their actions they deny him. They are detestable, disobedient and unfit for doing anything good.

[a]5 Or *ordain*   [b]7 Traditionally *bishop*   [c]12 From the Cretan philosopher Epimenides

Doing Good for the Sake of the Gospel

2 You, however, must teach what is appropriate to sound doctrine. [2]Teach the older men to be temperate, worthy of respect, self-controlled, and sound in faith, in love and in endurance.

[3]Likewise, teach the older women to be reverent in the way they live, not to be slanderers or addicted to much wine, but to teach what is good. [4]Then they can urge the younger women to love their husbands and children, [5]to be self-controlled and pure, to be busy at home, to be kind, and to be subject to their husbands, so that no one will malign the word of God.

[6]Similarly, encourage the young men to be self-controlled. [7]In everything set them an example by doing what is good. In your teaching show integrity, seriousness [8]and soundness of speech that cannot be condemned, so that those who oppose you may be ashamed because they have nothing bad to say about us.

[9]Teach slaves to be subject to their masters in everything, to try to please them, not to talk back to them, [10]and not to steal from them, but to show that they can be fully trusted, so that in every way they will make the teaching about God our Savior attractive.

[11]For the grace of God has appeared that offers salvation to all people. [12]It teaches us to say "No" to ungodliness and worldly passions, and to live self-controlled, upright and godly lives in this present age, [13]while we wait for the blessed hope—the appearing of the glory of our great God and Savior, Jesus Christ, [14]who gave himself for us to redeem us from all wickedness and to purify for himself a people that are his very own, eager to do what is good.

[15]These, then, are the things you should teach. Encourage and rebuke with all authority. Do not let anyone despise you.

Saved in Order to Do Good

3 Remind the people to be subject to rulers and authorities, to be obedient, to be ready to do whatever is good, [2]to slander no one, to be peaceable and considerate, and always to be gentle toward everyone.

[3]At one time we too were foolish, disobedient, deceived and enslaved by all kinds of passions and pleasures. We lived in malice and envy, being hated and hating one another. [4]But when the kindness and love of God our Savior appeared, [5]he saved us, not because of righteous things we had done, but because of his mercy. He saved us through the washing of rebirth and renewal by the Holy Spirit, [6]whom he poured out on us generously through Jesus Christ our Savior, [7]so that, having been justified by his grace, we might become heirs having the hope of eternal life. [8]This is a trustworthy saying. And I want you to stress these things, so that those who have trusted in God may be careful to devote themselves to doing what is good. These things are excellent and profitable for everyone.

[9]But avoid foolish controversies and genealogies and arguments and quarrels about the law, because these are unprofitable and useless. [10]Warn divisive people once, and then warn them a second time. After that, have nothing to do with them. [11]You may be sure that such people are warped and sinful; they are self-condemned.

Final Remarks

¹²As soon as I send Artemas or Tychicus to you, do your best to come to me at Nicopolis, because I have decided to winter there. ¹³Do everything you can to help Zenas the lawyer and Apollos on their way and see that they have everything they need. ¹⁴Our people must learn to devote themselves to doing what is good, in order to provide for urgent needs and not live unproductive lives.

¹⁵Everyone with me sends you greetings. Greet those who love us in the faith.

Grace be with you all.

PHILEMON

¹Paul, a prisoner of Christ Jesus, and Timothy our brother,

To Philemon our dear friend and fellow worker, ²—also to Apphia our sister and Archippus our fellow soldier—and to the church that meets in your home:

³Grace and peace to you*a* from God our Father and the Lord Jesus Christ.

Thanksgiving and Prayer

⁴I always thank my God as I remember you in my prayers, ⁵because I hear about your love for all God's people and your faith in the Lord Jesus. ⁶I pray that your partnership with us in the faith may be effective in deepening your understanding of every good thing we share for the sake of Christ. ⁷Your love has given me great joy and encouragement, because you, brother, have refreshed the hearts of God's people.

Paul's Plea for Onesimus

⁸Therefore, although in Christ I could be bold and order you to do what you ought to do, ⁹yet I prefer to appeal to you on the basis of love. It is as none other than Paul—an old man and now also a prisoner of Christ Jesus— ¹⁰that I appeal to you for my son Onesimus,*b* who became my son while I was in chains. ¹¹Formerly he was useless to you, but now he has become useful both to you and to me.

¹²I am sending him—who is my very heart—back to you. ¹³I would have liked to keep him with me so that he could take your place in helping me while I am in chains for the gospel. ¹⁴But I did not want to do anything without your consent, so that any favor you do should not seem forced but would be voluntary. ¹⁵Perhaps the reason he was separated from you for a little while was that you might have him back forever— ¹⁶no longer as a slave, but better than a slave, as a dear brother. He is very dear to me but even dearer to you, both as a fellow man and as a brother in the Lord.

¹⁷So if you consider me a partner, welcome him as you would welcome me. ¹⁸If he has done you any wrong or owes you anything, charge it to me. ¹⁹I, Paul, am writing this with my own hand. I will pay it back—not to mention that you owe me your very self. ²⁰I do wish, brother, that I may have some benefit from you in the Lord; refresh my heart in Christ. ²¹Confident of your obedience, I write to you, knowing that you will do even more than I ask.

---

a 3 The Greek is plural; also in verses 22 and 25.   *b* 10 *Onesimus* means *useful.*

[22]And one thing more: Prepare a guest room for me, because I hope to be restored to you in answer to your prayers.

[23]Epaphras, my fellow prisoner in Christ Jesus, sends you greetings. [24]And so do Mark, Aristarchus, Demas and Luke, my fellow workers.

[25]The grace of the Lord Jesus Christ be with your spirit.

HEBREWS

God's Final Word: His Son

1 In the past God spoke to our ancestors through the prophets at many times and in various ways, ²but in these last days he has spoken to us by his Son, whom he appointed heir of all things, and through whom also he made the universe. ³The Son is the radiance of God's glory and the exact representation of his being, sustaining all things by his powerful word. After he had provided purification for sins, he sat down at the right hand of the Majesty in heaven. ⁴So he became as much superior to the angels as the name he has inherited is superior to theirs.

The Son Superior to Angels

⁵For to which of the angels did God ever say,

> "You are my Son;
>   today I have become your Father*a" b*?

Or again,

> "I will be his Father,
>   and he will be my Son"*c*?

⁶And again, when God brings his firstborn into the world, he says,

> "Let all God's angels worship him."*d*

⁷In speaking of the angels he says,

> "He makes his angels spirits,
>   and his servants flames of fire."*e*

⁸But about the Son he says,

> "Your throne, O God, will last for ever and ever;
>   a scepter of justice will be the scepter of your kingdom.
> ⁹You have loved righteousness and hated wickedness;
>   therefore God, your God, has set you above your companions
>   by anointing you with the oil of joy."*f*

¹⁰He also says,

---

a 5 Or *have begotten you*   *b* 5 Psalm 2:7   *c* 5 2 Samuel 7:14; 1 Chron. 17:13   *d* 6 Deut. 32:43 (see Dead Sea Scrolls and Septuagint)   *e* 7 Psalm 104:4   *f* 9 Psalm 45:6,7

"In the beginning, Lord, you laid the foundations of the earth,
   and the heavens are the work of your hands.
11 They will perish, but you remain;
   they will all wear out like a garment.
12 You will roll them up like a robe;
   like a garment they will be changed.
But you remain the same,
   and your years will never end." [a]

13 To which of the angels did God ever say,

"Sit at my right hand
   until I make your enemies
   a footstool for your feet" [b]?

14 Are not all angels ministering spirits sent to serve those who will inherit salvation?

Warning to Pay Attention

2 We must pay the most careful attention, therefore, to what we have heard, so that we do not drift away. 2 For since the message spoken through angels was binding, and every violation and disobedience received its just punishment, 3 how shall we escape if we ignore so great a salvation? This salvation, which was first announced by the Lord, was confirmed to us by those who heard him. 4 God also testified to it by signs, wonders and various miracles, and by gifts of the Holy Spirit distributed according to his will.

Jesus Made Like His Brothers and Sisters

5 It is not to angels that he has subjected the world to come, about which we are speaking. 6 But there is a place where someone has testified:

"What are mere mortals that you are mindful of them,
   human beings that you care for them?
7 You made them a little lower than the angels;
   you crowned them with glory and honor
8   and put everything under their feet." [c]

In putting everything under them, [d] God left nothing that is not subject to them. [d] Yet at present we do not see everything subject to them. [d] 9 But we do see Jesus, who was made lower than the angels for a little while, now crowned with glory and honor because he suffered death, so that by the grace of God he might taste death for everyone.

10 In bringing many sons and daughters to glory, it was fitting that God, for whom and through whom everything exists, should make the author of their salvation perfect through what he suffered. 11 Both the one who makes people holy and those who are made holy are of the same family. So Jesus is not ashamed to call them brothers and sisters. 12 He says,

---

[a] 12 Psalm 102:25–27   [b] 13 Psalm 110:1   [c] 6–8 Psalm 8:4–6; or *"What is a human being that you are mindful of him,/ the son of man that you care for him?/ 7 You made him lower than the angels for a little while;/ you crowned him with glory and honor/ 8 and put everything under his feet."*   [d] 8 Or *him*

"I will declare your name to my brothers and sisters;
in the congregation I will sing your praises."[a]

13And again,

"I will put my trust in him."[b]

And again he says,

"Here am I, and the children God has given me."[c]

14Since the children have flesh and blood, he too shared in their humanity so that by his death he might break the power of him who holds the power of death—that is, the devil— 15and free those who all their lives were held in slavery by their fear of death. 16For surely it is not angels he helps, but Abraham's descendants. 17For this reason he had to be made like his brothers and sisters in every way, in order that he might become a merciful and faithful high priest in service to God, and that he might make atonement for the sins of the people. 18Because he himself suffered when he was tempted, he is able to help those who are being tempted.

Jesus Greater Than Moses

3 Therefore, holy brothers and sisters, who share in the heavenly calling, fix your thoughts on Jesus, whom we acknowledge as our apostle and high priest. 2He was faithful to the one who appointed him, just as Moses was faithful in all God's house. 3Jesus has been found worthy of greater honor than Moses, just as the builder of a house has greater honor than the house itself. 4For every house is built by someone, but God is the builder of everything. 5"Moses was faithful as a servant in all God's house,"[d] bearing witness to what would be spoken by God in the future. 6But Christ is faithful as the Son over God's house. And we are his house, if indeed we hold firmly to our confidence and the hope in which we glory.

Warning Against Unbelief

7So, as the Holy Spirit says:

"Today, if you hear his voice,
8   do not harden your hearts
as you did in the rebellion,
during the time of testing in the desert,
9where your ancestors tested and tried me,
though for forty years they saw what I did.
10That is why I was angry with that generation;
I said, 'Their hearts are always going astray,
and they have not known my ways.'
11So I declared on oath in my anger,
'They shall never enter my rest.' "[e]

12See to it, brothers and sisters, that none of you has a sinful, unbelieving heart that turns away from the living God. 13But encourage one another daily,

[a] 12 Psalm 22:22   [b] 13 Isaiah 8:17   [c] 13 Isaiah 8:18   [d] 5 Num. 12:7   [e] 11 Psalm 95:7–11

as long as it is called "today," so that none of you may be hardened by sin's deceitfulness. [14]We have come to share in Christ, if indeed we hold firmly till the end our original conviction. [15]As has just been said:

> "Today, if you hear his voice,
> do not harden your hearts
> as you did in the rebellion."[a]

[16]Who were they who heard and rebelled? Were they not all those Moses led out of Egypt? [17]And with whom was he angry for forty years? Was it not with those who sinned, whose bodies perished in the desert? [18]And to whom did God swear that they would never enter his rest if not to those who disobeyed? [19]So we see that they were not able to enter, because of their unbelief.

A Sabbath-Rest for the People of God

4 Therefore, since the promise of entering his rest still stands, let us be careful that none of you be found to have fallen short of it. [2]For we also have had the good news proclaimed to us, just as they did; but the message they heard was of no value to them, because they did not share the faith of those who obeyed.[b] [3]Now we who have believed enter that rest, just as God has said,

> "So I declared on oath in my anger,
> 'They shall never enter my rest.' "[c]

And yet his work has been finished since the creation of the world. [4]For somewhere he has spoken about the seventh day in these words: "On the seventh day God rested from all his work."[d] [5]And again in the passage above he says, "They shall never enter my rest."

[6]Therefore since it still remains for some to enter that rest, and since those who formerly had the good news proclaimed to them did not go in because of their disobedience, [7]God again set a certain day, calling it "today." This he did when a long time later he spoke through David, as in the passage already quoted:

> "Today, if you hear his voice,
> do not harden your hearts."[a]

[8]For if Joshua had given them rest, God would not have spoken later about another day. [9]There remains, then, a Sabbath-rest for the people of God; [10]for those who enter God's rest also rest from their own work, just as God did from his. [11]Let us, therefore, make every effort to enter that rest, so that no one will perish by following their example of disobedience.

[12]For the word of God is alive and active. Sharper than any double-edged sword, it penetrates even to dividing soul and spirit, joints and marrow; it judges the thoughts and attitudes of the heart. [13]Nothing in all creation is hidden from God's sight. Everything is uncovered and laid bare before the eyes of him to whom we must give account.

---

[a] 15,7 Psalm 95:7,8   [b] 2 Some manuscripts *because those who heard did not combine it with faith*
[c] 3 Psalm 95:11; also in verse 5   [d] 4 Gen. 2:2

Jesus the Great High Priest

14Therefore, since we have a great high priest who has ascended into heaven,*a* Jesus the Son of God, let us hold firmly to the faith we profess. 15For we do not have a high priest who is unable to empathize with our weaknesses, but we have one who has been tempted in every way, just as we are—yet he did not sin. 16Let us then approach God's throne of grace with confidence, so that we may receive mercy and find grace to help us in our time of need.

5 Every high priest is selected from among the people and is appointed to represent them in matters related to God, to offer gifts and sacrifices for sins. 2He is able to deal gently with those who are ignorant and are going astray, since he himself is subject to weakness. 3This is why he has to offer sacrifices for his own sins, as well as for the sins of the people. 4And no one takes this honor upon himself, but he receives it when called by God, just as Aaron was.

5In the same way, Christ did not take upon himself the glory of becoming a high priest. But God said to him,

"You are my Son;
    today I have become your Father.*b" c*

6And he says in another place,

"You are a priest forever,
    in the order of Melchizedek."*d*

7During the days of Jesus' life on earth, he offered up prayers and petitions with fervent cries and tears to the one who could save him from death, and he was heard because of his reverent submission. 8Son though he was, he learned obedience from what he suffered 9and, once made perfect, he became the source of eternal salvation for all who obey him 10and was designated by God to be high priest in the order of Melchizedek.

Warning Against Falling Away

11We have much to say about this, but it is hard to make it clear to you because you no longer try to understand. 12In fact, though by this time you ought to be teachers, you need someone to teach you the elementary truths of God's word all over again. You need milk, not solid food! 13Anyone who lives on milk, being still an infant, is not acquainted with the teaching about righteousness. 14But solid food is for the mature, who by constant use have trained themselves to distinguish good from evil.

6 Therefore let us move beyond the elementary teachings about Christ and be taken forward to maturity, not laying again the foundation of repentance from acts that lead to death,*e* and of faith in God, 2instruction about cleansing rites,*f* the laying on of hands, the resurrection of the dead, and eternal judgment. 3And God permitting, we will do so.

4It is impossible for those who have once been enlightened, who have tasted the heavenly gift, who have shared in the Holy Spirit, 5who have tasted the goodness of the word of God and the powers of the coming age 6and who

---

a 14 Greek *has gone through the heavens*   *b 5* Or *have begotten you*   *c 5* Psalm 2:7   *d 6* Psalm 110:4
e 1 Or *from useless rituals*   *f 2* Or *about baptisms*

have fallen[a] away, to be brought back to repentance. To their loss they are crucifying the Son of God all over again and subjecting him to public disgrace. [7]Land that drinks in the rain often falling on it and that produces a crop useful to those for whom it is farmed receives the blessing of God. [8]But land that produces thorns and thistles is worthless and is in danger of being cursed. In the end it will be burned.

[9]Even though we speak like this, dear friends, we are convinced of better things in your case—the things that have to do with salvation. [10]God is not unjust; he will not forget your work and the love you have shown him as you have helped his people and continue to help them. [11]We want each of you to show this same diligence to the very end, in order to make your hope sure. [12]We do not want you to become lazy, but to imitate those who through faith and patience inherit what has been promised.

The Certainty of God's Promise

[13]When God made his promise to Abraham, since there was no one greater for him to swear by, he swore by himself, [14]saying, "I will surely bless you and give you many descendants."[b] [15]And so after waiting patiently, Abraham received what was promised.

[16]People swear by someone greater than themselves, and the oath confirms what is said and puts an end to all argument. [17]Because God wanted to make the unchanging nature of his purpose very clear to the heirs of what was promised, he confirmed it with an oath. [18]God did this so that, by two unchangeable things in which it is impossible for God to lie, we who have fled to take hold of the hope set before us may be greatly encouraged. [19]We have this hope as an anchor for the soul, firm and secure. It enters the inner sanctuary behind the curtain, [20]where our forerunner, Jesus, has entered on our behalf. He has become a high priest forever, in the order of Melchizedek.

Melchizedek the Priest

7 This Melchizedek was king of Salem and priest of God Most High. He met Abraham returning from the defeat of the kings and blessed him, [2]and Abraham gave him a tenth of everything. First, the name Melchizedek means "king of righteousness"; then also, "king of Salem" means "king of peace." [3]Without father or mother, without genealogy, without beginning of days or end of life, resembling the Son of God, he remains a priest forever.

[4]Just think how great he was: Even the patriarch Abraham gave him a tenth of the plunder! [5]Now the law requires the descendants of Levi who become priests to collect a tenth from the people—that is, from their kindred—even though their kindred are descended from Abraham. [6]This man, however, did not trace his descent from Levi, yet he collected a tenth from Abraham and blessed him who had the promises. [7]And without doubt the lesser is blessed by the greater. [8]In the one case, the tenth is collected by those who die; but in the other case, by him who is declared to be living. [9]One might even say that Levi, who collects the tenth, paid the tenth through Abraham, [10]because when Melchizedek met Abraham, Levi was still in the body of his ancestor.

[a] 6 Or *age*, [6]*if they fall*   [b] 14 Gen. 22:17

Jesus Like Melchizedek

11If perfection could have been attained through the Levitical priesthood—and indeed the law given to the people established that priesthood—why was there still need for another priest to come, one in the order of Melchizedek, not in the order of Aaron? 12For when the priesthood is changed, the law must be changed also. 13He of whom these things are said belonged to a different tribe, and no one from that tribe has ever served at the altar. 14For it is clear that our Lord descended from Judah, and in regard to that tribe Moses said nothing about priests. 15And what we have said is even more clear if another priest like Melchizedek appears, 16one who has become a priest not on the basis of a regulation as to his ancestry but on the basis of the power of an indestructible life. 17For it is declared:

> "You are a priest forever,
>   in the order of Melchizedek." [a]

18The former regulation is set aside because it was weak and useless 19(for the law made nothing perfect), and a better hope is introduced, by which we draw near to God.

20And it was not without an oath! Others became priests without any oath, 21but he became a priest with an oath when God said to him:

> "The Lord has sworn
>   and will not change his mind:
>   'You are a priest forever.' " [a]

22Because of this oath, Jesus has become the guarantor of a better covenant.

23Now there have been many of those priests, since death prevented them from continuing in office; 24but because Jesus lives forever, he has a permanent priesthood. 25Therefore he is able to save completely [b] those who come to God through him, because he always lives to intercede for them.

26Such a high priest truly meets our need—one who is holy, blameless, pure, set apart from sinners, exalted above the heavens. 27Unlike the other high priests, he does not need to offer sacrifices day after day, first for his own sins, and then for the sins of the people. He sacrificed for their sins once for all when he offered himself. 28For the law appoints as high priests men in all their weakness; but the oath, which came after the law, appointed the Son, who has been made perfect forever.

The High Priest of a New Covenant

8 Now the main point of what we are saying is this: We do have such a high priest, who sat down at the right hand of the throne of the Majesty in heaven, 2and who serves in the sanctuary, the true tabernacle set up by the Lord, not by a mere human being.

3Every high priest is appointed to offer both gifts and sacrifices, and so it was necessary for this one also to have something to offer. 4If he were on earth, he would not be a priest, for there are already priests who offer the gifts prescribed by the law. 5They serve at a sanctuary that is a copy and shadow of

a 17,21 Psalm 110:4   b 25 Or forever

what is in heaven. This is why Moses was warned when he was about to build the tabernacle: "See to it that you make everything according to the pattern shown you on the mountain."[a] [6]But in fact the ministry Jesus has received is as superior to theirs as the covenant of which he is mediator is superior to the old one, since the new covenant is established on better promises.

[7]For if there had been nothing wrong with that first covenant, no place would have been sought for another. [8]But God found fault with the people and said[b]:

> "The days are coming, declares the Lord,
>   when I will make a new covenant
> with the house of Israel
>   and with the house of Judah.
> [9]It will not be like the covenant
>   I made with their ancestors
> when I took them by the hand
>   to lead them out of Egypt,
> because they did not remain faithful to my covenant,
>   and I turned away from them,
>   declares the Lord.
> [10]This is the covenant I will establish with the house of Israel
>   after that time, declares the Lord.
> I will put my laws in their minds
>   and write them on their hearts.
> I will be their God,
>   and they will be my people.
> [11]No longer will they teach their neighbors,
>   or say to one another, 'Know the Lord,'
> because they will all know me,
>   from the least of them to the greatest.
> [12]For I will forgive their wickedness
>   and will remember their sins no more."[c]

[13]By calling this covenant "new," he has made the first one obsolete; and what is obsolete and outdated will soon disappear.

Worship in the Earthly Tabernacle

9 Now the first covenant had regulations for worship and also an earthly sanctuary. [2]A tabernacle was set up. In its first room were the lampstand and the table with its consecrated bread; this was called the Holy Place. [3]Behind the second curtain was a room called the Most Holy Place, [4]which had the golden altar of incense and the gold-covered ark of the covenant. This ark contained the gold jar of manna, Aaron's staff that had budded, and the stone tablets of the covenant. [5]Above the ark were the cherubim of the Glory, overshadowing the atonement cover.[d] But we cannot discuss these things in detail now.

[a]5 Exodus 25:40   [b]8 Some manuscripts may be translated *fault and said to the people.*
[c]12 Jer. 31:31–34   [d]5 Traditionally *the mercy seat*

⁶When everything had been arranged like this, the priests entered regularly into the outer room to carry on their ministry. ⁷But only the high priest entered the inner room, and that only once a year, and never without blood, which he offered for himself and for the sins the people had committed in ignorance. ⁸The Holy Spirit was showing by this that the way into the Most Holy Place had not yet been disclosed as long as the first tabernacle was still functioning. ⁹This is an illustration for the present time, indicating that the gifts and sacrifices being offered were not able to clear the conscience of the worshiper. ¹⁰They are only a matter of food and drink and various ceremonial washings—external regulations applying until the time of the new order.

The Blood of Christ

¹¹But when Christ came as high priest of the good things that are now already here,ᵃ he went through the greater and more perfect tabernacle that is not made with human hands, that is to say, is not a part of this creation. ¹²He did not enter by means of the blood of goats and calves; but he entered the Most Holy Place once for all by his own blood, thus obtainingᵇ eternal redemption. ¹³The blood of goats and bulls and the ashes of a heifer sprinkled on those who are ceremonially unclean sanctify them so that they are outwardly clean. ¹⁴How much more, then, will the blood of Christ, who through the eternal Spirit offered himself unblemished to God, cleanse our consciences from acts that lead to death,ᶜ so that we may serve the living God!

¹⁵For this reason Christ is the mediator of a new covenant, that those who are called may receive the promised eternal inheritance—now that he has died as a ransom to set them free from the sins committed under the first covenant.

¹⁶In the case of a will,ᵈ it is necessary to prove the death of the one who made it, ¹⁷because a will is in force only when somebody has died; it never takes effect while the one who made it is living. ¹⁸This is why even the first covenant was not put into effect without blood. ¹⁹When Moses had proclaimed every commandment of the law to all the people, he took the blood of calves, together with water, scarlet wool and branches of hyssop, and sprinkled the scroll and all the people. ²⁰He said, "This is the blood of the covenant, which God has commanded you to keep."ᵉ ²¹In the same way, he sprinkled with the blood both the tabernacle and everything used in its ceremonies. ²²In fact, the law requires that nearly everything be cleansed with blood, and without the shedding of blood there is no forgiveness.

²³It was necessary, then, for the copies of the heavenly things to be purified with these sacrifices, but the heavenly things themselves with better sacrifices than these. ²⁴For Christ did not enter a sanctuary made with human hands that was only a copy of the true one; he entered heaven itself, now to appear for us in God's presence. ²⁵Nor did he enter heaven to offer himself again and again, the way the high priest enters the Most Holy Place every year with blood that is not his own. ²⁶Otherwise Christ would have had to suffer many times since the creation of the world. But he has appeared once for all at the

---

ᵃ 11 Some early manuscripts *are to come*   ᵇ 12 Or *blood, having obtained*   ᶜ 14 Or *from useless rituals*
ᵈ 16 Same Greek word as *covenant*; also in verse 17   ᵉ 20 Exodus 24:8

culmination of the ages to do away with sin by the sacrifice of himself. [27]Just as people are destined to die once, and after that to face judgment, [28]so Christ was sacrificed once to take away the sins of many; and he will appear a second time, not to bear sin, but to bring salvation to those who are waiting for him.

Christ's Sacrifice Once for All

10 The law is only a shadow of the good things that are coming—not the realities themselves. For this reason it can never, by the same sacrifices repeated endlessly year after year, make perfect those who draw near to worship. [2]Otherwise, would they not have stopped being offered? For the worshipers would have been cleansed once for all, and would no longer have felt guilty for their sins. [3]But those sacrifices are an annual reminder of sins. [4]It is impossible for the blood of bulls and goats to take away sins.

[5]Therefore, when Christ came into the world, he said:

> "Sacrifice and offering you did not desire,
> but a body you prepared for me;
> [6]with burnt offerings and sin offerings
> you were not pleased.
> [7]Then I said, 'Here I am—it is written about me in the scroll—
> I have come to do your will, O God.' "[a]

[8]First he said, "Sacrifices and offerings, burnt offerings and sin offerings you did not desire, nor were you pleased with them"—though they were offered in accordance with the law. [9]Then he said, "Here I am, I have come to do your will." He sets aside the first to establish the second. [10]And by that will, we have been made holy through the sacrifice of the body of Jesus Christ once for all.

[11]Day after day every priest stands and performs his religious duties; again and again he offers the same sacrifices, which can never take away sins. [12]But when this priest had offered for all time one sacrifice for sins, he sat down at the right hand of God, [13]and since that time he waits for his enemies to be made his footstool. [14]For by one sacrifice he has made perfect forever those who are being made holy.

[15]The Holy Spirit also testifies to us about this. First he says:

> [16]"This is the covenant I will make with them
> after that time, says the Lord.
> I will put my laws in their hearts,
> and I will write them on their minds."[b]

[17]Then he adds:

> "Their sins and lawless acts
> I will remember no more."[c]

[18]And where these have been forgiven, sacrifice for sin is no longer necessary.

[a]7 Psalm 40:6–8 (see Septuagint)   [b]16 Jer. 31:33   [c]17 Jer. 31:34

A Call to Persevere in Faith

[19]Therefore, brothers and sisters, since we have confidence to enter the Most Holy Place by the blood of Jesus, [20]by a new and living way opened for us through the curtain, that is, his body, [21]and since we have a great priest over the house of God, [22]let us draw near to God with a sincere heart in full assurance of faith, having our hearts sprinkled to cleanse us from a guilty conscience and having our bodies washed with pure water. [23]Let us hold unswervingly to the hope we profess, for he who promised is faithful. [24]And let us consider how we may spur one another on toward love and good deeds, [25]not giving up meeting together, as some are in the habit of doing, but encouraging one another—and all the more as you see the Day approaching.

[26]If we deliberately keep on sinning after we have received the knowledge of the truth, no sacrifice for sins is left, [27]but only a fearful expectation of judgment and of raging fire that will consume the enemies of God. [28]Anyone who rejected the law of Moses died without mercy on the testimony of two or three witnesses. [29]How much more severely do you think those deserve to be punished who have trampled the Son of God underfoot, who have treated as an unholy thing the blood of the covenant that sanctified them, and who have insulted the Spirit of grace? [30]For we know him who said, "It is mine to avenge; I will repay,"[a] and again, "The Lord will judge his people."[b] [31]It is a dreadful thing to fall into the hands of the living God.

[32]Remember those earlier days after you had received the light, when you endured in a great conflict full of suffering. [33]Sometimes you were publicly exposed to insult and persecution; at other times you stood side by side with those who were so treated. [34]You suffered along with those in prison and joyfully accepted the confiscation of your property, because you knew that you yourselves had better and lasting possessions. [35]So do not throw away your confidence; it will be richly rewarded.

[36]You need to persevere so that when you have done the will of God, you will receive what he has promised. [37]For,

> "In just a little while,
>   he who is coming will come
>   and will not delay."

[38]And,

> "But my righteous one[c] will live by faith.
>   And I take no pleasure
>   in the one who shrinks back."[d]

[39]But we are not of those who shrink back and are destroyed, but of those who believe and are saved.

Faith in Action

11 Now faith is being sure of what we hope for and certain of what we do not see. [2]This is what the ancients were commended for.

---

[a] 30 Deut. 32:35   [b] 30 Deut. 32:36; Psalm 135:14   [c] 38 One early manuscript *But the righteous*
[d] 37,38 Isaiah 26:20; Hab. 2:3,4 (Septuagint)

³By faith we understand that the universe was formed at God's command, so that what is seen was not made out of what was visible.

⁴By faith Abel brought God a better offering than Cain did. By faith he was commended as righteous, when God spoke well of his offerings. And by faith Abel still speaks, even though he is dead.

⁵By faith Enoch was taken from this life, so that he did not experience death: "He could not be found, because God had taken him away."ᵃ For before he was taken, he was commended as one who pleased God. ⁶And without faith it is impossible to please God, because anyone who comes to him must believe that he exists and that he rewards those who earnestly seek him.

⁷By faith Noah, when warned about things not yet seen, in holy fear built an ark to save his family. By his faith he condemned the world and became heir of the righteousness that is in keeping with faith.

⁸By faith Abraham, when called to go to a place he would later receive as his inheritance, obeyed and went, even though he did not know where he was going. ⁹By faith he made his home in the promised land like a stranger in a foreign country; he lived in tents, as did Isaac and Jacob, who were heirs with him of the same promise. ¹⁰For he was looking forward to the city with foundations, whose architect and builder is God. ¹¹And by faith even Sarah, who was past age, was enabled to bear children because sheᵇ considered him faithful who had made the promise. ¹²And so from this one man, and he as good as dead, came descendants as numerous as the stars in the sky and as countless as the sand on the seashore.

¹³All these people were still living by faith when they died. They did not receive the things promised; they only saw them and welcomed them from a distance, admitting that they were foreigners and strangers on earth. ¹⁴People who say such things show that they are looking for a country of their own. ¹⁵If they had been thinking of the country they had left, they would have had opportunity to return. ¹⁶Instead, they were longing for a better country—a heavenly one. Therefore God is not ashamed to be called their God, for he has prepared a city for them.

¹⁷By faith Abraham, when God tested him, offered Isaac as a sacrifice. He who had embraced the promises was about to sacrifice his one and only son, ¹⁸even though God had said to him, "It is through Isaac that your offspringᶜ will be reckoned."ᵈ ¹⁹Abraham reasoned that God could even raise the dead, and so in a manner of speaking he did receive Isaac back from death.

²⁰By faith Isaac blessed Jacob and Esau in regard to their future.

²¹By faith Jacob, when he was dying, blessed each of Joseph's sons, and worshiped as he leaned on the top of his staff.

²²By faith Joseph, when his end was near, spoke about the exodus of the Israelites from Egypt and gave instructions concerning the burial of his bones.

²³By faith Moses' parents hid him for three months after he was born, because they saw he was no ordinary child, and they were not afraid of the king's edict.

²⁴By faith Moses, when he had grown up, refused to be known as the son of

---

ᵃ 5 Gen. 5:24   ᵇ 11 Or By faith Abraham, even though he was past age—and Sarah herself was not able to conceive—was enabled to become a father because he   ᶜ 18 Greek seed   ᵈ 18 Gen. 21:12

Pharaoh's daughter. [25]He chose to be mistreated along with the people of God rather than to enjoy the fleeting pleasures of sin. [26]He regarded disgrace for the sake of Christ as of greater value than the treasures of Egypt, because he was looking ahead to his reward. [27]By faith he left Egypt, not fearing the king's anger; he persevered because he saw him who is invisible. [28]By faith he kept the Passover and the application of blood, so that the destroyer of the firstborn would not touch the firstborn of Israel.

[29]By faith the people passed through the Red Sea[a] as on dry land; but when the Egyptians tried to do so, they were drowned.

[30]By faith the walls of Jericho fell, after the army had marched around them for seven days.

[31]By faith the prostitute Rahab, because she welcomed the spies, was not killed with those who were disobedient.[b]

[32]And what more shall I say? I do not have time to tell about Gideon, Barak, Samson and Jephthah, about David and Samuel and the prophets, [33]who through faith conquered kingdoms, administered justice, and gained what was promised; who shut the mouths of lions, [34]quenched the fury of the flames, and escaped the edge of the sword; whose weakness was turned to strength; and who became powerful in battle and routed foreign armies. [35]Women received back their dead, raised to life again. There were others who were tortured, refusing to be released so that they might gain an even better resurrection. [36]Some faced jeers and flogging, and even chains and imprisonment. [37]They were stoned[c]; they were sawed in two; they were put to death by the sword. They went about in sheepskins and goatskins, destitute, persecuted and mistreated— [38]the world was not worthy of them. They wandered in deserts and mountains, and in caves and holes in the ground.

[39]These were all commended for their faith, yet none of them received what had been promised. [40]God had planned something better for us so that only together with us would they be made perfect.

12 Therefore, since we are surrounded by such a great cloud of witnesses, let us throw off everything that hinders and the sin that so easily entangles. And let us run with perseverance the race marked out for us, [2]fixing our eyes on Jesus, the author and perfecter of our faith. For the joy set before him he endured the cross, scorning its shame, and sat down at the right hand of the throne of God. [3]Consider him who endured such opposition from sinners, so that you will not grow weary and lose heart.

God Disciplines His Children

[4]In your struggle against sin, you have not yet resisted to the point of shedding your blood. [5]And have you completely forgotten this word of encouragement that addresses you as children? It says,

> "My son, do not make light of the Lord's discipline,
>   and do not lose heart when he rebukes you,
> [6]because the Lord disciplines those he loves,
>   and he chastens everyone he accepts as his child."[d]

---

[a] 29 That is, Sea of Reeds   [b] 31 Or *unbelieving*   [c] 37 Some early manuscripts *stoned; they were put to the test;*   [d] 6 Prov. 3:11,12

[7]Endure hardship as discipline; God is treating you as his children. For what children are not disciplined by their parents? [8]If you are not disciplined—and everyone undergoes discipline—then you are not legitimate children at all. [9]Moreover, we have all had human parents who disciplined us and we respected them for it. How much more should we submit to the Father of spirits and live! [10]Our parents disciplined us for a little while as they thought best; but God disciplines us for our good, that we may share in his holiness. [11]No discipline seems pleasant at the time, but painful. Later on, however, it produces a harvest of righteousness and peace for those who have been trained by it.

[12]Therefore, strengthen your feeble arms and weak knees. [13]"Make level paths for your feet," [a] so that the lame may not be disabled, but rather healed.

Warning and Encouragement

[14]Make every effort to live in peace with everyone and to be holy; without holiness no one will see the Lord. [15]See to it that no one falls short of the grace of God and that no bitter root grows up to cause trouble and defile many. [16]See that no one is sexually immoral, or is godless like Esau, who for a single meal sold his inheritance rights as the oldest son. [17]Afterward, as you know, when he wanted to inherit this blessing, he was rejected. Even though he sought the blessing with tears, he could not change what he had done.

The Mountain of Fear and the Mountain of Joy

[18]You have not come to a mountain that can be touched and that is burning with fire; to darkness, gloom and storm; [19]to a trumpet blast or to such a voice speaking words that those who heard it begged that no further word be spoken to them, [20]because they could not bear what was commanded: "If even an animal touches the mountain, it must be stoned." [b] [21]The sight was so terrifying that Moses said, "I am trembling with fear." [c]

[22]But you have come to Mount Zion, to the city of the living God, the heavenly Jerusalem. You have come to thousands upon thousands of angels in joyful assembly, [23]to the church of the firstborn, whose names are written in heaven. You have come to God, the Judge of all, to the spirits of the righteous made perfect, [24]to Jesus the mediator of a new covenant, and to the sprinkled blood that speaks a better word than the blood of Abel.

[25]See to it that you do not refuse him who speaks. If they did not escape when they refused him who warned them on earth, how much less will we, if we turn away from him who warns us from heaven? [26]At that time his voice shook the earth, but now he has promised, "Once more I will shake not only the earth but also the heavens." [d] [27]The words "once more" indicate the removing of what can be shaken—that is, created things—so that what cannot be shaken may remain.

[28]Therefore, since we are receiving a kingdom that cannot be shaken, let us be thankful, and so worship God acceptably with reverence and awe, [29]for our "God is a consuming fire." [e]

---

[a] 13 Prov. 4:26   [b] 20 Exodus 19:12,13   [c] 21 See Deut. 9:19.   [d] 26 Haggai 2:6   [e] 29 Deut. 4:24

Concluding Exhortations

13 Keep on loving one another as brothers and sisters. [2]Do not forget to show hospitality to strangers, for by so doing some people have shown hospitality to angels without knowing it. [3]Continue to remember those in prison as if you were together with them in prison, and those who are mistreated as if you yourselves were suffering.

[4]Marriage should be honored by all, and the marriage bed kept pure, for God will judge the adulterer and all the sexually immoral. [5]Keep your lives free from the love of money and be content with what you have, because God has said,

> "Never will I leave you;
> never will I forsake you." [a]

[6]So we say with confidence,

> "The Lord is my helper; I will not be afraid.
> What can human beings do to me?" [b]

[7]Remember your leaders, who spoke the word of God to you. Consider the outcome of their way of life and imitate their faith. [8]Jesus Christ is the same yesterday and today and forever.

[9]Do not be carried away by all kinds of strange teachings. It is good for our hearts to be strengthened by grace, not by the eating of ceremonial foods, which is of no benefit to those who observe such rituals. [10]We have an altar from which those who minister at the tabernacle have no right to eat.

[11]The high priest carries the blood of animals into the Most Holy Place as a sin offering, but the bodies are burned outside the camp. [12]And so Jesus also suffered outside the city gate to make the people holy through his own blood. [13]Let us, then, go to him outside the camp, bearing the disgrace he bore. [14]For here we do not have an enduring city, but we are looking for the city that is to come.

[15]Through Jesus, therefore, let us continually offer to God a sacrifice of praise—the fruit of lips that openly profess his name. [16]And do not forget to do good and to share with others, for with such sacrifices God is pleased.

[17]Have confidence in your leaders and submit to their authority, because they keep watch over you as those who must give an account. Do this so that their work will be a joy, not a burden, for that would be of no benefit to you.

[18]Pray for us. We are sure that we have a clear conscience and desire to live honorably in every way. [19]I particularly urge you to pray so that I may be restored to you soon.

[20]Now may the God of peace, who through the blood of the eternal covenant brought back from the dead our Lord Jesus, that great Shepherd of the sheep, [21]equip you with everything good for doing his will, and may he work in us what is pleasing to him, through Jesus Christ, to whom be glory for ever and ever. Amen.

[a]5 Deut. 31:6   [b]6 Psalm 118:6,7

[22]Brothers and sisters, I urge you to bear with my word of exhortation, for in fact I have written to you quite briefly.

[23]I want you to know that our brother Timothy has been released. If he arrives soon, I will come with him to see you.

[24]Greet all your leaders and all God's people. Those from Italy send you their greetings.

[25]Grace be with you all.

JAMES

1 James, a servant of God and of the Lord Jesus Christ,

To the twelve tribes scattered among the nations:

Greetings.

Trials and Temptations

2Consider it pure joy, my brothers and sisters, whenever you face trials of many kinds, 3because you know that the testing of your faith produces perseverance. 4Let perseverance finish its work so that you may be mature and complete, not lacking anything. 5If any of you lacks wisdom, you should ask God, who gives generously to all without finding fault, and it will be given to you. 6But when you ask, you must believe and not doubt, because the one who doubts is like a wave of the sea, blown and tossed by the wind. 7Those who doubt should not think they will receive anything from the Lord; 8they are double-minded and unstable in all they do.

9Believers in humble circumstances ought to take pride in their high position. 10But the rich should take pride in their humiliation—they will pass away like a wild flower! 11For the sun rises with scorching heat and withers the plant; its blossom falls and its beauty is destroyed. In the same way, the rich will fade away even while they go about their business.

12Blessed are those who persevere under trial, because when they have stood the test, they will receive the crown of life that God has promised to those who love him.

13When tempted, no one should say, "God is tempting me." For God cannot be tempted by evil, nor does he tempt anyone; 14but each of you is tempted when you are dragged away by your own evil desire and enticed. 15Then, after desire has conceived, it gives birth to sin; and sin, when it is full-grown, gives birth to death.

16Don't be deceived, my dear brothers and sisters. 17Every good and perfect gift is from above, coming down from the Father of the heavenly lights, who does not change like shifting shadows. 18He chose to give us birth through the word of truth, that we might be a kind of firstfruits of all he created.

Listening and Doing

19My dear brothers and sisters, take note of this: Everyone should be quick to listen, slow to speak and slow to become angry, 20because our anger does not produce the righteousness that God desires. 21Therefore, get rid of all moral filth and the evil that is so prevalent and humbly accept the word planted in you, which can save you. [22]Do not merely listen to the word, and so deceive yourselves. Do what it says. [23]Those who listen to the word but do not do what it says are like people who look at their faces in a mirror [24]and, after looking at themselves, go away and immediately forget what they look like. [25]But those who look intently into the perfect law that gives freedom and continue in it—not forgetting what they have heard but doing it—they will be blessed in what they do.

[26]Those who consider themselves religious and yet do not keep a tight rein on their tongues deceive themselves, and their religion is worthless. [27]Religion that God our Father accepts as pure and faultless is this: to look after orphans and widows in their distress and to keep oneself from being polluted by the world.

Favoritism Forbidden

2 My brothers and sisters, believers in our glorious Lord Jesus Christ must not show favoritism. [2]Suppose someone comes into your meeting wearing a gold ring and fine clothes, and a poor person in filthy old clothes also comes in. [3]If you show special attention to the one wearing fine clothes and say, "Here's a good seat for you," but say to the one who is poor, "You stand there" or "Sit on the floor by my feet," [4]have you not discriminated among yourselves and become judges with evil thoughts?

[5]Listen, my dear brothers and sisters: Has not God chosen those who are poor in the eyes of the world to be rich in faith and to inherit the kingdom he promised those who love him? [6]But you have dishonored the poor. Is it not the rich who are exploiting you? Are they not the ones who are dragging you into court? [7]Are they not the ones who are blaspheming the noble name of him to whom you belong?

[8]If you really keep the royal law found in Scripture, "Love your neighbor as yourself,"[a] you are doing right. [9]But if you show favoritism, you sin and are convicted by the law as lawbreakers. [10]For whoever keeps the whole law and yet stumbles at just one point is guilty of breaking all of it. [11]For he who said, "Do not commit adultery,"[b] also said, "Do not murder."[c] If you do not commit adultery but do commit murder, you have become a lawbreaker.

[12]Speak and act as those who are going to be judged by the law that gives freedom, [13]because judgment without mercy will be shown to anyone who has not been merciful. Mercy triumphs over judgment.

Faith and Deeds

[14]What good is it, my brothers and sisters, if people claim to have faith but have no deeds? Can such faith save them? [15]Suppose a brother or sister is without clothes and daily food. [16]If one of you says to them, "Go in peace; keep warm and well fed," but does nothing about their physical needs, what good is it? [17]In the same way, faith by itself, if it is not accompanied by action, is dead.

[18]But someone will say, "You have faith; I have deeds."

[a]8 Lev. 19:18   [b]11 Exodus 20:14; Deut. 5:18   [c]11 Exodus 20:13; Deut. 5:17

Show me your faith without deeds, and I will show you my faith by what I do. 19You believe that there is one God. Good! Even the demons believe that—and shudder.

20You foolish person, do you want evidence that faith without deeds is useless*a*? 21Was not our father Abraham considered righteous for what he did when he offered his son Isaac on the altar? 22You see that his faith and his actions were working together, and his faith was made complete by what he did. 23And the scripture was fulfilled that says, "Abraham believed God, and it was credited to him as righteousness,"*b* and he was called God's friend. 24You see that people are justified by what they do and not by faith alone.

25In the same way, was not even Rahab the prostitute considered righteous for what she did when she gave lodging to the spies and sent them off in a different direction? 26As the body without the spirit is dead, so faith without deeds is dead.

Taming the Tongue

3 Not many of you should presume to be teachers, my brothers and sisters, because you know that we who teach will be judged more strictly. 2We all stumble in many ways. Those who are never at fault in what they say are perfect, able to keep their whole body in check.

3When we put bits into the mouths of horses to make them obey us, we can turn the whole animal. 4Or take ships as an example. Although they are so large and are driven by strong winds, they are steered by a very small rudder wherever the pilot wants to go. 5Likewise, the tongue is a small part of the body, but it makes great boasts. Consider what a great forest is set on fire by a small spark. 6The tongue also is a fire, a world of evil among the parts of the body. It corrupts the whole person, sets the whole course of one's life on fire, and is itself set on fire by hell.

7All kinds of animals, birds, reptiles and sea creatures are being tamed and have been tamed by human beings, 8but no one can tame the tongue. It is a restless evil, full of deadly poison.

9With the tongue we praise our Lord and Father, and with it we curse human beings, who have been made in God's likeness. 10Out of the same mouth come praise and cursing. My brothers and sisters, this should not be. 11Can both fresh water and salt*c* water flow from the same spring? 12My brothers and sisters, can a fig tree bear olives, or a grapevine bear figs? Neither can a salt spring produce fresh water.

Two Kinds of Wisdom

13Who is wise and understanding among you? Let them show it by their good life, by deeds done in the humility that comes from wisdom. 14But if you harbor bitter envy and selfish ambition in your hearts, do not boast about it or deny the truth. 15Such "wisdom" does not come down from heaven but is earthly, unspiritual, demonic. 16For where you have envy and selfish ambition, there you find disorder and every evil practice.

17But the wisdom that comes from heaven is first of all pure; then peace-lov-

---

a 20 Some early manuscripts *dead*   *b 23* Gen. 15:6   *c 11* Greek *bitter* (see also verse 14)

ing, considerate, submissive, full of mercy and good fruit, impartial and sincere. [18]Peacemakers who sow in peace reap a harvest of righteousness.

Submit Yourselves to God

4 What causes fights and quarrels among you? Don't they come from your desires that battle within you? [2]You desire but do not have, so you kill. You covet but you cannot get what you want, so you quarrel and fight. You do not have because you do not ask God. [3]When you ask, you do not receive, because you ask with wrong motives, that you may spend what you get on your pleasures.

[4]You adulterous people, don't you know that friendship with the world means enmity against God? Anyone who chooses to be a friend of the world becomes an enemy of God. [5]Or do you think Scripture says without reason that he jealously longs for the spirit he has caused to dwell in us?[a] [6]But he gives us more grace. That is why Scripture says:

> "God opposes the proud
> but shows favor to the humble and oppressed."[b]

[7]Submit yourselves, then, to God. Resist the devil, and he will flee from you. [8]Come near to God and he will come near to you. Wash your hands, you sinners, and purify your hearts, you double-minded. [9]Grieve, mourn and wail. Change your laughter to mourning and your joy to gloom. [10]Humble yourselves before the Lord, and he will lift you up.

[11]Brothers and sisters, do not slander one another. Anyone who speaks against a brother or sister or judges them speaks against the law and judges it. When you judge the law, you are not keeping it, but sitting in judgment on it. [12]There is only one Lawgiver and Judge, the one who is able to save and destroy. But you—who are you to judge your neighbor?

Boasting About Tomorrow

[13]Now listen, you who say, "Today or tomorrow we will go to this or that city, spend a year there, carry on business and make money." [14]Why, you do not even know what will happen tomorrow. What is your life? You are a mist that appears for a little while and then vanishes. [15]Instead, you ought to say, "If it is the Lord's will, we will live and do this or that." [16]As it is, you boast in your arrogant schemes. All such boasting is evil. [17]So then, if you know the good you ought to do and don't do it, you sin.

Warning to Rich Oppressors

5 Now listen, you rich people, weep and wail because of the misery that is coming upon you. [2]Your wealth has rotted, and moths have eaten your clothes. [3]Your gold and silver are corroded. Their corrosion will testify against you and eat your flesh like fire. You have hoarded wealth in the last days. [4]Look! The wages you failed to pay the workers who mowed your fields are crying out against you. The cries of the harvesters have reached the ears of the

---

[a] 5 Or that the spirit he caused to dwell in us envies intensely; or that the Spirit he caused to dwell in us longs jealously   [b] 6 Prov. 3:34

Lord Almighty. 5You have lived on earth in luxury and self-indulgence. You have fattened yourselves in the day of slaughter.*ª 6You have condemned and murdered the innocent one, who was not opposing you.

Patience in Suffering

7Be patient, then, brothers and sisters, until the Lord's coming. See how the farmer waits for the land to yield its valuable crop, patiently waiting for the autumn and spring rains. 8You too, be patient and stand firm, because the Lord's coming is near. 9Don't grumble against one another, brothers and sisters, or you will be judged. The Judge is standing at the door!

10Brothers and sisters, as an example of patience in the face of suffering, take the prophets who spoke in the name of the Lord. 11As you know, we consider blessed those who have persevered. You have heard of Job's perseverance and have seen what the Lord finally brought about. The Lord is full of compassion and mercy.

12Above all, my brothers and sisters, do not swear—not by heaven or by earth or by anything else. All you need to say is a simple "Yes" or "No." Otherwise you will be condemned.

The Prayer of Faith

13Is any one of you in trouble? You should pray. Is anyone happy? Sing songs of praise. 14Is any one of you sick? Call the elders of the church to pray over you and anoint you with oil in the name of the Lord. 15And the prayer offered in faith will make you well; the Lord will raise you up. If you have sinned, you will be forgiven. 16Therefore confess your sins to each other and pray for each other so that you may be healed. The prayer of a righteous person is powerful and effective.

17Elijah was human just as we are. He prayed earnestly that it would not rain, and it did not rain on the land for three and a half years. 18Again he prayed, and the heavens gave rain, and the earth produced its crops.

19My brothers and sisters, if one of you should wander from the truth and someone should bring them back, 20remember this: Whoever turns a sinner from the error of their way will save their soul from death and cover over a multitude of sins.

*ª 5 Or *yourselves as in a day of feasting*

1 PETER

1 Peter, an apostle of Jesus Christ,

To God's elect, strangers in the world, scattered throughout the provinces of Pontus, Galatia, Cappadocia, Asia and Bithynia, [2]who have been chosen according to the foreknowledge of God the Father, through the sanctifying work of the Spirit, to be obedient to Jesus Christ and sprinkled with his blood:

Grace and peace be yours in abundance.

Praise to God for a Living Hope

[3]Praise be to the God and Father of our Lord Jesus Christ! In his great mercy he has given us new birth into a living hope through the resurrection of Jesus Christ from the dead, [4]and into an inheritance that can never perish, spoil or fade. This inheritance is kept in heaven for you, [5]who through faith are shielded by God's power until the coming of the salvation that is ready to be revealed in the last time. [6]In all this you greatly rejoice, though now for a little while you may have had to suffer grief in all kinds of trials. [7]These have come so that your faith—of greater worth than gold, which perishes even though refined by fire—may be proved genuine and may result in praise, glory and honor when Jesus Christ is revealed. [8]Though you have not seen him, you love him; and even though you do not see him now, you believe in him and are filled with an inexpressible and glorious joy, [9]for you are receiving the end result of your faith, the salvation of your souls.

[10]Concerning this salvation, the prophets, who spoke of the grace that was to come to you, searched intently and with the greatest care, [11]trying to find out the time and circumstances to which the Spirit of Christ in them was pointing when he predicted the sufferings of Christ and the glories that would follow. [12]It was revealed to them that they were not serving themselves but you, when they spoke of the things that have now been told you by those who have preached the gospel to you by the Holy Spirit sent from heaven. Even angels long to look into these things.

Be Holy

[13]Therefore, with minds that are alert and fully sober, set your hope on the grace to be brought to you when Jesus Christ is revealed at his coming. [14]As obedient children, do not conform to the evil desires you had when you lived

in ignorance. [15]But just as he who called you is holy, so be holy in all you do; [16]for it is written: "Be holy, because I am holy."[a]

[17]Since you call on a Father who judges each person's work impartially, live out your time as strangers here in reverent fear. [18]For you know that it was not with perishable things such as silver or gold that you were redeemed from the empty way of life handed down to you from your ancestors, [19]but with the precious blood of Christ, a lamb without blemish or defect. [20]He was chosen before the creation of the world, but was revealed in these last times for your sake. [21]Through him you believe in God, who raised him from the dead and glorified him, and so your faith and hope are in God.

[22]Now that you have purified yourselves by obeying the truth so that you have sincere love for each other, love one another deeply, from the heart.[b] [23]For you have been born again, not of perishable seed, but of imperishable, through the living and enduring word of God. [24]For,

> "All people are like grass,
>   and all their glory is like the flowers of the field;
>   the grass withers and the flowers fall,
> [25]   but the word of the Lord endures forever."[c]

And this is the word that was preached to you.

2 Therefore, rid yourselves of all malice and all deceit, hypocrisy, envy, and slander of every kind. [2]Like newborn babies, crave pure spiritual milk, so that by it you may grow up in your salvation, [3]now that you have tasted that the Lord is good.

The Living Stone and a Chosen People

[4]As you come to him, the living Stone—rejected by human beings but chosen by God and precious to him— [5]you also, like living stones, are being built into a spiritual house[d] to be a holy priesthood, offering spiritual sacrifices acceptable to God through Jesus Christ. [6]For in Scripture it says:

> "See, I lay a stone in Zion,
>   a chosen and precious cornerstone,
>   and the one who trusts in him
>   will never be put to shame."[e]

[7]Now to you who believe, this stone is precious. But to those who do not believe,

> "The stone the builders rejected
>   has become the cornerstone,"[f]

[8]and,

> "A stone that causes people to stumble
>   and a rock that makes them fall."[g]

---

[a]16 Lev. 11:44,45; 19:2   [b]22 Some early manuscripts *from a pure heart*   [c]25 Isaiah 40:6–8
[d]5 Or *into a temple of the Spirit*   [e]6 Isaiah 28:16   [f]7 Psalm 118:22   [g]8 Isaiah 8:14

They stumble because they disobey the message—which is also what they were destined for.

⁹But you are a chosen people, a royal priesthood, a holy nation, God's special possession, that you may declare the praises of him who called you out of darkness into his wonderful light. ¹⁰Once you were not a people, but now you are the people of God; once you had not received mercy, but now you have received mercy.

Living Godly Lives in a Pagan Society

¹¹Dear friends, I urge you, as foreigners and strangers in the world, to abstain from sinful desires, which war against your soul. ¹²Live such good lives among the pagans that, though they accuse you of doing wrong, they may see your good deeds and glorify God on the day he visits us.

¹³Submit yourselves for the Lord's sake to every human authority: whether to the emperor, as the supreme authority, ¹⁴or to governors, who are sent by him to punish those who do wrong and to commend those who do right. ¹⁵For it is God's will that by doing good you should silence the ignorant talk of the foolish. ¹⁶Live as free people, but do not use your freedom as a cover-up for evil; live as God's slaves. ¹⁷Show proper respect to everyone, love your fellow believers, fear God, honor the emperor.

¹⁸Slaves, in reverent fear of God submit yourselves to your masters, not only to those who are good and considerate, but also to those who are harsh. ¹⁹For it is commendable if you bear up under the pain of unjust suffering because you are conscious of God. ²⁰But how is it to your credit if you receive a beating for doing wrong and endure it? But if you suffer for doing good and you endure it, this is commendable before God. ²¹To this you were called, because Christ suffered for you, leaving you an example, that you should follow in his steps.

> ²²"He committed no sin,
>   and no deceit was found in his mouth."ᵃ

²³When they hurled their insults at him, he did not retaliate; when he suffered, he made no threats. Instead, he entrusted himself to him who judges justly. ²⁴"He himself bore our sins" in his body on the tree, so that we might die to sins and live for righteousness; "by his wounds you have been healed." ²⁵For "you were like sheep going astray,"ᵇ but now you have returned to the Shepherd and Overseer of your souls.

3 Wives, in the same way submit yourselves to your own husbands so that, if any of them do not believe the word, they may be won over without words by the behavior of their wives, ²when they see the purity and reverence of your lives. ³Your beauty should not come from outward adornment, such as elaborate hairstyles and the wearing of gold jewelry and fine clothes. ⁴Rather, it should be that of your inner self, the unfading beauty of a gentle and quiet spirit, which is of great worth in God's sight. ⁵For this is the way the holy women of the past who put their hope in God used to adorn themselves. They submitted themselves to their own husbands, ⁶like Sarah, who

ᵃ 22 Isaiah 53:9   ᵇ 24,25 Isaiah 53:4,5,6

obeyed Abraham and called him her master. You are her daughters if you do what is right and do not give way to fear.

7Husbands, in the same way be considerate as you live with your wives, and treat them with respect as the weaker partner and as heirs with you of the gracious gift of life, so that nothing will hinder your prayers.

Suffering for Doing Good

8Finally, all of you, be like-minded, be sympathetic, love one another, be compassionate and humble. 9Do not repay evil with evil or insult with insult. On the contrary, repay evil with blessing, because to this you were called so that you may inherit a blessing. 10For,

> "Whoever among you would love life
> 　　and see good days
> must keep your tongue from evil
> 　　and your lips from deceitful speech.
> 11 Turn from evil and do good;
> 　　seek peace and pursue it.
> 12 For the eyes of the Lord are on the righteous
> 　　and his ears are attentive to their prayer,
> but the face of the Lord is against those who do evil."[a]

13Who is going to harm you if you are eager to do good? 14But even if you should suffer for what is right, you are blessed. "Do not fear their threats; do not be frightened."[b] 15But in your hearts revere Christ as Lord. Always be prepared to give an answer to everyone who asks you to give the reason for the hope that you have. But do this with gentleness and respect, 16keeping a clear conscience, so that those who speak maliciously against your good behavior in Christ may be ashamed of their slander. 17It is better, if it is God's will, to suffer for doing good than for doing evil. 18For Christ also suffered once for sins, the righteous for the unrighteous, to bring you to God. He was put to death in the body but made alive in the Spirit. 19In that state[c] he went and made proclamation to the imprisoned spirits— 20to those who were disobedient long ago when God waited patiently in the days of Noah while the ark was being built. In it only a few people, eight in all, were saved through water, 21and this water symbolizes baptism that now saves you also—not the removal of dirt from the body but the pledge of a clear conscience toward God.[d] It saves you by the resurrection of Jesus Christ, 22who has gone into heaven and is at God's right hand—with angels, authorities and powers in submission to him.

Living for God

4 Therefore, since Christ suffered in his body, arm yourselves also with the same attitude, because those who have suffered in their bodies are done with sin. 2As a result, they do not live the rest of their earthly lives for evil human desires, but rather for the will of God. 3For you have spent enough

---

[a] 12 Psalm 34:12–16　　[b] 14 Isaiah 8:12　　[c] 18,19 Or *alive in the spirit,* 19*in which also*　　[d] 21 Or *but an appeal to God for a clear conscience*

time in the past doing what pagans choose to do—living in debauchery, lust, drunkenness, orgies, carousing and detestable idolatry. [4]They are surprised that you do not join them in their reckless, wild living, and they heap abuse on you. [5]But they will have to give account to him who is ready to judge the living and the dead. [6]For this is the reason the gospel was preached even to those who are now dead, so that they might be judged according to human standards in regard to the body, but live according to God in regard to the spirit.

[7]The end of all things is near. Therefore be alert and of sober mind so that you may pray. [8]Above all, love each other deeply, because love covers over a multitude of sins. [9]Offer hospitality to one another without grumbling. [10]Each of you should use whatever gift you have received to serve others, as faithful stewards of God's grace in its various forms. [11]If you speak, you should do so as one who speaks the very words of God. If you serve, you should do so with the strength God provides, so that in all things God may be praised through Jesus Christ. To him be the glory and the power for ever and ever. Amen.

Suffering for Being a Christian

[12]Dear friends, do not be surprised at the fiery ordeal that has come on you to test you, as though something strange were happening to you. [13]But rejoice inasmuch as you participate in the sufferings of Christ, so that you may be overjoyed when his glory is revealed. [14]If you are insulted because of the name of Christ, you are blessed, for the Spirit of glory and of God rests on you. [15]If you suffer, it should not be as a murderer or thief or any other kind of criminal, or even as a meddler. [16]However, if you suffer as a Christian, do not be ashamed, but praise God that you bear that name. [17]For it is time for judgment to begin with God's household; and if it begins with us, what will the outcome be for those who do not obey the gospel of God? [18]And,

> "If it is hard for the righteous to be saved,
>   what will become of the ungodly and the sinner?"[a]

[19]So then, those who suffer according to God's will should commit themselves to their faithful Creator and continue to do good.

To the Elders and the Flock

5 To the elders among you, I appeal as a fellow elder and a witness of Christ's sufferings who also will share in the glory to be revealed: [2]Be shepherds of God's flock that is under your care, watching over them—not because you must, but because you are willing, as God wants you to be; not pursuing dishonest gain, but eager to serve; [3]not lording it over those entrusted to you, but being examples to the flock. [4]And when the Chief Shepherd appears, you will receive the crown of glory that will never fade away.

[5]In the same way, you who are younger, submit yourselves to your elders. All of you, clothe yourselves with humility toward one another, because,

> "God opposes the proud
>   but shows favor to the humble and oppressed."[b]

[a]18 Prov. 11:31   [b]5 Prov. 3:34

6Humble yourselves, therefore, under God's mighty hand, that he may lift you up in due time. 7Cast all your anxiety on him because he cares for you.

8Be alert and of sober mind. Your enemy the devil prowls around like a roaring lion looking for someone to devour. 9Resist him, standing firm in the faith, because you know that your fellow believers throughout the world are undergoing the same kind of sufferings.

10And the God of all grace, who called you to his eternal glory in Christ, after you have suffered a little while, will himself restore you and make you strong, firm and steadfast. 11To him be the power for ever and ever. Amen.

Final Greetings

12With the help of Silas,a whom I regard as a faithful brother, I have written to you briefly, encouraging you and testifying that this is the true grace of God. Stand fast in it.

13She who is in Babylon, chosen together with you, sends you her greetings, and so does my son Mark. 14Greet one another with a kiss of love.

Peace to all of you who are in Christ.

---

a 12 Greek *Silvanus*, a variant of *Silas*

2 PETER

1 Simon Peter, a servant and apostle of Jesus Christ,

To those who through the righteousness of our God and Savior Jesus Christ have received a faith as precious as ours:

2Grace and peace be yours in abundance through the knowledge of God and of Jesus our Lord.

Making One's Calling and Election Sure

3His divine power has given us everything we need for a godly life through our knowledge of him who called us by his own glory and goodness. 4Through these he has given us his very great and precious promises, so that through them you may participate in the divine nature, having escaped the corruption in the world caused by evil desires.

5For this very reason, make every effort to add to your faith goodness; and to goodness, knowledge; 6and to knowledge, self-control; and to self-control, perseverance; and to perseverance, godliness; 7and to godliness, mutual affection; and to mutual affection, love. 8For if you possess these qualities in increasing measure, they will keep you from being ineffective and unproductive in your knowledge of our Lord Jesus Christ. 9But if any of you do not have them, you are nearsighted and blind, and you have forgotten that you have been cleansed from your past sins.

10Therefore, my brothers and sisters, make every effort to confirm your calling and election. For if you do these things, you will never stumble, 11and you will receive a rich welcome into the eternal kingdom of our Lord and Savior Jesus Christ.

Prophecy of Scripture

12So I will always remind you of these things, even though you know them and are firmly established in the truth you now have. 13I think it is right to refresh your memory as long as I live in the tent of this body, 14because I know that I will soon put it aside, as our Lord Jesus Christ has made clear to me. 15And I will make every effort to see that after my departure you will always be able to remember these things.

16For we did not follow cleverly devised stories when we told you about the coming of our Lord Jesus Christ in power, but we were eyewitnesses of his majesty. 17He received honor and glory from God the Father when the voice came to him from the Majestic Glory, saying, "This is my Son, whom I love;

with him I am well pleased."[a] [18]We ourselves heard this voice that came from heaven when we were with him on the sacred mountain.

[19]We also have the prophetic message as something completely reliable, and you will do well to pay attention to it, as to a light shining in a dark place, until the day dawns and the morning star rises in your hearts. [20]Above all, you must understand that no prophecy of Scripture came about by the prophet's own interpretation of things. [21]For prophecy never had its origin in the human will, but prophets, though human, spoke from God as they were carried along by the Holy Spirit.

False Teachers and Their Destruction

2 But there were also false prophets among the people, just as there will be false teachers among you. They will secretly introduce destructive heresies, even denying the sovereign Lord who bought them—bringing swift destruction on themselves. [2]Many will follow their depraved conduct and will bring the way of truth into disrepute. [3]In their greed these teachers will exploit you with fabricated stories. Their condemnation has long been hanging over them, and their destruction has not been sleeping.

[4]For if God did not spare angels when they sinned, but sent them to hell,[b] putting them in chains of darkness[c] to be held for judgment; [5]if he did not spare the ancient world when he brought the flood on its ungodly people, but protected Noah, a preacher of righteousness, and seven others; [6]if he condemned the cities of Sodom and Gomorrah by burning them to ashes, and made them an example of what is going to happen to the ungodly; [7]and if he rescued Lot, a righteous man, who was distressed by the depraved conduct of the lawless [8](for that righteous man, living among them day after day, was tormented in his righteous soul by the lawless deeds he saw and heard)— [9]if this is so, then the Lord knows how to rescue the godly from trials and to hold the unrighteous for punishment on the day of judgment. [10]This is especially true of those who follow the corrupt desire of the sinful nature[d] and despise authority.

Bold and arrogant, they are not afraid to heap abuse on celestial beings; [11]yet even angels, although they are stronger and more powerful, do not heap abuse on such beings when bringing judgment on them from[e] the Lord. [12]But these people blaspheme in matters they do not understand. They are like unreasoning animals, creatures of instinct, born only to be caught and destroyed, and like animals they too will perish.

[13]They will be paid back with harm for the harm they have done. Their idea of pleasure is to carouse in broad daylight. They are blots and blemishes, reveling in their pleasures while they feast with you.[f] [14]With eyes full of adultery, they never stop sinning; they seduce the unstable; they are experts in greed— an accursed brood! [15]They have left the straight way and wandered off to follow the way of Balaam son of Bezer,[g] who loved the wages of wickedness. [16]But he was rebuked for his wrongdoing by a donkey—an animal without

---

[a] 17 Matt. 17:5; Mark 9:7; Luke 9:35   [b] 4 Greek *Tartarus*   [c] 4 Some manuscripts *in gloomy dungeons*   [d] 10 Or *the flesh*   [e] 11 Many manuscripts *beings in the presence of*   [f] 13 Some manuscripts *in their love feasts*   [g] 15 Greek *Bosor*

speech—who spoke with a human voice and restrained the prophet's madness. [17]These people are springs without water and mists driven by a storm. Blackest darkness is reserved for them. [18]For they mouth empty, boastful words and, by appealing to the lustful desires of sinful human nature, they entice people who are just escaping from those who live in error. [19]They promise them freedom, while they themselves are slaves of depravity—for "people are slaves to whatever has mastered them." [20]If they have escaped the corruption of the world by knowing our Lord and Savior Jesus Christ and are again entangled in it and are overcome, they are worse off at the end than they were at the beginning. [21]It would have been better for them not to have known the way of righteousness, than to have known it and then to turn their backs on the sacred command that was passed on to them. [22]Of them the proverbs are true: "A dog returns to its vomit,"[a] and, "A sow that is washed returns to her wallowing in the mud."

The Day of the Lord

3 Dear friends, this is now my second letter to you. I have written both of them as reminders to stimulate you to wholesome thinking. [2]I want you to recall the words spoken in the past by the holy prophets and the command given by our Lord and Savior through your apostles.

[3]Above all, you must understand that in the last days scoffers will come, scoffing and following their own evil desires. [4]They will say, "Where is this 'coming' he promised? Ever since our ancestors died, everything goes on as it has since the beginning of creation." [5]But they deliberately forget that long ago by God's word the heavens came into being and the earth was formed out of water and by water. [6]By these waters also the world of that time was deluged and destroyed. [7]By the same word the present heavens and earth are reserved for fire, being kept for the day of judgment and destruction of the ungodly.

[8]But do not forget this one thing, dear friends: With the Lord a day is like a thousand years, and a thousand years are like a day. [9]The Lord is not slow in keeping his promise, as some understand slowness. Instead he is patient with you, not wanting anyone to perish, but everyone to come to repentance.

[10]But the day of the Lord will come like a thief. The heavens will disappear with a roar; the elements will be destroyed by fire, and the earth and everything done in it will be laid bare.[b]

[11]Since everything will be destroyed in this way, what kind of people ought you to be? You ought to live holy and godly lives [12]as you look forward to the day of God and speed its coming.[c] That day will bring about the destruction of the heavens by fire, and the elements will melt in the heat. [13]But in keeping with his promise we are looking forward to a new heaven and a new earth, where righteousness dwells.

[14]So then, dear friends, since you are looking forward to this, make every effort to be found spotless, blameless and at peace with him. [15]Bear in mind

---

[a]22 Prov. 26:11   [b]10 Some manuscripts *be burned up*   [c]12 Or *as you wait eagerly for the day of God to come*

that our Lord's patience means salvation, just as our dear brother Paul also wrote you with the wisdom that God gave him. 16He writes the same way in all his letters, speaking in them of these matters. His letters contain some things that are hard to understand, which ignorant and unstable people distort, as they do the other Scriptures, to their own destruction.

17Therefore, dear friends, since you have been forewarned, be on your guard so that you may not be carried away by the error of the lawless and fall from your secure position. 18But grow in the grace and knowledge of our Lord and Savior Jesus Christ. To him be glory both now and forever! Amen.

1 JOHN

The Incarnation of the Word of Life

1 That which was from the beginning, which we have heard, which we have seen with our eyes, which we have looked at and our hands have touched—this we proclaim concerning the Word of life. [2]The life appeared; we have seen it and testify to it, and we proclaim to you the eternal life, which was with the Father and has appeared to us. [3]We proclaim to you what we have seen and heard, so that you also may have fellowship with us. And our fellowship is with the Father and with his Son, Jesus Christ. [4]We write this to make our[a] joy complete.

Light and Darkness, Sin and Forgiveness

[5]This is the message we have heard from him and declare to you: God is light; in him there is no darkness at all. [6]If we claim to have fellowship with him and yet walk in the darkness, we lie and do not live out the truth. [7]But if we walk in the light, as he is in the light, we have fellowship with one another, and the blood of Jesus, his Son, purifies us from all[b] sin.

[8]If we claim to be without sin, we deceive ourselves and the truth is not in us. [9]If we confess our sins, he is faithful and just and will forgive us our sins and purify us from all unrighteousness. [10]If we claim we have not sinned, we make him out to be a liar and his word is not in us.

2 My dear children, I write this to you so that you will not sin. But if anybody does sin, we have an advocate with the Father—Jesus Christ, the Righteous One. [2]He is the atoning sacrifice for our sins, and not only for ours but also for the sins of the whole world.

Love and Hatred for Fellow Believers

[3]We know that we have come to know him if we keep his commands. [4]Those who say, "I know him," but do not do what he commands are liars, and the truth is not in them. [5]But if anyone obeys his word, love for God[c] is truly made complete in them. This is how we know we are in him: [6]Whoever claims to live in him must walk as Jesus did.

[7]Dear friends, I am not writing you a new command but an old one, which you have had since the beginning. This old command is the message you have heard. [8]Yet I am writing you a new command; its truth is seen in him and in you, because the darkness is passing and the true light is already shining.

[a]4 Some manuscripts *your*   [b]7 Or *every*   [c]5 Or *word, God's love*

⁹Those who claim to be in the light but hate a fellow believer are still in the darkness. ¹⁰Those who love their fellow believers live in the light, and there is nothing in them to make them stumble. ¹¹But those who hate a fellow believer are in the darkness and walk around in the darkness; they do not know where they are going, because the darkness has blinded them.

Reasons for Writing

¹²I am writing to you, dear children,
　　because your sins have been forgiven on account of his name.
¹³I am writing to you, fathers,
　　because you know him who is from the beginning.
I am writing to you, young people,
　　because you have overcome the evil one.

¹⁴I write to you, dear children,
　　because you know the Father.
I write to you, fathers,
　　because you know him who is from the beginning.
I write to you, young people,
　　because you are strong,
　　and the word of God lives in you,
　　and you have overcome the evil one.

On Not Loving the World

¹⁵Do not love the world or anything in the world. If you love the world, love for the Father[a] is not in you. ¹⁶For everything in the world—the cravings of sinful people, the lust of their eyes and their boasting about what they have and do—comes not from the Father but from the world. ¹⁷The world and its desires pass away, but whoever does the will of God lives forever.

Warnings Against Denying the Son

¹⁸Dear children, this is the last hour; and as you have heard that the antichrist is coming, even now many antichrists have come. This is how we know it is the last hour. ¹⁹They went out from us, but they did not really belong to us. For if they had belonged to us, they would have remained with us; but their going showed that none of them belonged to us. ²⁰But you have an anointing from the Holy One, and all of you know the truth.[b] ²¹I do not write to you because you do not know the truth, but because you do know it and because no lie comes from the truth. ²²Who is the liar? It is whoever denies that Jesus is the Messiah.[c] Such a person is the antichrist—denying the Father and the Son. ²³No one who denies the Son has the Father; whoever acknowledges the Son has the Father also.

²⁴As for you, see that what you have heard from the beginning remains in you. If it does, you also will remain in the Son and in the Father. ²⁵And this is what he promised us—eternal life.

²⁶I am writing these things to you about those who are trying to lead you

---

[a] 15 Or *world, the Father's love*　　[b] 20 Some manuscripts *and you know all things*　　[c] 22 Greek *Christ*

astray. [27]As for you, the anointing you received from him remains in you, and you do not need anyone to teach you. But as his anointing teaches you about all things and as that anointing is real, not counterfeit—just as it has taught you, remain in him.

God's Children and Sin

[28]And now, dear children, continue in him, so that when he appears we may be confident and unashamed before him at his coming. [29]If you know that he is righteous, you know that everyone who does what is right has been born of him.

3 See what great love the Father has lavished on us, that we should be called children of God! And that is what we are! The reason the world does not know us is that it did not know him. [2]Dear friends, now we are children of God, and what we will be has not yet been made known. But we know that when Christ appears,[a] we shall be like him, for we shall see him as he is. [3]All who have this hope in them purify themselves, just as he is pure.

[4]Everyone who sins breaks the law; in fact, sin is lawlessness. [5]But you know that he appeared so that he might take away our sins. And in him is no sin. [6]No one who lives in him keeps on sinning. No one who continues to sin has either seen him or known him.

[7]Dear children, do not let anyone lead you astray. The one who does what is right is righteous, just as he is righteous. [8]The one who does what is sinful is of the devil, because the devil has been sinning from the beginning. The reason the Son of God appeared was to destroy the devil's work. [9]Those who are born of God will not continue to sin, because God's seed remains in them; they cannot go on sinning, because they have been born of God. [10]This is how we know who the children of God are and who the children of the devil are: Those who do not do what is right are not God's children; nor are those who do not love their brothers and sisters.

More on Love and Hatred

[11]For this is the message you heard from the beginning: We should love one another. [12]Do not be like Cain, who belonged to the evil one and murdered his brother. And why did he murder him? Because his own actions were evil and his brother's were righteous. [13]Do not be surprised, my brothers and sisters, if the world hates you. [14]We know that we have passed from death to life, because we love each other. Anyone who does not love remains in death. [15]Anyone who hates a fellow believer is a murderer, and you know that no murderers have eternal life in them.

[16]This is how we know what love is: Jesus Christ laid down his life for us. And we ought to lay down our lives for one another. [17]If any one of you has material possessions and sees a brother or sister in need but has no pity on them, how can the love of God be in you? [18]Dear children, let us not love with words or tongue but with actions and in truth.

[19]This is how we know that we belong to the truth and how we set our hearts at rest in his presence: [20]If our hearts condemn us, we know that God

a 2 Or *when it is made known*

is greater than our hearts, and he knows everything. 21Dear friends, if our hearts do not condemn us, we have confidence before God 22and receive from him anything we ask, because we keep his commands and do what pleases him. 23And this is his command: to believe in the name of his Son, Jesus Christ, and to love one another as he commanded us. 24Those who keep his commands live in him, and he in them. And this is how we know that he lives in us: We know it by the Spirit he gave us.

On Denying the Incarnation

4 Dear friends, do not believe every spirit, but test the spirits to see whether they are from God, because many false prophets have gone out into the world. 2This is how you can recognize the Spirit of God: Every spirit that acknowledges that Jesus Christ has come in the flesh is from God, 3but every spirit that does not acknowledge Jesus is not from God. This is the spirit of the antichrist, which you have heard is coming and even now is already in the world.

4You, dear children, are from God and have overcome them, because the one who is in you is greater than the one who is in the world. 5They are from the world and therefore speak from the viewpoint of the world, and the world listens to them. 6We are from God, and whoever knows God listens to us; but whoever is not from God does not listen to us. This is how we recognize the Spirit*a* of truth and the spirit of falsehood.

God's Love and Ours

7Dear friends, let us love one another, for love comes from God. Everyone who loves has been born of God and knows God. 8Whoever does not love does not know God, because God is love. 9This is how God showed his love among us: He sent his one and only Son into the world that we might live through him. 10This is love: not that we loved God, but that he loved us and sent his Son as an atoning sacrifice for our sins. 11Dear friends, since God so loved us, we also ought to love one another. 12No one has ever seen God; but if we love one another, God lives in us and his love is made complete in us.

13This is how we know that we live in him and he in us: He has given us of his Spirit. 14And we have seen and testify that the Father has sent his Son to be the Savior of the world. 15If any acknowledge that Jesus is the Son of God, God lives in them and they in God. 16And so we know and rely on the love God has for us.

God is love. Those who live in love live in God, and God in them. 17This is how love is made complete among us so that we will have confidence on the day of judgment: In this world we are like Jesus. 18There is no fear in love. But perfect love drives out fear, because fear has to do with punishment. The one who fears is not made perfect in love.

19We love because he first loved us. 20If we say we love God yet hate a fellow believer, we are liars. For if we do not love a brother or sister whom we have seen, we cannot love God, whom we have not seen. 21And he has given us this command: Those who love God must also love one another.

a 6 Or *spirit*

Faith in the Incarnate Son of God

5 Everyone who believes that Jesus is the Messiah[a] is born of God, and everyone who loves the father loves his child as well. [2]This is how we know that we love the children of God: by loving God and carrying out his commands. [3]In fact, this is love for God: to keep his commands. And his commands are not burdensome, [4]for everyone born of God overcomes the world. This is the victory that has overcome the world, even our faith. [5]Who is it that overcomes the world? Only the one who believes that Jesus is the Son of God.

[6]This is the one who came by water and blood—Jesus Christ. He did not come by water only, but by water and blood. And it is the Spirit who testifies, because the Spirit is the truth. [7]For there are three that testify: [8]the[b] Spirit, the water and the blood; and the three are in agreement. [9]We accept human testimony, but God's testimony is greater because it is the testimony of God, which he has given about his Son. [10]Those who believe in the Son of God accept this testimony. Those who do not believe God have made him out to be a liar, because they have not believed the testimony God has given about his Son. [11]And this is the testimony: God has given us eternal life, and this life is in his Son. [12]Those who have the Son have life; those who do not have the Son of God do not have life.

Concluding Affirmations

[13]I write these things to you who believe in the name of the Son of God so that you may know that you have eternal life. [14]This is the confidence we have in approaching God: that if we ask anything according to his will, he hears us. [15]And if we know that he hears us—whatever we ask—we know that we have what we asked of him.

[16]If you see any brother or sister commit a sin that does not lead to death, you should pray and God will give them life. I refer to those whose sin does not lead to death. There is a sin that leads to death. I am not saying that you should pray about that. [17]All wrongdoing is sin, and there is sin that does not lead to death.

[18]We know that those who are born of God do not continue to sin; the One who was born of God keeps them safe, and the evil one cannot harm them. [19]We know that we are children of God, and that the whole world is under the control of the evil one. [20]We know also that the Son of God has come and has given us understanding, so that we may know him who is true. And we are in him who is true by being in his Son Jesus Christ. He is the true God and eternal life.

[21]Dear children, keep yourselves from idols.

---

[a] 1 Or *Christ*   [b] 7,8 Late manuscripts of the Vulgate *testify in heaven: the Father, the Word and the Holy Spirit, and these three are one. [8]And there are three that testify on earth: the* (not found in any Greek manuscript before the fourteenth century)

2 JOHN

¹The elder,

To the lady chosen by God and to her children, whom I love in the truth—and not I only, but also all who know the truth— ²because of the truth, which lives in us and will be with us forever:

³Grace, mercy and peace from God the Father and from Jesus Christ, the Father's Son, will be with us in truth and love.

⁴It has given me great joy to find some of your children walking in the truth, just as the Father commanded us. ⁵And now, dear lady, I am not writing you a new command but one we have had from the beginning. I ask that we love one another. ⁶And this is love: that we walk in obedience to his commands. As you have heard from the beginning, his command is that you walk in love.

⁷Many deceivers, who do not acknowledge Jesus Christ as coming in the flesh, have gone out into the world. Any such person is the deceiver and the antichrist. ⁸Watch out that you do not lose what we[a] have worked for, but that you may be rewarded fully. ⁹Anyone who runs ahead and does not continue in the teaching of Christ does not have God; whoever continues in the teaching has both the Father and the Son. ¹⁰If anyone comes to you and does not bring this teaching, do not take them into your house or welcome them. ¹¹Anyone who welcomes them shares in their wicked work.

¹²I have much to write to you, but I do not want to use paper and ink. Instead, I hope to visit you and talk with you face to face, so that our joy may be complete.

¹³The children of your sister, who is chosen by God, send their greetings.

ᵃ 8 Some manuscripts you

3 JOHN

[1]The elder,

To my dear friend Gaius, whom I love in the truth.

[2]Dear friend, I pray that you may enjoy good health and that all may go well with you, even as your soul is getting along well. [3]It gave me great joy to have some believers come and testify to your faithfulness to the truth, telling how you continue to walk in it. [4]I have no greater joy than to hear that my children are walking in the truth.

[5]Dear friend, you are faithful in what you are doing for the brothers and sisters, even though they are strangers to you. [6]They have told the church about your love. You will do well to send them on their way in a manner worthy of God. [7]It was for the sake of the Name that they went out, receiving no help from the pagans. [8]We ought therefore to show hospitality to such people so that we may work together for the truth.

[9]I wrote to the church, but Diotrephes, who loves to be first, will have nothing to do with us. [10]So when I come, I will call attention to what he is doing, spreading malicious nonsense about us. Not satisfied with that, he refuses to welcome other believers. He also stops those who want to do so and puts them out of the church.

[11]Dear friend, do not imitate what is evil but what is good. Anyone who does what is good is from God. Anyone who does what is evil has not seen God. [12]Demetrius is well spoken of by everyone—and even by the truth itself. We also speak well of him, and you know that our testimony is true.

[13]I have much to write you, but I do not want to do so with pen and ink. [14]I hope to see you soon, and we will talk face to face.

Peace to you. The friends here send their greetings. Greet the friends there by name.

JUDE

¹Jude, a servant of Jesus Christ and a brother of James,

To those who have been called, who are loved in God the Father and kept for*a* Jesus Christ:

²Mercy, peace and love be yours in abundance.

The Sin and Doom of Ungodly People

³Dear friends, although I was very eager to write to you about the salvation we share, I felt compelled to write and urge you to contend for the faith that the Lord has once for all entrusted to us, his people. ⁴For certain individuals whose condemnation was written about*b* long ago have secretly slipped in among you. They are ungodly people, who pervert the grace of our God into a license for immorality and deny Jesus Christ our only Sovereign and Lord.

⁵Though you already know all this, I want to remind you that the Lord*c* at one time delivered his people out of Egypt, but later destroyed those who did not believe. ⁶And the angels who did not keep their positions of authority but abandoned their proper dwelling—these he has kept in darkness, bound with everlasting chains for judgment on the great Day. ⁷In a similar way, Sodom and Gomorrah and the surrounding towns gave themselves up to sexual immorality and perversion. They serve as an example of those who suffer the punishment of eternal fire.

⁸In the very same way, on the strength of their dreams these ungodly people pollute their own bodies, reject authority and heap abuse on celestial beings. ⁹But even the archangel Michael, when he was disputing with the devil about the body of Moses, did not himself dare to condemn him for slander but said, "The Lord rebuke you!"*d* ¹⁰Yet these people speak abusively against whatever they do not understand; and what things they do understand by instinct, like unreasoning animals—these are the very things that destroy them.

¹¹Woe to them! They have taken the way of Cain; they have rushed for profit into Balaam's error; they have been destroyed in Korah's rebellion.

¹²These people are blemishes at your love feasts, eating with you without the slightest qualm—shepherds who feed only themselves. They are clouds without rain, blown along by the wind; autumn trees, without fruit and uprooted—twice dead. ¹³They are wild waves of the sea, foaming up their

---

a 1 Or *by; or in*   *b* 4 Or *individuals who were marked out for condemnation*   *c* 5 Some early manuscripts *Jesus*   *d* 9 Jude is alluding to the Jewish *Testament of Moses* (approximately the first century A.D.).

shame; wandering stars, for whom blackest darkness has been reserved forever.

[14]Enoch, the seventh from Adam, prophesied about them: "See, the Lord is coming with thousands upon thousands of his holy ones [15]to judge everyone, and to convict all the ungodly of all the ungodly acts they have done in an ungodly way, and of all the defiant words ungodly sinners have spoken against him."[a] [16]These people are grumblers and faultfinders; they follow their own evil desires; they boast about themselves and flatter others for their own advantage.

A Call to Persevere

[17]But, dear friends, remember what the apostles of our Lord Jesus Christ foretold. [18]They said to you, "In the last times there will be scoffers who will follow their own ungodly desires." [19]These are the people who divide you, who follow mere natural instincts and do not have the Spirit.

[20]But you, dear friends, by building yourselves up in your most holy faith and praying in the Holy Spirit, [21]keep yourselves in God's love as you wait for the mercy of our Lord Jesus Christ to bring you to eternal life.

[22]Be merciful to those who doubt; [23]save others by snatching them from the fire; to others show mercy, mixed with fear—hating even the clothing stained by corrupted flesh.[b]

Doxology

[24]To him who is able to keep you from stumbling and to present you before his glorious presence without fault and with great joy— [25]to the only God our Savior be glory, majesty, power and authority, through Jesus Christ our Lord, before all ages, now and forevermore! Amen.

[a] 14,15 From the Jewish *First Book of Enoch* (approximately the first century B.C.)   [b] 22,23 The Greek manuscripts of these verses vary at several points.

REVELATION

Prologue

1 The revelation from Jesus Christ, which God gave him to show his servants what must soon take place. He made it known by sending his angel to his servant John, ²who testifies to everything he saw—that is, the word of God testified to by Jesus Christ. ³Blessed is the one who reads the words of this prophecy, and blessed are those who hear it and take to heart what is written in it, because the time is near.

Greetings and Doxology

⁴John,

To the seven churches in the province of Asia:

Grace and peace to you from him who is, and who was, and who is to come, and from the seven spirits *a* before his throne, ⁵and from Jesus Christ, who is the faithful witness, the firstborn from the dead, and the ruler of the kings of the earth.

To him who loves us and has freed us from our sins by his blood, ⁶and has made us to be a kingdom and priests to serve his God and Father—to him be glory and power for ever and ever! Amen.

⁷"Look, he is coming with the clouds," *b*
    and "every eye will see him,
even those who pierced him";
    and all peoples on earth "will mourn because of him." *c*
                So shall it be! Amen.

⁸"I am the Alpha and the Omega," says the Lord God, "who is, and who was, and who is to come, the Almighty."

John's Vision of Christ

⁹I, John, your brother and companion in the suffering and kingdom and patient endurance that are ours in Jesus, was on the island of Patmos because of the word of God testified to by Jesus. ¹⁰On the Lord's Day I was in the Spirit, and I heard behind me a loud voice like a trumpet, ¹¹which said: "Write on a

---

a 4 That is, the sevenfold Spirit   *b* 7 Daniel 7:13   *c* 7 Zech. 12:10

scroll what you see and send it to the seven churches: to Ephesus, Smyrna, Pergamum, Thyatira, Sardis, Philadelphia and Laodicea."

[12]I turned around to see the voice that was speaking to me. And when I turned I saw seven golden lampstands, [13]and among the lampstands was someone like a son of man,[a] dressed in a robe reaching down to his feet and with a golden sash around his chest. [14]The hair on his head was white like wool, as white as snow, and his eyes were like blazing fire. [15]His feet were like bronze glowing in a furnace, and his voice was like the sound of rushing waters. [16]In his right hand he held seven stars, and coming out of his mouth was a sharp, double-edged sword. His face was like the sun shining in all its brilliance.

[17]When I saw him, I fell at his feet as though dead. Then he placed his right hand on me and said: "Do not be afraid. I am the First and the Last. [18]I am the Living One; I was dead, and now look, I am alive for ever and ever! And I hold the keys of death and Hades.

[19]"Write, therefore, what you have seen: both what is now and what will take place later. [20]The mystery of the seven stars that you saw in my right hand and of the seven golden lampstands is this: The seven stars are the angels[b] of the seven churches, and the seven lampstands are the seven churches.

To the Church in Ephesus

2 "To the angel[c] of the church in Ephesus write:

These are the words of him who holds the seven stars in his right hand and walks among the seven golden lampstands: [2]I know your deeds, your hard work and your perseverance. I know that you cannot tolerate wicked people, that you have tested those who claim to be apostles but are not, and have found them false. [3]You have persevered and have endured hardships for my name, and have not grown weary.

[4]Yet I hold this against you: You have forsaken the love you had at first. [5]Consider how far you have fallen! Repent and do the things you did at first. If you do not repent, I will come to you and remove your lampstand from its place. [6]But you have this in your favor: You hate the practices of the Nicolaitans, which I also hate.

[7]Whoever has ears, let them hear what the Spirit says to the churches. To those who are victorious, I will give the right to eat from the tree of life, which is in the paradise of God.

To the Church in Smyrna

[8]"To the angel of the church in Smyrna write:

These are the words of him who is the First and the Last, who died and came to life again. [9]I know your afflictions and your poverty—yet you are rich! I know about the slander of those who say they are Jews and are not, but are a synagogue of Satan. [10]Do not be afraid of what you are about to suffer. I tell you, the devil will put some of you in prison to test you, and you will suffer persecution for ten days. Be faithful, even to the point of death, and I will give you life as your victor's crown.

[a] 13 See Daniel 7:13.   [b] 20 Or *messengers*   [c] 1 Or *messenger*; also in verses 8, 12 and 18

¹¹Whoever has ears, let them hear what the Spirit says to the churches. Those who are victorious will not be hurt at all by the second death.

To the Church in Pergamum

¹²"To the angel of the church in Pergamum write:

These are the words of him who has the sharp, double-edged sword. ¹³I know where you live—where Satan has his throne. Yet you remain true to my name. You did not renounce your faith in me, not even in the days of Antipas, my faithful witness, who was put to death in your city— where Satan lives.

¹⁴Nevertheless, I have a few things against you: There are some among you who hold to the teaching of Balaam, who taught Balak to entice the Israelites to sin so that they ate food sacrificed to idols and committed sexual immorality. ¹⁵Likewise, you also have those who hold to the teaching of the Nicolaitans. ¹⁶Repent therefore! Otherwise, I will soon come to you and will fight against them with the sword of my mouth.

¹⁷Whoever has ears, let them hear what the Spirit says to the churches. To those who are victorious, I will give some of the hidden manna. I will also give each of them a white stone with a new name written on it, known only to the one who receives it.

To the Church in Thyatira

¹⁸"To the angel of the church in Thyatira write:

These are the words of the Son of God, whose eyes are like blazing fire and whose feet are like burnished bronze. ¹⁹I know your deeds, your love and faith, your service and perseverance, and that you are now doing more than you did at first.

²⁰Nevertheless, I have this against you: You tolerate that woman Jezebel, who calls herself a prophet. By her teaching she misleads my servants into sexual immorality and the eating of food sacrificed to idols. ²¹I have given her time to repent of her immorality, but she is unwilling. ²²So I will cast her on a bed of suffering, and I will make those who commit adultery with her suffer intensely, unless they repent of her ways. ²³I will strike her children dead. Then all the churches will know that I am he who searches hearts and minds, and I will repay each of you according to your deeds. ²⁴Now I say to the rest of you in Thyatira, to you who do not hold to her teaching and have not learned Satan's so-called deep secrets, 'I will not impose any other burden on you, ²⁵except to hold on to what you have until I come.'

²⁶To those who are victorious and do my will to the end, I will give authority over the nations— ²⁷they 'will rule them with an iron scepter and will dash them to pieces like pottery'ᵃ—just as I have received authority from my Father. ²⁸I will also give them the morning star. ²⁹Whoever has ears, let them hear what the Spirit says to the churches.

ᵃ 27 Psalm 2:9

To the Church in Sardis

3 "To the angel[a] of the church in Sardis write:

These are the words of him who holds the seven spirits[b] of God and the seven stars. I know your deeds; you have a reputation of being alive, but you are dead. [2]Wake up! Strengthen what remains and is about to die, for I have found your deeds unfinished in the sight of my God. [3]Remember, therefore, what you have received and heard; hold it fast, and repent. But if you do not wake up, I will come like a thief, and you will not know at what time I will come to you.

[4]Yet you have a few people in Sardis who have not soiled their clothes. They will walk with me, dressed in white, for they are worthy. [5]Those who are victorious will, like them, be dressed in white. I will never blot out their names from the book of life, but will acknowledge their names before my Father and his angels. [6]Whoever has ears, let them hear what the Spirit says to the churches.

To the Church in Philadelphia

[7]"To the angel of the church in Philadelphia write:

These are the words of him who is holy and true, who holds the key of David. What he opens no one can shut, and what he shuts no one can open. [8]I know your deeds. See, I have placed before you an open door that no one can shut. I know that you have little strength, yet you have kept my word and have not denied my name. [9]I will make those who are of the synagogue of Satan, who claim to be Jews though they are not, but are liars—I will make them come and fall down at your feet and acknowledge that I have loved you. [10]Since you have kept my command to endure patiently, I will also keep you from the hour of trial that is going to come upon the whole world to test those who live on the earth.

[11]I am coming soon. Hold on to what you have, so that no one will take your crown. [12]Those who are victorious I will make pillars in the temple of my God. Never again will they leave it. I will write on them the name of my God and the name of the city of my God, the new Jerusalem, which is coming down out of heaven from my God; and I will also write on them my new name. [13]Whoever has ears, let them hear what the Spirit says to the churches.

To the Church in Laodicea

[14]"To the angel of the church in Laodicea write:

These are the words of the Amen, the faithful and true witness, the ruler of God's creation. [15]I know your deeds, that you are neither cold nor hot. I wish you were either one or the other! [16]So, because you are lukewarm—neither hot nor cold—I am about to spit you out of my mouth. [17]You say, 'I am rich; I have acquired wealth and do not need a thing.' But you do not realize that you are wretched, pitiful, poor, blind and naked.

[a]1 Or *messenger*; also in verses 7 and 14   [b]1 That is, the sevenfold Spirit

¹⁸I counsel you to buy from me gold refined in the fire, so you can become rich; and white clothes to wear, so you can cover your shameful nakedness; and salve to put on your eyes, so you can see. ¹⁹Those whom I love I rebuke and discipline. So be earnest, and repent. ²⁰Here I am! I stand at the door and knock. If anyone hears my voice and opens the door, I will come in and eat with them, and they with me.

²¹To those who are victorious, I will give the right to sit with me on my throne, just as I was victorious and sat down with my Father on his throne. ²²Whoever has ears, let them hear what the Spirit says to the churches."

The Throne in Heaven

4 After this I looked, and there before me was a door standing open in heaven. And the voice I had first heard speaking to me like a trumpet said, "Come up here, and I will show you what must take place after this." ²At once I was in the Spirit, and there before me was a throne in heaven with someone sitting on it. ³And the one who sat there had the appearance of jasper and ruby. A rainbow that shone like an emerald encircled the throne. ⁴Surrounding the throne were twenty-four other thrones, and seated on them were twenty-four elders. They were dressed in white and had crowns of gold on their heads. ⁵From the throne came flashes of lightning, rumblings and peals of thunder. Before the throne, seven lamps were blazing. These are the seven spirits*a* of God. ⁶Also before the throne there was what looked like a sea of glass, clear as crystal.

In the center, around the throne, were four living creatures, and they were covered with eyes, in front and in back. ⁷The first living creature was like a lion, the second was like an ox, the third had a face like a man, the fourth was like a flying eagle. ⁸Each of the four living creatures had six wings and was covered with eyes all around, even under his wings. Day and night they never stop saying:

" 'Holy, holy, holy
is the Lord God Almighty,'*b*
who was, and is, and is to come."

⁹Whenever the living creatures give glory, honor and thanks to him who sits on the throne and who lives for ever and ever, ¹⁰the twenty-four elders fall down before him who sits on the throne and worship him who lives for ever and ever. They lay their crowns before the throne and say:

¹¹"You are worthy, our Lord and God,
to receive glory and honor and power,
for you created all things,
and by your will they were created
and have their being."

The Scroll and the Lamb

5 Then I saw in the right hand of him who sat on the throne a scroll with writing on both sides and sealed with seven seals. ²And I saw a mighty

*a 5 That is, the sevenfold Spirit   b 8 Isaiah 6:3

angel proclaiming in a loud voice, "Who is worthy to break the seals and open the scroll?" [3]But no one in heaven or on earth or under the earth could open the scroll or even look inside it. [4]I wept and wept because no one was found who was worthy to open the scroll or look inside. [5]Then one of the elders said to me, "Do not weep! See, the Lion of the tribe of Judah, the Root of David, has triumphed. He is able to open the scroll and its seven seals."

[6]Then I saw a Lamb, looking as if it had been slain, standing in the center before the throne, encircled by the four living creatures and the elders. The Lamb had seven horns and seven eyes, which are the seven spirits[a] of God sent out into all the earth. [7]He went and took the scroll from the right hand of him who sat on the throne. [8]And when he had taken it, the four living creatures and the twenty-four elders fell down before the Lamb. Each one had a harp and they were holding golden bowls full of incense, which are the prayers of God's people. [9]And they sang a new song, saying:

> "You are worthy to take the scroll
>   and to open its seals,
> because you were slain,
>   and with your blood you purchased for God
>   members of every tribe and language and people and nation.
> [10]You have made them to be a kingdom and priests to serve our God,
>   and they will reign[b] on the earth."

[11]Then I looked and heard the voice of many angels, numbering thousands upon thousands, and ten thousand times ten thousand. They encircled the throne and the living creatures and the elders. [12]In a loud voice they were saying:

> "Worthy is the Lamb, who was slain,
>   to receive power and wealth and wisdom and strength
>   and honor and glory and praise!"

[13]Then I heard every creature in heaven and on earth and under the earth and on the sea, and all that is in them, saying:

> "To him who sits on the throne and to the Lamb
>   be praise and honor and glory and power,
>   for ever and ever!"

[14]The four living creatures said, "Amen," and the elders fell down and worshiped.

The Seals

6 I watched as the Lamb opened the first of the seven seals. Then I heard one of the four living creatures say in a voice like thunder, "Come!" [2]I looked, and there before me was a white horse! Its rider held a bow, and he was given a crown, and he rode out as a conqueror bent on conquest.

[3]When the Lamb opened the second seal, I heard the second living creature say, "Come!" [4]Then another horse came out, a fiery red one. Its rider was

---

[a] 6 That is, the sevenfold Spirit   [b] 10 Some manuscripts *they reign*

given power to take peace from the earth and to make people slay each other. To him was given a large sword.

⁵When the Lamb opened the third seal, I heard the third living creature say, "Come!" I looked, and there before me was a black horse! Its rider was holding a pair of scales in his hand. ⁶Then I heard what sounded like a voice among the four living creatures, saying, "A quart*ᵃ* of wheat for a day's wages,*ᵇ* and three quarts of barley for a day's wages,*ᵇ* and do not damage the oil and the wine!"

⁷When the Lamb opened the fourth seal, I heard the voice of the fourth living creature say, "Come!" ⁸I looked, and there before me was a pale horse! Its rider was named Death, and Hades was following close behind him. They were given power over a fourth of the earth to kill by sword, famine and plague, and by the wild beasts of the earth.

⁹When he opened the fifth seal, I saw under the altar the souls of those who had been slain because of the word of God and the testimony they had maintained. ¹⁰They called out in a loud voice, "How long, Sovereign Lord, holy and true, until you judge the inhabitants of the earth and avenge our blood?" ¹¹Then each of them was given a white robe, and they were told to wait a little longer, until the full number of their fellow servants and brothers and sisters were killed just as they had been.

¹²I watched as he opened the sixth seal. There was a great earthquake. The sun turned black like sackcloth made of goat hair, the whole moon turned blood red, ¹³and the stars in the sky fell to earth, as figs drop from a fig tree when shaken by a strong wind. ¹⁴The sky receded like a scroll, rolling up, and every mountain and island was removed from its place.

¹⁵Then the kings of the earth, the princes, the generals, the rich, the mighty, and everyone else, both slave and free, hid in caves and among the rocks of the mountains. ¹⁶They called to the mountains and the rocks, "Fall on us and hide us*ᶜ* from the face of him who sits on the throne and from the wrath of the Lamb! ¹⁷For the great day of their*ᵈ* wrath has come, and who can withstand it?"

144,000 Sealed

7 After this I saw four angels standing at the four corners of the earth, holding back the four winds of the earth to prevent any wind from blowing on the land or on the sea or on any tree. ²Then I saw another angel coming up from the east, having the seal of the living God. He called out in a loud voice to the four angels who had been given power to harm the land and the sea: ³"Do not harm the land or the sea or the trees until we put a seal on the foreheads of the servants of our God." ⁴Then I heard the number of those who were sealed: 144,000 from all the tribes of Israel.

⁵From the tribe of Judah 12,000 were sealed,
　from the tribe of Reuben 12,000,
　from the tribe of Gad 12,000,
⁶from the tribe of Asher 12,000,
　from the tribe of Naphtali 12,000,
　from the tribe of Manasseh 12,000,

---

*ᵃ*6 About a liter　*ᵇ*6 Greek *a denarius*　*ᶜ*16 See Hosea 10:8.　*ᵈ*17 Some manuscripts *his*

7 from the tribe of Simeon 12,000,
   from the tribe of Levi 12,000,
   from the tribe of Issachar 12,000,
8 from the tribe of Zebulun 12,000,
   from the tribe of Joseph 12,000,
   from the tribe of Benjamin 12,000.

The Great Multitude in White Robes

9 After this I looked and there before me was a great multitude that no one could count, from every nation, tribe, people and language, standing before the throne and in front of the Lamb. They were wearing white robes and were holding palm branches in their hands. 10 And they cried out in a loud voice:

> "Salvation belongs to our God,
> who sits on the throne,
> and to the Lamb."

11 All the angels were standing around the throne and around the elders and the four living creatures. They fell down on their faces before the throne and worshiped God, 12 saying:

> "Amen!
> Praise and glory
> and wisdom and thanks and honor
> and power and strength
> be to our God for ever and ever.
> Amen!"

13 Then one of the elders asked me, "These in white robes—who are they, and where did they come from?"

14 I answered, "Sir, you know."

And he said, "These are they who have come out of the great tribulation; they have washed their robes and made them white in the blood of the Lamb.
15 Therefore,

> "they are before the throne of God
> and serve him day and night in his temple;
> and he who sits on the throne
> will spread his tent over them.
> 16 'Never again will they hunger;
> never again will they thirst.
> The sun will not beat upon them,'[a]
> nor any scorching heat.
> 17 For the Lamb at the center before the throne
> will be their shepherd;
> 'he will lead them to springs of living water.'[a]
> 'And God will wipe away every tear from their eyes.'[b]"

[a] 16,17 Isaiah 49:10   [b] 17 Isaiah 25:8

The Seventh Seal and the Golden Censer

8 When he opened the seventh seal, there was silence in heaven for about half an hour.

2And I saw the seven angels who stand before God, and seven trumpets were given to them.

3Another angel, who had a golden censer, came and stood at the altar. He was given much incense to offer, with the prayers of all God's people, on the golden altar before the throne. 4The smoke of the incense, together with the prayers of the saints, went up before God from the angel's hand. 5Then the angel took the censer, filled it with fire from the altar, and hurled it on the earth; and there came peals of thunder, rumblings, flashes of lightning and an earthquake.

The Trumpets

6Then the seven angels who had the seven trumpets prepared to sound them.

7The first angel sounded his trumpet, and there came hail and fire mixed with blood, and it was hurled down upon the earth. A third of the earth was burned up, a third of the trees were burned up, and all the green grass was burned up.

8The second angel sounded his trumpet, and something like a huge mountain, all ablaze, was thrown into the sea. A third of the sea turned into blood, 9a third of the living creatures in the sea died, and a third of the ships were destroyed.

10The third angel sounded his trumpet, and a great star, blazing like a torch, fell from the sky on a third of the rivers and on the springs of water— 11the name of the star is Wormwood.ᵃ A third of the waters turned bitter, and many people died from the waters that had become bitter.

12The fourth angel sounded his trumpet, and a third of the sun was struck, a third of the moon, and a third of the stars, so that a third of them turned dark. A third of the day was without light, and also a third of the night.

13As I watched, I heard an eagle that was flying in midair call out in a loud voice: "Woe! Woe! Woe to the inhabitants of the earth, because of the trumpet blasts about to be sounded by the other three angels!"

9 The fifth angel sounded his trumpet, and I saw a star that had fallen from the sky to the earth. The star was given the key to the shaft of the Abyss. 2When he opened the Abyss, smoke rose from it like the smoke from a gigantic furnace. The sun and sky were darkened by the smoke from the Abyss. 3And out of the smoke locusts came down upon the earth and were given power like that of scorpions of the earth. 4They were told not to harm the grass of the earth or any plant or tree, but only those people who did not have the seal of God on their foreheads. 5They were not allowed to kill them but only to torture them for five months. And the agony they suffered was like that of the sting of a scorpion when it strikes. 6During those days people will seek death but will not find it; they will long to die, but death will elude them.

7The locusts looked like horses prepared for battle. On their heads they wore something like crowns of gold, and their faces resembled human faces. 8Their hair was like women's hair, and their teeth were like lions' teeth. 9They

ᵃ 11 That is, Bitterness

had breastplates like breastplates of iron, and the sound of their wings was like the thundering of many horses and chariots rushing into battle. ¹⁰They had tails with stingers, like scorpions, and in their tails they had power to torment people for five months. ¹¹They had as king over them the angel of the Abyss, whose name in Hebrew is Abaddon, and in Greek, Apollyon.ᵃ

¹²The first woe is past; two other woes are yet to come.

¹³The sixth angel sounded his trumpet, and I heard a voice coming from the four horns of the golden altar that is before God. ¹⁴It said to the sixth angel who had the trumpet, "Release the four angels who are bound at the great river Euphrates." ¹⁵And the four angels who had been kept ready for this very hour and day and month and year were released to kill a third of the world's people. ¹⁶The number of the mounted troops was two hundred million. I heard their number.

¹⁷The horses and riders I saw in my vision looked like this: Their breastplates were fiery red, dark blue, and yellow as sulfur. The heads of the horses resembled the heads of lions, and out of their mouths came fire, smoke and sulfur. ¹⁸A third of the people were killed by the three plagues of fire, smoke and sulfur that came out of their mouths. ¹⁹The power of the horses was in their mouths and in their tails; for their tails were like snakes, having heads with which they inflict injury.

²⁰The rest of the people who were not killed by these plagues still did not repent of the work of their hands; they did not stop worshiping demons, and idols of gold, silver, bronze, stone and wood—idols that cannot see or hear or walk. ²¹Nor did they repent of their murders, their magic arts, their sexual immorality or their thefts.

The Angel and the Little Scroll

10 Then I saw another mighty angel coming down from heaven. He was robed in a cloud, with a rainbow above his head; his face was like the sun, and his legs were like fiery pillars. ²He was holding a little scroll, which lay open in his hand. He planted his right foot on the sea and his left foot on the land, ³and he gave a loud shout like the roar of a lion. When he shouted, the voices of the seven thunders spoke. ⁴And when the seven thunders spoke, I was about to write; but I heard a voice from heaven say, "Seal up what the seven thunders have said and do not write it down."

⁵Then the angel I had seen standing on the sea and on the land raised his right hand to heaven. ⁶And he swore by him who lives for ever and ever, who created the heavens and all that is in them, the earth and all that is in it, and the sea and all that is in it, and said, "There will be no more delay! ⁷But in the days when the seventh angel is about to sound his trumpet, the mystery of God will be accomplished, just as he announced to his servants the prophets."

⁸Then the voice that I had heard from heaven spoke to me once more: "Go, take the scroll that lies open in the hand of the angel who is standing on the sea and on the land."

⁹So I went to the angel and asked him to give me the little scroll. He said to me, "Take it and eat it. It will turn your stomach sour, but 'in your mouth it

---

ᵃ 11 *Abaddon* and *Apollyon* mean *Destroyer.*

will be as sweet as honey.'ᵃ" ¹⁰I took the little scroll from the angel's hand and ate it. It tasted as sweet as honey in my mouth, but when I had eaten it, my stomach turned sour. ¹¹Then I was told, "You must prophesy again about many peoples, nations, languages and kings."

The Two Witnesses

11 I was given a reed like a measuring rod and was told, "Go and measure the temple of God and the altar, with its worshipers. ²But exclude the outer court; do not measure it, because it has been given to the Gentiles. They will trample on the holy city for 42 months. ³And I will appoint my two witnesses, and they will prophesy for 1,260 days, clothed in sackcloth." ⁴They are "the two olive trees" and the two lampstands, and "they stand before the Lord of the earth."ᵇ ⁵If anyone tries to harm them, fire comes from their mouths and devours their enemies. This is how anyone who wants to harm them must die. ⁶They have power to shut up the sky so that it will not rain during the time they are prophesying; and they have power to turn the waters into blood and to strike the earth with every kind of plague as often as they want.

⁷Now when they have finished their testimony, the beast that comes up from the Abyss will attack them, and overpower and kill them. ⁸Their bodies will lie in the public square of the great city, which is figuratively called Sodom and Egypt, where also their Lord was crucified. ⁹For three and a half days many from every people, tribe, language and nation will gaze on their bodies and refuse them burial. ¹⁰The inhabitants of the earth will gloat over them and will celebrate by sending each other gifts, because these two prophets had tormented those who live on the earth.

¹¹But after the three and a half days the breathᶜ of life from God entered them, and they stood on their feet, and terror struck those who saw them. ¹²Then they heard a loud voice from heaven saying to them, "Come up here." And they went up to heaven in a cloud, while their enemies looked on.

¹³At that very hour there was a severe earthquake and a tenth of the city collapsed. Seven thousand people were killed in the earthquake, and the survivors were terrified and gave glory to the God of heaven.

¹⁴The second woe has passed; the third woe is coming soon.

The Seventh Trumpet

¹⁵The seventh angel sounded his trumpet, and there were loud voices in heaven, which said:

> "The kingdom of the world has become
>   the kingdom of our Lord and of his Messiah,ᵈ
>   and he will reign for ever and ever."

¹⁶And the twenty-four elders, who were seated on their thrones before God, fell on their faces and worshiped God, ¹⁷saying:

> "We give thanks to you, Lord God Almighty,

ᵃ 9 Ezek. 3:3   ᵇ 4 See Zech. 4:3,11,14.   ᶜ 11 Or *Spirit* (see Ezek. 37:5,14)   ᵈ 15 Or *Christ*. "Messiah" (Hebrew) and "Christ" (Greek) both mean "Anointed One" (see Psalm 2:2).

the One who is and who was,
because you have taken your great power
and have begun to reign.
[18] The nations were angry,
and your wrath has come.
The time has come for judging the dead,
and for rewarding your servants the prophets
and your people who revere your name,
both great and small—
and for destroying those who destroy the earth."

[19] Then God's temple in heaven was opened, and within his temple was seen the ark of his covenant. And there came flashes of lightning, rumblings, peals of thunder, an earthquake and a great hailstorm.

The Woman and the Dragon

12 A great and wondrous sign appeared in heaven: a woman clothed with the sun, with the moon under her feet and a crown of twelve stars on her head. [2] She was pregnant and cried out in pain as she was about to give birth. [3] Then another sign appeared in heaven: an enormous red dragon with seven heads and ten horns and seven crowns on its heads. [4] Its tail swept a third of the stars out of the sky and flung them to the earth. The dragon stood in front of the woman who was about to give birth, so that it might devour her child the moment he was born. [5] She gave birth to a son, a male child, who "will rule all the nations with an iron scepter."[a] And her child was snatched up to God and to his throne. [6] The woman fled into the desert to a place prepared for her by God, where she might be taken care of for 1,260 days.

[7] And there was war in heaven. Michael and his angels fought against the dragon, and the dragon and his angels fought back. [8] But he was not strong enough, and they lost their place in heaven. [9] The great dragon was hurled down—that ancient serpent called the devil, or Satan, who leads the whole world astray. He was hurled to the earth, and his angels with him.

[10] Then I heard a loud voice in heaven say:

"Now have come the salvation and the power
and the kingdom of our God,
and the authority of his Messiah.
For the accuser of our brothers and sisters,
who accuses them before our God day and night,
has been hurled down.
[11] They triumphed over him
by the blood of the Lamb
and by the word of their testimony;
they did not love their lives so much
as to shrink from death.
[12] Therefore rejoice, you heavens
and you who dwell in them!

[a] 5 Psalm 2:9

But woe to the earth and the sea,
  because the devil has gone down to you!
He is filled with fury,
  because he knows that his time is short."

13When the dragon saw that he had been hurled to the earth, he pursued the woman who had given birth to the male child. 14The woman was given the two wings of a great eagle, so that she might fly to the place prepared for her in the desert, where she would be taken care of for a time, times and half a time, out of the serpent's reach. 15Then from his mouth the serpent spewed water like a river, to overtake the woman and sweep her away with the torrent. 16But the earth helped the woman by opening its mouth and swallowing the river that the dragon had spewed out of his mouth. 17Then the dragon was enraged at the woman and went off to make war against the rest of her offspring—those who keep God's commandments and hold to Jesus' testimony.

The Beast out of the Sea

13 The dragon*a* stood on the shore of the sea. And I saw a beast coming out of the sea. It had ten horns and seven heads, with ten crowns on its horns, and on each head a blasphemous name. 2The beast I saw resembled a leopard, but had feet like those of a bear and a mouth like that of a lion. The dragon gave the beast his power and his throne and great authority. 3One of the heads of the beast seemed to have had a fatal wound, but the fatal wound had been healed. The whole world was filled with wonder and followed the beast. 4People worshiped the dragon because he had given authority to the beast, and they also worshiped the beast and asked, "Who is like the beast? Who can make war against it?"

5The beast was given a mouth to utter proud words and blasphemies and to exercise its authority for forty-two months. 6It opened its mouth to blaspheme God, and to slander his name and his dwelling place and those who live in heaven. 7It was given power to make war against God's holy people and to conquer them. And it was given authority over every tribe, people, language and nation. 8All inhabitants of the earth will worship the beast—all whose names have not been written in the Lamb's book of life, the Lamb who was slain from the creation of the world.*b*

9Whoever has ears, let them hear.

10 "If any are to go into captivity,
  into captivity they will go.
If any are to be killed*c* with the sword,
  with the sword they will be killed."*d*

This calls for patient endurance and faithfulness on the part of God's people.

The Beast out of the Earth

11Then I saw another beast, coming out of the earth. It had two horns like a lamb, but it spoke like a dragon. 12It exercised all the authority of the first

---

*a*1 Some manuscripts *And I*   *b*8 Or *written from the creation of the world in the book of life belonging to the Lamb who was slain*   *c*10 Some manuscripts *any kill*   *d*10 Jer. 15:2

beast on its behalf, and made the earth and its inhabitants worship the first beast, whose fatal wound had been healed. [13]And it performed great and miraculous signs, even causing fire to come down from heaven to the earth in full view of everyone. [14]Because of the signs it was given power to do on behalf of the first beast, it deceived the inhabitants of the earth. It ordered them to set up an image in honor of the beast who was wounded by the sword and yet lived. [15]It was given power to give breath to the image of the first beast, so that it could speak and cause all who refused to worship the image to be killed. [16]It also forced all people, great and small, rich and poor, free and slave, to receive a mark on their right hands or on their foreheads, [17]so that they could not buy or sell unless they had the mark, which is the name of the beast or the number of its name.

[18]This calls for wisdom. Let those who have insight calculate the number of the beast, for it is the number of a man.[a] That number is 666.

The Lamb and the 144,000

14 Then I looked, and there before me was the Lamb, standing on Mount Zion, and with him 144,000 who had his name and his Father's name written on their foreheads. [2]And I heard a sound from heaven like the roar of rushing waters and like a loud peal of thunder. The sound I heard was like that of harpists playing their harps. [3]And they sang a new song before the throne and before the four living creatures and the elders. No one could learn the song except the 144,000 who had been redeemed from the earth. [4]These are those who did not defile themselves with women, for they remained virgins. They follow the Lamb wherever he goes. They were purchased from among the human race and offered as firstfruits to God and the Lamb. [5]No lie was found in their mouths; they are blameless.

The Three Angels

[6]Then I saw another angel flying in midair, and he had the eternal gospel to proclaim to those who live on the earth—to every nation, tribe, language and people. [7]He said in a loud voice, "Fear God and give him glory, because the hour of his judgment has come. Worship him who made the heavens, the earth, the sea and the springs of water."

[8]A second angel followed and said, " 'Fallen! Fallen is Babylon the Great,'[b] which made all the nations drink the maddening wine of her adulteries."

[9]A third angel followed them and said in a loud voice: "If any worship the beast and its image and receive its mark on the forehead or on the hand, [10]they, too, will drink of the wine of God's fury, which has been poured full strength into the cup of his wrath. They will be tormented with burning sulfur in the presence of the holy angels and of the Lamb. [11]And the smoke of their torment will rise for ever and ever. There will be no rest day or night for those who worship the beast and its image, or for anyone who receives the mark of its name." [12]This calls for patient endurance on the part of the people of God who keep his commandments and remain faithful to Jesus.

[a]18 Or *is humanity's number*   [b]8 Isaiah 21:9

[13]Then I heard a voice from heaven say, "Write: Blessed are the dead who die in the Lord from now on."

"Yes," says the Spirit, "they will rest from their labor, for their deeds will follow them."

Harvesting the Earth and Trampling the Winepress

[14]I looked, and there before me was a white cloud, and seated on the cloud was one like a son of man[a] with a crown of gold on his head and a sharp sickle in his hand. [15]Then another angel came out of the temple and called in a loud voice to him who was sitting on the cloud, "Take your sickle and reap, because the time to reap has come, for the harvest of the earth is ripe." [16]So he who was seated on the cloud swung his sickle over the earth, and the earth was harvested.

[17]Another angel came out of the temple in heaven, and he too had a sharp sickle. [18]Still another angel, who had charge of the fire, came from the altar and called in a loud voice to him who had the sharp sickle, "Take your sharp sickle and gather the clusters of grapes from the earth's vine, because its grapes are ripe." [19]The angel swung his sickle on the earth, gathered its grapes and threw them into the great winepress of God's wrath. [20]They were trampled in the winepress outside the city, and blood flowed out of the press, rising as high as the horses' bridles for a distance of 1,600 stadia.[b]

Seven Angels With Seven Plagues

15 I saw in heaven another great and marvelous sign: seven angels with the seven last plagues—last, because with them God's wrath is completed. [2]And I saw what looked like a sea of glass glowing with fire and, standing beside the sea, those who had been victorious over the beast and its image and over the number of its name. They held harps given them by God [3]and sang the song of God's servant Moses and of the Lamb:

> "Great and marvelous are your deeds,
>   Lord God Almighty.
> Just and true are your ways,
>   King of the nations.[c]
> [4]Who will not fear you, Lord,
>   and bring glory to your name?
> For you alone are holy.
> All nations will come
>   and worship before you,
> for your righteous acts have been revealed."[d]

[5]After this I looked, and in heaven the temple—the tabernacle of the covenant law—was opened. [6]Out of the temple came the seven angels with the seven plagues. They were dressed in clean, shining linen and wore golden sashes around their chests. [7]Then one of the four living creatures gave to the seven angels seven golden bowls filled with the wrath of God, who lives for

---

[a] 14 See Daniel 7:13.   [b] 20 That is, about 180 miles (about 300 kilometers)   [c] 3 Some manuscripts ages   [d] 3,4 Phrases in this song are drawn from Psalm 111:2,3; Deut. 32:4; Jer. 10:7; Psalms 86:9; 98:2.

ever and ever. [8]And the temple was filled with smoke from the glory of God and from his power, and no one could enter the temple until the seven plagues of the seven angels were completed.

The Seven Bowls of God's Wrath

16 Then I heard a loud voice from the temple saying to the seven angels, "Go, pour out the seven bowls of God's wrath on the earth."

[2]The first angel went and poured out his bowl on the land, and ugly, festering sores broke out on the people who had the mark of the beast and worshiped its image.

[3]The second angel poured out his bowl on the sea, and it turned into blood like that of a dead person, and every living thing in the sea died.

[4]The third angel poured out his bowl on the rivers and springs of water, and they became blood. [5]Then I heard the angel in charge of the waters say:

"You are just in these judgments,
    you who are and who were, the Holy One,
    because you have so judged;
  [6]for they have shed the blood of your people and your prophets,
    and you have given them blood to drink as they deserve."

[7]And I heard the altar respond:

"Yes, Lord God Almighty,
    true and just are your judgments."

[8]The fourth angel poured out his bowl on the sun, and the sun was allowed to scorch people with fire. [9]They were seared by the intense heat and they cursed the name of God, who had control over these plagues, but they refused to repent and glorify him.

[10]The fifth angel poured out his bowl on the throne of the beast, and its kingdom was plunged into darkness. People gnawed their tongues in agony [11]and cursed the God of heaven because of their pains and their sores, but they refused to repent of what they had done.

[12]The sixth angel poured out his bowl on the great river Euphrates, and its water was dried up to prepare the way for the kings from the East. [13]Then I saw three evil[a] spirits that looked like frogs; they came out of the mouth of the dragon, out of the mouth of the beast and out of the mouth of the false prophet. [14]They are spirits of demons performing miraculous signs, and they go out to the kings of the whole world, to gather them for the battle on the great day of God Almighty.

[15]"Look, I come like a thief! Blessed are those who stay awake and keep their clothes on, so that they may not go naked and be shamefully exposed."

[16]Then they gathered the kings together to the place that in Hebrew is called Armageddon.

[17]The seventh angel poured out his bowl into the air, and out of the temple came a loud voice from the throne, saying, "It is done!" [18]Then there came

[a] 13 Greek *unclean*

flashes of lightning, rumblings, peals of thunder and a severe earthquake. No earthquake like it has ever occurred since the human race has been on earth, so tremendous was the quake. [19]The great city split into three parts, and the cities of the nations collapsed. God remembered Babylon the Great and gave her the cup filled with the wine of the fury of his wrath. [20]Every island fled away and the mountains could not be found. [21]From the sky huge hailstones of about a hundred pounds each fell upon people. And they cursed God on account of the plague of hail, because the plague was so terrible.

Babylon, the Prostitute on the Beast

17 One of the seven angels who had the seven bowls came and said to me, "Come, I will show you the punishment of the great prostitute, who sits by many waters. [2]With her the kings of the earth committed adultery and the inhabitants of the earth were intoxicated with the wine of her adulteries."

[3]Then the angel carried me away in the Spirit into a desert. There I saw a woman sitting on a scarlet beast that was covered with blasphemous names and had seven heads and ten horns. [4]The woman was dressed in purple and scarlet, and was glittering with gold, precious stones and pearls. She held a golden cup in her hand, filled with abominable things and the filth of her adulteries. [5]This title was written on her forehead:

MYSTERY
BABYLON THE GREAT
THE MOTHER OF PROSTITUTES
AND OF THE ABOMINATIONS OF THE EARTH.

[6]I saw that the woman was drunk with the blood of God's people, the blood of those who bore testimony to Jesus.

When I saw her, I was greatly astonished. [7]Then the angel said to me: "Why are you astonished? I will explain to you the mystery of the woman and of the beast she rides, which has the seven heads and ten horns. [8]The beast, which you saw, once was, now is not, and will come up out of the Abyss and go to its destruction. The inhabitants of the earth whose names have not been written in the book of life from the creation of the world will be astonished when they see the beast, because it once was, now is not, and yet will come.

[9]"This calls for a mind with wisdom. The seven heads are seven hills on which the woman sits. [10]They are also seven kings. Five have fallen, one is, the other has not yet come; but when he does come, he must remain for a little while. [11]The beast who once was, and now is not, is an eighth king. He belongs to the seven and is going to his destruction.

[12]"The ten horns you saw are ten kings who have not yet received a kingdom, but who for one hour will receive authority as kings along with the beast. [13]They have one purpose and will give their power and authority to the beast. [14]They will make war against the Lamb, but the Lamb will triumph over them because he is Lord of lords and King of kings—and with him will be his called, chosen and faithful followers."

[15]Then the angel said to me, "The waters you saw, where the prostitute sits, are peoples, multitudes, nations and languages. [16]The beast and the ten horns you saw will hate the prostitute. They will bring her to ruin and leave her

naked; they will eat her flesh and burn her with fire. [17]For God has put it into their hearts to accomplish his purpose by agreeing to give the beast their power to rule, until God's words are fulfilled. [18]The woman you saw is the great city that rules over the kings of the earth."

Lament Over Fallen Babylon

18 After this I saw another angel coming down from heaven. He had great authority, and the earth was illuminated by his splendor. [2]With a mighty voice he shouted:

" 'Fallen! Fallen is Babylon the Great!'[a]
    She has become a dwelling for demons
and a haunt for every evil[b] spirit,
    a haunt for every unclean bird,
    a haunt for every unclean and detestable animal.
[3]For all the nations have drunk
    the maddening wine of her adulteries.
The kings of the earth committed adultery with her,
    and the merchants of the earth grew rich from her excessive
        luxuries."

Warning to Escape Babylon's Judgment

[4]Then I heard another voice from heaven say:

" 'Come out of her, my people,'[c]
    so that you will not share in her sins,
    so that you will not receive any of her plagues;
[5]for her sins are piled up to heaven,
    and God has remembered her crimes.
[6]Give back to her as she has given;
    pay her back double for what she has done.
    Pour her a double portion from her own cup.
[7]Give her as much torment and grief
    as the glory and luxury she gave herself.
In her heart she boasts,
    'I sit enthroned as queen.
I am not a widow;[d]
    I will never mourn.'
[8]Therefore in one day her plagues will overtake her:
    death, mourning and famine.
She will be consumed by fire,
    for mighty is the Lord God who judges her.

Threefold Woe Over Babylon's Fall

[9]"When the kings of the earth who committed adultery with her and shared her luxury see the smoke of her burning, they will weep and mourn over her. [10]Terrified at her torment, they will stand far off and cry:

---

[a] 2 Isaiah 21:9   [b] 2 Greek *unclean*   [c] 4 Jer. 51:45   [d] 7 See Isaiah 47:7,8.

> " 'Woe! Woe to you, great city,
>   you mighty city of Babylon!
>   In one hour your doom has come!'

11 "The merchants of the earth will weep and mourn over her because no one buys their cargoes anymore— 12cargoes of gold, silver, precious stones and pearls; fine linen, purple, silk and scarlet cloth; every sort of citron wood, and articles of every kind made of ivory, costly wood, bronze, iron and marble; 13cargoes of cinnamon and spice, of incense, myrrh and frankincense, of wine and olive oil, of fine flour and wheat; cattle and sheep; horses and carriages; and human beings sold as slaves.

14 "They will say, 'The fruit you longed for is gone from you. All your luxury and splendor have vanished, never to be recovered.' 15The merchants who sold these things and gained their wealth from her will stand far off, terrified at her torment. They will weep and mourn 16and cry out:

> " 'Woe! Woe to you, great city,
>   dressed in fine linen, purple and scarlet,
>   and glittering with gold, precious stones and pearls!
>   17 In one hour such great wealth has been brought to ruin!'

"Every sea captain, and all who travel by ship, the sailors, and all who earn their living from the sea, will stand far off. 18When they see the smoke of her burning, they will exclaim, 'Was there ever a city like this great city?' 19They will throw dust on their heads, and with weeping and mourning cry out:

> " 'Woe! Woe to you, great city,
>   where all who had ships on the sea
>   became rich through her wealth!
>   In one hour she has been brought to ruin!'

> 20 "Rejoice over her, you heavens!
>   Rejoice, saints and apostles and prophets!
>   For God has judged her
>   with the judgment she imposed on you."

The Finality of Babylon's Doom

21Then a mighty angel picked up a boulder the size of a large millstone and threw it into the sea, and said:

> "With such violence
>   the great city of Babylon will be thrown down,
>   never to be found again.
> 22 The music of harpists and musicians, flute players and trumpeters,
>   will never be heard in you again.
>   No worker of any trade
>   will ever be found in you again.
>   The sound of a millstone
>   will never be heard in you again.
> 23 The light of a lamp

will never shine in you again.
The voice of bridegroom and bride
will never be heard in you again.
Your merchants were the world's important people.
By your magic spell all the nations were led astray.
24 In her was found the blood of prophets and of God's people,
of all who have been slaughtered on the earth."

Threefold Hallelujah Over Babylon's Fall

19 After this I heard what sounded like the roar of a great multitude in heaven shouting:

"Hallelujah!
Salvation and glory and power belong to our God,
2 for true and just are his judgments.
He has condemned the great prostitute
who corrupted the earth by her adulteries.
He has avenged on her the blood of his servants."

3 And again they shouted:

"Hallelujah!
The smoke from her goes up for ever and ever."

4 The twenty-four elders and the four living creatures fell down and worshiped God, who was seated on the throne. And they cried:

"Amen, Hallelujah!"

5 Then a voice came from the throne, saying:

"Praise our God,
all you his servants,
you who fear him,
both great and small!"

6 Then I heard what sounded like a great multitude, like the roar of rushing waters and like loud peals of thunder, shouting:

"Hallelujah!
For our Lord God Almighty reigns.
7 Let us rejoice and be glad
and give him glory!
For the wedding of the Lamb has come,
and his bride has made herself ready.
8 Fine linen, bright and clean,
was given her to wear."
(Fine linen stands for the righteous acts of God's people.)

9 Then the angel said to me, "Write: 'Blessed are those who are invited to the wedding supper of the Lamb!' " And he added, "These are the true words of God."

¹⁰At this I fell at his feet to worship him. But he said to me, "Don't do that! I am a fellow servant with you and with your brothers and sisters who hold to Jesus' testimony. Worship God! For the testimony of Jesus is the Spirit of prophecy."

The Heavenly Warrior Defeats the Beast

¹¹I saw heaven standing open and there before me was a white horse, whose rider is called Faithful and True. With justice he judges and makes war. ¹²His eyes are like blazing fire, and on his head are many crowns. He has a name written on him that no one knows but he himself. ¹³He is dressed in a robe dipped in blood, and his name is the Word of God. ¹⁴The armies of heaven were following him, riding on white horses and dressed in fine linen, white and clean. ¹⁵Coming out of his mouth is a sharp sword with which to strike down the nations. "He will rule them with an iron scepter."ᵃ He treads the winepress of the fury of the wrath of God Almighty. ¹⁶On his robe and on his thigh he has this name written:

KING OF KINGS AND LORD OF LORDS.

¹⁷And I saw an angel standing in the sun, who cried in a loud voice to all the birds flying in midair, "Come, gather together for the great supper of God, ¹⁸so that you may eat the flesh of kings, generals, and the mighty, of horses and their riders, and the flesh of all people, free and slave, great and small." ¹⁹Then I saw the beast and the kings of the earth and their armies gathered together to make war against the rider on the horse and his army. ²⁰But the beast was captured, and with him the false prophet who had performed the miraculous signs on his behalf. With these signs he had deluded those who had received the mark of the beast and worshiped his image. The two of them were thrown alive into the fiery lake of burning sulfur. ²¹The rest were killed with the sword coming out of the mouth of the rider on the horse, and all the birds gorged themselves on their flesh.

The Thousand Years

20 And I saw an angel coming down out of heaven, having the key to the Abyss and holding in his hand a great chain. ²He seized the dragon, that ancient serpent, who is the devil, or Satan, and bound him for a thousand years. ³He threw him into the Abyss, and locked and sealed it over him, to keep him from deceiving the nations anymore until the thousand years were ended. After that, he must be set free for a short time.

⁴I saw thrones on which were seated those who had been given authority to judge. And I saw the souls of those who had been beheaded because they held to the testimony of Jesus and to the word of God. They had not worshiped the beast or his image and had not received his mark on their foreheads or their hands. They came to life and reigned with Christ a thousand years. ⁵(The rest of the dead did not come to life until the thousand years were ended.) This is the first resurrection. ⁶Blessed and holy are those who have part in the first resurrection. The second death has no power over them, but

ᵃ 15 Psalm 2:9

they will be priests of God and of Christ and will reign with him for a thousand years.

The Judgment of Satan

7When the thousand years are over, Satan will be released from his prison 8and will go out to deceive the nations in the four corners of the earth—Gog and Magog—and to gather them for battle. In number they are like the sand on the seashore. 9They marched across the breadth of the earth and surrounded the camp of God's people, the city he loves. But fire came down from heaven and devoured them. 10And the devil, who deceived them, was thrown into the lake of burning sulfur, where the beast and the false prophet had been thrown. They will be tormented day and night for ever and ever.

The Judgment of the Dead

11Then I saw a great white throne and him who was seated on it. The earth and the heavens fled from his presence, and there was no place for them. 12And I saw the dead, great and small, standing before the throne, and books were opened. Another book was opened, which is the book of life. The dead were judged according to what they had done as recorded in the books. 13The sea gave up the dead that were in it, and death and Hades gave up the dead that were in them, and everyone was judged according to what they had done. 14Then death and Hades were thrown into the lake of fire. The lake of fire is the second death. 15All whose names were not found written in the book of life were thrown into the lake of fire.

A New Heaven and a New Earth

21 Then I saw "a new heaven and a new earth," *a* for the first heaven and the first earth had passed away, and there was no longer any sea. 2I saw the Holy City, the new Jerusalem, coming down out of heaven from God, prepared as a bride beautifully dressed for her husband. 3And I heard a loud voice from the throne saying, "Look! God's dwelling place is now among the people, and he will dwell with them. They will be his people, and God himself will be with them and be their God. 4'He will wipe every tear from their eyes. There will be no more death'*b* or mourning or crying or pain, for the old order of things has passed away."

5He who was seated on the throne said, "I am making everything new!" Then he said, "Write this down, for these words are trustworthy and true."

6He said to me: "It is done. I am the Alpha and the Omega, the Beginning and the End. To the thirsty I will give water without cost from the spring of the water of life. 7Those who are victorious will inherit all this, and I will be their God and they will be my children. 8But the cowardly, the unbelieving, the vile, the murderers, the sexually immoral, those who practice magic arts, the idolaters and all liars—they will be consigned to the fiery lake of burning sulfur. This is the second death."

a 1 Isaiah 65:17   *b* 4 Isaiah 25:8

The New Jerusalem, the Bride of the Lamb

⁹One of the seven angels who had the seven bowls full of the seven last plagues came and said to me, "Come, I will show you the bride, the wife of the Lamb." ¹⁰And he carried me away in the Spirit to a mountain great and high, and showed me the Holy City, Jerusalem, coming down out of heaven from God. ¹¹It shone with the glory of God, and its brilliance was like that of a very precious jewel, like a jasper, clear as crystal. ¹²It had a great, high wall with twelve gates, and with twelve angels at the gates. On the gates were written the names of the twelve tribes of Israel. ¹³There were three gates on the east, three on the north, three on the south and three on the west. ¹⁴The wall of the city had twelve foundations, and on them were the names of the twelve apostles of the Lamb.

¹⁵The angel who talked with me had a measuring rod of gold to measure the city, its gates and its walls. ¹⁶The city was laid out like a square, as long as it was wide. He measured the city with the rod and found it to be 12,000 stadia*ᵃ* in length, and as wide and high as it is long. ¹⁷He measured its wall and it was 144 cubits*ᵇ* thick,*ᶜ* by human measurement, which the angel was using. ¹⁸The wall was made of jasper, and the city of pure gold, as pure as glass. ¹⁹The foundations of the city walls were decorated with every kind of precious stone. The first foundation was jasper, the second sapphire, the third agate, the fourth emerald, ²⁰the fifth onyx, the sixth ruby, the seventh chrysolite, the eighth beryl, the ninth topaz, the tenth turquoise, the eleventh jacinth, and the twelfth amethyst.*ᵈ* ²¹The twelve gates were twelve pearls, each gate made of a single pearl. The great street of the city was of gold, as pure as transparent glass.

²²I did not see a temple in the city, because the Lord God Almighty and the Lamb are its temple. ²³The city does not need the sun or the moon to shine on it, for the glory of God gives it light, and the Lamb is its lamp. ²⁴The nations will walk by its light, and the kings of the earth will bring their splendor into it. ²⁵On no day will its gates ever be shut, for there will be no night there. ²⁶The glory and honor of the nations will be brought into it. ²⁷Nothing impure will ever enter it, nor will anyone who does what is shameful or deceitful, but only those whose names are written in the Lamb's book of life.

Eden Restored

22 Then the angel showed me the river of the water of life, as clear as crystal, flowing from the throne of God and of the Lamb ²down the middle of the great street of the city. On each side of the river stood the tree of life, bearing twelve crops of fruit, yielding its fruit every month. And the leaves of the tree are for the healing of the nations. ³No longer will there be any curse. The throne of God and of the Lamb will be in the city, and his servants will serve him. ⁴They will see his face, and his name will be on their foreheads. ⁵There will be no more night. They will not need the light of a lamp

---

ᵃ16 That is, about 1,400 miles (about 2,200 kilometers)   *ᵇ17* That is, about 200 feet (about 65 meters)   *ᶜ17* Or *high*   *ᵈ20* The precise identification of some of these precious stones is uncertain.

or the light of the sun, for the Lord God will give them light. And they will reign for ever and ever.

John and the Angel

6The angel said to me, "These words are trustworthy and true. The Lord, the God who inspires the prophets, sent his angel to show his servants the things that must soon take place."

7"Look, I am coming soon! Blessed are those who keep the words of the prophecy in this scroll."

8I, John, am the one who heard and saw these things. And when I had heard and seen them, I fell down to worship at the feet of the angel who had been showing them to me. 9But he said to me, "Don't do that! I am a fellow servant with you and with your fellow prophets and with all who keep the words of this scroll. Worship God!"

10Then he told me, "Do not seal up the words of the prophecy of this scroll, because the time is near. 11Let those who do wrong continue to do wrong; let those who are vile continue to be vile; let those who do right continue to do right; and let those who are holy continue to be holy."

Epilogue: Invitation and Warning

12"Look, I am coming soon! My reward is with me, and I will give to everyone according to what they have done. 13I am the Alpha and the Omega, the First and the Last, the Beginning and the End.

14"Blessed are those who wash their robes, that they may have the right to the tree of life and may go through the gates into the city. 15Outside are the dogs, those who practice magic arts, the sexually immoral, the murderers, the idolaters and everyone who loves and practices falsehood.

16"I, Jesus, have sent my angel to give you*a* this testimony for the churches. I am the Root and the Offspring of David, and the bright Morning Star."

17The Spirit and the bride say, "Come!" And let those who hear say, "Come!" Let those who are thirsty come; and let all who wish take the free gift of the water of life.

18I warn everyone who hears the words of the prophecy of this scroll: If any one of you adds anything to them, God will add to you the plagues described in this scroll. 19And if any one of you takes words away from this scroll of prophecy, God will take away from you your share in the tree of life and in the Holy City, which are described in this scroll.

20He who testifies to these things says, "Yes, I am coming soon."
Amen. Come, Lord Jesus.
21The grace of the Lord Jesus be with God's people. Amen.

a 16 The Greek is plural.

CONCORDANCE
TO THE NEW TESTAMENT OF
TODAY'S NEW INTERNATIONAL VERSION

The Concordance to the New Testament of the TNIV has been developed specifically for use with Today's New International Version. Like all concordances, it is a special index that contains an alphabetical listing of words used in the Bible text. By looking up key words, readers can find verses and passages for which they remember a word or two but not their location.

This concordance contains 2,104 word entries, with some 6,400 Scripture references. Each word entry is followed by the Scripture references in which that particular word is found, as well as by a brief excerpt from the surrounding context. The entry word is abbreviated and in bold type to conserve space and to allow for a longer context excerpt. Variant spellings due to number and tense and compound forms follow the entry in parentheses, and direct the reader to check other forms of that word in locating a passage.

This concordance contains 104 "block entries," which highlight some of the key events and characteristics in the lives of certain NT figures. The descriptive phrases replace the brief context surrounding each occurrence of the name. In those instances where more than one Bible character has the same name, that name is placed under one block entry, and each person is given a number (1), (2), etc.

Several word entries direct the reader to "See" another entry. These entries point out some key word changes between the NIV and the TNIV, such as "CAPSTONE See CORNERSTONE," "FISHERS See CATCH" and "MAN See also HUMAN PEOPLE."

This concordance is a valuable tool for Bible study. While one of its key purposes is to help the reader find forgotten references to verses, it can also be used to do word studies and to locate and trace biblical themes. Be sure to use this concordance as more than just a verse finder. Whenever you look up a verse, aim to discover the intended meaning of the verse in context. Give special attention to the flow of thought from the beginning of the passage to the end.

John R. Kohlenberger III

ABBREVIATIONS

Ac	Acts	2Jn	2 John	Phm	Philemon
1Co	1 Corinthians	3Jn	3 John	Php	Philippians
2Co	2 Corinthians	Jn	John	Rev	Revelation
Col	Colossians	Jude	Jude	Ro	Romans
Eph	Ephesians	Lk	Luke	1Th	1 Thessalonians
Gal	Galatians	Mk	Mark	2Th	2 Thessalonians
Heb	Hebrews	Mt	Matthew	1Ti	1 Timothy
Jas	James	1Pe	1 Peter	2Ti	2 Timothy
1Jn	1 John	2Pe	2 Peter	Tit	Titus

AARON
Priesthood of (Heb 5:1-4; 7). Built golden calf (Ac 7:40-41).

ABANDON
1Ti   4: 1 in later times some will a the faith

ABBA
Ro   8:15 And by him we cry, "*A*, Father."
Gal   4: 6 the Spirit who calls out, "*A*, Father."

ABEL
Offered proper sacrifice (Heb 11:4). Murdered by Cain (Mt 23:35; Lk 11:51; 1Jn 3:12).

ABILITY (ABLE)
2Co   1: 8 far beyond our a to endure,
         8: 3 were able, and even beyond their a.

ABLE (ABILITY ENABLE ENABLED ENABLES)
Ro   8:39 will be a to separate us
      14: 4 the Lord is a to make them stand.
      16:25 to him who is a to establish you
2Co   9: 8 God is a to bless you abundantly,
Eph   3:20 to him who is a to do immeasurably
2Ti   1:12 that he is a to guard what I have
         3:15 which are a to make you wise
Heb   7:25 Therefore he is a to save completely
Jude   :24 To him who is a to keep you
Rev   5: 5 He is a to open the scroll and its

ABOLISH
Mt   5:17 think that I have come to a the Law

ABOMINATION
Mk   13:14 see 'the a that causes desolation'

ABOUND (ABOUNDS)
2Co   9: 8 you will a in every good work.
Php   1: 9 that your love may a more and more

ABOUNDS (ABOUND)
2Co   1: 5 also our comfort a through Christ.

ABRAHAM
Covenant relation with the Lord (Lk 1:68-75; Ro 4; Heb 6:13-15).
Called from Ur, via Haran, to Canaan (Ac 7:2-4; Heb 11:8-10). Blessed by Melchizedek (Heb 7:1-20). Declared righteous by faith (Ro 4:3; Gal 3:6-9). Circumcised (Ro 4:9-12). Fathered Isaac by Sarah (Ac 7:8; Heb 11:11-12); sent away Hagar and Ishmael (Gal 4:22-30). Tested by offering Isaac (Heb 11:17-19; Jas 2:21-24).

ABSTAIN
Ro   14: 6 those who a do so to the Lord
1Pe   2:11 the world, to a from sinful desires,

ABUNDANCE (ABUNDANT)
Lk   12:15 not consist in an a of possessions."
Jude   : 2 peace and love be yours in a.

ABUNDANT (ABUNDANCE)
Ro   5:17 those who receive God's a provision

ABUSE
2Pe   2:11 do not heap a on such beings

ACCEPT (ACCEPTED ACCEPTS)
Ro   15: 7 A one another, then, just as Christ
Jas   1:21 humbly a the word planted in you,

ACCEPTED (ACCEPT)
Lk   4:24 "prophets are not a in their

ACCEPTS (ACCEPT)
Jn   13:20 whoever a anyone I send a me;
      13:20 whoever a me a the one who

ACCOMPANY
Mk   16:17 And these signs will a those who

ACCORD
Jn   10:18 me, but I lay it down of my own a.

ACCOUNT (ACCOUNTABLE)
Mt   12:36 will have to give a on the day
Ro   14:12 we will all give an a of ourselves
Heb   4:13 of him to whom we must give a.

ACCOUNTABLE (ACCOUNT)
Ro   3:19 and the whole world held a to God.

ACCUSATION (ACCUSE)
1Ti   5:19 not entertain an a against an elder

ACCUSE (ACCUSATION)
Lk   3:14 don't a people falsely—be content

ACKNOWLEDGE
Mt   10:32 also a before my Father in heaven.
Php   2:11 every tongue a that Jesus Christ is Lord,
1Th   5:12 to a those who work hard among you,
1Jn   4: 3 spirit that does not a Jesus is not

ACTION (ACTIONS ACTIVE ACTS)
Jas   2:17 if it is not accompanied by a,

ACTIONS (ACTION)
Mt   11:19 wisdom is proved right by her a."
Gal   6: 4 Each of you should test your own a.
Tit   1:16 God, but by their a they deny him.

ACTIVE (ACTION)
Heb   4:12 For the word of God is alive and a.

ACTS (ACTION)
Mt   6: 1 not to do your 'a of righteousness'

ADAM
First man (Ro 5:14; 1Ti 2:13). Sin of (Ro 5:12-21). Death of (Ro 5:12-21; 1Co 15:22).

ADD
Lk   12:25 you by worrying can a a single hour
Rev   22:18 them, God will a to you the plagues

ADMIRABLE
Php   4: 8 whatever is a—if anything is excellent

ADMONISH
Col   3:16 and a one another with all wisdom

ADOPTION
Ro   8:23 as we wait eagerly for our a,
Gal   4: 5 that we might receive a to sonship
Eph   1: 5 he predestined us for a to sonship

ADORN (ADORNMENT)
1Pe   3: 5 put their hope in God used to a

ADORNMENT (ADORN)
1Pe   3: 3 should not come from outward a,

ADULTERY
Mt   5:27 that it was said, 'Do not commit a.'
         5:28 lustfully has already committed a
         5:32 the divorced woman commits a.
      15:19 murder, a, sexual immorality, theft,

ADULTS
1Co 14:20 be infants, but in your thinking be **a**.

ADVANTAGE
1Th 4: 6 should wrong or take **a** of a brother

ADVOCATE
Jn 14:16 another **a** to help you and be with you
14:26 the **A**, the Holy Spirit,
1Jn 2: 1 we have an **a** with the Father—Jesus Christ,

AFFECTION
2Pe 1: 7 mutual **a**; and to mutual **a**, love.

AFFLICTION
Ro 12:12 hope, patient in **a**, faithful in prayer.

AFRAID (FEAR)
Mt 8:26 of little faith, why are you so **a**?"
10:28 Do not be **a** of those who kill
10:28 be **a** of the One who can destroy
10:31 So don't be **a**; you are worth more
Mk 5:36 they said, Jesus told him, "Don't be **a**;
Jn 14:27 hearts be troubled and do not be **a**.
Heb 13: 6 Lord is my helper; I will not be **a**.

AGREE
Mt 18:19 earth **a** about anything you ask for,
Ro 7:16 want to do, I **a** that the law is good.

AGRIPPA
Descendant of Herod; king before whom Paul pled his case in Caesarea (Ac 25:13-26:32).

AIM
1Co 7:34 Her **a** is to be devoted to the Lord

AIR
1Co 9:26 not fight like a boxer beating the **a**.
Eph 2: 2 of the ruler of the kingdom of the **a**,
1Th 4:17 the clouds to meet the Lord in the **a**.

ALABASTER
Mt 26: 7 him with an **a** jar of very expensive

ALERT
Mk 13:33 Be **a**! You do not know
Eph 6:18 be **a** and always keep on praying
1Pe 1:13 with minds that are **a** and fully sober,

ALIENATED (ALIEN)
Gal 5: 4 by law have been **a** from Christ;

ALIVE (LIVE)
Ac 1: 3 convincing proofs that he was **a**.
Ro 6:11 to sin but **a** to God in Christ Jesus.
1Co 15:22 die, so in Christ all will be made **a**.
Heb 4:12 For the word of God is **a** and active.

ALMIGHTY (MIGHT)
Rev 4: 8 'Holy, holy, holy is the Lord God **A**,'

ALTAR
Mt 5:23 if you are offering your gift at the **a**
Rev 6: 9 I saw under the **a** the souls of those

ALWAYS
Mt 26:11 The poor you will **a** have with you, but you will not **a** have me.
28:20 And surely I am with you **a**,
1Co 13: 7 It **a** protects, **a** trusts, **a** hopes,
Php 4: 4 Rejoice in the Lord **a**. I will say it
1Pe 3:15 **A** be prepared to give an answer

AMBASSADORS
2Co 5:20 We are therefore Christ's **a**,

AMBITION
Ro 15:20 It has always been my **a** to preach
1Th 4:11 to make it your **a** to lead a quiet life:

ANANIAS
1. Husband of Sapphira; died for lying to God (Ac 5:1-11).
2. Disciple who baptized Saul (Ac 9:10-19).
3. High priest at Paul's arrest (Ac 22:30-24:1).

ANCESTORS
Heb 1: 1 In the past God spoke to our **a**

ANCHOR
Heb 6:19 We have this hope as an **a**

ANDREW
Apostle; brother of Simon Peter (Mt 4:18; 10:2; Mk 1:16-18, 29; 3:18; 13:3; Lk 6:14; Jn 1:35-44; 6:8-9; 12:22; Ac 1:13).

ANGEL (ANGELS ARCHANGEL)
Ac 6:15 his face was like the face of an **a**.
2Co 11:14 Satan himself masquerades as an **a**
Gal 1: 8 or an **a** from heaven should preach

ANGELS (ANGEL)
Mt 18:10 that their **a** in heaven always see
25:41 fire prepared for the devil and his **a**.
Lk 20:36 longer die; for they are like the **a**.
1Co 6: 3 you not know that we will judge **a**?
Heb 1: 4 the **a** as the name he has inherited is
1:14 Are not all **a** ministering spirits sent
2: 7 made them a little lower than the **a**;
13: 2 hospitality to **a** without knowing it.
1Pe 1:12 Even **a** long to look into these
2Pe 2: 4 if God did not spare **a** when they

ANGER (ANGERED ANGRY)
Eph 4: 6 "In your **a** do not sin": Do not let

ANGERED (ANGER)
1Co 13: 5 it is not easily **a**, it keeps no record

ANGRY (ANGER)
Jas 1:19 to speak and slow to become **a**,

ANOINT
Jas 5:14 **a** you with oil in the name

ANTICHRIST
1Jn 2:18 you have heard that the **a** is coming,
2Jn : 7 person is the deceiver and the **a**.

ANTIOCH
Ac 11:26 were called Christians first at **A**.

ANXIETY (ANXIOUS)
1Pe 5: 7 Cast all your **a** on him because he

ANXIOUS (ANXIETY)
Php 4: 6 Do not be **a** about anything,

APOLLOS
Christian from Alexandria, learned in the Scriptures; instructed by Aquila and Priscilla (Ac 18:24-28). Ministered at Corinth (Ac 19:1; 1Co 1:12; 3; Tit 3:13).

APOSTLES
See also Andrew, Bartholomew, James, John, Judas, Matthew, Nathanael, Paul, Peter, Philip, Simon, Thaddaeus, Thomas.
Mt 10: 2 These are the names of the twelve **a**:
Ac 1:26 so he was added to the eleven **a**.
2:43 and miraculous signs done by the **a**.
1Co 12:28 placed in the church first of all **a**,
15: 9 For I am the least of the **a** and do

2Co 11:13 For such persons are false **a**,
11:13 masquerading as **a** of Christ.
Eph 2:20 built on the foundation of the **a**

APPEAR (APPEARANCE APPEARING)
Mk 13:22 false prophets will **a** and perform
2Co 5:10 we must all **a** before the judgment
Col 3: 4 you also will **a** with him in glory.
Heb 9:24 now to **a** for us in God's presence.
9:28 and he will **a** a second time,

APPEARANCE (APPEAR)
Php 2: 8 being found in **a** as a human being,

APPEARING (APPEAR)
2Ti 4: 8 to all who have longed for his **a**.
Tit 2:13 the blessed hope—the **a** of the glory

APPROACH
Eph 3:12 in him we may **a** God with freedom
Heb 4:16 us then **a** God's throne of grace

APPROVED
2Ti 2:15 to present yourself to God as one **a**,

AQUILA
Husband of Priscilla; co-worker with Paul, instructor of Apollos (Ac 18; Ro 16:3; 1Co 16:19; 2Ti 4:19).

ARCHANGEL (ANGEL)
1Th 4:16 with the voice of the **a**
Jude : 9 But even the **a** Michael, when he

ARCHITECT
Heb 11:10 whose **a** and builder is God.

ARK
Lk 17:27 up to the day Noah entered the **a**.
Heb 9: 4 the gold-covered **a** of the covenant.

ARM (ARMY)
1Pe 4: 1 **a** yourselves also with the same

ARMAGEDDON
Rev 16:16 the place that in Hebrew is called **A**.

ARMOR (ARMY)
Eph 6:11 Put on the full **a** of God, so that you
6:13 Therefore put on the full **a** of God,

ARMS (ARMY)
Mk 10:16 And he took the children in his **a**,

ARMY (ARM ARMOR ARMS)
Rev 19:19 the rider on the horse and his **a**.

AROMA
2Co 2:15 to God the pleasing **a** of Christ
2:16 to the other, an **a** that brings life.

ARROGANT
Ro 11:20 by faith. Do not be **a**, but tremble.

ARROWS
Eph 6:16 you can extinguish all the flaming **a**

ASCENDED
Eph 4: 8 "When he **a** on high, he led captives

ASHAMED (SHAME)
Lk 9:26 If any of you are **a** of me and my
9:26 the Son of Man will be **a** of you
Ro 1:16 I am not **a** of the gospel, because it
2Ti 1: 8 So do not be **a** of the testimony
2:15 a worker who does not need to be **a**

ASHER
Rev 7: 6 from the tribe of **A** 12,000,

ASSIGNED
Mk 13:34 each with an **a** task, and tells
1Co 3: 5 believe—as the Lord has **a** to each his
7:17 whatever situation the Lord has **a**

ASSOCIATE
Ro 12:16 be willing to **a** with people of low
1Co 5:11 you must not **a** with any who claim
2Th 3:14 Do not **a** with them, in order

ASSURANCE
Heb 10:22 a sincere heart in full **a** of faith,

ASTRAY
1Pe 2:25 For "you were like sheep going **a**,"
1Jn 3: 7 do not let anyone lead you **a**.

ATHLETE
2Ti 2: 5 competes as an **a** does not receive

ATONEMENT
Ro 3:25 presented Christ as a sacrifice of **a**,
Heb 2:17 that he might make **a** for the sins

ATTENTION
Tit 1:14 and will pay no **a** to Jewish myths

ATTITUDE (ATTITUDES)
Eph 4:23 made new in the **a** of your minds;
Php 2: 5 have the same **a** of mind Christ
1Pe 4: 1 yourselves also with the same **a**,

ATTITUDES (ATTITUDE)
Heb 4:12 the thoughts and **a** of the heart.

ATTRACTIVE
Tit 2:10 teaching about God our Savior **a**.

AUTHORITIES (AUTHORITY)
Ro 13: 5 it is necessary to submit to the **a**,
13: 6 for the **a** are God's servants,
Tit 3: 1 people to be subject to rulers and **a**,
1Pe 3:22 **a** and powers in submission to him.

AUTHORITY (AUTHORITIES)
Mt 7:29 because he taught as one who had **a**,
9: 6 the Son of Man has **a** on earth
28:18 "All **a** in heaven and on earth has
Ro 13: 1 for there is no **a** except
13: 2 rebels against the **a** is rebelling
1Co 11:10 ought to have **a** over her own head.
1Ti 2: 2 for kings and all those in **a**, that we
2:12 to teach or to have **a** over a man;
Heb 13:17 your leaders and submit to their **a**,
1Pe 2:13 for the Lord's sake to every human **a**:

AVENGE (REVENGE)
Ro 12:19 "It is mine to **a**; I will repay,"

AVOID
1Th 4: 3 you should **a** sexual immorality;
2Ti 2:16 **A** godless chatter, because those
Tit 3: 9 But **a** foolish controversies

AWAKE
1Th 5: 6 but let us be **a** and sober.

AWE
Mt 9: 8 saw this, they were filled with **a**;
Lk 7:16 They were all filled with **a**
Ac 2:43 Everyone was filled with **a**
Heb 12:28 acceptably with reverence and **a**,

BAAL
Ro 11: 4 who have not bowed the knee to **B**."

BABIES (BABY)
Lk 18:15 also bringing **b** to Jesus to have him
1Pe 2: 2 Like newborn **b**, crave pure spiritual

BABY (BABIES)
Lk 1:44 the **b** in my womb leaped for joy.
2:12 You will find a **b** wrapped in cloths
Jn 16:21 her **b** is born she forgets the anguish

BABYLON
Rev 14: 8 Fallen is **B** the Great,' which made
17: 5 MYSTERY **B** THE GREAT THE MOTHER

BAGS
Mt 25:15 To one he gave five **b** of gold,

BALAAM
Prophet who attempted to curse Israel (2Pe 2:15; Jude 11; Rev 2:14).

BANQUET
Lk 14:13 But when you give a **b**,

BAPTIZE (BAPTIZED)
Mt 3:11 "I **b** you with water for repentance.
3:11 He will **b** you with the Holy Spirit
Mk 1: 8 I **b** you with water, but he will **b** you
1Co 1:17 For Christ did not send me to **b**,

BAPTIZED (BAPTIZE)
Mt 3: 6 they were **b** by him in the Jordan
Mk 1: 9 and was **b** by John in the Jordan.
10:38 be **b** with the baptism I am **b** with?"
16:16 believes and is **b** will be saved,
Jn 4: 2 in fact it was not Jesus who **b**,
Ac 1: 5 For John **b** with water, but in a few
1: 5 you will be **b** with the Holy Spirit."

BARABBAS
Mt 27:16 prisoner whose name was Jesus **B**.
27:26 Then he released **B** to them. But he

BARAK
Judge who fought with Deborah against Canaanites (Heb 11:32).

BARE
Heb 4:13 and laid **b** before the eyes of him

BARNABAS
Disciple, originally Joseph (Ac 4:36), prophet (Ac 13:1), apostle (Ac 14:14). Brought Paul to apostles (Ac 9:27), Antioch (Ac 11:22-29; Gal 2:1-13), on the first missionary journey (Ac 13-14). Together at Jerusalem Council, they separated over John Mark (Ac 15). Later co-workers (1Co 9:6; Col 4:10).

BARREN
Gal 4:27 "Be glad, **b** woman, you who bear

BARTHOLOMEW
Apostle (Mt 10:3; Mk 3:18; Lk 6:14; Ac 1:13). Possibly also known as Nathanael (Jn 1:45-49; 21:2).

BATH
Jn 13:10 "Those who have had a **b** need only

BATTLE
Rev 20: 8 Magog—and to gather them for **b**.

BEAR (BEARING BIRTH BIRTHRIGHT BORN FIRSTBORN NEWBORN)
Mt 7:18 A good tree cannot **b** bad fruit,

Jn 15: 2 branch that does **b** fruit he prunes so
15:16 might go and **b** fruit—fruit that will
Ro 15: 1 We who are strong ought to **b**
1Co 10:13 be tempted beyond what you can **b**.
Col 3:13 **B** with each other and forgive one

BEARING (BEAR)
Eph 4: 2 patient, **b** with one another in love.
Col 1:10 **b** fruit in every good work,

BEAST
Rev 13:18 calculate the number of the **b**, for it

BEAT (BEATING)
Mk 14:65 And the guards took him and **b** him.

BEATING (BEAT)
1Co 9:26 I do not fight like a boxer **b** the air.
1Pe 2:20 if you receive a **b** for doing wrong

BEAUTIFUL (BEAUTY)
Mt 23:27 which look **b** on the outside
26:10 She has done a **b** thing to me.
Ro 10:15 "How **b** are the feet of those who

BEAUTY (BEAUTIFUL)
1Pe 3: 4 the unfading **b** of a gentle and quiet

BED
Heb 13: 4 and the marriage **b** kept pure,

BEELZEBUL
Lk 11:15 "By **B**, the prince of demons,

BEGINNING
Jn 1: 1 In the **b** was the Word,
1Jn 1: 1 That which was from the **b**,
Rev 21: 6 and the Omega, the **B** and the End.

BEHAVE
Ro 13:13 Let us **b** decently, as in the daytime,

BELIEVE (BELIEVED BELIEVER BELIEVERS BELIEVES BELIEVING)
Mt 18: 6 of these little ones—those who **b**
21:22 If you **b**, you will receive whatever
Mk 1:15 near. Repent and **b** the good news!"
9:24 the boy's father exclaimed, "I do **b**;
11:23 but **b** that what you say will happen,
16:17 signs will accompany those who **b**:
Lk 8:50 just **b**, and she will be healed."
24:25 how slow to **b** all that the prophets
Jn 1: 7 so that through him all might **b**.
3:18 does not **b** stands condemned
6:29 is this: to **b** in the one he has sent."
10:38 even though you do not **b** me,
11:27 him, "I **b** that you are the Messiah,
14:11 **B** me when I say that I am
14:11 or at least **b** on the evidence
16:30 This makes us **b** that you came
16:31 "Do you now **b**?" Jesus replied.
17:21 the world may **b** that you have sent
20:27 it into my side. Stop doubting and **b**."
20:31 you may **b** that Jesus is the Messiah,
Ac 16:31 They replied, "**B** in the Lord Jesus,
24:14 I **b** everything that is in accordance
Ro 3:22 faith in Jesus Christ to all who **b**.
4:11 he is the father of all who **b**
10: 9 **b** in your heart that God raised him
10:14 how can they **b** in the one of whom
1Th 4:14 We **b** that Jesus died and rose again,
2Th 2:11 delusion so that they will **b** the lie
1Ti 4:10 and especially of those who **b**.
Tit 1: 6 a man whose children **b** and are not
Heb 11: 6 comes to him must **b** that he exists
Jas 2:19 You **b** that there is one God. Good!

Jas 2:19 Even the demons **b** that—and shudder.
1Jn 4: 1 Dear friends, do not **b** every spirit,

BELIEVED (BELIEVE)
Jn 1:12 to those who **b** in his name, he gave
2:22 Then they **b** the scripture
3:18 already because they have not **b**
20: 8 also went inside. He saw and **b**.
20:29 you have seen me, you have **b**;
20:29 who have not seen and yet have **b**."
Ac 13:48 were appointed for eternal life **b**.
Ro 4: 3 "Abraham **b** God, and it was credited
10:14 call on the one they have not **b** in?
1Co 15: 2 you. Otherwise, you have **b** in vain.
Gal 3: 6 So also Abraham "**b** God, and it was
2Ti 1:12 because I know whom I have **b**,
Jas 2:23 fulfilled that says, "Abraham **b** God,

BELIEVER (BELIEVE)
1Co 7:12 brother has a wife who is not a **b**
2Co 6:15 what does a **b** have in common

BELIEVERS (BELIEVE)
Ac 4:32 All the **b** were one in heart
5:12 all the **b** used to meet together
1Co 6: 5 to judge a dispute between **b**?
1Ti 4:12 set an example for the **b** in speech,
1Pe 2:17 love your fellow **b**, fear God,

BELIEVES (BELIEVE)
Mk 9:23 is possible for one who **b**."
16:16 Whoever **b** and is baptized will be
Jn 3:16 whoever **b** in him shall not perish
3:36 Whoever **b** in the Son has eternal
5:24 **b** him who sent me has eternal life
6:35 and whoever **b** in me will never be
6:40 and **b** in him shall have eternal life,
6:47 tell you, whoever **b** has eternal life.
7:38 Whoever **b** in me, as Scripture has
11:26 lives and **b** in me will never die.
Ro 1:16 brings salvation to everyone who **b**:
9:33 who **b** in him will never be put
10: 4 righteousness for everyone who **b**.
1Jn 5: 1 Everyone who **b** that Jesus is
5: 5 Only the one who **b** that Jesus is

BELIEVING (BELIEVE)
Jn 20:31 by **b** you may have life in his name.

BELONG (BELONGS)
Jn 8:44 You **b** to your father, the devil,
15:19 As it is, you do not **b** to the world,
Ro 1: 6 those Gentiles who are called to **b**
7: 4 that you might **b** to another, to him
14: 8 we live or die, we **b** to the Lord.
Gal 5:24 Those who **b** to Christ Jesus have
1Th 5: 8 But since we **b** to the day, let us be

BELONGS (BELONG)
Jn 8:47 Whoever **b** to God hears what God
Ro 12: 5 and each member **b** to all the others.

BELOVED See LOVE

BELT
Eph 6:14 the **b** of truth buckled around your

BENEFIT (BENEFITS)
Ro 6:22 the **b** you reap leads to holiness,
2Co 4:15 All this is for your **b**,

BENEFITS (BENEFIT)
Jn 4:38 you have reaped the **b** of their labor."

BENJAMIN
Rev 7: 8 from the tribe of **B** 12,000.

BEREAN
Ac 17:11 the **B** Jews were of more noble character

BETHLEHEM
Mt 2: 1 After Jesus was born in **B** in Judea,

BETRAY
Mt 26:25 Judas, the one who would **b** him,
Mk 13:12 "Brother will **b** brother to death,

BIND
Mt 16:19 whatever you **b** on earth will be

BIRDS
Mt 8:20 "Foxes have holes and **b** have nests,

BIRTH (BEAR)
Mt 1:18 This is how the **b** of Jesus Christ
1Pe 1: 3 great mercy he has given us new **b**

BLAMELESS
1Co 1: 8 so that you will be **b** on the day
Eph 5:27 any other blemish, but holy and **b**
Php 2:15 so that you may become **b** and pure,
1Th 3:13 your hearts so that you will be **b**
5:23 body be kept **b** at the coming of our
Tit 1: 6 An elder must be **b**, faithful to his
Heb 7:26 meets our need—one who is holy, **b**,
2Pe 3:14 spotless, **b** and at peace with him.

BLASPHEMES
Mk 3:29 whoever **b** against the Holy Spirit

BLEMISH
1Pe 1:19 Christ, a lamb without **b** or defect.

BLESS (BLESSED BLESSING BLESSINGS)
Ro 12:14 **B** those who persecute you;
2Co 9: 8 God is able to **b** you abundantly,

BLESSED (BLESS)
Mt 5: 3 "**B** are the poor in spirit, for theirs is
5: 4 **B** are those who mourn, for they
5: 5 **B** are the meek, for they will inherit
5: 6 **B** are those who hunger and thirst
5: 7 **B** are the merciful, for they will be
5: 8 **B** are the pure in heart, for they will
5: 9 **B** are the peacemakers, for they will
5:10 **B** are those who are persecuted
5:11 "**B** are you when people insult you,
Lk 1:48 on all generations will call me **b**,
Jn 12:13 "**B** is he who comes in the name
12:13 "**B** is the king of Israel!"
Ac 20:35 'It is more **b** to give than to receive.' "
Tit 2:13 we wait for the **b** hope—the appearing
Jas 1:12 **B** are those who persevere under
Rev 1: 3 **B** is the one who reads the words
1: 3 and **b** are those who hear it and take
22:14 "**B** are those who wash their robes,

BLESSING (BLESS)
Eph 1: 3 with every spiritual **b** in Christ.
1Pe 3: 9 On the contrary, repay evil with **b**,

BLESSINGS (BLESS)
Ro 15:27 have shared in the Jews' spiritual **b**,

BLIND
Mt 15:14 Leave them; they are **b** guides.
15:14 If the **b** lead the **b**, both will fall
23:16 "Woe to you, **b** guides! You say,
Jn 9:25 I do know. I was **b** but now I see!"

BLOOD
Mt 26:28 This is my **b** of the covenant,
Ro 3:25 atonement, through the shedding of his **b**—

Ro 5: 9 we have now been justified by his **b**,
1Co 11:25 cup is the new covenant in my **b**;
Eph 1: 7 we have redemption through his **b**,
2:13 brought near by the **b** of Christ.
Col 1:20 by making peace through his **b**,
Heb 9:12 Place once for all by his own **b**,
9:22 everything be cleansed with **b**,
9:22 of **b** there is no forgiveness.
1Pe 1:19 but with the precious **b** of Christ,
1Jn 1: 7 another, and the **b** of Jesus, his Son,
Rev 1: 5 has freed us from our sins by his **b**,
5: 9 with your **b** you purchased for God
7:14 them white in the **b** of the Lamb.
12:11 over him by the **b** of the Lamb

BLOT
Rev 3: 5 I will never **b** out their names

BLOWN
Eph 4:14 and **b** here and there by every wind
Jas 1: 6 of the sea, **b** and tossed by the wind.

BOAST
1Co 1:31 "Let those who **b b** in the Lord."
Gal 6:14 May I never **b** except in the cross
Eph 2: 9 not by works, so that no one can **b**.

BOAZ
Wealthy Bethlehemite who showed favor to Ruth; ancestor of Jesus (Mt 1:5-16; Lk 3:23-32).

BODIES (BODY)
Ro 12: 1 to offer your **b** as living sacrifices,
1Co 6:15 not know that your **b** are members
6:19 your **b** are temples of the Holy Spirit,
Eph 5:28 to love their wives as their own **b**.

BODY (BODIES)
Mt 10:28 can destroy both soul and **b** in hell.
26:26 saying, "Take and eat; this is my **b**."
Jn 13:10 their feet; their whole **b** is clean.
Ro 12: 4 us has one **b** with many members,
1Co 11:24 said, "This is my **b**, which is for you;
12:12 Just as a **b**, though one, has many
12:12 but all its many parts form one **b**,
Eph 5:30 for we are members of his **b**.

BOLD (BOLDNESS)
2Co 3:12 have such a hope, we are very **b**.

BOLDNESS (BOLD)
Ac 4:29 to speak your word with great **b**.

BONDAGE
Ro 8:21 be liberated from its **b** to decay

BOOK (BOOKS)
Jn 20:30 which are not recorded in this **b**.
Php 4: 3 whose names are in the **b** of life.
Rev 21:27 are written in the Lamb's **b** of life.

BOOKS (BOOK)
Jn 21:25 world would not have room for the **b**

BORN (BEAR)
Jn 3: 7 at my saying, 'You must be **b** again.'
1Pe 1:23 For you have been **b** again,
1Jn 4: 7 Everyone who loves has been **b**
5: 1 Jesus is the Messiah is **b** of God,

BOUGHT
Ac 20:28 which he **b** with his own blood.
1Co 6:20 you were **b** at a price.
7:23 You were **b** at a price; do not
2Pe 2: 1 Lord who **b** them—bringing swift

BOW
Ro 14:11 Lord, 'every knee will **b** before me;
Php 2:10 name of Jesus every knee should **b**,

BRANCH (BRANCHES)
Jn 15: 4 No **b** can bear fruit by itself;

BRANCHES (BRANCH)
Jn 15: 5 "I am the vine; you are the **b**. If you

BREAD
Mt 4: 4 'People do not live on **b** alone,
6:11 Give us today our daily **b**.
Jn 6:35 Jesus declared, "I am the **b** of life.
21:13 took the **b** and gave it to them,
1Co 11:23 the night he was betrayed, took **b**,

BREAK (BREAKING BROKEN)
Mt 12:20 A bruised reed he will not **b**,

BREAKING (BREAK)
Jas 2:10 just one point is guilty of **b** all of it.

BREASTPLATE
Eph 6:14 with the **b** of righteousness in place,
1Th 5: 8 putting on faith and love as a **b**,

BREATHED (GOD-BREATHED)
Jn 20:22 with that he **b** on them and said,

BRIDE
Rev 19: 7 and his **b** has made herself ready.

BROAD
Mt 7:13 gate and **b** is the road that leads

BROKEN (BREAK)
Jn 10:35 God came—and Scripture cannot be **b**—

BROTHER (BROTHERS)
Mt 5:23 **b** or sister has something against you,
18:15 "If a **b** or sister sins, go and point
Mk 3:35 Whoever does God's will is my **b**
Lk 17: 3 "If any **b** or sister sins against you,
1Co 8:13 if what I eat causes my **b** or sister
1Jn 4:20 we love God yet hate a **b** or sister

BROTHERS (BROTHER)
Mt 25:40 did for one of the least of these **b**
Mk 10:29 "no one who has left home or **b**
Heb 13: 1 Keep on loving one another as **b**
1Jn 3:10 who do not love their **b** and sisters.

BUILD (BUILDING BUILDS BUILT)
Mt 16:18 and on this rock I will **b** my church,
Ac 20:32 which can **b** you up and give you
1Co 3:10 But each one should **b** with care.
14:12 excel in those that **b** up the church.
1Th 5:11 one another and **b** each other up,

BUILDING (BUILD)
1Co 3: 9 you are God's field, God's **b**.
2Co 10: 8 authority the Lord gave us for **b** you
Eph 4:29 only what is helpful for **b** others

BUILDS (BUILD)
8: 1 puffs up while love **b** up.

BUILT (BUILD)
Mt 7:24 is like a wise man who **b** his house
1Co 14:26 so that the church may be **b** up.
Eph 2:20 **b** on the foundation of the apostles
4:12 that the body of Christ may be **b**

BURDEN (BURDENED BURDENS)
Mt 11:30 my yoke is easy and my **b** is light."

BURDENED (BURDEN)
Gal 5: 1 do not let yourselves be **b** again

BURDENS (BURDEN)
Gal 6: 2 Carry each other's **b**, and in this way

BURIED
Ro   6: 4 We were therefore **b** with him
1Co 15: 4 that he was **b**, that he was raised

BURNING
Ro 12:20 you will heap **b** coals on his head."

BUSINESS
1Th 4:11 You should mind your own **b**

BUSY
2Th 3:11 They are not **b**; they are busybodies.
Tit   2: 5 pure, to be **b** at home, to be kind,

CAESAR
Mt 22:21 "Give back to **C** what is Caesar's,

CAIN
Firstborn of Adam; murdered his brother Abel (1Jn 3:12).

CALF
Lk 15:23 Bring the fattened **c** and kill it.

CALL (CALLED CALLING CALLS)
Mt   9:13 I have not come to **c** the righteous,
Ro 10:12 and richly blesses all who **c** on him,
    11:29 God's gifts and his **c** are irrevocable.
1Th 4: 7 For God did not **c** us to be impure,

CALLED (CALL)
Mt 21:13 " 'My house will be **c** a house
Ro   8:30 And those he predestined, he also **c**;
     8:30 those he **c**, he also justified;
1Co 7:15 God has **c** us to live in peace.
Gal 5:13 and sisters, were **c** to be free. But do
1Pe 2: 9 the praises of him who **c** you

CALLING (CALL)
Jn   1:23 "I am the voice of one **c** in the desert,
Ac 22:16 wash your sins away, **c** on his name.'
Eph 4: 1 worthy of the **c** you have received.
2Pe 1:10 make every effort to confirm your **c**

CALLS (CALL)
Jn 10: 3 He **c** his own sheep by name
Ro 10:13 "Everyone who **c** on the name

CAMEL
Mt 19:24 easier for a **c** to go through the eye
    23:24 strain out a gnat but swallow a **c**.

CANCELED
Col 2:14 having **c** the statement

CAPSTONE See CORNERSTONE

CARE (CAREFUL CARES CARING)
Lk 10:34 him to an inn and took **c** of him.
Jn 21:16 Jesus said, "Take **c** of my sheep."
1Co 3:10 But each one should build with **c**.
Eph 5:29 bodies, but they feed and **c** for them,
Heb 2: 6 human beings that you **c** for them?
1Pe 5: 2 of God's flock that is under your **c**,

CAREFUL (CARE)
Mt   6: 1 "Be **c** not to do your 'acts
Ro 12:17 Be **c** to do what is right in the eyes
1Co 8: 9 Be **c**, however, that the exercise
Eph 5:15 Be very **c**, then, how you live—not as

CARES (CARE)
1Th 2: 7 as a nursing mother **c** for her children,
1Pe 5: 7 on him because he **c** for you.

CARING (CARE)
1Ti 5: 4 practice by **c** for their own family

CARRIED (CARRY)
Heb 13: 9 Do not be **c** away by all kinds
2Pe 1:21 God as they were **c** along

CARRY (CARRIED CARRIES)
Lk 14:27 those who do not **c** their cross
Gal 6: 2 **C** each other's burdens, and in this
     6: 5 each of you should **c** your own load.

CAST
Jn 19:24 them and **c** lots for my garment."
1Pe 5: 7 **C** all your anxiety on him because

CATCH (CAUGHT)
Mk   1:17 I will send you out to **c** people."
Lk   5:10 from now on you will **c** people."

CAUGHT (CATCH)
1Th 4:17 are left will be **c** up together

CAUSE (CAUSES)
Mt 18: 7 the things that **c** people to stumble!
Ro 14:21 else that will **c** your brother or sister
1Co 10:32 Do not **c** anyone to stumble,

CAUSES (CAUSE)
Mt 18: 6 "If anyone **c** one of these little

CEASE
1Co 13: 8 there are prophecies, they will **c**;

CENTURION
Mt   8: 5 Capernaum, a **c** came to him,

CERTAIN (CERTAINTY)
Heb 11: 1 and **c** of what we do not see.

CERTAINTY (CERTAIN)
Lk   1: 4 you may know the **c** of the things
Jn 17: 8 They knew with **c** that I came

CHAFF
Lk   3:17 burn up the **c** with unquenchable fire."

CHAINED
2Ti 2: 9 the point of being **c** like a criminal. But God's
         word is not **c**.

CHANGE (CHANGED)
Mt 18: 3 unless you **c** and become like little
Heb 7:21 has sworn and will not **c** his mind:
Jas 1:17 lights, who does not **c** like shifting

CHANGED (CHANGE)
1Co 15:51 not all sleep, but we will all be **c**—

CHARACTER
Ro   5: 4 perseverance, **c**; and **c**, hope.
1Co 15:33 "Bad company corrupts good **c**."

CHARGE
Ro   8:33 will bring any **c** against those whom
2Co 11: 7 the gospel of God to you free of **c**?
2Ti 4: 1 and his kingdom, I give you this **c**:

CHASTENS
Heb 12: 6 he **c** everyone he accepts as his

CHATTER
1Ti 6:20 Turn away from godless c
2Ti 2:16 Avoid godless c, because those who

CHEAT (CHEATED)
1Co 6: 8 you yourselves c and do wrong,

CHEATED (CHEAT)
Lk 19: 8 if I have c anybody out of anything,
1Co 6: 7 be wronged? Why not rather be c?

CHEEK
Mt 5:39 If anyone slaps you on the right c, turn to them the other c also.

CHEERFUL
2Co 9: 7 compulsion, for God loves a c giver.

CHILD (CHILDHOOD CHILDREN)
Mt 18: 2 He called a little c whom he placed
Lk 1:42 and blessed is the c you will bear!
1:80 And the c grew and became strong
1Co 13:11 When I was a c, I talked like a c,
1Jn 5: 1 loves the father loves his c as well.

CHILDHOOD (CHILD)
1Co 13:11 I put the ways of c behind me.

CHILDREN (CHILD)
Mt 7:11 how to give good gifts to your c,
11:25 and revealed them to little c.
18: 3 you change and become like little c,
19:14 said, "Let the little c come to me,
21:16 " 'From the lips of c and infants you
Mk 9:37 these little c in my name welcomes
10:14 to them, "Let the little c come to me,
10:16 And he took the c in his arms,
13:12 C will rebel against their parents
Lk 10:21 and revealed them to little c.
18:16 and said, "Let the little c come to me,
Jn 12:36 so that you may become c of light."
Ro 8:14 by the Spirit of God are the c of God.
8:16 with our spirit that we are God's c.
2Co 12:14 their parents, but parents for their c.
Eph 6: 1 C, obey your parents in the Lord,
6: 4 Fathers, do not exasperate your c;
Col 3:20 C, obey your parents in everything,
3:21 do not embitter your c, or they will
1Ti 3: 4 well and see that his c obey him,
3:12 wife and must manage his c and his
5:10 such as bringing up c,
Heb 12: 7 God is treating you as his c. For what c are not disciplined
1Jn 3: 1 that we should be called c of God!

CHOOSE (CHOOSES CHOSE CHOSEN)
Jn 15:16 You did not c me, but I chose you
Ac 15:14 to c a people for his name

CHOOSES (CHOOSE)
Jn 7:17 Anyone who c to do the will of God

CHOSE (CHOOSE)
Jn 15:16 but I c you and appointed you so
1Co 1:27 But God c the foolish things
1:27 God c the weak things of the world
Eph 1: 4 For he c us in him before
2Th 2:13 because God c you as firstfruits

CHOSEN (CHOOSE)
Mt 22:14 "For many are invited, but few are c."
Lk 10:42 Mary has c what is better, and it
23:35 if he is God's Messiah, the C One."
Jn 15:19 but I have c you out of the world.
1Pe 1:20 He was c before the creation
2: 9 But you are a c people, a royal

CHRIST (CHRIST'S CHRISTIAN MESSIAH)
Jn 1:41 found the Messiah" (that is, the C).
Ro 3:22 faith in Jesus C to all who believe.
5: 6 powerless, C died for the ungodly.
5: 8 we were still sinners, C died for us.
5:17 life through the one man, Jesus C!
6: 4 just as C was raised from the dead
8: 1 for those who are in C Jesus,
8: 9 does not have the Spirit of C, they do not belong to C.
8:35 separate us from the love of C?
10: 4 C is the culmination of the law so
14: 9 C died and returned to life so that he
15: 3 even C did not please himself but,
1Co 1:23 but we preach C crucified:
2: 2 while I was with you except Jesus C
3:11 one already laid, which is Jesus C.
5: 7 For C, our Passover lamb, has been
8: 6 Jesus C, through whom all things
10: 4 them, and that rock was C.
10: 9 We should not test C, as some
11: 1 as I follow the example of C.
11: 3 that the head of every man is C,
11: 3 and the head of C is God.
12:27 Now you are the body of C,
15: 3 that C died for our sins according
15:14 And if C has not been raised,
15:22 die, so in C all will be made alive.
15:57 victory through our Lord Jesus C.
2Co 3: 3 show that you are a letter from C,
4: 5 but Jesus C as Lord, and ourselves
5:10 before the judgment seat of C,
5:17 if anyone is in C, there is a new
11: 2 to C, so that I might present you as
Gal 2:20 I have been crucified with C and I
2:20 I no longer live, but C lives in me.
3:13 C redeemed us from the curse
6:14 in the cross of our Lord Jesus C,
Eph 1: 3 with every spiritual blessing in C.
3: 8 Gentiles the boundless riches of C,
4:13 whole measure of the fullness of C.
5: 2 just as C loved us and gave himself
5:23 the head of the wife as C is the head
5:25 just as C loved the church and gave
Php 1:21 to me, to live is C and to die is gain.
1:27 a manner worthy of the gospel of C.
4:19 to the riches of his glory in C Jesus.
Col 1:27 which is C in you, the hope
1:28 present everyone fully mature in C.
2: 6 as you received C Jesus as Lord,
2:17 the reality, however, is found in C.
3:15 Let the peace of C rule in your
2Th 2: 1 the coming of our Lord Jesus C
1Ti 1:15 C Jesus came into the world to save
2: 5 God and human beings, C Jesus,
2Ti 2: 3 like a good soldier of C Jesus.
3:15 salvation through faith in C Jesus.
Tit 2:13 our great God and Savior, Jesus C,
Heb 3:14 We have come to share in C,
9:14 will the blood of C, who through
9:15 For this reason C is the mediator
9:28 so C was sacrificed once to take
10:10 of the body of Jesus C once for all.
13: 8 Jesus C is the same yesterday
1Pe 1:19 but with the precious blood of C,
2:21 called, because C suffered for you,
3:18 For C also suffered once for sins,
4:14 insulted because of the name of C,
1Jn 3:16 is: Jesus C laid down his life for us.
Rev 20: 4 reigned with C a thousand years.

CHRIST'S (CHRIST)
2Co 5:14 For C love compels us, because we
5:20 We are therefore C ambassadors,
5:20 We implore you on C behalf:

2Co 12: 9 so that **C** power may rest on me.

CHRISTIAN (CHRIST)
1Pe 4:16 if you suffer as a **C**, do not be

CHURCH
Mt 16:18 and on this rock I will build my **c**,
 18:17 to listen to them, tell it to the **c**;
 18:17 if they refuse to listen even to the **c**,
Ac 20:28 Be shepherds of the **c** of God,
1Co 5:12 mine to judge those outside the **c**?
 14: 4 but those who prophesy edify the **c**.
 14:12 to excel in those that build up the **c**.
 14:26 done so that the **c** may be built up.
Eph 5:23 wife as Christ is the head of the **c**,
Col 1:24 the sake of his body, which is the **c**.

CIRCUMCISED
Ac 15: 1 "Unless you are **c**, according to the
Ro 3:30 God, who will justify the **c** by faith
Col 2:11 In him you were also **c** with a

CIRCUMSTANCES
Php 4:11 to be content whatever the **c**.
1Th 5:18 give thanks in all **c**; for this is God's

CITIZENS (CITIZENSHIP)
Eph 2:19 but fellow **c** with God's people

CITIZENSHIP (CITIZENS)
Php 3:20 But our **c** is in heaven. And we

CITY
Mt 5:14 A **c** on a hill cannot be hidden.
Heb 13:14 here we do not have an enduring **c**,

CIVILIAN
2Ti 2: 4 a soldier gets involved in **c** affairs;

CLAIM (CLAIMS)
Jas 2:14 if people **c** to have faith but have no
1Jn 1: 6 If we **c** to have fellowship with him
 1: 8 If we **c** to be without sin,
 1:10 If we **c** we have not sinned,
 2: 9 who **c** to be in the light but hate

CLAIMS (CLAIM)
1Jn 2: 6 Whoever **c** to live in him must walk

CLAY
Ro 9:21 the same lump of **c** some pottery
2Co 4: 7 this treasure in jars of **c** to show
2Ti 2:20 and silver, but also of wood and **c**;

CLEAN
Mt 12:44 swept **c** and put in order.
 23:25 You **c** the outside of the cup
Mk 7:19 this, Jesus declared all foods **c**.)
Jn 13:10 And you are **c**, though not every one
 15: 3 You are already **c** because
Ac 10:15 impure that God has made **c**."
Ro 14:20 All food is **c**, but it is wrong

CLING
Ro 12: 9 Hate what is evil; **c** to what is good.

CLOAK
Mt 9:21 only touch his **c**, I will be healed."

CLOTHE (CLOTHED CLOTHES CLOTHING)
Ro 13:14 **c** yourselves with the Lord Jesus
Col 3:12 **c** yourselves with compassion,
1Pe 5: 5 **c** yourselves with humility toward

CLOTHED (CLOTHE)
Lk 24:49 the city until you have been **c**

CLOTHES (CLOTHE)
Mt 6:25 the body more important than **c**?
 6:28 "And why do you worry about **c**?
Jn 11:44 "Take off the grave **c** and let him go."

CLOTHING (CLOTHE)
Mt 7:15 They come to you in sheep's **c**,

CLOUD (CLOUDS)
Lk 21:27 of Man coming in a **c** with power
Heb 12: 1 by such a great **c** of witnesses, let us

CLOUDS (CLOUD)
Mk 13:26 Man coming in **c** with great power
1Th 4:17 them in the **c** to meet the Lord

CO-HEIRS (INHERIT)
Ro 8:17 heirs—heirs of God and **c** with Christ,

COALS
Ro 12:20 you will heap burning **c** on his head."

COLD
Mt 10:42 anyone gives even a cup of **c** water
 24:12 the love of most will grow **c**,

COMFORT (COMFORTED COMFORTS)
1Co 14: 3 encouragement and **c**.
2Co 1: 4 so that we can **c** those in any trouble
 2: 7 you ought to forgive and **c** him,

COMFORTED (COMFORT)
Mt 5: 4 those who mourn, for they will be **c**.

COMFORTS (COMFORT)
2Co 1: 4 who **c** us in all our troubles,
 7: 6 But God, who **c** the downcast,

COMMAND (COMMANDED COMMANDING
COMMANDMENT COMMANDMENTS
COMMANDS)
Jn 13:34 "A new **c** I give you: Love one another.
 15:12 My **c** is this: Love each other as I
1Co 14:37 I am writing to you is the Lord's **c**.
Gal 5:14 is fulfilled in keeping this one **c**:
1Ti 1: 5 The goal of this **c** is love,
Heb 11: 3 the universe was formed at God's **c**,
1Jn 3:23 And this is his **c**: to believe
2Jn : 6 his **c** is that you walk in love.

COMMANDED (COMMAND)
Mt 28:20 to obey everything I have **c** you.
1Co 9:14 way, the Lord has **c** that those who
1Jn 3:23 and to love one another as he **c** us.

COMMANDING (COMMAND)
2Ti 2: 4 they try to please their **c** officer.

COMMANDMENT (COMMAND)
Mt 22:38 This is the first and greatest **c**.
Ro 7:12 and the **c** is holy,
Eph 6: 2 is the first **c** with a promise—

COMMANDMENTS (COMMAND)
Mt 5:19 sets aside one of the least of these **c**
 22:40 the Prophets hang on these two **c**."

COMMANDS (COMMAND)
Mt 5:19 teaches these **c** will be called great
Jn 14:15 "If you love me, keep my **c**.
 14:21 Whoever has my **c** and keeps them
Ac 17:30 now he **c** all people everywhere
1Co 7:19 Keeping God's **c** is what counts.
1Jn 5: 3 this is love for God: to keep his **c**. And his **c**
 are not burdensome,

COMMEND (COMMENDED COMMENDS)
1Pe 2:14 wrong and to c those who do right.

COMMENDED (COMMEND)
Ro 13: 3 do what is right and you will be c.
Heb 11:39 These were all c for their faith,

COMMENDS (COMMEND)
2Co 10:18 but those whom the Lord c.

COMMIT (COMMITS COMMITTED)
Mt 5:27 that it was said, 'Do not c adultery.'
Lk 23:46 into your hands I c my spirit."
Ac 20:32 "Now I c you to God and to the word
1Co 10: 8 We should not c sexual immorality,
1Pe 4:19 to God's will should c themselves

COMMITS (COMMIT)
Mt 19: 9 marries another woman c adultery."

COMMITTED (COMMIT)
Mt 5:28 lustfully has already c adultery
2Co 5:19 And he has c to us the message
1Pe 2:22 "He c no sin, and no deceit was

COMMON
1Co 10:13 has overtaken you except what is c
2Co 6:14 and wickedness have in c? Or what

COMPANY
1Co 15:33 "Bad c corrupts good character."

COMPARED (COMPARING)
Ro 5:16 Nor can the gift of God be c with

COMPARING (COMPARED)
Ro 8:18 present sufferings are not worth c
2Co 8: 8 of your love by c it
Gal 6: 4 without c yourself to somebody

COMPASSION (COMPASSIONATE)
Mt 9:36 saw the crowds, he had c on them,
Mk 8: 2 "I have c for these people; they have
Ro 9:15 and I will have c on whom I have c."
Col 3:12 clothe yourselves with c, kindness,
Jas 5:11 The Lord is full of c and mercy.

COMPASSIONATE (COMPASSION)
Eph 4:32 Be kind and c to one another,
1Pe 3: 8 love one another, be c and humble.

COMPELL (COMPELLED COMPELS)
Lk 14:23 c them to come in, so that my house

COMPELLED (COMPEL)
Ac 20:22 "And now, c by the Spirit, I am
1Co 9:16 cannot boast, since I am c to preach.

COMPELS (COMPELL)
2Co 5:14 For Christ's love c us, because we

COMPETENCE (COMPETENT)
2Co 3: 5 but our c comes from God.

COMPETENT (COMPETENCE)
Ro 15:14 and c to instruct one another.
1Co 6: 2 are you not c to judge trivial cases?
2Co 3: 5 Not that we are c in ourselves
3: 6 He has made us c as ministers

COMPETES
1Co 9:25 Everyone who c in the games goes
2Ti 2: 5 anyone who c as an athlete does not
2: 5 anyone who c as an athlete does not

COMPLETE
Jn 15:11 in you and that your joy may be c.
16:24 will receive, and your joy will be c.
17:23 that they may be brought to c unity.
Ac 20:24 c the task the Lord Jesus has given
Php 2: 2 then make my joy c by being
Col 4:17 you c the work you have received
Jas 1: 4 so that you may be mature and c,
2:22 his faith was made c by what he did.

CONCEALED
Mt 10:26 There is nothing c that will not be
Mk 4:22 whatever is c is meant to be brought

CONCEITED
Gal 5:26 Let us not become c,
1Ti 6: 4 they are c and understand nothing.

CONCEIVE (CONCEIVED)
Mt 1:23 "The virgin will c and give birth

CONCEIVED (CONCEIVE)
Mt 1:20 because what is c in her is
1Co 2: 9 human mind has c— these things God

CONCERN (CONCERNED)
1Co 7:32 I would like you to be free from c.
12:25 that its parts should have equal c
2Co 11:28 of my c for all the churches.

CONCERNED (CONCERN)
1Co 7:32 An unmarried man is c

CONDEMN (CONDEMNATION CONDEMNED
    CONDEMNING)
Lk 6:37 Do not c, and you will not be
Jn 3:17 Son into the world to c the world,
12:48 words I have spoken will c them
Ro 2:27 yet obeys the law will c you who,
8:34 Who then can c? No one.
1Jn 3:20 If our hearts c us, we know that God

CONDEMNATION (CONDEMN)
Ro 5:18 just as one trespass resulted in c
8: 1 there is now no c for those who are
2Co 3: 9 If the ministry that brought c

CONDEMNED (CONDEMN)
Mt 12:37 and by your words you will be c."
23:33 How will you escape being c
Jn 3:18 Whoever believes in him is not c,
3:18 not believe stands c already because
16:11 prince of this world now stands c.
Ro 14:23 those who have doubts are c if they
1Co 11:32 that we will not be finally c
Heb 11: 7 By his faith he c the world

CONDEMNING (CONDEMN)
Ro 2: 1 you are c yourself, because you who

CONDUCT
1Ti 3:15 how people ought to c themselves

CONFESS (CONFESSION)
Jas 5:16 Therefore c your sins to each other
1Jn 1: 9 If we c our sins, he is faithful

CONFESSION (CONFESS)
2Co 9:13 accompanies your c of the gospel

CONFIDENCE
Php 3: 3 Jesus, and who put no c in the flesh—
Heb 4:16 God's throne of grace with c,
10:19 since we have c to enter the Most
10:35 So do not throw away your c; it will
13:17 Have c in your leaders and submit

1Jn 5:14 This is the c we have

CONFIRM
2Pe 1:10 make every effort to c your calling

CONFORM (CONFORMED)
Ro 12: 2 Do not c to the pattern of this world,
1Pe 1:14 do not c to the evil desires you had

CONFORMED (CONFORM)
Ro 8:29 predestined to be c to the likeness

CONQUERORS
Ro 8:37 are more than c through him who

CONSCIENCE (CONSCIENCES)
Ro 13: 5 but also as a matter of c.
1Co 8: 7 idol, and since their c is weak, it is
     8:12 in this way and wound their weak c,
     10:25 without raising questions of c,
     10:29 being judged by another's c?
Heb 10:22 to cleanse us from a guilty c
1Pe 3:16 keeping a clear c, so that those who

CONSCIENCES (CONSCIENCE)
Ro 2:15 hearts, their c also bearing witness,
1Ti 4: 2 whose c have been seared as
Tit 1:15 their minds and c are corrupted.
Heb 9:14 cleanse our c from acts that lead

CONSCIOUS
Ro 3:20 through the law we become c of our
1Pe 2:19 unjust suffering because you are c

CONSECRATED
1Ti 4: 5 because it is c by the word of God

CONSIDER (CONSIDERATE CONSIDERED)
Lk 12:24 C the ravens: They do not sow
     12:27 "C how the lilies grow. They do not
Ro 14: 5 Some c one day more sacred
Php 3: 8 I c everything a loss because
Heb 10:24 And let us c how we may spur one
Jas 1: 2 C it pure joy, my brothers
     1:26 Those who c themselves religious

CONSIDERATE (CONSIDER)
Tit 3: 2 to be peaceable and c, and always
Jas 3:17 then peace-loving, c, submissive,
1Pe 2:18 only to those who are good and c,
     3: 7 the same way be c as you live

CONSIDERED (CONSIDER)
Ro 8:36 we are c as sheep to be slaughtered."

CONSIST
Lk 12:15 life does not c in an abundance

CONSTRUCTIVE
1Co 10:23 do anything"—but not everything is c.

CONSUME (CONSUMING)
Jn 2:17 "Zeal for your house will c me."

CONSUMING (CONSUME)
Heb 12:29 for our "God is a c fire."

CONTAIN
2Pe 3:16 His letters c some things that are

CONTAMINATES
2Co 7: 1 from everything that c body

CONTEMPLATE
2Co 3:18 unveiled faces c the Lord's glory,

CONTEMPT
Ro 2: 4 do you show c for the riches of his
Gal 4:14 you did not treat me with c or scorn.
1Th 5:20 Do not treat prophecies with c

CONTEND
Jude : 3 urge you to c for the faith

CONTENT (CONTENTMENT)
Php 4:11 to be c whatever the circumstances.
     4:12 learned the secret of being c in any
1Ti 6: 8 and clothing, we will be c with that.
Heb 13: 5 and be c with what you have,

CONTENTMENT (CONTENT)
1Ti 6: 6 But godliness with c is great gain.

CONTINUE
Php 2:12 now much more in my a to work
2Ti 3:14 c in what you have learned and have
1Jn 5:18 who are born of God do not c to sin;
Rev 22:11 let those who are holy c to be holy."

CONTROL (CONTROLLED SELF-CONTROL SELF-CONTROLLED)
1Co 7: 9 But if they cannot c themselves,
     7:37 but has c over his own will,
1Th 4: 4 should learn to c your own body

CONTROLLED (CONTROL)
Ro 8: 6 The mind c by the sinful nature is
     8: 6 but the mind c by the Spirit is life
     8: 8 Those c by the sinful nature cannot

CONTROVERSIES
Tit 3: 9 But avoid foolish c and genealogies

CONVERSATION
Col 4: 6 Let your c be always full of grace,

CONVERT
1Ti 3: 6 He must not be a recent c, or he

CONVICT
Jude :15 to c all the ungodly of all the

CONVICTION
Heb 3:14 hold firmly till the end our original c.

CONVINCED (CONVINCING)
Ro 8:38 I am c that neither death nor life,
2Ti 1:12 am c that he is able to guard what I
     3:14 have learned and have become c of,

CONVINCING (CONVINCED)
Ac 1: 3 and gave many c proofs that he was

CORNELIUS
Roman to whom Peter preached; first Gentile Christian (Ac 10).

CORNERSTONE (STONE)
Mk 12:10 builders rejected has become the c;
Eph 2:20 Christ Jesus himself as the chief c.
1Pe 2: 6 a chosen and precious c, and the one

CORRECT (CORRECTING)
2Ti 4: 2 c, rebuke and encourage—with great

CORRECTING (CORRECT)
2Ti 3:16 c and training in righteousness,

CORRUPT (CORRUPTS)
Ac 2:40 yourselves from this c generation."

CORRUPTS (CORRUPT)
1Co 15:33 "Bad company **c** good character."
Jas 3: 6 It **c** the whole person, sets the whole

COST
Rev 21: 6 thirsty I will give water without **c**

COUNSEL
Rev 3:18 I **c** you to buy from me gold refined

COUNSELOR See ADVOCATE

COUNT (COUNTING COUNTS)
Ro 4: 8 the Lord will never **c** against them."
     6:11 **c** yourselves dead to sin but alive

COUNTING (COUNT)
2Co 5:19 not **c** people's sins against them.

COUNTRY
Jn 4:44 have no honor in their own **c**.)

COUNTS (COUNT)
Jn 6:63 gives life; the flesh **c** for nothing.
1Co 7:19 Keeping God's commands is what **c**.
Gal 5: 6 **c** is faith expressing itself through

COURAGE (COURAGEOUS)
Ac 23:11 stood near Paul and said, "Take **c**!

COURAGEOUS (COURAGE)
1Co 16:13 stand firm in the faith; be **c**;

COVENANT (COVENANTS)
1Co 11:25 "This cup is the new **c** in my blood;
Gal 4:24 One **c** is from Mount Sinai
Heb 9:15 Christ is the mediator of a new **c**,

COVENANTS (COVENANT)
Ro 9: 4 the **c**, the receiving of the law,
Gal 4:24 for the women represent two **c**.

COVER (COVER-UP COVERED COVERS)
Jas 5:20 death and **c** over a multitude of sins.

COVER-UP (COVER)
1Pe 2:16 do not use your freedom as a **c**

COVERED (COVER)
Ro 4: 7 are forgiven, whose sins are **c**.
1Co 11: 4 with his head **c** dishonors his head.

COVERS (COVER)
1Pe 4: 8 because love **c** over a multitude

COVET
Ro 13: 9 steal," "Do not **c**," and whatever other

COWARDLY
Rev 21: 8 But the **c**, the unbelieving, the vile,

CRAFTINESS (CRAFTY)
1Co 3:19 "He catches the wise in their **c**";

CRAFTY (CRAFTINESS)
2Co 12:16 Yet, **c** fellow that I am, I caught you

CRAVE
1Pe 2: 2 babies, **c** pure spiritual milk,

CREATE (CREATED CREATION CREATOR)
Eph 2:15 to **c** in himself one new humanity

CREATED (CREATE)
Ro 1:25 and served **c** things rather than
1Co 11: 9 neither was man **c** for woman,

Col 1:16 For in him all things were **c**:
1Ti 4: 4 For everything God **c** is good,
Rev 10: 6 who **c** the heavens and all that is

CREATION (CREATE)
Mk 16:15 world and preach the gospel to all **c**.
Jn 17:24 because you loved me before the **c**
Ro 8:19 The **c** waits in eager expectation
     8:39 nor anything else in all **c**, will be
2Co 5:17 anyone is in Christ, there is a new **c**:
Col 1:15 God, the firstborn over all **c**.
1Pe 1:20 He was chosen before the **c**
Rev 13: 8 was slain from the **c** of the world.

CREATOR (CREATE)
Ro 1:25 served created things rather than the **C**—

CREDIT (CREDITED)
Ro 4:24 whom God will **c**
1Pe 2:20 it to your **c** if you receive a beating

CREDITED (CREDIT)
Ro 4: 5 their faith is **c** as righteousness.
Gal 3: 6 and it was **c** to him as righteousness."
Jas 2:23 and it was **c** to him as righteousness,"

CRIPPLED
Mk 9:45 to enter life **c** than to have two feet

CRITICISM
2Co 8:20 want to avoid any **c** of the way we

CROOKED
Php 2:15 fault in a warped and **c** generation."

CROSS
Mt 10:38 Those who do not take up their **c**
Lk 9:23 take up their **c** daily and follow me.
Ac 2:23 him to death by nailing him to the **c**.
1Co 1:17 lest the **c** of Christ be emptied of its
Gal 6:14 in the **c** of our Lord Jesus Christ,
Php 2: 8 obedient to death— even death on a **c**!
Col 1:20 through his blood, shed on the **c**.
     2:14 has taken it away, nailing it to the **c**.
     2:15 triumphing over them by the **c**.
Heb 12: 2 joy set before him he endured the **c**,

CROWN (CROWNED CROWNS)
Mt 27:29 then twisted together a **c** of thorns
1Co 9:25 do it to get a **c** that will last forever.
2Ti 4: 8 store for me the **c** of righteousness,
Rev 2:10 I will give you life as your victor's **c**.

CROWNED (CROWN)
Heb 2: 7 you **c** them with glory and honor

CROWNS (CROWN)
Rev 4:10 They lay their **c** before the throne
     19:12 fire, and on his head are many **c**.

CRUCIFIED (CRUCIFY)
Mt 20:19 to be mocked and flogged and **c**.
     27:38 Two rebels were **c** with him,
Lk 24: 7 be **c** and on the third day be raised
Jn 19:18 Here they **c** him, and with him two
Ac 2:36 Jesus, whom you **c**, both Lord
Ro 6: 6 that our old self was **c** with him so
1Co 1:23 but we preach Christ **c**: a stumbling
     2: 2 you except Jesus Christ and him **c**.
Gal 2:20 I have been **c** with Christ and I no
     5:24 Christ Jesus have **c** the sinful nature

CRUCIFY (CRUCIFIED CRUCIFYING)
Mt 27:22 asked. They all answered, "**C** him!"
     27:31 Then they led him away to **c** him.

CRUCIFYING (CRUCIFY)
Heb 6: 6 their loss they are **c** the Son of God

CRUSH (CRUSHED)
Ro 16:20 peace will soon **c** Satan under your

CRUSHED (CRUSH)
2Co 4: 8 pressed on every side, but not **c**;

CULMINATION
Ro 10: 4 Christ is the **c** of the law

CUP
Mt 10:42 anyone gives even a **c** of cold water
23:25 You clean the outside of the **c**
26:39 may this **c** be taken from me.
1Co 11:25 "This **c** is the new covenant in my

CURSE (CURSED)
Lk 6:28 bless those who **c** you,
Gal 1: 8 let that person be under God's **c**!
3:13 redeemed us from the **c** of the law by
becoming a **c** for us,
Rev 22: 3 No longer will there be any **c**.

CURSED (CURSE)
Ro 9: 3 I could wish that I myself were **c**
Gal 3:10 written: "**C** is everyone who does not

CURTAIN
Lk 23:45 the **c** of the temple was torn in two.
Heb 10:20 way opened for us through the **c**,

CYMBAL
1Co 13: 1 a resounding gong or a clanging **c**.

DANCE
Mt 11:17 the flute for you, and you did not **d**;

DANGER
Ro 8:35 famine or nakedness or **d** or sword?

DANIEL
Mt 24:15 spoken of through the prophet **D**—

DARK (DARKNESS)
Ro 2:19 a light for those who are in the **d**,
2Pe 1:19 it, as to a light shining in a **d** place,

DARKNESS (DARK)
Jn 3:19 but people loved **d** instead of light
2Co 6:14 fellowship can light have with **d**?
Eph 5: 8 For you were once **d**, but now you
1Pe 2: 9 out of **d** into his wonderful light.
1Jn 1: 5 is light; in him there is no **d** at all.
2: 9 a fellow believer are still in the **d**.

DAUGHTERS
Ac 2:17 Your sons and **d** will prophesy,
21: 9 four unmarried **d** who prophesied.
2Co 6:18 and you will be my sons and **d**,

DAVID
Son of Jesse, ancestor of Jesus (Mt 1:1-17; Lk 3:31; Ro 1:3;
Rev 5:5; 22:16).
Psalmist (Mt 22:43-45), prophet (Ac 1:16; 2:30).

DAY (DAYS)
Lk 11: 3 Give us each **d** our daily bread.
Ac 17:11 examined the Scriptures every **d**
2Co 4:16 we are being renewed **d** by **d**.
1Th 5: 2 the **d** of the Lord will come like
2Pe 3: 8 With the Lord a **d** is like a thousand

DAYS (DAY)
Heb 1: 2 in these last **d** he has spoken to us

2Pe 3: 3 that in the last **d** scoffers will come,

DEACONS
1Ti 3: 8 way, **d** are to be worthy of respect,

DEAD (DIE)
Mt 28: 7 'He has risen from the **d** and is going
Ro 6:11 count yourselves **d** to sin but alive
Eph 2: 1 you were **d** in your transgressions
1Th 4:16 and the **d** in Christ will rise first.
Jas 2:17 is not accompanied by action, is **d**.
2:26 As the body without the spirit is **d**, so faith
without deeds is **d**.

DEATH (DIE)
Jn 5:24 but has crossed over from **d** to life.
Ro 5:12 and **d** through sin, and in this way **d**
6:23 For the wages of sin is **d**,
8:13 the Spirit you put to **d** the misdeeds
1Co 15:21 For since **d** came through a human
15:31 I face **d** every day—yes, just as surely
15:55 "Where, O **d**, is your victory? Where, O **d**, is
your sting?"
1Pe 3:18 He was put to **d** in the body but made
Rev 1:18 And I hold the keys of **d** and Hades.
20: 6 The second **d** has no power over
20:14 Then **d** and Hades were thrown
20:14 The lake of fire is the second **d**.
21: 4 eyes. There will be no more **d'**

DEBAUCHERY
Ro 13:13 not in sexual immorality and **d**,
Eph 5:18 get drunk on wine, which leads to **d**.

DEBT (DEBTORS DEBTS)
Ro 13: 8 Let no **d** remain outstanding, except the
continuing **d** to love one

DEBTORS (DEBT)
Mt 6:12 as we also have forgiven our **d**.

DEBTS (DEBT)
Mt 6:12 And forgive us our **d**, as we

DECAY
Ac 2:27 will not let your Holy One see **d**.

DECEIT (DECEIVE)
Mk 7:22 greed, malice, **d**, lewdness, envy,
1Pe 2: 1 yourselves of all malice and all **d**,
2:22 and no **d** was found in his mouth."

DECEITFUL (DECEIVE)
2Co 11:13 are false apostles, **d** workers,

DECEITFULNESS (DECEIVE)
Mk 4:19 the **d** of wealth and the desires
Heb 3:13 of you may be hardened by sin's **d**.

DECEIVE (DECEIT DECEITFUL DECEITFULNESS
DECEIVED DECEIVES DECEPTIVE)
Mt 24: 5 'I am the Messiah,' and will **d** many.
Ro 16:18 flattery they **d** the minds of naive
1Co 3:18 Do not **d** yourselves. If any of you
Gal 6: 3 you are nothing, you **d** yourselves.
Eph 5: 6 Let no one **d** you with empty words,
Jas 1:22 to the word, and so **d** yourselves.
1:26 rein on their tongues **d** themselves,
1Jn 1: 8 we **d** ourselves and the truth is not

DECEIVED (DECEIVE)
Gal 6: 7 Do not be **d**: God cannot be
1Ti 2:14 And Adam was not the one **d**; it was the
woman who was **d**
2Ti 3:13 to worse, deceiving and being **d**.
Jas 1:16 Don't be **d**, my dear brothers

DECEIVES (DECEIVE)
Mk 13: 5 "Watch out that no one **d** you.

DECENCY
1Ti 2: 9 modestly, with **d** and propriety,

DECEPTIVE (DECEIVE)
Col 2: 8 through hollow and **d** philosophy,

DECLARE (DECLARED DECLARING)
Ro 10: 9 **d** with your mouth, "Jesus is Lord,"

DECLARED (DECLARE)
Mk 7:19 saying this, Jesus **d** all foods clean.)
Ro 2:13 the law who will be **d** righteous.
3:20 Therefore no one will be **d** righteous

DECLARING (DECLARE)
Ac 2:11 Arabs—we hear them **d** the wonders

DECREED (DECREES)
Lk 22:22 Son of Man will go as it has been **d**.

DEDICATION
1Ti 5:11 sensual desires overcome their **d**

DEED (DEEDS)
Col 3:17 whether in word or **d**, do it all

DEEDS (DEED)
Mt 5:16 that they may see your good **d**
Ac 26:20 their repentance by their deeds.
Jas 2:14 claim to have faith but have no **d**?
2:20 that faith without **d** is useless?
1Pe 2:12 they may see your good **d**

DEEP (DEPTH)
1Co 2:10 all things, even the **d** things of God.
1Ti 3: 9 They must keep hold of the **d** truths

DEFEND (DEFENSE)
Lk 12:11 do not worry about how you will **d**

DEFENSE (DEFEND)
Php 1:16 I am put here for the **d** of the gospel.

DEFILE
Mt 15:11 What goes into your mouth does not **d**

DEITY
Col 2: 9 Christ all the fullness of the **D** lives

DELIGHT
Mt 12:18 chosen, the one I love, in whom I **d**;
1Co 13: 6 Love does not **d** in evil but rejoices
2Co 12:10 for Christ's sake, I **d** in weaknesses,

DELIVER (DELIVERED DELIVERER)
Mt 6:13 but **d** us from the evil one.'
2Co 1:10 hope that he will continue to **d** us,

DELIVERED (DELIVER)
Ro 4:25 He was **d** over to death for our sins

DELIVERER (DELIVER)
Ro 11:26 "The **d** will come from Zion;

DEMANDED
Lk 12:20 This very night your life will be **d**
12:48 been given much, much will be **d**;

DEMONS
Mt 12:27 And if I drive out **d** by Beelzebul,
Mk 5:15 been possessed by the legion of **d**,
Ro 8:38 life, neither angels nor **d**,
Jas 2:19 Even the **d** believe that—and shudder.

DEMONSTRATE (DEMONSTRATES)
Ac 26:20 **d** their repentance by their deeds.
Ro 3:26 he did it to **d** his justice

DEMONSTRATES (DEMONSTRATE)
Ro 5: 8 God **d** his own love for us in this:

DEN
Mt 21:13 but you are making it 'a **d** of robbers.'"

DENARIUS
Mk 12:15 "Bring me a **d** and let me look at it."

DENIED (DENY)
1Ti 5: 8 has **d** the faith and is worse than

DENIES (DENY)
1Jn 2:23 No one who **d** the Son has

DENY (DENIED DENIES DENYING)
Lk 9:23 be my disciples must **d** themselves
Tit 1:16 but by their actions they **d** him.

DENYING (DENY)
2Ti 3: 5 a form of godliness but **d** its power.
2Pe 2: 1 even **d** the sovereign Lord who

DEPART (DEPARTED)
Mt 25:41 say to those on his left, '**D** from me,
Php 1:23 I desire to **d** and be with Christ,

DEPARTED (DEPART)
1Ti 6:21 in so doing have **d** from the faith.

DEPOSIT
2Co 1:22 put his Spirit in our hearts as a **d**,
5: 5 who has given us the Spirit as a **d**,
Eph 1:14 who is a **d** guaranteeing our
2Ti 1:14 Guard the good **d** that was entrusted

DEPRAVED (DEPRAVITY)
Ro 1:28 so God gave them over to a **d** mind,
2Pe 2: 7 who was distressed by the **d** conduct

DEPRAVITY (DEPRAVED)
Ro 1:29 of wickedness, evil, greed and **d**.

DEPRIVE
1Co 7: 5 Do not **d** each other except perhaps

DEPTH (DEEP)
Ro 8:39 neither height nor **d**, nor anything
11:33 the **d** of the riches of the wisdom

DESERT
Mk 1:13 and he was in the **d** forty days,

DESERTED (DESERTING)
Mt 26:56 all the disciples **d** him and fled.
2Ti 1:15 in the province of Asia has **d** me,

DESERTING (DESERTED)
Gal 1: 6 you are so quickly **d** the one who

DESERVE
Mt 22: 8 those I invited did not **d** to come.
Lk 10: 7 for workers **d** their wages.
Ro 1:32 those who do such things **d** death,
1Ti 5:18 and "Workers **d** their wages."

DESIRE (DESIRES)
Mt 9:13 this means: 'I **d** mercy, not sacrifice.'
Ro 7:18 For I have the **d** to do what is good,
1Co 12:31 Now eagerly **d** the greater gifts.
14: 1 of love and eagerly **d** spiritual gifts,
Php 1:23 I **d** to depart and be with Christ,

Heb 13:18 **d** to live honorably in every way.
Jas 1:15 after **d** has conceived, it gives birth

DESIRES (DESIRE)
Mk 4:19 and the **d** for other things come
Ro 8: 5 minds set on what that nature **d;**
8: 5 their minds set on what the Spirit **d.**
13:14 to gratify the **d** of the sinful nature.
Gal 5:16 and you will not gratify the **d**
5:17 the sinful nature **d** what is contrary
1Ti 3: 1 to be an overseer **d** a noble task.
6: 9 harmful **d** that plunge people
2Ti 2:22 Flee the evil **d** of youth and pursue
Jas 1:20 the righteousness that God **d.**
4: 1 from your **d** that battle within you?
1Pe 2:11 to abstain from sinful **d,** which war
1Jn 2:17 The world and its **d** pass away,

DESPAIR
2Co 4: 8 not crushed; perplexed, but not in **d;**

DESPISE (DESPISED DESPISES)
Lk 16:13 devoted to the one and **d** the other.
Tit 2:15 authority. Do not let anyone **d** you.

DESPISED
1Co 1:28 the **d** things—and the things that are

DESTINED
Lk 2:34 "This child is **d** to cause the falling

DESTITUTE
Heb 11:37 in sheepskins and goatskins, **d,**

DESTROY (DESTROYED DESTROYS DESTRUCTION)
Mt 10:28 of the One who can **d** both soul

DESTROYED (DESTROY)
1Co 8:11 Christ died, is **d** by your knowledge.
15:26 The last enemy to be **d** is death.
2Co 5: 1 if the earthly tent we live in is **d,**
Heb 10:39 of those who shrink back and are **d,**
2Pe 3:10 the elements will be **d** by fire,

DESTROYS (DESTROY)
1Co 3:17 If anyone **d** God's temple, God will

DESTRUCTION (DESTROY)
Mt 7:13 and broad is the road that leads to **d,**
Gal 6: 8 nature, from that nature will reap **d;**
2Th 1: 9 will be punished with everlasting **d**
1Ti 6: 9 that plunge people into ruin and **d.**
2Pe 2: 1 who bought them—bringing swift **d**
3:16 the other Scriptures, to their own **d.**

DETERMINES
1Co 12:11 them to each one, just as he **d.**

DETESTABLE
Lk 16:15 What people value highly is **d**
Tit 1:16 They are **d,** disobedient and unfit

DEVIL (DEVIL'S)
Mt 13:39 the enemy who sows them is the **d.**
25:41 the eternal fire prepared for the **d**
Lk 4: 2 forty days he was tempted by the **d.**
8:12 then the **d** comes and takes away
Eph 4:27 and do not give the **d** a foothold.
2Ti 2:26 and escape from the trap of the **d,**
Jas 4: 7 Resist the **d,** and he will flee
1Pe 5: 8 Your enemy the **d** prowls around
1Jn 3: 8 who does what is sinful is of the **d,**
3: 8 because the **d** has been sinning
Rev 12: 9 ancient serpent called the **d,**

DEVIL'S (DEVIL)
Eph 6:11 your stand against the **d** schemes.
1Ti 3: 7 fall into disgrace and into the **d** trap.
1Jn 3: 8 appeared was to destroy the **d** work.

DEVOTE (DEVOTED DEVOTING DEVOTION DEVOUT)
Col 4: 2 **D** yourselves to prayer,
1Ti 4:13 **d** yourself to the public reading
Tit 3: 8 God may be careful to **d** themselves

DEVOTED (DEVOTE)
Ac 2:42 They **d** themselves to the apostles'
Ro 12:10 Be **d** to one another in love.
1Co 7:34 Her aim is to be **d** to the Lord

DEVOTING (DEVOTE)
1Ti 5:10 **d** herself to all kinds of good deeds.

DEVOTION (DEVOTE)
1Co 7:35 way in undivided **d** to the Lord.
2Co 11: 3 your sincere and pure **d** to Christ.

DEVOUR
Mk 12:40 They **d** widows' houses
1Pe 5: 8 lion looking for someone to **d.**

DEVOUT (DEVOTE)
Lk 2:25 Simeon, who was righteous and **d.**

DIE (DEAD DEATH DIED DIES)
Mt 26:52 "for all who draw the sword will **d**
Jn 11:26 and believes in me will never **d.**
Ro 5: 7 someone might possibly dare to **d.**
14: 8 and if we **d,** we **d** to the Lord.
1Co 15:22 For as in Adam all **d,** so in Christ all
Php 1:21 me, to live is Christ and to **d** is gain.
Heb 9:27 as people are destined to **d** once,
Rev 14:13 Blessed are the dead who **d**

DIED (DIE)
Ro 5: 6 powerless, Christ **d** for the ungodly.
6: 2 We are those who have **d** to sin;
6: 8 Now if we **d** with Christ, we believe
14:15 brother or sister for whom Christ **d.**
1Co 8:11 for whom Christ **d,** is destroyed
15: 3 that Christ **d** for our sins according
2Co 5:14 one **d** for all, and therefore all **d.**
Col 3: 3 For you **d,** and your life is now
1Th 5:10 He **d** for us so that, whether we are
2Ti 2:11 If we **d** with him, we will also live
Heb 9:15 that he has **d** as a ransom to set
Rev 2: 8 Last, who **d** and came to life again.

DIES (DIE)
1Co 15:36 does not come to life unless it **d.**

DIFFERENCE (DIFFERENT)
Ro 10:12 For there is no **d** between Jew

DIFFERENT (DIFFERENCE)
1Co 12: 4 There are **d** kinds of gifts,
2Co 11: 4 or a **d** gospel from the one you

DILIGENCE (DILIGENT)
Heb 6:11 to show this same **d** to the very end,

DILIGENT (DILIGENCE)
1Ti 4:15 Be **d** in these matters; give yourself

DIRECT
2Th 3: 5 May the Lord **d** your hearts

DIRGE
Mt 11:17 we sang a **d,** and you did not mourn.'

DISAPPEAR
Mt 5:18 until heaven and earth **d**, not the
Lk 16:17 earth to **d** than for the least stroke

DISCERN (DISCERNING)
Php 1:10 you may be able to **d** what is best

DISCERNING (DISCERN)
1Co 11:29 drink without **d** the body of Christ

DISCIPLE (DISCIPLES)
Mt 10:42 little ones who is known to be my **d**,

DISCIPLES (DISCIPLE)
Mt 28:19 go and make **d** of all nations,
Lk 14:27 and follow me cannot be my **d**.
Jn 8:31 to my teaching, you are really my **d**.
 13:35 will know that you are my **d**, if you
Ac 11:26 The **d** were called Christians first

DISCIPLINE (DISCIPLINED DISCIPLINES)
Heb 12: 5 do not make light of the Lord's **d**,
 12: 7 Endure hardship as **d**; God is
 12:11 No **d** seems pleasant at the time,
Rev 3:19 Those whom I love I rebuke and **d**.

DISCIPLINED (DISCIPLINE)
1Co 11:32 we are being **d** so that we will not
Col 2: 5 delight to see how **d** you are
Tit 1: 8 self-controlled, upright, holy and **d**.
Heb 12: 7 For what children are not **d** by their

DISCIPLINES (DISCIPLINE)
Heb 12: 6 because the Lord **d** those he loves,
 12:10 but God **d** us for our good, that we

DISCLOSED
Lk 8:17 is nothing hidden that will not be **d**,

DISCOURAGED
Col 3:21 children, or they will become **d**.

DISCREDITED
2Co 6: 3 so that our ministry will not be **d**.

DISCRIMINATED
Jas 2: 4 have you not **d** among yourselves

DISGRACE
Ac 5:41 worthy of suffering **d** for the Name.
Heb 13:13 the camp, bearing the **d** he bore.

DISHONEST
Lk 16:10 whoever is **d** with very little will
1Ti 3: 8 much wine, and not pursuing **d** gain.

DISHONOR (DISHONORS)
1Co 13: 5 It does not **d** others, it is not
 15:43 it is sown in **d**, it is raised in glory;

DISHONORS (DISHONOR)
1Co 11: 4 with his head covered **d** his head.

DISOBEDIENCE (DISOBEY)
Ro 5:19 just as through the **d** of the one man
 11:32 has bound everyone over to **d** so
Heb 2: 2 and **d** received its just punishment,
 4: 6 did not go in because of their **d**,
 4:11 by following their example of **d**.

DISOBEDIENT (DISOBEY)
2Ti 3: 2 proud, abusive, **d** to their parents,
Tit 1: 6 to the charge of being wild and **d**.
 1:16 **d** and unfit for doing anything good.

DISOBEY (DISOBEDIENCE DISOBEDIENT)
Ro 1:30 of doing evil; they **d** their parents;

DISORDER
1Co 14:33 For God is not a God of **d**
2Co 12:20 slander, gossip, arrogance and **d**.
Jas 3:16 there you find **d** and every evil

DISOWN
Mt 10:33 me I will **d** before my Father
 26:35 to die with you, I will never **d** you."
2Ti 2:12 him. If we **d** him, he will also **d** us;

DISPLAY
1Ti 1:16 Christ Jesus might **d** his immense

DISPUTE
1Co 6: 1 If any of you has a **d** with another,

DISQUALIFIED
1Co 9:27 I myself will not be **d** for the prize.

DISREPUTE
2Pe 2: 2 will bring the way of truth into **d**.

DISSENSION
Ro 13:13 debauchery, not in **d** and jealousy.

DISSIPATION
Lk 21:34 hearts will be weighed down with **d**,

DISTINGUISH
Heb 5:14 have trained themselves to **d** good

DISTORT
2Co 4: 2 nor do we **d** the word of God.
2Pe 3:16 ignorant and unstable people **d**,

DISTRESS (DISTRESSED)
Jas 1:27 and widows in their **d** and to keep

DISTRESSED (DISTRESS)
Ro 14:15 sister is **d** because of what you eat,

DIVIDED (DIVISION)
Mt 12:25 "Every kingdom **d** against itself will
Lk 23:34 they **d** up his clothes by casting lots.
1Co 1:13 Is Christ **d**? Was Paul crucified

DIVINE
Ro 1:20 and **d** nature—have been clearly seen,
2Co 10: 4 they have **d** power to demolish
2Pe 1: 4 you may participate in the **d** nature,

DIVISION (DIVIDED DIVISIONS DIVISIVE)
Lk 12:51 peace on earth? No, I tell you, but **d**.
1Co 12:25 there should be no **d** in the body,

DIVISIONS (DIVISION)
Ro 16:17 to watch out for those who cause **d**
1Co 1:10 and that there be no **d** among you,
 11:18 as a church, there are **d** among you,

DIVISIVE (DIVISION)
Tit 3:10 Warn **d** people once, and then warn

DIVORCE
Mt 19: 3 for a man to **d** his wife for any
1Co 7:11 And a husband must not **d** his wife.

DOCTOR
Mt 9:12 "It is not the healthy who need a **d**,

DOCTRINE
1Ti 4:16 Watch your life and **d** closely.
Tit 2: 1 what is appropriate to sound **d**.

DOMINION
Eph 1:21 all rule and authority, power and **d**,

DOOR
Mt   6: 6 close the **d** and pray to your Father,
      7: 7 and the **d** will be opened to you.
Rev 3:20 I stand at the **d** and knock.

DOUBLE-EDGED
Heb 4:12 active. Sharper than any **d** sword,
Rev 1:16 of his mouth was a sharp, **d** sword.
      2:12 of him who has the sharp, **d** sword.

DOUBLE-MINDED (MIND)
Jas   1: 8 they are **d** and unstable in all they

DOUBT
Mt 14:31 little faith," he said, "why did you **d**?"
     21:21 if you have faith and do not **d**,
Mk 11:23 sea,' and do not **d** in your heart
Jas   1. 6 you must believe and not **d**,
Jude :22 Be merciful to those who **d**;

DOWNCAST
2Co 7: 6 who comforts the **d**, comforted us

DRAW (DRAWING DRAWS)
Mt 26:52 "for all who **d** the sword will die
Jn 12:32 earth, will **d** all people to myself."
Heb 10:22 let us **d** near to God with a sincere

DRAWING (DRAW)
Lk 21:28 because your redemption is **d** near."

DRAWS (DRAW)
Jn   6:44 the Father who sent me **d** them,

DREADFUL
Heb 10:31 It is a **d** thing to fall into the hands

DRESS
1Ti   2: 9 also want the women to **d** modestly,

DRINK (DRUNK DRUNKARDS DRUNKENNESS)
Lk 12:19 Take life easy; eat, **d** and be merry." '
Jn   7:37 who is thirsty come to me and **d**.
1Co 12:13 were all given the one Spirit to **d**.

DRIVES
1Jn   4:18 But perfect love **d** out fear,

DRUNK (DRINK)
Eph 5:18 Do not get **d** on wine, which leads

DRUNKARDS (DRINK)
1Co 6:10 the greedy nor **d** nor slanderers nor

DRUNKENNESS (DRINK)
Lk 21:34 **d** and the anxieties of life,
Ro 13:13 not in carousing and **d**, not in sexual
Gal 5:21 and envy; **d**, orgies, and the like.
1Pe 4: 3 in debauchery, lust, **d**, orgies,

DUST
Mk   6:11 shake the **d** off your feet when you
Ac 13:51 So they shook the **d** off their feet
1Co 15:47 first man was of the **d** of the earth;

DUTY
Ac 23: 1 I have fulfilled my **d** to God in all
1Co 7: 3 husband should fulfill his marital **d**

DWELL (DWELLING DWELLS)
Ro   7:18 that good itself does not **d** in me,
Eph 3:17 Christ may **d** in your hearts through
Col 1:19 to have all his fullness **d** in him,

Col 3:16 of Christ **d** among you richly as you

DWELLING (DWELL)
Eph 2:22 built together to become a **d**

DWELLS (DWELL)
1Co 3:16 that God's Spirit **d** in your midst?

EAGER
1Pe 5: 2 dishonest gain, but **e** to serve;

EAR (EARS)
1Co 2: 9 eye has seen, what no **e** has heard,
     12:16 And if the **e** should say, "Because I

EARS (EAR)
2Ti   4: 3 to say what their itching **e** want

EARTH (EARTHLY)
Mt   6:10 your will be done on **e** as it is
     16:19 you bind on **e** will be bound
     24:35 Heaven and **e** will pass away,
     28:18 and on **e** has been given to me.
Lk   2:14 on **e** peace to those on whom his
1Co 10:26 for, "The **e** is the Lord's,
Php 2:10 in heaven and on **e** and under the **e**,
2Pe 3:13 to a new heaven and a new **e**,

EARTHLY (EARTH)
Php 3:19 Their mind is set on **e** things.
Col 3: 2 on things above, not on **e** things.

EASY
Mt 11:30 For my yoke is **e** and my burden is

EAT (EATING)
Mt 26:26 to his disciples, saying, "Take and **e**;
Ro 14: 2 faith allows him to **e** everything,
1Co 8:13 if what I **e** causes my brother
     10:31 So whether you **e** or drink
2Th 3:10 who will not work shall not **e**."

EATING (EAT)
Ro 14:17 kingdom of God is not a matter of **e**

EDICT
Heb 11:23 they were not afraid of the king's **e**.

EDIFY
1Co 14: 4 Those who speak in a t edify themselves,

EFFECT
Heb 9:18 was not put into **e** without blood.

EFFORT
Lk 13:24 "Make every **e** to enter through
Ro   9:16 depend on human desire or **e**,
     14:19 Let us therefore make every **e** to do
Eph 4: 3 Make every **e** to keep the unity
Heb 4:11 make every **e** to enter that rest,
     12:14 Make every **e** to live in peace
2Pe 1: 5 make every **e** to add to your faith
      3:14 make every **e** to be found spotless,

ELDERS
1Ti   5:17 The **e** who direct the affairs

ELECTION
Ro   9:11 that God's purpose in **e** might stand:
2Pe 1:10 effort to confirm your calling and **e**.

ELI
Mt 27:46 "**E, E,** lema sabachthani?"—which

ELIJAH
     Prophet; predicted famine in Israel (Jas 5:17). Equated

with John the Baptist (Mt 17:9-13; Mk 9:9-13; Lk 1:17). Appeared with Moses in transfiguration of Jesus (Mt 17:1-8; Mk 9:1-8).

ELISHA
Lk   4:27 in the time of E the prophet,

ELIZABETH
Mother of John the Baptist, relative of Mary (Lk 1:5-58).

EMBITTER
Col   3:21 Fathers, do not e your children,

EMPEROR
1Pe   2:17 believers, fear God, honor the e.

EMPTY
Mt   12:36 the day of judgment for every e word
Eph   5: 6 no one deceive you with e words,
1Pe   1:18 you were redeemed from the e way

ENABLE (ABLE)
Lk   1:74 and to e us to serve him without fear
Ac   4:29 e your servants to speak your word

ENABLED (ABLE)
Jn   6:65 to me unless the Father has e them."

ENABLES (ABLE)
Php   3:21 by the power that e him to bring

ENCOURAGE (ENCOURAGEMENT
ENCOURAGING)
Ac   15:32 said much to e and strengthen
Ro   12: 8 if it is to e, then give
1Th   4:18 Therefore e one another with these
2Ti   4: 2 correct, rebuke and e—with great patience
Tit   2: 6 Similarly, e the young men to be
Heb   3:13 But e one another daily, as long as it

ENCOURAGEMENT (ENCOURAGE)
Ac   4:36 Barnabas (which means Son of E),
Ro   15: 4 the e they provide we might have
     15: 5 e give you the same attitude of mind
1Co 14: 3 their strengthening, e and comfort.
Heb 12: 5 completely forgotten this word of e

ENCOURAGING (ENCOURAGE)
Heb 10:25 e one another—and all the more as

END
Mt   10:22 stand firm to the e will be saved.
Lk   21: 9 but the e will not come right away."
1Co 15:24 Then the e will come, when he

ENDURANCE (ENDURE)
Ro   15: 4 so that through the e taught
     15: 5 May the God who gives e
2Co   1: 6 you patient e of the same sufferings
Col   1:11 might so that you may have great e
1Ti   6:11 faith, love, e and gentleness.
Tit   2: 2 and sound in faith, in love and in e.

ENDURE (ENDURANCE ENDURES)
1Co 10:13 a way out so that you can e it.
2Ti   2:12 if we e, we will also reign with him.
Heb 12: 7 E hardship as discipline; God is
Rev   3:10 kept my command to e patiently,

ENDURES (ENDURE)
1Pe   1:25 the word of the Lord e forever."

ENEMIES (ENEMY)
Mt   5:44 love your e and pray for those who
Lk   20:43 until I make your e a footstool

ENEMY (ENEMIES ENMITY)
1Co 15:26 The last e to be destroyed is death.
1Ti   5:14 and to give the e no opportunity

ENJOY (JOY)
Eph   6: 3 and that you may e long life
Heb 11:25 than to e the fleeting pleasures

ENJOYMENT (JOY)
1Ti   6:17 us with everything for our e.

ENLIGHTENED (LIGHT)
Eph   1:18 eyes of your heart may be e in order
Heb   6: 4 for those who have once been e,

ENMITY (ENEMY)
Jas   4: 4 with the world means e against God?

ENOCH
Walked with God and taken by him (Heb 11:5). Prophet (Jude 14).

ENTANGLED (ENTANGLES)
2Pe   2:20 Jesus Christ and are again e in it

ENTANGLES (ENTANGLED)
Heb 12: 1 hinders and the sin that so easily e.

ENTER (ENTERED ENTERS ENTRANCE)
Mt   5:20 you will certainly not e the kingdom
     7:13 "E through the narrow gate. For wide
   18: 8 It is better for you to e life maimed
Mk 10:15 God like a little child will never e it."
   10:23 the rich to e the kingdom of God!"

ENTERED (ENTER)
Ro   5:12 just as sin e the world through one
Heb   9:12 he e the Most Holy Place once

ENTERS (ENTER)
Mk   7:18 nothing that e you from the outside
Jn   10: 2 The one who e by the gate is

ENTERTAIN
1Ti   5:19 Do not e an accusation against

ENTICE
2Pe   2:18 they e people who are just escaping

ENTIRE
Gal   5:14 For the e law is fulfilled in keeping

ENTRUSTED (TRUST)
1Ti   6:20 guard what has been e to your care.
2Ti   1:12 to guard what I have e to him until
     1:14 deposit that was e to you—guard it
Jude   : 3 the Lord has once for all e to us,

ENVY
1Co 13: 4 It does not e, it does not boast, it is

EQUAL
Jn   5:18 Father, making himself e with God.
1Co 12:25 its parts should have e concern

EQUIP (EQUIPPED)
Eph   4:12 to e God's people for works of service,
Heb 13:21 e you with everything good

EQUIPPED (EQUIP)
2Ti   3:17 God's people may be thoroughly e

ERROR
Jas   5:20 the e of their way will save their

ESAU
Firstborn of Isaac, twin of Jacob to Jacob; "hated" by God (Ro 9:13), example of godlessness (Heb 12:16).

ESCAPE (ESCAPING)
Ro 2: 3 think you will e God's judgment?
Heb 2: 3 how shall we e if we ignore so great

ESCAPING (ESCAPE)
1Co 3:15 only as one e through the flames.

ESTABLISH
Ro 10: 3 of God and sought to e their own,

ETERNAL
Mt 19:16 good thing must I do to get e life?"
25:41 into the e fire prepared for the devil
25:46 they will go away to e punishment, but the righteous to e life."
Jn 3:15 who believes may have e life
3:16 him shall not perish but have e life.
3:36 believes in the Son has e life,
4:14 spring of water welling up to e life."
5:24 believes him who sent me has e life
6:47 whoever believes has e life.
6:68 go? You have the words of e life.
10:28 I give them e life, and they shall
17: 3 Now this is e life: that they know
Ro 1:20 God's invisible qualities—his e power
6:23 of God is e life in Christ Jesus our
2Co 4:17 for us an e glory that far outweighs
4:18 temporary, but what is unseen is e.
1Ti 1:16 believe on him and receive e life.
1:17 Now to the King e, immortal,
Heb 9:12 blood, thus obtaining e redemption.
1Jn 5:11 God has given us e life, and this life
5:13 you may know that you have e life.

ETHIOPIAN
Ac 8:27 on his way he met an E eunuch,

EUNUCHS
Mt 19:12 some are e because they were born

EVANGELIST (EVANGELISTS)
2Ti 4: 5 do the work of an e, discharge all

EVANGELISTS (EVANGELIST)
Eph 4:11 the e, the pastors and teachers,

EVE
2Co 11: 3 afraid that just as E was deceived
1Ti 2:13 For Adam was formed first, then E.

EVER (EVERLASTING FOREVER)
Mk 4:12 that, " 'they may be e seeing but never
Jn 1:18 No one has e seen God, but the one
Rev 1:18 now look, I am alive for e and e!
22: 5 And they will reign for e and e.

EVER-INCREASING (INCREASE)
Ro 6:19 to impurity and to e wickedness,
2Co 3:18 into his likeness with e glory,

EVERLASTING (EVER)
2Th 1: 9 will be punished with e destruction
Jude : 6 bound with e chains for judgment

EVIDENCE (EVIDENT)
Jn 14:11 on the e of the works themselves.

EVIDENT (EVIDENCE)
Php 4: 5 Let your gentleness be e to all.

EVIL
Mt 5:45 He causes his sun to rise on the e

Mt 6:13 but deliver us from the e one.'
7:11 though you are e, know how to give
12:35 e people bring e things out of the e
Jn 17:15 you protect them from the e one.
Ro 2: 9 for every human being who does e:
12: 9 Hate what is e; cling to what is
12:17 Do not repay anyone e for e.
16:19 good, and innocent about what is e.
1Co 13: 6 Love does not delight in e
14:20 In regard to e be infants, but in your
Eph 6:16 all the flaming arrows of the e one.
1Ti 6:10 of money is a root of all kinds of e.
2Ti 2:22 Flee the e desires of youth
Jas 1:13 For God cannot be tempted by e,
1Pe 2:16 your freedom as a cover-up for e;
3: 9 Do not repay e with e or insult
3: 9 the contrary, repay e with blessing,

EXACT
Heb 1: 3 the e representation of his being,

EXALT (EXALTED)
Mt 23:12 those who e themselves will be humbled,

EXALTED (EXALT)
Mt 23:12 who humble themselves will be e.
Php 1:20 now as always Christ will be e
2: 9 Therefore God e him to the highest

EXAMINE (EXAMINED)
1Co 11:28 ought to e ourselves before we eat
2Co 13: 5 E yourselves to see whether you are

EXAMINED (EXAMINE)
Ac 17:11 e the Scriptures every day to see

EXAMPLE (EXAMPLES)
Jn 13:15 I have set you an e that you should
1Co 11: 1 Follow my e, as I follow the e
Eph 5: 1 Follow God's e, therefore, as dearly
1Ti 4:12 set an e for the believers in speech,
Tit 2: 7 everything set them an e by doing
1Pe 2:21 leaving you an e, that you should

EXAMPLES (EXAMPLE)
1Co 10: 6 Now these things occurred as e
10:11 These things happened to them as e
1Pe 5: 3 to you, but being e to the flock.

EXASPERATE
Eph 6: 4 Fathers, do not e your children;

EXCEL (EXCELLENT)
1Co 14:12 try to e in those that build
2Co 8: 7 you also e in this grace of giving.

EXCELLENT (EXCEL)
1Co 12:31 yet I will show you the most e way.
Php 4: 8 is admirable—if anything is e
1Ti 3:13 have served well gain an e standing
Tit 3: 8 These things are e and profitable

EXCHANGED
Ro 1:23 e the glory of the immortal God
1:25 They e the truth about God for a lie,

EXCUSE (EXCUSES)
Jn 15:22 but now they have no e for their sin.
Ro 1:20 made, so that people are without e.

EXCUSES (EXCUSE)
Lk 14:18 "But they all alike began to make e.

EXISTS
Heb 2:10 and through whom everything e,
11: 6 comes to him must believe that he e

EXPECT (EXPECTATION)
Mt 24:44 at an hour when you do not **e** him.

EXPECTATION (EXPECT)
Ro 8:19 waits in eager **e** for the children
Heb 10:27 but only a fearful **e** of judgment

EXPEL
1Co 5:13 "E the wicked person from among

EXPENSIVE
1Ti 2: 9 or gold or pearls or **e** clothes,

EXPLOIT
2Co 12:17 Did I **e** you through any of the men

EXPOSE
1Co 4: 5 will **e** the motives of people's hearts.
Eph 5:11 of darkness, but rather **e** them.

EXTENDS
Lk 1:50 His mercy **e** to those who fear him,

EXTORT
Lk 3:14 "Don't **e** money and don't accuse

EYE (EYES)
Mt 5:29 If your right **e** causes you
5:38 have heard that it was said, 'E for **e**,
7: 3 speck of sawdust in someone else's **e**
7: 3 to the plank in your own **e**?
1Co 2: 9 "What no **e** has seen, what no ear has
Col 3:22 not only when their **e** is on you
Rev 1: 7 and "every **e** will see him, even those

EYES (EYE)
Jn 4:35 open your **e** and look at the fields!
2Co 4:18 So we fix our **e** not on what is seen,
Heb 12: 2 fixing our **e** on Jesus, the author
Jas 2: 5 who are poor in the **e** of the world
1Pe 3:12 For the **e** of the Lord are
Rev 7:17 wipe away every tear from their **e**.'"
21: 4 'He will wipe every tear from their **e**.

FACE (FACES)
Mt 17: 2 His **f** shone like the sun, and his
1Co 13:12 in a mirror; then we shall see **f** to **f**.
2Co 4: 6 glory displayed in the **f** of Christ.
1Pe 3:12 but the **f** of the Lord is against those
Rev 1:16 His **f** was like the sun shining in all

FACES (FACE)
2Co 3:18 unveiled **f** contemplate the Lord's

FACTIONS
Gal 5:20 rage, selfish ambition, dissensions,

FADE
1Pe 5: 4 of glory that will never **f** away.

FAIL (FAILINGS FAILS)
Lk 1:37 For no word from God will ever **f**."
2Co 13: 5 you—unless, of course, you **f** the test?

FAILINGS (FAIL)
Ro 15: 1 ought to bear with the **f** of the weak

FAILS (FAIL)
1Co 13: 8 Love never **f**. But where there are

FAIR
Col 4: 1 your slaves with what is right and **f**,

FAITH (FAITHFUL FAITHFULNESS FAITHLESS)
Mt 9:29 "According to your **f** let it be done
17:20 replied, "Because you have so little **f**.

17:20 if you have **f** as small as a mustard
24:10 time many will turn away from the **f**
Mk 11:22 "Have **f** in God," Jesus answered.
Lk 7: 9 I have not found such great **f** even
12:28 will he clothe you—you of little **f**!
17: 5 said to the Lord, "Increase our **f**!"
18: 8 comes, will he find **f** on the earth?"
Ac 14: 9 him, saw that he had **f** to be healed
14:27 how he had opened a door of **f**
Ro 1:12 encouraged by each other's **f**.
1:17 righteousness that is by **f** from first
1:17 written: "The righteous will live by **f**."
3:22 righteousness is given through **f**
3:25 of his blood—to be received by **f**.
4: 5 their **f** is credited as righteousness.
5: 1 we have been justified through **f**,
10:17 **f** comes from hearing the message,
14: 1 Accept those whose **f** is weak,
14:23 because their eating is not from **f**;
14:23 that does not come from **f** is sin.
16:26 that all the Gentiles might come to **f**
1Co 13: 2 I have a **f** that can move mountains,
13:13 these three remain: **f**, hope and love.
16:13 stand firm in the **f**; be courageous;
2Co 5: 7 We live by **f**, not by sight.
13: 5 to see whether you are in the **f**;
Gal 2:16 the law, but by **f** in Jesus Christ.
2:16 have put our **f** in Christ Jesus
2:16 we may be justified by **f** in Christ
2:20 body, I live by **f** in the Son of God,
3:11 because "the righteous will live by **f**."
3:24 came that we might be justified by **f**.
Eph 2: 8 by grace you have been saved, through **f**—
4: 5 one Lord, one **f**, one baptism;
6:16 take up the shield of **f**,
Col 1:23 if you continue in your **f**,
1Th 5: 8 be sober, putting on **f** and love as
1Ti 2:15 childbearing—if they continue in **f**,
4: 1 later times some will abandon the **f**
5: 8 has denied the **f** and is worse than
6:12 Fight the good fight of the **f**.
2Ti 3:15 salvation through **f** in Christ Jesus.
4: 7 finished the race, I have kept the **f**.
Phm : 6 with us in the **f** may be effective
Heb 10:38 "But my righteous one will live by **f**.
11: 1 Now **f** is being sure of what we
11: 3 By **f** we understand that the universe
11: 5 By **f** Enoch was taken from this life,
11: 6 without **f** it is impossible to please
11: 7 By **f** Noah, when warned
11: 7 By his **f** he condemned the world
11: 7 that is in keeping with **f**.
11: 8 By **f** Abraham, when called to go
11:17 By **f** Abraham, when God tested
11:20 By **f** Isaac blessed Jacob and Esau
11:21 By **f** Jacob, when he was dying,
11:22 By **f** Joseph, when his end was near,
11:24 By **f** Moses, when he had grown up,
11:31 By **f** the prostitute Rahab,
12: 2 the author and perfecter of our **f**.
Jas 2:14 people claim to have **f** but have no deeds?
Can such **f** save them?
2:17 In the same way, **f** by itself, if it is
2:26 is dead, so **f** without deeds is dead.
2Pe 1: 5 effort to add to your **f** goodness;
1Jn 5: 4 has overcome the world, even our **f**.
Jude : 3 for the **f** that the Lord has once

FAITHFUL (FAITH)
Mt 25:21 'Well done, good and **f** servant!
Ro 12:12 patient in affliction, **f** in prayer.
1Co 4: 2 been given a trust must prove **f**.
10:13 And God is **f**; he will not let you be
1Th 5:24 The one who calls you is **f**, and he
1Ti 3: 2 above reproach, **f** to his wife,

2Ti 2:13 he remains f, for he cannot disown
Heb 3: 6 But Christ is f as the Son over God's
10:23 profess, for he who promised is f.
1Pe 4:10 as f stewards of God's grace
4:19 themselves to their f Creator
1Jn 1: 9 he is f and just and will forgive us
Rev 1: 5 who is the f witness, the firstborn
2:10 Be f, even to the point of death,
19:11 whose rider is called F and True.

FAITHFULNESS (FAITH)
Ro 3: 3 their unfaithfulness nullify God's f?
Gal 5:22 patience, kindness, goodness, f,

FAITHLESS (FAITH)
2Ti 2:13 if we are f, he remains faithful,

FALL (FALLEN FALLS)
Lk 11:17 a house divided against itself will f.
Jn 16: 1 told you so that you will not f away.
Ro 3:23 and f short of the glory of God,
14: 4 To their own master they stand or f.

FALLEN (FALL)
1Co 15:20 of those who have f asleep.
Gal 5: 4 Christ; you have f away from grace.
1Th 4:15 precede those who have f asleep.
Heb 6: 6 who have f away, to be brought back

FALLS (FALL)
Jn 12:24 a kernel of wheat f to the ground

FALSE (FALSEHOOD FALSELY)
Mt 7:15 "Watch out for f prophets.
19:18 do not steal, do not give f testimony,
24:11 and many f prophets will appear
Php 1:18 whether from f motives or true,
1Ti 1: 3 not to teach f doctrines any longer
2Pe 2: 1 also f prophets among the people,
2: 1 there will be f teachers among you.

FALSEHOOD (FALSE)
Eph 4:25 Therefore each of you must put off f

FALSELY (FALSE)
Lk 3:14 extort money and don't accuse people f—
1Ti 6:20 ideas of what is f called knowledge,

FAMILY
Lk 9:61 go back and say good-by to my f."
12:52 in one f divided against each other,
1Ti 3: 4 He must manage his own f well
3: 5 not know how to manage his own f,
5: 4 practice by caring for their own f
5: 8 for their immediate f members,

FAMINE
Ro 8:35 or persecution or f or nakedness

FAN
2Ti 1: 6 this reason I remind you to f

FAST
Mt 6:16 "When you f, do not look somber as
1Pe 5:12 the true grace of God. Stand f in it.

FATHER (FATHER'S FATHERLESS FATHERS)
Mt 6: 9 " 'Our F in heaven, hallowed be your
10:37 "Anyone who loves their f or mother
15: 4 said, 'Honor your f and mother'
15: 4 and 'Anyone who curses their f
19: 5 this reason a man will leave his f
Lk 12:53 f against son and son against f,
23:34 Jesus said, "F, forgive them, for they
Jn 6:44 me unless the F who sent me draws
6:46 No one has seen the F except

8:44 You belong to your f, the devil,
10:30 I and the F are one."
14: 6 comes to the F except through me.
14: 9 who has seen me has seen the F.
Ro 4:11 he is the f of all who believe
2Co 6:18 And, "I will be a F to you, and you
Eph 6: 2 "Honor your f and mother"—which is

FATHER'S (FATHER)
Lk 2:49 know I had to be in my F house?"
Jn 2:16 Stop turning my F house
10:29 can snatch them out of my F hand.
14: 2 My F house has plenty of room;

FATHERS (FATHER)
Lk 11:11 "Which of you f, if your son asks
Eph 6: 4 F, do not exasperate your children;
Col 3:21 F, do not embitter your children,

FATHOM
1Co 13: 2 of prophecy and can f all mysteries

FAULT
Mt 18:15 go and point out the f, just between
Php 2:15 of God without f in a warped
Jas 1: 5 generously to all without finding f,
Jude :24 his glorious presence without f

FAULTFINDERS
Jude :16 These people are grumblers and f;

FAVORITISM
Ac 10:34 true it is that God does not show f
Ro 2:11 For God does not show f.
Gal 2: 6 God does not show f—
Eph 6: 9 heaven, and there is no f with him.
Col 3:25 for their wrongs, and there is no f.
1Ti 5:21 partiality, and to do nothing out of f.
Jas 2: 1 Lord Jesus Christ must not show f.
2: 9 But if you show f, you sin and are

FEAR (AFRAID FEARS)
Lk 12: 5 I will show you whom you should f:
Php 2:12 to work out your salvation with f
1Jn 4:18 There is no f in love. But perfect love drives
out f,

FEARS (FEAR)
1Jn 4:18 The one who f is not made perfect

FEED
Jn 21:15 I love you." Jesus said, "F my lambs."
21:17 I love you." Jesus said, "F my sheep.
Ro 12:20 "If your enemy is hungry, f him; if he
Jude :12 slightest qualm—shepherds who f only

FEET (FOOT)
Ro 10:15 "How beautiful are the f of those
1Co 12:21 And the head cannot say to the f,
15:25 has put all his enemies under his f.
Heb 12:13 "Make level paths for your f,"

FELIX
Governor before whom Paul was tried (Ac 23:23-24:27).

FELLOWSHIP
2Co 6:14 what f can light have with darkness?
13:14 the f of the Holy Spirit be with you
1Jn 1: 6 If we claim to have f with him
1: 7 light, we have f with one another,

FEMALE
Gal 3:28 neither male nor f, for you are all

FERVOR
Ro 12:11 but keep your spiritual f,

FESTUS
Successor of Felix; sent Paul to Caesar (Ac 25-26).

FIDELITY
Ro 1:31 they have no understanding, no f,

FIELD (FIELDS)
Mt 6:28 See how the lilies of the f grow.
    13:38 The f is the world, and the good
1Co 3: 9 you are God's f, God's building.

FIELDS (FIELD)
Lk 2: 8 shepherds living out in the f nearby,
Jn 4:35 open your eyes and look at the f!

FIERY (FIRE)
1Pe 4:12 do not be surprised at the f ordeal

FIG (FIGS)
Mk 11:21 "Rabbi, look! The f tree you cursed
Lk 13: 6 this parable: "A man had a f tree

FIGHT (FOUGHT)
Jn 18:36 my servants would f to prevent my
1Co 9:26 I do not f like a boxer beating
2Co 10: 4 The weapons we f with are not
1Ti 1:18 them you may f the battle well,
     6:12 F the good f of the faith. Take hold
2Ti 4: 7 I have fought the good f, I have

FIGS (FIG)
Lk 6:44 own fruit. People do not pick f

FILL (FILLED FILLS FULL FULLNESS FULLY)
Jn 6:26 you ate the loaves and had your f.
Ac 2:28 life; you will f me with joy in your
Ro 15:13 May the God of hope f you with all

FILLED (FILL)
Lk 1:15 and he will be f with the Holy Spirit
     1:41 Elizabeth was f with the Holy Spirit.
Jn 12: 3 the house was f with the fragrance
Ac 2: 4 of them were f with the Holy Spirit
     4: 8 Then Peter, f with the Holy Spirit,
     9:17 again and be f with the Holy Spirit."
    13: 9 called Paul, f with the Holy Spirit,
Eph 5:18 Instead, be f with the Spirit,
Php 1:11 f with the fruit of righteousness

FILLS (FILL)
Eph 1:23 him who f everything in every way.

FILTHY
Col 3: 8 and f language from your lips.

FIND (FINDS FOUND)
Mt 7: 7 seek and you will f;
    10:39 who f their life will lose it,
    11:29 and you will f rest for your souls.
    16:25 who lose their life for me will f it.
Lk 18: 8 comes, will he f faith on the earth?"
Jn 10: 9 come in and go out, and f pasture.

FINDS (FIND)
Lk 12:37 whose master f them watching
    15: 4 go after the lost sheep until he f it?

FINISH (FINISHED)
Jn 4:34 him who sent me and to f his work.
     5:36 works that the Father has given me to f—
Ac 20:24 me; my only aim is to f the race
Gal 3: 3 now trying to f by human effort?
2Co 8:11 Now f the work, so that your eager
Jas 1: 4 Let perseverance f its work so

FINISHED (FINISH)
Jn 19:30 received the drink, Jesus said, "It is f."
2Ti 4: 7 the good fight, I have f the race,

FIRE (FIERY)
Mt 3:11 you with the Holy Spirit and f.
     5:22 will be in danger of the f of hell.
    25:41 the eternal f prepared for the devil
Mk 9:43 into hell, where the f never goes out.
Ac 2: 3 to be tongues of f that separated
1Co 3:13 It will be revealed with f, and the f
1Th 5:19 Do not put out the Spirit's f.
Heb 12:29 for our "God is a consuming f."
Jas 3: 5 what a great forest is set on f
2Pe 3:10 the elements will be destroyed by f,
Jude :23 others by snatching them from the f;
Rev 20:14 were thrown into the lake of f. The lake of f is
          the second death.

FIRM
Mk 13:13 those who stand f to the end will be
1Co 16:13 on your guard; stand f in the faith;
2Co 1:24 because it is by faith you stand f.
Eph 6:14 Stand f then, with the belt of truth
Col 4:12 that you may stand f in all the will
2Th 2:15 stand f and hold fast to the teachings
2Ti 2:19 God's solid foundation stands f,
Heb 6:19 an anchor for the soul, f and secure.
1Pe 5: 9 Resist him, standing f in the faith,

FIRST
Mt 5:24 altar. F go and be reconciled
     6:33 But seek f his kingdom and his
     7: 5 f take the plank out of your own
    20:27 wants to be f must be your slave—
    22:38 This is the f and greatest
    23:26 F clean the inside of the cup
Mk 13:10 the gospel must f be preached to all
Ac 11:26 disciples were called Christians f
Ro 1:16 f to the Jew, then to the Gentile.
1Co 12:28 in the church f of all apostles,
2Co 8: 5 having given themselves f of all
1Ti 2:13 For Adam was formed f, then Eve.
Jas 3:17 comes from heaven is f of all pure;
1Jn 4:19 We love because he f loved us.
3Jn : 9 who loves to be f, will have nothing
Rev 1:17 be afraid. I am the F and the Last.
     2: 4 have forsaken the love you had at f.

FIRSTBORN (BEAR)
Lk 2: 7 she gave birth to her f, a son.
Col 1:15 the f over all creation.
Rev 1: 5 witness, the f from the dead.

FIRSTFRUITS
Ro 8:23 who have the f of the Spirit,
1Co 15:23 Christ, the f; then, when he comes,

FISHERS See CATCH

FITTING
1Co 14:40 everything should be done in a f
Col 3:18 own husbands, as is f in the Lord.
Heb 2:10 to glory, it was f that God,

FIX (FIXING)
2Co 4:18 So we f our eyes not on what is
Heb 3: 1 calling, f your thoughts on Jesus,

FIXING (FIX)
Heb 12: 2 f our eyes on Jesus, the author

FLAME (FLAMES FLAMING)
2Ti 1: 6 you to fan into f the gift of God,

FLAMES (FLAME)
1Co 3:15 only as one escaping through the f.

FLAMING (FLAME)
Eph 6:16 you can extinguish all the f arrows

FLASH
1Co 15:52 in a f, in the twinkling of an eye,

FLATTER (FLATTERY)
Jude :16 f others for their own advantage.

FLATTERY (FLATTER)
Ro 16:18 f they deceive the minds of naive
1Th 2: 5 You know we never used f, nor did

FLEE
1Co 6:18 F from sexual immorality. All other
     10:14 my dear friends, f from idolatry.
1Ti 6:11 man of God, f from all this,
2Ti 2:22 F the evil desires of youth
Jas 4: 7 the devil, and he will f from you.

FLESH
Mt 26:41 spirit is willing, but the f is weak."
Mk 10: 8 and the two will become one f.'
Jn   1:14 The Word became f and made his
     6:51 This bread is my f, which I will give
1Co 6:16 is said, "The two will become one f."
Eph 5:31 wife, and the two will become one f."
     6:12 For our struggle is not against f

FLOCK (FLOCKS)
Mt 26:31 the sheep of the f will be scattered.'
Ac 20:28 all the f of which the Holy Spirit has
1Pe 5: 2 of God's f that is under your care,

FLOCKS (FLOCK)
Lk   2: 8 keeping watch over their f at night.

FLOG
Ac 22:25 to f a Roman citizen who hasn't even

FLOW
Jn   7:38 of living water will f from within

FLOWERS
1Pe 1:24 the grass withers and the f fall,

FOLLOW (FOLLOWS)
Mt 16:24 and take up their cross and f me.
Jn 10: 4 his sheep f him because they know
1Co 14: 1 F the way of love and eagerly desire
Rev 14: 4 They f the Lamb wherever he goes.

FOLLOWS (FOLLOW)
Jn   8:12 Whoever f me will never walk

FOOD (FOODS)
Jn   6:27 Do not work for f that spoils,
1Co 8: 8 But f does not bring us near to God;
1Ti 6: 8 But if we have f and clothing,
Jas 2:15 sister is without clothes and daily f.

FOODS (FOOD)
Mk   7:19 this, Jesus declared all f clean.)

FOOL (FOOLISH FOOLISHNESS FOOLS)
Mt   5:22 And anyone who says, 'You f!'

FOOLISH (FOOL)
Mt   7:26 practice is like a f man who built his
     25: 2 Five of them were f and five were
1Co 1:27 God chose the f things of the world

FOOLISHNESS (FOOL)
1Co 1:18 of the cross is f to those who are
     1:25 the f of God is wiser than human
     2:14 Spirit of God but considers them f,
     3:19 of this world is f in God's sight. As it

FOOLS (FOOL)
1Co 4:10 We are f for Christ, but you are so

FOOT (FEET FOOTHOLD)
1Co 12:15 Now if the f should say, "Because I

FOOTHOLD (FOOT)
Eph 4:27 and do not give the devil a f.

FORBEARANCE
Ro   3:25 his f he had left the sins committed

FORBID
1Co 14:39 and do not f speaking in tongues.

FOREKNEW (KNOW)
Ro   8:29 For those God f he also predestined
     11: 2 did not reject his people, whom he f.

FOREVER (EVER)
Jn   6:51 eats of this bread will live f.
     14:16 to help you and be with you f—
1Co 9:25 do it to get a crown that will last f.
1Th 4:17 And so we will be with the Lord f.
Heb 13: 8 the same yesterday and today and f.
1Pe 1:25 but the word of the Lord endures f."
1Jn 2:17 does the will of God lives f.

FORFEIT
Lk   9:25 and yet lose or f your very self?

FORGAVE (FORGIVE)
Lk   7:42 so he f the debts of both.
Eph 4:32 other, just as in Christ God f you.
Col 2:13 with Christ. He f us all our sins,
     3:13 Forgive as the Lord f you.

FORGET (FORGETS FORGETTING)
Heb 6:10 he will not f your work and the love
Jas 1:24 and immediately f what they look like.

FORGETS (FORGET)
Jn 16:21 is born she f the anguish because

FORGETTING (FORGET)
Php 3:13 I do: F what is behind and straining

FORGIVE (FORGAVE FORGIVENESS FORGIVING)
Mt   6:12 And f us our debts, as we also have
     6:14 if you f others when they sin against
     6:14 heavenly Father will also f you.
     18:21 times shall I f someone who sins
Mk 11:25 anything against anyone, f them,
Lk 11: 4 F us our sins, for we also f everyone
     23:34 "Father, f them, for they do not know
Col 3:13 F as the Lord forgave you.
1Jn 1: 9 just and will f us our sins and purify

FORGIVENESS (FORGIVE)
Ac 10:43 in him receives f of sins through his
Eph 1: 7 through his blood, the f of sins,
Col 1:14 we have redemption, the f of sins.
Heb 9:22 the shedding of blood there is no f.

FORGIVING (FORGIVE)
Eph 4:32 to one another, f each other, just as

FORMED
Ro   9:20 "Shall what is f say to the one who f
1Ti 2:13 For Adam was f first, then Eve.

Heb 11: 3 that the universe was **f** at God's

FORSAKE (FORSAKEN)
Heb 13: 5 will I leave you; never will I **f** you."

FORSAKEN (FORSAKE)
Mt 27:46 God, my God, why have you **f** me?"
Rev 2: 4 You have **f** the love you had at first.

FOUGHT (FIGHT)
2Ti 4: 7 I have **f** the good fight, I have

FOUND (FIND)
Lk 15: 6 with me; I have **f** my lost sheep.'
    15: 9 with me; I have **f** my lost coin.'
Ac 4:12 Salvation is **f** in no one else,

FOUNDATION
1Co 3:11 one can lay any **f** other than the one
Eph 2:20 built on the **f** of the apostles
2Ti 2:19 God's solid **f** stands firm,

FOXES
Mt 8:20 "**F** have holes and birds have nests,

FRANKINCENSE
Mt 2:11 with gifts of gold, **f** and myrrh.

FREE (FREED FREEDOM FREELY)
Jn 8:32 the truth, and the truth will set you **f.**"
Ro 6:18 You have been set **f** from sin
Gal 3:28 neither slave nor **f**, neither male nor
1Pe 2:16 Live as **f** people, but do not use your

FREED (FREE)
Rev 1: 5 has **f** us from our sins by his blood,

FREEDOM (FREE)
Ro 8:21 brought into the **f** and glory
2Co 3:17 the Spirit of the Lord is, there is **f.**
Gal 5:13 But do not use your **f** to indulge
1Pe 2:16 do not use your **f** as

FREELY (FREE)
Mt 10: 8 **F** you have received, **f** give.
Ro 3:24 and all are justified **f** by his grace
Eph 1: 6 which he has **f** given us in the One

FRIEND (FRIENDS)
Jas 4: 4 to be a **f** of the world becomes

FRIENDS (FRIEND)
Jn 15:13 to lay down one's life for one's **f.**

FRUIT (FRUITFUL)
Mt 7:16 By their **f** you will recognize them.
Jn 15: 2 every branch in me that bears no **f,**
Gal 5:22 But the **f** of the Spirit is love, joy,
Rev 22: 2 bearing twelve crops of **f,**

FRUITFUL (FRUIT)
Jn 15: 2 prunes so that it will be even more **f.**

FULFILL (FULFILLED FULFILLMENT)
Mt 5:17 come to abolish them but to **f** them.
1Co 7: 3 The husband should **f** his marital

FULFILLED (FULFILL)
Mk 14:49 me. But the Scriptures must be **f.**"
Ro 13: 8 whoever loves others has **f** the law.

FULFILLMENT (FULFILL)
Ro 13:10 Therefore love is the **f** of the law.

FULL (FILL)
Jn 10:10 may have life, and have it to the **f.**

Ac 6: 3 who are known to be **f** of the Spirit

FULLNESS (FILL)
Col 1:19 to have all his **f** dwell in him,
    2: 9 in Christ all the **f** of the Deity lives

FULLY (FILL)
1Co 15:58 you. Always give yourselves **f**

FUTURE
Ro 8:38 neither the present nor the **f**, nor any

GABRIEL
   Angel who announced births of John (Lk 1:11-20) and
Jesus (Lk 1:26-38).

GAD
Rev 7: 5 from the tribe of **G** 12,000,

GAIN (GAINED)
Mk 8:36 is it for you to **g** the whole world,
1Co 13: 3 but do not have love, I **g** nothing.
Php 1:21 me, to live is Christ and to die is **g.**
    3: 8 them garbage, that I may **g** Christ
1Ti 6: 6 with contentment is great **g.**
1Pe 5: 2 not pursuing dishonest **g**, but eager

GAINED (GAIN)
Ro 5: 2 through whom we have **g** access

GALILEE
Mk 1: 9 Jesus came from Nazareth in **G**

GALL
Mt 27:34 Jesus wine to drink, mixed with **g;**

GARBAGE
Php 3: 8 I consider them **g**, that I may gain

GARDENER
Jn 15: 1 true vine, and my Father is the **g.**

GARMENT
Mt 9:16 patch of unshrunk cloth on an old **g,**
Jn 19:23 This **g** was seamless, woven in one
    19:24 and cast lots for my **g.**"

GATE (GATES)
Mt 7:13 "Enter through the narrow **g.**
Jn 10: 9 I am the **g;** whoever enters through

GATES (GATE)
Mt 16:18 the **g** of death will not overcome it.

GATHER (GATHERS)
Mt 12:30 whoever does not **g** with me
    23:37 longed to **g** your children together,

GATHERS (GATHER)
Mt 23:37 as a hen **g** her chicks under her

GAVE (GIVE)
Jn 3:16 so loved the world that he **g** his one
2Co 8: 5 they **g** themselves by the will
Gal 2:20 who loved me and **g** himself for me.
1Ti 2: 6 who **g** himself as a ransom for all

GENEALOGIES
1Ti 1: 4 themselves to myths and endless **g.**

GENERATIONS
Lk 1:48 now on all **g** will call me blessed,
Eph 3: 5 other **g** as it has now been revealed

GENEROUS
2Co 9: 5 for the **g** gift you had promised.

1Ti 6:18 and to be g and willing to share.

GENTILE (GENTILES)
Ro 1:16 first to the Jew, then to the G.
10:12 no difference between Jew and G—

GENTILES (GENTILE)
Ro 3: 9 G alike are all under the power
11:13 as I am the apostle to the G, I make
1Co 1:23 block to Jews and foolishness to G,

GENTLE (GENTLENESS)
Mt 11:29 me, for I am g and humble in heart,
21: 5 to you, g and riding on a donkey,
1Co 4:21 I come in love and with a g spirit?
Tit 3: 2 always to be g toward everyone.
1Pe 3: 4 the unfading beauty of a g and quiet

GENTLENESS (GENTLE)
2Co 10: 1 By the meekness and g of Christ,
Gal 5:23 g and self-control. Against such
Php 4: 5 Let your g be evident to all.
Col 3:12 kindness, humility, g and patience.
1Ti 6:11 faith, love, endurance and g.
1Pe 3:15 have. But do this with g and respect,

GETHSEMANE
Mt 26:36 his disciples to a place called G,

GIDEON
Israelite judge (Heb 11:32).

GIFT (GIFTS)
Mt 5:23 if you are offering your g at the altar
Ac 2:38 you will receive the g of the Holy
Ro 6:23 the g of God is eternal life in Christ
1Co 7: 7 of you has your own g from God;
2Co 8:12 the g is acceptable according
9:15 be to God for his indescribable g!
Eph 2: 8 from yourselves, it is the g of God—
1Ti 4:14 Do not neglect your g, which was
2Ti 1: 6 you to fan into flame the g of God,
Jas 1:17 good and perfect g is from above,
1Pe 4:10 you should use whatever g you have

GIFTS (GIFT)
Ro 11:29 for God's g and his call are
12: 6 We have different g,
1Co 12: 4 There are different kinds of g,
12:31 Now eagerly desire the greater g.
14: 1 love and eagerly desire spiritual g,
14:12 you. Since you are eager for g

GIVE (GAVE GIVEN GIVER GIVES GIVING)
Mt 6:11 G us today our daily bread.
10: 8 Freely you have received, freely g.
22:21 "G back to Caesar what is Caesar's,
Mk 8:37 Or what can you g in exchange
Lk 6:38 G, and it will be given to you.
11:13 Father in heaven g the Holy Spirit
Jn 10:28 I g them eternal life, and they shall
13:34 "A new command I g you: Love one
Ac 20:35 said: 'It is more blessed to g
Ro 12: 8 if it is giving, then g generously;
13: 7 G to everyone what you owe: If you
14:12 So then, we will all g an account
2Co 9: 7 you should g what you have decided
Rev 14: 7 "Fear God and g him glory,

GIVEN (GIVE)
Mt 6:33 all these things will be g to you as
7: 7 "Ask and it will be g to you;
Lk 22:19 saying, "This is my body g for you;
Jn 3:27 "A person can receive only what is g
Ro 5: 5 Holy Spirit, who has been g to us.
1Co 4: 2 those who have been g a trust must

1Co 12:13 we were all g the one Spirit
Eph 4: 7 one of us grace has been g as Christ

GIVER (GIVE)
2Co 9: 7 for God loves a cheerful g.

GIVES (GIVE)
Mt 10:42 if anyone g even a cup of cold water
Jn 6:63 The Spirit g life; the flesh counts
1Co 15:57 He g us the victory through our
2Co 3: 6 the letter kills, but the Spirit g life.

GIVING (GIVE)
Mt 6: 4 so that your g may be in secret.
2Co 8: 7 you also excel in this grace of g.

GLAD
Mt 5:12 Rejoice and be g, because great is

GLORIFIED (GLORY)
Jn 13:31 Son of Man g and God is g in him.
Ro 8:30 those he justified, he also g
2Th 1:10 he comes to be g in his holy people

GLORIFY (GLORY)
Jn 13:32 God will g the Son in himself,
17: 1 G your Son, that your Son may g

GLORIOUS (GLORY)
Mt 19:28 the Son of Man sits on his g throne,
Lk 9:31 appeared in g splendor,
Ac 2:20 of the great and g day of the Lord.
2Co 3: 8 of the Spirit be even more g?
Php 3:21 so that they will be like his g body.
Jude :24 you before his g presence without

GLORY (GLORIFIED GLORIFY GLORIOUS)
Mt 24:30 of the sky, with power and great g.
25:31 the Son of Man comes in his g,
Mk 8:38 his Father's g with the holy angels."
13:26 in clouds with great power and g.
Lk 2: 9 and the g of the Lord shone around
2:14 "G to God in the highest heaven,
Jn 1:14 We have seen his g, the g of the one
12:43 for they loved human g more than the g of
God.
17: 5 your presence with the g I had
17:24 am, and to see my g, the g you have
Ac 7: 2 The God of g appeared to our father
Ro 1:23 exchanged the g of the immortal
3:23 and fall short of the g of God,
8:18 with the g that will be revealed
9: 4 theirs the divine g, the covenants,
1Co 10:31 you do, do it all for the g of God.
11: 7 since he is the image and g of God;
11: 7 but the woman is the g of man.
15:43 is sown in dishonor, it is raised in g;
2Co 3:10 what was glorious has no g now
3:10 comparison with the surpassing g.
3:18 faces contemplate the Lord's g,
3:18 his likeness with ever-increasing g,
4:17 us an eternal g that far outweighs
Php 4:19 according to the riches of his g
Col 1:27 is Christ in you, the hope of g.
3: 4 you also will appear with him in g.
1Ti 3:16 on in the world, was taken up in g.
Tit 2:13 appearing of the g of our great God
Heb 1: 3 The Son is the radiance of God's g
2: 7 you crowned them with g and honor
1Pe 1:24 all their g is like the flowers
Rev 4:11 to receive g and honor and power,
21:23 for the g of God gives it light,

GLUTTONS
Tit 1:12 are always liars, evil brutes, lazy g."

GNASHING
Mt 8:12 there will be weeping and **g** of teeth."

GNAT
Mt 23:24 You strain out a **g** but swallow

GOAL
2Co 5: 9 So we make it our **g** to please him,
Php 3:14 on toward the **g** to win the prize

GOATS
Mt 25:32 separates the sheep from the **g**.

GOD (GOD'S GODLINESS GODLY GODS)
Mt 1:23 Immanuel"—which means, "G with us."
5: 8 pure in heart, for they will see G.
6:24 You cannot faithfully serve both G
19: 6 one. Therefore what G has joined
19:26 but with G all things are possible."
22:21 is Caesar's, and to G what is God's."
22:37 " 'Love the Lord your G with all your
27:46 means, "My G, my G, why have you
Mk 12:29 the Lord our G, the Lord is one.
16:19 and he sat at the right hand of G.
Lk 1:37 For no word from G will ever fail."
1:47 my spirit rejoices in G my Savior,
10: 9 The kingdom of G has come near
10:27 " 'Love the Lord your G with all your
18:19 "No one is good—except G alone.
Jn 1: 1 and the Word was with G, and the Word was
G.
1:18 No one has ever seen G, but the one
1:18 who is himself G and is in closest
3:16 For G so loved the world that he
4:24 G is spirit, and his worshipers must
7:17 Anyone who chooses to do the will of G
14: 1 Trust in G; trust also in me.
20:28 said to him, "My Lord and my G!"
Ac 2:24 But G raised him from the dead,
5: 4 lied just to human beings but to G."
5:29 "We must obey G rather than human
7:55 to heaven and saw the glory of G,
17:23 this inscription: TO AN UNKNOWN G.
20:27 proclaim to you the whole will of G.
20:32 "Now I commit you to G
Ro 1:17 of G is revealed—a righteousness
2:11 For G does not show favoritism.
3: 4 all! Let G be true, and every human
3:23 and fall short of the glory of G,
4:24 also for us, to whom G will credit
5: 8 G demonstrates his own love for us
6:23 the gift of G is eternal life in Christ
8:28 in all things G works for the good
11:22 the kindness and sternness of G:
14:12 give an account of ourselves to G.
1Co 1:20 Has not G made foolish the wisdom
2: 9 these things G has prepared
3: 6 it, but G has been making it grow.
6:20 price. Therefore honor G with your
7:24 the situation in which G called you.
8: 8 food does not bring us near to G;
10:13 And G is faithful; he will not let you
10:31 you do, do it all for the glory of G.
14:33 For G is not a G of disorder
15:28 him, so that G may be all in all.
2Co 1: 9 not rely on ourselves but on G,
2:14 But thanks be to G, who always
3: 5 but our competence comes from G.
4: 7 this all-surpassing power is from G
5:19 that G was reconciling the world
5:21 G made him who had no sin to be
6:16 we are the temple of the living G.
6:16 and I will be their G, and they will
9: 7 for G loves a cheerful giver.
9: 8 G is able to bless you abundantly,

Gal 2: 6 me; G does not show favoritism—they
6: 7 be deceived: G cannot be mocked.
Eph 2:10 which G prepared in advance for us
4: 6 one G and Father of all, who is over
Php 2: 6 being in very nature G, did not consider
equality with G something
4:19 And my G will meet all your needs
1Th 2: 4 we speak as those approved by G
2: 4 not trying to please people but G,
4: 7 For G did not call us to be impure,
4: 9 yourselves have been taught by G
5: 9 For G did not appoint us to suffer
1Ti 2: 5 For there is one G and one mediator between
G and human
4: 4 For everything G created is good,
5: 4 for this is pleasing to G.
Tit 2:13 of the glory of our great G
Heb 1: 1 In the past G spoke to our ancestors
4:12 For the word of G is alive
6:10 G is not unjust; he will not forget
10:31 to fall into the hands of the living G.
11: 6 faith it is impossible to please G,
12:10 but G disciplines us for our good,
12:29 for our "G is a consuming fire."
13:15 us continually offer to G a sacrifice
Jas 1:13 one should say, "G is tempting me."
1:13 For G cannot be tempted by evil,
2:19 You believe that there is one G.
2:23 "Abraham believed G, and it was
4: 4 the world means enmity against G?
4: 8 Come near to G and he will come
1Pe 4:11 who speaks the very words of G.
2Pe 1:21 from G as they were carried along
1Jn 1: 5 him and declare to you: G is light;
2: 5 love for G is truly made complete
3:20 that G is greater than our hearts,
4: 7 one another, for love comes from G.
4: 9 This is how G showed his love
4:11 Dear friends, since G so loved us,
4:12 No one has ever seen G; but if we
4:16 and rely on the love G has for us.
4:16 Those who live in love live in G, and G in
them.
Rev 4: 8 holy is the Lord G Almighty,'
7:17 G will wipe away every tear
19: 6 For our Lord G Almighty reigns.

GOD-BREATHED (BREATHED)
2Ti 3:16 All Scripture is G and is useful

GOD'S (GOD)
Mk 3:35 Whoever does G will is my brother
Jn 10:36 because I said, 'I am G Son'?
Ro 2: 3 think you will escape G judgment?
2: 4 realizing that G kindness is intended
3: 3 nullify G faithfulness?
7:22 my inner being I delight in G law;
9:16 desire or effort, but on G mercy.
11:29 for G gifts and his call are
12: 2 and approve what G will is—his good,
12:13 Share with G people who are
13: 6 for the authorities are G servants,
1Co 7:19 Keeping G commands is what
2Co 6: 2 now is the time of G favor, now is
Eph 1: 7 with the riches of G grace
5: 1 Follow G example, therefore,
1Th 4: 3 It is G will that you should be
5:18 for this is G will for you in Christ
1Ti 6: 1 so that G name and our teaching
2Ti 2:19 G solid foundation stands firm,
Tit 1: 7 an overseer manages G household,
Heb 1: 3 The Son is the radiance of G glory
9:24 now to appear for us in G presence.
11: 3 was formed at G command,
1Pe 2:15 For it is G will that by doing good

1Pe 3: 4 which is of great worth in G sight.

GODLINESS (GOD)
1Ti 2: 2 and quiet lives in all **g** and holiness.
     4: 8 value, but **g** has value for all things,
     6: 6 **g** with contentment is great gain.
     6:11 and pursue righteousness, **g**, faith,

GODLY (GOD)
2Co 7:10 **G** sorrow brings repentance
     11: 2 jealous for you with a **g** jealousy.
2Ti 3:12 live a **g** life in Christ Jesus will be
2Pe 3:11 You ought to live holy and **g** lives

GODS (GOD)
Ac 19:26 says that **g** made by human hands

GOLD
Mt   2:11 gifts of **g**, frankincense and myrrh.
Ac   3. 6 said, "Silver or **g** I do not have,
Rev 21:21 great street of the city was of **g**,

GOLGOTHA
Jn 19:17 (which in Aramaic is called **G**).

GOOD
Mt   5:45 his sun to rise on the evil and the **g**,
     7:17 Likewise, every **g** tree bears **g** fruit,
     12:35 **G** people bring **g** things out of the **g**
     19:17 "There is only One who is **g**. If you
     25:21 'Well done, **g** and faithful servant!
Mk   3: 4 to do **g** or to do evil, to save life
     8:36 What **g** is it for you to gain
Lk   6:27 do **g** to those who hate you,
Jn 10:11 "I am the **g** shepherd. The **g** shepherd
Ro   8:28 for the **g** of those who love him,
     10:15 the feet of those who bring **g** news!"
     12: 9 Hate what is evil; cling to what is **g**.
1Co 10:24 No one should seek their own **g**, but the **g** of
     others.
     15:33 "Bad company corrupts **g** character."
2Co 9: 8 you will abound in every **g** work.
Gal 6: 9 Let us not become weary in doing **g**,
     6:10 let us do **g** to all people,
Eph 2:10 in Christ Jesus to do **g** works,
Php 1: 6 he who began a **g** work in you will
1Th 5:15 always strive to do what is **g** for
     5:21 test them all; hold on to what is **g**,
2Th 3:13 never tire of doing what is **g**.
1Ti 3: 7 have a **g** reputation with outsiders,
     4: 4 For everything God created is **g**,
     6:12 Fight the **g** fight of the faith.
     6:18 Command them to do **g**, to be rich in **g** deeds,
2Ti 3:17 equipped for every **g** work.
     4: 7 I have fought the **g** fight, I have
Heb 12:10 but God disciplines us for our **g**,
1Pe 2: 3 you have tasted that the Lord is **g**.
     2:12 Live such **g** lives among the pagans

GOSPEL
Mk 13:10 the **g** must first be preached to all
Ro   1:16 I am not ashamed of the **g**,
     15:16 duty of proclaiming the **g** of God,
1Co 1:17 to baptize, but to preach the **g**—
     9:16 Woe to me if I do not preach the **g**!
     15: 1 to remind you of the **g** I preached
Gal 1: 7 which is really no **g** at all.
     1: 7 are trying to pervert the **g** of Christ.
Php 1:27 a manner worthy of the **g** of Christ.

GOSSIP
2Co 12:20 slander, **g**, arrogance and disorder.

GRACE
Jn   1:17 **g** and truth came through Jesus
Ac 20:32 you to God and to the word of his **g**,

Ro   3:24 by his **g** through the redemption
     5:15 how much more did God's **g**
     5:15 that came by the **g** of the one man,
     5:17 God's abundant provision of **g**
     5:20 increased, **g** increased all the more,
     6:14 are not under the law, but under **g**.
     11: 6 And if by **g**, then it cannot be based
     11: 6 if it were, **g** would no longer be **g**.
2Co 6: 1 you not to receive God's **g** in vain.
     8: 9 you know the **g** of our Lord Jesus
     12: 9 to me, "My **g** is sufficient for you,
Gal 2:21 I do not set aside the **g** of God,
     5: 4 you have fallen away from **g**.
Eph 1: 7 with the riches of God's **g**
     2: 5 is by **g** you have been saved.
     2: 7 the incomparable riches of his **g**,
     2: 8 For it is by **g** you have been saved,
Php 1: 7 all of you share in God's **g** with me.
Col 4: 6 conversation be always full of **g**,
2Th 2:16 his **g** gave us eternal encouragement
2Ti 2: 1 be strong in the **g** that is in Christ
Tit 2:11 For the **g** of God has appeared
     3: 7 having been justified by his **g**,
Heb 2: 9 by the **g** of God he might taste death
     4:16 approach God's throne of **g**
     4:16 find **g** to help us in our time of need.
Jas 4: 6 But he gives us more **g**. That is why
2Pe 3:18 grow in the **g** and knowledge of our

GRAIN
1Co 9: 9 an ox while it is treading out the **g**."

GRANTED
Php 1:29 For it has been **g** to you on behalf

GRASS
1Pe 1:24 the **g** withers and the flowers fall,

GRAVE (GRAVES)
Ac   2:31 he was not abandoned to the **g**

GRAVES (GRAVE)
Jn   5:28 are in their **g** will hear his voice
Ro   3:13 "Their throats are open **g**;

GREAT (GREATER GREATEST)
Mk 10:43 become **g** among you must be your
Lk 21:27 in a cloud with power and **g** glory.
1Ti 6: 6 with contentment is **g** gain.
Tit 2:13 appearing of the glory of our **g** God
Heb 2: 3 if we ignore so **g** a salvation?
1Jn 3: 1 See what **g** love the Father has

GREATER (GREAT)
Mk 12:31 is no commandment **g** than these."
Jn   1:50 You shall see **g** things than that."
     15:13 **G** love has no one than this: to lay
1Co 12:31 Now eagerly desire the **g** gifts.
Heb 11:26 as of **g** value than the treasures
1Jn 3:20 know that God is **g** than our hearts,
     4: 4 is in you is **g** than the one who is

GREATEST (GREAT)
Mt 22:38 is the first and **g** commandment.
Lk   9:48 is least among you all is the **g**."
1Co 13:13 and love. But the **g** of these is love.

GREED (GREEDY)
Lk 12:15 on your guard against all kinds of **g**;
Ro   1:29 wickedness, evil, **g** and depravity.
Eph 5: 3 or of **g**, because these are improper
Col 3: 5 evil desires and **g**, which is idolatry.
2Pe 2:14 experts in **g**—an accursed brood!

GREEDY (GREED)
1Co 6:10 thieves nor the **g** nor drunkards nor

Eph 5: 5 or **g** person—such a person is

GREW (GROW)
Lk   2:52 And as Jesus **g** up, he increased
Ac   16: 5 in the faith and **g** daily in numbers.

GRIEF (GRIEVE)
Jn   16:20 grieve, but your **g** will turn to joy.
1Pe   1: 6 may have had to suffer **g** in all kinds

GRIEVE (GRIEF)
Eph 4:30 do not **g** the Holy Spirit of God,
1Th 4:13 so that you do not **g** like the rest,

GROUND
Eph 6:13 you may be able to stand your **g,**

GROW (GREW)
1Co 3: 6 it, but God has been making it **g.**
2Pe 3:18 But **g** in the grace and knowledge

GRUMBLE (GRUMBLING)
1Co 10:10 And do not **g,** as some of them
Jas   5: 9 Don't **g** against one another,

GRUMBLING (GRUMBLE)
Jn   6:43 "Stop **g** among yourselves,"
Php 2:14 Do everything without **g** or arguing,
1Pe   4: 9 hospitality to one another without **g.**

GUARANTEEING (GUARANTOR)
2Co 1:22 as a deposit, **g** what is to come.
Eph 1:14 is a deposit **g** our inheritance until

GUARANTOR (GUARANTEEING)
Heb 7:22 Jesus has become the **g** of a better

GUARD
Mk 13:33 Be on **g**! Be alert! You do not know
1Co 16:13 Be on your **g;** stand firm
Php 4: 7 will **g** your hearts and your minds
1Ti   6:20 **g** what has been entrusted to your

GUIDE
Jn   16:13 he will **g** you into all the truth.

GUILTY
Jn   8:46 Can any of you prove me **g** of sin?
Heb 10:22 to cleanse us from a **g** conscience
Jas   2:10 at just one point is **g** of breaking all

HADES
Lk   16:23 In **H,** where he was in torment,
Rev 20:14 and **H** were thrown into the lake of fire.

HAGAR
   Servant of Sarah, wife of Abraham, mother of Ishmael;
figurative of slavery to law (Gal 4:21-31).

HAIR (HAIRS)
Lk   21:18 But not a **h** of your head will perish.
1Co 11: 6 for a woman to have her **h** cut off

HAIRS (HAIR)
Mt 10:30 even the very **h** of your head are all

HALLELUJAH
Rev 19: 1, multitude in heaven shouting: "**H**!

HALLOWED (HOLY)
Mt   6: 9 Father in heaven, **h** be your name,

HAND (HANDS)
Mt   6: 3 not let your left **h** know what your right **h** is
                 doing,
Jn   10:28 one will snatch them out of my **h.**

1Co 12:15 say, "Because I am not a **h,** I do not

HANDIWORK (WORK)
Eph 2:10 we are God's **h,** created in Christ

HANDS (HAND)
Lk   23:46 into your **h** I commit my spirit."
1Th 4:11 own business and work with your **h,**
1Ti   2: 8 lifting up holy **h** without anger
          5:22 not be hasty in the laying on of **h,**

HAPPY
Jas   5:13 Is anyone **h**? Sing songs of praise.

HARD (HARDEN HARDSHIP)
Mt 19:23 you, it is **h** for the rich to enter
1Co 4:12 We work **h** with our own hands.
1Th 5:12 those who work **h** among you,

HARDEN (HARD)
Ro   9:18 and he hardens whom he wants to **h.**
Heb 3: 8 do not **h** your hearts as you did

HARDSHIP (HARD)
Ro   8:35 Shall trouble or **h** or persecution
2Ti   4: 5 endure **h,** do the work
Heb 12: 7 Endure **h** as discipline; God is

HARM (HARMFUL)
Ro   13:10 Love does no **h** to its neighbor.
1Jn   5:18 and the evil one cannot **h** them.

HARMFUL (HARM)
1Th 5:22 reject whatever is **h.**

HARMONY
Ro   12:16 Live in **h** with one another. Do not
2Co 6:15 What **h** is there between Christ

HARVEST
Mt   9:37 "The **h** is plentiful but the workers
Jn   4:35 at the fields! They are ripe for **h.**
Gal   6: 9 at the proper time we will reap a **h**
Heb 12:11 it produces a **h** of righteousness

HASTY
1Ti   5:22 Do not be **h** in the laying

HATE (HATED HATES)
Mt   5:43 your neighbor and **h** your enemy.'
          10:22 Everyone will **h** you because of me,
Lk   6:27 do good to those who **h** you,
Jn   3:20 All those who do evil **h** the light,
Ro   12: 9 **H** what is evil; cling to what is
1Jn   2: 9 claim to be in the light but **h**

HATED (HATE)
Ro   9:13 written: "Jacob I loved, but Esau I **h.**"
Eph 5:29 all, people have never **h** their own
Heb 1: 9 righteousness and **h** wickedness;

HATES (HATE)
1Jn   3:15 who hates a fellow **b** is a murderer,

HAY
1Co 3:12 costly stones, wood, **h** or straw,

HEAD (HEADS)
Mt   8:20 of Man has no place to lay his **h.**"
Ro   12:20 will heap burning coals on his **h.**"
1Co 11: 3 that the **h** of every man is Christ, and the **h** of
                 the woman is man, and the **h** of Christ is
                 God.
          12:21 And the **h** cannot say to the feet,
Eph 5:23 the husband is the **h** of the wife as Christ is
                 the **h**

2Ti 4: 5 you, keep your **h** in all situations,
Rev 19:12 fire, and on his **h** are many crowns.

HEADS (HEAD)
Rev 12: 3 an enormous red dragon with seven **h**

HEAL (HEALED HEALING)
Mt 10: 8 **H** the sick, raise the dead,
Lk 4:23 to me: 'Physician, **h** yourself!'
     5:17 Lord was with Jesus to **h** the sick.

HEALED (HEAL)
Mt 9:22 he said, "your faith has **h** you."
    14:36 and all who touched him were **h**.
Ac 4:10 that this man stands before you **h**.
    14: 9 at him, saw that he had faith to be **h**
Jas 5:16 for each other so that you may be **h**.
1Pe 2:24 "by his wounds you have been **h**."

HEALING (HEAL)
1Co 12: 9 to another gifts of **h** by that one
    12:30 Do all have gifts of **h**? Do all speak
Rev 22: 2 the tree are for the **h** of the nations.

HEALTH (HEALTHY)
3Jn   : 2 I pray that you may enjoy good **h**

HEALTHY (HEALTH)
Mk 2:17 "It is not the **h** who need a doctor,

HEAR (HEARD HEARING HEARS)
Mt 11:15 Whoever has ears, let them **h**.
Jn 8:47 The reason you do not **h** is that you
2Ti 4: 3 what their itching ears want to **h**.

HEARD (HEAR)
Mt 5:21 "You have **h** that it was said
     5:27 "You have **h** that it was said, 'Do not
     5:33 you have **h** that it was said
     5:38 "You have **h** that it was said,
     5:43 "You have **h** that it was said,
1Co 2: 9 what no ear has **h**, and what no
1Th 2:13 which you **h** from us, you accepted
2Ti 1:13 What you **h** from me, keep as
Jas 1:25 in it—not forgetting what they have **h**

HEARING (HEAR)
Ro 10:17 faith comes from **h** the message,

HEARS (HEAR)
Jn 5:24 whoever **h** my word and believes
1Jn 5:14 according to his will, he **h** us.
Rev 3:20 If anyone **h** my voice and opens

HEART (HEARTS WHOLEHEARTEDLY)
Mt 5: 8 Blessed are the pure in **h**, for they
     6:21 treasure is, there your **h** will be also.
    12:34 overflow of the **h** the mouth speaks.
    22:37 the Lord your God with all your **h**
Lk 6:45 out of the good stored in their **h**,
     6:45 overflow of the **h** the mouth speaks.
Ro 2:29 is circumcision of the **h**,
    10:10 For it is with your **h** that you believe
Eph 5:19 music from your **h** to the Lord,
     6: 6 doing the will of God from your **h**.
Col 3:23 you do, work at it with all your **h**,
1Pe 1:22 love one another deeply, from the **h**.

HEARTS (HEART)
Lk 16:15 of others, but God knows your **h**.
    24:32 "Were not our **h** burning within us
Jn 14: 1 "Do not let your **h** be troubled.
Ac 15: 9 for he purified their **h** by faith.
Ro 2:15 of the law are written on their **h**,
1Co 14:25 the secrets of their **h** are laid bare.
2Co 3: 2 written on our **h**, known and read

2Co 3: 3 of stone but on tablets of human **h**.
     4: 6 shine in our **h** to give us the light
Eph 3:17 may dwell in your **h** through faith.
Col 3: 1 Christ, set your **h** on things above,
Heb 3: 8 do not harden your **h** as you did
    10:16 I will put my laws in their **h**, and I
1Jn 3:20 know that God is greater than our **h**,

HEAT
2Pe 3:12 and the elements will melt in the **h**.

HEAVEN (HEAVENLY HEAVENS)
Mt 6: 9 " 'Our Father in **h**, hallowed be your
     6:20 up for yourselves treasures in **h**,
    16:19 you the keys of the kingdom of **h**;
    19:23 the rich to enter the kingdom of **h**.
    24:35 **H** and earth will pass away, but my
    26:64 One and coming on the clouds of **h**."
    28:18 "All authority in **h** and on earth has
Mk 16:19 he was taken up into **h** and he sat
Lk 15: 7 **h** over one sinner who repents than
    18:22 and you will have treasure in **h**.
Ro 10: 6 your heart, 'Who will ascend into **h**?'"
2Co 5: 1 an eternal house in **h**, not built
    12: 2 ago was caught up to the third **h**.
Php 2:10 in **h** and on earth and under
     3:20 But our citizenship is in **h**. And we
1Th 1:10 and to wait for his Son from **h**,
Heb 8: 5 a copy and shadow of what is in **h**.
     9:24 he entered **h** itself, now to appear
2Pe 3:13 we are looking forward to a new **h**
Rev 21: 1 Then I saw "a new **h** and a new earth,"

HEAVENLY (HEAVEN)
2Co 5: 2 to be clothed with our **h** dwelling,
Eph 1: 3 who has blessed us in the **h** realms
     1:20 at his right hand in the **h** realms,
2Ti 4:18 bring me safely to his **h** kingdom.
Heb 12:22 of the living God, the **h** Jerusalem.

HEAVENS (HEAVEN)
Eph 4:10 who ascended higher than all the **h**,
2Pe 3:10 The **h** will disappear with a roar;

HEEL
Jn 13:18 has lifted up his **h** against me.'

HEIRS (INHERIT)
Ro 8:17 then we are **h** of God and c
Gal 3:29 and **h** according to the promise.
Eph 3: 6 gospel the Gentiles are **h** together
1Pe 3: 7 as **h** with you of the gracious gift

HELL
Mt 5:22 will be in danger of the fire of **h**.
2Pe 2: 4 but sent them to **h**, putting them

HELMET
Eph 6:17 Take the **h** of salvation
1Th 5: 8 and the hope of salvation as a **h**.

HELP (HELPER HELPING HELPS)
Mk 9:24 **h** me overcome my unbelief!"
Ac 16: 9 "Come over to Macedonia and **h** us."

HELPER (HELP)
Heb 13: 6 with confidence, "The Lord is my **h**;

HELPING (HELP)
Ac 9:36 always doing good and **h** the poor.
1Co 12:28 gifts of healing, of **h**, of guidance,
1Ti 5:10 **h** those in trouble and devoting

HELPS (HELP)
Ro 8:26 the Spirit **h** us in our weakness.

HEN
Mt 23:37 as a **h** gathers her chicks under her

HEROD
1. King of Judea who tried to kill Jesus (Mt 2; Lk 1:5).
2. Son of 1. Tetrarch of Galilee who arrested and beheaded John the Baptist (Mt 14:1-12; Mk 6:14-29; Lk 3:1, 19-20; 9:7-9); tried Jesus (Lk 23:6-15).
3. Grandson of 1. King of Judea who killed James (Ac 12:2); arrested Peter (Ac 12:3-19). Death (Ac 12:19-23).

HERODIAS
Wife of Herod the Tetrarch who persuaded her daughter to ask for John the Baptist's head (Mt 14:1-12; Mk 6:14-29).

HID (HIDDEN)
Heb 11:23 faith Moses' parents **h** him for three

HIDDEN (HID)
Mt 5:14 world. A city on a hill cannot be **h**.
   13:44 heaven is like treasure **h** in a field.
Col 1:26 that has been kept **h** for ages
   2: 3 in whom are **h** all the treasures
   3: 3 and your life is now **h** with Christ

HILL
Mt 5:14 A city on a **h** cannot be hidden.

HINDER (HINDERS)
Mt 19:14 and do not **h** them, for the kingdom
1Co 9:12 anything rather than **h** the gospel
1Pe 3: 7 so that nothing will **h** your prayers.

HINDERS (HINDER)
Heb 12: 1 let us throw off everything that **h**

HINT
Eph 5: 3 you there must not be even a **h**

HOLD
Mk 11:25 if you **h** anything against anyone,
Php 2:16 as you **h** firmly to the word of life.
   3:12 for which Christ Jesus took **h** of me.
Col 1:17 and in him all things **h** together.
1Th 5:21 test them all; **h** on to what is good,
1Ti 6:12 Take **h** of the eternal life
Heb 10:23 Let us **h** unswervingly to the hope

HOLINESS (HOLY)
Ro 6:19 slaves to righteousness leading to **h**.
2Co 7: 1 perfecting **h** out of reverence
Eph 4:24 God in true righteousness and **h**.
Heb 12:10 good, that we may share in his **h**.
   12:14 without **h** no one will see the Lord.

HOLY (HALLOWED HOLINESS)
Ac 2:27 will not let your **H** One see decay.
Ro 7:12 the law is **h**, and the commandment is **h**,
   12: 1 **h** and pleasing to God—this is your
Eph 5: 3 are improper for God's **h** people.
2Th 1:10 comes to be glorified in his **h** people
2Ti 1: 9 called us to a **h** life—not because
   3:15 you have known the **H** Scriptures,
Tit 1: 8 upright, **h** and disciplined.
1Pe 1:15 who called you is **h**, so be **h**
   1:16 it is written: "Be **h**, because I am **h**."
   2: 9 a royal priesthood, a **h** nation,
2Pe 3:11 You ought to live **h** and godly lives
Rev 4: 8 " '**H, h, h** is the Lord God Almighty,'

HOME (HOMES)
Mk 10:29 "no one who has left **h** or brothers
Jn 14:23 to them and make our **h** with them.
Tit 2: 5 and pure, to be busy at **h**, to be kind,

HOMES (HOME)
1Ti 5:14 to manage their **h** and to give

HOMOSEXUALITY (HOMOSEXUALS)
1Ti 1:10 sexually immoral, for those practicing **h**,

HOMOSEXUALS (HOMOSEXUALITY)
1Co 6: 9 nor male prostitutes nor practicing **h**

HONEY
Mk 1: 6 and he ate locusts and wild **h**.
Rev 10: 9 mouth it will be as sweet as **h**." '

HONOR (HONORABLE HONORABLY HONORED)
Mt 15: 4 said, '**H** your father and mother'
Ro 12:10 **H** one another above yourselves.
1Co 6:20 Therefore **h** God with your bodies.
Eph 6: 2 "**H** your father and mother"—which is
1Ti 5:17 church well are worthy of double **h**,
Heb 2: 7 you crowned them with glory and **h**
Rev 4: 9 **h** and thanks to him who sits

HONORABLE (HONOR)
1Th 4: 4 body in a way that is holy and **h**,

HONORABLY (HONOR)
Heb 13:18 and desire to live **h** in every way.

HONORED (HONOR)
1Co 12:26 if one part is **h**, every part rejoices
Heb 13: 4 Marriage should be **h** by all,

HOPE (HOPES)
Ro 5: 4 character; and character, **h**.
   8:24 For in this **h** we were saved. But **h** that is seen is no **h** at all.
   12:12 Be joyful in **h**, patient in affliction,
   15: 4 they provide we might have **h**.
1Co 13:13 these three remain: faith, **h** and love.
   15:19 for this life we have **h** in Christ,
Col 1:27 is Christ in you, the **h** of glory.
1Th 5: 8 and the **h** of salvation as a helmet.
1Ti 6:17 arrogant nor to put their **h** in wealth,
   6:17 but to put their **h** in God, who richly
Tit 2:13 while we wait for the blessed **h**—
Heb 6:19 We have this **h** as an anchor
   11: 1 faith is being sure of what we **h**
1Jn 3: 3 All who have this **h** in them purify

HOPES (HOPE)
1Co 13: 7 trusts, always **h**, always perseveres.

HORSE
Rev 6: 2 and there before me was a white **h**!
   6: 4 Then another **h** came out, a fiery red
   6: 5 and there before me was a black **h**!
   6: 8 and there before me was a pale **h**!
   19:11 and there before me was a white **h**,

HOSANNA
Mt 21: 9 shouted, "**H** to the Son of David!"

HOSEA
Ro 9:25 As he says in **H**: "I will call

HOSPITABLE (HOSPITALITY)
1Ti 3: 2 respectable, **h**, able to teach,
Tit 1: 8 he must be **h**, one who loves what is

HOSPITALITY (HOSPITABLE)
Ro 12:13 people who are in need. Practice **h**.
1Ti 5:10 showing **h**, washing the feet
Heb 13: 2 shown **h** to angels without knowing it.
1Pe 4: 9 Offer **h** to one another without

HOSTILE
Ro 8: 7 the sinful mind is **h** to God. It does

HOT
1Ti 4: 2 have been seared as with a **h** iron.
Rev 3:15 that you are neither cold nor **h**.

HOUR
Mt 6:27 worrying add a single **h** to your life?
Lk 12:40 at an **h** when you do not expect him."
Jn 12:23 "The **h** has come for the Son of Man
12:27 'Father, save me from this **h**'?
12:27 for this very reason I came to this **h**.

HOUSE (HOUSEHOLD)
Mt 7:24 is like a wise man who built his **h**
12:29 can anyone enter a strong man's **h**
21:13 " 'My **h** will be called a **h** of prayer,'
Mk 3:25 If a **h** is divided against itself, that **h**
Lk 11:17 a **h** divided against itself will fall.
Jn 2:16 Stop turning my Father's **h**
12: 3 the **h** was filled with the fragrance
14: 2 My Father's **h** has plenty of room;
Heb 3: 3 of a **h** has greater honor than the **h**

HOUSEHOLD (HOUSE)
Mt 10:36 will be the members of your own **h**.'
12:25 or **h** divided against itself will not
1Ti 3:12 manage his children and his **h** well.
3:15 to conduct themselves in God's **h**,

HUMAN (HUMANITY)
Ac 5:29 must obey God rather than **h** beings!
Ro 6:19 because of your **h** limitations.
Gal 3: 3 you now trying to finish by **h** effort?
Php 2: 8 being found in appearance as a **h** being,
1Ti 2: 5 one mediator between God and **h** beings,
Christ Jesus, himself **h**,
2Pe 1:21 prophecy never had its origin in the **h**

HUMANITY (HUMAN)
Heb 2:14 he too shared in their **h** so

HUMBLE (HUMBLED HUMILIATING HUMILITY)
Mt 11:29 for I am gentle and **h** in heart,
18: 4 whoever takes a **h** place—becoming
Eph 4: 2 Be completely **h** and gentle;
Jas 4:10 **H** yourselves before the Lord,
1Pe 5: 6 **H** yourselves, therefore, under God's

HUMBLED (HUMBLE)
Mt 23:12 who exalt themselves will be **h**,
Php 2: 8 he **h** himself by becoming obedient

HUMILIATING (HUMBLE)
1Co 11:22 by **h** those who have nothing?

HUMILITY (HUMBLE)
Php 2: 3 in **h** value others above yourselves,
1Pe 5: 5 with **h** toward one another, because,

HUNGRY
Mt 25:35 For I was **h** and you gave me
Lk 1:53 He has filled the **h** with good things
Jn 6:35 comes to me will never go **h**,
Ro 12:20 "If your enemy is **h**, feed him; if he is

HURT
Mk 16:18 poison, it will not **h** them at all;
Rev 2:11 who are victorious will not be **h**

HUSBAND (HUSBANDS)
1Co 7: 3 The **h** should fulfill his marital duty
7: 3 wife, and likewise the wife to her **h**.
7: 4 the **h** does not have authority over
7:10 wife must not separate from her **h**.

1Co 7:11 And a **h** must not divorce his wife.
7:13 And if a woman has a **h** who is not
7:39 But if her **h** dies, she is free
2Co 11: 2 I promised you to one **h**, to Christ,
Eph 5:23 For the **h** is the head of the wife as
5:33 and the wife must respect her **h**.

HUSBANDS (HUSBAND)
Eph 5:22 yourselves to your own **h** as you do
5:25 **H**, love your wives, just as Christ
Tit 2: 4 the younger women to love their **h**
1Pe 3: 1 yourselves to your own **h** so that,
3: 7 **H**, in the same way be considerate

HYMN
1Co 14:26 each of you has a **h**, or a word

HYPOCRISY (HYPOCRITE HYPOCRITES)
Mt 23:28 on the inside you are full of **h**
1Pe 2: 1 of all malice and all deceit, **h**, envy,

HYPOCRITE (HYPOCRISY)
Mt 7: 5 You **h**, first take the plank

HYPOCRITES (HYPOCRISY)
Mt 6: 5 do not be like the **h**, for they love

HYSSOP
Jn 19:29 sponge on a stalk of the **h** plant,

IDLE
1Th 5:14 warn those who are **i** and disruptive,
2Th 3: 6 away from every believer who is **i**
1Ti 5:13 they get into the habit of being **i**

IDOL (IDOLATRY IDOLS)
1Co 8: 4 We know that "An **i** is nothing at all

IDOLATRY (IDOL)
Col 3: 5 evil desires and greed, which is **i**

IDOLS (IDOL)
1Co 8: 1 Now about food sacrificed to **i**:

IGNORANT (IGNORE)
1Co 15:34 for there are some who are **i** of God—I
Heb 5: 2 to deal gently with those who are **i**
1Pe 2:15 good you should silence the **i** talk
2Pe 3:16 which **i** and unstable people distort,

IGNORE (IGNORANT IGNORES)
Heb 2: 3 escape if we **i** so great a salvation?

ILLUMINATED
Rev 18: 1 and the earth was **i** by his splendor.

IMAGE
1Co 11: 7 since he is the **i** and glory of God;
Col 1:15 The Son is the **i** of the invisible
3:10 in knowledge in the **i** of its Creator.

IMAGINE
Eph 3:20 more than all we ask or **i**,

IMITATE (IMITATORS)
1Co 4:16 Therefore I urge you to **i** me.
Heb 6:12 but to **i** those who through faith
13: 7 of their way of life and **i** their faith.
3Jn :11 do not **i** what is evil but what is

IMITATORS (IMITATE)
1Th 1: 6 You became **i** of us and of the Lord,
2:14 became **i** of God's churches

IMMANUEL
Mt 1:23 and they will call him **I** means,

IMMORAL (IMMORALITY)
1Co 5: 9 to associate with sexually i people—
       5:10 the people of this world who are i,
       5:11 but are sexually i or greedy,
        6: 9 Neither the sexually i nor idolaters
Eph 5: 5 No i, impure or greedy person—such
Heb 12:16 See that no one is sexually i, or is
       13: 4 the adulterer and all the sexually i.
Rev 21: 8 the sexually i, those who practice
       22:15 arts, the sexually i, the murderers,

IMMORALITY (IMMORAL)
Mt 5:32 divorces his wife, except for sexual i,
       19: 9 divorces his wife, except for sexual i,
1Co 6:13 is not meant for sexual i
        6:18 Flee from sexual i. All other sins
       10: 8 We should not commit sexual i,
Gal 5:19 sexual i, impurity and debauchery;
Eph 5: 3 must not be even a hint of sexual i,
1Th 4: 3 that you should avoid sexual i;
Jude : 4 grace of our God into a license for i

IMMORTAL (IMMORTALITY)
Ro 1:23 exchanged the glory of the i God
1Ti 1:17 Now to the King eternal, i,
        6:16 who alone is i and who lives

IMMORTALITY (IMMORTAL)
Ro 2: 7 honor and i, he will give eternal life.
1Co 15:53 imperishable, and the mortal with i.
2Ti 1:10 life and i to light through the gospel.

IMPERISHABLE
1Pe 1:23 seed, but of i, through the living

IMPORTANCE (IMPORTANT)
1Co 15: 3 I passed on to you as of first i:

IMPORTANT (IMPORTANCE)
Mt 6:25 Is not life more i than food,
       23:23 have neglected the more i matters
Mk 12:29 "The most i one," answered Jesus,
       12:33 as yourself is more i than all burnt
Php 1:18 The i thing is that in every way,

IMPOSSIBLE
Mt 17:20 move. Nothing will be i for you."
Lk 18:27 "What is humanly i is possible
Heb 6:18 things in which it is i for God to lie,
       11: 6 without faith it is i to please God,

IMPRISONED (PRISON)
1Pe 3:19 made proclamation to the i spirits—

IMPROPER
Eph 5: 3 because these are i for God's holy

IMPURE (IMPURITY)
Ac 10:15 "Do not call anything i that God has
Eph 5: 5 i or greedy person—such a person is
1Th 4: 7 For God did not call us to be i,
Rev 21:27 Nothing i will ever enter it, nor will

IMPURITY (IMPURE)
Ro 1:24 hearts to sexual i for the degrading
Eph 5: 3 or of any kind of i, or of greed,

INCENSE
Rev 5: 8 full of i, which are the prayers

INCOME
1Co 16: 2 of money in keeping with your i,

INCOMPARABLE
Eph 2: 7 ages he might show the i riches

INCREASE (EVER-INCREASING INCREASED
INCREASING)
Lk 17: 5 apostles said to the Lord, "I our faith!"
1Th 3:12 May the Lord make your love i

INCREASED (INCREASE)
Ac 6: 7 of disciples in Jerusalem i rapidly,
Ro 5:20 But where sin i, grace i all the more,

INCREASING (INCREASE)
Ac 6: 1 when the number of disciples was i,
2Th 1: 3 all of you have for one another is i.
2Pe 1: 8 possess these qualities in i measure,

INDEPENDENT
1Co 11:11 in the Lord woman is not i of man, nor is
         man i of woman.

INDESCRIBABLE
2Co 9:15 Thanks be to God for his i gift!

INDISPENSABLE
1Co 12:22 body that seem to be weaker are i,

INEFFECTIVE
2Pe 1: 8 they will keep you from being i

INEXPRESSIBLE
2Co 12: 4 up to paradise and heard i things,
1Pe 1: 8 are filled with an i and glorious joy,

INFANTS
Mt 21:16 and i you have ordained praise'?"
1Co 14:20 In regard to evil be i, but in your

INFIRMITIES
Mt 8:17 "He took up our i and carried our

INHERIT (CO-HEIRS HEIRS INHERITANCE)
Mt 5: 5 the meek, for they will i the earth.
Mk 10:17 "what must I do to i eternal life?"
1Co 15:50 blood cannot i the kingdom of God,

INHERITANCE (INHERIT)
Eph 1:14 deposit guaranteeing our i until
       5: 5 a person is an idolater—has any i
Heb 9:15 may receive the promised eternal i—
1Pe 1: 4 and into an i that can never perish,

INNOCENT
Mt 10:16 shrewd as snakes and as i as doves.
       27: 4 he said, "for I have betrayed i blood."
1Co 4: 4 clear, but that does not make me i.

INSCRIPTION
Mt 22:20 portrait is this? And whose i?"

INSOLENT
Ro 1:30 God-haters, i, arrogant and boastful;

INSTITUTED
Ro 13: 2 is rebelling against what God has i,

INSTRUCT (INSTRUCTION)
Ro 15:14 and competent to i one another.

INSTRUCTED (INSTRUCTION)
2Ti 2:25 Opponents must be gently i,

INSTRUCTION (INSTRUCT INSTRUCTED)
1Co 14: 6 or prophecy or word of i?
       14:26 a hymn, or a word of i, a revelation,
Eph 6: 4 up in the training and i of the Lord.
1Th 4: 8 who rejects this i does not reject
2Th 3:14 those who do not obey our i in this
1Ti 6: 3 the sound i of our Lord Jesus Christ

2Ti 4: 2 great patience and careful i.

INSULT
Mt   5:11 "Blessed are you when people i you,
Lk   6:22 when they exclude you and i you
1Pe 3: 9 not repay evil with evil or i with i.

INTEGRITY
Tit   2: 7 In your teaching show i,

INTELLIGENCE
1Co 1:19 wise; the i of the intelligent I will

INTELLIGIBLE
1Co 14:19 I would rather speak five i words

INTERCEDE (INTERCEDES INTERCESSION)
Heb 7:25 him, because he always lives to i

INTERCEDES (INTERCEDE)
Ro   8:26 the Spirit himself i for us through

INTERCESSION (INTERCEDE)
1Ti   2: 1 i and thanksgiving be made

INTERESTS
1Co 7:34 and his i are divided. An unmarried
Php 2: 4 not looking to your own i but each of you to
          the i of the others.

INVESTIGATED
Lk   1: 3 I myself have carefully i everything

INVISIBLE
Ro   1:20 the world God's i qualities—his eternal
Col 1:15 The Son is the image of the i God,
1Ti 1:17 eternal, immortal, i, the only God,

INVITE (INVITED INVITES)
Lk 14:13 when you give a banquet, i the poor,

INVITED (INVITE)
Mt 22:14 "For many are i, but few are chosen."
    25:35 I was a stranger and you i me in,

INVITES (INVITE)
1Co 10:27 If an unbeliever i you to a meal

INVOLVED
2Ti   2: 4 No one serving as a soldier gets i

IRON
1Ti   4: 2 have been seared as with a hot i.
Rev 2:27 they 'will rule them with an i scepter

IRREVOCABLE
Ro 11:29 for God's gifts and his call are i.

ISAAC
    Son of Abraham by Sarah (Ac 7:8). Father of Israel (Ro
9:10). Offered up by Abraham (Heb 11:17-19).

ISAIAH
    Prophet frequently quoted in NT (Mt 3:3; 4:14; 8:17;
12:17; 13:14; 15:7).

ISRAEL (ISRAELITES)
    1. Name given to Jacob (see JACOB).
    2. Corporate name of Jacob's descendants; often specif-
ically Northern Kingdom.
Mk 12:29 'Hear, O I, the Lord our God,
Lk 22:30 judging the twelve tribes of I.
Ro   9: 6 all who are descended from I are I.
    11:26 and in this way all I will be saved.
Eph 3: 6 Gentiles are heirs together with I,

ISRAELITES (ISRAEL)
Ro   9:27 the number of the I be like the sand

ISSACHAR
Rev 7: 7 from the tribe of I 12,000,

ITCHING
2Ti 4: 3 to say what their i ears want to hear.

JACOB
    Second son of Isaac, twin of Esau (Heb 11:20), renamed
Israel. Synopsis of his life (Ac 7:8-16).

JAIRUS
    Synagogue ruler whose daughter Jesus raised (Mk 5:22-
43; Lk 8:41-56).

JAMES
    1. Apostle; brother of John (Mt 4:21-22; 10:2; Mk 3:17; Lk
5:1-10). At transfiguration (Mt 17:1-13; Mk 9:1-13; Lk 9:28-
36). Killed by Herod (Ac 12:2).
    2. Apostle; son of Alphaeus (Mt 10:3; Mk 3:18; Lk 6:15).
    3. Brother of Jesus (Mt 13:55; Mk 6:3; Lk 24:10; Gal 1:19)
and Judas (Jude 1). With believers before Pentecost (Ac
1:13). Leader of church at Jerusalem (Ac 12:17; 15; 21:18;
Gal 2:9, 12). Author of epistle (Jas 1:1).

JARS
2Co 4: 7 we have this treasure in j of clay

JEALOUS (JEALOUSY)
2Co 11: 2 I am j for you with a godly jealousy.

JEALOUSY (JEALOUS)
1Co 3: 3 For since there is j and quarreling
2Co 11: 2 I am jealous for you with a godly j.
Gal 5:20 hatred, discord, j, fits of rage,

JEPHTHAH
    Israelite judge (Heb 11:32).

JEREMIAH
    Prophet to Judah (Mt 2:17; 16:14; 27:9).

JERUSALEM
Mt 23:37 "J, J, you who kill the prophets
Lk 13:34 "J, J, you who kill the prophets
    21:24 nations. J will be trampled
Jn   4:20 where we must worship is in J."
Ac   1: 8 and you will be my witnesses in J,
Gal 4:25 corresponds to the present city of J,
Rev 21: 2 the new J, coming down

JESUS
    1. The Messiah.
    LIFE: Genealogy (Mt 1:1-17; Lk 3:21-37). Birth an-
nounced (Mt 1:18-25; Lk 1:26-45). Birth (Mt 2:1-12; Lk 2:1-
40). Escape to Egypt (Mt 2:13-23). As a boy in the temple
(Lk 2:41-52). Baptism (Mt 3:13-17; Mk 1:9-11; Lk 3:21-22; Jn
1:32-34). Temptation (Mt 4:1-11; Mk 1:12-13; Lk 4:1-13).
Ministry in Galilee (Mt 4:12-18:35; Mk 1:14-9:50; Lk 4:14-
13:9; Jn 1:35-2:11; 4; 6), Transfiguration (Mt 17:1-8; Mk 9:2-
8; Lk 9:28-36), on the way to Jerusalem (Mt 19-20; Mk 10;
Lk 13:10-19:27), in Jerusalem (Mt 21-25; Mk 11-13; Lk 19:28-
21:38; Jn 2:13-3:36; 5; 7-12). Last supper (Mt 26:17-35; Mk
14:12-31; Lk 22:1-38; Jn 13-17). Arrest and trial (Mt 26:36-
27:31; Mk 14:43-15:20; Lk 22:39-23:25; Jn 18:1-19:16). Cru-
cifixion (Mt 27:32-66; Mk 15:21-47; Lk 23:26-55; Jn 19:28-
42). Resurrection and appearances (Mt 28; Mk 16; Lk 24; Jn
20-21; Ac 1:1-11; 7:56; 9:3-6; 1Co 15:1-8; Rev 1:1-20).
    MIRACLES. Healings: official's son (Jn 4:43-54), demo-
niac in Capernaum (Mk 1:23-26; Lk 4:33-35), Peter's mother-in-law (Mt 8:14-17; Mk 1:29-31; Lk 4:38-39), leper (Mt
8:2-4; Mk 1:40-45; Lk 5:12-16), paralytic (Mt 9:1-8; Mk 2:1-
12; Lk 5:17-26), cripple (Jn 5:1-9), shriveled hand (Mt 12:10-
13; Mk 3:1-5; Lk 6:6-11), centurion's servant (Mt 8:5-13; Lk

7:1-10), widow's son raised (Lk 7:11-17), demoniac (Mt 12:22-23; Lk 11:14), Gadarene demoniacs (Mt 8:28-34; Mk 5:1-20; Lk 8:26-39), woman's bleeding and Jairus' daughter (Mt 9:18-26; Mk 5:21-43; Lk 8:40-56), blind man (Mt 9:27-31), mute man (Mt 9:32-33), Canaanite woman's daughter (Mt 15:21-28; Mk 7:24-30), deaf man (Mk 7:31-37), blind man (Mk 8:22-26), demoniac boy (Mt 17:14-18; Mk 9:14-29; Lk 9:37-43), ten lepers (Lk 17:11-19), man born blind (Jn 9:1-7), Lazarus raised (Jn 11), crippled woman (Lk 13:11-17), man with dropsy (Lk 14:1-6), two blind men (Mt 20:29-34; Mk 10:46-52; Lk 18:35-43), Malchus' ear (Lk 22:50-51). Other Miracles: water to wine (Jn 2:1-11), catch of fish (Lk 5:1-11), storm stilled (Mt 8:23-27; Mk 4:37-41; Lk 8:22-25), 5,000 fed (Mt 14:15-21; Mk 6:35-44; Lk 9:10-17; Jn 6:1-14), walking on water (Mt 14:25-33; Mk 6:48-52; Jn 6:15-21), 4,000 fed (Mt 15:32-39; Mk 8:1-9), money from fish (Mt 17:24-27), fig tree cursed (Mt 21:18-22; Mk 11:12-14), catch of fish (Jn 21:1-14).

MAJOR TEACHING: Sermon on the Mount (Mt 5-7; Lk 6:17-49), to Nicodemus (Jn 3), to Samaritan woman (Jn 4), Bread of Life (Jn 6:22-59), at Feast of Tabernacles (Jn 7-8), woes to Pharisees (Mt 23; Lk 11:37-54), Good Shepherd (Jn 10:1-18), Olivet Discourse (Mt 24-25; Mk 13; Lk 21:5-36), Upper Room Discourse (Jn 13-16).

PARABLES: Sower (Mt 13:3-23; Mk 4:3-25; Lk 8:5-18), seed's growth (Mk 4:26-29), wheat and weeds (Mt 13:24-30, 36-43), mustard seed (Mt 13:31-32; Mk 4:30-32), yeast (Mt 13:33; Lk 13:20-21), hidden treasure (Mt 13:44), valuable pearl (Mt 13:45-46), net (Mt 13:47-51), house owner (Mt 13:52), good Samaritan (Lk 10:25-37), unmerciful servant (Mt 18:15-35), lost sheep (Mt 18:10-14; Lk 15:4-7), lost coin (Lk 15:8-10), prodigal son (Lk 15:11-32), dishonest manager (Lk 16:1-13), rich man and Lazarus (Lk 16:19-31), persistent widow (Lk 18:1-8), Pharisee and tax collector (Lk 18:9-14), payment of workers (Mt 20:1-16), tenants and the vineyard (Mt 21:28-46; Mk 12:1-12; Lk 20:9-19), wedding banquet (Mt 22:1-14), faithful servant (Mt 24:45-51), ten virgins (Mt 25:1-13), talents (Mt 25:1-30; Lk 19:12-27).

DISCIPLES see APOSTLES. Call of (Jn 1:35-51; Mt 4:18-22; 9:9; Mk 1:16-20; 2:13-14; Lk 5:1-11, 27-28). Named Apostles (Mk 3:13-19; Lk 6:12-16). Twelve sent out (Mt 10; Mk 6:7-11; Lk 9:1-5). Seventy sent out (Lk 10:1-24). Defection of (Jn 6:60-71; Mt 26:56; Mk 14:50-52). Final commission (Mt 28:16-20; Jn 21:15-23; Ac 1:3-8).

Ac   2:32 God has raised this J to life, and we
       9: 5 "I am J, whom you are persecuting,"
       15:11 of our Lord J that we are saved,
       16:31 "Believe in the Lord J, and you will
Ro   3:24 redemption that came by Christ J.
       5:17 life through the one man, J Christ!
       8: 1 for those who are in Christ J,
1Co   2: 2 I was with you except J Christ
       8: 6 and there is but one Lord, J Christ,
       12: 3 the Spirit of God says, "J be cursed,"
       12: 3 and no one can say, "J is Lord,"
2Co   4: 5 but J Christ as Lord, and ourselves
Gal   2:16 the law, but by faith in J Christ.
       3:28 for you are all one in Christ J.
       5: 6 in Christ J neither circumcision nor
Eph   2:10 in Christ J to do good works,
       2:20 with Christ J himself as the chief
Php   1: 6 completion until the day of Christ J.
       2: 5 same attitude of mind Christ J had:
       2:10 name of J every knee should bow,
Col   3:17 do it all in the name of the Lord J,
2Th   2: 1 the coming of our Lord J Christ
1Ti   1:15 Christ J came into the world to save
2Ti   3:12 life in Christ J will be persecuted,
Tit   2:13 our great God and Savior, J Christ,
Heb   2: 9 But we do see J, who was made
       3: 1 fix your thoughts on J, whom we
       4:14 into heaven, J the Son of God, let us
       7:22 J has become the guarantor
       7:24 but because J lives forever, he has
       12: 2 fixing our eyes on J, the author

2Pe   1:16 of our Lord J Christ in power,
1Jn   1: 7 another, and the blood of J, his Son,
       2: 1 have an advocate with the F Christ,
       2: 6 to live in him must walk as J did.
       4:15 If any acknowledge that J is the Son
Rev   22:20 coming soon." Amen. Come, Lord J.
       2. Jesus Barabbas, a criminal (Mt 27:16-21).
       3. Jesus Justus, an associate of Paul (Col 4:11).

JEW (JEWS JUDAISM)
Ro   1:16 first to the J, then to the Gentile.
       10:12 For there is no difference between J
1Co   9:20 To the Jews I became like a J,
Gal   3:28 There is neither J nor Greek,

JEWELRY
1Pe   3: 3 and the wearing of gold j and fine

JEWS (JEW)
Mt   2: 2 who has been born king of the J?
       27:11 him, "Are you the king of the J?"
Jn   4:22 do know, for salvation is from the J.
Ro   3:29 Is God the God of J only? Is he not
1Co   1:22 J demand signs and Greeks look
       9:20 To the J I became like a Jew, to win
       12:13 so as to form one body—whether J
Gal   2: 8 work in Peter as an apostle to the J,
Rev   3: 9 claim to be J though they are not,

JEZEBEL
Rev   2:20 You tolerate that woman J,

JOANNA
An early disciple (Lk 8:3; 24:10).

JOB
Righteous man from Uz; his suffering an example of perseverance (Jas 5:11).

JOEL
Ac   2:16 what was spoken by the prophet J:

JOHN
1. Son of Zechariah and Elizabeth (Lk 1). Called the Baptist (Mt 3:1-12; Mk 1:2-8). Witness to Jesus (Mt 3:11-12; Mk 1:7-8; Lk 3:15-18; Jn 1:6-35; 3:27-30; 5:33-36). Doubts about Jesus (Mt 11:2-6; Lk 7:18-23). Arrest (Mt 4:12; Mk 1:14). Execution (Mt 14:1-12; Mk 6:14-29; Lk 9:7-9). Ministry compared to Elijah (Mt 11:7-19; Mk 9:11-13; Lk 7:24-35).
2. Apostle; brother of James (Mt 4:21-22; 10:2; Mk 3:17; Lk 5:1-10). At transfiguration (Mt 17:1-13; Mk 9:1-13; Lk 9:28-36). Desire to be greatest (Mk 10:35-45). Leader of church at Jerusalem (Ac 4:1-3; Gal 2:9). Elder who wrote epistles (2Jn 1; 3Jn 1). Prophet who wrote Revelation (Rev 1:1; 22:8).
3. Cousin of Barnabas, co-worker with Paul, (Ac 12:12-13:13; 15:37), see MARK.

JOIN (JOINED)
Ro   15:30 to j me in my struggle by praying
2Ti   1: 8 But j with me in suffering
       2: 3 J with me in suffering, like a good

JOINED (JOIN)
Mt   19: 6 Therefore what God has j together,
Mk   10: 9 Therefore what God has j together,
Eph   2:21 him the whole building is j together
       4:16 body, j and held together by every

JOINTS
Heb   4:12 soul and spirit, j and marrow;

JOKING
Eph   5: 4 foolish talk or coarse j, which are

JONAH
Prophet who preached to Nineveh (Mt 12:41). Sign of (Mt 12:39-41; Lk 11:29-32).

JORDAN
Mt 3: 6 were baptized by him in the **J** River.

JOSEPH
1. Son of Jacob by Rachel; synopsis of his life (Ac 7:9-16; Heb 11:22). 12,000 from the tribe of (Rev 7:8).
2. Husband of Mary, mother of Jesus (Mt 1:16-24; 2:13-19; Lk 1:27; 2; Jn 1:45).
3. Disciple from Arimathea, who gave his tomb for Jesus' burial (Mt 27:57-61; Mk 15:43-47; Lk 24:50-52).
4. Original name of Barnabas (Ac 4:36).

JOSHUA
Succeeded Moses; led conquest of Canaan (Ac 7:45; Heb 4:8).

JOY (ENJOY ENJOYMENT JOYFUL OVERJOYED REJOICE REJOICES REJOICING)
Lk 1:44 the baby in my womb leaped for **j**.
  2:10 good news of great **j** that will be
Jn 15:11 told you this so that my **j** may be
  15:11 and that your **j** may be complete.
  16:20 grieve, but your grief will turn to **j**.
2Co 8: 2 trial, their overflowing **j** and their
Php 2: 2 then make my **j** complete by being
  4: 1 I love and long for, my **j** and crown,
1Th 2:19 our **j**, or the crown in which we will
Phm : 7 Your love has given me great **j**
Heb 12: 2 the **j** set before him he endured
Jas 1: 2 Consider it pure **j**, my brothers
1Pe 1: 8 with an inexpressible and glorious **j**,
2Jn : 4 It has given me great **j** to find some
3Jn : 4 I have no greater **j** than to hear

JOYFUL (JOY)
Ro 12:12 Be **j** in hope, patient in affliction,

JUDAH
1. Son of Jacob by Leah (Mt 1:2). Tribe of Jesus (Heb 7:14; Rev 5:5); 12,000 from (Rev 7:5).
2. Name used for people and land of Southern Kingdom (Mt 2:6; Heb 8:8).

JUDAISM (JEW)
Gal 1:13 of my previous way of life in **J**,

JUDAS
1. Apostle (Lk 6:16; Jn 14:22; Ac 1:13). Probably also called Thaddaeus (Mt 10:3; Mk 3:18).
2. Brother of James and Jesus (Mt 13:55; Mk 6:3), also called Jude (Jude 1).
3. Apostle, also called Iscariot, who betrayed Jesus (Mt 10:4; 26:14-56; Mk 3:19; 14:10-50; Lk 6:16; 22:3-53; Jn 6:71; 12:4; 13:2-30; 18:2-11). Suicide of (Mt 27:3-5; Ac 1:16-25).

JUDGE (JUDGED JUDGES JUDGING JUDGMENT)
Mt 7: 1 "Do not **j**, or you too will be judged.
Jn 7:24 appearances, but instead **j** correctly."
  12:47 For I did not come to **j** the world,
Ac 17:31 set a day when he will **j** the world
1Co 4: 3 indeed, I do not even **j** myself.
  6: 2 that God's people will **j** the world?
2Ti 4: 1 who will **j** the living and the dead,
  4: 8 the righteous **J**, will award to me
Jas 4:12 There is only one Lawgiver and **J**,
  4:12 you—who are you to **j** your neighbor?
Rev 20: 4 who had been given authority to **j**.

JUDGED (JUDGE)
Mt 7: 1 "Do not judge, or you too will be **j**.
Jn 5:24 will not be **j** but has crossed over
Jas 3: 1 we who teach will be **j** more strictly.

Rev 20:12 The dead were **j** according to what

JUDGES (JUDGE)
Ro 2:16 God **j** everyone's secrets through
Heb 4:12 it **j** the thoughts and attitudes
Rev 19:11 With justice he **j** and makes war.

JUDGING (JUDGE)
Mt 19:28 thrones, **j** the twelve tribes of Israel.
Jn 7:24 Stop **j** by mere appearances,
2Co 10: 7 You are **j** by appearances.

JUDGMENT (JUDGE)
Mt 5:21 who murders will be subject to **j**.'
  10:15 Gomorrah on the day of **j** than
  12:36 the day of **j** for every empty word
Jn 5:22 but has entrusted all **j** to the Son,
  16: 8 about sin and righteousness and **j**:
Ro 14:10 we will all stand before God's **j** seat.
  14:13 Therefore let us stop passing **j**
1Co 11:29 eat and drink **j** on themselves.
  11:31 we would not come under such **j**.
2Co 5:10 we must all appear before the **j** seat
Heb 9:27 to die once, and after that to face **j**,
  10:27 only a fearful expectation of **j**
1Pe 4:17 For it is time for **j** to begin
Jude : 6 everlasting chains for **j** on the great

JUST (JUSTICE JUSTIFICATION JUSTIFIED JUSTIFY)
Ro 3:26 time, so as to be **j** and the one who
Heb 2: 2 received its **j** punishment,
1Jn 1: 9 he is faithful and **j** and will forgive
Rev 16: 7 true and **j** are your judgments."

JUSTICE (JUST)
Lk 11:42 you neglect **j** and the love of God.
Ro 3:25 He did this to demonstrate his **j**,

JUSTIFICATION (JUST)
Ac 13:39 **j** you were not able to obtain under
Ro 4:25 sins and was raised to life for our **j**
  5:18 one righteous act resulted in **j**

JUSTIFIED (JUST)
Ro 3:24 all are **j** freely by his grace through
  3:28 that a person is **j** by faith apart
  5: 1 since we have been **j** through faith,
  5: 9 Since we have now been **j** by his
  8:30 those he called, he also **j**; those he **j**,
1Co 6:11 you were **j** in the name of the Lord
Gal 2:16 a person is not **j** by observing
  2:16 Jesus that we may be **j** by faith
  3:11 Clearly no one is **j** before God
  3:24 came that we might be **j** by faith.
Jas 2:24 see that people are **j** by what they do

JUSTIFY (JUST)
Gal 3: 8 that God would **j** the Gentiles

KEEP (KEEPING KEEPS KEPT)
Mt 10:10 staff, for workers are worth their **k**.
Lk 12:35 service and **k** your lamps burning,
Gal 5:25 let us **k** in step with the Spirit.
Eph 4: 3 Make every effort to **k** the unity
1Ti 5:22 the sins of others. **K** yourself pure.
2Ti 4: 5 you, **k** your head in all situations,
Heb 13: 5 **K** your lives free from the love
Jas 1:26 and yet do not **k** a tight rein on their
  2: 8 If you really **k** the royal law found
1Jn 5: 3 love for God: to **k** his commands.
Jude :24 To him who is able to **k** you

KEEPING (KEEP)
Mt 3: 8 Produce fruit in **k** with repentance.
Lk 2: 8 **k** watch over their flocks at night.
1Co 7:19 **K** God's commands is what counts.

2Pe 3: 9 Lord is not slow in **k** his promise,

KEEPS (KEEP)
1Co 13: 5 angered, it **k** no record of wrongs.
Jas 2:10 For whoever **k** the whole law

KEPT (KEEP)
2Ti 4: 7 finished the race, I have **k** the faith.
1Pe 1: 4 This inheritance is **k** in heaven

KEYS
Mt 16:19 I will give you the **k** of the kingdom

KILLED (KILLS)
Mt 17:23 He will be **k**, and on the third day he

KILLS (KILLED)
2Co 3: 6 for the letter **k**, but the Spirit gives

KIND (KINDNESS KINDS)
Lk 6:35 because he is **k** to the ungrateful
1Co 13: 4 Love is patient, love is **k**. It does not
15:35 what **k** of body will they come?"
Eph 4:32 Be **k** and compassionate to one
2Ti 2:24 but must be **k** to everyone,
Tit 2: 5 to be **k**, and to be subject to their

KINDNESS (KIND)
Ac 14:17 He has shown **k** by giving you rain
Ro 11:22 Consider therefore the **k**
Gal 5:22 joy, peace, patience, **k**, goodness,
Eph 2: 7 expressed in his **k** to us in Christ

KINDS (KIND)
1Co 12: 4 There are different **k** of gifts,
1Ti 6:10 of money is a root of all **k** of evil.

KING (KINGDOM KINGS)
1Ti 6:15 the **K** of kings and Lord of lords,
Rev 19:16 written: K OF KINGS AND LORD OF LORDS.

KINGDOM (KING)
Mt 3: 2 for the **k** of heaven has come near."
5: 3 spirit, for theirs is the **k** of heaven.
6:10 your **k** come, your will be done
6:33 But seek first his **k** and his
7:21 Lord,' will enter the **k** of heaven,
11:11 in the **k** of heaven is greater than he.
13:24 "The **k** of heaven is like a man who
13:31 "The **k** of heaven is like a mustard
13:33 "The **k** of heaven is like yeast
13:44 "The **k** of heaven is like treasure
13:45 the **k** of heaven is like a merchant
13:47 the **k** of heaven is like a net that was
16:19 you the keys of the **k** of heaven;
18:23 the **k** of heaven is like a king who
19:24 for the rich to enter the **k** of God."
24: 7 rise against nation, and **k** against **k**.
24:14 this gospel of the **k** will be preached
25:34 the **k** prepared for you since
Mk 9:47 you to enter the **k** of God with one
10:14 for the **k** of God belongs to such as
10:23 is for the rich to enter the **k** of God!"
Lk 10: 9 'The **k** of God has come near to you.'
12:31 But seek his **k**, and these things will
17:21 it is,' because the **k** of God is in your
Jn 3: 5 you, no one can enter the **k** of God
18:36 Jesus said, "My **k** is not of this world.
1Co 6: 9 wrongdoers will not inherit the **k**
15:24 when he hands over the **k** to God
Rev 1: 6 has made us to be a **k** and priests
11:15 "The **k** of the world has become the **k**

KINGS (KING)
1Ti 2: 2 for **k** and all those in authority,
Rev 1: 5 and the ruler of the **k** of the earth.

KISS
Lk 22:48 betraying the Son of Man with a **k**?"

KNEE (KNEES)
Ro 14:11 Lord, 'every **k** will bow before me;
Php 2:10 name of Jesus every **k** should bow,

KNEES (KNEE)
Heb 12:12 your feeble arms and weak **k**.

KNEW (KNOW)
Mt 7:23 will tell them plainly, 'I never **k** you.

KNOCK
Mt 7: 7 **k** and the door will be opened
Rev 3:20 I stand at the door and **k**. If anyone

KNOW (FOREKNEW KNEW KNOWING
KNOWLEDGE KNOWN KNOWS)
Mt 6: 3 let your left hand **k** what your right
24:42 because you do not **k** on what day
Lk 1: 4 so that you may **k** the certainty
Jn 3:11 you, we speak of what we **k**, and we
4:22 worship what you do not **k**; we worship what
we do **k**,
9:25 One thing I do **k**. I was blind
10:14 I **k** my sheep and my sheep **k** me—
17: 3 that they **k** you, the only true God,
21:24 We **k** that his testimony is true.
Ac 1: 7 "It is not for you to **k** the times
Ro 6: 6 we **k** that our old self was crucified
7:18 I **k** that good itself does not dwell
8:28 we **k** that in all things God works
1Co 2: 2 I resolved to **k** nothing while I was
6:15 Do you not **k** that your bodies are
6:19 Do you not **k** that your bodies are
8: 2 think they **k** something do not yet **k**
13:12 Now I **k** in part; then I shall **k** fully,
15:58 because you **k** that your labor
Php 3:10 I want to **k** Christ—yes, to **k** the power
2Ti 1:12 because I **k** whom I have believed,
Jas 4:14 you do not even **k** what will happen
1Jn 2: 4 Those who say, "I **k** him," but do not
3:14 We **k** that we have passed
3:16 This is how we **k** what love is:
5: 2 This is how we **k** that we love
5:13 you may **k** that you have eternal life.

KNOWING (KNOW)
Php 3: 8 worth of **k** Christ Jesus my Lord,

KNOWLEDGE (KNOW)
Ro 11:33 riches of the wisdom and **k** of God!
1Co 8: 1 But **k** puffs up while love builds up.
8:11 Christ died, is destroyed by your **k**.
13: 2 can fathom all mysteries and all **k**,
2Co 2:14 aroma of the **k** of him everywhere.
4: 6 of the **k** of God's glory displayed
Eph 3:19 to know this love that surpasses **k**—
Col 2: 3 all the treasures of wisdom and **k**.
1Ti 6:20 ideas of what is falsely called **k**,
2Pe 3:18 grow in the grace and **k** of our Lord

KNOWN (KNOW)
Mt 10:26 or hidden that will not be made **k**.
Ro 1:19 since what may be **k** about God is
11:34 "Who has **k** the mind of the Lord?
15:20 the gospel where Christ was not **k**,
2Co 3: 2 our hearts, **k** and read by everyone.
2Pe 2:21 than to have **k** it and then to turn

KNOWS (KNOW)
Mt 6: 8 your Father **k** what you need before
24:36 "But about that day or hour no one **k**,
Ro 8:27 who searches our hearts **k** the mind
2Ti 2:19 "The Lord **k** those who are his," and,

LABOR
Mt   6:28 field grow. They do not l or spin.
1Co 3: 8 rewarded according to their own l.
    15:58 know that your l in the Lord is not

LACK (LACKING LACKS)
Lk 18:22 "You still l one thing. Sell
Col 2:23 but they l any value in restraining

LACKING (LACK)
Ro 12:11 Never be l in zeal, but keep your
Jas 1: 4 and complete, not l anything.

LACKS (LACK)
Jas 1: 5 If any of you l wisdom, you should

LAID (LAY)
1Co 3:11 other than the one already l,
1Jn 3:16 Jesus Christ l down his life for us.

LAKE
Rev 19:20 into the fiery l of burning sulfur.
    20:14 The l of fire is the second death.

LAMB (LAMB'S LAMBS)
Jn   1:29 "Look, the L of God, who takes away
1Co 5: 7 our Passover l, has been sacrificed.
1Pe 1:19 a l without blemish or defect.
Rev 5: 6 The L had seven horns and seven
     5:12 "Worthy is the L, who was slain,
    14: 4 They follow the L wherever he

LAMB'S (LAMB)
Rev 21:27 names are written in the L book

LAMBS (LAMB)
Lk 10: 3 you out like l among wolves.
Jn 21:15 I love you." Jesus said, "Feed my l."

LAMP (LAMPS)
Lk   8:16 "No one lights a l and hides it
Rev 21:23 gives it light, and the Lamb is its l.

LAMPS (LAMP)
Mt 25: 1 be like ten virgins who took their l
Lk 12:35 for service and keep your l burning,

LANGUAGE
Jn   8:44 he speaks his native l, for he is a liar
Ac   2: 6 one heard their own l being spoken.
Col 3: 8 slander, and filthy l from your lips.
Rev 5: 9 God members of every tribe and l

LAST (LASTING LASTS)
Mt 19:30 But many who are first will be l,
Mk 10:31 first will be l, and the l first."
Jn 15:16 and bear fruit—fruit that will l—
Ro   1:17 that is by faith from first to l, just as
2Ti 3: 1 will be terrible times in the l days.
2Pe 3: 3 that in the l days scoffers will come,
Rev 1:17 be afraid. I am the First and the L.
    22:13 the First and the L, the Beginning

LASTING (LAST)
Heb 10:34 had better and l possessions.

LASTS (LAST)
2Co 3:11 greater is the glory of that which l!

LAUGH
Lk   6:21 you who weep now, for you will l.

LAVISHED
Eph 1: 8 that he l on us. With all wisdom
1Jn 3: 1 See what great love the Father has l

LAW (LAWS)
Mt   5:17 that I have come to abolish the L
     7:12 you, for this sums up the L
    22:40 All the L and the Prophets hang
Lk 16:17 stroke of a pen to drop out of the L.
Jn   1:17 For the l was given through Moses;
Ro   2:12 All who sin apart from the l will also perish
              apart from the l,
     2:15 the requirements of the l are written
     5:13 anyone's account where there is no l.
     5:20 The l was brought in so
     6:14 because you are not under the l,
     7: 6 we have been released from the l so
     7:12 So then, the l is holy,
     8: 3 For what the l was powerless to do
    10: 4 Christ is the culmination of the l so
    13:10 love is the fulfillment of the l.
Gal 3:13 curse of the l by becoming a curse
     3:24 So the l was put in charge of us
     5: 3 he is obligated to obey the whole l.
     5: 4 be justified by l have been alienated
     5:14 For the entire l is fulfilled
Heb 7:19 (for the l made nothing perfect),
    10: 1 The l is only a shadow of the good
Jas 1:25 into the perfect l that gives freedom
     2:10 For whoever keeps the whole l

LAWLESSNESS
2Th 2: 3 occurs and the man of l is revealed,
     2: 7 the secret power of l is already
1Jn 3: 4 sins breaks the law; in fact, sin is l.

LAWS (LAW)
Heb 8:10 I will put my l in their minds
    10:16 I will put my l in their hearts, and I

LAY (LAID LAYING)
Mt   8:20 of Man has no place to l his head."
Jn 10:15 I l down my life for the sheep.
    15:13 to l down one's life for one's friends.
1Co 3:11 no one can l any foundation other
1Jn 3:16 we ought to l down our lives for one
Rev 4:10 ever. They l their crowns before

LAYING (LAY)
1Ti 5:22 Do not be hasty in the l on of hands,
Heb 6: 1 not l again the foundation

LAZARUS
1. Poor man in Jesus' parable (Lk 16:19-31).
2. Brother of Mary and Martha whom Jesus raised from
the dead (Jn 11:1-12:19).

LAZY
Heb 6:12 We do not want you to become l,

LEAD (LEADERS LEADS LED)
Mt   6:13 And l us not into temptation,
    15:14 If the blind l the blind,
Ro 12: 8 if it is to l, do it diligently;
1Jn 3: 7 do not let anyone l you astray.

LEADERS (LEAD)
Heb 13: 7 Remember your l, who spoke
    13:17 Have confidence in your l

LEADS (LEAD)
Mt   7:13 gate and broad is the road that l
Jn 10: 3 own sheep by name and l them out.
Ro 14:19 every effort to do what l to peace
2Co 2:14 God, who always l us as captives

LEARN (LEARNED LEARNING)
Mt 11:29 my yoke upon you and l from me,

LEARNED (LEARN)
Php 4:11 I have l to be content whatever
2Ti 3:14 you know those from whom you l it,

LEARNING (LEARN)
2Ti 3: 7 always l but never able

LED (LEAD)
Ro 8:14 For those who are l by the Spirit
Eph 4: 8 he l captives in his train and gave

LEFT
Mt 6: 3 do not let your l hand know what
25:33 on his right and the goats on his l.

LEGION
Mk 5: 9 "My name is L," he replied, "for we are

LEND (LENDS)
Lk 6:34 Even 'sinners' l to 'sinners,'

LEPROSY
Lk 7:22 those who have l are cleansed,

LETTER (LETTERS)
Mt 5:18 not the smallest l, not the least
2Co 3: 2 You yourselves are our l,
3: 6 for the l kills, but the Spirit gives
2Th 3:14 do not obey our instruction in this l.

LETTERS (LETTER)
2Co 3: 7 which was engraved in l on stone,
10:10 say, "His l are weighty and forceful,
2Pe 3:16 His l contain some things that are

LEVEL
Heb 12:13 "Make l paths for your feet,"

LEVI
1. Son of Jacob by Leah; tribe of chosen as priests (Heb 7:5-13); 12,000 from (Rev 7:7).
2. See MATTHEW.

LEWDNESS
Mk 7:22 malice, deceit, l, envy, slander,

LIAR (LIE)
Jn 8:44 for he is a l and the father of lies.
Ro 3: 4 be true, and every human being a l.

LIBERATED
Ro 8:21 the creation itself will be l from its

LIE (LIAR LIED LIES)
Ro 1:25 the truth about God for a l,
Col 3: 9 Do not l to each other, since you
Heb 6:18 which it is impossible for God to l,

LIED (LIE)
Ac 5: 4 You have not l just to human beings

LIES (LIE)
Jn 8:44 for he is a liar and the father of l.

LIFE (LIVE)
Mt 6:25 Is not l more important than food,
7:14 and narrow the road that leads to l,
10:39 those who lose their l for my sake
16:25 who want to save their l will lose it,
20:28 to give his l as a ransom for many."
Mk 10:45 to give his l as a ransom for many."
Lk 12:15 l does not consist in an abundance
12:22 do not worry about your l, what you
14:26 even l itself—such a person cannot be
Jn 1: 4 In him was l, and that l was the light
3:15 who believes may have eternal l

Jn 3:36 believes in the Son has eternal l,
3:36 rejects the Son will not see l,
4:14 of water welling up to eternal l."
5:24 but has crossed over from death to l.
6:35 Jesus declared, "I am the bread of l.
6:47 you, whoever believes has eternal l.
6:68 go? You have the words of eternal l.
10:10 I have come that they may have l,
10:15 I lay down my l for the sheep.
10:28 I give them eternal l, and they shall
11:25 her, "I am the resurrection and the l.
14: 6 "I am the way and the truth and the l.
15:13 to lay down one's l for one's friends.
20:31 by believing you may have l in his
Ac 13:48 appointed for eternal l believed.
Ro 4:25 was raised to l for our justification.
6:13 have been brought from death to l;
6:23 God is eternal l in Christ Jesus our
8:38 convinced that neither death nor l,
1Co 15:19 If only for this l we have hope
2Co 3: 6 the letter kills, but the Spirit gives l.
Gal 2:20 The l I now live in the body, I live
Eph 4: 1 to live a l worthy of the calling you
Php 2:16 as you hold firmly to the word of l.
Col 1:10 you may live a l worthy of the Lord
1Th 4:12 your daily l may win the respect
1Ti 4: 8 both the present l and the l to come.
4:16 Watch your l and doctrine closely.
6:19 may take hold of the l that is truly l.
2Ti 3:12 live a godly l in Christ Jesus will be
Jas 1:12 they will receive the crown of l
3:13 Let them show it by their good l,
1Pe 3:10 "Whoever among you would love l
2Pe 1: 3 for a godly l through our knowledge
1Jn 3:14 that we have passed from death to l,
5:11 God has given us eternal l, and this l
Rev 13: 8 been written in the Lamb's book of l,
20:12 was opened, which is the book of l.
21:27 are written in the Lamb's book of l.
22: 2 side of the river stood the tree of l,

LIFTED (LIFTING)
Jn 3:14 Just as Moses l up the snake
3:14 so the Son of Man must be l up,
12:32 I, when I am l up from the earth,

LIFTING (LIFTED)
1Ti 2: 8 l up holy hands without anger

LIGHT (ENLIGHTENED)
Mt 4:16 the shadow of death a l has dawned."
5:16 way, let your l shine before others,
11:30 my yoke is easy and my burden is l."
Jn 3:19 L has come into the world,
8:12 he said, "I am the l of the world.
2Co 4: 6 made his l shine in our hearts
6:14 Or what fellowship can l have
11:14 masquerades as an angel of l.
1Ti 6:16 and who lives in unapproachable l,
1Pe 2: 9 out of darkness into his wonderful l.
1Jn 1: 5 God is l; in him there is no darkness
1: 7 But if we walk in the l, as he is
Rev 21:23 for the glory of God gives it l,

LIGHTNING
Mt 24:27 For as l that comes from the east is
28: 3 His appearance was like l, and his

LIKE-MINDED (MIND)
1Pe 3: 8 all of you, be l, be sympathetic,

LIKENESS
Ro 8: 3 own Son in the l of sinful humanity
8:29 to be conformed to the l of his Son,
2Co 3:18 into his l with ever-increasing glory,

Php 2: 7 of a servant, being made in human l.
Jas 3: 9 who have been made in God's l.

LILIES
Lk 12:27 "Consider how the l grow. They do

LION
1Pe 5: 8 around like a roaring l looking
Rev 5: 5 See, the L of the tribe of Judah,

LIPS
Mt 21:16 " 'From the l of children and infants
Col 3: 8 and filthy language from your l.

LISTEN (LISTENS)
Jn 10:27 My sheep l to my voice; I know
Jas 1:19 Everyone should be quick to l,
1:22 Do not merely l to the word, and so

LISTENS (LISTEN)
Lk 10:16 "Whoever l to you l to me;
Jn 18:37 on the side of truth l to me."

LIVE (ALIVE LIFE LIVES LIVING)
Mt 4: 4 'People do not l on bread alone,
Ac 17:24 does not l in temples built by hands.
17:28 'For in him we l and move and have
Ro 1:17 "The righteous will l by faith."
14: 7 For we do not l to ourselves alone
2Co 5: 7 We l by faith, not by sight.
Gal 2:20 with Christ and I no longer l,
5:25 Since we l by the Spirit, let us keep
Php 1:21 to l is Christ and to die is gain.
1:27 l in a manner worthy of the gospel
1Th 5:13 work. L in peace with each other.
2Ti 3:12 everyone who wants to l a godly life
Heb 12:14 Make every effort to l in peace
1Pe 1:17 l out your time as strangers here
1Jn 4:16 Those who l in love l in God,

LIVES (LIVE)
Jn 14:17 for he l with you and will be in you.
Gal 2:20 I no longer live, but Christ l in me.
Heb 13: 5 Keep your l free from the love
2Pe 3:11 You ought to live holy and godly l
1Jn 3:16 to lay down our l for one another.

LIVING (LIVE)
Mt 22:32 not the God of the dead but of the l."
Jn 7:38 streams of l water will flow
Ro 12: 1 to offer your bodies as l sacrifices,
Heb 10:31 to fall into the hands of the l God.
Rev 1:18 I am the L One; I was dead,

LOAD
Gal 6: 5 of you should carry your own l.

LOCKED
Jn 20:26 Though the doors were l, Jesus came
Gal 3:22 Scripture has l up everything under

LOCUSTS
Mt 3: 4 His food was l and wild honey.

LONG (LENGTH LONGED LONGING)
Jn 9: 4 As l as it is day, we must do
Eph 3:18 to grasp how wide and l and high
1Pe 1:12 Even angels l to look into these

LONGED (LONG)
Mt 13:17 righteous people l to see what you
23:37 how often I have l to gather your
2Ti 4: 8 to all who have l for his appearing.

LONGING (LONG)
2Co 5: 2 l to be clothed with our heavenly

LOOK (LOOKING LOOKS)
Mk 13:21 is the Messiah!' or, 'L, there he is!'
Lk 24:39 L at my hands and my feet. It is I
Jn 1:36 by, he said, "L, the Lamb of God!"
4:35 open your eyes and l at the fields!
19:37 "They will l on the one they have
Jas 1:27 to l after orphans and widows
1Pe 1:12 Even angels long to l into these

LOOKING (LOOK)
Rev 5: 6 saw a Lamb, l as if it had been slain,

LOOKS (LOOK)
Lk 9:62 and l back is fit for service
Php 2:21 For everyone l out for their own

LORD (LORD'S LORDING)
Mt 3: 3 'Prepare the way for the L,
4: 7 'Do not put the L your God
7:21 "Not everyone who says to me, 'L, L,'
22:37 " 'Love the L your God with all your
22:44 " 'The L said to my L: "Sit at my right
Mk 12:11 the L has done this, and it is
12:29 O Israel, the L our God, the L is
Lk 2: 9 An angel of the L appeared to them,
2: 9 glory of the L shone around them,
6:46 "Why do you call me, 'L, L,' and do
10:27 " 'Love the L your God with all your
Ac 2:21 on the name of the L will be saved.'
16:31 "Believe in the L Jesus, and you will
Ro 10: 9 "Jesus is L," and believe in your heart
10:13 on the name of the L will be saved."
12:11 your spiritual fervor, serving the L.
14: 8 we live or die, we belong to the L.
1Co 1:31 "Let those who boast boast in the L."
3: 5 to believe—as the L has assigned
7:34 to be devoted to the L in both body
11:23 The L Jesus, on the night he was
12: 3 say, "Jesus is L," except by the Holy
15:57 victory through our L Jesus Christ
16:22 If anyone does not love the L,
2Co 3:17 Now the L is the Spirit, and where
8: 5 themselves first of all to the L,
10:17 "Let those who boast boast in the L."
Gal 6:14 in the cross of our L Jesus Christ,
Eph 4: 5 one L, one faith, one baptism;
5:10 and find out what pleases the L.
5:19 music from your heart to the L,
Php 2:11 acknowledge that Jesus Christ is L,
3: 1 brothers and sisters, rejoice in the L!
4: 4 Rejoice in the L always. I will say it
Col 2: 6 as you received Christ Jesus as L,
3:17 do it all in the name of the L Jesus,
3:23 as working for the L, not for human
4:17 the work you have received in the L."
1Th 3:12 May the L make your love increase
5: 2 day of the L will come like a thief
5:23 at the coming of our L Jesus Christ.
2Th 2: 1 the coming of our L Jesus Christ
2Ti 2:19 "The L knows those who are his,"
Heb 12:14 holiness no one will see the L.
13: 6 confidence, "The L is my helper;
Jas 4:10 Humble yourselves before the L,
1Pe 1:25 the word of the L endures forever."
2: 3 you have tasted that the L is good.
3:15 in your hearts revere Christ as L.
2Pe 1:16 the coming of our L Jesus Christ
2: 1 the sovereign L who bought
3: 9 The L is not slow in keeping his
Jude :14 "See, the L is coming with thousands
Rev 4: 8 holy is the L God Almighty,'
4:11 "You are worthy, our L and God,
17:14 triumph over them because he is L
22:20 soon." Amen. Come, L Jesus.

LORD'S (LORD)
Ac 21:14 up and said, "The **L** will be done."
1Co 10:26 "The earth is the **L**, and everything
11:26 you proclaim the **L** death until he
2Co 3:18 faces contemplate the **L** glory,
2Ti 2:24 And the **L** servant must not be
Jas 4:15 "If it is the **L** will, we will live

LORDING (LORD)
1Pe 5: 3 not l it over those entrusted to you,

LOSE (LOSES LOSS LOST)
Mt 10:39 those who l their life for my sake
Lk 9:25 and yet l or forfeit your very self?
Jn 6:39 that I shall l none of all those he has
Heb 12: 3 you will not grow weary and l heart.
12: 5 do not l heart when he rebukes you,

LOSES (LOSE)
Mt 5:13 But if the salt l its saltiness,
Lk 15: 4 a hundred sheep and l one of them.
15: 8 has ten silver coins and l one.

LOSS (LOSE)
Ro 11:12 their l means riches for the Gentiles,
1Co 3:15 the builder will suffer l but yet will
Php 3: 8 I consider everything a l because

LOST (LOSE)
Lk 15: 4 go after the l sheep until he finds it?
15: 6 with me; I have found my l sheep.'
15: 9 with me; I have found my l coin.'
15:24 is alive again; he was l and is found.'
19:10 to seek and to save what was l."
Php 3: 8 for whose sake I have l all things.

LOT (LOTS)
Nephew of Abraham; rescued from Sodom (Lk 17:28-29; 2Pe 2:7).
Ac 1:26 cast lots, and the l fell to Matthias;

LOTS (LOT)
Mt 27:35 divided up his clothes by casting l.

LOVE (BELOVED LOVED LOVELY LOVER LOVERS LOVES LOVING)
Mt 3:17 said, "This is my Son, whom I l;
5:44 l your enemies and pray for those
6:24 will hate the one and l the other,
17: 5 said, "This is my Son, whom I l;
19:19 and 'l your neighbor as yourself.'"
22:37 " 'L the Lord your God with all your
Lk 6:32 "If you l those who l you, what credit
6:32 Even 'sinners' l those who l them.
7:42 which of them will l him more?"
20:13 I do? I will send my son, whom I l;
Jn 12:25 Those who l their life will lose it,
13:34 command I give you: l one another.
13:35 my disciples, if you l one another."
14:15 "If you l me, keep my commands.
15:13 Greater l has no one than this: to lay
15:17 This is my command: L each other.
21:15 do you l me more than these?"
21:15 Lord," he said, "you know that I l you."
Ro 5: 5 because God's l has been poured
5: 8 God demonstrates his own l for us
8:28 for the good of those who l him,
8:35 separate us from the l of Christ?
8:39 separate us from the l of God that is
12: 9 L must be sincere. Hate what is evil;
12:10 Be devoted to one another in l.
13: 8 the continuing debt to l one another,
13: 9 "L your neighbor as yourself."
13:10 L does no harm to its neighbor.
13:10 Therefore l is the fulfillment

1Co 2: 9 has prepared for those who l him"—
8: 1 puffs up while l builds up.
13: 1 but do not have l, I am only
13: 2 but do not have l, I am nothing.
13: 3 but do not have l, I gain nothing.
13: 4 L is patient, l is kind. It does not
13: 4 L is patient, l is kind. It does not
13: 6 L does not delight in evil
13: 8 L never fails. But where there are
13:13 these three remain: faith, hope and l. But the greatest of these is l.
14: 1 Follow the way of l and eagerly
16:14 Do everything in l.
2Co 5:14 For Christ's l compels us,
8: 8 sincerity of your l by comparing it
8:24 show these men the proof of your l
Gal 5: 6 is faith expressing itself through l.
5:13 serve one another humbly in l.
5:22 But the fruit of the Spirit is l, joy,
Eph 1: 4 holy and blameless in his sight. In l
2: 4 But because of his great l for us,
3:17 being rooted and established in l,
3:18 and high and deep is the l of Christ,
3:19 and to know this l that surpasses
4: 2 bearing with one another in l.
4:15 speaking the truth in l, we will in all
5: 2 and walk in the way of l, just as
5:25 Husbands, l your wives, just as
5:28 to l their wives as their own bodies.
5:33 must l his wife as he loves himself,
Php 1: 9 that your l may abound more
2: 2 having the same l, being one
Col 1: 5 l that spring from the hope stored
2: 2 encouraged in heart and united in l,
3:14 And over all these virtues put on l,
3:19 l your wives and do not be harsh
1Th 1: 3 your labor prompted by l, and your
4: 9 been taught by God to l each other.
5: 8 on faith and l as a breastplate,
2Th 3: 5 Lord direct your hearts into God's l
1Ti 1: 5 The goal of this command is l,
2:15 faith, l and holiness with propriety.
4:12 conduct, in l, in faith and in purity.
6:10 For the l of money is a root of all
6:11 faith, l, endurance and gentleness.
2Ti 1: 7 us power, l and self-discipline.
2:22 faith, l and peace, along with those
3:10 faith, patience, l, endurance,
Tit 2: 4 younger women to l their husbands
Phm : 9 to appeal to you on the basis of l.
Heb 6:10 the l you have shown him as you
10:24 may spur one another on toward l
13: 5 your lives free from the l of money
Jas 1:12 has promised to those who l him.
2: 5 he promised those who l him?
2: 8 "L your neighbor as yourself," you are
1Pe 1:22 you have sincere l for each other,
1:22 you have sincere l for each other,
2:17 to everyone, l your fellow believers,
3: 8 be sympathetic, l one another,
3:10 "Whoever among you would l life
4: 8 because l covers over a multitude
5:14 Greet one another with a kiss of l.
2Pe 1: 7 affection; and to mutual affection, l.
1:17 saying, "This is my Son, whom I l;
1Jn 2: 5 l for God is truly made complete
2:10 who l their fellow believers live
2:15 Do not l the world or anything
2:15 If you l the world, l for the Father
3: 1 See what great l the Father has
3:10 are those who do not l their brothers
3:11 beginning: We should l one another.
3:14 to life, because we l each other.
3:16 This is how we know what l is:
3:18 let us not l with words or tongue

1Jn 3:23 l one another as he commanded us.
4: 7 Dear friends, let us l one another, for l comes from God.
4: 8 Whoever does not l does not know God, because God is l.
4: 9 is how God showed his l among us:
4:10 This is l: not that we loved God,
4:11 us, we also ought to l one another.
4:12 but if we l one another, God lives
4:16 God is l. Those who live in l live
4:17 This is how l is made complete
4:18 There is no fear in l. But perfect l
4:19 We l because he first loved us.
4:20 we say we l God yet hate a brother
4:21 Those who l God must also l one
5: 2 how we know that we l the children
5: 3 In fact, this is l for God: to keep his
2Jn : 5 I ask that we l one another.
: 6 his command is that you walk in l.
Jude :12 are blemishes at your l feasts,
:21 yourselves in God's l as you wait
Rev 2: 4 You have forsaken the l you had
3:19 Those whom I l I rebuke
12:11 they did not l their lives so much as

LOVED (LOVE)
Mk 12: 6 one left to send, a son, whom he l.
Jn 3:16 For God so l the world that he gave
3:19 people l darkness instead of light
11: 5 Now Jesus l Martha and her sister
12:43 they l human glory more than
13: 1 in the world, he l them to the end.
13:23 the disciple whom Jesus l,
13:34 As I have l you, so you must love
14:21 Anyone who loves me will be l
15: 9 "As the Father has l me, so have I l
15:12 Love each other as I have l you.
19:26 disciple whom he l standing nearby,
Ro 8:37 conquerors through him who l us.
9:13 written: "Jacob I l, but Esau I hated "
9:25 I will call her 'my l one' who is not
11:28 they are l on account
Gal 2:20 who l me and gave himself for me.
Eph 5: 2 just as Christ l us and gave himself
5:25 just as Christ l the church and gave
2Th 2:16 who l us and by his grace gave us
2Ti 4:10 for Demas, because he l this world,
Heb 1: 9 You have l righteousness and hated
1Jn 4:10 not that we l God, but that he l us
4:11 since God so l us, we also ought
4:19 We love because he first l us.

LOVELY (LOVE)
Php 4: 8 is pure, whatever is l, whatever is

LOVER (LOVE)
1Ti 3: 3 not quarrelsome, not a l of money.

LOVERS (LOVE)
2Ti 3: 2 People will be l of themselves,
3: 3 brutal, not l of the good,
3: 4 l of pleasure rather than l of God—

LOVES (LOVE)
Mt 10:37 "Anyone who l their father or mother
Lk 7:47 has been forgiven little l little."
Jn 3:35 The Father l the Son and has placed
10:17 The reason my Father l me is that I
14:21 Anyone who l me will be loved
14:23 "Anyone who l me will obey my
Ro 13: 8 for whoever l others has fulfilled
2Co 9: 7 for God l a cheerful giver.
Eph 5:28 bodies. He who l his wife l himself.
5:33 must love his wife as he l himself,
Heb 12: 6 the Lord disciplines those he l,

1Jn 4: 7 Everyone who l has been born
5: 1 everyone who l the father l his child
3Jn : 9 but Diotrephes, who l to be first,
Rev 1: 5 To him who l us and has freed us

LOVING (LOVE)
Heb 13: 1 Keep on l one another as brothers
1Jn 5: 2 God: by l God and carrying out his

LOWLY
1Co 1:28 He chose the l things of this world

LUKE
Co-worker with Paul (Col 4:14; 2Ti 4:11; Phm 24).

LUKEWARM
Rev 3:16 you are l—neither hot nor cold—

LUST
Col 3: 5 impurity, l, evil desires and greed,
1Th 4: 5 not in passionate l like the pagans,
1Jn 2:16 the l of their eyes and their boasting

MACEDONIA
Ac 16: 9 had a vision of a man of M standing

MADE (MAKE)
Mk 2:27 "The Sabbath was m for people,
Jn 1: 3 Through him all things were m;
Ac 17:24 "The God who m the world
Heb 1: 2 whom also he m the universe,
Rev 14: 7 Worship him who m the heavens,

MAGI
Mt 2: 1 M from the east came to Jerusalem

MAGOG
Rev 20: 8 four corners of the earth—Gog and M—

MAIMED
Mt 18: 8 It is better for you to enter life m

MAJESTIC (MAJESTY)
2Pe 1:17 came to him from the M Glory,

MAJESTY (MAJESTIC)
2Pe 1:16 but we were eyewitnesses of his m.
Jude :25 only God our Savior be glory, m,

MAKE (MADE MAKES MAKING)
Mt 3: 3 the Lord, m straight paths for him.' "
28:19 go and m disciples of all nations,
Lk 13:24 "M every effort to enter through
Ro 14:19 Let us therefore m every effort to do
2Co 5: 9 So we m it our goal to please him,
Eph 4: 3 M every effort to keep the unity
Col 4: 5 m the most of every opportunity.
1Th 4:11 to m it your ambition to lead a quiet
Heb 4:11 m every effort to enter that rest,
12:14 M every effort to live in peace
2Pe 1: 5 m every effort to add to your faith
3:14 m every effort to be found spotless,

MAKES (MAKE)
1Co 3: 7 but only God, who m things grow.

MAKING (MAKE)
Jn 5:18 Father, m himself equal with God.
Eph 5:16 m the most of every opportunity,

MALE
Gal 3:28 slave nor free, neither m nor female,

MALICE (MALICIOUS)
Ro 1:29 envy, murder, strife, deceit and m.
Col 3: 8 anger, rage, m, slander, and filthy

1Pe 2: 1 rid yourselves of all **m** and all

MALICIOUS (MALICE)
1Ti 3:11 not **m** talkers but temperate
     6: 4 envy, strife, **m** talk, evil suspicions

MAN (MEN WOMAN WOMEN; See also HUMAN
PEOPLE SON [of MAN])
Mt 19: 5 this reason a **m** will leave his father
Ro 5:12 entered the world through one **m**,
1Co 7: 2 each **m** should have sexual relations
    11: 3 that the head of every **m** is Christ,
    11: 3 and the head of the woman is **m**,
    13:11 When I became a **m**, I put the ways
1Ti 2:12 or to have authority over a **m**;

MANAGE
1Ti 3: 4 He must **m** his own family well
     3:12 to his wife and must **m** his children
     5:14 to **m** their homes and to give

MANASSEH
Rev 7: 6 from the tribe of **M** 12,000,

MANGER
Lk 2:12 wrapped in cloths and lying in a **m**."

MANNA
Jn 6:49 Your ancestors ate the **m**
Rev 2:17 I will give some of the hidden **m**.

MANNER
1Co 11:27 in an unworthy **m** will be guilty
Php 1:27 of heaven live in a **m** worthy

MARITAL (MARRY)
1Co 7: 3 husband should fulfill his **m** duty

MARK (MARKED MARKS)
    Cousin of Barnabas (Col 4:10; 2Ti 4:11; Phm 24; 1Pe 5:13),
    see JOHN.
Rev 13:16 to receive a **m** on their right hands

MARKED (MARK)
Ac 17:26 he **m** out their appointed times in history

MARKS (MARK)
Jn 20:25 "Unless I see the nail **m** in his hands
Gal 6:17 I bear on my body the **m** of Jesus.

MARRIAGE (MARRY)
Mt 22:30 neither marry nor be given in **m**;
    24:38 marrying and giving in **m**,
Heb 13: 4 **M** should be honored by all,

MARRIED (MARRY)
Ro 7: 2 by law a **m** woman is bound to her
1Co 7:33 But a **m** man is concerned
     7:36 is not sinning. They should get **m**.

MARRIES (MARRY)
Mt 5:32 anyone who **m** the divorced woman
    19: 9 and **m** another woman commits
Lk 16:18 wife and **m** another woman commits

MARRY (INTERMARRY MARITAL MARRIAGE
MARRIED MARRIES)
Mt 22:30 people will neither **m** nor be given
1Co 7: 9 they should **m**, for it is better to **m**
1Ti 5:14 So I counsel younger widows to **m**,

MARTHA
    Sister of Mary and Lazarus (Lk 10:38-42; Jn 11; 12:2).

MARVELED
Lk 2:33 mother **m** at what was said

MARY
    1. Mother of Jesus (Mt 1:16-25; Lk 1:27-56; 2:1-40). With
Jesus at temple (Lk 2:41-52), at the wedding in Cana (Jn
2:1-5), questioning his sanity (Mk 3:21), at the cross (Jn
19:25-27). Among disciples after Ascension (Ac 1:14).
    2. Magdalene; former demoniac (Lk 8:2). Helped sup-
port Jesus' ministry (Lk 8:1-3). At the cross (Mt 27:56; Mk
15:40; Jn 19:25), burial (Mt 27:61; Mk 15:47). Saw angel after
resurrection (Mt 28:1-10; Mk 16:1-9; Lk 24:1-12); also Jesus
(Jn 20:1-18).
    3. Sister of Martha and Lazarus (Jn 11). Washed Jesus'
feet (Jn 12:1-8).

MASQUERADES
2Co 11:14 for Satan himself **m** as an angel

MASTER (MASTERED MASTERS)
Mt 10:24 teacher, nor servants above their **m**.
    23: 8 for you have only one **M** and you
    24:46 servant whose **m** finds him doing so
    25:21 "His **m** replied, 'Well done,
Ro 6:14 For sin shall no longer be your **m**,
    14: 4 To their own **m** they stand or fall.
2Ti 2:21 useful to the **M** and prepared to do

MASTERED (MASTER)
1Co 6:12 I will not be **m** by anything.
2Pe 2:19 are slaves to whatever has **m** them."

MASTERS (MASTER)
Mt 6:24 one can be a loyal servant to two **m**.
Eph 6: 5 obey your earthly **m** with respect
     6: 9 And **m**, treat your slaves in the same
Tit 2: 9 be subject to their **m** in everything,

MATTHEW
    Apostle; former tax collector (Mt 9:9-13; 10:3; Mk 3:18;
Lk 6:15; Ac 1:13). Also called Levi (Mk 2:14-17; Lk 5:27-32).

MATTHIAS
Ac 1:26 they cast lots, and the lot fell to **M**;

MATURE (MATURITY)
Eph 4:13 of the Son of God and become **m**,
Php 3:15 who are **m** should take such a view
Col 1:28 present everyone fully **m** in Christ.
Heb 5:14 But solid food is for the **m**,
Jas 1: 4 finish its work so that you may be **m**

MATURITY (MATURE)
Heb 6: 1 Christ and be taken forward to **m**,

MEAL
1Co 10:27 If an unbeliever invites you to a **m**
Heb 12:16 a single **m** sold his inheritance rights

MEANS
1Co 9:22 by all possible **m** I might save some.

MEAT
Ro 14: 6 Those who eat **m** do so to the Lord,
    14:21 It is better not to eat **m** or drink

MEDIATOR
1Ti 2: 5 is one God and one **m** between God
Heb 8: 6 which he is **m** is superior to the old
     9:15 this reason Christ is the **m** of a new
    12:24 to Jesus the **m** of a new covenant,

MEEK (MEEKNESS)
Mt 5: 5 Blessed are the **m**, for they will

MEEKNESS (MEEK)
2Co 10: 1 By the **m** and gentleness of Christ,

MEET (MEETING)
1Th 4:17 the clouds to **m** the Lord in the air.

MEETING (MEET)
Heb 10:25 not giving up **m** together, as some

MELCHIZEDEK
Heb 7:11 one in the order of **M**,

MELT
2Pe 3:12 and the elements will **m** in the heat.

MEMBERS
Ro 12: 4 of us has one body with many **m**,
     12: 4 these **m** do not all have the same
1Co 6:15 your bodies are **m** of Christ himself?
     6:15 Shall I then take the **m** of Christ
Eph 4:25 for we are all **m** of one body.
Col 3:15 since as **m** of one body you were

MEN (MAN See also HUMAN PEOPLE)
Ro 1:27 **M** committed shameful acts with other **m**,
1Ti 2: 8 I want the **m** everywhere to pray,

MERCIFUL (MERCY)
Mt 5: 7 Blessed are the **m**, for they will be
Lk 6:36 Be **m**, just as your Father is **m**.
Heb 2:17 in order that he might become a **m**
Jude :22 Be **m** to those who doubt;

MERCY (MERCIFUL)
Mt 12: 7 mean, 'I desire **m**, not sacrifice,'
     23:23 the law—justice, **m** and faithfulness.
Ro 9:15 "I will have **m** on whom I have **m**,
Eph 2: 4 love for us, God, who is rich in **m**,
Jas 2:13 **M** triumphs over judgment.
1Pe 1: 3 In his great **m** he has given us new

MESSAGE
Jn 12:38 who has believed our **m**
Ro 10:17 faith comes from hearing the **m**,
1Co 1:18 For the **m** of the cross is foolishness
2Co 5:19 to us the **m** of reconciliation.
Col 3:16 Let the **m** of Christ dwell among you
2Pe 1:19 We also have the prophetic **m** as

MESSIAH (CHRIST MESSIAHS)
Mt 1:16 mother of Jesus who is called the **M**.
     16:16 "You are the **M**, the Son
     22:42 the **M**? Whose son is he?"
Jn 1:41 "We have found the **M**"
     4:25 that **M**" (called Christ) "is coming.
     20:31 may believe that Jesus is the **M**,
Ac 2:36 whom you crucified, both Lord and **M**."
     5:42 the good news that Jesus is the **M**.
     9:22 by proving that Jesus is the **M**.
     17: 3 the **M** had to suffer and rise
     18:28 the Scriptures that Jesus was the **M**.
     26:23 that the **M** would suffer
1Jn 2:22 whoever denies that Jesus is the **M**.
     5: 1 who believes that Jesus is the **M**

MESSIAHS (MESSIAH)
Mt 24:24 For false **m** and false prophets will appear

MICHAEL
Archangel (Jude 9); warrior in angelic realm, protector of Israel (Rev 12:7).

MIGHT (ALMIGHTY MIGHTY)
1Ti 6:16 see. To him be honor and **m** forever.

MIGHTY (MIGHT)
Eph 6:10 in the Lord and in his **m** power.

MILE
Mt 5:41 If anyone forces you to go one **m**,

MILK
1Co 3: 2 I gave you **m**, not solid food,
Heb 5:12 again. You need **m**, not solid food!
1Pe 2: 2 crave pure spiritual **m**, so that by it

MILLSTONE (STONE)
Lk 17: 2 with a **m** tied around your neck than

MIND (DOUBLE-MINDED LIKE-MINDED MINDFUL MINDS)
Mt 22:37 all your soul and with all your **m**.'
Ac 4:32 believers were one in heart and **m**.
Ro 7:25 then, I myself in my **m** am a slave
     8: 7 the sinful **m** is hostile to God.
     12: 2 by the renewing of your **m**.
     15: 5 give you the same attitude of **m**
1Co 2: 9 what no human **m** has conceived—
     14:14 spirit prays, but my **m** is unfruitful.
2Co 13:11 another, be of one **m**, live in peace.
Php 2: 2 being one in spirit and of one **m**.
     3:19 Their **m** is set on earthly things.
     4: 2 to be of the same **m** in the Lord.
1Th 4:11 You should **m** your own business
Heb 7:21 sworn and will not change his **m**:

MINDFUL (MIND)
Lk 1:48 he has been **m** of the humble state
Heb 2: 6 mortals that you are **m** of them,

MINDS (MIND)
Eph 4:23 made new in the attitude of your **m**;
Col 3: 2 Set your **m** on things above,
Heb 8:10 I will put my laws in their **m**
Rev 2:23 I am he who searches hearts and **m**,

MINISTERING (MINISTRY)
Heb 1:14 Are not all angels **m** spirits sent

MINISTRY (MINISTERING)
Ac 6: 4 to prayer and the **m** of the word."
2Co 5:18 and gave us the **m** of reconciliation:
2Ti 4: 5 discharge all the duties of your **m**.

MIRACLES (MIRACULOUS)
Mt 11:20 most of his **m** had been performed,
     11:21 If the **m** that were performed in you
Mk 6: 2 What are these remarkable **m** he is
Ac 2:22 man accredited by God to you by **m**,
     19:11 did extraordinary **m** through Paul,
1Co 12:28 then **m**, then gifts of healing,
Heb 2: 4 wonders and various **m**, and by gifts

MIRACULOUS (MIRACLES)
Jn 3: 2 could perform the **m** signs you are
     9:16 "How can a sinner do such **m** signs?"
     20:30 Jesus did many other **m** signs

MIRROR
Jas 1:23 who look at their faces in a **m**

MISERY
Ro 3:16 ruin and **m** mark their ways,
Jas 5: 1 wail because of the **m** that is coming

MISLED
1Co 15:33 Do not be **m**: "Bad company corrupts

MIST
Jas 4:14 You are a **m** that appears for a little

MOCK (MOCKED)
Mk 10:34 who will **m** him and spit on him,

MOCKED (MOCK)
Mt 27:29 knelt in front of him and **m** him.
27:41 of the law and the elders **m** him.
Gal 6: 7 not be deceived: God cannot be **m**.

MODEL
1Th 1: 7 And so you became a **m** to all
2Th 3: 9 to offer ourselves as a **m** for you

MOMENT
Gal 2: 5 We did not give in to them for a **m**,

MONEY
Mt 6:24 faithfully serve both God and **M**.
Lk 9: 3 bag, no bread, no **m**, no extra shirt.
1Co 16: 2 you should set aside a sum of **m**
1Ti 3: 3 not quarrelsome, not a lover of **m**.
6:10 the love of **m** is a root of all kinds
2Ti 3: 2 of themselves, lovers of **m**, boastful,
Heb 13: 5 your lives free from the love of **m**

MOON
1Co 15:41 the **m** another and the stars another;

MORNING
2Pe 1:19 and the **m** star rises in your hearts.
Rev 22:16 of David, and the bright **M** Star."

MORTAL
1Co 15:53 and the **m** with immortality.

MOSES
Levite; brother of Aaron; called by the Lord to deliver Israel from Egypt (Ac 7:20-44). Received Law at Sinai (Jn 1:17). Appeared at Jesus' transfiguration (Mk 9:4-5). "Law of Moses" (Lk 24:44; Jn 7:23). "Book of Moses" (Mk 12:26). "Song of Moses" (Rev 15:3).

MOTH
Mt 6:19 on earth, where **m** and rust destroy,

MOTHER
Mt 10:37 or **m** more than me is not worthy
15: 4 said, 'Honor your father and **m'**
19: 5 a man will leave his father and **m**
Mk 7:10 'Honor your father and your **m**,' and,
10:19 defraud, honor your father and **m.'''**
Jn 19:27 and to the disciple, "Here is your **m**."

MOTIVES
1Co 4: 5 will expose the **m** of people's hearts.
Php 1:18 way, whether from false **m** or true,
1Th 2: 3 not spring from error or impure **m**,
Jas 4: 3 because you ask with wrong **m**,

MOUNTAIN (MOUNTAINS)
Mt 17:20 you can say to this **m**,

MOUNTAINS (MOUNTAIN)
1Co 13: 2 if I have a faith that can move **m**,

MOURN (MOURNING)
Mt 5: 4 Blessed are those who **m**, for they
Ro 12:15 who rejoice; **m** with those who **m**.

MOURNING (MOURN)
Rev 21: 4 There will be no more death' or **m**

MOUTH
Mt 12:34 overflow of the heart the **m** speaks.
15:11 into your **m** does not defile you,
Ro 10: 9 If you declare with your **m**, "Jesus is

MUD
2Pe 2:22 returns to her wallowing in the **m**."

MULTITUDE
1Pe 4: 8 because love covers over a **m**
Rev 7: 9 there before me was a great **m**

MURDER (MURDERER MURDERERS)
Mt 15:19 of the heart come evil thoughts, **m**,
Ro 13: 9 adultery," "Do not **m**," "Do not steal,"
Jas 2:11 adultery," also said, "Do not **m**." If you

MURDERER (MURDER)
Jn 8:44 He was a **m** from the beginning,
1Jn 3:15 who hates a fellow believer is a **m**,

MURDERERS (MURDER)
1Ti 1: 9 kill their fathers or mothers, for **m**,
Rev 21: 8 vile, the **m**, the sexually immoral,

MUSIC
Eph 5:19 make **m** from your heart to the Lord,

MUSTARD
Mt 13:31 kingdom of heaven is like a **m** seed,
17:20 you have faith as small as a **m** seed,

MUZZLE
1Co 9: 9 "Do not **m** an ox while it is treading

MYRRH
Mt 2:11 gifts of gold, frankincense and **m**.
Mk 15:23 offered him wine mixed with **m**,

MYSTERY
Ro 16:25 the revelation of the **m** hidden
1Co 15:51 Listen, I tell you a **m**: We will not
Eph 5:32 This is a profound **m**—but I am
Col 1:26 the **m** that has been kept hidden
1Ti 3:16 the **m** from which true godliness

MYTHS
1Ti 4: 7 Have nothing to do with godless **m**

NAIL (NAILING)
Jn 20:25 "Unless I see the **n** marks in his

NAILING (NAIL)
Ac 2:23 him to death by **n** him to the cross.
Col 2:14 has taken it away, **n** it to the cross.

NAKED
2Co 5: 3 are clothed, we will not be found **n**.

NAME (NAMES)
Mt 1:21 and you are to give him the **n** Jesus,
6: 9 in heaven, hallowed be your **n**,
18:20 two or three come together in my **n**,
Jn 10: 3 He calls his own sheep by **n**
16:24 not asked for anything in my **n**.
Ac 4:12 is no other **n** given under heaven
Ro 10:13 on the **n** of the Lord will be saved."
Php 2: 9 him the **n** that is above every **n**,
Col 3:17 do it all in the **n** of the Lord Jesus,
Heb 1: 4 the angels as the **n** he has inherited

NAMES (NAME)
Lk 10:20 that your **n** are written in heaven."
Rev 20:15 All whose **n** were not found written

NAPHTALI
Rev 7: 6 from the tribe of **N** 12,000,

NARROW
Mt 7:13 "Enter through the **n** gate. For wide

NATHANAEL
Apostle (Jn 1:45-49; 21:2). Probably also called Bartholomew (Mt 10:3).

NATION (NATIONS)
1Pe 2: 9 a holy **n**, God's special possession,
Rev 7: 9 could count, from every **n**, tribe,

NATIONS (NATION)
Mt 28:19 go and make disciples of all **n**,
Rev 21:24 The **n** will walk by its light,

NATURAL (NATURE)
1Co 15:44 it is sown a **n** body, it is raised

NATURE (NATURAL)
Ro 8: 4 do not live according to the sinful **n**
8: 8 by the sinful **n** cannot please God.
Gal 5:19 The acts of the sinful **n** are obvious:
5:24 Jesus have crucified the sinful **n**
Php 2: 6 Who, being in very **n** God, did not

NAZARENE
Mt 2:23 the prophets: "He will be called a N "

NECESSARY
Ro 13: 5 it is **n** to submit to the authorities,

NEED (NEEDS NEEDY)
Mt 6: 8 knows what you **n** before you ask
Ro 12:13 with God's people who are in **n**.
1Co 12:21 say to the hand, "I don't **n** you!"
1Jn 3:17 sister in **n** but has no pity on them,

NEEDLE
Mt 19:24 to go through the eye of a **n** than

NEEDS (NEED)
Php 4:19 God will meet all your **n** according

NEEDY (NEED)
Mt 6: 2 "So when you give to the **n**, do not

NEGLECT (NEGLECTED)
Ac 6: 2 for us to **n** the ministry of the word
1Ti 4:14 Do not **n** your gift, which was given

NEGLECTED (NEGLECT)
Mt 23:23 But you have **n** the more important

NEIGHBOR
Mt 19:19 mother,' and 'love your **n** as yourself."'
Lk 10:29 he asked Jesus, "And who is my **n**?"
Ro 13:10 Love does no harm to its **n**.

NEW
Mt 9:17 they pour **n** wine into **n** wineskins,
Lk 22:20 "This cup is the **n** covenant in my
2Co 5:17 is in Christ, there is a **n** creation:
Eph 4:24 and to put on the **n** self,
2Pe 3:13 forward to a **n** heaven and a **n** earth,
1Jn 2: 8 Yet I am writing you a **n** command;

NEWBORN (BEAR)
1Pe 2: 2 Like **n** babies, crave pure spiritual

NEWS
Mk 1:15 Repent and believe the good **n**!"
Lk 2:10 I bring you good **n** of great joy
Ac 5:42 proclaiming the good **n** that Jesus is
17:18 Paul was preaching the good **n**
Ro 10:15 the feet of those who bring good **n**!"

NICODEMUS
Pharisee who visited Jesus at night (Jn 3). Argued fair treatment of Jesus (Jn 7:50-52). With Joseph, prepared Jesus for burial (Jn 19:38-42).

NIGHT
Jn 3: 2 He came to Jesus at **n** and said,

1Th 5: 2 Lord will come like a thief in the **n**.
5: 5 We do not belong to the **n**
Rev 21:25 be shut, for there will be no **n** there.

NOAH
Righteous man called to build the ark to save his family from the flood (Mt 24:37-39; Heb 11:7; 1Pe 3:20; 2Pe 2:5).

NOBLE
Lk 8:15 good soil stands for those with a **n**
Ro 9:21 of clay some pottery for **n** purposes
Php 4: 8 whatever is **n**, whatever is right,
2Ti 2:20 some are for **n** purposes and some

NOTHING
Jn 15: 5 fruit; apart from me you can do **n**.

NULLIFY
Ro 3:31 Do we, then, **n** the law by this faith?

OATH
Heb 7:21 became a priest with an **o** when God

OBEDIENCE (OBEY)
Ro 1: 5 to faith and **o** for his name's sake.
6:16 to death, or to **o**, which leads
2Jn : 6 that we walk in **o** to his commands.

OBEDIENT (OBEY)
Lk 2:51 with them and was **o** to them.
Php 2: 8 by becoming **o** to death— even death
1Pe 1:14 As **o** children, do not conform

OBEY (OBEDIENCE OBEDIENT OBEYED)
Mt 28:20 to **o** everything I have commanded
Jn 14:23 who loves me will **o** my teaching.
Ac 5:29 "We must **o** God rather than human
Ro 6:16 you are slaves of the one you **o**—
Ro 6:17 you have come to **o** from your heart
Gal 5: 3 he is obligated to **o** the whole law.
Eph 6: 1 **o** your parents in the Lord, for this
6: 5 **o** your earthly masters with respect
Col 3:20 **o** your parents in everything,
1Ti 3: 4 well and see that his children **o** him,

OBEYED (OBEY)
Jn 17: 6 to me and they have **o** your word.
Heb 11: 8 as his inheritance, **o** and went,
1Pe 3: 6 who **o** Abraham and called him her

OBLIGATED
Ro 1:14 I am **o** both to Greeks
Gal 5: 3 that he is **o** to obey the whole law.

OBSCENITY
Eph 5: 4 Nor should there be **o**, foolish talk

OBSOLETE
Heb 8:13 "new," he has made the first one **o**;

OBTAINED (OBTAINING)
Ro 9:30 not pursue righteousness, have **o** it,
Php 3:12 Not that I have already **o** all this,

OBTAINING (OBTAINED)
Heb 9:12 blood, thus **o** eternal redemption.

OFFER (OFFERED OFFERING OFFERINGS)
Ro 12: 1 to **o** your bodies as living sacrifices,
Heb 13:15 let us continually **o** to God

OFFERED (OFFER)
Heb 7:27 sins once for all when he **o** himself.

OFFERING (OFFER)
Mt 5:23 if you are **o** your gift at the altar

Eph 5: 2 himself up for us as a fragrant **o**
Heb 10: 5 "Sacrifice and **o** you did not desire,
    11: 4 By faith Abel brought God a better **o**

OFFERINGS (OFFER)
Mk 12:33 is more important than all burnt **o**

OFFICER
2Ti 2: 4 try to please their commanding **o**.

OFFSPRING
Ac 3:25 'Through your **o** all peoples on earth
Rev 22:16 I am the Root and the **O** of David,

OIL
Heb 1: 9 by anointing you with the **o** of joy."

OLIVE (OLIVES)
Ro 11:17 and you, though a wild **o** shoot,
Rev 11: 4 They are "the two **o** trees" and the two

OLIVES (OLIVE)
Jas 3:12 can a fig tree bear **o**, or a grapevine

OMEGA
Rev 1: 8 "I am the Alpha and the **O**,"

ONE
Mk 12:29 the Lord our God, the Lord is **o**.
1Co 12:12 as a body, though **o**, has many parts,

ONESIMUS
Col 4: 9 He is coming with **O**, our faithful
Phm :10 that I appeal to you for my son **O**,

ONESIPHORUS
2Ti 1:16 show mercy to the household of **O**,
    4:19 and Aquila and the household of **O**.

OPPORTUNITY
Ro 7:11 sin, seizing the **o** afforded
Gal 6:10 as we have **o**, let us do good to all
Eph 5:16 making the most of every **o**,
Col 4: 5 outsiders; make the most of every **o**.
1Ti 5:14 to give the enemy no **o** for slander.

OPPOSES
Jas 4: 6 "God **o** the proud but shows favor
1Pe 5: 5 "God **o** the proud but shows favor

OPPRESSED
Lk 4:18 for the blind, to release the **o**,
Jas 4: 6 shows favor to the humble and **o**."

ORDERLY
1Co 14:40 be done in a fitting and **o** way.

ORGIES
Gal 5:21 envy; drunkenness, **o**, and the like.
1Pe 4: 3 lust, drunkenness, **o**,

ORIGIN
2Pe 1:21 For prophecy never had its **o**

ORPHANS
Jn 14:18 I will not leave you as **o**; I will
Jas 1:27 to look after **o** and widows in their

OUTCOME
Heb 13: 7 Consider the **o** of their way of life
1Pe 4:17 what will the **o** be for those who do

OUTSIDERS
Col 4: 5 wise in the way you act toward **o**;
1Th 4:12 daily life may win the respect of **o**
1Ti 3: 7 also have a good reputation with **o**,

OUTSTANDING
Ro 13: 8 Let no debt remain **o**, except

OUTWEIGHS
2Co 4:17 an eternal glory that far **o** them all.

OVERCOME (OVERCOMES)
Mt 16:18 and the gates of death will not **o** it.
Mk 9:24 "I do believe; help me **o** my unbelief!"
Jn 16:33 But take heart! I have **o** the world."
Ro 12:21 Do not be **o** by evil, but **o** evil
1Jn 5: 4 is the victory that has **o** the world,

OVERCOMES (OVERCOME See also VICTORIOUS)
1Jn 5: 4 everyone born of God **o** the world.
    5: 5 Who is it that **o** the world?

OVERFLOW
Lk 6:45 the **o** of the heart the mouth speaks.
Ro 15:13 so that you may **o** with hope
2Co 4:15 people may cause thanksgiving to **o**
1Th 3:12 love increase and **o** for each other

OVERJOYED (JOY)
Mt 2:10 they saw the star, they were **o**.
Jn 20:20 The disciples were **o** when they saw
Ac 12:14 she was so **o** she ran back without
1Pe 4:13 that you may be **o** when his glory is

OVERSEER (OVERSEERS)
1Ti 3: 1 to be an **o** desires a noble task.
    3: 2 Now the **o** is to be above reproach,
Tit 1: 7 Since an **o** manages God's

OVERSEERS (OVERSEER)
Ac 20:28 the Holy Spirit has made you **o**.
Php 1: 1 together with the **o** and deacons:

OVERWHELMED
Mt 26:38 "My soul is **o** with sorrow
Mk 7:37 People were **o** with amazement.

OWE
Ro 13: 7 Give to everyone what you **o**: If you
Phm :19 that you **o** me your very self.

OX
1Co 9: 9 "Do not muzzle an **o** while it is

PAGANS
Mt 5:47 than others? Do not even **p** do that?
1Pe 2:12 such good lives among the **p** that,

PAIN (PAINFUL)
Jn 16:21 to a child has **p** because her time has

PAINFUL (PAIN)
Heb 12:11 seems pleasant at the time, but **p**.

PALM
Jn 12:13 They took **p** branches and went out

PARABLES
    See also JESUS: PARABLES
Mt 13:35 "I will open my mouth in **p**, I will
Lk 8:10 but to others I speak in **p**, so that,

PARADISE
Lk 23:43 you, today you will be with me in **p**."
2Co 12: 4 was caught up to **p** and heard
Rev 2: 7 tree of life, which is in the **p** of God.

PARALYZED
Mk 2: 3 bringing to him a **p** man, carried by

PARENTS

Lk 18:29 sisters or **p** or children for the sake
   21:16 You will be betrayed even by **p**,
Ro   1:30 of doing evil; they disobey their **p**;
2Co 12:14 not have to save up for their **p**, but **p**
Eph 6: 1 Children, obey your **p** in the Lord,
Col 3:20 Children, obey your **p** in everything,
Heb12: 7 children are not disciplined by their **p**?
2Ti   3: 2 disobedient to their **p**, ungrateful,

PARTIALITY

Lk 20:21 that you do not show **p** but teach

PARTICIPATION

1Co 10:16 we give thanks a **p** in the blood
   10:16 bread that we break a **p** in the body
Php 3:10 resurrection and **p** in his sufferings,

PASS

Lk 21:33 Heaven and earth will **p** away,
  21:33 but my words will never **p** away.
1Co 13: 8 there is knowledge, it will **p** away.

PASSION (PASSIONS)

1Co 7: 9 better to marry than to burn with **p**.

PASSIONS (PASSION)

Gal 5:24 crucified the sinful nature with its **p**
Tit   2:12 "No" to ungodliness and worldly **p**,

PASSOVER

1Co 5: 7 For Christ, our **P** lamb, has been

PAST

Ro 15: 4 was written in the **p** was written
Heb 1: 1 In the **p** God spoke to our ancestors

PASTORS

Eph 4:11 the evangelists, the **p** and teachers,

PASTURE

Jn 10: 9 will come in and go out, and find **p**.

PATCH

Mt   9:16 "No one sews a **p** of unshrunk cloth

PATH (PATHS)

Lk   1:79 to guide our feet into the **p** of peace."
2Co 6: 3 no stumbling block in anyone's **p**,

PATHS (PATH)

Ro 11:33 and his **p** beyond tracing out!
Heb12:13 "Make level **p** for your feet,"

PATIENCE (PATIENT)

2Co 6: 6 understanding, **p** and kindness;
Gal 5:22 joy, peace, **p**, kindness, goodness,
Col 1:11 may have great endurance and **p**,
   3:12 humility, gentleness and **p**.

PATIENT (PATIENCE PATIENTLY)

Ro 12:12 Be joyful in hope, **p** in affliction,
1Co 13: 4 Love is **p**, love is kind. It does not
Eph 4: 2 be **p**, bearing with one another
1Th 5:14 help the weak, be **p** with everyone.

PATIENTLY (PATIENT)

Ro   8:25 we do not yet have, we wait for it **p**.

PATTERN

Ro 5:14 who is a **p** of the one to come.
  12: 2 not conform to the **p** of this world,
2Ti   1:13 me, keep as the **p** of sound teaching,

PAUL

Also called Saul (Ac 13:9). Pharisee from Tarsus (Ac 9:11;

Php 3:5). Apostle (Gal 1). At stoning of Stephen (Ac 8:1). Persecuted Church (Ac 9:1-2; Gal 1:13). Vision of Jesus on road to Damascus (Ac 9:4-9; 26:12-18). In Arabia (Gal 1:17). Preached in Damascus; escaped death through the wall in a basket (Ac 9:19-25). In Jerusalem; sent back to Tarsus (Ac 9:26-30).

Brought to Antioch by Barnabas (Ac 11:22-26). First missionary journey to Cyprus and Galatia (Ac 13-14). Stoned at Lystra (Ac 14:19-20). At Jerusalem council (Ac 15). Split with Barnabas over Mark (Ac 15:36-41).

Second missionary journey with Silas (Ac 16-20). Called to Macedonia (Ac 16:6-10). Freed from prison in Philippi (Ac 16:16-40). In Thessalonica (Ac 17:1-9). Speech in Athens (Ac 17:16-33). In Corinth (Ac 18). In Ephesus (Ac 19). Return to Jerusalem (Ac 21). Farewell to Ephesian elders (Ac 20:13-38). Arrival in Jerusalem (Ac 21:1-26). Arrested (Ac 21:27-36). Addressed crowds (Ac 22), Sanhedrin (Ac 23:1-11). Transferred to Caesarea (Ac 23:12-35). Trial before Felix (Ac 24), Festus (Ac 25:1-12). Before Agrippa (Ac 25:13-26:32). Voyage to Rome; shipwreck (Ac 27). Arrival in Rome (Ac 28).

Letters: Romans, 1 and 2 Corinthians, Galatians, Ephesians, Philippians, Colossians, 1 and 2 Thessalonians, 1 and 2 Timothy, Titus, Philemon.

PAY (REPAID REPAY)

Mt 22:17 Is it right to **p** the poll tax to Caesar
Ro 13: 6 This is also why you **p** taxes,
2Pe 1:19 you will do well to **p** attention to it,

PEACE (PEACEMAKERS)

Mt 10:34 I did not come to bring **p**,
Lk   2:14 and on earth **p** to those on whom his
Jn 14:27 **P** I leave with you; my **p** I give you.
  16:33 so that in me you may have **p**.
Ro   5: 1 we have **p** with God through our
1Co 7:15 God has called us to live in **p**.
  14:33 God is not a God of disorder but of **p**—
Gal 5:22 of the Spirit is love, joy, **p**, patience,
Eph 2:14 For he himself is our **p**, who has
Php 4: 7 And the **p** of God, which transcends
Col 1:20 by making **p** through his blood,
   3:15 Let the **p** of Christ rule in your
   3:15 of one body you were called to **p**.
1Th 5: 3 people are saying, "**P** and safety,"
2Th 3:16 the Lord of **p** himself give you **p**
2Ti   2:22 love and **p**, along with those who
1Pe 3:11 and do good; seek **p** and pursue it.
Rev 6: 4 given power to take **p** from the earth

PEACEMAKERS (PEACE)

Mt   5: 9 Blessed are the **p**, for they will be
Jas 3:18 **P** who sow in peace reap a harvest

PEARL (PEARLS)

Rev 21:21 pearls, each gate made of a single **p**.

PEARLS (PEARL)

Mt   7: 6 sacred; do not throw your **p** to pigs.
  13:45 is like a merchant looking for fine **p**.
1Ti   2: 9 or gold or **p** or expensive clothes,
Rev 21:21 The twelve gates were twelve **p**,

PEN

Mt   5:18 not the least stroke of a **p**,

PENTECOST

Ac   2: 1 When the day of **P** came, they were

PEOPLE (PEOPLES)

Mt   4:19 I will send you out to catch **p**."
  12:36 **p** will have to give account on
Lk   2:10 of great joy that will be for all the **p**.
   4: 4 '**P** do not live on bread alone.'"
Jn 12:32 will draw all **p** to myself."
Ac 15:14 to choose a **p** for his name

Ro   5:12 in this way death came to all **p**,
     8:27 the Spirit intercedes for God's **p**
1Co   9:22 I have become all things to all **p**
2Co   5:11 fear the Lord, we try to persuade **p**.
     6:16 be their God, and they will be my **p**."
Eph   1:18 of his glorious inheritance in his **p**,
     6:18 always keep on praying for all God's **p**.
1Ti   2: 4 who wants all **p** to be saved
2Ti   2: 2 entrust to reliable **p** who will also
Tit   2:14 himself a **p** that are his very own,
Heb   9:27 Just as **p** are destined to die once,
1Pe   2: 9 But you are a chosen **p**, a royal
Rev   5: 8 which are the prayers of God's **p**.
     19: 8 the righteous acts of God's **p**.)
     21: 3 dwelling place is now among the **p**,
     21: 3 They will be his **p**, and God himself

PEOPLES (PEOPLE)
Ac   3:25 all **p** on earth will be blessed.'
Rev   1: 7 all **p** on earth "will mourn

PERFECT (PERFECTER PERFECTION)
Mt   5:48 Be **p**, therefore, as your heavenly Father is **p**.
Ro   12: 2 will is—his good, pleasing and **p** will.
2Co   12: 9 my power is made **p** in weakness."
Col   3:14 binds them all together in **p** unity.
Heb   9:11 more **p** tabernacle that is not made
     10:14 he has made **p** forever those who
Jas   1:17 good and **p** gift is from above,
     1:25 who look intently into the **p** law
     3: 2 never at fault in what they say are **p**,
1Jn   4:18 But **p** love drives out fear,

PERFECTER (PERFECT)
Heb 12: 2 Jesus, the author and **p** of our faith.

PERFECTION (PERFECT)
Heb   7:11 **p** could have been attained through

PERISH (PERISHABLE)
Mt   18:14 that any of these little ones should **p**.
Lk   13: 3 unless you repent, you too will all **p**.
Jn   10:28 eternal life, and they shall never **p**;
Col   2:22 that are all destined to **p** with use,
Heb   1:11 They will **p**, but you remain;
2Pe   3: 9 you, not wanting anyone to **p**,

PERISHABLE (PERISH)
1Co 15:42 The body that is sown is **p**, it is

PERJURERS
1Ti   1:10 for slave traders and liars and **p**.

PERMIT
1Ti   2:12 I do not **p** a woman to teach

PERSECUTE (PERSECUTED PERSECUTION)
Mt   5:11 **p** you and falsely say all kinds
Jn   15:20 persecuted me, they will **p** you also.
Ac   9: 4 him, "Saul, Saul, why do you **p** me?"
Ro   12:14 Bless those who **p** you; bless and do

PERSECUTED (PERSECUTE)
1Co   4:12 bless; when we are **p**, we endure it;
2Ti   3:12 godly life in Christ Jesus will be **p**,

PERSECUTION (PERSECUTE)
Ro   8:35 trouble or hardship or **p** or famine

PERSEVERANCE (PERSEVERE)
Ro   5: 3 we know that suffering produces **p**;
     5: 4 **p**, character; and character, hope.
Heb 12: 1 let us run with **p** the race marked
Jas   1: 3 the testing of your faith produces **p**.
2Pe   1: 6 and to self-control, **p**; and to **p**,

PERSEVERE (PERSEVERANCE PERSEVERED PERSEVERES)
1Ti   4:16 **P** in them, because if you do,
Heb 10:36 You need to **p** so that when you
Jas   1:12 Blessed are those who **p** under trial,

PERSEVERED (PERSEVERE)
Heb 11:27 he **p** because he saw him who is
Jas   5:11 consider blessed those who have **p**.
Rev   2: 3 You have **p** and have endured

PERSEVERES (PERSEVERE)
1Co 13: 7 trusts, always hopes, always **p**.

PERSUADE
2Co   5:11 to fear the Lord, we try to **p** people.

PERVERSION (PERVERT)
Jude   : 7 up to sexual immorality and **p**.

PERVERT (PERVERSION)
Gal   1: 7 are trying to **p** the gospel of Christ.

PETER
     Apostle, brother of Andrew, also called Simon (Mt 10:2; Mk 3:16; Lk 6:14; Ac 1:13), and Cephas (Jn 1:42). Confession of Christ (Mt 16:13-20; Mk 8:27-30; Lk 9:18-27). At transfiguration (Mt 17:1-8; Mk 9:2-8; Lk 9:28-36; 2Pe 1:16-18). Caught fish with coin (Mt 17:24-27). Denial of Jesus predicted (Mt 26:31-35; Mk 14:27-31; Lk 22:31-34; Jn 13:31-38). Denied Jesus (Mt 26:69-75; Mk 14:66-72; Lk 22:54-62; Jn 18:15-27). Commissioned by Jesus to shepherd his flock (Jn 21:15-23).
     Speech at Pentecost (Ac 2). Healed beggar (Ac 3:1-10). Speech at temple (Ac 3:11-26), before Sanhedrin (Ac 4:1-22). In Samaria (Ac 8:14-25). Sent by vision to Cornelius (Ac 10). Announced salvation of Gentiles in Jerusalem (Ac 11; 15). Freed from prison (Ac 12). Inconsistency at Antioch (Gal 2:11-21). At Jerusalem Council (Ac 15).
     Letters: 1-2 Peter.

PHARISEES
Mt   5:20 surpasses that of the **P**

PHILIP
     1. Apostle (Mt 10:3; Mk 3:18; Lk 6:14; Jn 1:43-48; 14:8; Ac 1:13).
     2. Deacon (Ac 6:1-7); evangelist in Samaria (Ac 8:4-25), to Ethiopian (Ac 8:26-40).

PHILOSOPHY
Col   2: 8 through hollow and deceptive **p**,

PHYLACTERIES
Mt   23: 5 see: They make their **p** wide

PHYSICAL
1Ti   4: 8 For **p** training is of some value,
Jas   2:16 does nothing about their **p** needs,

PIERCED
Jn   19:37 will look on the one they have **p**."

PIGS
Mt   7: 6 do not throw your pearls to **p**. If you

PILATE
     Governor of Judea. Questioned Jesus (Mt 27:1-26; Mk 15:15; Lk 22:66-23:25; Jn 18:28-19:16); sent him to Herod (Lk 23:6-12); consented to his crucifixion when crowds chose Barabbas (Mt 27:15-26; Mk 15:6-15; Lk 23:13-25; Jn 19:1-10).

PILLAR
1Ti   3:15 the **p** and foundation of the truth.

PIT
Mt 15:14 lead the blind, both will fall into a **p**."

PITIED
1Co 15:19 we are to be **p** more than all others.

PLAIN
Ro 1:19 be known about God is **p** to them,

PLAN (PLANNED)
Eph 1:11 to the **p** of him who works

PLANK
Mt 7: 3 attention to the **p** in your own eye?
Lk 6:41 attention to the **p** in your own eye?

PLANNED (PLAN)
Heb 11:40 God had **p** something better for us

PLANTED (PLANTS)
Mt 15:13 Father has not **p** will be pulled
1Co 3: 6 I **p** the seed, Apollos watered it,

PLANTS (PLANTED)
1Co 3: 7 neither the one who **p** nor the one
9· 7 Who **p** a vineyard and does not eat

PLATTER
Mk 6:25 the head of John the Baptist on a **p**."

PLAYED
Lk 7:32 " 'We **p** the flute for you, and you did
1Co 14: 7 what tune is being **p** unless there is

PLEADED
2Co 12: 8 Three times I **p** with the Lord

PLEASANT (PLEASE)
Heb 12:11 No discipline seems **p** at the time,

PLEASE (PLEASANT PLEASED PLEASES PLEASING
PLEASURE PLEASURES)
Jn 5:30 for I seek not to **p** myself but him
Ro 8: 8 by the sinful nature cannot **p** God.
15: 2 We should all **p** our neighbors
1Co 7:32 Lord's affairs—how he can **p** the Lord.
10:33 even as I try to **p** everyone in every
2Co 5: 9 So we make it our goal to **p** him,
Gal 1:10 Or am I trying to **p** people? If I were
1Th 4: 1 you how to live in order to **p** God,
2Ti 2: 4 try to **p** their commanding officer.
Heb 11: 6 faith it is impossible to **p** God,

PLEASED (PLEASE)
Mt 3:17 whom I love; with him I am well **p**."
1Co 1:21 God was **p** through the foolishness
Col 1:19 God was **p** to have all his fullness
Heb 11: 5 was commended as one who **p** God.
2Pe 1:17 whom I love; with him I am well **p**."

PLEASES (PLEASE)
Jn 3: 8 The wind blows wherever it **p**.
8:29 alone, for I always do what **p** him."
Col 3:20 in everything, for this **p** the Lord.
1Ti 2: 3 This is good, and **p** God our Savior,
1Jn 3:22 his commands and do what **p** him.

PLEASING (PLEASE)
Ro 12: 1 **p** to God—this is your proper worship
Php 4:18 an acceptable sacrifice, **p** to God.
Heb 13:21 may he work in us what is **p** to him,

PLEASURE (PLEASE)
Eph 1: 5 in accordance with his **p** and will—
1: 9 of his will according to his good **p**,
2Ti 3: 4 lovers of **p** rather than lovers of God—

PLEASURES (PLEASE)
Heb 11:25 than to enjoy the fleeting **p** of sin.
2Pe 2:13 reveling in their **p** while they feast

PLENTIFUL
Mt 9:37 "The harvest is **p** but the workers are

PLOW
Lk 9:62 "No one who puts a hand to the **p**

POINT
Jas 2:10 yet stumbles at just one **p** is guilty

POISON
Mk 16:18 and when they drink deadly **p**,
Jas 3: 8 It is a restless evil, full of deadly **p**.

POLLUTE (POLLUTED)
Jude : 8 these ungodly people **p** their own

POLLUTED (POLLUTE)
Ac 15:20 to abstain from food **p** by idols,
Jas 1:27 oneself from being **p** by the world.

POOR (POVERTY)
Mt 5: 3 "Blessed are the **p** in spirit, for theirs
11: 5 good news is proclaimed to the **p**.
19:21 your possessions and give to the **p**,
26:11 The **p** you will always have
Mk 12:42 But a **p** widow came and put in two
Ac 10: 4 and gifts to the **p** have come up as
1Co 13: 3 If I give all I possess to the **p**
2Co 8: 9 yet for your sake he became **p**,
Jas 2: 2 and a **p** person in filthy old clothes

POSSESS (POSSESSING POSSESSION
POSSESSIONS)
Jn 5:39 think that in them you **p** eternal life.

POSSESSING (POSSESS)
2Co 6:10 nothing, and yet **p** everything.

POSSESSION (POSSESS)
Eph 1:14 redemption of those who are God's **p**—

POSSESSIONS (POSSESS)
Lk 12:15 not consist in an abundance of **p**."
2Co 12:14 because what I want is not your **p**
1Jn 3:17 If any one of you has material **p**

POSSIBLE
Mt 19:26 but with God all things are **p**."
Mk 9:23 Jesus. "Everything is **p** for one who
10:27 with God; all things are **p** with God."
Ro 12:18 If it is **p**, as far as it depends on you,
1Co 9:22 by all **p** means I might save some.

POTTER (POTTERY)
Ro 9:21 Does not the **p** have the right

POTTERY (POTTER)
Ro 9:21 of clay some **p** for noble purposes

POUR (POURED)
Ac 2:17 I will **p** out my Spirit on all people.

POURED (POUR)
Ac 10:45 the Holy Spirit had been **p** out even
Ro 5: 5 because God's love has been **p**

POVERTY (POOR)
Mk 12:44 out of her **p**, put in everything—all she
2Co 8: 2 their extreme **p** welled up in rich
8: 9 you through his **p** might become

POWER (POWERFUL POWERS)
Mt 22:29 know the Scriptures or the **p** of God.
    24:30 of the sky, with **p** and great glory.
Ac   1: 8 you will receive **p** when the Holy
    4:33 With great **p** the apostles continued
  10:38 Nazareth with the Holy Spirit and **p**,
Ro   1:16 because it is the **p** of God
1Co 1:18 us who are being saved it is the **p**
  15:56 is sin, and the **p** of sin is the law.
2Co 12: 9 for you, for my **p** is made perfect
   12: 9 so that Christ's **p** may rest on me.
Eph 1:19 his incomparably great **p** for us who
Php 3:10 to know the **p** of his resurrection
Col   1:11 strengthened with all **p** according
2Ti   1: 7 us timid, but gives us **p**,
Heb 7:16 of the **p** of an indestructible life.
Rev 4:11 to receive glory and honor and **p**,
  19: 1 and glory and **p** belong to our God,
  20: 6 second death has no **p** over them,

POWERFUL (POWER)
Lk 24:19 **p** in word and deed before God
2Th 1: 7 in blazing fire with his **p** angels.
Heb 1: 3 sustaining all things by his **p** word.
Jas 5:16 prayer of a righteous person is **p**

POWERLESS
Ro 5: 6 when we were still **p**, Christ died
  8: 3 what the law was **p** to do because it

POWERS (POWER)
Ro 8:38 the present nor the future, nor any **p**,
1Co 12:10 to another miraculous **p**, to another
Col 1:16 whether thrones or **p** or rulers
  2:15 And having disarmed the **p**

PRACTICE
Mt 23: 3 for they do not **p** what they preach.
Lk   8:21 hear God's word and put it into **p**."
Ro 12:13 who are in need. **P** hospitality.
1Ti   5: 4 to put their religion into **p** by caring

PRAISE (PRAISED PRAISES PRAISING)
Mt 5:16 deeds and **p** your Father in heaven.
  21:16 and infants you have ordained **p**'?"
Eph 1: 6 to the **p** of his glorious grace,
  1:12 might be for the **p** of his glory.
  1:14 possession—to the **p** of his glory.
Heb 13:15 offer to God a sacrifice of **p**—
Jas 5:13 Is anyone happy? Sing songs of **p**.

PRAISED (PRAISE)
Ro 9: 5 who is God over all, forever **p**!
1Pe 4:11 God may be **p** through Jesus Christ.

PRAISES (PRAISE)
Ro 15:11 Gentiles, and sing **p** to him,

PRAISING (PRAISE)
Ac 10:46 speaking in tongues and **p** God.
1Co 14:16 when you are **p** God in the Spirit,

PRAY (PRAYED PRAYER PRAYERS PRAYING)
Mt 5:44 and **p** for those who persecute you,
  6: 5 "And when you **p**, do not be like
  6: 9 "This, then, is how you should **p**:
  26:36 "Sit here while I go over there and **p**."
Lk   6:28 you, **p** for those who mistreat you.
  18: 1 them that they should always **p**
  22:40 to them, "**P** that you will not fall
Ro 8:26 do not know what we ought to **p** for,
1Co 14:13 in a tongue should **p** that they may
1Th 5:17 **p** continually,
Jas 5:13 You should **p**. Is anyone happy?
  5:16 **p** for each other so that you may be

PRAYED (PRAY)
Mk 14:35 and **p** that if possible the hour might

PRAYER (PRAY)
Mt 21:13 house will be called a house of **p**,'
Mk 11:24 whatever you ask for in **p**,
Jn 17:15 My **p** is not that you take them
Ac 6: 4 will give our attention to **p**
Php 4: 6 in every situation, by **p** and petition,
Jas 5:15 the **p** offered in faith will make you
1Pe 3:12 and his ears are attentive to their **p**,

PRAYERS (PRAY)
Mk 12:40 and for a show make lengthy **p**.
1Pe 3: 7 so that nothing will hinder your **p**.
Rev 5: 8 which are the **p** of God's people.

PRAYING (PRAY)
Mk 11:25 And when you stand **p**, if you hold
Jn 17: 9 I am not **p** for the world,
Ac 16:25 Silas were **p** and singing hymns
Eph 6:18 and always keep on **p** for all God's

PREACH (PREACHED PREACHING)
Mt 23: 3 for they do not practice what they **p**.
Mk 16:15 and **p** the gospel to all creation.
Ac 9:20 At once he began to **p**
Ro 10:15 how can anyone **p** unless they are
  15:20 to **p** the gospel where Christ was not
1Co 1:17 but to **p** the gospel—not with wisdom
  1:23 but we **p** Christ crucified:
  9:14 that those who **p** the gospel should
  9:16 Woe to me if I do not **p** the gospel!
2Co 10:16 so that we can **p** the gospel
Gal 1: 8 heaven should **p** a gospel other than
2Ti 4: 2 **P** the word; be prepared in season

PREACHED (PREACH)
Mk 13:10 And the gospel must first be **p** to all
Ac 8: 4 who had been scattered **p** the word
1Co 9:27 slave so that after I have **p** to others,
  15: 1 remind you of the gospel I **p** to you,
2Co 11: 4 a Jesus other than the Jesus we **p**,
Gal 1: 8 a gospel other than the one we **p**
Php 1:18 false motives or true, Christ is **p**.
1Ti 3:16 by angels, was **p** among the nations,

PREACHING (PREACH)
Ro 10:14 can they hear without someone **p**
1Co 9:18 in **p** the gospel I may offer it free
1Ti 4:13 of Scripture, to **p** and to teaching.
  5:17 especially those whose work is **p**

PRECIOUS
1Pe 1:19 but with the **p** blood of Christ,
  2: 6 a chosen and **p** cornerstone,
2Pe 1: 4 us his very great and **p** promises,

PREDESTINED (DESTINY)
Ro 8:29 **p** to be conformed to the likeness
  8:30 And those he **p**, he also called;
Eph 1: 5 he **p** us for adoption to sonship
  1:11 having been **p** according to the plan

PREPARE (PREPARED)
Jn 14: 2 that I am going there to **p** a place

PREPARED (PREPARE)
Mt 25:34 the kingdom **p** for you since
1Co 2: 9 conceived— these things God has **p**
Eph 2:10 which God **p** in advance for us
2Ti 4: 2 be **p** in season and out of season;
1Pe 3:15 Always be **p** to give an answer

PRESENCE (PRESENT)
Heb 9:24 now to appear for us in God's **p**.

Jude :24 before his glorious **p** without fault

PRESENT (PRESENCE)
2Co 11: 2 that I might **p** you as a pure virgin
Eph 5:27 and to **p** her to himself as a radiant
2Ti 2:15 Do your best to **p** yourself to God as

PRESS (PRESSED PRESSURE)
Php 3:14 I **p** on toward the goal to win

PRESSED (PRESS)
Lk 6:38 A good measure, **p** down,

PRESSURE (PRESS)
2Co 1: 8 We were under great **p**, far beyond
11:28 I face daily the **p** of my concern

PRICE
1Co 6:20 you were bought at a **p**.
7:23 You were bought at a **p**, do not

PRIDE (PROUD)
Gal 6: 4 Then you can take **p** in yourself,
Jas 1: 9 to take **p** in their high position.

PRIEST (PRIESTHOOD PRIESTS)
Heb 4:14 a great high **p** who has ascended
4:15 do not have a high **p** who is unable
7:26 Such a high **p** truly meets our
8: 1 We do have such a high **p**, who sat

PRIESTHOOD (PRIEST)
Heb 7:24 lives forever, he has a permanent **p**.
1Pe 2: 5 into a spiritual house to be a holy **p**,
2: 9 people, a royal **p**, a holy nation,

PRIESTS (PRIEST)
Rev 5:10 a kingdom and **p** to serve our God,

PRINCE
Jn 12:31 now the **p** of this world will be
Ac 5:31 him to his own right hand as **P**

PRISCILLA
Wife of Aquila; co-worker with Paul (Ac 18; Ro 16:3; 1Co 16:19; 2Ti 4:19); instructor of Apollos (Ac 18:24-28).

PRISON (IMPRISONED PRISONER)
Mt 25:36 I was in **p** and you came to visit me.'
Rev 20: 7 Satan will be released from his **p**

PRISONER (PRISON)
Ro 7:23 making me a **p** of the law of sin
Eph 3: 1 the **p** of Christ Jesus for the sake

PRIVILEGE
2Co 8: 4 us for the **p** of sharing in this service

PRIZE
1Co 9:24 Run in such a way as to get the **p**.
Php 3:14 on toward the goal to win the **p**

PROCLAIM (PROCLAIMED)
Ac 20:27 I have not hesitated to **p** to you
Ro 10: 8 the message concerning faith that we **p**:
1Co 11:26 cup, you **p** the Lord's death until he

PROCLAIMED (PROCLAIM)
Ro 15:19 I have fully **p** the gospel of Christ.
Col 1:23 has been **p** to every creature under

PRODUCE (PRODUCES)
Mt 3: 8 **P** fruit in keeping with repentance.
3:10 that does not **p** good fruit will be cut

PRODUCES (PRODUCE)
Ro 5: 3 know that suffering **p** perseverance;
Heb 12:11 it **p** a harvest of righteousness

PROFESS
1Ti 2:10 for women who **p** to worship God.
Heb 4:14 let us hold firmly to the faith we **p**.
10:23 hold unswervingly to the hope we **p**,

PROMISE (PROMISED PROMISES)
Ac 2:39 The **p** is for you and your children
Gal 3:14 faith we might receive the **p**
1Ti 4: 8 holding **p** for both the present life
2Pe 3: 9 Lord is not slow in keeping his **p**,

PROMISED (PROMISE)
Ro 4:21 God had power to do what he had **p**.
Heb 10:23 we profess, for he who **p** is faithful.
2Pe 3: 4 will say, "Where is this 'coming' he **p**?

PROMISES (PROMISE)
Ro 9: 4 law, the temple worship and the **p**.
2Pe 1: 4 us his very great and precious **p**,

PROMPTED
1Th 1: 3 by faith, your labor **p** by love,
2Th 1:11 and your every deed **p** by faith.

PROPER
Ro 12: 1 your **p** worship as rational beings.

PROPHECIES (PROPHESY)
1Co 13: 8 But where there are **p**, they will
1Th 5:20 Do not treat **p** with contempt

PROPHECY (PROPHESY)
1Co 14: 1 gifts, especially the gift of **p**.
2Pe 1:20 that no **p** of Scripture came

PROPHESY (PROPHECIES PROPHECY PROPHESYING PROPHET PROPHETIC PROPHETS)
Mt 7:22 did we not **p** in your name
1Co 14:39 be eager to **p**, and do not forbid

PROPHESYING (PROPHESY)
Ro 12: 6 us. If your gift is **p**, then prophesy

PROPHET (PROPHESY)
Mt 10:41 to be a **p** will receive a prophet's

PROPHETIC (PROPHESY)
2Pe 1:19 We also have the **p** message as

PROPHETS (PROPHESY)
Mt 5:17 come to abolish the Law or the **P**;
7:12 for this sums up the Law and the **P**.
24:24 messiahs and false **p** will appear
Lk 4:24 "**p** are not accepted in their
24:25 believe all that the **p** have spoken!
Ac 10:43 All the **p** testify about him
1Co 12:28 apostles, second **p**, third teachers,
14:32 The spirits of **p** are subject to the control of **p**.
Eph 2:20 the foundation of the apostles and **p**,
Heb 1: 1 our ancestors through the **p** at many
1Pe 1:10 the **p**, who spoke of the grace

PROSTITUTE (PROSTITUTES)
1Co 6:15 of Christ and unite them with a **p**?

PROSTITUTES (PROSTITUTE)
Lk 15:30 your property with **p** comes home,
1Co 6: 9 adulterers nor male **p** nor practicing

PROTECT (PROTECTS)
Jn 17:11 **p** them by the power of your name,

PROTECTS (PROTECT)
1Co 13: 7 It always **p**, always trusts,

PROUD (PRIDE)
Ro 12:16 Do not be **p**, but be willing
1Co 13: 4 envy, it does not boast, it is not **p**.

PROVE
Jn 16: 8 he will **p** the world to be in the wrong
1Co 4: 2 been given a trust must **p** faithful.

PROVIDE (PROVIDES)
1Ti 5: 8 Anyone who does not **p** for their

PROVIDES (PROVIDE)
1Ti 6:17 who richly **p** us with everything
1Pe 4:11 do so with the strength God **p**,

PRUNES
Jn 15: 2 branch that does bear fruit he **p**

PSALMS
Eph 5:19 speaking to one another with **p**,
Col 3:16 another with all wisdom through **p**,

PUBLICLY
Ac 20:20 have taught you **p** and from house
1Ti 5:20 Those who sin are to be rebuked **p**,

PUFFS
1Co 8: 1 knowledge **p** up while love builds

PUNISH (PUNISHED)
1Pe 2:14 by him to **p** those who do wrong

PUNISHED (PUNISH)
2Th 1: 9 They will be **p** with everlasting
Heb 10:29 to be **p** who have trampled the Son

PURE (PURIFIES PURIFY PURITY)
Mt 5: 8 Blessed are the **p** in heart, for they
2Co 11: 2 I might present you as a **p** virgin
Php 4: 8 whatever is **p**, whatever is lovely,
1Ti 5:22 the sins of others. Keep yourself **p**.
Tit 1:15 To the **p**, all things are **p**,
2: 5 to be self-controlled and **p**, to be
Heb 13: 4 all, and the marriage bed kept **p**,
1Jn 3: 3 purify themselves, just as he is **p**.

PURIFIES (PURE)
1Jn 1: 7 of Jesus, his Son, **p** us from all sin.

PURIFY (PURE)
Tit 2:14 to **p** for himself a people that are his
1Jn 1: 9 and **p** us from all unrighteousness.
3: 3 who have this hope in them **p** themselves,

PURITY (PURE)
2Co 6: 6 in **p**, understanding,
1Ti 4:12 in conduct, in love, in faith and in **p**.

PURPOSE
Ro 8:28 have been called according to his **p**.

PURSES
Lk 12:33 Provide **p** for yourselves that will

PURSUE
2Ti 2:22 of youth and **p** righteousness, faith,
1Pe 3:11 and do good; seek peace and **p** it.

QUALITIES (QUALITY)
2Pe 1: 8 if you possess these **q** in increasing

QUALITY (QUALITIES)
1Co 3:13 and the fire will test the **q** of each

QUARRELSOME
1Ti 3: 3 gentle, not **q**, not a lover of money.
2Ti 2:24 the Lord's servant must not be **q**

QUEEN
Mt 12:42 The **Q** of the South will rise
Rev 18: 7 she boasts, 'I sit enthroned as **q**.

QUICK-TEMPERED
Tit 1: 7 not **q**, not given to drunkenness,

QUIET (QUIETNESS)
Lk 19:40 "if they keep **q**, the stones will cry
1Ti 2: 2 peaceful and **q** lives in all godliness
1Pe 3: 4 beauty of a gentle and **q** spirit,

QUIETNESS (QUIET)
1Ti 2:11 A woman should learn in **q** and full

RACE
1Co 9:24 know that in a **r** all the runners run,
2Ti 4: 7 I have finished the **r**, I have kept
Heb 12: 1 with perseverance the **r** marked

RADIANCE (RADIANT)
Heb 1: 3 The Son is the **r** of God's glory

RADIANT (RADIANCE)
Eph 5:27 present her to himself as a **r** church,

RAHAB
Prostitute of Jericho who hid Israelite spies (Heb 11:31; Jas 2:25). Ancestor of Jesus (Mt 1:5).

RAIN (RAINBOW)
Mt 5:45 and sends **r** on the righteous

RAINBOW (RAIN)
Rev 4: 3 **r** that shone like an emerald

RAISED (RISE)
Ro 4:25 was **r** to life for our justification.
10: 9 your heart that God **r** him
1Co 15: 4 he was **r** on the third day according

RANSOM
Mt 20:28 and to give his life as a **r** for many."
Heb 9:15 he has died as a **r** to set them free

RAVENS
Lk 12:24 Consider the **r**: They do not sow

READ (READS)
2Co 3: 2 hearts, known and **r** by everyone.

READS (READ)
Rev 1: 3 Blessed is the one who **r** the words

REAL (REALITIES REALITY)
Jn 6:55 For my flesh is **r** food and my blood is **r** drink.

REALITIES (REAL)
1Co 2:13 by the Spirit, explaining spiritual **r**

REALITY (REAL)
Col 2:17 the **r**, however, is found in Christ.

REAP (REAPS)
2Co 9: 6 sows sparingly will also **r** sparingly,
9: 6 generously will also **r** generously.
Gal 6: 7 People **r** what they sow.

REAPS (REAP)
Jn 4:37 saying 'One sows and another **r**'

REASON
1Pe 3:15 asks you to give the r for the hope

REBEKAH
Wife of Isaac, mother of Esau and Jacob (Ro 9:10-13).

REBEL (REBELS)
Mt 10:21 children will r against their parents

REBELS (REBEL)
Mk 15:27 They crucified two r with him,

REBUKE (REBUKED REBUKING)
Lk 17: 3 sins against you, r the offender;
2Ti   4: 2 r and encourage—with great patience
Rev 3:19 Those whom I love I r

REBUKED (REBUKE)
1Ti   5:20 Those who sin are to be r publicly,

REBUKING (REBUKE)
2Ti   3:16 and is useful for teaching, r,

RECALLING
1Ti   1·18 by r them you may fight the battle

RECEIVE (RECEIVED RECEIVES)
Ac   1: 8 But you will r power when the Holy
  20.35 'It is more blessed to give than to r.' "
2Co 6:17 no unclean thing, and I will r you."
Rev 4:11 to r glory and honor and power,

RECEIVED (RECEIVE)
Mt   6: 2 you, they have r their reward in full.
  10: 8 Freely you have r, freely give.
1Co 11:23 For I r from the Lord what I
Col   2: 6 just as you r Christ Jesus as Lord,
1Pe 4:10 should use whatever gift you have r

RECEIVES (RECEIVE)
Mt   7: 8 For everyone who asks r; those who
Ac 10:43 who believes in him r forgiveness

RECOGNIZE (RECOGNIZED)
Mt   7:16 By their fruit you will r them.

RECOGNIZED (RECOGNIZE)
Mt 12:33 be bad, for a tree is r by its fruit.
Ro   7:13 in order that sin might be r as sin,

RECONCILE (RECONCILED RECONCILIATION)
Eph 2:16 and in one body to r both of them

RECONCILED (RECONCILE)
Mt   5:24 First go and be r to that person;
Ro   5:10 we were r to him through the death
2Co 5:18 who r us to himself through Christ

RECONCILIATION (RECONCILE)
Ro   5:11 whom we have now received r.
  11:15 For if their rejection brought r
2Co 5:18 Christ and gave us the ministry of r:
  5:19 committed to us the message of r.

RED
Heb 11:29 through the R Sea as on dry land;
Rev 12: 3 an enormous r dragon with seven

REDEEM (REDEEMED REDEMPTION)
Gal 4: 5 to r those under the law, that we

REDEEMED (REDEEM)
Gal 3:13 Christ r us from the curse of the law
1Pe 1:18 that you were r from the empty way

REDEMPTION (REDEEM)
Lk 21:28 because your r is drawing near."
Ro   8:23 our adoption, the r of our bodies.
Eph 1: 7 In him we have r through his blood,
Col 1:14 in whom we have r, the forgiveness
Heb 9:12 own blood, thus obtaining eternal r.

REFLECTION
1Co 13:12 we see only a r as in a mirror;

REIGN
Ro   6:12 Therefore do not let sin r in your
1Co 15:25 For he must r until he has put all his
2Ti 2:12 we endure, we will also r with him.
Rev 20: 6 will r with him for a thousand years.

REJECT (REJECTED REJECTS)
1Th 5:22 r whatever is harmful.

REJECTED (REJECT)
1Ti   4: 4 nothing is to be r if it is received
1Pe 2: 4 the living S by human beings
  2: 7 stone the builders r has become

REJECTS (REJECT)
Lk 10:16 listens to me; whoever r you r me;
  10:16 whoever r me r him who sent me."
Jn   3:36 whoever r the Son will not see life,

REJOICE (JOY)
Lk 10:20 do not r that the spirits submit
  10:20 but r that your names are written
  15: 6 together and says, 'R with me; I have
Ro 12:15 R with those who r;
Php 4: 4 R in the Lord always. I will say it
1Th 5:16 R always,

REJOICES (JOY)
Lk   1:47 and my spirit r in God my Savior,
1Co 12:26 part is honored, every part r with it.
  13: 6 delight in evil but r with the truth.

REJOICING (JOY)
Lk 15: 7 the same way there will be more r
Ac   5:41 r because they had been counted

RELEASED
1Co 7:27 pledged to a woman? Do not seek to be r.

RELIABLE
2Ti 2: 2 entrust to r people who will also be
2Pe 1:19 prophetic message as something completely r,

RELIGION
1Ti   5: 4 of all to put their r into practice
Jas 1:27 R that God our Father accepts as

REMAIN (REMAINS)
Jn 15: 7 If you r in me and my words r
Ro 13: 8 Let no debt r outstanding,
1Co 13:13 And now these three r: faith,

REMAINS (REMAIN)
2Ti   2:13 if we are faithless, he r faithful,
Heb 7: 3 Son of God, he r a priest forever.

REMEMBER (REMEMBRANCE)
Gal 2:10 we should continue to r the poor,
Php 1: 3 I thank my God every time I r you.
Heb 8:12 and will r their sins no more."

REMEMBRANCE (REMEMBER)
1Co 11:24 which is for you; do this in r of me."

REMIND
Jn 14:26 will r you of everything I have said

REMOVED
Jn 20: 1 that the stone had been r

RENEWED (RENEWING)
2Co 4:16 yet inwardly we are being r day

RENEWING (RENEWED)
Ro 12: 2 transformed by the r of your mind.

REPAID (PAY)
Lk 14:14 you will be r at the resurrection
Col 3:25 Those who do wrong will be r

REPAY (PAY)
Ro 12:19 to avenge; I will r," says the Lord.
1Pe 3: 9 Do not r evil with evil or insult
      3: 9 the contrary, r evil with blessing,

REPENT (REPENTANCE REPENTS)
Mt 4:17 time on Jesus began to preach, "R,
Lk 13: 3 But unless you r, you too will all
      17: 3 and if they r, forgive them.
Ac 2:38 Peter replied, "R and be baptized,
      17:30 all people everywhere to r.

REPENTANCE (REPENT)
Lk 3: 8 Produce fruit in keeping with r.
      5:32 call the righteous, but sinners to r."
Ac 26:20 demonstrate their r by their deeds.
2Co 7:10 Godly sorrow brings r that leads

REPENTS (REPENT)
Lk 15:10 of God over one sinner who r."

REPROACH
1Ti 3: 2 Now the overseer is to be above r,

REPUTATION
1Ti 3: 7 also have a good r with outsiders,

REQUESTS
Php 4: 6 thanksgiving, present your r to God.

RESCUE (RESCUES)
2Pe 2: 9 the Lord knows how to r the godly

RESCUES (RESCUE)
1Th 1:10 who r us from the coming wrath.

RESIST
Jas 4: 7 R the devil, and he will flee
1Pe 5: 9 R him, standing firm in the faith,

RESOLVED
1Co 2: 2 For I r to know nothing while I was

RESPECT (RESPECTABLE)
1Th 4:12 that your daily life may win the r
1Ti 3: 4 do so in a manner worthy of full r.
1Pe 2:17 Show proper r to everyone,
      3: 7 them with r as the weaker partner

RESPECTABLE (RESPECT)
1Ti 3: 2 self-controlled, r, hospitable,

REST
Mt 11:28 and burdened, and I will give you r.

RESTORATION
2Co 13:11 Strive for full r, encourage one

RESTORE (RESTORATION)
Gal 6: 1 by the Spirit should r that person

RESURRECTION
Mt 22:30 the r people will neither marry nor

Lk 14:14 be repaid at the r of the righteous."
Jn 11:25 said to her, "I am the r and the life.
Ro 1: 4 in power by his r from the dead:
1Co 15:12 say that there is no r of the dead?
Php 3:10 to know the power of his r
Rev 20: 5 were ended.) This is the first r.

REUBEN
Rev 7: 5 from the tribe of R 12,000,

REVEALED (REVELATION)
Mt 11:25 and r them to little children.
Ro 1:17 the righteousness of God is r—
      8:18 with the glory that will be r in us.

REVELATION (REVEALED)
Gal 1:12 I received it by r from Jesus Christ.
Rev 1: 1 The r from Jesus Christ, which God

REVENGE (AVENGE)
Ro 12:19 Do not take r, my dear friends,

REVERE (REVERENCE)
1Pe 3:15 in your hearts r Christ as Lord.

REVERENCE (REVERE)
Col 3:22 sincerity of heart and r for the Lord.
1Pe 3: 2 see the purity and r of your lives.

REWARD (REWARDED)
Mt 5:12 because great is your r in heaven,
      6: 5 they have received their r in full.
      16:27 then he will r everyone according
1Co 3:14 the builder will receive a r.
Rev 22:12 My r is with me, and I will give

REWARDED (REWARD)
1Co 3: 8 and they will each be r according

RICH (RICHES)
Mt 19:23 hard for the r to enter the kingdom
2Co 6:10 poor, yet making many r;
      8: 9 that though he was r, yet for your
1Ti 6:17 Command those who are r in this

RICHES (RICH)
Ro 9:23 to make the r of his glory known
      11:33 the depth of the r of the wisdom
Eph 2: 7 he might show the incomparable r
      3: 8 the boundless r of Christ,
Col 1:27 among the Gentiles the glorious r

RID
1Co 5: 7 Get r of the old yeast, so that you
Gal 4:30 "Get r of the slave woman and her

RIGHT (RIGHTS)
Mt 6: 3 know what your r hand is doing,
Jn 1:12 he gave the r to become children
Ro 9:21 Does not the potter have the r
      12:17 careful to do what is r in the eyes
1Co 10:23 the r to do anything," you say—
Eph 1:20 and seated him at his r hand
Php 4: 8 whatever is r, whatever is pure,

RIGHTEOUS (RIGHTEOUSNESS)
Mt 5:45 and sends rain on the r
      9:13 For I have not come to call the r,
      13:49 and separate the wicked from the r
      25:46 punishment, but the r to eternal life."
Ro 1:17 it is written: "The r will live by faith."
      3:10 "There is no one r, not even one;
1Ti 1: 9 that the law is made not for the r
1Pe 3:18 for sins, the r for the unrighteous,
1Jn 3: 7 The one who does what is right is r, just as he
         is r.

Rev 19: 8 (Fine linen stands for the **r** acts

RIGHTEOUSNESS (RIGHTEOUS)
Mt   5: 6 those who hunger and thirst for **r**,
     5:20 you that unless your **r** surpasses
     6:33 But seek first his kingdom and his **r**,
Ro   4: 3 God, and it was credited to him as **r**."
     4: 9 faith was credited to him as **r**.
     6:13 to him as an instrument of **r**.
2Co 5:21 him we might become the **r** of God.
Gal 2:21 if **r** could be gained through the law,
     3: 6 God, and it was credited to him as **r**."
Eph 6:14 with the breastplate of **r** in place,
Php 3: 9 him, not having a **r** of my own
2Ti 3:16 correcting and training in **r**,
     4: 8 is in store for me the crown of **r**,
Heb 11: 7 and became heir of the **r** that is
2Pe 2:21 not to have known the way of **r**,

RIGHTS (RIGHT)
1Co 8: 9 the exercise of your **r** does not

RISE (RAISED)
Mt 27:63 said, 'After three days I will **r** again.'
Jn   5:29 those who have done good will **r**
     5:29 those who have done evil will **r**
1Th 4:16 and the dead in Christ will **r** first.

ROAD
Mt   7:13 gate and broad is the **r** that leads

ROBBERS
Lk 19:46 but you have made it 'a den of **r**.'"
Jn 10: 8 come before me are thieves and **r**,

ROCK
Mt   7:24 man who built his house on the **r**.
  16:18 and on this **r** I will build my church,
Ro 9:33 and a **r** that makes them fall,
1Co 10: 4 the spiritual **r** that accompanied
  10: 4 them, and that **r** was Christ.

ROOM
Mt   6: 6 go into your **r**, close the door
Lk   2: 7 there was no guest **r** available
Jn 14: 2 My Father's house has plenty of **r**;
  21:25 the whole world would not have **r**

ROOT
1Ti 6:10 the love of money is a **r** of all kinds

ROYAL
Jas 2: 8 If you really keep the **r** law found
1Pe 2: 9 are a chosen people, a **r** priesthood,

RUIN (RUINS)
1Ti 6: 9 desires that plunge people into **r**

RUINS (RUIN)
2Ti 2:14 value, and only **r** those who listen.

RULE (RULER RULERS RULES)
Col 3:15 the peace of Christ **r** in your hearts,
Rev 2:27 they 'will **r** them with an iron scepter

RULER (RULE)
Eph 2: 2 of the **r** of the kingdom of the air,
1Ti 6:15 the blessed and only **R**, the King

RULERS (RULE)
Col 1:16 or powers or **r** or authorities;

RULES (RULE)
Lk 22:26 and the one who **r** like the one who
2Ti 2: 5 by competing according to the **r**.

RUMORS
Mt 24: 6 You will hear of wars and **r** of wars,

RUN
1Co 9:24 **R** in such a way as to get the prize.
Heb 12: 1 let us **r** with perseverance the race

RUST
Mt   6:19 where moth and **r** destroy,

RUTH
  Moabitess; ancestor of David and Jesus (Mt 1:5-6).

SABBATH
Col 2:16 a New Moon celebration or a **S** day.

SACKCLOTH
Mt 11:21 would have repented long ago in **s**

SACRED
Mt   7: 6 "Do not give dogs what is **s**; do not
1Co 3:17 for God's temple is **s**, and you

SACRIFICE (SACRIFICED SACRIFICES)
Mt   9:13 this means: 'I desire mercy, not **s**.'
Heb 9:26 away with sin by the **s** of himself.
  13:15 offer to God a **s** of praise—the fruit
1Jn 2: 2 He is the atoning **s** for our sins,

SACRIFICED (SACRIFICE)
1Co 5: 7 our Passover lamb, has been **s**.
     8: 1 Now about food **s** to idols:
Heb 9:28 so Christ was **s** once to take away

SACRIFICES (SACRIFICE)
Ro 12: 1 to offer your bodies as living **s**,

SADDUCEES
Mk 12:18 Then the **S**, who say there is no

SAFE (SAVE)
1Jn 5:18 who was born of God keeps them **s**,

SAFETY (SAVE)
1Th 5: 3 "Peace and **s**," destruction will come

SAINTS See also [GOD'S] PEOPLE
Rev 8: 4 together with the prayers of the **s**,

SAKE
Php 3: 7 consider loss for the **s** of Christ.
Heb 11:26 disgrace for the **s** of Christ as

SALT
Mt   5:13 "You are the **s** of the earth.

SALVATION (SAVE)
Lk 2:30 For my eyes have seen your **s**,
Jn   4:22 we do know, for **s** is from the Jews.
Ac 4:12 **S** is found in no one else, for there is
  13:47 that you may bring **s** to the ends
Ro 11:11 **s** has come to the Gentiles to make
2Co 7:10 brings repentance that leads to **s**
Eph 6:17 Take the helmet of **s** and the sword
Php 2:12 to work out your **s** with fear
1Th 5: 8 and the hope of **s** as a helmet.
2Ti 3:15 make you wise for **s** through faith
Heb 2: 3 we escape if we ignore so great a **s**?
     6: 9 things that have to do with **s**.
1Pe 1:10 Concerning this **s**, the prophets,
     2: 2 by it you may grow up in your **s**,

SAMARITAN
Lk 10:33 But a **S**, as he traveled, came where

SAMSON
Israelite judge (Heb 11:32).

SAMUEL
Israelite judge and prophet (Ac 3:24; 13:20; Heb 11:32).

SANCTIFIED (SANCTIFY)
Ac 20:32 among all those who are s.
Ro 15:16 to God, s by the Holy Spirit.
1Co 6:11 you were s, you were justified
7:14 husband has been s through his
7:14 wife has been s through her
Heb 10:29 blood of the covenant that s them,

SANCTIFY (SANCTIFIED SANCTIFYING)
1Th 5:23 peace, s you through and through.

SANCTIFYING (SANCTIFY)
2Th 2:13 be saved through the s work

SANCTUARY
Heb 9:24 Christ did not enter a s made

SAND
Mt 7:26 man who built his house on s.

SANDALS
Mt 3:11 whose s I am not fit to carry.

SANG (SING)
Rev 5: 9 And they s a new song, saying:

SARAH
Wife of Abraham (1Pe 3:6). Bore Isaac at advanced age (Ro 9:9; Heb 11:11).

SATAN
Mk 4:15 it, S comes and takes away the word
2Co 11:14 S himself masquerades as an angel
12: 7 a messenger of S, to torment me.
Rev 12: 9 or S, who leads the whole world
20: 2 or S, and bound him for a thousand
20: 7 S will be released from his prison

SAUL See PAUL

SAVE (SAFE SAFETY SALVATION SAVED SAVIOR)
Mt 1:21 because he will s his people
16:25 who want to s their life will lose it,
Lk 19:10 came to seek and to s what was lost."
Jn 3:17 but to s the world through him.
1Ti 1:15 the world to s sinners—of whom I am
Jas 5:20 of their way will s their soul

SAVED (SAVE)
Mk 13:13 who stand firm to the end will be s.
16:16 believes and is baptized will be s,
Jn 10: 9 enters through me will be s.
Ac 4:12 heaven by which we must be s."
16:30 asked, "Sirs, what must I do to be s?"
Ro 9:27 the sea, only the remnant will be s.
10: 9 him from the dead, you will be s.
1Co 3:15 suffer loss but yet will be s—
15: 2 By this gospel you are s, if you hold
Eph 2: 5 is by grace you have been s.
2: 8 For it is by grace you have been s,
1Ti 2: 4 who wants all people to be s

SAVIOR (SAVE)
Lk 1:47 and my spirit rejoices in God my S,
2:11 the town of David a S has been born
Jn 4:42 this man really is the S of the world."
Eph 5:23 his body, of which he is the S.
1Ti 4:10 God, who is the S of all people,
Tit 2:10 teaching about God our S attractive.
2:13 of the glory of our great God and S,

Tit 3: 4 and love of God our S appeared,
1Jn 4:14 his Son to be the S of the world.
Jude :25 to the only God our S be glory,

SCALES
Ac 9:18 like s fell from Saul's eyes,
Rev 6: 5 Its rider was holding a pair of s

SCARLET
Mt 27:28 and put a s robe on him,
Rev 17: 3 a woman sitting on a s beast

SCATTERED
Ac 8: 4 who had been s preached the word

SCEPTER
Rev 19:15 "He will rule them with an iron s."

SCHEMES
2Co 2:11 us. For we are not unaware of his s.
Eph 6:11 take your stand against the devil's s.

SCOFFERS
2Pe 3: 3 that in the last days s will come,

SCORPION
Rev 9: 5 of the sting of a s when it strikes.

SCRIPTURE (SCRIPTURES)
Jn 10:35 of God came—and S cannot be broken—
1Ti 4:13 yourself to the public reading of S,
2Ti 3:16 All S is God-breathed and is useful
2Pe 1:20 that no prophecy of S came

SCRIPTURES (SCRIPTURE)
Lk 24:27 said in all the S concerning himself.
Jn 5:39 diligently study the S because you
5:39 These are the very S that testify
Ac 17:11 examined the S every day to see

SCROLL
Lk 4:17 the s of the prophet Isaiah was
Rev 5: 2 break the seals and open the s?"

SEA
Jas 1: 6 who doubts is like a wave of the s,
Rev 13: 1 I saw a beast coming out of the s.

SEAL (SEALS)
Jn 6:27 him God the Father has placed his s
2Co 1:22 set his s of ownership on us, and put
Eph 1:13 you were marked in him with a s,

SEALS (SEAL)
Rev 5: 2 "Who is worthy to break the s
6: 1 opened the first of the seven s.

SEARCH (SEARCHES)
Lk 15: 8 and s carefully until she finds it?

SEARCHES (SEARCH)
Ro 8:27 he who s our hearts knows the mind
1Co 2:10 The Spirit s all things, even the deep

SEARED
1Ti 4: 2 whose consciences have been s as

SEASON
2Ti 4: 2 word; be prepared in s and out of s;

SEAT (SEATED SEATS)
2Co 5:10 all appear before the judgment s

SEATED (SEAT)
Col 3: 1 where Christ is s at the right hand

SEATS (SEAT)
Lk 11:43 you love the most important **s**

SECRET (SECRETS)
Mt 6: 4 so that your giving may be in **s**.
2Co 4: 2 we have renounced **s** and shameful
Php 4:12 I have learned the **s** of being content

SECRETS (SECRET)
1Co 14:25 as the **s** of their hearts are laid bare.

SECURE
Heb 6:19 as an anchor for the soul, firm and **s**.

SEED (SEEDS)
Lk 8:11 parable: The **s** is the word of God.
1Co 3: 6 I planted the **s**, Apollos watered it,
2Co 9:10 Now he who supplies **s** to the sower
Gal 3:29 then you are Abraham's **s**, and heirs
1Pe 1:23 again, not of perishable **s**,

SEEDS (SEED)
Jn 12:24 But if it dies, it produces many **s**.
Gal 3:16 Scripture does not say "and to **s**,"

SEEK (SEEKS SELF-SEEKING)
Mt 6:33 But **s** first his kingdom and his
Lk 19:10 For the Son of Man came to **s**
Ro 10:20 found by those who did not **s** me;
1Co 7:27 a woman? Do not **s** to be released.

SEEKS (SEEK)
Jn 4:23 the kind of worshipers the Father **s**.

SELF-CONTROL (CONTROL)
1Co 7: 5 tempt you because of your lack of **s**.
Gal 5:23 gentleness and **s**. Against such
2Pe 1: 6 and to knowledge, **s**; and to **s**,

SELF-CONTROLLED (CONTROL See also SOBER)
1Ti 3: 2 his wife, temperate, **s**, respectable,
Tit 1: 8 what is good, who is **s**, upright,
2: 2 worthy of respect, **s**, and sound
2: 5 to be **s** and pure, to be busy
2: 6 encourage the young men to be **s**.
2:12 and to live **s**, upright and godly lives

SELF-INDULGENCE
Mt 23:25 inside they are full of greed and **s**.

SELF-SEEKING (SEEK)
1Co 13: 5 it is not **s**, it is not easily angered,

SELFISH
Gal 5:20 fits of rage, **s** ambition, dissensions,
Php 1:17 preach Christ out of **s** ambition,
2: 3 Do nothing out of **s** ambition
Jas 3:14 envy and **s** ambition in your hearts,
3:16 you have envy and **s** ambition,

SEND (SENDING SENT)
Mt 9:38 to **s** out workers into his harvest
Mk 1:17 I will **s** you out to catch people."
Jn 16: 7 but if I go, I will **s** him to you.

SENDING (SEND)
Jn 20:21 the Father has sent me, I am **s** you."

SENSES
Lk 15:17 "When he came to his **s**, he said,
1Co 15:34 Come back to your **s** as you ought,
2Ti 2:26 that they will come to their **s**

SENSUAL
Col 2:23 value in restraining **s** indulgence.

SENT (SEND)
Mt 10:40 me welcomes the one who **s** me.
Jn 4:34 "is to do the will of him who **s** me
Ro 10:15 anyone preach unless they are **s**?
1Jn 4:10 **s** his Son as an atoning sacrifice

SEPARATE
Mt 19: 6 has joined together, let no one **s**."
Ro 8:35 Who shall **s** us from the love
1Co 7:10 Lord): A wife must not **s** from her
2Co 6:17 "Come out from them and be **s**,

SERPENT
Rev 12: 9 down—that ancient **s** called the devil,

SERVANT (SERVANTS)
Mt 20:26 great among you must be your **s**,
25:21 'Well done, good and faithful **s**!
Php 2: 7 by taking the very nature of a **s**,
2Ti 2:24 the Lord's **s** must not be quarrelsome

SERVANTS (SERVANT)
Lk 17:10 do, should say, 'We are unworthy **s**;
Jn 15:15 I no longer call you **s**, because **s** do

SERVE (SERVICE SERVING)
Mt 4:10 the Lord your God, and **s** him only.'"
6:24 You cannot faithfully **s** both God
20:28 but to **s**, and to give his life as
Eph 6: 7 **s** wholeheartedly, as if you were

SERVICE (SERVE)
1Co 12: 5 There are different kinds of **s**,
Eph 4:12 to equip God's people for works of **s**,

SERVING (SERVE)
Ro 12:11 your spiritual fervor, **s** the Lord
Eph 6: 7 as if you were **s** the Lord,
Col 3:24 It is the Lord Christ you are **s**.
2Ti 2: 4 No one **s** as a soldier gets involved

SEVEN
Mt 18:21 who sins against me? Up to **s** times?"
Lk 11:26 takes **s** other spirits more wicked
Ro 11: 4 for myself **s** thousand who have not
Rev 1: 4 To the **s** churches in the province
1: 4 from the **s** spirits before his throne,
6: 1 Lamb opened the first of the **s** seals.
8: 2 I saw the **s** angels who stand before
8: 2 and **s** trumpets were given to them.
10: 4 And when the **s** thunders spoke,
15: 7 to the **s** angels **s** golden bowls filled

SEXUAL (SEXUALLY)
Mt 5:32 divorces his wife, except for **s**
19: 9 divorces his wife, except for **s**
1Co 6:13 is not meant for **s** immorality. All other
6:18 Flee from **s** immorality. All other
7: 1 for a man not to have **s** relations
10: 8 should not commit **s** immorality,
Eph 5: 3 not be even a hint of **s** immorality,
1Th 4: 3 that you should avoid **s** immorality;

SEXUALLY (SEXUAL)
1Co 5: 9 to associate with **s** immoral people—
6:18 but those who sin **s** sin against their

SHADOW
Heb 10: 1 The law is only a **s** of the good

SHAME (ASHAMED)
Ro 5: 5 And hope does not put us to **s**,
Heb 12: 2 scorning its **s**, and sat down

SHARE (SHARED)
Lk 3:11 "Anyone who has two shirts should **s**

Gal 4:30 the slave woman's son will never **s**
6: 6 in the word should **s** all good things
Eph 4:28 they may have something to **s**
1Ti 6:18 and to be generous and willing to **s.**
Heb 12:10 good, that we may **s** in his holiness.
13:16 to do good and to **s** with others,

SHARED (SHARE)
Heb 2:14 he too **s** in their humanity so

SHARPER
Heb 4:12 **S** than any double-edged sword,

SHED (SHEDDING)
Col 1:20 through his blood, **s** on the cross.

SHEDDING (SHED)
Heb 9:22 without the **s** of blood there is no

SHEEP
Mt 9:36 helpless, like **s** without a shepherd.
Jn 10: 3 He calls his own **s** by name
10:15 I lay down my life for the **s.**
10:27 My **s** listen to my voice; I know
21:17 I love you." Jesus said, "Feed my **s.**
1Pe 2:25 For "you were like **s** going astray,"

SHEPHERD (SHEPHERDS)
Mt 9:36 and helpless, like sheep without a **s.**
Jn 10:11 "I am the good **s.** The good **s** lays
10:16 there shall be one flock and one **s.**
1Pe 5: 4 And when the Chief **S** appears,

SHEPHERDS (SHEPHERD)
Lk 2: 8 there were **s** living out in the fields
Ac 20:28 Be **s** of the church of God, which he
1Pe 5: 2 Be **s** of God's flock that is under

SHIELD
Eph 6:16 take up the **s** of faith,

SHINE (SHONE)
Mt 5:16 let your light **s** before others,
13:43 the righteous will **s** like the sun
2Co 4: 6 made his light **s** in our hearts to give
Eph 5:14 the dead, and Christ will **s** on you."

SHIPWRECK (SHIPWRECKED)
1Ti 1:19 rejected these and so have suffered **s**

SHIPWRECKED (SHIPWRECK)
2Co 11:25 three times I was **s,** I spent a night

SHIRT
Lk 6:29 your coat, do not withhold your **s.**

SHONE (SHINE)
Mt 17: 2 His face **s** like the sun, and his
Lk 2: 9 the glory of the Lord **s** around them,
Rev 21:11 It **s** with the glory of God, and its

SHORT
Ro 3:23 and fall **s** of the glory of God,

SHOULDERS
Lk 15: 5 finds it, he joyfully puts it on his **s**

SHOWED
1Jn 4: 9 This is how God **s** his love among

SHREWD
Mt 10:16 Therefore be as **s** as snakes and as

SICK
Mt 9:12 who need a doctor, but the **s.**
25:36 I was **s** and you looked after me,

Jas 5:14 Is any one of you **s?** Call the elders

SICKLE
Rev 14:15 "Take your **s** and reap, because

SIDE
2Ti 4:17 the Lord stood at my **s** and gave me

SIGHT
2Co 5: 7 We live by faith, not by **s.**
1Pe 3: 4 which is of great worth in God's **s.**

SIGN (SIGNS)
Mt 12:39 adulterous generation asks for a **s!**
1Co 14:22 Tongues, then, are a **s,** not for

SIGNS (SIGN)
Mk 16:17 these **s** will accompany those who
Jn 20:30 Jesus did many other miraculous **s**
1Co 1:22 Jews demand **s** and Greeks look for

SILAS
Prophet (Ac 15:22-32); co-worker with Paul on second
missionary journey (Ac 16-18; 2Co 1:19). Co-writer with
Paul (1Th 1:1; 2Th 1:1); Peter (1Pe 5:12).

SILENT
1Co 14:34 Women should remain **s**
1Ti 2:12 authority over a man; she must be **s.**

SILVER
1Co 3:12 on this foundation using gold, **s,**

SIMON
1. See PETER.
2. Apostle, called the Zealot (Mt 10:4; Mk 3:18; Lk 6:15;
Ac 1:13).
3. Samaritan sorcerer (Ac 8:9-24).

SIN (SINFUL SINNED SINNER SINNERS SINNING
SINS)
Jn 1:29 who takes away the **s** of the world!
8:34 everyone who sins is a slave to **s.**
Ro 5:12 just as **s** entered the world through
5:12 and death through **s,** and in this way
5:20 But where **s** increased,
6:11 count yourselves dead to **s** but alive
6:23 For the wages of **s** is death,
14:23 that does not come from faith is **s.**
1Co 14:24 they are convicted of **s** and are
2Co 5:21 God made him who had no **s** to be **s**
Gal 6: 1 if someone is caught in a **s,** you who
Heb 9:26 to do away with **s** by the sacrifice
11:25 to enjoy the fleeting pleasures of **s.**
12: 1 and the **s** that so easily entangles.
Jas 4:17 ought to do and don't do it, you **s.**
1Pe 2:22 "He committed no **s,** and no deceit
1Jn 1: 8 If we claim to be without **s,**
3: 4 the law; in fact, **s** is lawlessness.
3: 5 away our sins. And in him is no **s.**
3: 9 born of God will not continue to **s,**
5:18 born of God do not continue to **s;**

SINCERE
Ro 12: 9 Love must be **s.** Hate what is evil;
Heb 10:22 God with a **s** heart in full assurance

SINFUL (SIN)
Ro 7: 5 we were controlled by our **s** nature,
7: 5 the **s** passions aroused by the law
8: 4 do not live according to the **s** nature
8: 9 are not controlled by the **s** nature
Gal 5:19 The acts of the **s** nature are obvious:
5:24 Jesus have crucified the **s** nature
1Pe 2:11 to abstain from **s** desires, which war

SING (SANG SINGING SONG SONGS)
Eph 5:19 **S** and make music from your heart

SINGING (SING)
Ac 16:25 were praying and **s** hymns to God,

SINNED (SIN)
Lk 15:18 I have **s** against heaven and against
Ro 3:23 for all have **s** and fall short
1Jn 1:10 If we claim we have not **s**, we make

SINNER (SIN)
Lk 15: 7 heaven over one **s** who repents than
18:13 said, 'God, have mercy on me, a **s**.'
Jas 5:20 Whoever turns a **s** from the error
1Pe 4:18 become of the ungodly and the **s**?"

SINNERS (SIN)
Mt 9:13 not come to call the righteous, but **s**."
Ro 5: 8 While we were still **s**, Christ died
1Ti 1:15 Jesus came into the world to save **s**—

SINNING (SIN)
1Co 15:34 senses as you ought, and stop **s**;
Heb 10:26 If we deliberately keep on **s** after we
1Jn 3: 6 No one who lives in him keeps on **s**.
3: 9 they cannot go on **s**, because they

SINS (SIN)
Mt 1:21 he will save his people from their **s**."
18:15 "If a brother or sister **s**, go and point
Lk 11: 4 Forgive us our **s**, for we also forgive everyone
who **s** against us.
17: 3 any brother or sister **s** against you,
Ac 22:16 be baptized and wash your **s** away,
1Co 15: 3 Christ died for our **s** according
Eph 2: 1 dead in your transgressions and **s**,
Col 2:13 When you were dead in your **s**
2:13 with Christ. He forgave us all our **s**,
Heb 1: 3 he had provided purification for **s**,
7:27 He sacrificed for their **s** once for all
8:12 and will remember their **s** no more."
10:12 for all time one sacrifice for **s**,
Jas 5:16 Therefore confess your **s** to each
5:20 and cover over a multitude of **s**.
1Pe 2:24 "He himself bore our **s**" in his body
3:18 For Christ also suffered once for **s**,
1Jn 1: 9 If we confess our **s**, he is faithful
1: 9 will forgive us our **s** and purify us
Rev 1: 5 freed us from our **s** by his blood,

SITS
Mt 19:28 Son of Man **s** on his glorious throne,
Rev 4: 9 thanks to him who **s** on the throne

SLAIN
Rev 5:12 who was **s**, to receive power

SLANDER (SLANDERED SLANDERERS)
1Ti 5:14 give the enemy no opportunity for **s**.
Tit 3: 2 to **s** no one, to be peaceable

SLANDERED (SLANDER)
1Co 4:13 when we are **s**, we answer kindly.

SLANDERERS (SLANDER)
Ro 1:30 **s**, God-haters, insolent,
1Co 6:10 nor drunkards nor **s** nor swindlers
Tit 2: 3 live, not to be **s** or addicted to much

SLAPS
Mt 5:39 If anyone **s** you on the right cheek,

SLAVE (SLAVERY SLAVES)
Mt 20:27 wants to be first must be your **s**—
Lk 16:13 "No one can be a **s** to two masters.

Jn 8:34 you, everyone who sins is a **s** to sin.
1Co 12:13 **s** or free—and we were all given
Gal 3:28 Jew nor Greek, neither **s** nor free,
4:30 "Get rid of the **s** woman and her son,

SLAVERY (SLAVE)
Gal 4: 3 in **s** under the elemental spiritual

SLAVES (SLAVE)
Ro 6: 6 that we should no longer be **s** to sin—
6:19 to offer yourselves as **s** to impurity
6:22 from sin and have become **s** of God,
2Pe 2:19 "people are **s** to whatever has

SLEEP (SLEEPING)
1Co 15:51 We will not all **s**, but we will all be

SLEEPING (SLEEP)
Mk 13:36 suddenly, do not let him find you **s**.

SLOW
Jas 1:19 **s** to speak and **s** to become angry,
2Pe 3: 9 The Lord is not **s** in keeping his

SLUMBER
Ro 13:11 for you to wake up from your **s**,

SNAKE (SNAKES)
Jn 3:14 Moses lifted up the **s** in the desert,

SNAKES (SNAKE)
Mt 10:16 Therefore be as shrewd as **s** and as
Mk 16:18 they will pick up **s** with their hands;

SNATCH (SNATCHING)
Jn 10:28 no one will **s** them out of my hand.

SNATCHING (SNATCH)
Jude :23 save others by **s** them from the fire;

SOBER
1Th 5: 6 but let us be awake and **s**
5: 8 we belong to the day, let us be **s**,
1Pe 1:13 with minds that are alert and fully **s**,
4: 7 Therefore be alert and of **s** mind
5: 8 Be alert and of **s** mind. Your enemy

SODOM
Ro 9:29 we would have become like **S**,

SOIL
Mt 13:23 But seed falling on good **s** refers

SOLDIER
1Co 9: 7 Who serves as a **s** at his own
2Ti 2: 3 like a good **s** of Christ Jesus.

SOLID
2Ti 2:19 God's **s** foundation stands firm,
Heb 5:12 again. You need milk, not **s** food!

SOLOMON
Son of David by Bathsheba; king of Judah (Mt 1:6-7).
Built temple (Ac 7:47). Wisdom of (Lk 11:31).

SON (SONS SONSHIP)
Mt 2:15 prophet: "Out of Egypt I called my **s**."
3:17 said, "This is my **S**, whom I love;
11:27 one knows the **S** except the Father,
16:16 Messiah, the **S** of the living God."
17: 5 said, "This is my **S**, whom I love;
20:18 the **S** of Man will be delivered over
24:30 the sign of the **S** of Man will appear
24:30 They will see the **S** of Man coming
24:44 because the **S** of Man will come
27:54 "Surely he was the **S** of God!"

Mt 28:19 and of the **S** and of the Holy Spirit,
Mk 10:45 For even the **S** of Man did not come
14:62 you will see the **S** of Man sitting
Lk 9:58 the **S** of Man has no place to lay his
18: 8 when the **S** of Man comes, will he
19:10 For the **S** of Man came to seek
Jn 3:14 so the **S** of Man must be lifted up,
3:16 that he gave his one and only **S**,
17: 1 Glorify your **S**, that your **S** may
Ro 8:29 conformed to the likeness of his **S**,
8:32 He who did not spare his own **S**,
1Co 15:28 the **S** himself will be made subject
Gal 4:30 rid of the slave woman and her **s**,
4:30 inheritance with the free woman's **s**."
1Th 1:10 and to wait for his **S** from heaven,
Heb 1: 2 days he has spoken to us by his **S**,
10:29 punished who have trampled the **S**
1Jn 1: 7 Jesus, his **S**, purifies us from all sin.
4: 9 only **S** into the world that we might
5: 5 believes that Jesus is the **S** of God.
5:11 eternal life, and this life is in his **S**.

SONG (SING)
Rev 5: 9 And they sang a new **s**, saying:
15: 3 sang the **s** of God's servant Moses

SONGS (SING)
Eph 5:19 hymns and **s** from the Spirit.
Jas 5:13 Is anyone happy? Sing **s** of praise.

SONS (SON See also CHILDREN)
2Co 6:18 and you will be my **s** and daughters,

SONSHIP (SON)
Gal 4: 5 that we might receive adoption to **s**.

SORROW
Ro 9: 2 I have great **s** and unceasing
2Co 7:10 Godly **s** brings repentance that leads
7:10 regret, but worldly **s** brings death.

SOUL (SOULS)
Mt 10:28 kill the body but cannot kill the **s**.
16:26 the whole world, yet forfeit your **s**?
16:26 you give in exchange for your **s**?
22:37 and with all your **s** and with all your
Heb 4:12 it penetrates even to dividing **s**

SOULS (SOUL)
Mt 11:29 and you will find rest for your **s**.

SOUND
1Co 14: 8 if the trumpet does not **s** a clear call,
15:52 For the trumpet will **s**, the dead will
2Ti 4: 3 will not put up with **s** doctrine.

SOW (SOWS)
Mt 6:26 they do not **s** or reap or store away
Gal 6: 7 mocked. People reap what they **s**.
2Pe 2:22 "A **s** that is washed returns to her

SOWS (SOW)
2Co 9: 6 Whoever **s** sparingly will also reap
9: 6 and whoever **s** generously will

SPARE
Ro 8:32 He who did not **s** his own Son,
11:21 God did not **s** the natural branches, he will
not **s** you either.

SPEAR
Jn 19:34 pierced Jesus' side with a **s**,

SPECTACLE
1Co 4: 9 We have been made a **s** to the whole
Col 2:15 he made a public **s** of them,

SPIN
Mt 6:28 field grow. They do not labor or **s**.

SPIRIT (SPIRIT'S SPIRITS SPIRITUAL)
Mt 1:18 to be pregnant through the Holy **S**.
3:11 He will baptize you with the Holy **S**
3:16 he saw the **S** of God descending like
4: 1 was led by the **S** into the desert
5: 3 "Blessed are the poor in **s**, for theirs
26:41 The **s** is willing, but the flesh is
28:19 and of the Son and of the Holy **S**,
Lk 1:80 child grew and became strong in **s**;
11:13 in heaven give the Holy **S** to those
Jn 4:24 God is **s**, and his worshipers must worship in
the **S**
7:39 By this he meant the **S**, whom those
7:39 that time the **S** had not been given,
14:26 the Holy **S**, whom the Father will
16:13 But when he, the **S** of truth, comes,
20:22 them and said, "Receive the Holy **S**.
Ac 1: 5 will be baptized with the Holy **S**."
2: 4 of them were filled with the Holy **S**
2: 4 other tongues as the **S** enabled them.
2:38 will receive the gift of the Holy **S**.
6: 3 who are known to be full of the **S**
19: 2 "Did you receive the Holy **S**
Ro 8: 9 if indeed the **S** of God lives in you.
8: 9 if anyone does not have the **S**
8:26 the **S** helps us in our weakness.
8:26 but the **S** himself intercedes for us
1Co 2:10 has revealed them to us by his **S**.
2:10 The **S** searches all things,
2:14 person without the **S** does not accept things
that come from the **S** of God
6:19 bodies are temples of the Holy **S**,
12: 1 Now about the gifts of the **S**,
12:13 we were all baptized by one **S** so as
2Co 3: 6 the letter kills, but the **S** gives life.
5: 5 who has given us the **S** as a deposit,
Gal 5:16 say, walk by the **S**, and you will not
5:22 But the fruit of the **S** is love, joy,
5:25 Since we live by the **S**, let us keep in step
with the **S**.
6: 1 you who live by the **S** should restore
Eph 1:13 with a seal, the promised Holy **S**,
4:30 do not grieve the Holy **S** of God,
5:18 Instead, be filled with the **S**,
5:19 psalms, hymns and songs from the **S**.
6:17 of salvation and the sword of the **S**,
2Th 2:13 the sanctifying work of the **S**
Heb 4:12 even to dividing soul and **s**,
1Pe 3: 4 beauty of a gentle and quiet **s**,
2Pe 1:21 were carried along by the Holy **S**.
1Jn 4: 1 do not believe every **s**, but test

SPIRIT'S (SPIRIT)
1Th 5:19 Do not put out the **S** fire.

SPIRITS (SPIRIT)
1Co 12:10 to another distinguishing between **s**,
14:32 The **s** of prophets are subject
1Jn 4: 1 but test the **s** to see whether they are

SPIRITUAL (SPIRIT)
Pr 12:11 but keep your **s** fervor,
1Co 2:13 the Spirit, explaining **s** realities
3: 1 I could not address you as **s** but as
14: 1 of love and eagerly desire **s** gifts,
15:44 a natural body, it is raised a **s** body.
Eph 1: 3 realms with every **s** blessing
6:12 against the **s** forces of evil
1Pe 2: 2 crave pure **s** milk, so that by it you
2: 5 are being built into a **s** house to be

SPLENDOR
Lk   9:31 appeared in glorious **s**,
2Th 2: 8 and destroy by the **s** of his coming.

SPOTLESS
2Pe 3:14 make every effort to be found **s**,

SPREAD (SPREADING)
Ac 12:24 of God continued to increase and **s**.
    19:20 way the word of the Lord **s** widely

SPREADING (SPREAD)
1Th 3: 2 in God's service in **s** the gospel

SPRING
Jn   4:14 become in them a **s** of water welling
Jas 3:12 can a salt **s** produce fresh water.

SPUR
Heb 10:24 consider how we may **s** one another

STAND (STANDING STANDS)
Mt 10:22 who **s** firm to the end will be saved.
    12:25 divided against itself will not **s**.
Ro 14:10 we will all **s** before God's judgment
1Co 15:58 my dear brothers and sisters, **s** firm.
Eph 6:14 **S** firm then, with the belt of truth
2Th 2:15 **s** firm and hold fast to the teachings
Jas   5: 8 be patient and **s** firm,
Rev 3:20 I am! I **s** at the door and knock.

STANDING (STAND)
1Pe 5: 9 Resist him, **s** firm in the faith,

STANDS (STAND)
2Ti 2:19 God's solid foundation **s** firm,

STAR (STARS)
Rev 22:16 of David, and the bright Morning **S**."

STARS (STAR)
Php 2:15 you will shine among them like **s**

STEADFAST
1Pe 5:10 and make you strong, firm and **s**.

STEAL
Mt 19:18 adultery, do not **s**, do not give false
Eph 4:28 have been stealing must **s** no longer,

STEP (STEPS)
Gal 5:25 let us keep in **s** with the Spirit.

STEPHEN
    Early church leader (Ac 6:5). Arrested (Ac 6:8-15).
Speech to Sanhedrin (Ac 7). Stoned (Ac 7:54-60; 22:20).

STEPS (STEP)
1Pe 2:21 that you should follow in his **s**.

STONE (CAPSTONE CORNERSTONE MILLSTONE)
Mk 16: 3 "Who will roll the **s** away
Lk   4: 3 of God, tell this **s** to become bread."
Jn   8: 7 sin be the first to throw a **s** at her."
2Co 3: 3 not on tablets of **s** but on tablets

STORE
Mt   6:19 "Do not **s** up for yourselves treasures

STORIES
2Pe 1:16 we did not follow cleverly devised **s**

STRAIGHT
Jn   1:23 'Make **s** the way for the Lord.' "

STRAIN
Mt 23:24 You **s** out a gnat but swallow

STRANGER (STRANGERS)
Mt 25:35 I was a **s** and you invited me in,
Jn   10: 5 But they will never follow a **s**;

STRANGERS (STRANGER)
1Pe 2:11 as foreigners and **s** in the world,

STREAMS
Jn   7:38 **s** of living water will flow

STRENGTH (STRONG)
Mk 12:30 all your mind and with all your **s**.'
1Co 1:25 of God is stronger than human **s**.
Php 4:13 all this through him who gives me **s**.
1Pe 4:11 do so with the **s** God provides,

STRENGTHEN (STRONG)
Eph 3:16 of his glorious riches he may **s** you
2Th 2:17 hearts and **s** you in every good deed
Heb 12:12 **s** your feeble arms and weak knees.

STRIKE (STRIKES)
Mt 26:31 " 'I will **s** the shepherd, and the sheep
1Co 9:27 I **s** a blow to my body and make it my slave

STRIVE (STRIVING)
2Co 13:11 **S** for full restoration, encourage one
1Th 5:15 always **s** to do what is good for each other

STRIVING (STRIVE)
Php 1:27 **s** together with one accord for the faith

STRONG (STRENGTH STRENGTHEN)
Lk   2:40 And the child grew and became **s**;
Ro 15: 1 We who are **s** ought to bear
1Co 1:27 things of the world to shame the **s**.
    16:13 in the faith; be courageous; be **s**.
2Co 12:10 For when I am weak, then I am **s**.
Eph 6:10 be **s** in the Lord and in his mighty

STRUGGLE
Ro 15:30 join me in my **s** by praying to God
Eph 6:12 For our **s** is not against flesh
Heb 12: 4 In your **s** against sin, you have not

STUDY
Jn   5:39 You diligently **s** the Scriptures

STUMBLE (STUMBLING)
Mt 18: 6 those who believe in me—to **s**,
1Co 10:32 Do not cause anyone to **s**,
1Pe 2: 8 "A stone that causes people to **s**
    2: 8 They **s** because they disobey

STUMBLING (STUMBLE)
Ro 14:13 up your mind not to put any **s** block
1Co 8: 9 rights does not become a **s** block
2Co 6: 3 We put no **s** block in anyone's path,
Jude :24 To him who is able to keep you from **s**

SUBJECT (SUBJECTED)
Ro 13: 1 be **s** to the governing authorities,
1Co 14:32 of prophets are **s** to the control
    15:28 the Son himself will be made **s**
Tit   2: 5 and to be **s** to their husbands,
    2: 9 Teach slaves to be **s** to their masters
    3: 1 Remind the people to be **s** to rulers

SUBJECTED (SUBJECT)
Ro   8:20 For the creation was **s** to frustration,

SUBMISSION (SUBMIT)
1Co 14:34 but must be in **s**, as the law says.

1Ti 2:11 should learn in quietness and full **s.**

SUBMISSIVE (SUBMIT)
Jas 3:17 considerate, **s,** full of mercy

SUBMIT (SUBMISSION SUBMISSIVE SUBMITS)
Ro 13: 5 it is necessary to **s** to the authorities,
1Co 16:16 to **s** to such as these and to everyone
Eph 5:21 **S** to one another out of reverence
Col 3:18 **s** yourselves to your own husbands,
Heb 12: 9 How much more should we **s**
     13:17 your leaders and **s** to their authority,
Jas   4: 7 **S** yourselves, then, to God.
1Pe 2:18 reverent fear of God **s** yourselves
      3: 1 Wives, in the same way **s** yourselves
      5: 5 you who are younger, **s** yourselves

SUBMITS (SUBMIT)
Eph 5:24 Now as the church **s** to Christ,

SUFFER (SUFFERED SUFFERING SUFFERINGS SUFFERS)
Mk 8:31 the Son of Man must **s** many things
Lk 24:26 the Messiah have to **s** these things
     24:46 The Messiah will **s** and rise
Php 1:29 on him, but also to **s** for him,
1Pe 4:16 if you **s** as a Christian, do not be

SUFFERED (SUFFER)
Heb 2: 9 glory and honor because he **s** death,
      2:10 perfect through what he **s.**
      2:18 Because he himself **s** when he was
1Pe 2:21 called, because Christ **s** for you,

SUFFERING (SUFFER)
Ac   5:41 been counted worthy of **s** disgrace
2Ti 1: 8 But join with me in **s** for the gospel,
      2: 3 Join with me in **s,** like a good soldier

SUFFERINGS (SUFFER)
Ro   8:17 if indeed we share in his **s** in order
      8:18 that our present **s** are not worth
2Co 1: 5 share abundantly in the **s** of Christ,
Php 3:10 and participation in his **s,**

SUFFERS (SUFFER)
1Co 12:26 If one part **s,** every part **s** with it;

SUFFICIENT
2Co 12: 9 he said to me, "My grace is **s** for you,

SUN
Mt   5:45 He causes his **s** to rise on the evil
     17: 2 His face shone like the **s,** and his
Rev 1:16 His face was like the **s** shining in all
     21:23 The city does not need the **s**

SUPERIOR
Ro 12:16 Do not think you are **s.**
Heb 1: 4 So he became as much **s**
      1: 4 as the name he has inherited is **s**
      8: 6 ministry Jesus has received is as **s**
      8: 6 he is mediator is **s** to the old one,

SUPERVISION
Gal 3:25 we are no longer under the **s**

SUPREMACY
Col 1:18 in everything he might have the **s.**

SURE
Heb 11: 1 Now faith is being **s** of what we

SURPASSES (SURPASSING)
Mt   5:20 that unless your righteousness **s**
Eph 3:19 know this love that **s**

SURPASSING (SURPASSED)
2Co 3:10 now in comparison with the **s** glory.
      9:14 of the **s** grace God has given you.
Php 3: 8 a loss because of the **s** worth

SURROUNDED
Heb 12: 1 since we are **s** by such a great cloud

SUSTAINING
Heb 1: 3 **s** all things by his powerful word.

SWALLOWED
1Co 15:54 true: "Death has been **s** up in victory."
2Co 5: 4 so that what is mortal may be **s**

SWEAR
Mt   5:34 But I tell you, do not **s** at all:

SWORD
Mt 10:34 did not come to bring peace, but a **s.**
     26:52 all who draw the **s** will die by the **s.**
Lk   2:35 a **s** will pierce your own soul too."
Ro 13: 4 for rulers do not bear the **s** for no
Eph 6:17 of salvation and the **s** of the Spirit,
Heb 4:12 Sharper than any double-edged **s,**
Rev 1:16 mouth was a sharp, double-edged **s.**

SYMPATHETIC
1Pe 3: 8 like-minded, be **s,** love one another,

SYNAGOGUE
Lk   4:16 the Sabbath day he went into the **s,**
Ac 17: 2 Paul went into the **s,** and on three

TABERNACLE
Heb 8: 2 the true **t** set up by the Lord,
Rev 15: 5 in heaven the temple—the **t** of

TABLE (TABLES)
1Co 10:21 the Lord's **t** and the **t** of demons.

TABLES (TABLE)
Ac   6: 2 word of God in order to wait on **t.**

TABLETS
2Co 3: 3 not on **t** of stone but on **t** of human

TAKE (TAKEN TAKES TAKING TOOK)
Mt 10:38 Those who do not **t** up their cross
     11:29 **T** my yoke upon you and learn
     16:24 deny themselves and **t** up their cross

TAKEN (TAKE)
Mt 24:40 one will be **t** and the other left.
Mk 16:19 he was **t** up into heaven and he sat
1Ti 3:16 on in the world, was **t** up in glory.

TAKES (TAKE)
Jn   1:29 who **t** away the sin of the world!
Rev 22:19 if any one of you **t** words away

TAKING (TAKE)
Php 2: 7 himself nothing by **t** the very nature

TALENT See BAGS

TAME
Jas 3: 8 but no one can **t** the tongue. It is

TASK
Mk 13:34 each with an assigned **t,** and tells
Ac 20:24 complete the **t** the Lord Jesus has
1Co 3: 5 the Lord has assigned to each his **t.**
2Co 2:16 life. And who is equal to such a **t?**

TASTE (TASTED)
Col 2:21 handle! Do not t! Do not touch!"?
Heb 2: 9 God he might t death for everyone.

TASTED (TASTE)
1Pe 2: 3 you have t that the Lord is good.

TAUGHT (TEACH)
Mt 7:29 because he t as one who had
1Co 2:13 not in words t us by human wisdom but in
         words t by the Spirit,
Gal 1:12 any human source, nor was I t it;

TAX (TAXES)
Mt 22:17 right to pay the poll t to Caesar

TAXES (TAX)
Ro 13: 7 what you owe: If you owe t, pay t;

TEACH (TAUGHT TEACHER TEACHERS TEACHES
TEACHING)
Lk 11: 1 him, "Lord, t us to pray, just as John
Jn 14:26 will t you all things and will remind
1Ti 2:12 I do not permit a woman to t
     3: 2 respectable, hospitable, able to t,
Tit 2: 1 must t what is appropriate to sound
Heb 8:11 longer will they t their neighbors,
Jas 3: 1 that we who t will be judged more
1Jn 2:27 you do not need anyone to t you.

TEACHER (TEACH)
Mt 10:24 "Students are not above their t,
Jn 13:14 your Lord and T, have washed your

TEACHERS (TEACH)
1Co 12:28 prophets, third t, then miracles,
Eph 4:11 the evangelists, the pastors and t,
Heb 5:12 by this time you ought to be t,

TEACHES (TEACH)
1Ti 6: 3 If anyone t otherwise and does not

TEACHING (TEACH)
Mt 28:20 t them to obey everything I have
Jn 7:17 out whether my t comes from God
    14:23 who loves me will obey my t.
1Ti 4:13 of Scripture, to preaching and to t.
2Ti 3:16 is God-breathed and is useful for t,
Tit 2: 7 In your t show integrity,

TEAR (TEARS)
Rev 7:17 God will wipe away every t

TEARING
2Co 10: 8 building you up rather than t you down,

TEARS (TEAR)
Php 3:18 and now tell you again even with t,

TEETH (TOOTH)
Mt 8:12 will be weeping and gnashing of t."

TEMPERATE
1Ti 3: 2 reproach, faithful to his wife, t,
    3:11 not malicious talkers but t
Tit 2: 2 Teach the older men to be t,

TEMPLE (TEMPLES)
1Co 3:16 know that you yourselves are God's t
2Co 6:16 For we are the t of the living God.

TEMPLES (TEMPLE)
Ac 17:24 and does not live in t built by hands.
1Co 6:19 your bodies are t of the Holy Spirit,

TEMPT (TEMPTATION TEMPTED)
1Co 7: 5 Satan will not t you because of your

TEMPTATION (TEMPT)
Mt 6:13 And lead us not into t, but deliver us
    26:41 pray so that you will not fall into t.
1Co 10:13 No t has overtaken you except what

TEMPTED (TEMPT)
Mt 4: 1 into the desert to be t by the devil.
1Co 10:13 not let you be t beyond what you
Heb 2:18 he himself suffered when he was t,
    2:18 able to help those who are being t.
    4:15 but we have one who has been t
Jas 1:13 When t, no one should say, "God is
    1:13 For God cannot be t by evil,

TEN (TENTH)
Mt 25:28 give it to the one who has t bags.
Lk 15: 8 suppose a woman has t silver coins

TENTH (TEN)
Lk 11:42 Pharisees, because you give God a t
Heb 7: 2 Abraham gave him a t of everything.

TERRIBLE (TERROR)
2Ti 3: 1 this: There will be t times in the last

TERROR (TERRIBLE)
Lk 21:26 People will faint from t,
Ro 13: 3 rulers hold no t for those who do

TEST (TESTED TESTS)
Ro 12: 2 you will be able to t and approve
1Co 3:13 and the fire will t the quality of each
1Jn 4: 1 t the spirits to see whether they are

TESTED (TEST)
1Ti 3:10 They must first be t;

TESTIFY (TESTIMONY)
Jn 5:39 These are the very Scriptures that t

TESTIMONY (TESTIFY)
Lk 18:20 steal, do not give false t, honor your
2Ti 1: 8 not be ashamed of the t about our Lord

TESTS (TEST)
1Th 2: 4 people but God, who t our hearts.

THADDAEUS
    Apostle (Mt 10:3; Mk 3:18); probably also known as
Judas son of James (Lk 6:16; Ac 1:13).

THANKFUL (THANKS)
Heb 12:28 let us be t, and so worship God

THANKS (THANKFUL THANKSGIVING)
1Co 15:57 But t be to God! He gives us
2Co 2:14 But t be to God, who always leads
    9:15 T be to God for his indescribable
1Th 5:18 give t in all circumstances; for this

THANKSGIVING (THANKS)
Php 4: 6 with t, present your requests to God.
1Ti 4: 3 to be received with t by those who

THIEF (THIEVES)
1Th 5: 2 of the Lord will come like a t
Rev 16:15 "Look, I come like a t! Blessed are

THIEVES (THIEF)
1Co 6:10 nor t nor the greedy nor drunkards

THINK (THOUGHT THOUGHTS)
Ro 12: 3 Do not t of yourself more highly

Php 4: 8 is excellent or **p** about such things.

THIRST (THIRSTY)
Mt 5: 6 who hunger and **t** for righteousness,
Jn 4:14 the water I give them will never **t**.

THIRSTY (THIRST)
Jn 7:37 "Let anyone who is **t** come to me
Rev 21: 6 the **t** I will give water without cost
22:17 Let those who are **t** come; and let all

THOMAS
Apostle (Mt 10:3; Mk 3:18; Lk 6:15; Jn 11:16; 14:5; 21:2; Ac 1:13). Doubted resurrection (Jn 20:24-28).

THONGS
Mk 1: 7 I, the **t** of whose sandals I am not

THORN (THORNS)
2Co 12: 7 I was given a **t** in my flesh,

THORNS (THORN)
Mt 27:29 twisted together a crown of **t** and set
Heb 6: 8 land that produces **t** and thistles is

THOUGHT (THINK)
1Co 13:11 I talked like a child, I **t** like a child,

THOUGHTS (THINK)
Heb 4:12 it judges the **t** and attitudes

THREE
Mt 12:40 For as Jonah was **t** days and **t** nights
12:40 so the Son of Man will be **t** days
18:20 two or **t** come together in my name,
27:63 said, 'After **t** days I will rise again.'
1Co 13:13 And now these **t** remain: faith,
14:27 two—or at the most **t**—should speak,
2Co 13: 1 the testimony of two or **t** witnesses."

THRONE
Heb 4:16 then approach God's **t** of grace
12: 2 at the right hand of the **t** of God.
Rev 4:10 They lay their crowns before the **t**
20:11 I saw a great white **t** and him who
22: 3 The **t** of God and of the Lamb will

THROW
Jn 8: 7 is without sin be the first to **t** a stone
Heb 10:35 So do not **t** away your confidence;
12: 1 let us **t** off everything that hinders

TIME (TIMES)
Ro 9: 9 "At the appointed **t** I will return,
Heb 9:28 and he will appear a second **t**,
10:12 had offered for all **t** one sacrifice
1Pe 4:17 For it is **t** for judgment to begin

TIMES (TIME)
Mt 18:21 how many **t** shall I forgive someone
Ac 1: 7 "It is not for you to know the **t**
Rev 12:14 care of for a time, **t** and half a time,

TIMID
2Ti 1: 7 Spirit God gave us does not make us **t**,

TIMOTHY
Believer from Lystra (Ac 16:1). Joined Paul on second missionary journey (Ac 16-20). Sent to settle problems at Corinth (1Co 4:17; 16:10). Led church at Ephesus (1Ti 1:3). Co-writer with Paul (1Th 1:1; 2Th 1:1; Phm 1).

TIRE
2Th 3:13 never **t** of doing what is good.

TITUS
Gentile co-worker of Paul (Gal 2:1-3; 2Ti 4:10); sent to Corinth (2Co 2:13; 7-8; 12:18), Crete (Tit 1:4-5).

TODAY
Mt 6:11 Give us **t** our daily bread.
Lk 23:43 **t** you will be with me in paradise."
Heb 3:13 as long as it is called "**t**," so that none
13: 8 Christ is the same yesterday and **t**

TOLERATE
Rev 2: 2 that you cannot **t** wicked people,

TOMB
Mt 27:65 make the **t** as secure as you know
Lk 24: 2 the stone rolled away from the **t**,

TOMORROW
Mt 6:34 Therefore do not worry about **t**, for **t**
Jas 4:13 "Today or **t** we will go to this

TONGUE (TONGUES)
1Co 14: 2 those who speak in a **t** do not speak
14: 4 who speak in a **t** edify themselves,
14:13 those who speak in a **t** should pray
14:19 than ten thousand words in a **t**.
Php 2:11 and every **t** acknowledge that Jesus
Jas 3: 8 but no one can tame the **t**. It is

TONGUES (TONGUE)
Mk 16:17 demons; they will speak in new **t**;
Ac 2: 4 in other **t** as the Spirit enabled them.
10:46 For they heard them speaking in **t**
19: 6 and they spoke in **t** and prophesied.
1Co 12:30 Do all speak in **t**? Do all interpret?
14:18 I speak in **t** more than all of you.
14:39 and do not forbid speaking in **t**.
Jas 1:26 not keep a tight rein on their **t**

TOOK (TAKE)
1Co 11:23 the night he was betrayed, **t** bread,
Php 3:12 for which Christ Jesus **t** hold of me.

TOOTH (TEETH)
Mt 5:38 it was said, 'Eye for eye, and **t** for **t**.'

TORMENTED
Rev 20:10 They will be **t** day and night

TORN
Gal 4:15 you would have **t** out your eyes
Php 1:23 I am **t** between the two: I desire

TOUCH (TOUCHED)
Lk 24:39 **T** me and see; a ghost does not have
2Co 6:17 Lord. **T** no unclean thing, and I will
Col 2:21 not handle! Do not taste! Do not **t**!"?

TOUCHED (TOUCH)
Mt 14:36 and all who **t** him were healed.

TRACING
Ro 11:33 and his paths beyond **t** out!

TRADITION
Mt 15: 6 word of God for the sake of your **t**.
Col 2: 8 which depends on human **t**

TRAIN (TRAINING)
Eph 4: 8 he led captives in his **t** and gave

TRAINING (TRAIN)
1Co 9:25 in the games goes into strict **t**.
2Ti 3:16 correcting and **t** in righteousness,

TRAMPLED
Lk 21:24 Jerusalem will be t
Heb 10:29 be punished who have t the Son

TRANCE
Ac 10:10 was being prepared, he fell into a t.

TRANSCENDS
Php 4: 7 God, which t all understanding,

TRANSFIGURED
Mt 17: 2 There he was t before them.

TRANSFORM (TRANSFORMED)
Php 3:21 will t our lowly bodies so that they

TRANSFORMED (TRANSFORM)
Ro 12: 2 be t by the renewing of your mind.
2Co 3:18 are being t into his likeness

TRANSGRESSION (TRANSGRESSIONS TRANSGRESSORS)
Ro 4:15 where there is no law there is no t.

TRANSGRESSIONS (TRANSGRESSION)
Eph 2: 1 you were dead in your t and sins,

TRANSGRESSORS (TRANSGRESSION)
Lk 22:37 he was numbered with the t';

TREADING
1Co 9: 9 "Do not muzzle an ox while it is t

TREASURE (TREASURED TREASURES)
Mt 6:21 For where your t is, there your heart
2Co 4: 7 But we have this t in jars of clay

TREASURED (TREASURE)
Lk 2:19 But Mary t up all these things

TREASURES (TREASURE)
Mt 6:19 store up for yourselves t on earth,
Col 2: 3 in whom are hidden all the t
Heb 11:26 of greater value than the t of Egypt,

TREAT
1Ti 5: 1 father. T younger men as brothers,
1Pe 3: 7 t them with respect as the weaker

TREE
Mt 3:10 every t that does not produce good
12:33 bad, for a t is recognized by its fruit.
Gal 3:13 is everyone who is hung on a t."
Rev 22:14 may have the right to the t of life

TREMBLING
Php 2:12 out your salvation with fear and t,

TRESPASS
Ro 5:17 if, by the t of the one man,

TRIALS
1Th 3: 3 one would be unsettled by these t.
Jas 1: 2 whenever you face t of many kinds,
2Pe 2: 9 how to rescue the godly from t

TRIBES
Mt 19:28 judging the twelve t of Israel.

TRIBULATION
Rev 7:14 who have come out of the great t;

TRIUMPH (TRIUMPHAL TRIUMPHING)
Rev 17:14 the Lamb will t over them because

TRIUMPHAL (TRIUMPH)
2Co 2:14 as captives in Christ's t procession

TRIUMPHING (TRIUMPH)
Col 2:15 of them, t over them by the cross.

TROUBLE (TROUBLED TROUBLES)
Mt 6:34 Each day has enough t of its own.
Jn 16:33 In this world you will have t.
Ro 8:35 Shall t or hardship or persecution

TROUBLED (TROUBLE)
Jn 14: 1 "Do not let your hearts be t.
14:27 Do not let your hearts be t and do

TROUBLES (TROUBLE)
1Co 7:28 those who marry will face many t
2Co 1: 4 who comforts us in all our t,
4:17 momentary t are achieving for us

TRUE (TRUTH)
Jn 17: 3 the only t God, and Jesus Christ,
Ro 3: 4 all! Let God be t, and every human
Php 4: 8 whatever is t, whatever is noble,
Rev 22: 6 "These words are trustworthy and t.

TRUMPET
1Co 14: 8 if the t does not sound a clear call,
15:52 the twinkling of an eye, at the last t.

TRUST (ENTRUSTED TRUSTED TRUSTS TRUSTWORTHY)
Jn 14: 1 be troubled. T in God; t also in me.
1Co 4: 2 been given a t must prove faithful.

TRUSTED (TRUST)
Lk 16:10 "Whoever can be t with very little

TRUSTS (TRUST)
Mt 27:43 He t in God. Let God rescue him
1Pe 2: 6 who t in him will never be put to

TRUSTWORTHY (TRUST)
Rev 22: 6 to me, "These words are t and true.

TRUTH (TRUE TRUTHFUL TRUTHS)
Jn 4:23 the Father in spirit and in t,
8.32 Then you will know the t, and the t
8:32 Then you will know the t, and the t
14: 6 "I am the way and the t and the life.
16:13 But when he, the Spirit of t, comes,
16:13 he will guide you into all the t.
18:38 "What is t?" retorted Pilate. With this
Ro 1:25 They exchanged the t about God
1Co 13: 6 in evil but rejoices with the t.
2Co 13: 8 we cannot do anything against the t, but only for the t.
Eph 4:15 Instead, speaking the t in love,
6:14 belt of t buckled around your waist,
2Th 2:10 because they refused to love the t
1Ti 2: 4 and to come to a knowledge of the t.
3:15 the pillar and foundation of the t.
2Ti 2:15 who correctly handles the word of t.
3: 7 but never able to acknowledge the t.
Heb 10:26 received the knowledge of the t,
1Pe 1:22 by obeying the t so that you have
2Pe 2: 2 and will bring the way of t
1Jn 1: 6 we lie and do not live out the t.
1: 8 ourselves and the t is not in us.

TRUTHFUL (TRUTH)
Jn 3:33 it has certified that God is t.

TRUTHS (TRUTH)
1Ti 3: 9 keep hold of the deep t of the faith
Heb 5:12 teach you the elementary t of God's

TRY (TRYING)
1Co 14:12 **t** to excel in those that build
2Co 5:11 the Lord, we **t** to persuade people.

TRYING (TRY)
2Co 5:12 We are not **t** to commend ourselves
1Th 2: 4 We are not **t** to please people

TUNICSee SHIRT

TURN (TURNED TURNS)
Mt 5:39 **t** to them the other cheek also.
    10:35 come to **t** " 'a man against his father,
Jn 12:40 nor **t**—and I would heal them."
Ac 3:19 and **t** to God, so that your sins may
    26:18 and **t** them from darkness to light,
1Ti 6:20 **T** away from godless chatter
1Pe 3:11 **T** from evil and do good; seek peace

TURNED (TURN)
Ro 3:12 All have **t** away, they have together

TURNS (TURN)
Jas 5:20 Whoever **t** a sinner from the error

TWELVE
Mt 10: 1 He called his **t** disciples to him

TWINKLING
1Co 15:52 a flash, in the **t** of an eye, at the last

UNAPPROACHABLE
1Ti 6:16 is immortal and who lives in **u** light,

UNBELIEF (UNBELIEVER UNBELIEVERS
UNBELIEVING)
Mk 9:24 believe; help me overcome my **u**!"
Ro 11:20 they were broken off because of **u**,
Heb 3:19 not able to enter, because of their **u**.

UNBELIEVER (UNBELIEF)
1Co 7:15 But if the **u** leaves, let it be so.
    10:27 If an **u** invites you to a meal
    14:24 if an **u** or an inquirer comes in while
2Co 6:15 believer have in common with an **u**?
1Ti 5: 8 the faith and is worse than an **u**.

UNBELIEVERS (UNBELIEF)
1Co 6: 6 against another—and this in front of **u**!
2Co 6:14 Do not be yoked together with **u**.

UNBELIEVING (UNBELIEF)
1Co 7:14 the **u** husband has been sanctified
    7:14 and the **u** wife has been sanctified
Rev 21: 8 But the cowardly, the **u**, the vile,

UNCERTAIN
1Ti 6:17 which is so **u**, but to put their hope

UNCHANGEABLE
Heb 6:18 that, by two **u** things in which it is

UNCIRCUMCISED
Col 3:11 or Jew, circumcised or **u**, barbarian,

UNCIRCUMCISION
1Co 7:19 is nothing and **u** is nothing.
Gal 5: 6 neither circumcision nor **u** has any

UNCLEAN
Ro 14:14 Jesus, that nothing is **u** in itself.
2Co 6:17 Touch no **u** thing, and I will receive

UNCOVERED
1Co 11: 5 prays or prophesies with her head **u**
Heb 4:13 Everything is **u** and laid bare before

UNDERSTAND (UNDERSTANDING)
Lk 24:45 so they could **u** the Scriptures.
Ac 8:30 "Do you **u** what you are reading?"
Ro 7:15 I do not **u** what I do. For what I
1Co 2:14 and cannot **u** them because they are
Eph 5:17 foolish, but **u** what the Lord's will is.
1Ti 6: 4 they are conceited and **u** nothing.
2Pe 3:16 some things that are hard to **u**,

UNDERSTANDING (UNDERSTAND)
Mk 4:12 and ever hearing but never **u**;
    12:33 with all your **u** and with all your
Php 4: 7 which transcends all **u**, will guard

UNDIVIDED
1Co 7:35 in a right way in **u** devotion

UNDYING
Eph 6:24 Lord Jesus Christ with an **u** love.

UNFADING
1Pe 3: 4 the **u** beauty of a gentle and quiet

UNFAITHFUL
Ro 3: 3 What if some were **u**? Will their

UNFAITHFULNESSSee SEXUAL IMMORALITY

UNGODLINESS
Tit 2:12 It teaches us to say "No" to **u**

UNITED (UNITY)
Ro 6: 5 If we have been **u** with him
Php 2: 1 from being **u** with Christ, if any
Col 2: 2 encouraged in heart and **u** in love,

UNITY (UNITED)
Eph 4: 3 keep the **u** of the Spirit through
    4:13 until we all reach **u** in the faith
Col 3:14 binds them all together in perfect **u**.

UNIVERSE
Heb 1: 2 through whom also he made the **u**.

UNKNOWN
Ac 17:23 with this inscription: TO AN **u** GOD.

UNLEAVENED
Mk 14:22 first day of the Feast of **U** Bread,
1Co 5: 7 so that you may be a new **u** batch—

UNPROFITABLE
Tit 3: 9 because these are **u** and useless.

UNREPENTANT
Ro 2: 5 your stubbornness and your **u** heart,

UNRIGHTEOUS
Mt 5:45 rain on the righteous and the **u**.
1Pe 3:18 the righteous for the **u**, to bring you
2Pe 2: 9 to hold the **u** for punishment

UNSEARCHABLE
Ro 11:33 How **u** his judgments, and his paths

UNSEEN
2Co 4:18 temporary, but what is **u** is eternal.

UNSTABLE
Jas 1: 8 double-minded and **u** in all they do.
2Pe 2:14 they seduce the **u**; they are experts
    3:16 which ignorant and **u** people distort,

UNVEILED
2Co 3:18 **u** faces contemplate the Lord's glory,

UNWORTHY
Lk 17:10 do, should say, 'We are **u** servants;

UPRIGHT
Tit   1: 8 who is self-controlled, **u**,
       2:12 **u** and godly lives in this present age,

UPROOTED
Jude :12 without fruit and **u**—twice dead.

USEFUL
2Ti   2:21 **u** to the Master and prepared to do
       3:16 God-breathed and is **u** for teaching,

USELESS
1Co 15:14 our preaching is **u** and so is your
Jas   2:20 that faith without deeds is **u**?

VAIN
1Co 15: 2 Otherwise, you have believed in **v**.
      15:58 your labor in the Lord is not in **v**.
2Co   6: 1 you not to receive God's grace in **v**.

VALUABLE (VALUE)
Lk 12:24 And how much more **v** you are than

VALUE (VALUABLE)
Mt 13:46 When he found one of great **v**,
Php 2: 3 in humility **v** others above yourselves,
1Ti   4: 8 For physical training is of some **v**, but
              godliness has **v** for all things,
Heb 11:26 as of greater **v** than the treasures

VEIL
2Co 3:14 to this day the same **v** remains

VICTORIOUS (VICTORY)
Rev 2: 7 those who are **v**, I will give
       2:11 Those who are **v** will not be hurt at
       2:17 those who are **v**, I will give
       2:26 those who are **v** and do my will
       3: 5 Those who are **v** will, like them,
       3:12 who are **v** I will make pillars
       3:21 those who are **v**, I will give
      21: 7 who are **v** will inherit all this,

VICTORY (VICTORIOUS)
1Co 15:54 "Death has been swallowed up in **v**."
      15:57 He gives us the **v** through our Lord
1Jn   5: 4 This is the **v** that has overcome

VINDICATED
1Ti   3:16 in a body, was **v** by the Spirit,

VINE
Jn   15: 1 "I am the true **v**, and my Father is

VINEGAR
Mk 15:36 filled a sponge with wine **v**, put it

VIOLATION
Heb 2: 2 every **v** and disobedience received

VIPERS
Ro   3:13 "The poison of **v** is on their lips."

VIRGIN
Mt   1:23 "The **v** will conceive and give birth
2Co 11: 2 I might present you as a pure **v**

VIRTUES
Col   3:14 And over all these **v** put on love,

VISION
Ac 26:19 disobedient to the **v** from heaven.

VOICE
Jn   5:28 are in their graves will hear his **v**
      10: 3 him, and the sheep listen to his **v**.
Heb 3: 7 Spirit says: "Today, if you hear his **v**,
Rev 3:20 If anyone hears my **v** and opens

VOMIT
2Pe 2:22 "A dog returns to its **v**," and, "A sow

WAGES
Lk 10: 7 you, for workers deserve their **w**.
Ro   4: 4 their **w** are not credited to them as
       6:23 For the **w** of sin is death, but the gift

WAIST
Mt   3: 4 he had a leather belt around his **w**.

WAIT (WAITS)
Ac   1: 4 **w** for the gift my Father promised,
Ro   8:23 groan inwardly as we **w** eagerly
1Th 1:10 and to **w** for his Son from heaven,
Tit   2:13 while we **w** for the blessed

WAITS (WAIT)
Ro   8:19 The creation **w** in eager expectation

WALK (WALKED)
Mk 2: 9 to say, 'Get up, take your mat and **w**'?
Jn   8:12 Whoever follows me will never **w**
1Jn 1: 7 But if we **w** in the light, as he is
2Jn   : 6 his command is that you **w** in love.

WALKED (WALK)
Mt 14:29 **w** on the water and came toward

WALL
Rev 21:12 a great, high **w** with twelve gates,

WALLOWING
2Pe 2:22 washed returns to her **w** in the mud."

WANT (WANTED WANTING WANTS)
Mk 8:35 who **w** to save their life will lose
Lk 19:14 'We don't **w** this man to be our king.'
Ro   7:15 For what I **w** to do I do not do,
Php 3:10 I **w** to know Christ—yes, to know

WANTED (WANT)
1Co 12:18 of them, just as he **w** them to be.

WANTING (WANT)
2Pe 3: 9 with you, not **w** anyone to perish,

WANTS (WANT)
Mt 20:26 whoever **w** to become great among
Ro   9:18 on whom he **w** to have mercy,
1Ti   2: 4 who **w** all people to be saved

WAR (WARS)
2Co 10: 3 we do not wage **w** as the world
Rev 19:11 With justice he judges and makes **w**.

WARNINGS
1Co 10:11 and were written down as **w** for us,

WARS (WAR)
Mt 24: 6 You will hear of **w** and rumors of **w**,

WASH (WASHED WASHING)
Jn   13: 5 and began to **w** his disciples' feet,
Ac 22:16 be baptized and **w** your sins away,
Rev 22:14 "Blessed are those who **w** their robes,

WASHED (WASH)
1Co 6:11 were. But you were **w**, you were
Rev 7:14 they have **w** their robes and made

WASHING (WASH)
Eph 5:26 the **w** with water through the word,
Tit 3: 5 He saved us through the **w** of rebirth

WATCH (WATCHING)
Mt 24:42 "Therefore keep **w**, because you do
26:41 "**W** and pray so that you will not fall
Lk 2: 8 keeping **w** over their flocks at night.
1Ti 4:16 **W** your life and doctrine closely.

WATCHING (WATCH)
Lk 12:37 servants whose master finds them **w**
1Pe 5: 2 under your care, **w** over them—

WATER (WATERED WATERS)
Mk 9:41 anyone who gives you a cup of **w**
Jn 4:10 he would have given you living **w**."
7:38 streams of living **w** will flow
Eph 5:26 washing with **w** through the word,
1Pe 3:21 this **w** symbolizes baptism that now
Rev 21: 6 the thirsty I will give **w** without cost

WATERED (WATER)
1Co 3: 6 I planted the seed, Apollos **w** it,

WATERS (WATER)
1Co 3: 7 nor the one who **w** is anything,

WAVE (WAVES)
Jas 1: 6 the one who doubts is like a **w**

WAVES (WAVE)
Mt 8:27 Even the winds and the **w** obey him!"
Eph 4:14 tossed back and forth by the **w**,

WAY (WAYS)
Mt 3: 3 desert, 'Prepare the **w** for the Lord,
Jn 14: 6 "I am the **w** and the truth and the life.
1Co 10:13 also provide a **w** out so that you can
12:31 will show you the most excellent **w**.
Heb 4:15 who has been tempted in every **w**,
9: 8 the **w** into the Most Holy Place had
10:20 living **w** opened for us through

WAYS (WAY)
Jas 3: 2 We all stumble in many **w**.

WEAK (WEAKER WEAKNESS)
Mt 26:41 spirit is willing, but the flesh is **w**."
Ro 14: 1 Accept those whose faith is **w**,
1Co 1:27 God chose the **w** things of the world
8: 9 become a stumbling block to the **w**.
9:22 To the **w** I became **w**, to win the **w**.
2Co 12:10 For when I am **w**, then I am strong.
Heb 12:12 your feeble arms and **w** knees.

WEAKER (WEAK)
1Co 12:22 that seem to be **w** are indispensable,
1Pe 3: 7 them with respect as the **w** partner

WEAKNESS (WEAK)
Ro 8:26 way, the Spirit helps us in our **w**.
1Co 1:25 the **w** of God is stronger than human
2Co 12: 9 for my power is made perfect in **w**."
Heb 5: 2 since he himself is subject to **w**.

WEALTH
Mk 10:22 away sad, because he had great **w**.
Lk 15:13 and there squandered his **w** in wild

WEAPONS
2Co 10: 4 The **w** we fight with are not the **w**

WEARY
Mt 11:28 all you who are **w** and burdened,
Gal 6: 9 Let us not become **w** in doing good,

WEDDING
Mt 22:11 who was not wearing **w** clothes.
Rev 19: 7 For the **w** of the Lamb has come,

WEEP (WEEPING WEPT)
Lk 6:21 Blessed are you who **w** now, for you

WEEPING (WEEP)
Mt 8:12 where there will be **w** and gnashing

WELCOMES
Mt 10:40 who **w** you **w** me, and anyone who **w** me **w**
the one who sent me.
18: 5 whoever **w** one such child in my name **w** me.
2Jn :11 Anyone who **w** them shares in their

WELL
Lk 17:19 and go; your faith has made you **w**."
Jas 5:15 offered in faith will make you **w**;

WEPT (WEEP)
Jn 11:35 Jesus **w**.

WHITE
Rev 1:14 hair on his head was **w** like wool,
3: 4 dressed in **w**, for they are worthy.
20:11 I saw a great **w** throne and him who

WHOLE
Mt 16:26 it be for you to gain the **w** world,
24:14 in the **w** world as a testimony to all
Jn 13:10 their feet; their **w** body is clean.
21:25 even the **w** world would not have
Ac 20:27 proclaim to you the **w** will of God.
Ro 3:19 and the **w** world held accountable
8:22 the **w** creation has been groaning as
Gal 5: 3 he is obligated to obey the **w** law.
Eph 4:13 attaining to the **w** measure
Jas 2:10 For whoever keeps the **w** law
1Jn 2: 2 but also for the sins of the **w** world.

WHOLEHEARTEDLY (HEART)
Eph 6: 7 Serve **w**, as if you were serving

WICKED (WICKEDNESS)
Mt 12:39 "A **w** and adulterous generation asks
Lk 6:35 he is kind to the ungrateful and **w**.

WICKEDNESS (WICKED)
Heb 8:12 For I will forgive their **w** and

WIDE
Mt 7:13 For **w** is the gate and broad is
Eph 3:18 to grasp how **w** and long and high

WIDOW (WIDOWS)
Lk 21: 2 saw a poor **w** put in two very small

WIDOWS (WIDOW)
Jas 1:27 after orphans and **w** in their distress

WIFE (WIVES)
Mt 19: 3 for a man to divorce his **w** for any
1Co 7: 2 sexual relations with his own **w**,
7:33 this world—how he can please his **w**—
Eph 5:23 head of the **w** as Christ is the head
5:33 must love his **w** as he loves himself,
5:33 and the **w** must respect her husband.
1Ti 3: 2 faithful to his **w**, temperate,
Rev 21: 9 you the bride, the **w** of the Lamb."

WILD
Lk 15:13 squandered his wealth in **w** living.
Ro 11:17 and you, though a **w** olive shoot,
1Pe 4: 4 not join them in their reckless, **w** living,

WILL (WILLING WILLINGNESS)
Mt 6:10 your **w** be done on earth as it is
26:39 me. Yet not as I **w**, but as you **w**."
Jn 7:17 chooses to do the **w** of God **w** find
Ac 20:27 to you the whole **w** of God.
Ro 12: 2 approve what God's **w** is—his good,
1Co 7:37 but has control over his own **w**,
Eph 5:17 but understand what the Lord's **w** is.
Php 2:13 for it is God who works in you to **w**
1Th 4: 3 It is God's **w** that you should be
5:18 for this is God's **w** for you in Christ
Heb 9:16 In the case of a **w**, it is necessary
10: 7 the scroll— I have come to do your **w**,
Jas 4:15 "If it is the Lord's **w**, we **w** live
1Jn 5:14 we ask anything according to his **w**,
Rev 4:11 by your **w** they were created

WILLING (WILL)
Mt 18:14 Father in heaven is not **w** that any
23:37 her wings, and you were not **w**.
26:41 The spirit is **w**, but the flesh is

WILLINGNESS (WILL)
2Co 8:12 For if the **w** is there, the gift is

WIN (WINS)
Php 3:14 on toward the goal to **w** the prize
1Th 4:12 your daily life may **w** the respect

WIND
Jas 1: 6 the sea, blown and tossed by the **w**.

WINE
Mt 9:17 No, they pour new **w** into new
Lk 23:36 him. They offered him **w** vinegar
Ro 14:21 drink **w** or to do anything else
Eph 5:18 Do not get drunk on **w**, which leads

WINESKINS
Mt 9:17 they pour new wine into new **w**,

WINGS
Lk 13:34 hen gathers her chicks under her **w**,

WIPE
Rev 7:17 God will **w** away every tear

WISDOM (WISE)
Mt 11:19 But **w** is proved right by her actions."
Lk 2:52 he increased in **w** and in favor
Ro 11:33 the depth of the riches of the **w**
Col 2: 3 are hidden all the treasures of **w**
Jas 1: 5 If any of you lacks **w**, you should

WISE (WISDOM WISER)
Mt 11:25 have hidden these things from the **w**
1Co 1:27 things of the world to shame the **w**;
2Ti 3:15 to make you **w** for salvation through

WISER (WISE)
1Co 1:25 of God is **w** than human wisdom,

WITHERS
1Pe 1:24 the grass **w** and the flowers fall,

WITNESS (WITNESSES)
Jn 1: 8 he came only as a **w** to the light.

WITNESSES (WITNESS)
Ac 1: 8 and you will be my **w** in Jerusalem,

WIVES (WIFE)
Eph 5:22 **W**, submit yourselves to your own
5:25 love your **w**, just as Christ loved
Col 3:19 Husbands, love your **w** and do not
1Pe 3: 1 **W**, in the same way submit

1Pe 3: 7 considerate as you live with your **w**,

WOMAN (MAN)
Mt 5:28 a **w** lustfully has already committed
Jn 8: 3 the Pharisees brought in a **w** caught
Ro 7: 2 by law a married **w** is bound to her
1Co 11: 3 and the head of the **w** is man,
11:13 Is it proper for a **w** to pray to God
1Ti 2:11 A **w** should learn in quietness

WOMEN (MAN)
Lk 1:42 "Blessed are you among **w**,
1Co 14:34 **W** should remain silent
1Ti 2: 9 I also want the **w** to dress modestly,
Tit 2: 3 teach the older **w** to be reverent
1Pe 3: 5 this is the way the holy **w** of the past

WOMB
Lk 1:44 the baby in my **w** leaped for joy.

WONDERFUL (WONDERS)
1Pe 2. 9 you out of darkness into his **w** light.

WONDERS (WONDERFUL)
Mt 24:24 perform great signs and **w** to deceive,
Ac 2:19 I will show **w** in the heaven

WOOD
1Co 3:12 costly stones, **w**, hay or straw,

WORD (WORDS)
Jn 1: 1 In the beginning was the **W**, and the **W** was
with God, and the **W**
1:14 The **W** became flesh and made his
2Co 2:17 we do not peddle the **w** of God
4: 2 nor do we distort the **w** of God.
Eph 6:17 of the Spirit, which is the **w** of God.
Php 2:16 as you hold firmly to the **w** of life.
2Ti 2:15 and who correctly handles the **w**
Heb 4:12 For the **w** of God is alive and active.
Jas 1:22 Do not merely listen to the **w**,

WORDS (WORD)
Mt 24:35 but my **w** will never pass away.
Jn 6:68 go? You have the **w** of eternal life.
15: 7 in me and my **w** remain in you,
1Co 14:19 rather speak five intelligible **w**
Rev 22:19 of you takes **w** away from this scroll

WORK (HANDIWORK WORKER WORKERS
WORKING WORKMAN WORKS)
Jn 6:27 Do not **w** for food that spoils,
9: 4 is coming, when no one can **w**.
1Co 3:13 test the quality of each person's **w**.
Php 1: 6 he who began a good **w** in you will
2:12 my absence—continue to **w** out your
Col 3:23 you do, **w** at it with all your heart,
1Th 5:12 those who **w** hard among you,
2Th 3:10 who will not **w** shall not eat."
2Ti 3:17 equipped for every good **w**.
Heb 6:10 he will not forget your **w**

WORKER (WORK)
2Ti 2:15 a **w** who does not need to be ashamed

WORKERS (WORK)
Mt 9:37 is plentiful but the **w** are few.
Lk 10: 7 give you, for **w** deserve their wages.
1Co 3: 9 For we are God's **c**; you are God's
1Ti 5:18 and "**W** deserve their wages."

WORKING (WORK)
Col 3:23 all your heart, as **w** for the Lord,

WORKS (WORK)
Jn 10:32 shown you many good **w** from the Father.

Jn 14:11 believe on the evidence of the **w**
Ro 8:28 in all things God **w** for the good
Eph 2: 9 not by **w**, so that no one can boast.
4:12 equip God's people for **w** of service,

WORLD (WORLDLY)
Mt 5:14 "You are the light of the **w**. A city
16:26 it be for you to gain the whole **w**,
Mk 16:15 "Go into all the **w** and preach
Jn 1:29 who takes away the sin of the **w**!
3:16 God so loved the **w** that he gave his
8:12 he said, "I am the light of the **w**.
15:19 If you belonged to the **w**, it would
15:19 but I have chosen you out of the **w**.
16:33 In this **w** you will have trouble.
16:33 take heart! I have overcome the **w**."
18:36 said, "My kingdom is not of this **w**.
Ro 3:19 and the whole **w** held accountable
1Co 3:19 the wisdom of this **w** is foolishness
2Co 5:19 that God was reconciling the **w**
10: 3 we do not wage war as the **w** does.
1Ti 6: 7 For we brought nothing into the **w**,
1Jn 2: 2 but also for the sins of the whole **w**.
2:15 Do not love the **w** or anything in the **w**.
Rev 13: 8 was slain from the creation of the **w**.

WORLDLY (WORLD)
Tit 2:12 "No" to ungodliness and **w** passions,

WORM
Mk 9:48 where " 'their **w** does not die,

WORRY (WORRYING)
Mt 6:25 I tell you, do not **w** about your life,
10:19 do not **w** about what to say or how

WORRYING (WORRY)
Mt 6:27 you by **w** add a single hour to your

WORSHIP
Mt 2: 2 it rose and have come to **w** him."
Jn 4:24 his worshipers must **w** in the Spirit
Ro 12: 1 is your proper **w** as rational beings.

WORTH (WORTHY)
Mt 10:31 afraid; you are **w** more than many
Ro 8:18 sufferings are not **w** comparing
Php 3: 8 the surpassing **w** of knowing Christ
1Pe 1: 7 your faith—of greater **w** than gold,
3: 4 which is of great **w** in God's sight.

WORTHLESS
Jas 1:26 themselves, and their religion is **w**.

WORTHY (WORTH)
Eph 4: 1 live a life **w** of the calling you have
Php 1:27 live in a manner **w** of the gospel
3Jn : 6 on their way in a manner **w** of God.
Rev 5: 2 "Who is **w** to break the seals

WOUNDS
1Pe 2:24 "by his **w** you have been healed."

WRATH
Ro 1:18 The **w** of God is being revealed

Ro 5: 9 be saved from God's **w** through him!
1Th 5: 9 God did not appoint us to suffer **w**
Rev 6:16 throne and from the **w** of the Lamb!

WRITE (WRITING WRITTEN)
Heb 8:10 minds and **w** them on their hearts.

WRITING (WRITE)
1Co 14:37 that what I am **w** to you is the Lord's

WRITTEN (WRITE)
Lk 10:20 that your names are **w** in heaven."
Jn 20:31 these are **w** that you may believe
1Co 4: 6 saying, "Do not go beyond what is **w**."
2Co 3: 3 **w** not with ink but with the Spirit
Heb 12:23 whose names are **w** in heaven.

WRONG (WRONGDOING WRONGED WRONGS)
1Th 5:15 sure that nobody pays back **w** for **w**,

WRONGDOING (WRONG)
1Jn 5:17 All **w** is sin, and there is sin

WRONGED (WRONG)
1Co 6: 7 Why not rather be **w**? Why not

WRONGS (WRONG)
1Co 13: 5 angered, it keeps no record of **w**.

YEARS
2Pe 3: 8 the Lord a day is like a thousand **y**, and a thousand **y** are like a day.
Rev 20: 2 and bound him for a thousand **y**.

YESTERDAY
Heb 13: 8 Jesus Christ is the same **y** and today

YOKE (YOKED)
Mt 11:29 Take my **y** upon you and learn

YOKED (YOKE)
2Co 6:14 Do not be **y** together

YOUNG (YOUTH)
1Ti 4:12 down on you because you are **y**,

YOUTH (YOUNG)
2Ti 2:22 Flee the evil desires of **y** and pursue

ZEAL
Ro 12:11 Never be lacking in **z**, but keep your

ZEBEDEE
Father of Hames and John (Mk 1:19-20).

ZECHARIAH
Father of John the Baptist (Lk 1:13; 3:2).

ZEBULUN
Rev 7: 8 from the tribe of **Z** 12,000,

ZION
Ro 9:33 I lay in **Z** a stone that causes people
11:26 "The deliverer will come from **Z**;